Computer Networks And Internets

With Internet Applications

THIRD EDITION

Computer Networks
And Internets

With Internet Applications

THIRD EDITION

DOUGLAS E. COMER

Department of Computer Sciences
Purdue University
West Lafayette, IN 47907

PRENTICE HALL
Upper Saddle River, New Jersey 07458

Library of Congress Cataloging-in-Publication Data

Comer, Douglas.
    Computer networks and internets / Douglas E. Comer.
    p.cm.
    Includes bibliographical references and index.
    ISBN 0-13-091449-5
    1.Computer networking 2. Telecommunications.
    I. Title.
    CIP DATA AVAILABLE.

Vice President and Editorial Director of ECS: MARCIA HORTON
Publisher: ALAN APT
Associate Editor: TONI HOLM
Editorial Assistant: AMY TODD
Vice President and Director of Production and Manufacturing, ESM: DAVID W. RICCARDI
Executive Managing Editor: VINCE O'BRIEN
Managing Editor: DAVID A. GEORGE
Production Editor: IRWIN ZUCKER
Manufacturing Manager: TRUDY PISCIOTTI
Manufacturing Buyer: PAT BROWN
Director of Creative Services: PAUL BELFANTI
Creative Director: CAROLE ANSON
Art Director: HEATHER SCOTT
Assistant to Art Director: JOHN CHRISTIANA
Senior Marketing Manager: JENNIE BURGER
Marketing Assistant: CYNTHIA SZOLLOSE

© 2001, 1999, 1997 by Prentice Hall
Prentice-Hall, Inc.
Upper Saddle River, New Jersey 07458

The author and publisher of this book have used their best efforts in preparing this book. These efforts include the development, research, and testing of the theories and programs to determine their effectiveness. The author and publisher make no warranty of any kind, expressed or implied, with regard to these programs or the documentation contained in this book. The author and publisher shall not be liable in any event for incidental or consequential damages in connection with, or arising out of, the furnishing, performance, or use of these programs.

TRADEMARK INFORMATION: UNIX is a registered trademark of The Open Group in the U.S. and other countries. Microsoft Windows, Windows 95, Windows 98, and Windows NT are trademarks of Microsoft Corporation. Microsoft is a registered trademark of Microsoft Corporation. Solaris, Sparc, Java, and JavaScript are trademarks of Sun Microsystems, Incorporated. Sniffer is a trademark of Network General Corporation. AdaMagic is a trademark of Intermetrics, Incorporated. Alpha is a trademark of Digital Equipment Corporation. Pentium is a trademark of Intel Corporation. X Window System is a trademark of X Consortium, Inc.

Printed in the United States of America

10 9 8 7 6 5 4 3 2 1

ISBN 0-13-091449-5

Prentice-Hall International (UK) Limited, *London*
Prentice-Hall of Australia Pty. Limited, *Sydney*
Prentice-Hall Canada Inc., *Toronto*
Prentice-Hall Hispanoamericana, S.A., *Mexico*
Prentice-Hall of India Private Limited, *New Delhi*
Prentice-Hall of Japan, Inc., *Tokyo*
Pearson Education Asia Pte. Ltd., *Singapore*
Editora Prentice-Hall do Brasil, Ltda., *Rio de Janeiro*

To Packets Everywhere

Contents

PART I   Data Transmission

PART II   Packet Transmission

Chapter 7   Packets, Frames, And Error Detection   81

Chapter 8   LAN Technologies And Network Topology   99

Chapter 9   Hardware Addressing And Frame Type Identification   121

Chapter 10   LAN Wiring, Physical Topology, And Interface Hardware   139

Chapter 11   Extending LANs: Fiber Modems, Repeaters, Bridges, and   155
                Switches

Chapter 12   Long-Distance Digital Connection Technologies   173

Chapter 13   WAN Technologies And Routing   197

Chapter 14   Connection-Oriented Networking And ATM   217

Chapter 15   Network Characteristics: Ownership, Service Paradigm,   231
             And Performance

Chapter 16   Protocols And Layering   247

PART III   Internetworking

Chapter 17   Internetworking: Concepts, Architecture, and Protocols   269

Chapter 18   IP: Internet Protocol Addresses   **281**

Chapter 19   Binding Protocol Addresses (ARP)   **301**

Chapter 20   IP Datagrams And Datagram Forwarding   317

Chapter 21   IP Encapsulation, Fragmentation, And Reassembly   329

Chapter 22   The Future IP (IPv6)   339

Chapter 23   An Error Reporting Mechanism (ICMP)   351

Chapter 24   TCP: Reliable Transport Service   361

PART IV Network Applications

Chapter 27   The Socket Interface   411

Chapter 28   Example Of A Client And A Server   425

Chapter 29   Naming With The Domain Name System   439

Chapter 30 Electronic Mail Representation And Transfer   455

Chapter 31 File Transfer And Remote File Access   471

Chapter 32   World Wide Web Pages And Browsing   489

Chapter 33   Dynamic Web Document Technologies (CGI, ASP, JSP,   509
            PHP, ColdFusion)

Chapter 34   Technology For Active Web Documents (Java, JavaScript)   527

Chapter 35   RPC and Middleware   549

Preface

I am extremely pleased that *Computer Networks And Internets* is generating such excitement. In addition to the hundreds of U.S. schools using it in their networking courses, many professionals have written to say that it is being used in industry, and enthusiastic comments have arrived about the foreign translations. The success is especially satisfying in a market glutted with networking books. This book stands out because of its breadth of coverage, logical organization, explanation of concepts, focus on the Internet, and wealth of supplemental materials for both students and instructors on the CD-ROM and on the web site:

http://www.netbook.cs.purdue.edu

The new edition has been completely revised and updated, with three new chapters (3, 14, and 25), many new sections, and over 80 additional glossary entries. The CD-ROM and Web site have also been reorganized and expanded.

Each new chapter responds to requests from instructors and readers. Chapter 3 responds to those who requested an early introduction to network applications and programming. The chapter explains how to build applications that operate across the Internet before one acquires knowledge of the underlying technologies or protocol facilities. The chapter presents a simplified API (code is available), and shows examples of Internet applications that use the API to communicate. Even readers who are not interested in programming will be able to appreciate how much functionality can be achieved with a handful of procedures.

Chapter 14 was written in response to those who requested expanded coverage of connection-oriented networking. The chapter explores the connection-oriented paradigm, and uses ATM as an example. In addition to explaining concepts and details such as label switching, the chapter provides an assessment of the technology, and discusses why ATM has failed to live up to its ambitious design goals.

Chapter 25 was written in response to those who requested a chapter on Internet routing and Internet routing protocols. The chapter discusses both static and automatic routing. It covers the autonomous system concept and specific protocols such as RIP, OSPF, and BGP. Finally, the chapter examines the difficult problem of multicast route propagation.

The text answers the basic question "how do computer networks and internets operate?" in the broadest sense. It provides a comprehensive, self-contained tour through all of networking from the lowest levels of data transmission and wiring to the highest levels of application software. At each level, it shows how the facilities and services provided by lower levels are used and extended in the next level. Thus, after describing how a modem uses a carrier to encode data, the text shows how packet-switching systems like the Internet use modems to send frames. After describing how technologies like Ethernet transfer frames, the text shows how a protocol like TCP uses such transmission facilities to transfer data reliably. Ultimately, the text explains how Internet applications like the World Wide Web operate over the resulting infrastructure.

The text is intended for upper-division undergraduates, or beginning graduate students, who have little or no background in networking. It does not use sophisticated mathematics, nor does it assume a knowledge of operating systems. Instead, the text defines concepts clearly, uses examples and drawings to illustrate how the technology operates, and states results of analysis without providing mathematical proofs.

After an introduction (Chapters 1—3), the body of the text is organized into four sections. The first section (Chapters 4—6) provides a brief explanation of how the underlying hardware works. The section explains the concept of a carrier signal, discusses modulating a carrier, and shows how a modem encodes data on a carrier wave for transfer. The section also discusses asynchronous, character-oriented data transmission and defines terms such as *bandwidth* and *baud* that arise in later chapters.

The second section (Chapters 7—16) focuses on packet switching. The section introduces the motivation for using packets, and then describes characteristics used to categorize networks as LANs, WANs, local loops, public or private, connection-oriented or connectionless, as well as basic network topologies and wiring schemes. The section also introduces the concepts of next-hop routing, switching, and protocol layering, with the terminology used for each. Finally, the section uses several common network technologies as examples, including Ethernet, FDDI, Token Ring, ATM, and ADSL.

The third section (Chapters 17—25) focuses on the Internet protocols. After discussing the motivation for internetworking, the section describes internet architecture and routers, internet addressing, address binding, and the TCP/IP protocols. Protocols such as IP, TCP, ICMP, and ARP are reviewed in more detail, allowing students to understand how the concepts relate to practice. Chapter 24 on TCP covers the important and deep topic of reliability in transport protocols. Appendix 5 shows how to put theory into practice by building a home network that connects multiple computers to the Internet through a single IP address.

The final section (Chapters 26—38) examines network applications. As with other sections of the text, coverage is quite broad — the section includes a discussion of both general principles and specific applications. The section begins by describing the client-server model that network applications use to communicate. The section then describes the socket API, and shows code from an example client and server that use sockets for communication. The section describes name resolution with the domain name system and applications such as e-mail, file transfer, and Web browsing, including an explanation of dynamic and active documents along with examples using CGI, Java, and JavaScript. In each case, the text describes the structure of the software, and explains how a client and server interact to provide the service. Chapter 35 discusses middleware, including both procedural and object oriented middleware technologies. Later chapters in the section discuss network security and explain how application software can be used for network management. Finally, Chapter 38 considers the interesting problem of initialization. The chapter shows how application-level software can achieve what seems to be impossible — use of protocol software to obtain the information needed to initialize the protocol software being used.

The text is ideally suited for a one-semester introductory course on networking taught at the senior level. Designed for a comprehensive course, it covers the entire subject from wiring to applications. In the course at Purdue, for example, students have weekly lab assignments to reinforce the concepts and provide hands-on experience. By the time they finish our course, each student is expected to: know how an IP router uses a routing table to forward IP datagrams; describe how a datagram crosses the Internet; explain the difference between a hub and a layer 2 switch; know how TCP identifies a connection and why a concurrent web server can handle multiple connections to port 80; describe the conceptual differences between a bridge and an IP router; compute the length of a single bit as it travels across a 100BaseT network; explain why TCP is classified as end-to-end; distinguish between the CSMA/CD media access mechanism used by Ethernet and a token passing scheme; and know how DSL uses multiplexing to send data at high speed.

The goal of a single course is breadth, not depth — to cover the subject, one cannot focus on a few technologies or a few concepts. Thus, the key to a successful course lies in maintaining a quick pace. To cover the fundamental topics in a semester, the lower-layer material in Section 1 can be condensed into a week, and the sections on networks and internetworking can be allocated five weeks each, leaving a few weeks for the section on applications and topics such as network management and security.

Instructors should impress on students the importance of concepts and principles: specific technologies may become obsolete in a few years, but the principles will remain. In addition, instructors should give students a feeling for the excitement that pervades networking.

Although no single topic is challenging, students may find the quantity of material daunting. In particular, students are faced with a plethora of new terms. Networking acronyms and jargon can be especially confusing; students spend much of the time becoming accustomed to using proper terms. To help students master terminology, Appendix 1 contains a glossary of terms and acronyms. To provide additional clarification, definitions in the glossary have been written independently rather than being taken verbatim from the text.

Because programming and experimentation are crucial to helping students learn about networks, laboratory experience is an essential part of any networking course. Appendix 6 describes the architecture of the undergrad networking lab at Purdue, and shows how inexpensive hardware can be used to create a useful lab environment. Our lab curriculum at Purdue emphasizes two main aspects of networking: socket programming and packet analysis. We begin the semester by having students construct client software to access the web and extract data (e.g., write a program to print the current temperature). Chapter 3 explains the simple API that we give students; with our API, students can write working code before they learn about protocols, addresses, or sockets. Later in the semester, of course, students learn to use the socket API. Eventually, they write a concurrent web server (CGI support is optional). In addition to application programming, students also use the lab facilities to capture packets from a live network. They write programs that decode packet headers (Ethernet/IP/TCP).

Giving students access to a network builds enthusiasm and encourages experimentation — our experience shows that students who have access to a live network understand and appreciate the subject better. Thus, if a dedicated packet analyzer is not available, an inexpensive analyzer can be configured by installing appropriate software on a standard PC. For students without access to networking facilities, the CD-ROM contains examples of packet traces; students can write programs that read a trace and process packets as if they have been captured from the network.

The CD-ROM included with the text and the Web site both contain materials that will make teaching easier and help readers understand the material. For instructors, the CD-ROM contains course materials, figures from the text that can be used in presentations, and animated figures that help clarify the concepts. The CD-ROM also contains materials not in the text, including photographs of network wiring and equipment as well as files of data that can be used as input to student projects.

To help both professors and students locate information, the CD-ROM includes a keyword search mechanism. When given a term, the search mechanism locates a definition from the online glossary as well as other items related to the term. Finally, the CD-ROM contains links to the Web site, which is updated continuously. Two electronic mailing lists have been established for the text: general information can be obtained from *netbook@cs.purdue.edu*; discussions about teaching the material occur on *netbook-inst@cs.purdue.edu*. To join either list, send an e-mail message to the list name *-request* with a body that consists of the word *subscribe*. To avoid having the mail server send multiple copies of each message over the Internet, instructors are requested to establish a single local alias for all students at their site.

I thank all the people who have contributed to this edition of the book. Dennis Brylow, and John Lin, proofread chapters throughout the text. Jennifer Seitzer, Abdullah Abonamah, and George Varghese reviewed an earlier edition and made valuable comments. Mike Evangelista wrote the client and server application code in Chapter 3 as well as the API; he ported the API to Linux, Solaris, and Windows platforms. Ralph Droms prepared the CD-ROM, and manages the Web materials. Jim Griffioen reviewed drafts of the three new chapters and offered global perspective as well as technical details. Special thanks go to my wife and partner, Chris, whose careful editing and helpful suggestions made many improvements throughout.

Douglas E. Comer

January, 2001

About The Author

Dr. Douglas Comer is an internationally recognized expert on TCP/IP protocols, computer networking, and the Internet. One of the researchers who contributed to the Internet as it was being formed in the late 1970s and 1980s, he was a member of the Internet Architecture Board, the group responsible for guiding the Internet's development. He was also chairman of the CSNET technical committee and a member of the CSNET executive committee.

Comer consults for industry on the design of computer networks. In addition to talks in universities, each year Comer teaches many onsite courses to networking professionals around the world. His operating system, Xinu, and implementation of TCP/IP protocols (both documented in his textbooks), have been used in commercial products.

Comer is a professor of computer science at Purdue University, where he teaches courses and does research on computer networking, internetworking, and operating systems. In addition to writing a series of best-selling technical books, he serves as the North American editor of the journal *Software — Practice and Experience*. Comer is a Fellow of the ACM.

Additional information can be found at:

www.cs.purdue.edu/people/comer

What Others Have Said About
Computer Networks And Internets

"The book is one of the best that I have ever read. Thank you."

Gokhan Mutlu
Ege University, Turkey

"An excellent book for beginners and professionals alike — well written, comprehensive coverage, and easy to follow."

John Lin
Bell Labs

"The breadth is astonishing."

George Varghese
University of California at San Diego

"I just could not put it down before I finished it. It was simply superb."

Lalit Y. Raju
Regional Engineering College, India

"The miniature webserver in Chapter 3 is brilliant — readers will get a big thrill out of it."

Dennis Brylow
Purdue University

"Despite the plethora of acronyms that infest the discipline of networking, this book is not intimidating. Comer is an excellent writer, who expands and explains the terminology. The text covers the entire scope of networking from wires to the web. I find it outstanding."

Jennifer Seitzer
University of Dayton

Other Books In the Internetworking Series
from Douglas Comer and Prentice Hall

Internetworking With TCP/IP Volume I: Principles, Protocols and Architectures, 4th edition: 2000, ISBN 0-13-01830-6

The classic reference in the field for anyone who wants to understand Internet technology, Volume I surveys the TCP/IP protocol suite and describes each component. The highly accessible text presents the scientific principles used in the construction of TCP/IP, and shows how the components were designed to work together. The text covers protocols such as IP, ICMP, TCP, UDP, ARP, SNMP, and RTP, as well as concepts such as Virtual Private Networks and Network Address Translation.

Internetworking With TCP/IP Volume II: Design, Implementation, and Internals (with David Stevens), 3rd edition: 1999, ISBN 0-13-973843-6

Volume II continues the discussion of Volume I by using code from a running implementation of TCP/IP to illustrate all the details. The text shows, for example, how TCP's slow start algorithm interacts with the Partridge-Karn exponential retransmission backoff algorithm and how routing updates interact with datagram forwarding.

Internetworking With TCP/IP Volume III: Client-Server Programming and Applications (with David Stevens)

> **Linux/POSIX sockets version: 2000, ISBN 0-13-032071-4**
> **AT&T TLI Version: 1994, ISBN 0-13-474230-3**
> **Windows Sockets Version: 1997, ISBN 0-13-848714-6**

Volume III describes the fundamental concept of client-server computing used to build all distributed computing systems. The text discusses various server designs as well as the tools and techniques used to build clients and servers, including Remote Procedure Call (RPC). It contains examples of running programs that illustrate each of the designs and tools. Three versions of Volume III are available for the socket API (Linux/POSIX), the TLI API (AT&T System V), and the Windows Sockets API (Microsoft).

The Internet Book: Everything you need to know about computer networking and how the Internet works, 3rd edition: 2000, ISBN 0-13-030852-8, paperback

A gentle introduction to networking and the Internet, *The Internet Book* does not assume the reader has a technical background. It explains the Internet, how it works, and services available in general terms, without focusing on a particular computer or a particular brand of software. Ideal for someone who wants to become Internet and computer networking literate, *The Internet Book* explains the terminology as well as the concepts; an extensive glossary of terms and abbreviations is included.

**To order, visit the Prentice Hall Web page at www.prenhall.com/
or contact your local bookstore or Prentice Hall representative.
In North America, call 1-515-284-6751, or send a FAX to 1-515-284-6719.**

Computer Networks And Internets

With Internet Applications

THIRD EDITION

Chapter Contents

1

Introduction

1.1 Growth Of Computer Networking

Computer networks have been growing explosively. Two decades ago, few people had access to a network. Now, computer communication has become an essential part of our infrastructure. Networking is used in every aspect of business, including advertising, production, shipping, planning, billing, and accounting. Consequently, most corporations have multiple networks. Schools, at all grade levels from elementary through post-graduate, are using computer networks to provide students and teachers with instantaneous access to information in online libraries around the world. Federal, state, and local government offices use networks, as do military organizations. In short, computer networks are everywhere.

Continued growth of the global Internet is one of the most interesting and exciting phenomena in networking. Twenty years ago, the Internet was a research project that involved a few dozen sites. Today, the Internet has grown into a production communication system that reaches millions of people in all populated countries of the world. In the United States, the Internet connects corporations, colleges and universities, as well as federal, state, and local government offices, and schools. In addition, private residences have low-speed access to the Internet through the dial-up telephone system and high-speed access through cable modems, satellites, DSL, and wireless technologies. Evidence of the Internet's impact on society can be seen in advertisements in magazines and on television, which contain references to Internet Web sites that provide additional information about the advertiser's products and services.

The growth in networking has an economic impact as well. Data networks have made telecommuting available to individuals and have changed business communication. In addition, an entire industry has emerged that develops networking technologies, products, and services. The popularity and importance of computer networking has produced a strong demand in all jobs for people with more networking expertise. Companies need workers to plan, acquire, install, operate, and manage the hardware and software systems that comprise computer networks and internets. In addition, computer programming is no longer restricted to individual computers; programmers are expected to design and implement application software that can communicate with software on other computers.

1.2 Complexity In Network Systems

Computer networking is a complex subject. Many technologies exist, and each technology has features that distinguish it from the others. Multiple organizations have created networking standards independently, which are not all compatible. Many companies have created commercial networking products and services that use the technologies in unconventional ways. Finally, networking is complex because multiple technologies exist that can be used to interconnect two or more networks. As a result, many combinations of networks are possible.

Networking can be especially confusing to a beginner because there is no single underlying theory that explains the relationship among all parts. In fact, various organizations and research groups have attempted to define conceptual models that can be used to explain the differences and similarities among network hardware and software systems. Unfortunately, the set of technologies is diverse and changing rapidly; models are either so simplistic that they do not distinguish among details, or so complex that they do not help simplify the subject.

The lack of an underlying theory has produced another challenge for beginners: there is no simple and uniform terminology for networking concepts. Because multiple organizations define networking technologies and standards, multiple terms exist for a given concept. Professionals often use a technical term from one technology when referring to an analogous feature of another technology. In addition, technical terms are sometimes confused with the names of popular products. Consequently, in addition to a large set of terms and acronyms that contains many synonyms, networking jargon contains terms that are often abbreviated, misused, or associated with products.

1.3 Mastering The Complexity

To master the complexity, one must look beyond the details and concentrate on understanding concepts. For example, although it is not important to understand the details of wires used to connect computers to a specific network, it is important to understand the few basic categories of wiring schemes that exist and the advantages of each. Similarly, although it is not important to learn the details of how a particular communication protocol handles a congested network, it is important to know what congestion is and why it must be handled.

1.4 Concepts And Terminology

This text is written to help overcome the complexity. The text focuses on concepts and avoids unnecessary detail. It explains the purpose of each networking technology, gives the advantages and disadvantages, and describes some of the consequences of using the technology. Whenever possible, the text uses analogies and illustrations to simplify explanations.

In addition to covering concepts and technologies, the text introduces networking terminology. When a new concept is introduced, terminology for that concept is defined. The text also notes popular abbreviations and synonyms that professionals use. The terminology is summarized in a Glossary in Appendix *1* that serves as a quick reference for the many terms and acronyms defined throughout the text.

1.5 Organization Of The Text

Following the introductory chapters, the text is divided into four major parts. The first part describes data transmission. It explains that at the lowest level, electrical signals traveling across wires are used to carry information, and shows how data can be encoded using electrical signals. The chapters in the first part do not provide details for engineers who design networking hardware. Instead, they provide general descriptions of the principles and practical realities of data transmission and their consequences for computer networks.

The second part of the text focuses on packet transmission. It explains why computer networks use packets, and shows how data is grouped into packets for transmission. This section introduces the two basic categories of computer networks: Local Area Networks and Wide Area Networks. It explains the differences between the two categories and reviews example technologies. Finally, the section discusses the important concepts of addressing and routing. It explains how a network routes a packet to its destination.

The third part of the text covers internetworking — the important idea that allows heterogeneous network technologies to be combined into a large, seamless communication system. The text explains TCP/IP, the protocol technology used in the global Internet.

The fourth part of the text explains networking applications. It focuses on how applications use the underlying network to communicate. The chapters begin by explaining the client-server model of interaction. Later chapters use the model to explain how application programs provide services such as electronic mail and Web browsing.

1.6 Summary

The large set of technologies, products, and interconnection schemes make networking a complex subject. Many organizations have defined competing standards, and most networks incorporate components that use multiple standards. Furthermore, no single theory exists that can be used to explain how the pieces fit together. Consequently, the terminology and jargon used in networking are complex and confusing. To master such complexity, it is important to focus on understanding concepts and terminology.

The text, which focuses on concepts, is divided into four parts. Chapters in the first part describe data transmission and modems, those in the second part cover packet communication, those in the third explain internetworking, and those in the fourth examine how network applications operate.

Chapter Contents

2

Motivation And Tools

2.1 Introduction

Before examining underlying network technologies, it will be instructive to consider the motivation for networking and internetworking, and to examine some of the services that such systems provide. In addition to reviewing some of the early motivations, this chapter discusses the size and rapid growth of the Internet, and introduces a few basic tools that can be used to explore networks.

2.2 Resource Sharing

Some of the earliest computer networks were built to extend existing computing facilities. For example, networks were devised that allowed multiple computers to access a shared peripheral device such as a printer or a disk. That is, instead of attaching a peripheral device to a single computer, the device was attached to a network, which allowed access from any computer attached to the network. The motivations for large-scale data networking did not arise from the desire to share peripheral devices or even to provide communication that humans would use directly. Instead, the first networks were designed to share large-scale computational power.

To understand the problem, it is important to know that early digital computers were extremely expensive and scarce. As computer technologies evolved, new computers with more computational power and larger storage capabilities emerged. The U.S. government, which funds much of the science and engineering research, realized that computers were crucial to advances in science and technology. Because computers were used to analyze data from experiments, the programs often ran for hours or even days. The government budget for research was insufficient to provide computers for all scientists and engineers.

The U.S. Department of Defense *Advanced Research Projects Agency* (*ARPA*) was especially concerned about the lack of high-powered computers. Many of the ARPA research projects needed access to the latest equipment. Each research group wanted one of each new computer type. By the latter 1960s, it became obvious that the ARPA budget could not keep up with demand. As an alternative, ARPA started investigating data networking. Instead of placing multiple computers at each research site, the agency decided to give each group one computer, interconnect the computer with a data network, and devise software that would allow a researcher to use whichever computer was best suited to perform a given task.

When ARPA began its networking project, it faced many challenges. No one knew how to build a large, efficient data network or the application programs to use such a network. In fact, many people thought it was impossible. Others said that even if it were possible, doing so would be a waste of government research money. Even some computer scientists were skeptical.

The ARPA networking research turned out to be revolutionary. ARPA had chosen to follow a relatively new approach that became the basis for all future data networks†. ARPA gathered some of the best minds available, focused them on networking research, and hired contractors to turn the designs into a working system called the *ARPANET*. Finally, ARPA continued the project by funding research on alternative technologies, network applications, and a technology known as *internetworking*.

By the 1970s, internetworking had become the focus of ARPA research, and the early *Internet* had emerged. Research continued into the 1980s, with the Internet becoming a commercial success in the 1990s. Today, most businesses use the Internet for communication with other businesses as well as communication with customers.

2.3 Growth Of The Internet

The Internet has grown from the early research prototype to a global communication system that reaches all countries of the world. However, the size is not as surprising as the rate of growth. For example, Figure 2.1 illustrates how the Internet has grown. The figure contains a graph of the number of computers attached to the Internet as a function of the years from 1981 through 2000.

The graph in Figure 2.1 uses a linear scale in which the y-axis represents values from zero through eighty million. Linear plots can be deceptive because they hide small details. For example, the graph in Figure 2.1 hides details about early Internet growth, making it appear that the Internet did not start to grow until approximately 1990, and that all growth occurred in the last few years, with the biggest change occurring in 2000. In fact, the average rate of new computers being added to the Internet reached more than one per second in 1998.

Despite the graph, the growth did not start in recent years. To understand the early growth rate, look at the plot in Figure 2.2.

---

†The approach is known as *packet switching*; Chapter 7 introduces the concept, and later chapters examine it in great detail.

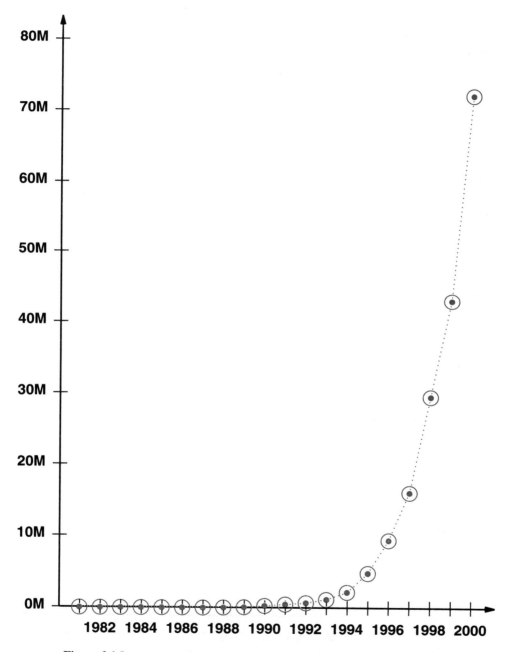

Figure 2.1 Internet growth measured by the number of computers attached to
the Internet in each year from 1981 though 2000. The y-axis is
labeled in millions of computers.

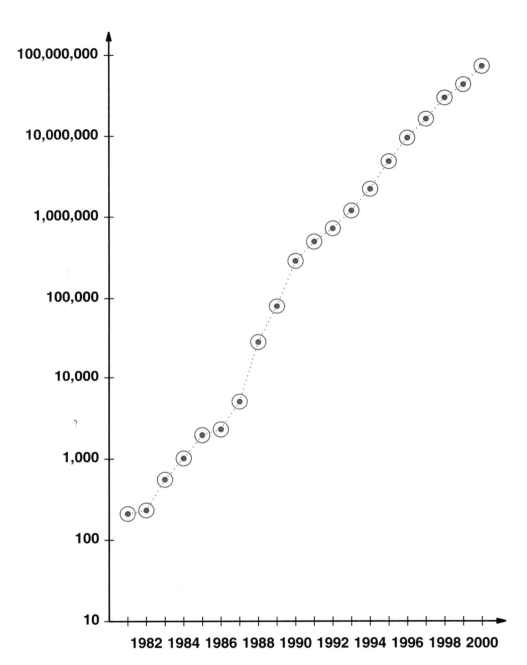

Figure 2.2 Internet growth from 1981 through 2000 plotted on a log scale illustrates the exponential growth.

The graph in Figure 2.2 uses a log scale in which the position on the y-axis is proportional to the log of the number being represented. That is, values along the axis represent powers of ten, with the first tick mark representing *10*, the second representing *100*, and so on.

When plotted on log-scale as in Figure 2.2, the growth appears approximately linear, meaning that the Internet has experienced exponential growth over two decades. That is, the Internet has been doubling in size every nine to twelve months.

2.4 Probing The Internet

How are the plots in Figures 2.1 and 2.2 obtained? In the early days when the Internet consisted of a dozen sites, the size could be determined manually. Now, an automated tool is required (i.e., a computer program that sends messages to remote hosts and evaluates the responses). The program begins by walking through the Domain Name System — the system that stores names for computers such as www.yahoo.com along with the computer's address — and then uses a program that tests to see whether the computer is currently online. Tools used to probe the Internet are also available to users.

One of the simplest probing tools consists of a program known as *ping*†. When a user invokes ping, the user must specify an argument that gives the name or the numeric address of a remote computer on the Internet. For example, a user might invoke ping with an argument that specifies computer *www.netbook.cs.purdue.edu*:

```
ping www.netbook.cs.purdue.edu
```

The ping program sends a message to the specified computer and then waits a short time for a response. If a response arrives, ping reports to the user that the computer is alive; otherwise, ping reports that the computer is not responding. For example, the following output may appear‡:

```
leo.eg.bucknell.edu is alive
```

Some versions of ping provide options that allow the user to specify the size of the packet sent, compute the round trip time (i.e., the time between sending a message and receiving a response), and repeatedly send one message per second until the program is stopped. Figure 2.3 shows an example of ping output with the timing and repetition options turned on. The example was run from the author's workstation to destination *www.sears.com*.

---

†Chapter 23 explains the exact details and the protocols used by the ping program and others tools described in this chapter.

‡The domain name that appears in the output differs from the name the user entered because *www.netbook.cs.purdue.edu* is merely an alias for *leo.eg.bucknell.edu*.

```
PING sears.com: 56 data bytes
64 bytes from 32.97.168.129: icmp_seq=0. time=49. ms
64 bytes from 32.97.168.129: icmp_seq=1. time=50. ms
64 bytes from 32.97.168.129: icmp_seq=2. time=48. ms
64 bytes from 32.97.168.129: icmp_seq=3. time=50. ms
64 bytes from 32.97.168.129: icmp_seq=4. time=48. ms
----sears.com PING Statistics----
5 packets transmitted, 5 packets received, 0% packet loss
round-trip (ms)   min/avg/max = 48/49/50
```

> **Figure 2.3** Example output from the ping program run on the author's works-
> tation. The destination was www.sears.com, and the program was
> manually interrupted after five responses were received.

2.5 Interpreting A Ping Response

In Figure 2.3, ping sends one request each second, and produces one line of output for each response received. The output tells the size of the packet received, the sequence number, and the round-trip time in milliseconds. When the user interrupts the program, ping produces a summary that specifies the number of packets sent and received, packet loss, and the minimum, mean, and maximum round-trip times.

The output in the figure also shows another interesting feature. Although the author specified *www.sears.com* as the destination computer, ping lists the computer's name as *sears.com*. Chapter 29 discusses computer names in detail. For now, it is sufficient to know that *www.sears.com* is merely an alias for computer *sears.com*.

The output in Figure 2.3 shows an average round-trip time of 49 milliseconds, typical when the Internet is not congested. As a comparison, Figure 2.4 shows the round-trip time from the author's workstation to a site on the west coast (the University of California at Berkeley), and Figure 2.5 shows the round-trip time for a site on the east coast (MIT in Cambridge, Massachusetts), all taken on the same day at nearly the same time. When the measurement was taken, the path to MIT was experiencing congestion which increased delays substantially; measurements a few hours later produced a much lower round-trip time to the same destination.

```
PING amber.Berkeley.EDU: 56 data bytes
64 bytes from amber.Berkeley.EDU (128.32.25.12): icmp_seq=0. time=53. ms
64 bytes from amber.Berkeley.EDU (128.32.25.12): icmp_seq=1. time=53. ms
64 bytes from amber.Berkeley.EDU (128.32.25.12): icmp_seq=2. time=54. ms
64 bytes from amber.Berkeley.EDU (128.32.25.12): icmp_seq=3. time=53. ms
64 bytes from amber.Berkeley.EDU (128.32.25.12): icmp_seq=4. time=55. ms
----amber.Berkeley.EDU PING Statistics----
5 packets transmitted, 5 packets received, 0% packet loss
round-trip (ms)  min/avg/max = 53/53/55
```

Figure   2.4 Example output from the ping program for destination
www.berkeley.edu, which is located on the west coast. Round-
trip times are only slightly higher than those reported in Figure
2.3.

```
PING DANDELION-PATCH.MIT.EDU: 56 data bytes
64 bytes from DANDELION-PATCH.MIT.EDU (18.181.0.31): icmp_seq=0. time=176. ms
64 bytes from DANDELION-PATCH.MIT.EDU (18.181.0.31): icmp_seq=1. time=234. ms
64 bytes from DANDELION-PATCH.MIT.EDU (18.181.0.31): icmp_seq=2. time=302. ms
64 bytes from DANDELION-PATCH.MIT.EDU (18.181.0.31): icmp_seq=3. time=165. ms
64 bytes from DANDELION-PATCH.MIT.EDU (18.181.0.31): icmp_seq=4. time=208. ms
----DANDELION-PATCH.MIT.EDU PING Statistics----
5 packets transmitted, 5 packets received, 0% packet loss
round-trip (ms)  min/avg/max = 165/217/302
```

Figure   2.5 Example output from the ping program for destination
www.mit.edu, a location on the east coast. Round-trip times are
significantly higher than in previous examples.

It may seem that the ping program is too simplistic to be useful. Even with options turned on, the round-trip times provide little information to the average user. For
example, ping cannot explain why the time required to reach MIT is higher than the
time to reach other distant locations. More important, it appears ping has little to offer
as a tool to debug network failures because output occurs only when a computer
responds successfully. When no response is received, ping cannot help determine the
reason. The remote computer could be turned off, disconnected from the network, its
network interface could have failed, or it could be running software that does not
respond to ping. The local computer could be disconnected from the network, the network to which the remote computer attaches could have failed, or the problem could be
caused by the failure of an intermediate computer or network. Finally, ping sometimes
fails because the network has become so congested with traffic that delays are unreason-
ably long. Ping has no way to determine the cause of the problem.

Another reason why ping may fail to generate a response is less subtle: some companies configure their site to reject ping packets. The motivation for disabling ping is security — if a corporation allows ping traffic to enter its site, the site becomes susceptible to a *denial-of-service* or *flooding* attack in which so many ping packets arrive that the company's networks and computers cannot respond to legitimate requests. To avoid such attacks, the company merely rejects ping packets before they enter.

You may be surprised to learn that despite its limitations, ping is heavily used as a diagnostic tool. In fact, network administrators often run ping as soon as they learn of a failure. They use ping to determine which parts of the network are still operating correctly and which have failed. The results help them pinpoint the failure quickly.

2.6 Tracing A Route

Network administrators use another tool, *traceroute*, to determine the intermediate computers along the path to a remote destination. Like ping, traceroute takes an argument that specifies a remote computer name or address. For example, the following command will trace a path from the user's computer to *www.netbook.cs.purdue.edu*:

```
traceroute www.netbook.cs.purdue.edu
```

Traceroute determines the intermediate computers along a path to the destination†, and prints one line for each. For example, Figure 2.6 shows the output from traceroute with the destination www.mit.edu.

```
traceroute to DANDELION-PATCH.MIT.EDU (18.181.0.31), 40 byte packets
 1  cisco1 (128.10.2.250)   2 ms   1 ms   2 ms
 2  cisco-tel-252.tcom.purdue.edu (128.210.252.22)   2 ms   1 ms   1 ms
 3  abilene.tcom.purdue.edu (192.5.40.10)   6 ms   8 ms   7 ms
 4  clev-ipls.abilene.ucaid.edu (198.32.8.26)   14 ms   14 ms   12 ms
 5  nycm-clev.abilene.ucaid.edu (198.32.8.30)   24 ms   27 ms   24 ms
 6  192.5.89.45 (192.5.89.45)   31 ms   34 ms   35 ms
 7  192.5.89.10 (192.5.89.10)   33 ms   33 ms   33 ms
 8  NW12-RTR-FDDI.MIT.EDU (18.168.0.16)   59 ms   34 ms   33 ms
 9  DANDELION-PATCH.MIT.EDU (18.181.0.31)   62 ms   *   79 ms
```

Figure 2.6 Example output from traceroute run on the author's workstation to destination www.mit.edu, which is an alias for computer dandelion-patch.mit.edu.

Traceroute provides more information than ping. For example, the figure shows nine lines of output for the path between the author's workstation and the destination computer at MIT. One line corresponds to each of eight intermediate computers, and one corresponds to the final destination itself. In network jargon, we say that the destination is nine *hops* away from the source. Traceroute determined that computer *www* at U.C. Berkeley is thirteen hops away from the author's computer. Interestingly, tra-

---

†We will learn in Chapter 17 that the intermediate computers are called *routers*.

ceroute cannot be used for all destinations because some network administrators choose to disable it to prevent outsiders from obtaining detailed information about their architecture.

2.7 Summary

The Advanced Research Projects Agency (ARPA) funded much of the early investigations into networking as a way to share computation resources among ARPA researchers. Later, ARPA shifted its focus to internetworking and started the Internet, which has been growing exponentially for many years.

Some of the tools used to probe the Internet are available to users. The ping program sends a message to a remote computer and reports whether the computer responds; the traceroute program identifies intermediate computers along a path to a remote destination.

Ping and traceroute software is included in many operating systems; source code for more advanced versions is as well. For example, one can find several versions for the Windows operating system on site:

http://www.shareware.com/

To access traceroute via the Web, contact:

http://www.net.cmu.edu/cgi-bin/netops.cgi

EXERCISES

2.1 Use the ping program to test whether you can reach computers on your local network.

2.2 If your version of ping reports the time required to obtain a response, experiment to find out if the network delays vary during the day.

2.3 Use ping to measure the round-trip times to destinations on the Internet (e.g., to Web sites). What is the maximum round-trip time you encounter?

2.4 Experiment with the packet size option in ping. How does packet size affect round-trip time?

2.5 Compare output from the ping program for a computer that is turned off with the output for a non-existent address (e.g., *10.0.0.50*). Do they differ?

2.6 Use the traceroute program to find the number of hops between your computer and remote destinations (e.g., to well-known web sites). What is the maximum number of hops you can find?

2.7 Compare round-trip times reported by ping to the number of hops reported by traceroute to a set of destinations. Is there a correlation between a longer delay and a higher hop count?

2.8 Internet technology is documented in a series of reports known as *Request For Comments* (*RFC*). RFC 2151, which can be found on the CD-ROM that accompanies this text, describes tools available on the Internet. What tools does the RFC document describe that are not described in this chapter?

Chapter Contents

3

Network Programming And Applications

3.1 Introduction

The previous chapter mentions some of the services that a network provides, discusses the size and growth of the Internet, and explains some of the measurement tools. Although this text is not about programming, this chapter describes computer networks from a programmer's point of view. After briefly outlining the network facilities available to a programmer, the chapter examines example applications that use a network. Later chapters explain how the underlying network supports these applications.

A single chapter cannot cover all aspects of network programming. However, this chapter will demonstrate an important idea:

> *A programmer can create Internet application software without understanding the underlying network technology or communication protocols.*

To demonstrate the point, the chapter introduces a small set of library functions that a programmer can use, and shows how the library functions can be used to write network applications. The example code from the chapter is available on the CD-ROM and the Web site, and students are encouraged to modify the examples or write additional applications. Later chapters explain the underlying details and show how to create applications without using our library code.

3.2 Network Communication

Although a data network transfers data from one point to another, the network it-self is passive. That is, the network neither generates nor understands the data being sent. In fact, the network does not contain any facilities to process information. In-stead, all data processing is performed by application programs.

When applications use a network, they do so in pairs — the pair uses the network merely to exchange messages. For example, imagine a distributed database service that allows remote users to access a central database. Such a service requires two applica-tions, one running on the computer that has the database and the other running on a re-mote computer. The application on the remote computer sends a request to the applica-tion running on the database computer. When the request arrives, the application run-ning on the database computer consults the database and returns a response. Only the two applications understand the message format and meaning.

3.3 Client-Server Computing

How can a pair of programs find each other in a network as large as the Internet? Like most networks, the Internet uses a straightforward mechanism: one application starts first and waits for the other application to contact it. The second application must know the location where the first application is waiting.

The arrangement in which a network application waits for contact from another ap-plication is known as the *client-server paradigm* or as *client-server computing*. Chapter 26 explains client-server interaction in more detail, and Chapter 27 discusses a set of functions available to client and server software on many operating systems. For now, it is sufficient to understand the concept and basic terminology.

The program that waits for contact is called a *server* and the program that initiates contact is known as a *client*. To initiate contact, a client must know where the server is running, and must specify the location to the network software.

How does a client specify the location of a server? In the Internet, a location is given by a pair of identifiers:

(computer, application)

where *computer* identifies the computer on which the server is running, and *application* identifies a particular application program on that computer. When sent across the In-ternet, the two values are represented as binary numbers. However, humans do not deal with the binary representation directly. Instead, the values are also given alphabetic names. Humans enter the names, and the network software includes functions that translate each name to a corresponding binary value automatically.

3.4 Communication Paradigm

Most Internet applications follow the same basic sequence of operations when they communicate.

- The server application starts first, and waits for contact from a client.
- The client contacts the server by specifying its location and requesting communication.
- The client and server exchange messages.
- After they finish sending data, the client and server each send an *end-of-file* to terminate communication.

Our library contains functions that make each of these steps possible.

3.5 An Example Application Program Interface

So far, we have discussed the interaction between two applications at a conceptual level. We will now consider a detailed implementation. Computer scientists use the term *Application Program Interface (API)* to describe the set of operations available to an application programmer. The API specifies the arguments for each operation as well as the semantics.

To demonstrate network programming, we have devised a straightforward API for network communication. After describing the API, we will consider applications that use it. Figure 3.1 lists the seven functions that an application can call.

Operation	Meaning
await_contact	used by a server to wait for contact from a client
make_contact	used by a client to contact a server
cname_to_comp	used to translate a computer name to an equivalent internal binary value
appname_to_appnum	used to translate a program name to an equivalent internal binary value
send	used by either client or server to send data
recv	used by either client or server to receive data
send_eof	used by both client and server after they have finished sending data

Figure 3.1 An example API consisting of seven operations. These seven functions are sufficient for most network applications.†

---

†Functions *send* and *recv* are supplied directly by the operating system; other functions in the API consist of library routines that we have written.

3.6 An Intuitive Look At The API

A server begins by calling *await_contact* to wait for contact from a client. The client begins by calling *make_contact* to establish contact. Once the client has contacted the server, the two can exchange messages with *send* and *recv*. The two applications must be programmed to know whether to send or receive — if both sides try to receive without sending, they will block forever.

After it finishes sending data, an application calls *send_eof* to send the end-of-file condition. On the other side, *recv* returns a value of zero to indicate that the end-of-file has been reached. For example, if the client calls *send_eof*, the server will find a zero return value from its call to *recv*. Once both sides have invoked *send_eof*, communication is terminated.

A trivial example will help explain the example API. Consider an application in which the client contacts a server, sends a single request, and receives a single reply. Figure 3.2 illustrates the sequence of API calls that the client and server make for such an interaction.

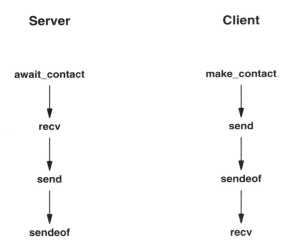

Figure 3.2 Illustration of the API calls used for a trivial interaction. The client sends one request and receives one reply.

3.7 Definition Of The API

To keep our API independent of particular operating systems and network software, we define three data types, and use those types throughout the code. Figure 3.3 lists the type names and their meanings.

Type Name	Meaning
appnum	A binary value used to identify an application
computer	A binary value used to identify a computer
connection	A value used to identify the connection between a client and server

Figure 3.3 The three type names used in our example API. On a given computer these types are defined to be integers of a specific size.

Using the three type names in Figure 3.3 we can precisely define the example API. For each function, the C-like declarations below list the type of each argument as well as the type the function returns.

3.7.1 The Await_Contact Function

A server calls function *await_contact* to wait for contact from a client.

```
connection await_contact(appnum a)
```

The call takes one argument of type *appnum* and returns a value of type *connection*. The argument specifies a number that identifies the server application; a client must specify the same number when contacting the server. The server uses the return value (type *connection*) to transfer data.

3.7.2 The Make_Contact Function

A client calls function *make_contact* to establish contact with a server.

```
connection make_contact(computer c, appnum a)
```

The call takes two arguments that identify a computer on which the server is running and the application number that the server is using on that computer. The client uses the return value, which is of type *connection*, to transfer data.

3.7.3 The Appname_to_appnum Function

Clients and servers both use *appname_to_appnum* to translate from a human-readable name for a service to an internal binary value. The service names are standardized throughout the Internet (e.g., www denotes the World Wide Web).

```
appnum appname_to_appnum(char *a)
```

The call takes one argument of type string (C uses the declaration *char* * to denote a string) and returns an equivalent binary value of type *appnum*.

3.7.4 The Cname_to_comp Function

Clients call *cname_to_comp* to convert from a human-readable computer name to the internal binary value.

> computer cname_to_comp(char *c)

The call takes one argument of type string (*char* *), and returns an equivalent binary value of type *computer*.

3.7.5 The Send Function

Both clients and servers use *send* to transfer data across the network.

> int send(connection con, char *buffer, int length, int flags)

The call takes four arguments. The first argument specifies a connection previously established with *await_contact* or *make_contact*, the second is the address of a buffer containing data to send, the third argument gives the length of the data in bytes (octets), and the fourth argument is zero for normal transfer. *Send* returns the number of bytes transferred, or a negative value if an error occurred. Also see *send_eof*, which is used to send *end-of-file* after all data has been sent.

3.7.6 The Recv And Recvln Functions

Both clients and servers use *recv* to access data that arrives across the network.

> int recv(connection con, char *buffer, int length, int flags)

The call takes four arguments. The first argument specifies a connection previously established with *await_contact* or *make_contact*, the second is the address of a buffer into which the data should be placed, the third argument gives the size of the buffer in bytes (octets), and the fourth argument is zero for normal transfer. *Recv* returns the number of bytes that were placed in the buffer, zero to indicate that *end-of-file* has been reached, or a negative value to indicate that an error occurred.

In the example code, we also use a library function *recvln* that repeatedly calls *recv* until an entire line of text has been received. The definition of *recvln* is:

> int recvln(connection con, char *buffer, int length)

3.7.7 The Send_eof Function

Both the client and server must use *send_eof* after sending data to inform the other side that no further transmission will occur. On the other side, the *recv* function returns zero when it receives the end-of-file.

> int send_eof(connection con)

The call has one argument that specifies a connection previously established with *await_contact* or *make_contact*. The function returns a negative value to indicate that an error occurred, and a non-negative value otherwise.

3.7.8 Summary Of API Types

Figure 3.4 summarizes the arguments used for each function in the example API. The table shows the type of each argument as well as the return type.

Function Name	Type Returned	Type of arg 1	Type of arg 2	Type of args 3 & 4
await_contact	connection	appnum		
make_contact	connection	computer	appnum	
appname_to_appnum	appnum	char *		
cname_to_comp	computer	char *		
send	int	connection	char *	int
recv	int	connection	char *	int
send_eof	int	connection		

Figure 3.4 A summary of argument and return types for the example API.

The next sections contain examples of application programs that illustrate how client and server software uses our API to communicate†.

3.8 Code For An Echo Application

The first application we will consider is trivial: the server merely echoes back all the data it receives. The client repeatedly prompts the user for a line of input, sends the line to the server, and then displays whatever the server sends back.

Like all the applications described in this chapter, the echo application operates across a network. That is, the client and server programs can run on separate comput-

---

†To reduce the size and make the code easier to read, the programs in this chapter use command-line arguments without checking their validity.

ers. As Figure 3.5 illustrates, the software can be used on arbitrary computers connected to the Internet.

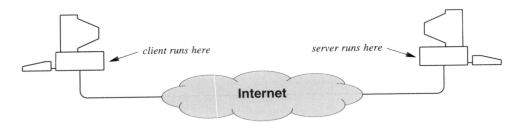

Figure 3.5 Illustration of the echo application, which can be used on any two
computers connected to the Internet. The client program runs on
one computer and the server program runs on another.

To invoke the server, a user must choose an application number between 1 and
32767 that is not being used by any other applications, and specify the number as a
command line argument. For example, suppose someone using computer
lancelot.cs.purdue.edu chooses 20000 as the application number. The server is invoked
by the command:

echoserver 20000

If some other application is using number 20000, the server emits an appropriate error
message and exits; the user must choose another number.

Once the server has been invoked, the client is invoked by specifying the name of
the computer on which the server is running and the application number the server is
using. For example, to contact the server described above, a user on an arbitrary computer in the Internet can enter the command:

echoclient lancelot.cs.purdue.edu 20000

3.8.1 Example Echo Server Code

File *echoserver.c* contains code for the echo server.

```
/* echoserver.c */

#include <stdlib.h>
#include <stdio.h>
#include <cnaiapi.h>
```

```
#define BUFFSIZE                     256

/*-------------------------------------------------------------------------
 *
 * Program: echoserver
 * Purpose: wait for a connection from an echoclient and echo data
 * Usage:   echoserver <appnum>
 *
 *-------------------------------------------------------------------------
 */
int
main(int argc, char *argv[])
{
        connection      conn;
        int             len;
        char            buff[BUFFSIZE];

        if (argc != 2) {
                (void) fprintf(stderr, "usage: %s <appnum>\n", argv[0]);
                exit(1);
        }


        /* wait for a connection from an echo client */

        conn = await_contact((appnum) atoi(argv[1]));
        if (conn < 0)
                exit(1);

        /* iterate, echoing all data received until end of file */

        while((len = recv(conn, buff, BUFFSIZE, 0)) > 0)
                (void) send(conn, buff, len, 0);
        send_eof(conn);
        return 0;
}
```

As we have seen, the server takes a single command-line argument that specifies the application number to use. In C, command-line arguments are passed to the program as an array of strings (*argv*), along with an integer count of arguments (*argc*). The code extracts the command-line argument from *argv[1]*, and calls the standard C function *atoi* to convert the value from an ASCII string to binary. It then passes the result as an argument to *await_contact*. Once the call to *await_contact* returns, the server repeatedly calls *recv* to receive data from the client and *send* to transmit the same data back. The iteration terminates when *recv* finds an end-of-file and returns zero. At that time, the server sends an end-of-file and exits.

3.8.2 Example Echo Client Code

File *echoclient.c* contains code for an echo client application.

```
/* echoclient.c */

#include <stdlib.h>
#include <stdio.h>
#include <cnaiapi.h>


#define BUFFSIZE            256
#define INPUT_PROMPT        "Input   > "
#define RECEIVED_PROMPT     "Received> "

int readln(char *, int);

/*----------------------------------------------------------------------
 *
 * Program: echoclient
 * Purpose: contact echoserver, send user input and print server response
 * Usage:   echoclient <compname> [appnum]
 * Note:    Appnum is optional. If not specified the standard echo appnum
 *          (7) is used.
 *
 *----------------------------------------------------------------------
 */
int
main(int argc, char *argv[])
{
        computer          comp;
        appnum            app;
        connection        conn;
        char              buff[BUFFSIZE];
        int               expect, received, len;

        if (argc < 2 || argc > 3) {
                (void) fprintf(stderr, "usage: %s <compname> [appnum]\n",
                                argv[0]);
                exit(1);
        }
```

```
/* convert the arguments to binary format comp and appnum */

comp = cname_to_comp(argv[1]);
if (comp == -1)
        exit(1);

if (argc == 3)
        app = (appnum) atoi(argv[2]);
else
        if ((app = appname_to_appnum("echo")) == -1)
                exit(1);

/* form a connection with the echoserver */

conn = make_contact(comp, app);
if (conn < 0)
        exit(1);

(void) printf(INPUT_PROMPT);
(void) fflush(stdout);

/* iterate: read input from the user, send to the server,        */
/*          receive reply from the server, and display for user */

while((len = readln(buff, BUFFSIZE)) > 0) {

        /* send the input to the echoserver */

        (void) send(conn, buff, len, 0);
        (void) printf(RECEIVED_PROMPT);
        (void) fflush(stdout);

        /* read and print same no. of bytes from echo server */

        expect = len;
        for (received = 0; received < expect;) {
           len = recv(conn, buff, (expect - received) < BUFFSIZE ?
                        (expect - received) : BUFFSIZE, 0);
                if (len < 0) {
                        send_eof(conn);
                        return 1;
                }
                (void) write(STDOUT_FILENO, buff, len);
                received += len;
```

```
              }
              (void) printf("\n");
              (void) printf(INPUT_PROMPT);
              (void) fflush(stdout);
        }

        /* iteration ends when EOF found on stdin */

        (void) send_eof(conn);
        (void) printf("\n");
        return 0;
}
```

The client program takes either one or two arguments. The first argument specifies the name of a computer on which the server is running. If present, the second argument specifies the application number the server is using. If the second argument is missing, the client calls appname_to-appnum with argument *echo*.

After converting the arguments to binary form, the client passes them to *make_contact*, which contacts the server. Once contact has been established, the client issues a prompt to the user and enters a loop that reads a line of input, sends the line to the server, reads the reply from the server, and prints the reply for the user followed by a new prompt. When the client reaches the end of input (i.e., *readln* returns a zero value), the client calls *send_eof* to inform the server, and exits.

Several details complicate the code. First, the client calls a function, *readln*, to read one line of input. Second, the client tests the return value from each function call, and exits when the value indicates an error occurred. Third, the client calls *fflush* to ensure that output is displayed immediately rather than being accumulated in a buffer. Fourth, and most significant, the client does not merely issue one call to *recv* each time it receives data from the server. Instead, the client enters a loop that repeatedly calls *recv* until it has received as many bytes as it sent.

The use of multiple calls to *recv* brings up a key point about our API:

> *A receiver cannot assume that data will arrive in the same size pieces as it was sent; a call to* recv *may return less data than was sent in a call to* send.

Later chapters explain why *recv* behaves as it does: networks divide data into small ''packets''. Thus, an application may receive the data from one packet at a time. Surprisingly, the opposite is also true: even if a sender calls *send* repeatedly, the network software may receive data from many packets before the application calls *recv*. In such cases, *recv* will return all the data at once.

3.9 Code For A Chat Application

The second application we will consider is a simplified form of the *chat* facility. On the Internet, chat allows a group of users to communicate by entering text messages that are displayed on each others' screens. Our software provides a simplified version of chat that works between a single pair of users — when one user enters text, the text is displayed on the other user's screen, and vice versa. Furthermore, like the echo application described earlier, our chat software can be used between any computers connected to the Internet. One user begins by choosing an application number and running the server. For example, suppose a user on computer *excalibur.cs.purdue.edu* runs the server:

chatserver 25000

A user on another computer can invoke the client, which contacts the server:

chatclient excalibur.cs.purdue.edu 25000

To keep the code as small as possible, we have chosen a scheme that requires users to take turns entering text. Both the client and server issue a prompt when the user on that side is expected to enter a line of text. The user on the client side is prompted for input first. When a line of text has been received, the client sends the line to the server and the roles reverse. Users alternate entering text until one of them sends an end-of-file.

The code itself is straightforward. The server begins by waiting for contact from the client. It then enters a loop in which it obtains and displays a line of text from the client, prompts the local user, reads a line of input from the keyboard, and sends the line to the client side. Thus, until it receives an end-of-file, the server iterates between displaying output from the client and sending keyboard input to the client.

The client begins by contacting the server. Once communication has been established, the client also enters a loop. During each iteration, the client prompts the local user to enter a line of text, reads a line from the keyboard, sends the line to the server, and then receives and displays a line of text from the server. Thus, the client continues to alternate between sending a line of text that the user enters and displaying a line of text from the server.

3.9.1 Example Chat Server Code

File *chatserver.c* contains the code for the chat server.

```
/* chatserver.c */

#include <stdlib.h>
#include <stdio.h>
#include <cnaiapi.h>

#define BUFFSIZE                256
#define INPUT_PROMPT            "Input   > "
#define RECEIVED_PROMPT         "Received> "

int recvln(connection, char *, int);
int readln(char *, int);

/*----------------------------------------------------------------------
 *
 * Program: chatserver
 * Purpose: wait for a connection from a chatclient & allow users to chat
 * Usage:   chatserver <appnum>
 *
 *----------------------------------------------------------------------
 */
int
main(int argc, char *argv[])
{
        connection      conn;
        int             len;
        char            buff[BUFFSIZE];

        if (argc != 2) {
                (void) fprintf(stderr, "usage: %s <appnum>\n", argv[0]);
                exit(1);
        }

        (void) printf("Chat Server Waiting For Connection.\n");

        /* wait for a connection from a chatclient */

        conn = await_contact((appnum) atoi(argv[1]));
        if (conn < 0)
                exit(1);

        (void) printf("Chat Connection Established.\n");
```

```
/* iterate, reading from the client and the local user */

while((len = recvln(conn, buff, BUFFSIZE)) > 0) {
        (void) printf(RECEIVED_PROMPT);
        (void) fflush(stdout);
        (void) write(STDOUT_FILENO, buff, len);

        /* send a line to the chatclient */

        (void) printf(INPUT_PROMPT);
        (void) fflush(stdout);
        if ((len = readln(buff, BUFFSIZE)) < 1)
                break;
        buff[len - 1] = '\n';
        (void) send(conn, buff, len, 0);
}

/* iteration ends when EOF found on stdin or chat connection */

(void) send_eof(conn);
(void) printf("\nChat Connection Closed.\n\n");
return 0;
}
```

Functions, *recvln* and *readln*, simplify the code — they each consist of a loop that iterates until an entire line or end-of-file is encountered. *Recvln* calls *recv* to receive from a network connection, and *readln* calls *read* to read characters from a keyboard.

The overall structure of the chat server is similar to the echo server we examined earlier. Like the echo server, the chat server expects a single command-line argument that is the application number to use. Once contact arrives from a client, the chat server prints a message for the local user, and enters a loop. At each iteration, the server receives a line of text from the network connection, prints the line on the user's screen, reads a line of input from the keyboard, and sends the line over the network. When it detects an end-of-file, the server sends an end-of-file and exits.

3.9.2 Example Chat Client Code

File *chatclient.c* contains the code for the chat client.

```
/* chatclient.c */

#include <stdlib.h>
#include <stdio.h>
#include <cnaiapi.h>

#define BUFFSIZE                256
#define INPUT_PROMPT            "Input    > "
#define RECEIVED_PROMPT         "Received> "

int recvln(connection, char *, int);
int readln(char *, int);

/*-------------------------------------------------------------------------
 *
 * Program: chatclient
 * Purpose: contact a chatserver and allow users to chat
 * Usage:    chatclient <compname> <appnum>
 *
 *-------------------------------------------------------------------------
 */
int
main(int argc, char *argv[])
{
        computer        comp;
        connection      conn;
        char            buff[BUFFSIZE];
        int             len;

        if (argc != 3) {
                (void) fprintf(stderr, "usage: %s <compname> <appnum>\n",
                                argv[0]);
                exit(1);
        }

        /* convert the compname to binary form comp */

        comp = cname_to_comp(argv[1]);
        if (comp == -1)
                exit(1);

        /* make a connection to the chatserver */

        conn = make_contact(comp, (appnum) atoi(argv[2]));
```

```
if (conn < 0)
        exit(1);


(void) printf("Chat Connection Established.\n");
(void) printf(INPUT_PROMPT);
(void) fflush(stdout);


/* iterate, reading from local user and then from chatserver */

while((len = readln(buff, BUFFSIZE)) > 0) {
        buff[len - 1] = '\n';
        (void) send(conn, buff, len, 0);

        /* receive and print a line from the chatserver */
        if ((len = recvln(conn, buff, BUFFSIZE)) < 1)
                break;
        (void) printf(RECEIVED_PROMPT);
        (void) fflush(stdout);
        (void) write(STDOUT_FILENO, buff, len);

        (void) printf(INPUT_PROMPT);
        (void) fflush(stdout);
}


/* iteration ends when stdin or the connection indicates EOF */

(void) printf("\nChat Connection Closed.\n");
(void) send_eof(conn);
exit(0);
}
```

The client begins by contacting a server. Once communication has been established, the client enters a loop that reads from the keyboard, sends the data to the server, receives a line from the server, and displays the line on the user's screen. The iteration continues until the client receives an end-of-file condition from the server or an end-of-file from the keyboard (a return value of zero). At that time, the client sends an end-of-file and exits.

3.10 Code For A Web Application

The final example application we will consider consists of a client and server for the World Wide Web. To run the server, a user chooses an application number and invokes the server program. For example, if a user on computer *merlin.cs.purdue.edu* chooses application number 27000, the server can be invoked with the command:

> webserver 27000

As usual, the client specifies a computer, a path name, and an application number:

> webclient merlin.cs.purdue.edu /index.html 27000

Although extremely small, our web server follows the standard protocols. Thus, it is possible to use a conventional (i.e., commercially available) web browser to access the server. For example, to use a commercial browser instead of our webclient in the example above, one enters the URL:

> http://merlin.cs.purdue.edu:27000/index.html

To keep our code a short as possible, we make a few simplifying assumptions. For example, the server only supplies three web pages, and none of the pages contains anything except text. Furthermore, each page is hard-wired into the code; the page can only be changed by recompiling the server†.

The most significant limitation of our web application lies in the client. Unlike a conventional web browser, our client code does not understand how to format and display web pages. Instead, the client merely prints the source of the page. Despite the limitation, the client does interoperate with a commercial web server — it can be used to print the source of any page available on the World Wide Web.

3.10.1 Example Web Client Code

File *webclient.c* contains the code for the web client.

```
/* webclient.c */

#include <stdlib.h>
#include <stdio.h>
#include <cnaiapi.h>

#define BUFFSIZE        256


/*----------------------------------------------------------------------
 *
 * Program: webclient
 * Purpose: fetch page from webserver and dump to stdout with headers
 * Usage:   webclient <compname> <path> [appnum]
```

---

†Exercises suggest extending the server code to overcome some of the limitations.

```
 * Note:      Appnum is optional. If not specified the standard www appnum
 *            (80) is used.
 *
 *-----------------------------------------------------------------------
 */
int
main(int argc, char *argv[])
{

        computer        comp;
        appnum          app;
        connection      conn;
        char            buff[BUFFSIZE];
        int             len;

        if (argc < 3 || argc > 4) {
                (void) fprintf(stderr, "%s%s%s", "usage: ", argv[0],
                                " <compane> <path> [appnum]\n");
                exit(1);
        }

        /* convert arguments to binary computer and appnum */

        comp = cname_to_comp(argv[1]);
        if (comp == -1)
                exit(1);

        if (argc == 4)
                app = (appnum) atoi(argv[3]);
        else
                if ((app = appname_to_appnum("www")) == -1)
                        exit(1);

        /* contact the web server */

        conn = make_contact(comp, app);
        if (conn < 0)
                exit(1);

        /* send an HTTP/1.0 request to the webserver */

        len = sprintf(buff, "GET %s HTTP/1.0\r\n\r\n", argv[2]);
        (void) send(conn, buff, len, 0);
```

```
        /* dump all data received from the server to stdout */

        while((len = recv(conn, buff, BUFFSIZE, 0)) > 0)
                (void) write(STDOUT_FILENO, buff, len);

        return 0;
}
```

The client code is extremely simple — after establishing communication with the
web server, it sends a request, which must have the form†:

$$\text{GET } /path \text{ HTTP}/1.0 \text{ } CRLF \text{ } CRLF$$

where *path* denotes the name of an item such as *index.html*, and *CRLF* denotes the two
characters carriage return and line feed. After sending the request, the client receives
and prints output from the server.

3.10.2 Example Web Server Code

File *webserver.c* contains the code for a (miniature) web server.

```
/* webserver.c */

#include <stdio.h>
#include <stdlib.h>
#include <time.h>
#include <cnaiapi.h>

#if defined(LINUX) || defined(SOLARIS)
#include <sys/time.h>
#endif

#define BUFFSIZE        256
#define SERVER_NAME     "CNAI Demo Web Server"

#define ERROR_400       "<head></head><body><html><h1>Error 400</h1><p>Th\
e server couldn't understand your request.</html></body>\n"

#define ERROR_404       "<head></head><body><html><h1>Error 404</h1><p>Do\
cument not found.</html></body>\n"

#define HOME_PAGE       "<head></head><body><html><h1>Welcome to the CNAI\
```

---

†Later chapters explain the format in more detail.

```
 Demo Server</h1><p>Why not visit: <ul><li><a href=\"http://netbook.cs.pu\
rdue.edu\">Netbook Home Page</a><li><a href=\"http://www.comerbooks.com\"\
>Comer Books Home Page<a></ul></html></body>\n"

#define TIME_PAGE        "<head></head><body><html><h1>The current date is\
: %s</h1></html></body>\n"

int     recvln(connection, char *, int);
void    send_head(connection, int, int);


/*------------------------------------------------------------------------
 *
 * Program: webserver
 * Purpose: serve hard-coded webpages to web clients
 * Usage:   webserver <appnum>
 *
 *------------------------------------------------------------------------
 */
int
main(int argc, char *argv[])
{

        connection      conn;
        int             n;
        char            buff[BUFFSIZE], cmd[16], path[64], vers[16];
        char            *timestr;
#if defined(LINUX) || defined(SOLARIS)
        struct timeval  tv;
#elif defined(WIN32)
        time_t          tv;
#endif

        if (argc != 2) {
                (void) fprintf(stderr, "usage: %s <appnum>\n", argv[0]);
                exit(1);
        }

        while(1) {

                /* wait for contact from a client on specified appnum */

                conn = await_contact((appnum) atoi(argv[1]));
                if (conn < 0)
                        exit(1);
```

```
        /* read and parse the request line */

        n = recvln(conn, buff, BUFFSIZE);
        sscanf(buff, "%s %s %s", cmd, path, vers);

        /* skip all headers - read until we get \r\n alone */

        while((n = recvln(conn, buff, BUFFSIZE)) > 0) {
                if (n == 2 && buff[0] == '\r' && buff[1] == '\n')
                        break;
        }

        /* check for unexpected end of file */

        if (n < 1) {
                (void) send_eof(conn);
                continue;
        }

        /* check for a request that we cannot understand */

        if (strcmp(cmd, "GET") || (strcmp(vers, "HTTP/1.0") &&
                                    strcmp(vers, "HTTP/1.1"))) {
                send_head(conn, 400, strlen(ERROR_400));
                (void) send(conn, ERROR_400, strlen(ERROR_400),0);
                (void) send_eof(conn);
                continue;
        }

        /* send the requested web page or a "not found" error */

        if (strcmp(path, "/") == 0) {
                send_head(conn, 200, strlen(HOME_PAGE));
                (void) send(conn, HOME_PAGE, strlen(HOME_PAGE),0);
        } else if (strcmp(path, "/time") == 0) {
#if defined(LINUX) || defined(SOLARIS)
                gettimeofday(&tv, NULL);
                timestr = ctime(&tv.tv_sec);
#elif defined(WIN32)
                time(&tv);
                timestr = ctime(&tv);
#endif
                (void) sprintf(buff, TIME_PAGE, timestr);
                send_head(conn, 200, strlen(buff));
```

```
                        (void) send(conn, buff, strlen(buff), 0);
                } else { /* not found */
                        send_head(conn, 404, strlen(ERROR_404));
                        (void) send(conn, ERROR_404, strlen(ERROR_404),0);
                }
                (void) send_eof(conn);
        }
}


/*-----------------------------------------------------------------
 * send_head - send an HTTP 1.0 header with given status and content-len
 *-----------------------------------------------------------------
 */
void
send_head(connection conn, int stat, int len)
{
        char    *statstr, buff[BUFFSIZE];

        /* convert the status code to a string */

        switch(stat) {
        case 200:
                statstr = "OK";
                break;
        case 400:
                statstr = "Bad Request";
                break;
        case 404:
                statstr = "Not Found";
                break;
        default:
                statstr = "Unknown";
                break;
        }

        /*
         * send an HTTP/1.0 response with Server, Content-Length,
         * and Content-Type headers.
         */

        (void) sprintf(buff, "HTTP/1.0 %d %s\r\n", stat, statstr);
        (void) send(conn, buff, strlen(buff), 0);

        (void) sprintf(buff, "Server: %s\r\n", SERVER_NAME);
```

```
        (void) send(conn, buff, strlen(buff), 0);

        (void) sprintf(buff, "Content-Length: %d\r\n", len);
        (void) send(conn, buff, strlen(buff), 0);

        (void) sprintf(buff, "Content-Type: text/html\r\n");
        (void) send(conn, buff, strlen(buff), 0);

        (void) sprintf(buff, "\r\n");
        (void) send(conn, buff, strlen(buff), 0);
}
```

Although the web server may seem more complex than previous examples, most of the complexity results from Web details rather than networking details. In addition to reading and parsing a request, the server must send both a ''header'' and data in the response. The header consists of several lines of text that are terminated by the carriage return and linefeed characters. The header lines are of the form:

> HTTP/1.0 status *status_string CRLF*
> Server: CNAI Demo Server *CRLF*
> Content-Length: *datasize CRLF*
> Content-Type: text/html *CRLF*
> *CRLF*

where *datasize* denotes the size of the data that follows measured in bytes.

Procedure *send_head* handles the chore of generating a header. When *send_head* is called, argument *stat* contains an integer status code and argument *len* specifies the content length. The *switch* statement uses the code to choose an appropriate text message, which is assigned to variable *statstr*. *Send_head* uses the C function *sprintf* to generate the complete header in a buffer, and then calls *send* to transmit the header lines over the connection to the client.

The code is also complicated by error handling — error messages must be sent in a form that a browser can understand. If a request is incorrectly formed, our server generates a *400* error message; if the item specified in the request cannot be found (i.e., the *path* is incorrect), the server generates a *404* message.

Our web server does differs from the previous examples in a significant way: the server program does not exit after satisfying one request. Instead, the server remains running, ready to accept additional requests. That is, the server program consists of an infinite loop that calls *await_contact* to wait for contact from a client. When contact arrives, the server calls *recvln* to receive a request and calls *send* to send a response. The server then goes back to the top of the loop to wait for the next contact. Thus, once it is started, the server runs forever, just like a commercial web server.

3.11 Summary

It is possible for a programmer to create network applications that operate across the global Internet without understanding how networks operate or how the underlying technologies carry the data between computers. The programmer must be given a set of high-level functions that form an Application Program Interface (API). This chapter presented a network API that contains only seven primitives, and reviewed example applications that show the API is sufficient to construct software that correctly interoperates with commercial software.

EXERCISES

3.1   The *echo* service is a standard service available throughout the Internet. It has been assigned application number 7. Use the echo client to test computers in your organization to see if they run a standard echo server.

3.2   Modify the echo server so that instead of exiting after it handles one client, the server waits for another client. Hint: look at the web server.

3.3   Our chat software requires the users to take turns entering text. Rewrite the software to allow either user to type an arbitrary number of lines at any time. Hint: use threads.

3.4   Modify the chat client to send a user name with each message, and modify the server to identify a user when displaying a line of output.

3.5   Extend the above exercise so that instead of sending the user name with each message, the chat client and server exchange user names when they first make contact.

3.6   Why does the example code use a mixture of calls to *write* and various forms of *printf*? Hint: does Windows treat sockets, files, and pipes identically?

3.7   Devise software that permits an *n-way* chat session that allows users to join and leave the session at any time.

3.8   Try the web client program with well-known Internet web servers. To do so, give the server's name, a path of *index.html* or *index.htm*, and application number *80*.

3.9   Add another ''page'' to the web server.

3.10 Modify the web server so it extracts the contents of each page from a file instead of having them hard-wired into the code.

3.11 Expand the previous exercise to recognize file names that end in *.gif* and send them using a *Content-type* header with a value *image/gif* instead of the string *text/html*.

3.12 (advanced) Implement the Common Gateway Interface (CGI) from the specification found at:

http://hoohoo.ncsa.uiuc.edu/cgi/

3.13 (advanced) Extend the web server so it can handle multiple connections concurrently. Hint: use *fork* or *pthread_create*.

Data Transmission

The basics of media, signals, bits, carriers, and modems

Chapter Contents

4

Transmission Media

4.1 Introduction

At the lowest level, all computer communication involves encoding data in a form of energy, and sending the energy across a transmission medium. For example, electric current can be used to transfer data across a wire, or radio waves can be used to carry data through the air. Because hardware devices attached to a computer perform the encoding and decoding of data, programmers and users do not need to know the details of data transmission. However, because a major role of communication software is to handle errors and failures that arise in the underlying hardware, understanding such software requires knowledge of a few basic data transmission concepts.

This section covers the basics of data transmission. The first chapter examines the media that are used for transmission in modern network systems. The next two chapters explain how data can be transferred across such media. Later sections explain how transmission forms the basis of data networking.

4.2 Copper Wires

Conventional computer networks use wires as the primary medium to connect computers because wire is inexpensive and easy to install. Computer networks use copper wire almost exclusively because its low resistance to electric current means signals can travel farther. Thus, network professionals sometimes use the term *copper* as a synonym for *wire*.

The type of wiring used for computer networks is chosen to minimize interference. Interference arises because an electrical signal traveling across a wire acts like a miniature radio station — the wire emits a small amount of electromagnetic energy, which can travel through the air. Furthermore, whenever it encounters another wire, an electromagnetic wave generates a small electric current in the wire. The amount of current generated depends on the strength of the electromagnetic wave and the physical position of the wire. Usually, wires do not come close enough to make interference a problem. For example, if two wires lie near each other at right angles and a signal passes through one of the wires, the current generated in the other is almost undetectable. However, when two wires are placed close together and in parallel, a strong signal sent on one wire will generate a similar signal on the other. Because computers cannot distinguish between signals generated accidentally and normal transmissions, generated current can be strong enough to disrupt or prevent normal communication. Unfortunately, the problem of interference is severe because wires that comprise a data network often are placed in parallel with many other wires. For example, the wires from one computer may lie next to wires from other computers or wires for other networks.

To minimize interference, networks use one of two basic wiring types: *twisted pair* or *coaxial cable*. Twisted pair wiring is also used by telephone systems. The term arises because each wire is coated with an insulating material (e.g., plastic), and then a pair of wires is twisted together as Figure 4.1 shows.

Figure 4.1 Illustration of twisted pair wiring. A plastic coating on the surface of each wire prevents the metal in one wire from touching the metal in the other. The twists help reduce interference.

The simple twists change the electrical properties of the wire, and help make it suitable for use in a network. First, because they limit the electromagnetic energy the wire emits, the twists help prevent electric currents on the wire from radiating energy that interferes with other wires. Second, because they make the pair of wires less susceptible to electromagnetic energy, the twists help prevent signals on other wires from interfering with the pair.

The second type of copper wiring used in networks is coaxial cable (coax), the same type of wiring used for cable TV. Coax provides even more protection from interference than twisted pair. Instead of twisting wires around one another to limit interference, a coaxial cable consists of a single wire surrounded by a heavier metal shield as Figure 4.2 illustrates.

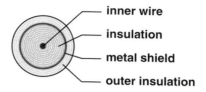

Figure 4.2 Enlarged cross-section of a coaxial cable with major parts identified. Although a coaxial cable is stiffer than a single wire, it can be bent.

The heavy metal shield in a coaxial cable forms a flexible cylinder around the inner wire that provides a barrier to electromagnetic radiation. The barrier isolates the inner wire in two ways: it protects the wire from incoming electromagnetic energy that could cause interference, and keeps signals on the inner wire from radiating electromagnetic energy that could affect other wires. Because it surrounds the center wire uniformly on all sides, the shield in a coaxial cable is especially effective. The cable can be placed parallel to other cables or bent and twisted around corners. The shield always stays in place.

The idea of using a shield to protect wires has also been applied to twisted pair. A *shielded twisted pair* cable consists of a pair of wires surrounded by a metal shield. Each wire is coated with an insulating material, so the metal in one wire does not touch the metal in another — the shield merely forms a barrier that prevents electromagnetic radiation from entering or escaping. The additional shielding provided by coaxial or shielded twisted pair cabling is often used when wires from a network pass near equipment that generates strong electric or magnetic fields (e.g., a large air conditioner).

4.3 Glass Fibers

Computer networks also use flexible glass fibers to transmit data. Known as an *optical fiber*, the medium uses light to transport data. The miniature glass fiber is encased in a plastic jacket which allows the fiber to bend without breaking†. A transmitter at one end of a fiber uses a *light emitting diode* (*LED*) or a *laser* to send pulses of light down the fiber. A receiver at the other end uses a light sensitive transistor to detect the pulses.

Optical fibers have four main advantages over wires. First, because they use light, optical fibers neither cause electrical interference in other cables nor are they susceptible to electrical interference. Second, because glass fibers can be manufactured to reflect most of the light inward, a fiber can carry a pulse of light much farther than a copper wire can carry a signal. Third, because light can encode more information than electrical signals, an optical fiber can carry more information than a wire. Fourth, unlike electricity, which always requires a pair of wires connected into a complete circuit, light can travel from one computer to another over a single fiber.

---

†Although an optical fiber cannot be bent at a right angle, it can be formed into a circle with a radius of less than two inches.

Despite their advantages, optical fibers do have some disadvantages. First, installing a fiber requires special equipment that polishes the ends to allow light to pass
through. Second, if a fiber breaks inside the plastic jacket (e.g., by being bent at a right
angle), finding the location of the problem is difficult. Third, repairing a broken fiber is
difficult because special equipment is needed to join two fibers so that light can pass
through the joint.

4.4 Radio

In addition to its uses for the public broadcast of radio and television programs and
for private communication with devices like portable phones, electromagnetic radiation
can be used to transmit computer data. Informally, a network that uses electromagnetic
radio waves is said to operate at *radio frequency*, and the transmissions are referred to
as *RF* transmissions. Unlike networks that use wires or optical fibers, networks using
RF transmissions do not require a direct physical connection between computers. Instead, each participating computer attaches to an antenna, which can both transmit and
receive RF.

Physically, the antennas used with RF networks may be large or small, depending
on the range desired. For example, an antenna designed to propagate signals several
miles across town may consist of a metal pole approximately two meters long that is
mounted vertically on top of a building. An antenna designed to permit communication
within a building may be small enough to fit inside a portable computer (e.g., less than
twenty centimeters).

4.5 Satellites

Although radio transmissions do not bend around the surface of the earth, RF technology can be combined with satellites to provide communication across longer distances. For example, Figure 4.3 illustrates how a communication satellite in orbit
around the earth can provide a network connection across an ocean. The satellite contains a *transponder* that consists of a radio receiver and transmitter. The transponder
accepts an incoming radio transmission, amplifies it, and transmits the amplified signal
back toward the ground at a slightly different angle than it arrived. A ground station on
one side of the ocean transmits a signal to the satellite, which then sends the signal to a
ground station on the other side. Because placing a communication satellite in orbit is
expensive, a single satellite usually contains multiple transponders that operate independently (typically six to twelve). Each transponder uses a different radio frequency (i.e.,
channel), making it possible for multiple communications to proceed simultaneously.
Furthermore, because a single satellite channel can be shared, it can serve many customers.

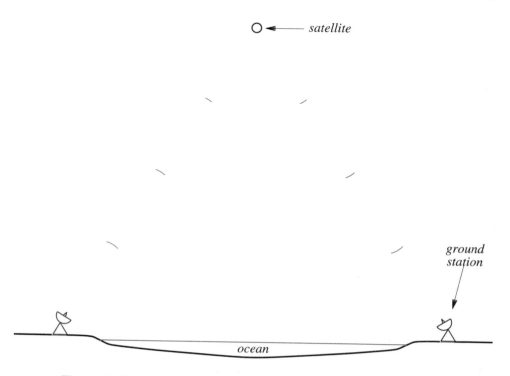

Figure 4.3 Illustration of a satellite used to provide communication across an ocean. The satellite receives radio signals from one ground station, and transmits them to another.

4.6 Geosynchronous Satellites

Communication satellites can be grouped into categories according to the height at which they orbit. The easiest type to understand are known as *geosynchronous* or *geostationary* satellites. The name arises because a geosynchronous satellite is placed in an orbit that is exactly synchronized with the rotation of the earth. Such an orbit is classified as a *Geostationary Earth Orbit (GEO)* because, when viewed from the ground, the satellite appears to remain at exactly the same point in the sky at all times. For example, a geostationary satellite in a circular orbit above the equator over the Atlantic Ocean can be used to relay transmissions between Europe and North America at all times because the satellite remains above the same spot over the ocean.

The laws of physics determine the exact distance from the earth that a satellite must orbit to remain synchronized with the earth's rotation†. The distance required for geosynchronous orbit is 35,785 kilometers or 22,236 miles‡. Engineers sometimes refer to the distance as *high earth orbit*.

---

†See *Kepler's Law* for details.
‡Geosynchronous orbit is about one tenth of the distance to the moon.

Interestingly, there is a limited amount of ''space'' available in the geosynchronous orbit above the equator because communication satellites using a given frequency must be separated from one another to avoid interference. The minimum separation depends on the power of the transmitters, but generally requires an angular separation of between *4* and *8* degrees. Thus, the entire *360*-degree circle above the equator can only hold *45* to *90* satellites.

4.7 Low Earth Orbit Satellites

A second category of communication satellites operate in what is called *Low Earth Orbit* (*LEO*), which means that they orbit a few hundred miles above the earth (typically 200 to 400 miles). The chief disadvantage of a low-altitude orbit lies in the rate at which a satellite must travel. Because their period of rotation is faster than the rotation of the earth, satellites in lower orbits do not stay above a single point on the earth's surface. Instead, an observer, who stands on the earth looking upward through a telescope, sees such satellites move across the sky. In fact, a single satellite can complete an entire orbit in approximately 1.5 hours.

From a communication provider's point of view, having a satellite that does not appear to remain stationary causes problems. First, the satellite can only be used during the time that its orbit passes between two ground stations. Second, maximal utilization requires complex control systems that continuously move the ground stations so they point directly at the satellite.

4.8 Low Earth Orbit Satellite Arrays

An interesting scheme has been invented that allows continuous communication through satellites in low earth orbit. Instead of focusing on one satellite, the scheme requires a communication company to launch a set of satellites into low earth orbits. Although a given satellite orbits quickly, the set of orbits is chosen so that each point on the ground has at least one satellite overhead at any time (sixty-six satellites are required to provide service over the entire surface of the earth). From the point of view of an observer on earth, it appears that a satellite emerges from a point on the horizon, flies overhead, and then disappears into a point on the opposite horizon. The key to the scheme lies in the set of orbits that guarantees at least one satellite is available at any time.

In addition to transponders used to communicate with ground stations, an array of satellites in low earth orbit contains radio equipment used to communicate with other satellites in the array. As they move through their orbits, the satellites communicate with one another and agree to forward data. For example, suppose that at a given point in time, a satellite traveling over Europe receives a transmission from a ground station in Germany intended for a location in the United States. The receiving satellite might forward the transmission to another satellite, which forwards it to one that can reach a ground station in the United States near the destination. As time passes, the satellites move on and new satellites take their place, meaning that a later transmission from Germany to the United States might go through three other satellites in the array.

4.9 Microwave

Electromagnetic radiation beyond the frequency range used for radio and television can also be used to transport information. In particular, many long-distance telephone companies use microwave transmissions to carry telephone conversations. A few large companies have also installed microwave communication systems as part of the company's network system.

Although microwaves are merely a higher frequency version of radio waves, they behave differently. Instead of broadcasting in all directions, a microwave transmission can be aimed in a single direction, preventing others from intercepting the signal. In addition, microwave transmission can carry more information than lower frequency RF transmissions. However, because microwaves cannot penetrate metal structures, microwave transmission works best when a clear path exists between the transmitter and receiver. As a result, most microwave installations consist of two towers that are taller than the surrounding buildings and vegetation, each with a microwave transmitter aimed directly at a microwave receiver on the other.

4.10 Infrared

The wireless remote controls used with appliances such as televisions and stereos communicate with *infrared* transmissions. Infrared is limited to a small area (e.g., a single room), and usually requires that the transmitter be pointed toward the receiver. Infrared hardware is inexpensive compared to other mechanisms, and does not require an antenna.

Computer networks can use infrared technology for data communication. For example, it is possible to equip a large room with a single infrared connection that provides network access to all computers in the room. Computers can remain in contact with the network while they are moved within the room. Infrared networks are especially convenient for small, portable computers because infrared offers the advantages of wireless communication without requiring the use of antennas. Thus, a portable computer that uses infrared can have all communication hardware built in.

4.11 Light From A Laser

We have already mentioned that light can be used to communicate through optical fibers. A beam of light can also be used to carry data through the air. Like a microwave communication system, a communication link that uses light consists of two sites that each have a transmitter and receiver. The equipment is mounted in a fixed position, often on a tower, and aligned so the transmitter at one location sends its beam of light directly to the receiver at the other. The transmitter uses a *laser* to generate the beam of light because a coherent laser beam will stay focused over a long distance.

Like a microwave transmission, light from a laser must travel in a straight line and must not be blocked. Unfortunately, a laser beam cannot penetrate vegetation or weather conditions such as snow and fog. Thus, laser transmission has limited use.

4.12 Summary

Computer networks use a variety of transmission media, including copper wires, optical fibers, radio and microwave transmissions, infrared, and laser beams. Each medium and transmission technology has advantages and costs. For example, although an infrared system can provide network connections for portable computers as they move within a room, a satellite in orbit may be needed to provide wireless transmission across an ocean.

EXERCISES

4.1 How strong is a coaxial cable? Find a piece of unused cable and remove the insulation from the end. Does the strength of the shield surprise you?

4.2 Investigate network connections used at your site. What types of media are used?

4.3 What media can be used for a network connection that passes near a powerful electric motor (e.g., near an air conditioner)?

4.4 Some commercial network services offer satellite network connections to individuals. Each subscriber is given a small dish antenna that is used to receive data; the subscriber is also given a dialup telephone modem that is used to send data. Find out why a subscriber cannot send data to the satellite. Hint: read about the size of antennas on ground stations that transmit to a satellite.

4.5 How flexible is optical fiber? To find out, see if a fiber breaks when bent around an arc of radius 25 cm, 5 cm, or 1 cm.

4.6 Higher number categories of twisted pair cable are capable of supporting higher data rates, with category 5 being the current standard for high speed. Find out whether your site uses category 5 twisted pair.

4.7 If a satellite is exactly 20,000 miles above the earth's surface, how long does it take a radio signal to reach the satellite and be transmitted back? If the satellite is at exactly 22,236 miles? (Assume the signal propagates at the speed of light and that the satellite takes 53 microseconds to retransmit a signal.)

Chapter Contents

5

Local Asynchronous Communication (RS-232)

5.1 Introduction

Because they are digital devices, computers use binary digits (bits) to represent data. Thus, transmitting data across a network from one computer to another means sending bits through the underlying transmission medium. Physically, communication systems use electric current, radio waves, or light to transfer information. This chapter explains how one of these forms, electric current, can be used to transfer digital information across short distances. It shows how bits can be encoded, and discusses a popular mechanism used to send characters. The next chapter explains why the mechanism described here cannot be used over long distances, and describes how long-distance communication is implemented.

In addition to discussing basic transmission, this chapter introduces the two primary properties of a network that can be measured quantitatively: bandwidth and delay. It discusses the motivation for using quantitative measures, and explains the relationship between bandwidth and network capacity. Later chapters explain how similar measurements can be applied to complete network systems.

5.2 The Need For Asynchronous Communication

In the broadest sense of the term, a communication is called *asynchronous* if a sender and receiver do not need to coordinate before data can be transmitted (i.e., the sender and receiver do not synchronize before each transmission). Thus, when using asynchronous communication, a sender can wait arbitrarily long between transmissions and can transmit whenever data becomes ready. In an asynchronous system, the receiver must be ready to accept data whenever it arrives. Asynchrony is especially useful for devices such as keyboards where the data is generated when a human touches a key and no data flows if the keyboard is idle.

In a more technical sense, communication hardware is classified as asynchronous if the electrical signal the transmitter sends does not contain information that the receiver can use to determine where individual bits begin and end. Instead, the receiving hardware must be built to accept and interpret the signal the sending hardware generates. This chapter will examine asynchrony that allows a sender to transmit at any time and requires the receiver to interpret the signal; the next chapter will describe synchronous communication hardware.

5.3 Using Electric Current To Send Bits

The simplest electronic communication systems use a small electric current to encode data. To understand how electricity can encode bits, imagine a wire that connects two electronic devices. Negative voltage might be used to represent a *1*, and positive voltage to represent a *0*. For example, to transmit a *0* bit, the sending device places a positive voltage on the wire for a short time, and then returns the wire to zero volts. The receiving device senses the positive voltage and records that a zero arrived. Similarly, to send a *1* bit, the sending devices places a negative voltage on the wire for a short time, and then returns the wire to zero volts. Figure 5.1 illustrates how the voltage on a wire might vary over time as a sending device transmits a sequence of bits.

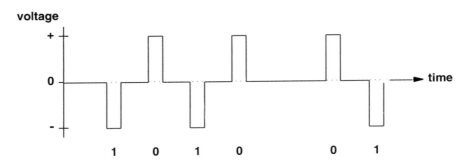

Figure 5.1 Illustration of how positive and negative voltage can be used to transmit bits across a wire. In this example, the sender applies a negative voltage to send a *1* bit or a positive voltage to send a *0* bit.

A plot like the one in Figure 5.1 is called a *waveform diagram*. Such diagrams provide a visual representation of how an electrical signal varies over time. For example, the diagram shows that a longer time elapsed between the transmission of the fourth and fifth bits than between others.

5.4 Standards For Communication

The example in Figure 5.1 shows one possible way to use voltage for digital transmission. However, several questions remain unanswered. For example, how long should the sender hold a voltage on the wire for a single bit? Although the sender must wait long enough for the receiving hardware to sense the voltage, waiting longer than necessary wastes time. What is the maximum rate at which hardware can change the voltage? How can a customer know that transmitting hardware purchased from one vendor will work correctly with receiving hardware purchased from another vendor? Is there a way to send more data in the same amount of time?

To ensure that communication hardware built by different vendors will interoperate, the specifications for communication systems are standardized. Organizations such as the International Telecommunications Union (*ITU*), the Electronic Industries Association (*EIA*), and the Institute for Electrical and Electronic Engineers (*IEEE*) publish specifications for communication equipment in documents known as *standards*. Standard documents answer questions about a particular communication technology — a standard specifies both the timing of signals and the electrical details of voltage and current. If two vendors follow a given standard, their equipment will interoperate. For example, Appendix 2 shows the bits assigned to each character by the ASCII standard.

One particular standard produced by the EIA has emerged as the most widely accepted way to transfer characters across copper wires between a computer and a device such as a modem, keyboard, or terminal. EIA standard *RS-232-C*, which is commonly abbreviated *RS-232*†, specifies the details of the physical connection (e.g., that the connection must be less than 50 feet long) as well as the electrical details (e.g., that the two voltages used to transmit data range from -15 volts to +15 volts). Because RS-232 is designed for use with devices such as modems and terminals, it specifies the transmission of *characters*. Although it can be used to send eight-bit characters, RS-232 is often configured so that each character consists of seven data bits.

RS-232 defines serial, asynchronous communication. The communication is called *serial*‡ because bits travel on the wire one after another as in the example above. RS-232 allows a sender to transmit a character at any time and to delay arbitrarily long before sending another. Furthermore, the transmission of a given character is asynchronous because the sender and receiver do not coordinate before transmission. However, once it begins sending a character, the sending hardware transmits all bits one after another with no delay between them. More important, RS-232 hardware never leaves zero volts on the wire — when the transmitter has nothing to send, it leaves the wire with a negative voltage that corresponds to bit value *1*.

---

†Although the later RS-422 standard provides slightly more functionality, equipment that uses RS-232 remains so prevalent that most professionals still use the older name.

‡The alternative is *parallel* communication, which uses multiple wires and allows one bit to travel on each wire at a given time; typical computers have both serial and parallel I/O ports.

Because the wire does not return to zero volts between each bit, a receiver cannot use the lack of voltage to mark the end of one bit and the start of the next. Instead, both the sender and receiver must agree on the exact length of time the voltage will be held for each bit. When the first bit of a character arrives, the receiver starts a timer and uses the timer to know when to measure the voltage for each of the successive bits. Because a receiver cannot distinguish between an idle line and an initial *1* bit, the RS-232 standard requires a sender to transmit an extra *0* bit before transmitting the bits of a character. The extra bit is known as a *start bit*.

Although the idle period between the end of one character and the start bit of the next character can last arbitrarily long, the RS-232 standard specifies that the sender must leave the line idle for a minimum time. The time chosen as a minimum is the time required to send one bit. Thus, one can think of a phantom *1* bit appended to each character. In RS-232 terminology, the phantom bit is called a *stop bit*. The waveform diagram in Figure 5.2 illustrates how the voltage on a wire varies when a character is sent using RS-232. Although the character shown in the example contains only seven bits, RS-232 adds both a start and stop bit when transmitting. Thus, the complete transmission requires nine bits.

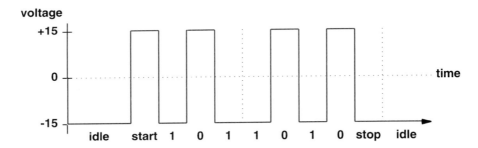

Figure 5.2 The voltage on a wire as a character is transmitted using RS-232†.
A start bit notifies the receiver that a character is starting, and
each bit transmission lasts the same length of time.

The figure shows that RS-232 uses negative *15* volts to represent a *1* bit and positive *15* volts to represent a *0* bit. In RS-232 terminology, a negative voltage places the wire in a *MARK* state, and a positive voltage places the wire in a *SPACE* state. The terms are seldom used with modern hardware‡.

We can summarize the main features of RS-232:

---

†For an example of an alternative to the encoding used by RS-232, see the Manchester encoding (used with Ethernet) described in Chapter 8.

‡The terminology used in the RS-232 standard originated with telegraph systems.

RS-232 is a popular standard used for asynchronous, serial communication over short distances between a computer and a modem or ASCII terminal. RS-232 precedes each character with a start bit, follows each character with an idle period at least one bit long (stop bit), and sends each bit in exactly the same length of time.

5.5 Baud Rate, Framing, And Errors

Recall that the sending and receiving hardware must agree on the length of time the voltage will be held for each bit. Instead of specifying the time per bit, which is a small fraction of a second, communication systems specify the number of bits that can be transferred in a second. For example, some early RS-232 connections operated at 300 bits per second; currently, 19200 bits per second and 33600 bits per second are more common.

Technically, transmission hardware is rated in *baud*, the number of changes in the signal per second that the hardware generates. For the simple RS-232 scheme presented, the baud rate is exactly equal to the number of bits per second. Thus, 9600 baud means 9600 bits per second. The next chapter shows an example of a scheme in which the number of bits per second being sent is greater than the baud rate.

To make RS-232 hardware more general, manufacturers usually design each piece of hardware to operate at a variety of baud rates. The baud rate can be configured, either manually (e.g., by physically setting switches on the hardware when it is installed in a computer) or automatically (e.g., by device driver software in a computer). If the sending and receiving hardware are not configured to use the same baud rate, errors will occur because the receiver's timer will not wait an appropriate length of time for each bit. To detect errors, a receiver measures the voltage for each bit multiple times and compares the measurements. If the voltages do not all agree or if the stop bit does not occur exactly at the time expected, the receiver reports an error. Such errors are called *framing errors* because the character is like an odd-size picture that does not fit into a standard picture frame.

RS-232 hardware can make use of framing errors. In particular, ASCII keyboards often include a *BREAK* key. *BREAK* does not generate an ASCII character. Instead, when a user presses *BREAK*, the keyboard places the outgoing connection in a *0* state much longer than it takes to send a single character (e.g., *2* seconds). When it detects that the line has moved to the *0* state, the receiver assumes a character has started to arrive, and begins to extract individual bits. However, after all bits of the character have arrived, the receiver expects the line to return to the *1* state (i.e., expects a stop bit). If it does not find a stop bit as expected, the receiver reports a framing error, which can be used by the receiving system. For example, some applications use *BREAK* as a way to abort an application — whenever a user presses *BREAK*, the system reports a framing error to the application that is using the keyboard. The application interprets the error as a request to abort.

5.6 Full Duplex Asynchronous Communication

Although we have described electric current flowing along a single wire, all electric circuits require a minimum of two wires — the current flows out on one wire and back on another. The second wire is often called a *ground*. Thus, when RS-232 is used with twisted pair wiring, one of the wires carries the signal and the other is a ground that provides a return path. Similarly, when a signal is sent along a coaxial cable, the signal travels down the center conductor, and the shield provides a return path.

In many RS-232 applications, data must flow in two directions at the same time. For example, when RS-232 is used to connect an ASCII terminal to a computer, characters travel from the keyboard to the computer at the same time characters travel from the computer to the terminal's display screen. Simultaneous transfer in two directions is known as *full duplex transmission* as distinguished from transfer in a single direction, which is known as *half duplex transmission* or *simplex transmission*. To accommodate full duplex transmission, RS-232 requires a wire for data traveling in one direction, a wire for data traveling in the reverse direction, and a single ground wire used to complete the electrical path in both directions. In fact, RS-232 defines a 25-pin connector†, and specifies how the hardware uses each of the *25* wires for control or data. For example, as long as it remains capable of receiving characters, a receiver supplies voltage on one of the control wires, which the sender interprets as *clear to send*. To reduce costs, RS-232 hardware can be configured to ignore the control wires and assume the other end is working. Full duplex connections that ignore control signals are often called *three wire circuits* because they require three wires to carry data (two for the signals traveling in each direction and a common ground for the return). Figure 5.3 illustrates a three wire circuit.

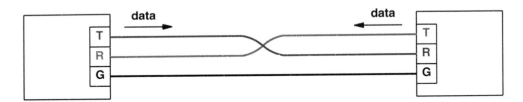

Figure 5.3 The minimal wiring required for full-duplex RS-232 communication. Although the two circuits carry data independently, it is possible for them to share a single ground wire.

As the figure shows, the ground wire connects directly from the ground on one device to the ground on the other. However, the other two wires cross: the wire connected to the transmitter on one device connects to the receiver on the other. To make cables simpler, the designers decided that computers and modems should use opposite pins on the standard *25*-pin connector — a computer transmits on pin *2* and receives on

---

†Technically, the connector is known as a *DB-25*.

pin *3*, while a modem transmits on pin *3* and receives on pin *2* (the ground wire uses pin *7*). Technically, the two types of connectors are associated with *Data Communication Equipment* (*DCE*) and *Data Terminal Equipment* (*DTE*). Thus, a cable that connects a computer to a modem has a wire from pin *2* to pin *2* and a wire from pin *3* to pin *3*. However, a cable used to connect two computers (i.e., two DCE devices) must have a wire from pin *2* to pin *3* and a wire from pin *3* to pin *2*. The exchange is often called a *2-3 swap*†.

5.7 Limitations Of Real Hardware

How fast can hardware transmit bits across a wire? The illustration in Figure 5.2 is an idealized case. In practice, no electronic device can produce an exact voltage or change from one voltage to another instantly. Furthermore, no wire conducts electricity perfectly — as electric current travels down the wire, the signal loses energy. As a result, it takes a small time for the voltage to rise or fall, and the signal received is not perfect. For example, Figure 5.4 illustrates how a bit might appear if the voltage changes on a real communication line are plotted.

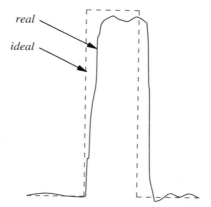

Figure 5.4 An illustration of the voltage emitted by a real device as it transmits a bit. In practice, voltages are often worse than this example.

Like most communication technologies, RS-232 recognizes that real hardware is imperfect. The standard specifies how close to a perfect waveform a transmitter must emit, and how tolerant of imperfection a receiver must be. For example, the standard does not specify that a receiver should measure the voltage exactly at the beginning of each bit. Instead, the standard recommends taking samples during the middle of the time allocated to the bit. Thus, a receiver will accept signals like the one Figure 5.4 illustrates.

---

†A cable that contains a 2-3 swap is called a *null modem*; the following chapter explains the concept of a modem.

5.8 Hardware Bandwidth And The Transmission Of Bits

Knowing that real hardware cannot change voltages instantly explains a fundamental property of transmission systems that is related to the speed at which bits can be sent. Each transmission system has a limited *bandwidth*, which is the maximum rate that the hardware can change a signal. If a sender attempts to transmit changes faster than the bandwidth, the hardware will not be able to keep up because it will not have sufficient time to complete one change before the sender attempts to make another. Thus, some of the changes will be lost.

Bandwidth is measured in *cycles per second* or *Hertz (Hz)*. It is easiest to think of the bandwidth as the fastest continuously oscillating signal that can be sent across the hardware. For example, if a transmission system has a bandwidth of 4000 Hz, then the underlying hardware in that system can transmit any signal that oscillates back and forth at a rate less than or equal to 4000 cycles per second. Note that because bandwidth limitations arise from the physical properties of matter and energy, every physical transmission system has a finite bandwidth. Thus, any transmission system that uses radio waves, sound, light, or electric current will have a limited bandwidth†.

In the 1920s, a researcher discovered a fundamental relationship between the bandwidth of a transmission system and the maximum number of bits per second that can be transferred over that system. Known as the *Nyquist Intersymbol Interference Theorem*, the relationship provides a theoretical bound on the maximum rate at which data can be sent. For a transmission scheme like RS-232 that uses two values of voltage to encode data, Nyquist's theorem states that the maximum data rate in bits per second that can be achieved over a transmission system of bandwidth B is $2B$. More generally, if the transmission system uses K possible values of voltage instead of two, Nyquist's theorem states that the maximum data rate in bits per second, D, is:

$$D = 2B log_2 K$$

5.9 The Effect Of Noise On Communication

Nyquist's theorem provides an absolute maximum that cannot be achieved in practice. In particular, engineers have observed that a real communication system is subject to small amounts of background interference called *noise*, and that such noise makes it impossible to achieve the theoretical maximum transmission rate. In 1948, Claude Shannon extended Nyquist's work to specify the maximum data rate that could be achieved over a transmission system that introduces noise. The result, called *Shannon's Theorem‡*, can be stated as:

$$C = B log_2 (1 + S/N)$$

where C is the effective limit on the channel capacity in bits per second, B is the hardware bandwidth, S is the average signal power, and N is the average noise power.

---

†In fact, biological systems have bandwidth limits as well. For example, dogs can hear sounds that are beyond the bandwidth limitation of human ears.

‡The result is also called the *Shannon-Hartley Law*.

Usually, *S/N*, which is known as the *signal-to-noise ratio,* is not represented directly. Instead, engineers cite the quantity $10 log_{10} S/N$, which is measured in *decibels* (abbreviated *dB*). For example, a ratio of *S/N* equal to *100* is *20 dB*, and ratio of *1000* is *30 dB*.

5.10 Significance For Data Networking

The theorems of Nyquist and Shannon that are described above have consequences for engineers who design networks. Nyquist's work has provided an incentive to explore complex ways to encode bits on signals:

> *Nyquist's theorem encourages engineers to explore ways to encode bits on a signal because a clever encoding allows more bits to be transmitted per unit time.*

In some sense, Shannon's Theorem is more fundamental because it represents an absolute limitation derived from the laws of physics. Much of the noise on a transmission line, for example, can be attributed to thermodynamics. Thus,

> *Shannon's Theorem informs engineers that no amount of clever encoding can overcome the laws of physics that place a fundamental limit on the number of bits per second that can be transmitted in a real communication system.*

In a practical sense, Shannon's Theorem helps explain how fast one can send data across a voice telephone call. The voice telephone system has a signal-to-noise ratio of approximately *30 dB* and a bandwidth of approximately *3000 Hz*. Thus, according to Shannon's Theorem, the maximum number of bits per second that can be transmitted across such a system is limited to:

$$C \ = \ 3000 \, log_2 (1 \ + \ 1000)$$

or approximately 30,000 bps. Engineers recognize this as a fundamental limit — faster transmission speeds will only be possible after the signal-to-noise ratio has been improved.

How can dialup modems achieve higher throughput than the Shannon Theorem allows? One possibility is compression — the data is compressed before transmission and decompressed after reception. Of course, compression only works if the data has been encoded inefficiently. For example, when an 8-bit ASCII encoding is used to transfer email that contains only upper and lower case English letters and digits, only 62 of the 256 possible 8-bit values are actually used. If the same data is encoded in 6-bit characters, 25% fewer bits are needed. It should be obvious, however, that although compression reduces the number of bits required to represent the data, Shannon's Theorem still bounds the rate at which the compressed data can be transmitted.

5.11 Summary

In the broadest sense, asynchronous communication allows a sender to transmit data at any time and to wait arbitrarily long before transmitting again. In a more technical sense, communication hardware is asynchronous if the electrical signal does not contain information that a receiver can use to locate the beginning and end of bits. Originally created to define the interaction between a computer and a modem, the RS-232 standard has become the most widely accepted standard for asynchronous transmission of characters over short distances. RS-232 is used for communication between a keyboard and a computer as well as for communication over a computer's serial ports.

According to the RS-232 standard, a transmitter must leave a negative voltage on the communication line when it does not have data to send. The transmitter precedes each character with a start bit and follows each character with a stop bit. The start bit informs the receiver that a character is arriving, and the stop bit allows a receiver to detect that all bits of the character arrived in the time allotted.

Because any physical system used for communication has limits on the speed at which it can change state, physical systems cannot transmit bits arbitrarily fast. For example, electronic components cannot change the voltage on a wire instantly. The speed at which hardware can change state is known as the hardware bandwidth; the bandwidth of a transmission system can be measured. Researchers have discovered two fundamental relationships. Nyquist's theorem defines the relationship between hardware bandwidth and the theoretical maximum rate at which data can be sent. Shannon's Theorem gives a limit on the rate at which data can be sent in the presence of noise.

EXERCISES

5.1   The term *baud* is named after Emile Baudot. Find out who Baudot was and what contribution he made to communication systems.

5.2   Draw the waveform diagram that results when the word *bit* is sent in ASCII across an RS-232 connection. Hint: Appendix 2 contains the 7-bit ASCII character codes.

5.3   Suppose one sent 10000 7-bit characters across an RS-232 connection that operated at 9600 baud. How long would the transmission require? (Hint: remember to allow for a start bit and a stop bit on each character.)

5.4   Use Nyquist's theorem to determine the maximum rate in bits per second at which data can be sent across a transmission system that has a bandwidth of 4000 Hz and uses four values of voltage to encode information.

5.5   Read about RS-232. What purpose is assigned to each of the 25 wires in a DB-25 connector?

5.6   The serial ports on some computers use connectors with fewer than 25 pins. Read about the *DB-9* connector used for serial ports on PCs. When RS-232 is used with a DB-9 connector, which signals are omitted?

5.7   Read about RS-232 hardware. How many times does the hardware sample each bit?

5.8   Extend the previous exercise by calculating how closely the hardware rates must match on RS-232 interfaces to allow them to transfer data successfully. If the sender's RS-232 hardware manufactures bits that are five percent smaller than the receiver's RS-232 hardware expects, will the receiver accept the resulting characters?

5.9   What happens if an RS-232 transmitter and receiver are programmed to send and receive at different baud rates? To find out, hook up a serial line between two computers and make the rates unequal (you will not harm the hardware).

5.10   Most RS-232 hardware allows the computer to which it attaches to specify the data rate to use as well as the number of stop bits to use. If a transmitter is programmed to use two stop bits, but a receiver is programmed to require only one, will data be received correctly? If so, what is the disadvantage of using an extra stop bit?

Chapter Contents

6

Long-Distance Communication (Carriers, Modulation, And Modems)

6.1 Introduction

The previous chapter describes how characters can be sent a short distance over copper wires by encoding each bit with a positive or negative voltage. This chapter explains why the same scheme does not work across long distances, and describes the hardware needed for long-distance communication.

In addition to describing the motivation for using a continuous carrier, the chapter discusses how a carrier can be used to send data. The chapter identifies the purpose of modem hardware, and shows how modems are used for long-distance communication. In addition, the chapter discusses point-to-point digital circuits and describes how computers use such circuits.

6.2 Sending Signals Across Long Distances

An electric current cannot be propagated an arbitrary distance over copper wire because the current becomes weaker as it travels. For example, although RS-232 connections work well in a single room, any attempt to use RS-232 over a connection to a remote city will result in electric currents too weak for a receiver to detect. Engineers term the problem *signal loss* — such loss occurs because resistance in the wire causes small amounts of the electrical energy to be converted to heat. Signal loss is important for communication systems because it means simple changes in electrical voltage like that used by RS-232 will not suffice for long-distance communication.

Researchers who study how to transmit signals have discovered an interesting property of long-distance transmission systems: a continuous, oscillating signal will propagate farther than other signals. That observation forms the basis for most long-distance communication systems. Instead of transmitting an electric current that only changes when the value of a bit changes, long-distance communication systems send a continuously oscillating signal, usually a sine wave, called a *carrier*. Figure 6.1 illustrates a carrier waveform.

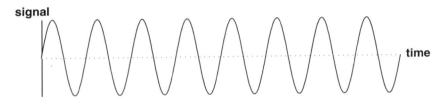

Figure 6.1 The waveform of a typical carrier. The carrier oscillates continuously, even when no data is being sent.

To send data, a transmitter modifies the carrier slightly. Collectively, such modifications are called *modulation*. The use of a modulated carrier wave for long-distance communication did not originate with computer networks — it was devised for use with telephone, radio, and television. For example, a radio station uses a continuous carrier wave that oscillates at an assigned frequency. Before it transmits the signal, the radio station uses an audio signal to modulate the carrier wave. When a radio receiver in range of the transmitter has been tuned to the frequency of the carrier wave, electronic circuits in the receiver monitor the carrier, detect the modulation, and use it to reconstruct the original audio signal. Note that a radio receiver is designed to extract and play only the modulation — the receiver discards the carrier after the sound has been extracted.

Whether they transmit over wires, optical fibers, microwaves, or radio frequencies, most long-distance computer networks use the same underlying scheme as a radio station. The transmitter generates a continuously oscillating carrier signal, which it modulates according to the data being sent. Like a radio receiver, the receiver on a long-distance communication link must be configured to recognize the carrier that the sender uses. The receiver monitors the incoming carrier, detects modulation, reconstructs the original data, and discards the carrier.

Network technologies use a variety of modulation techniques, including *amplitude* and *frequency modulation*, the techniques used by AM and FM radio stations†. Amplitude modulation varies the strength of the outgoing signal in proportion to the information being sent; frequency modulation varies the frequency of the underlying carrier in

---

†When referring to radio transmission, the term *AM* is an acronym for Amplitude Modulation, and the term *FM* is an abbreviation for Frequency Modulation.

proportion to the information being sent. For example, Figure 6.2 illustrates how a bit might be encoded using amplitude modulation.

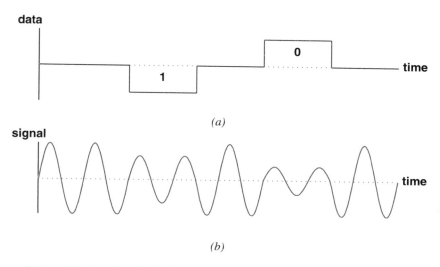

(a)

(b)

Figure 6.2 (a) a digital signal, and (b) the wave that results from amplitude modulation using the signal in (a). The carrier is reduced to 2/3 full strength to encode a *1* bit and 1/3 strength to encode a *0* bit.

Although amplitude and frequency modulation work well for audio, both require at least one cycle of a carrier wave to send a single bit. The Nyquist theorem described in Chapter 5 suggests that the number of bits sent per unit time can be increased if the encoding scheme permits multiple bits to be encoded in a single cycle of the carrier. Thus, computer networks often use other modulation techniques that can send more bits. In particular, *phase shift modulation* changes the timing of the carrier wave abruptly to encode data. Each such change is called a *phase shift*. After a phase shift, the carrier continues to oscillate, but it immediately jumps to a new point in its cycle. Figure 6.3 shows an example waveform produced by phase shift modulation.

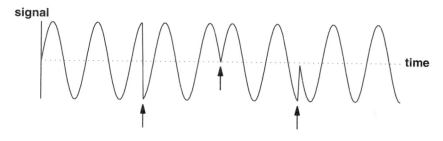

Figure 6.3 An illustration of phase shift modulation. Arrows indicate points at which the carrier abruptly jumps to a new point in the cycle.

Because hardware can measure the amount of shift in an oscillating wave, each phase shift can encode more than one bit of data. To do so, the sender takes the value of a group of bits to determine how much to shift the carrier. To understand a shift, observe in Figure 6.3 that horizontal sections of an ordinary sine wave have been removed, the remaining pieces pushed together, and the breaks joined with vertical lines at the points indicated by arrows. The size of the section that is removed determines the amount of the shift.

We said that the baud rate of a transmission system is the number of changes the hardware can make per second. The chief advantage of mechanisms like phase shift modulation arises from their ability to encode more than one bit value at a given change. For example, Figure 6.3 illustrates how the phase can shift by different amounts.

A complete cycle of the carrier wave consists of a positive arc followed by a negative arc. In Figure 6.3, the first two shifts each jump half of a complete cycle, while the third shift jumps three quarters of a cycle†. Usually, phase shifts are chosen so each shift represents a power of two possible values. The sender can then use bits of data to select the shift. For example, in a system that can shift the phase by eight possible amounts (i.e., 2^3), a transmitter uses three bits of data to select which of the eight shift values to use. The receiver determines how much the carrier shifted, and uses the shift to recreate the bits that produced the change. That is, if a transmitter uses T bits to create a phase shift, the receiver can extract all T bits by observing the amount of shift. Because each shift encodes T bits, the maximum data rate that can be sent using phase shift modulation is $2R log_2 2^T$, or $2RT$, where R is the number of signal changes per second. According to our definition, R is the *baud rate* of the hardware. Thus, when using phase shift modulation, the number of bits per second that the system can transfer is a multiple of the baud rate.

6.3 Modem Hardware Used For Modulation And Demodulation

A hardware circuit that accepts a sequence of data bits and applies modulation to a carrier wave according to the bits is called a *modulator*; a hardware circuit that accepts a modulated carrier wave and recreates the sequence of data bits that was used to modulate the carrier is called a *demodulator*. Thus, transmission of data across a long distance requires a modulator at one end of the transmission line and a demodulator at the other.

In practice, most network systems are full duplex (i.e., they permit data to flow in both directions). To support such full duplex communication, each location needs both a modulator, which is used to transmit data, and a demodulator, which is used to receive data. To keep costs low and make the pair of devices easy to install and operate, manufacturers combine both circuits into a single device called a *modem* (*mo*dulator and *dem*odulator). Figure 6.4 illustrates how a pair of modems can be used to connect two computers across a long distance.

---

†Mathematically, a sine wave completes a cycle in 2π radians. Thus, the first two shifts in Figure 6.3 are π radians each, and the third is $3\pi/2$ radians.

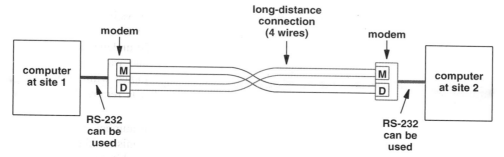

Figure 6.4 The use of two modems for long-distance communication across a
4-wire circuit. The modulator in one modem connects to the
demodulator in the other. A pair of wires is needed for each connection.

6.4 Leased Analog Data Circuits

Many companies use one or more 4-wire circuits as part of their data communication network. When the circuit connects two locations at a single site, the company can
install the necessary wires itself. Private companies cannot install circuits across long
distances, however, because government regulations only allow utility companies to run
wires across public property (e.g., across a street). Fortunately, the necessary wiring
can be obtained from a telephone company. In particular, telephone companies allow
companies to lease a circuit between any two locations.

To understand why the phone company can supply wiring, it is necessary to know
two facts. First, when a telephone company installs cables, each cable includes extra
wires that can be used for future expansion. Thus, the telephone cables already in place
contain wires that are not being used for telephone service. Second, although it does
not sell the wires in the cables, a telephone company agrees to lease the wires for a
monthly fee (the fee depends on the distance spanned and the bandwidth of the wires).
A leased circuit usually consists of four wires that do not connect to the dialup telephone system in any way — the wires can be used only with special modems as
described above. Because bits travel across such circuits one at a time, professionals
use the terms *serial data circuit*, *serial line*, or *leased serial line* to describe such a connection.

Once a connection has been leased from the phone company, a modem must be installed at each end before communication is possible. After that, the leased line is
available to send data. The chief advantage of such an arrangement arises from its constant availability — data can be sent at any time, twenty-four hours per day. The chief
disadvantages arise from the limited connectivity and cost — the leased line only connects two points, and whoever signs the lease must pay the monthly fee even if the line
is not being used to send data.

6.5 Optical, Radio Frequency, And Dialup Modems

In addition to dedicated wires, modems are also used with other media, including RF transmission, glass fibers, and conventional telephone connections. For example, a pair of *Radio Frequency (RF)* modems can be used to send data using a radio frequency signal, or a pair of *optical modems* can be used to send data across a pair of glass fibers using light. Although such modems use entirely different technology than modems that operate over dedicated wires, the principle remains the same: at the sending end, a modem transforms data into a modulated signal; at the receiving end, data is extracted from the modulated signal.

RF modems have become especially attractive because of the increased interest in *wireless networking*. A small RF modem attached to a notebook computer, for example, makes it possible to move the computer around in a building while maintaining network connectivity in the same way a portable phone can move around. More powerful RF modems make it possible to establish a wireless communication link over longer distances (e.g., kilometers).

Another interesting application of modems involves the dialup telephone system. As Figure 6.5 illustrates, a *dialup modem* connects to an ordinary telephone line.

Dialup modems differ in three significant ways from the 4-wire modems described earlier. First, in addition to circuitry for sending data, a dialup modem contains circuitry that mimics a telephone — the modem can simulate lifting the handset, dialing, or hanging up the phone. Second, because the telephone system is designed to carry sound, a dialup modem uses a carrier that is an audible tone†. Thus, a dialup modem must contain circuitry to send and receive audio over the telephone line (in addition to sending and receiving a carrier, a dialup modem can detect a dial tone). Third, although they send all data through a single voice channel, a pair of dialup modems offers full duplex communication. That is, a single telephone connection between two dialup modems usually allows data to flow in both directions. In practice, the modems must use different carrier tones or coordinate to avoid having both modems transmit at the same time.

Modems that coordinate sending data are called *half duplex* or *2-wire* modems to distinguish them from the 4-wire type described above. To coordinate, the pair of 2-wire modems agree to take turns sending data. One modem sends data, and then allows the other modem to send data. Such coordination occurs automatically; a user remains unaware that the modems are taking turns.

To use a pair of dialup modems, one modem must begin operation by waiting for a telephone call at a known telephone number, *T*. The waiting modem is said to be in *answer mode*. The other modem begins in *calling mode*, with the telephone number to dial. The calling modem simulates lifting the handset, listening for a dial tone, and then dials. When it detects the telephone is ringing, the modem that is in answer mode answers the call and sends a carrier wave, which initiates communication. The calling modem detects the carrier and responds by sending a carrier of its own. Once the two

---

†The carrier used by a dialup modem is the tone heard if one accidentally lifts the handset of a telephone while a modem is using the telephone line.

modems agree on the carriers, data can be sent in either direction by modulating the carrier as described above. After an application finishes communicating over a dialup modem, the application instructs the modem to terminate the call.

Figure 6.5 Illustration of dialup modems that use the voice telephone system to communicate. To the telephone system, a dialup modem appears to be a telephone.

Computers using modems do not know about the underlying media — a modem does not inform the computer whether it is using wires, optical fibers, a dialup telephone connection, or some other medium. An application that uses a modem might be able to deduce the underlying media by measuring the delay and bandwidth of the channel, but computer software seldom attempts to do so. Instead, most computer systems merely use modems as a way to send bits across long distances.

In summary,

> *A pair of modems is required for long-distance communication across a leased line; each modem contains separate circuitry to send and receive digital data. To send data, a modem emits a continuous carrier wave, which it then modulates according to the values of the bits being transferred. To receive data, a modem detects modulation in the incoming carrier, and uses it to recreate the data bits.*

6.6 Carrier Frequencies And Multiplexing

Computer networks that use a modulated carrier wave to transmit data are similar to television stations that use a modulated carrier wave to broadcast video. The similarities provide the intuition needed to understand a fundamental principle:

> *Two or more signals that use different carrier frequencies can be transmitted over a single medium simultaneously without interference.*

To understand the principle, consider how television transmission works. Each television station is assigned a channel number on which it broadcasts a signal. In fact, a channel number is merely shorthand for the frequency at which the station's carrier oscillates. To receive a transmission, a television receiver must be tuned to the same frequency as the transmitter. More important, a given city can contain many television stations that all broadcast on separate frequencies simultaneously. A receiver selects one to receive at any time.

Cable television illustrates that the principle applies to many signals traveling across a wire. Although a cable subscriber has only one physical wire that connects to the cable company, the subscriber receives many channels of information simultaneously. The signal for one channel does not interfere with the signal for another, making it possible to watch a show on Channel 6 without receiving any interference from signals on Channels 5 or 7.

Computer networks use the principle of separate channels to permit multiple communications to share a single, physical connection. Each sender transmits a signal using a particular carrier frequency. A receiver configured to accept a carrier at a given frequency will not be affected by signals sent at other frequencies. Thus, multiple carriers can pass over the same wire at the same time without interference.

Frequency division multiplexing (*FDM*) is the technical term applied to a network system that uses multiple carrier frequencies to allow independent signals to travel through a medium. FDM technology can be used when sending signals over wire, RF, or optical fiber. Figure 6.6 illustrates the concept, and shows the hardware components needed for FDM.

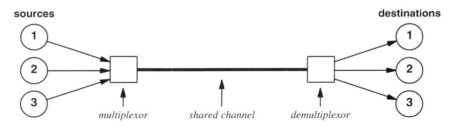

Figure 6.6 The concept of frequency division multiplexing. Each pair of source and destination can send data over the shared channel without interference. In practice, each end requires a multiplexor and demultiplexor for 2-way communication, and a multiplexor may need circuitry to generate the carrier waves.

In theory, as long as each carrier operates at a different frequency than the others, it remains independent. In practice, however, two carriers operating at almost the same frequency or at exact multiples of a frequency can interfere with one another. To avoid problems, engineers who design FDM network systems choose a minimum separation between the carriers†. The mandate for large gaps between the frequencies assigned to carriers means that underlying hardware used with FDM must tolerate a wide range of frequencies. Consequently, FDM is only used on high-bandwidth transmission systems (i.e., transmission systems that can send a wide range of frequencies). In summary,

> *Frequency division multiplexing (FDM) allows multiple pairs of senders and receivers to communicate over a shared medium simultaneously. The carrier used by each pair operates at a unique frequency that does not interfere with the others.*

6.7 Baseband And Broadband Technologies

Engineers have used frequency division multiplexing to build a variety of network technologies that permit independent communications to proceed simultaneously over a single underlying medium. For example, the transmitters and receivers used with some wireless networks can be tuned to a specific channel, making it possible to have two independent sets of computers in a single room communicating at the same time. One set communicates on Channel *1* at the same time that the other set communicates on Channel *2*.

The primary motivation for using frequency division multiplexing arises from the desire for high throughput. To achieve higher throughput, the underlying hardware uses a larger part of the electromagnetic spectrum (i.e., a larger bandwidth). Thus, the term *broadband technology* is used to characterize such technologies. The alternative, any technology that uses a small part of the electromagnetic spectrum and sends only one signal at a time over the medium, is known as a *baseband technology*.

6.8 Wave Division Multiplexing

The concept of frequency division multiplexing can be applied to optical transmission systems as well as to those that use radio frequencies. Technically, optical FDM is known as *wave division multiplexing*. When many wavelengths are used, the term is *Dense Wave Division Multiplexing (DWDM)*. Because humans see frequencies of visible light as colors, however, engineers sometimes use the informal term *color division multiplexing*, and joke about the carriers being ''red,'' ''orange,'' ''blue,'' and so on.

Wave division multiplexing operates by sending multiple light waves across a single optical fiber. At the receiving end, an optical prism is used to separate the frequencies. As in conventional FDM, the carriers can be mixed onto a single medium because light at a given frequency does not interfere with light at another frequency.

---

†The requirement for a minimum separation between carrier frequencies also applies to television and radio stations.

6.9 Spread Spectrum

A special case of frequency division multiplexing involves the use of multiple carriers to improve reliability. The technique is called *spread spectrum*, and is used for a variety of reasons. One chief reason for using spread spectrum is to improve reliability when the underlying transmission system has sporadic interference at some frequencies. For example, consider a network that uses radio waves. If the transmitter and receiver are close to sources of electromagnetic interference or if large objects move around in the area between the transmitter and receiver, the optimum carrier frequency may vary over time. At a given time, one carrier frequency may work while others do not. Later, a different carrier frequency may work while the original does not. Spread spectrum solves the problem by arranging for a transmitter to send the same signal on a set of carrier frequencies. A receiver is configured to check all carrier frequencies and to use whichever is working at present.

Some dialup modems also use a form of spread spectrum transmission to improve reliability. Instead of sending data on a single carrier frequency, such modems select a set of carrier frequencies and use them simultaneously. If interference damages one or more of the carriers, the modem can extract the data from the others.

6.10 Time Division Multiplexing

The general alternative to FDM is *time division multiplexing (TDM)*, in which sources sharing a medium "take turns". There are two types of TDM:

- *Synchronous Time Division Multiplexing (STDM)* which is also known as *Slotted Time Division Multiplexing*, arranges for sources to proceed in a *round-robin* manner. That is, the multiplexor sends a small amount of data from source *1*, then sends a small amount from source *2*, and so on. Such an approach provides an absolute guarantee on fairness because it gives each source an opportunity to use the shared medium before any source gains a second opportunity. STDM is especially well-suited to telephone voice transmission because each phone call generates data at exactly the same rate.

- *Statistical Multiplexing†*, used in most computer networks, works like STDM in that sources take turns sending. However, there is one small modification — if a given source does not have data to send, the multiplexor skips that source.

Later chapters will explore statistical multiplexing in detail, and will show several examples. We will learn that most computer networks use a form of statistical multiplexing because computers do not all generate data at exactly the same rate. Instead, most computers only generate data for a short time (e.g., to send a request), and then stop (e.g., while waiting for a response). Thus, statistical multiplexing is preferred because it does not make sense to waste a time slot if a computer does not have data to send.

_____

†The term is misleading at best.

6.11 Summary

Because a continuous signal can be propagated farther than a random signal, most long-distance communication systems transmit a continuous carrier wave, which is then modulated to convey data. A modem is a hardware device that contains two functional parts, a modulator used to send data across a carrier wave, and a demodulator used to extract data from an incoming carrier wave. The modulator uses digital data from a computer to modulate an outgoing carrier wave. The demodulator extracts data from the incoming carrier it receives, and then discards the carrier.

Modems are used in pairs, with the pair connected by a communication circuit. The modulator in one modem connects to the demodulator on the other, allowing data to be sent in either direction.

Although they can use the same modulation techniques as radio or television stations, most modems use techniques such as phase shift modulation, which work well for digital data. To implement phase shift modulation, the sending modem changes the carrier wave by abruptly jumping to a new point in the cycle. The chief advantage of phase shift modulation lies in its ability to encode more than one bit of data in each shift.

The concept of multiplexing is fundamental to computer networks. Multiplexing allows multiple sources to send to multiple destinations over a shared communication channel. Frequency division multiplexing works like cable television — multiple signals can travel across a wire simultaneously because each uses a unique carrier frequency. Time division multiplexing requires senders to take turns transmitting across the shared medium.

EXERCISES

6.1   Consider using amplitude modulation with a sine wave that operates at a frequency of 4000 Hz. How many bits per second can be encoded? Why? (Hint: information from Chapter 5 is needed to solve this problem.)

6.2   Explain why each radio station in an area must be assigned a unique carrier frequency.

6.3   Check with a local telephone company to find out how much it costs per year to lease a 4-wire data circuit that extends one mile.

6.4   Although dialup modems need sophisticated electronics to handle the details of dialing a telephone, they are usually much less expensive than equivalent 4-wire modems. Explain why. (Hint: think of economics.)

6.5   Survey commercial modem vendors to find the maximum data rate in bits per second available over a dialup telephone modem.

6.6   In the previous exercise, use Shannon's Theorem to calculate the signal-to-noise ratio required on a dialup phone line to obtain the maximum modem data rate. (Assume a bandwidth of 3,000 Hz.)

6.7   The author uses a multiplexor and demultiplexor that allows three separate sources of 8-bit data to send to three separate destinations over a single channel. The channel can only send 8-bit characters, and any source can transfer any possible 8-bit value at any time. Devise a multiplexing mechanism that works with 8-bit hardware to accept data from three sources and send it over a shared channel. (Hint: devise a way to tell the receiver which source sent each data item.)

6.8   Write two computer programs that implement the multiplexing scheme you designed for the previous exercise. Have one program simulate a multiplexor by reading characters from three files and producing a fourth file. To guarantee that data can be intermixed, read one character from the first file, one from the second file, one from the third file, and so on. Have the second program take the output from the first program and decode it into three output files (which should be identical to the input files).

6.9   Replacing a multiplexor that uses Time Division Multiplexing with one that uses Frequency Division Multiplexing can improve throughput. Explain why.

6.10 Read about research on *Wave Division Multiplexing* (*WDM*) for optical modems. How many frequencies of light have been sent across an optical fiber simultaneously using WDM?

Packet Transmission

Packets, frames,
Local Area Networks,
Wide Area Networks,
hardware addresses,
bridges, switches,
routing, and
protocols

Chapter Contents

7

Packets, Frames, And Error Detection

7.1 Introduction

Previous chapters describe how the lowest levels of hardware transmit individual bits across media such as copper wires or glass fibers. Although such details are interesting, only engineers who design hardware work with individual bits or modulation techniques. Most computer networks provide a more convenient interface that allows a computer to send multiple bytes of data across the network without handling individual bits and without knowing how the underlying hardware encodes bits in signals.

This chapter describes a fundamental idea in computer networking. It discusses the concept of packets, and explains how a sender and receiver coordinate to transfer a packet. The chapter also shows how packets can be implemented in a character-oriented network using a simple frame format. Finally, the chapter explains transmission errors, and discusses mechanisms that networks use to detect such errors.

Later chapters expand the packet concept and describe how particular network technologies handle packets. They show more examples and examine details.

7.2 The Concept Of Packets

Most computer networks do not transfer data as an arbitrary string of continuous bits. Instead, the network system divides data into small blocks called *packets*, which it sends individually. Computer networks are often called *packet networks* or *packet switching networks* because they use packet technology.

Two facts motivate the use of packets. First, a sender and receiver need to coordinate transmission to ensure that data arrives correctly. We will learn that when transmission errors occur, data can be lost. Dividing the data into small blocks helps a sender and receiver determine which blocks arrive intact and which do not. Second, because communication circuits and the associated modem hardware are expensive, multiple computers often share underlying connections and hardware. To ensure that all computers receive fair, prompt access to a shared communication facility, a network system cannot allow one computer to deny access to others. Using small packets helps ensure fairness. To see how, consider the alternative used in early computer networks.

The first networks did not guarantee fair access. Instead, networks allowed an application program to hold a shared communication resource arbitrarily long — an application was permitted to finish before another application could begin using the resource. To avoid having one computer hold a network for an arbitrary time, modern computer networks enforce the use of packets. The network permits one computer to send a packet, then blocks that computer from sending again. Meanwhile the network permits another computer to send a packet, and so on. A single computer can hold a shared resource only long enough to send a single packet, and must wait until other computers have a turn before sending a second packet.

To understand how using packets allows prompt service, suppose a network granted an application program exclusive use of a network until the application completed. For example, suppose the four computers in Figure 7.1 share a communication channel and that they use the channel to transfer files. While computer *A* sends a file to computer *D*, computers *B* and *C* must wait.

Figure 7.1 An illustration of one reason computer networks use packets. While one pair of computers communicate, others must wait.

How long does a file transfer require? If a file contains 5 megabytes (a typical large data file) and the communication system can transfer 56,000 bits per second (a typical long-distance network rate), the transfer will require almost *12* minutes. The example clearly shows that:

Any network system that grants an application exclusive use of shared resources will block other computers for intolerably long periods of time.

In contrast, consider the delays introduced when the network in Figure 7.1 requires computers to divide data into packets that each contain *1000* bytes of data. Suppose computer *A* begins sending data to *D*. Also suppose that after *A* begins sending, computer *B* needs to send data to *C*. After *A* finishes sending one packet, the network will allow *B* to send one packet. Because a packet contains only *8000* bits of data and the hardware can transfer data at 56,000 bits per second, a complete packet can be sent in only .143 seconds. Consequently, *B* waits at most *143* ms before it can start sending. We can summarize:

> *To allow the sender and receiver to coordinate and to ensure all computers that share a network resource have fair, prompt access, most computer networks divide data into small blocks called* packets. *Computers take turns sending packets over the shared resource. Because each packet is small, no computer experiences a long delay while waiting for access.*

7.3 Packets And Time-Division Multiplexing

Conceptually, a network that permits many sources to take turns accessing a shared communication resource is providing a form of time-division multiplexing. Figure 7.2 illustrates the idea.

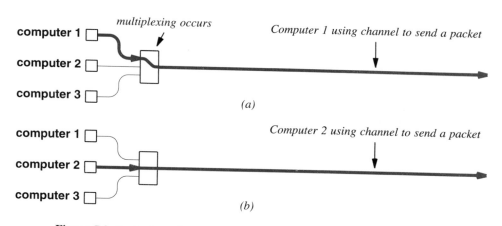

Figure 7.2 Illustration of multiplexing with packets. The sources take turns using the shared communication channel. (a) Computer *1* uses the resource to send a packet, and then (b) computer *2* uses the resource to send a packet.

Dividing data into small packets ensures that all sources receive prompt service because it prohibits one source from gaining exclusive access for an arbitrarily long time. In particular, if one source has a few packets to send and another has many, allowing both sources to take turns sending packets guarantees that the source with a small amount of data will finish promptly.

7.4 Packets And Hardware Frames

Although the term *packet* refers to the general concept of a small block of data, there is no universal agreement on the exact format of a packet. Instead, each hardware technology defines the details of packets that can be transferred on that hardware, and specifies how individual bits of the packet are transmitted. To help distinguish between the general idea of packet transmission and the specific definition of packets for a given hardware technology, we use the term *frame* to denote the definition of a packet used with a specific type of network. Thus, one might refer to the maximum amount of data a frame can hold or the order in which bits of a frame are sent across a network.

To understand how a network technology can specify a frame format, consider a simple example. Suppose one needs to send a block of data from one computer to another using a character-oriented transmission scheme such as the RS-232 mechanism described in Chapter 5. Although the RS-232 standard specifies how to encode bits and transmit an individual character, it does not include a mechanism that allows the sender to signal the end of a block of characters — the sending and receiving computers must agree on such details. That is, the sender and receiver must agree on how they will specify the beginning and end of each frame.

If the data characters being carried in a frame do not include all possible values, the network system can choose two unused values and use them to mark the beginning and end of each frame. For example, suppose RS-232 is being used to transmit a text document that is stored in ASCII†. Because ASCII includes codes for unprintable characters that do not appear in typical text documents, the network can use two of the unprintable ASCII characters to delimit the frame. Figure 7.3 illustrates how a frame would appear if the network used the ASCII characters *soh* and *eot*‡ to delimit the frame. The sender transmits *soh* followed by the characters of data followed by *eot*.

| soh | block of data in frame | eot |

Figure 7.3 An example frame that uses character *soh* to mark the beginning of the frame and *eot* to mark the end. The format is simple and unambiguous — a receiver can tell when the entire frame has arrived, even if there are delays between characters.

---

†The ASCII character codes can be found in Appendix 2.

‡In fact, ASCII includes these two characters primarily for framing — *soh* (hexadecimal *01*) is an abbreviation for *start of header*, and *eot* (hexadecimal *04*) is an abbreviation for *end of transmission*.

The example framing scheme has disadvantages and advantages. The chief disadvantage is overhead. To understand why, consider what happens when a sender transmits two frames with no delay between them. At the end of the first frame, the sender transmits *eot* and then, with no delay, the sender transmits *soh* to start the second frame. In such circumstances, only one character is needed to separate two blocks of data — a framing scheme that delimits both the beginning and end of each frame sends an extra, unnecessary character between blocks of data.

The chief advantage of sending a character at the beginning and end of a frame becomes clear when one considers large delays and computers that crash. Recall that an asynchronous transmission system permits arbitrary delay between characters. More important, a computer system can crash and reboot. Using two characters to delimit a frame handles such situations well. If the sending computer crashes before transmitting a complete frame, the *eot* will not arrive, and the receiver will know that the frame is incomplete. When the sender reboots and transmits a new frame, it will begin with *soh*, allowing the receiver to detect the problem. If a receiver crashes and reboots, it can use the *soh* at the beginning of a frame to distinguish between two possibilities: the reboot completed before the sender began to transmit a frame (in which case the *soh* arrives before any other characters from the frame) or the sender began to transmit before the reboot completed (in which case the *soh* will be lost, and another character will arrive first).

7.5 Byte Stuffing

Although using characters to mark the beginning and end of each frame has advantages, most computer networks cannot afford to reserve characters for use by the network. Instead, the network permits an application to transfer arbitrary characters across the network. In particular, an application may choose to send data that contains one or more occurrences of characters like *soh* and *eot* that are used for framing. Simply transmitting such characters in the data portion of a frame causes problems. For example, a receiver will interpret an *eot* character to mean that the entire frame has arrived. Similarly, if it encounters an *soh* character, a receiver will assume a new frame has started to arrive.

In general, to distinguish between data being sent and control information such as frame delimiters, network systems arrange for the sending side to change the data slightly before it is sent, and then arrange for the receiving side to restore the original data before passing it to the receiving application. Thus, although applications using the network can transfer arbitrary data, the network system never confuses data with control information.

Because network systems usually insert extra bits or bytes to change data for transmission, the technique is known as *data stuffing*. The terms *byte stuffing* and *character stuffing* refer to data stuffing used with character-oriented hardware, and *bit stuffing*, which is more common, refers to data stuffing used with bit-oriented hardware†.

---

†The *Point-to-Point Protocol* (*PPP*) that is used to send IP over dialup lines employs byte stuffing; the Frame Relay technology covered in Chapter 13 uses bit stuffing.

To understand how data stuffing can permit a frame to include arbitrary data values, consider the character-oriented frame format described above. Because a sender and receiver agree to use characters *soh* and *eot* to delimit the frame, those two characters must not appear in the data. Byte stuffing can solve the problem by reserving a third character to mark occurrences of reserved characters in the data. For example, suppose the ASCII character *esc* (hexadecimal value *1B*) has been selected as the third character. When any of the three special characters occur in the data, the sender inserts *esc* and replaces the character. The table in Figure 7.4 summarizes the mapping.

Character In Data	Characters Sent
soh	esc x
eot	esc y
esc	esc z

Figure 7.4 An example of byte stuffing. For each occurrence of a character listed in the left column in the data, the sender transmits the two characters in the right column.

To implement byte stuffing, a sender must scan an entire data block and perform the mapping before any data is sent. As the table specifies, the sender replaces each occurrence of *soh* by the two characters *esc* and *x*, each occurrence of *eot* by the characters *esc* and *y*, and each occurrence of *esc* by the combination *esc* and *z*. As characters arrive, the receiver must look for occurrences of *esc* followed by one of *x*, *y* or *z*, and replace the *2*-character combination by the appropriate single character. Figure 7.5 shows an example data block and the resulting frame after byte stuffing has occurred.

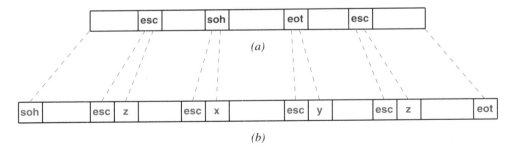

Figure 7.5 Illustration of byte stuffing, where (a) is an example of data that includes characters such as *soh*, and (b) is the frame after byte stuffing. The dashed lines show the locations in the original data where characters have been replaced or new characters added.

As the figure illustrates, the mapping has been chosen carefully to guarantee that after a sender finishes byte stuffing, the characters *soh* and *eot* do not occur in the data section of a frame. Thus, a receiver can be sure that *soh* always delimits the beginning of a frame and *eot* always delimits the end of a frame.

7.6 Transmission Errors

Lightning, power surges, and other electro-magnetic interference can introduce unwanted electrical currents in the electronic components or wires used for communication. Interference that is severe (especially lightning) can cause permanent damage to network equipment. More often, however, interference merely changes the signal used for transmission without damaging the equipment. A small change in the electrical signal can cause the receiver to misinterpret one or more bits of the data. In fact, interference can completely destroy a signal, meaning that although the sender transmits, the receiver does not detect that any data has arrived. Surprisingly, interference on a completely idle transmission circuit can create the opposite effect — although the sender does not transmit anything, a receiver might interpret the incoming interference as a valid sequence of bits or characters. Called *transmission errors*, the problems of lost, changed, or spuriously appearing bits account for much of the complexity needed in computer networks. We can summarize:

> *Much of the complexity in computer networks arises because digital transmission systems are susceptible to interference that can cause random data to appear or transmitted data to be lost or changed.*

7.7 Parity Bits And Parity Checking

Fortunately, few communication systems experience frequent interference. For example, local communication circuits often operate for years without serious problems. More important, the interference on a long-distance communication circuit may be so small that modems can handle all problems automatically. Despite the low probability of error, scientists and engineers who design networks understand that transmission errors do occur, and provide hardware and software mechanisms to detect and correct such problems.

Chapter 5 discusses one of the mechanisms RS-232 hardware uses to detect errors: when a character begins to arrive, the receiver starts a timer and uses the timer to check bits of the incoming character. If the signal does not remain at a fixed voltage for the expected duration of each bit or if a stop bit does not occur at the appropriate time, the hardware declares that interference caused an error. In addition, most RS-232 circuits use a second mechanism to help ensure that each character arrives intact. Known as a *parity check*, the mechanism requires the sender to compute an additional bit, called a *parity bit*, and to attach it to each character before sending. After all bits of a character arrive, the receiver removes the parity bit, performs the same computation as the sender, and verifies that the result agrees with the value of the parity bit. The parity computation is chosen such that if one of the bits in the character is damaged in transit, the receiver's computation will not agree with the parity bit and the receiver will report that an error occurred.

There are two forms of parity, *even* and *odd*; both the sender and receiver must agree on which form is being used. In either form, the computation of parity for a given character is straightforward. To achieve *even parity*, the sender sets the parity bit to *0* or *1* whichever will make the total number of *1* bits (including the parity bit) an even number. Thus, when using even parity, the parity bit for *0100101* is *1* because the character contains an odd number of *1* bits, and the parity bit for *0101101* is *0* because the character already contains an even number of *1* bits. Similarly, to achieve *odd parity*, the sender chooses a parity bit that will make the total number of *1* bits odd. As a character arrives, the receiver counts the number of *1* bits to check the parity. If all bits from the character arrive intact, the receiver's computation of parity will agree with the sender's. If interference changes one of the bits during transmission, the receiver's computation will not agree with the sender's and the receiver will report a parity error.

Parity illustrates an important idea implemented throughout network hardware and software:

> *To detect errors, network systems usually send a small amount of additional information with the data. A sender computes the value of the additional information from the data, and a receiver performs the same computation to verify that the packet was transmitted without error.*

7.8 Probability, Mathematics, And Error Detection

Although the parity mechanism discussed above works well to detect a single bit error, it cannot detect all possible errors. To see why, consider what happens if transmission errors change two bits of a character. For example, even parity means that the bits transmitted by the sender, including the parity bit, contain an even number of *1* bits. If transmission errors change two bits, there are three possible cases: both changed bits began as *0*, both changed bits began as *1*, or the changed bits began as a *0* and a *1*. If two *0* bits are changed to *1*, the total number of *1* bits increases by an even number, so even parity is preserved. Similarly, if two *1* bits are changed to *0*, even parity is preserved because the total number of *1* bits decreases by an even number. Finally, if a *1* is changed to a *0* and a *0* is changed to a *1*, parity is preserved because the total number of *1* bits remains the same.

The example above shows that parity cannot detect transmission errors that change two bits of a character. In fact, parity cannot detect any transmission error that changes an even number of bits. In the worst case, a character can have all *1* bits changed to *0* and still have even parity! We can summarize:

A parity scheme, which is designed to help detect transmission errors, sends one extra bit of information with each character. Although it allows a receiver to determine if a single bit has been changed, parity cannot detect transmission errors that change an even number of bits.

Statisticians and engineers have analyzed the problem of detecting transmission errors, and have invented several alternative mechanisms. In each mechanism, the sender transmits additional information along with the data, and the receiver uses the information to verify that the data arrived intact. Differences among the mechanisms arise in three ways: the size of the additional information (which determines the transmission overhead), the computational complexity of the algorithm (which determines the computational overhead required to create or verify the information), and the number of bit errors that can be detected (which determines how well the method can detect transmission errors). Of course, if the underlying transmission system scrambles bits at random, no amount of additional information can absolutely guarantee that data will arrive without error because the additional information could be changed as well as the original data. Thus, all error detection methods are approximate — the goal is to expend a reasonable effort to produce a low probability of accepting corrupted data.

7.9 Detecting Errors With Checksums

Although several error detection methods have been devised, only a few are used in practice. Many computer network systems send a *checksum* along with each packet to help the receiver detect errors. To compute a checksum, the sender treats the data as a sequence of binary integers and computes their sum. The data is not restricted to integer values — it can contain characters, floating point numbers, or an image. The network system merely treats the data as a sequence of integers for purposes of computing a checksum. For example, Figure 7.6 illustrates a *16*-bit checksum computation for a small text string. To compute a checksum, the sender treats each pair of characters as a *16*-bit integer and computes the sum. If the sum grows larger than *16* bits, the carry bits are added into the final sum.

H	e	l	l	o		w	o	r	l	d	.
48	65	6C	6C	6F	20	77	6F	72	6C	64	2E

4865 + 6C6C + 6F20 + 776F + 726C + 642E + carry = 71FC

Figure 7.6 An example 16-bit checksum computation for a string of 12 ASCII characters. Characters are grouped into 16-bit quantities, added together using 16-bit arithmetic, and the carry bits are added to the result.

Checksums have advantages and disadvantages. The chief advantages arise from the size and ease of computation. Most networks that employ a checksum technique use a *16*-bit or *32*-bit checksum, and compute a single checksum for an entire packet. The small size of the checksum means the cost of transmitting the checksum is usually much smaller than the cost of transmitting the data. Furthermore, because checksums only require addition, the computation required to create or verify a checksum is small.

Checksums have the disadvantage of not detecting all common errors. For example, the table in Figure 7.7 shows that a checksum is not sufficient to detect a transmission error that reverses a bit in each of four data items (to extend the example to an entire packet, imagine that the four changed items occur among several others). Despite the changes, a receiver will declare that the packet has a valid checksum.

Data Item In Binary	Checksum Value	Data Item In Binary	Checksum Value
0001	1	0011	3
0010	2	0000	0
0011	3	0001	1
0001	1	0011	3
totals	7		7

Figure 7.7 Illustration of how a checksum can fail to detect transmission errors. Reversing the value of the second bit in each data item produces the same checksum.

7.10 Detecting Errors With Cyclic Redundancy Checks

How can a network system detect more errors without increasing the amount of additional information in each packet? The answer lies in *Cyclic Redundancy Check* (*CRC*) techniques†, which can detect more errors than a checksum. Although they can be analyzed mathematically, the simplicity and elegance of CRC mechanisms can only be appreciated by understanding the hardware used to implement them. We will examine the basic hardware components briefly, and then show how they can be combined to produce a working system.

Hardware that calculates a CRC uses two simple components: a *shift register* and an *exclusive or* (*xor*) unit. Figure 7.8 shows the diagram we will use for hardware that produces an output equal to the *exclusive or* of two inputs.

---

†In addition to being used in computer networks, CRC techniques are also used to verify that data has been recorded correctly on storage devices such as magnetic disks.

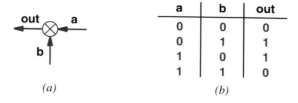

<table>
<tr><th>a</th><th>b</th><th>out</th></tr>
</table>

a	b	out
0	0	0
0	1	1
1	0	1
1	1	0

(a)   *(b)*

Figure 7.8 (a) A diagram of hardware that computes an *exclusive or*, and (b)
the output value for each of the four combinations of input
values. Such hardware units are used to calculate a CRC.

The second hardware device used to compute a CRC is a *shift register*. We can
think of a shift register as a tunnel through which bits move in single file from right to
left. The shift register holds a fixed number of bits (e.g., a shift register might contain
16 bits), so one bit must move out of the register each time a new bit enters. We will
also assume that each shift register has an output that gives the value of the leftmost bit.
Whenever the bit changes, the output changes.

In principle, a shift register has two operations: *initialize* and *shift*. When told to
initialize, a shift register sets all bits to zero. As a result, its output also becomes zero.
When told to shift, a shift register instantaneously moves all bits to the left one position,
sets the rightmost bit according to the current input, and sets the output according to the
leftmost bit. Figure 7.9 illustrates how bit values move during a shift operation and
how the output changes.

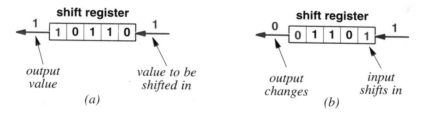

Figure 7.9 A shift register (a) before and (b) after a shift operation. During a
shift, each bit moves left one position, and the output becomes
equal to the leftmost bit.

It is important to understand that changing the input value of a shift register does
not cause a value to be entered — the shift register only reads its input at the instant a
shift operation occurs. For example, Figure 7.9a illustrates that although the input is *1*,
the rightmost bit in the shift register remains *0* until the instant the shift occurs.

7.11 Combining Building Blocks

Figure 7.10 illustrates how three shift registers and three exclusive or units can be combined to compute a 16-bit CRC. The hardware is inexpensive and easy to construct.

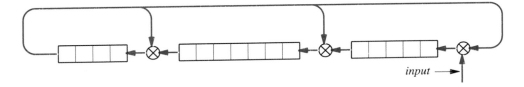

Figure 7.10 A diagram of the hardware used to compute a CRC. After bits
of a message have been shifted into the unit, the shift registers
contain the *16*-bit CRC for the message.

As the figure shows, the hardware consists of three shift registers interconnected by exclusive or units. Output from the leftmost exclusive or hardware unit goes to three places simultaneously: the three exclusive or units. In this example, the shift registers contain *5, 7,* and *4* bits. To compute a CRC, the values in all shift registers are initialized to zero, and the bits of a message are shifted in one at a time†. That is, one bit of the message is applied to the input of the rightmost exclusive or unit at the point labeled *input,* and all three shift registers are instructed to perform a shift operation simultaneously. The hardware repeats the procedure for each bit of the message. After an entire message has been shifted into the unit, the shift registers contain the *16*-bit CRC for the message. A receiver uses identical hardware to calculate the CRC for an incoming message and to verify that it agrees with the CRC the sender transmits.

To simplify checking a CRC, standard CRC algorithms use a small modification to the scheme described above — when computing a CRC, the sender temporarily appends an additional sixteen bits of zeroes to the message. Mathematically, the additional zeroes cause the resulting CRC to act as an inverse, a property useful to the receiver. Instead of computing a CRC over the incoming message and then comparing it to the incoming CRC, the receiver computes a CRC over the incoming message plus the incoming CRC. If all bits are received correctly, the computed value will be zero. The technique is beneficial because hardware can compare sixteen bits to zero efficiently.

Intuitively, there are two reasons a CRC can detect more errors than a simple checksum. First, because an input bit is shifted through all three registers, a single bit of the message affects the resulting CRC in dramatic ways. Second, because the hardware uses feedback in which the output from the leftmost shift register affects each exclusive or unit, the effect from a single bit of the message cycles through the shift registers more than one time.

---

†Several CRC algorithms exist; the algorithms differ in the number of bits allocated to each of the three shift registers and the initial values used.

Mathematically, a CRC uses a polynomial, usually expressed as powers of X, to divide the message. The polynomial used for the example in Figure 7.10 is:

$$P(X) = X^{16} + X^{12} + X^5 + 1$$

7.12 Burst Errors

It can be proved mathematically that a CRC computation detects more errors than a checksum. Two categories of common errors make CRCs especially useful. First, hardware failures sometimes cause a specific set of bits to be damaged. For example, a character-oriented I/O device that is damaged might set the first two bits of every character to zero. Such errors are sometimes called *vertical errors* because they appear in a vertical column when the characters are arranged in rows. CRCs detect vertical errors better than checksums.

Second, CRCs are especially useful for detecting errors that involve changes to a small set of bits near a single location. Such errors are called *burst errors*. Detecting burst errors is important because these errors account for many of the problems that network hardware must handle. For example, electrical interference, such as lightning, often produces burst errors as does electrical interference caused when an electric motor starts near a cable that carries data.

7.13 Frame Format And Error Detection Mechanisms

Networks usually associate error detection information with each frame. The sender calculates information such as a checksum or CRC, and transmits the additional information along with the data in the frame. The receiver calculates the same value and compares it to the additional information that arrives in the frame. For example, Figure 7.11 illustrates how the simple frame format shown in Figure 7.3 can be extended to include a *16*-bit checksum field following the *eot* character.

soh	block of data with byte stuffing	eot	CRC

Figure 7.11 A modification of the frame format from Figure 7.3 that includes a *16*-bit CRC.

Recall that the frame format uses byte stuffing to replace occurrences of the characters *soh*, *eot*, and *esc* in the data. Is byte stuffing required for the CRC as well? The answer depends on the types of error detection required. Because the CRC can contain arbitrary bit strings, one or both of the 8-bit values in the CRC might correspond to a special character (*soh*, *eot*, or *esc*). If characters can be damaged but not lost, a receiver can assume that the two characters immediately following the *eot* comprise a 16-bit CRC which should be used to verify the frame correctness. As an extra check, the receiver can examine the character following a CRC to verify that it is the *soh* at the beginning of the next frame. Thus, if no characters are lost, byte stuffing of the CRC is not required.

If characters can be lost, byte stuffing the CRC can add reliability. To understand how, consider the case where the second character of the CRC is lost. If the receiver assumes the two 8-bit characters following the *eot* form a CRC, the receiver will read the *soh* from the next frame as part of the CRC. Of course, when the receiver compares the computed CRC to the one read, it will find that they do not match and will reject the frame. Ironically, the receiver will then skip the following frame as it scans for an *soh*. Thus, when the CRC is not byte-stuffed, the loss of a single character can cause the receiver to discard two frames.

Should a CRC be computed over the original message or the stuffed frame? Because CRCs are usually computed by hardware, it makes little difference. The sending hardware can stuff the frame, calculate the CRC, and transmit the bytes continuously, with no extra delay for the CRC computation. Similarly, hardware in the receiver can unstuff the incoming frame without delay, and can compare the CRC before or after unstuffing. Thus, individual standards specify whether the CRC is computed on the message or the encoded frame.

7.14 Summary

To ensure that each computer receives prompt, fair service, computer networks require data to be divided into small blocks called *packets*. Conceptually, a network multiplexes packets from multiple sources over a shared communication channel, with the sources taking turns. A given source uses the shared channel to transmit a single packet and then allows another source to proceed. Thus, no single source can delay others for an arbitrarily long time.

To distinguish between the general concept of packets and the specific form of packets used with a given network, we use the term *frame* to refer to a specific packet format. Each network technology defines the exact details of frames the network can use, including the size and format.

We examined a specific frame format that can be used with a character-oriented communication system such as an RS-232 serial data circuit. The example frame format uses a character to mark the beginning of each frame and a different character to mark the end.

To permit a frame to carry arbitrary data, the data must be modified before transmission and restored after reception. Techniques used for modification are referred to as data stuffing because they involve inserting extra bits or bytes. We saw an example of byte stuffing that changes each occurrence of a reserved character into a two-character sequence.

Because electronic equipment and transmission lines are susceptible to electromagnetic interference, data transferred across a network can be mangled or lost. In addition, interference can cause a receiver to interpret electrical noise as data. Computer networks include a variety of mechanisms to detect such transmission errors — the mechanisms require a sender to compute and transmit additional information with the data, and require a receiver to verify that the additional information agrees with the data received. We examined three error detection mechanisms: parity bits, checksums, and cyclic redundancy checks. A parity bit is sent with each individual character; a checksum or cyclic redundancy check is sent with each frame.

No error detection scheme is perfect because transmission errors can affect the additional information as well as the data. A cyclic redundancy check, which is slightly more difficult to compute, can detect more errors than a parity or checksum mechanism. Although a CRC is mathematically complex, it can be implemented with simple, inexpensive hardware.

EXERCISES

7.1 Assume that two computers are using time division multiplexing to take turns sending 1000-byte packets over a shared channel that operates at 64000 bits per second. If the hardware takes 100 microseconds after one computer stops sending before the other can begin, how long will it take for each of the computers to send a one megabyte data file?

7.2 In the previous exercise, calculate the time required for transmission if the computers transmit serially. (Assume a minimum delay of 5 microseconds between two packets sent from the same computer.)

7.3 Consider byte stuffing as described in Section 7.5. Devise a formula that gives an upper bound on the size of data transferred as a function of the size of the original data.

7.4 Does the byte-stuffing technique described in this chapter apply to multiplexing? To find out, create a multiplexor and demultiplexor that use byte-stuffing. Arrange to accept 8-bit data streams from three sources, send the data across a shared interconnection, and then separate the data into three independent streams.

7.5 A byte stuffing system is *adaptive* if the sender can choose the escape character for each transfer. To inform the receiver about the scheme being used, the sender transmits a sequence such as *soh x*, where *x* denotes the escape character to be used. The value of *x* is chosen to minimize the size of the transfer. Design an algorithm that takes as input a file of data to be transmitted, and produces a byte stuffing scheme that minimizes the data transferred.

7.6 Write a computer program that does adaptive byte stuffing as described in the previous exercise. Run your program on binary files. How does the size of the data transferred compare to the data transferred with a non-adaptive scheme? Do you ever send more data?

7.7 Suppose malfunctioning hardware in a character-oriented transmission system sets all bits transferred to zero. Does a parity bit catch the problem? Why or why not?

7.8 Write a computer program that computes a 16-bit checksum over a file. The fastest method uses a 32-bit integer to accumulate the sum. Remember to handle carry bits (i.e., bits beyond the first 16) by adding them back into the sum.

7.9 In the previous exercise, what happens if adding carry bits causes another carry? How can the situation be handled efficiently?

7.10 Write a computer program to simulate the CRC hardware shown in Figure 7.10.

7.11 Checksum computation is often implemented with conventional computer software, but most CRC computations are performed with special-purpose hardware. Why?

Chapter Contents

8

LAN Technologies And Network Topology

8.1 Introduction

Early chapters explain how bits can be encoded in signals which are then transmitted over a communication channel, and discuss the modem hardware that interconnects two computers and performs the necessary encoding and decoding. Although modems are needed for long-distance communication, most networks are local — the network fits inside a building or a single room. Furthermore, small networks are often designed to permit multiple computers to share resources. For example, a local network that connects two computers and a printer allows either of the computers to access the printer.

The hardware technologies used for local networks do not consist of separate modems and cables. Instead, the technologies are designed for sharing. They allow multiple computers and devices like printers to attach directly to a single, shared network. Because the underlying medium is shared, the computers must take turns using it. This chapter describes the concepts underlying local network technologies, and explains why networks that use sharing have become popular. The chapter describes basic network topologies and examines examples of popular local network technologies. The next three chapters continue the discussion of networks used for local communication by describing additional details, including an explanation of wiring schemes.

8.2 Direct Point-to-Point Communication

The first computer communication systems all used the pattern described in previous chapters. Each communication channel (e.g., a leased data circuit) connected exactly two computers, and was available to those computers exclusively. Known as a *point-to-point network* or *mesh network*, the scheme has three useful properties. First, because each connection is installed independently, appropriate hardware can be used. For example, the transmission capacity (i.e., the bandwidth) of the underlying circuit and the modems used do not need to be the same on all connections. Second, because they have exclusive access, the connected computers can decide exactly how to send data across the connection. They can choose a frame format, an error detection mechanism, and a maximum frame size. More important, because each connection is independent of others, the details can be changed whenever the owners of the attached computers agree to make a change. Third, because only two computers have access to the channel, it is easy to enforce security and privacy. No other computers handle data, and no other computers can obtain access.

Of course, point-to-point connections have disadvantages as well. The main disadvantage becomes apparent when more than two computers need to communicate with one another. In a point-to-point scheme that provides a separate communication channel for each pair of computers, the number of connections grows quickly as the size of the set increases. For example, Figure 8.1 illustrates that two computers need only one connection, three computers need three connections, and four computers need six connections.

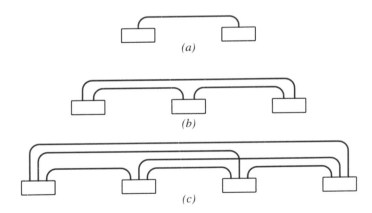

Figure 8.1 The independent point-to-point connections required for (a) two, (b) three, and (c) four computers. The number of connections grows rapidly as the number of computers increases.

As the figure illustrates, the total number of connections grows more rapidly than the total number of computers. Mathematically, the number of connections needed for N computers is proportional to the square of N:

$$direct\ connections\ required\ =\ \frac{(N^2 - N)}{2}$$

Intuitively, we can understand the effect by considering how expensive it becomes to add a new computer to an existing set: the new computer must have a connection to each of the existing computers. Thus, adding the Nth computer requires $N-1$ new connections.

In practice, the expense is especially high because many connections follow the same physical path. For example, suppose an organization has five computers, with two computers in one location (e.g., the ground floor of a building) and three computers in another (e.g., the top floor of the same building). Figure 8.2 illustrates that if each computer has a connection to all other computers, six connections pass between the two locations — in many cases such connections follow the same physical path.

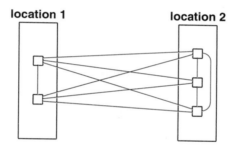

location 1   **location 2**

Figure 8.2 The disadvantage of a point-to-point network that requires a dedicated connection for each pair of computers: the total number of connections passing between two locations can exceed the total number of computers being connected.

The figure shows that in a point-to-point network, the number of connections passing between two locations usually exceeds the total number of computers. If another computer is added to the two computers at location *1*, the situation becomes worse: the total number of computers becomes six and the number of connections passing between the two locations increases to nine†.

---

†Chapter 13 describes how electronic switching can be used to reduce the number of connections.

8.3 Shared Communication Channels

The history of computer networking changed dramatically during the late 1960s and early 1970s when researchers developed a form of computer communication known as *Local Area Networks* (*LANs*). Devised as alternatives to expensive, dedicated point-to-point connections, the designs differ fundamentally from long-distance networks because they rely on sharing the network. Each LAN consists of a single shared medium, usually a cable, to which many computers attach. The computers take turns using the medium to send packets.

Several LAN designs emerged from the research. The designs differ in details such as the voltages and modulation techniques used, and the approach to sharing (i.e., the mechanisms used to coordinate access and transmit packets).

Because it eliminates duplication, sharing has an important economic impact on networking: it reduces cost. Consequently, Local Area Network technologies that allow a set of computers to share a medium have become popular. In fact,

> *Networks that allow multiple computers to share a communication medium are used for local communication. Point-to-point connections are used for long-distance networks and a few other special cases.*

If sharing reduces cost, why are shared networks used only for local communication? Both technical and economic reasons contribute to the answer. We said that the computers attached to a shared network must coordinate use of the network. Because coordination requires communication and the time required to communicate depends on distance, a large geographic separation between computers introduces longer delays. Thus, shared networks with long delays are inefficient because they spend more time coordinating use of the shared medium and less time sending data. In addition, engineers have learned that providing a high bandwidth communication channel over long distances is significantly more expensive than providing the same bandwidth communication over a short distance.

8.4 Significance Of LANs And Locality Of Reference

The significance of LANs can be stated simply:

> *Local Area Network technologies have become the most popular form of computer networks. LANs now connect more computers than any other type of network.*

One of the reasons so many LANs have been installed is economic: LAN technologies are both inexpensive and widely available. However, the main reason the demand for LANs is high can be attributed to a fundamental principle of computer networking known as *locality of reference*. The locality of reference principle states that communication among a set of computers is not random, but instead follows two patterns. First, if a pair of computers communicates once, the pair is likely to communicate again in the near future and then periodically. The pattern is called *temporal locality of reference* to imply a relationship over time. Second, a computer tends to communicate most often with other computers that are nearby. The second pattern is called *physical locality of reference*† to emphasize the geographic relationship. We can summarize:

> The locality of reference principle: *computer communication follows two distinct patterns. First, a computer is more likely to communicate with computers that are physically nearby than with computers that are far away. Second, a computer is more likely to communicate with the same set of computers repeatedly.*

The locality of reference principle is easy to understand because it applies to human communication. For example, people communicate most often with others who are physically nearby (e.g., working together). Furthermore, if an individual communicates with someone (e.g., a friend or family member), the individual is likely to communicate with the same person again.

8.5 LAN Topologies

Because many LAN technologies have been invented, it is important to know how specific technologies are similar and how they differ. To help understand similarities, each network is classified into a category according to its *topology* or general shape. This section describes the three topologies used most often with LANs; later sections add more detail and show specific examples.

8.5.1 Star Topology

A network uses a *star topology* if all computers attach to a central point. Figure 8.3 illustrates the concept.

---

†Physical locality of reference is sometimes referred to as *spatial locality of reference*.

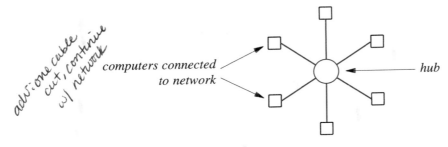

adv: one cable cut, continue w/ network

computers connected to network   *hub*

Figure 8.3 Illustration of the star topology in which each computer attaches to
a central point called a *hub*.

Because a star-shaped network resembles the spokes of a wheel, the center of a star
network is often called a *hub*. A typical hub consists of an electronic device that accepts data from a sending computer and delivers it to the appropriate destination.

Figure 8.3 illustrates an idealized star network. In practice, star networks seldom
have a symmetric shape in which the hub is located an equal distance from all computers. Instead, a hub often resides in a location separate from the computers attached to
it. For example, Chapter 10 will illustrate that computers can reside in individual offices, while the hub resides in a location accessible to an organization's networking
staff.

8.5.2 Ring Topology

A network that uses a *ring topology* arranges for computers to be connected in a
closed loop — a cable connects the first computer to a second computer, another cable
connects the second computer to a third, and so on, until a cable connects the final computer back to the first. The name *ring* arises because one can imagine the computers
and the cables connecting them arranged in a circle as Figure 8.4 illustrates.

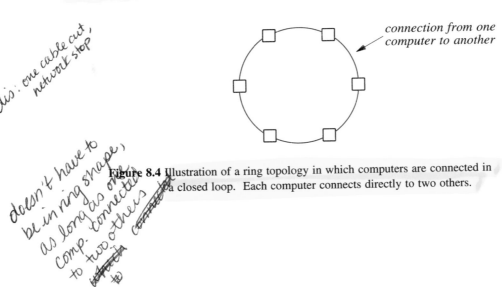

dis: one cable cut, network stop

doesn't have to be in ring shape, as long as comp. connected to two others

connection from one computer to another

Figure 8.4 Illustration of a ring topology in which computers are connected in
a closed loop. Each computer connects directly to two others.

It is important to understand that the *ring*, like the star topology, refers to logical connections among computers, not physical orientation — the computers and connections in a ring network need not be arranged in a circle. Instead, the cable between a pair of computers in a ring network may follow a hallway or rise vertically from one floor of a building to another. Furthermore, if one computer is far from others in the ring, the two cables that connect the distant computer may follow the same physical path.

8.5.3 Bus Topology

A network that uses a *bus topology* usually consists of a single, long cable to which computers attach†. Any computer attached to a bus can send a signal down the cable, and all computers receive the signal. Figure 8.5 illustrates the topology. Because all computers attached to the cable can sense an electrical signal, any computer can send data to any other computer. Of course, the computers attached to a bus network must coordinate to ensure that only one computer sends a signal at any time or chaos results.

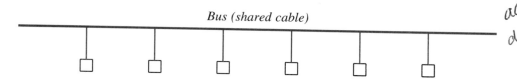

Bus (shared cable)

adv- less wire comp.
dis: one comp. cut, all out

Figure 8.5 Illustration of a bus topology in which all computers attach to a single cable.

8.5.4 The Reason For Multiple Topologies

Each topology has advantages and disadvantages. A ring topology makes it easy for computers to coordinate access and to detect whether the network is operating correctly. However, an entire ring network is disabled if one of the cables is cut. A star topology helps protect the network from damage to a single cable because each cable connects only one machine. A bus requires fewer wires than a star, but has the same disadvantage as a ring: a network is disabled if someone accidentally cuts the main cable. In addition to later sections in this chapter, other chapters provide detailed examples of network technologies that illustrate some of the differences.

We can summarize the major points about network topologies.

> *Networks are classified into broad categories according to their general shape. The primary topologies used with LANs are star, ring, and bus; each topology has advantages and disadvantages.*

---

†In practice, the ends of a bus network must be terminated to prevent electrical signals from reflecting back along the bus.

8.6 Example Bus Network: Ethernet

8.6.1 History Of The Ethernet

Ethernet is a well-known and widely used network technology that employs bus topology. Ethernet was invented at Xerox Corporation's Palo Alto Research Center in the early 1970s. Digital Equipment Corporation, Intel Corporation, and Xerox later cooperated to devise a production standard, which is informally called *DIX Ethernet* for the initials of the three companies. IEEE now controls Ethernet standards†. In its original version, an Ethernet LAN consisted of a single coaxial cable, called the *ether*, to which multiple computers connect. Engineers use the term *segment* to refer to the Ethernet coaxial cable. A given Ethernet segment is limited to *500* meters in length, and the standard requires a minimum separation of *3* meters between each pair of connections.

The original Ethernet hardware operated at a rate of 10 Megabits per second (Mbps); a later version known as *Fast Ethernet* operates at 100 Mbps, and the most recent version, which is known as *Gigabit Ethernet* operates at 1000 Mbps or 1 Gigabit per second (Gbps).

8.6.2 Ethernet Transmission And Manchester Encoding

The Ethernet standard specifies all details, including the format of frames that computers send across the ether‡, the voltage to be used, and the method used to modulate a signal. For example, the standard specifies that frames are sent using the *Manchester Encoding*.

To understand Manchester Encoding, it is necessary to know that hardware can detect a change in voltage more easily than a fixed value. As a result, instead of encoding digital values using two voltages like RS-232, values are encoded as a series of changes§. Technically, the hardware is said to be *edge triggered*, and the changes are known as *rising* or *falling* edges. Manchester Encoding uses rising and falling edges to encode data. The sender transmits a falling edge to encode a 0 and a rising edge to encode a 1. Figure 8.6 illustrates the encoding.

In the figure, the x-axis represents the time required to transmit the twelve bits 101011000101, and the y-axis represents the voltage. The x-axis is divided into twelve "slots" that each correspond to a single bit. The voltage change that encodes a digital value occurs exactly half-way through a time slot. For example, when transmission begins, the voltage is zero. Exactly half-way through the first time slot, the voltage becomes positive to encode a bit value of 1. Similarly, exactly half-way through the second time slot, the voltage falls to encode a value of 0. If two contiguous bits have the same value, an additional change in voltage occurs at the edge of the time slot. For example, because a rising edge encodes the value 1, when contiguous 1 bits occur, the voltage drops on the boundary between the bits.

---

†Several variations of Ethernet exist; Chapter 10 discusses alternatives.
‡Chapter 9 discusses Ethernet frames in more detail and shows an example.
§Figure 5.2 on page 58 illustrates the RS-232 encoding.

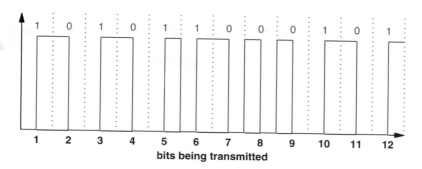

Figure 8.6 Illustration of Manchester Encoding used with Ethernet. A change
from positive voltage to zero encodes a 0 bit, and a change from
zero to positive voltage encodes a 1 bit.

To make sense of the incoming signal, a receiver must know exactly when each
time slot begins and ends. Manchester encoding uses a *preamble* to allow such synchronization. The preamble consists of sixty-four alternating 1's and 0's sent before the
frame. As the figure illustrates, alternating 1's and 0's produce a square wave with
transitions exactly at the middle of each slot. Receiving hardware uses the preamble to
synchronize its notion of time slots with the arriving signal. Once the preamble has
been processed, the receiver can correctly identify successive bits.

8.6.3 Sharing On An Ethernet

Because it uses a bus topology, Ethernet requires multiple computers to share access to a single medium. A sender transmits a signal, which propagates from the sender
toward both ends of the cable. Figure 8.7 illustrates how data flows across an Ethernet.

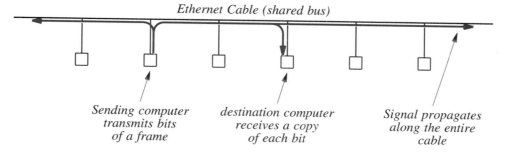

Figure 8.7 Conceptual flow of bits across an Ethernet. While transmitting a
frame, a computer has exclusive use of the cable.

As the figure shows, a signal propagates from the sending computer to both ends of the shared cable. It is important to understand that sharing in local area networks technologies does not mean that multiple frames are being sent at the same time. Instead, the sending computer has exclusive use of the entire cable during the transmission of a given frame — other computers must wait. After one computer finishes transmitting one frame, the shared cable becomes available for another computer to use. To summarize:

Ethernet is a bus network in which multiple computers share a single transmission medium. While one computer transmits a frame to another, all other computers must wait.

8.7 Carrier Sense On Multi-Access Networks (CSMA)

The most interesting aspect of Ethernet is the mechanism used to coordinate transmission. An Ethernet network does not have a centralized controller that tells each computer how to take turns using the shared cable. Instead, all computers attached to an Ethernet participate in a distributed coordination scheme called *Carrier Sense Multiple Access* (*CSMA*). The scheme uses electrical activity on the cable to determine status. When no computer is sending a frame, the ether does not contain electrical signals. During frame transmission, however, a sender transmits electrical signals used to encode bits. Although the signals differ slightly from the carrier waves described in Chapter 6, they are informally called a *carrier*. Thus, to determine whether the cable is currently being used, a computer can check for a carrier. If no carrier is present, the computer can transmit a frame. If a carrier is present, the computer must wait for the sender to finish before proceeding. Technically, checking for a carrier wave is called *carrier sense*, and the idea of using the presence of a signal to determine when to transmit is called *Carrier Sense Multiple Access* (*CSMA*).

8.8 Collision Detection And Backoff With CSMA/CD

Because CSMA allows each computer to determine whether a shared cable is already in use by another computer, it prevents a computer from interrupting an ongoing transmission. However, CSMA cannot prevent all possible conflicts. To understand why, imagine what happens if two computers at opposite ends of an idle cable both have a frame ready to send at the same time. When they check for a carrier, both stations find the cable idle, and both start to send frames simultaneously. The signals travel at approximately 70% of the speed of light, and when the signals transmitted by two computers reach the same point on the cable, they interfere with each other.

The interference between two signals is called a *collision*. Although a collision does not harm the hardware, it produces a garbled transmission that prevents either of the two frames from being received correctly. To ensure that no other computer transmits simultaneously, the Ethernet standard requires a sending station to monitor signals on the cable. If the signal on the cable differs from the signal that the station is sending, it means that a collision has occurred†. Whenever a collision is detected, a sending station immediately stops transmitting. Technically, monitoring a cable during transmission is known as *Collision Detect* (*CD*), and the Ethernet mechanism is known as *Carrier Sense Multiple Access with Collision Detect* (*CSMA/CD*).

CSMA/CD does more than merely detect collisions — it also recovers from them. After a collision occurs, a computer must wait for the cable to become idle again before transmitting a frame. However, if the computers begin to transmit as soon as the ether becomes idle, another collision will occur. To avoid multiple collisions, Ethernet requires each computer to delay after a collision before attempting to retransmit. The standard specifies a maximum delay, *d*, and forces each computer to choose a random delay less than *d*. In most cases, when a computer chooses a delay at random, it will select a value that differs from any of the values chosen by the other computers — the computer that chooses the smallest delay will proceed to send a frame and the network will return to normal operation.

If two or more computers happen to choose nearly the same amount of delay after a collision, they will both begin to transmit at nearly the same time, producing a second collision. To avoid a sequence of collisions, Ethernet requires each computer to double the range from which a delay is chosen after each collision. Thus, a computer chooses a random delay from *0* to *d* after one collision, a random delay between *0* and *2d* after a second collision, between *0* and *4d* after a third, and so on. After a few collisions, the range from which a random value is chosen becomes large, and the probability is high that some computer will choose a short delay and transmit without a collision.

Technically, doubling the range of the random delay after each collision is known as *binary exponential backoff*. In essence, exponential backoff means that an Ethernet can recover quickly after a collision because each computer agrees to wait longer times between attempts when the cable becomes busy. In the unlikely event that two or more computers choose delays that are approximately equal, exponential backoff guarantees that contention for the cable will be reduced after a few collisions. We can summarize:

> *Computers attached to an Ethernet use CSMA/CD in which a computer waits for the ether to be idle before transmitting a frame. If two computers transmit simultaneously, a collision occurs; the computers use exponential backoff to choose which computer will proceed. Each computer delays a random time before trying to transmit again, and then doubles the delay for each successive collision.*

---

†To guarantee that a collision has time to reach all stations before they stop transmitting, the Ethernet standard specifies both a maximum cable length and a minimum frame size.

8.9 802.11 Wireless LANs And CSMA/CA

A set of *wireless LAN* technologies are available that use a modified form of CSMA/CD. The products, which are manufactured by several companies are available under a variety of trade names. For example, Apple Computer Corporation sells an *Airport* device; Lucent Corporation sells *WaveLAN*; Solectek sells *AirLAN*; and Proxim Corporation sells *RangeLAN*. Older devices use 900 MHz frequencies to permit data to be sent at 2 Mbps; IEEE standard *802.11* defines wireless LANs that operate at 11 Mbps using a frequency in the 2.4 GHz range. A standard known as *bluetooth* specifies a wireless LAN technology designed for short distances.

Instead of transmitting signals across a cable, wireless LAN hardware uses antennas to broadcast RF signals through the air, which other computers receive. Like other LAN technologies, the wireless LANs use sharing. That is, all the computers participating in a given wireless LAN are configured to the same radio frequency. Thus, they must take turns sending packets.

One difference between the way wired and wireless LANs manage sharing arises because of the way wireless transmissions propagate. Although the electromagnetic energy radiates in all directions, wireless LAN transmitters use low power, meaning that a transmission only has enough power to travel a short distance. Furthermore, metallic obstructions can block the signal. Thus, wireless units located far apart or behind obstructions will not receive each other's transmissions.

The lack of full communication means that wireless LANs cannot use the same CSMA/CD mechanism that Ethernet uses. To understand why, consider three computers with wireless LAN hardware positioned far apart as Figure 8.8 illustrates.

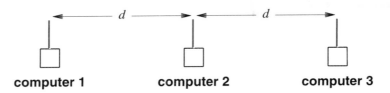

Figure 8.8 Three computers with wireless LAN hardware positioned at maximal transmission distance, *d*. Although computer *2* will receive all transmissions, computers *1* and *3* will not receive transmissions from each other

In the figure, the two outer computers are too far apart to receive each others' transmissions. In such situations, carrier sense and collision detection does not suffice. For example, suppose computer *1* is sending a packet to computer *2*. Because computer *3* cannot receive the transmission, it might proceed to transmit, resulting in a collision. Similarly, if both computer *1* and computer *3* transmit a frame at the same time, only computer *2* can detect a collision.

To ensure that they share the transmission media correctly, wireless LANs use a modified scheme known as *Carrier Sense Multiple Access With Collision Avoidance (CSMA/CA)*. Instead of depending on all other computers to receive all transmissions, the CSMA/CA used with wireless LANs triggers a brief transmission from the intended receiver before transmitting a packet. For example, suppose computer *1* in Figure 8.8 needs to send a frame to computer *2*. Before sending the frame, computer *1* first transmits a brief control message. When computer *2* receives the control message, it responds by sending another control message to indicate that it is ready to receive a transmission. When computer *1* receives the response from its intended recipient, it begins transmitting the frame.

The advantage of waiting for a response from the recipient becomes clear if we remember that transmission is asymmetric. In the figure, although computer *3* does not receive the transmission from computer *1*, it does receive the transmission from computer *2*. Thus, once computer *2* sends a response, all computers within range of its antenna will wait for the transmission of a packet (even if they cannot receive the transmission).

Collisions of control messages can occur when using CSMA/CA, but they can be handled easily. In the figure, for example, if computers *1* and *3* both generate a packet for computer *2* at exactly the same time, they each send a control message. The control messages will arrive at computer *2* simultaneously, causing a collision. When such collisions do occur, the sending stations apply random backoff before resending the control messages. Because control messages are much shorter than data frames, the probability of a second collision is much lower than with conventional Ethernet. Eventually, one of the two control messages arrives intact, and computer *2* transmits a response.

8.10 Another Example Bus Network: LocalTalk

Apple Computer Corporation also invented a LAN that employs bus topology. Called *LocalTalk*, the technology is designed for use with Apple's personal computers, and is especially popular in organizations that have many Apple computers. Each Apple Macintosh includes all the hardware needed to connect the computer to a LocalTalk network; LocalTalk hardware is also available for other brands of computers.

Although each LocalTalk network is a bus, attached computers use a version of CSMA/CA when accessing the medium. As with wireless LANs, a computer sends a small control message to reserve the bus. If a reservation succeeds (i.e., no collision results), all other computers refrain from using the medium while the sender transmits its frame. Because it is extremely small compared to a conventional data message, the time required to send the reservation is insignificant.

Compared to Ethernet, LocalTalk has both advantages and disadvantages. One disadvantage is throughput. LocalTalk network hardware can send 230.4 thousand bits per second (*Kbps*), which is only *2.3* percent of the throughput available on a 10 Mbps

Ethernet network. Lower throughput means it takes longer to transmit large volumes of data. LocalTalk also has distance limitations, and is not available on all computers.

Despite its limitations, LocalTalk has some advantages. The chief advantage arises from its price: LocalTalk is almost free because most of the hardware needed to connect the computer to a LocalTalk network is included with the computer. For example, only a single cable is needed to connect two Macintosh computers over LocalTalk. Furthermore, LocalTalk is easy to install — the technology uses simple connectors that allow one to attach or change connections without tools or special training. Finally, Local-Talk hardware is available on many printers, making it possible to attach a printer to a network, where it can be accessed by multiple computers.

8.11 Example Ring Network: IBM Token Ring

We said that a LAN using a ring topology connects computers in a loop. Most LANs that employ ring topology also use an access mechanism known as *token passing*, and the resulting networks are known as *token passing ring networks*, abbreviated *token ring*. A token ring operates as a single, shared medium. When a computer needs to send data, the computer must wait for permission before it can access the network. Once it obtains permission, the sending computer has complete control of the ring — no other transmissions occur simultaneously. As the sending computer transmits a frame, the bits pass from the sender to the next computer, then to the next computer and so on, until the bits pass completely around the ring and arrive back at the sender. Figure 8.9 illustrates the concept.

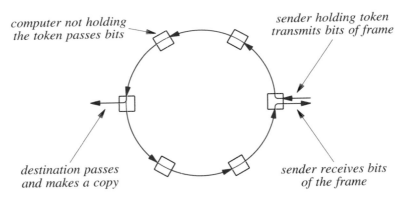

Figure 8.9 The conceptual flow of bits during a transmission on a token ring network. Except for the sender, computers on the network pass bits of the frame to the next station. The destination makes a copy.

As the figure shows, all stations except the sender forward bits around the ring. Thus, to verify that no transmission errors occurred, a sender can compare the data being received to the data being sent. Other stations monitor all transmissions. If a frame is destined for a given computer, that computer makes a copy of the frame as the bits pass around the ring.

How does a sender obtain permission to transmit on a token ring? Unlike an Ethernet, a token ring transmission does not rely on CSMA/CD. Instead, the token ring hardware coordinates among all connected computers to ensure that permission is passed to each computer in turn. The coordination uses a special, reserved message called a *token*. The token is a bit pattern that differs from normal data frames. To ensure that normal data cannot be interpreted as a token, some token ring technologies use bit stuffing† to temporarily change occurrences of the token in data for transmission on the ring. More important, the token ring hardware ensures that exactly one token exists on a token ring network.

In essence, a token gives a computer permission to send one frame. Thus, before it can send a frame, a computer must wait for the token to arrive. When a token arrives, the computer temporarily removes the token from the ring and uses the ring to transmit data. Although it may have more than one frame waiting to be sent, the computer only sends one frame, and then transmits the token. Unlike data frames, which pass completely around the ring while they are being sent, the token travels from one computer directly to an adjacent computer, which can then use the network to send a frame.

If all computers on a token ring network have data to send, the token passing scheme guarantees that they will take turns, with each computer sending one frame before passing the token. Note that the scheme guarantees fair access: as the token passes around the ring, each computer will have an opportunity to use the network. If a particular computer does not have any data to send when it receives the token, the interface hardware merely passes the token on without delay. In the extreme case where no station has any data to transmit, the token circulates continuously, with each station receiving the token and then immediately passing it on to the next computer. The time required for a token to make a complete trip around a ring of idle computers is extremely brief (e.g., a millisecond). A short time is possible for two reasons. First, because the token is small, it can be transmitted across a single wire quickly. Second, the token is handled by the ring hardware, which means that the speed does not depend on the computer's CPU. We can summarize:

> *Computers attached to a token ring network use a special, short message called a* token *to coordinate use of the ring. One token exists on the ring at any time. To send data, a computer must wait for the token to arrive, transmit exactly one frame, and then transmit the token to the next computer. When no computers have data to send, the token cycles around the ring at high speed.*

---

†Recall from Chapter 7 that bit stuffing encodes data bits so the receiver does not confuse them with a token.

IBM Corporation has developed one of the best-known token passing network technologies. Although it was not the first commercially-available token ring network, the *IBM Token Ring* became so popular that many professionals use the term *Token Ring* to denote IBM's technology†. IBM's Token Ring operates at 16 million bits per second, and can be used with computers from IBM, computers from other vendors, and peripheral devices such as printers.

8.12 Another Example Ring Network: FDDI

One of the chief disadvantages of the token ring networks arises from their susceptibility to failures. Because each computer attached to a ring must pass bits of a frame to the next computer, failure of a single machine can disable the entire network. Token ring hardware is usually designed to avoid such failures. For example the hardware that attaches a computer to the network is designed to overcome software failures — the hardware can continue to send each incoming bit on the outgoing connection despite software failures (e.g., a system crash). However, most token ring networks cannot recover from a broken connection such as those that result if the cable connecting two computers is accidentally cut.

Some ring network technologies have been designed to overcome severe failures. For example, *Fiber Distributed Data Interconnect* (*FDDI*) is a token ring technology that can transmit data at a rate of 100 million bits per second, eight times faster than an IBM Token Ring network, and ten times faster than the original Ethernet. To provide such high data rates, FDDI uses optical fibers to interconnect computers instead of copper cables‡.

FDDI also uses redundancy to overcome failures. An FDDI network contains two complete rings — one that is used to send data when everything is working correctly, and another that is used only when the first ring fails. Physically, the two fibers connecting a pair of computers are not completely separate. Instead, each fiber is covered with a flexible plastic jacket, and the jackets of the pair are joined in the same way as the plastic jacket on the wires in the power cord of a household applicance. Therefore, the fibers needed for two rings can be installed at the same time.

Interestingly, the rings in an FDDI network are called *counter rotating* because data flows around the second ring opposite of the direction data flows around the main ring. To understand the motivation for counter rotating rings, consider how catastrophic failures occur. First, because the pair of fibers connecting two stations usually follow the same physical path, an accident that breaks one fiber often breaks both. Second, if data always passes in the same direction across both rings, disconnecting one station from the ring (e.g., while moving a computer) will prevent other stations from communicating. However, if data travels in the reverse direction across the second ring, remaining stations can reconfigure the network to use the reverse path. Figure 8.10 illustrates the concept.

---

†Throughout this text, we will follow the accepted convention of writing *Token Ring* in uppercase to refer to the token ring technology developed by IBM.

‡A related technology, *Copper Distributed Data Interconnection* (*CDDI*) works like FDDI, but uses copper wires instead of optical fibers.

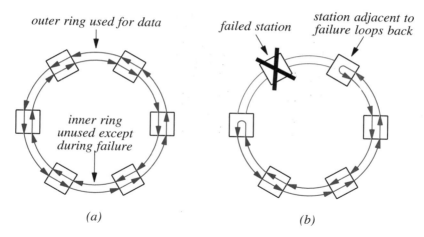

Figure 8.10 (a) An FDDI network with arrows showing the directions that data flows, and (b) the same network after a station has failed. Normally, data travels in one direction. After a station fails, adjacent stations use the reverse path to form a closed ring.

Although Figure 8.10a shows the directions data can travel in the counter rotating rings, only one of the two rings is normally used. For example, in the figure, a station always transmits and receives frames on the outer ring, while the network hardware forwards bits on the inner ring without interpreting them. Figure 8.10b illustrates the data path following a failure. Hardware in the stations adjacent to a failure detect the disconnection and reconfigure so they loop incoming bits back along the reverse path. Thus, the failed station is removed and the remaining stations are connected to a contiguous ring. The process of reconfiguring to avoid a failure is called *self-healing*, and FDDI is known as a *self-healing network*. We can summarize:

> *An FDDI network is called* self-healing *because the hardware can detect a catastrophic failure and recover automatically. To do so, FDDI uses a pair of counter rotating rings. One ring is used to transmit data. When a failure occurs that breaks the ring, stations adjacent to the failure automatically reconfigure, using the second ring to bypass the failure.*

8.13 Example Star Network: ATM

Telephone companies have developed a networking technology known as *Asynchronous Transfer Mode (ATM)*†. The basic element of an ATM network is an electronic switch to which several computers can connect. For example, Figure 8.11 illustrates six computers connected to an ATM switch.

---

†Chapter 14 covers ATM in more detail.

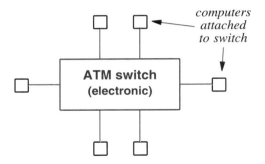

Figure 8.11 An ATM switch with six computers attached, and the star topology that results.

The figure shows why ATM is classified as a star topology. One or more interconnected switches form a central hub to which all computers attach. Unlike bus or ring topologies, a star network does not propagate data to any computers other than the communicating pair — the hub receives incoming data directly from the sender, and transmits outgoing data directly to the receiver. Note that the star topology makes an ATM network less dependent on the connections to individual computers than a network that uses a ring topology. If the connection between a computer and the switch breaks, only that computer is affected.

Because ATM is designed to provide high throughput, a typical connection between a computer and an ATM switch operates at a speed of 155 Mbps or faster. To carry such high data rates, the connection between a computer and an ATM switch usually uses optical fiber instead of copper cable. In fact, each connection uses a pair of fibers as Figure 8.12 illustrates; a given fiber is only used to carry data in one direction.

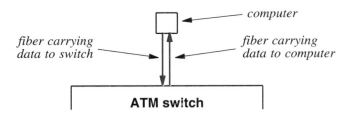

Figure 8.12 Details of a connection between an ATM switch and a computer. Each connection consists of a pair of optical fibers. One fiber carries data to the switch, and the other carries data to the computer.

Like the optical fibers used with FDDI, the pair of fibers used to connect a computer to an ATM switch are fastened together. Usually, the jacket on one fiber contains a colored stripe or is labeled; whoever installs a connection uses the label to ensure that the output of the switch connects to the input of the computer and vice versa.

To summarize:

> *An ATM network is formed from a switch to which multiple computers attach. The connection between a computer and an ATM switch consists of a pair of fibers, one carrying data in each direction.*

8.14 Summary

This chapter discusses an alternative to direct point-to-point communication called a Local Area Network (LAN). Designed for use over a small distance (e.g., in a building), a LAN does not need a separate wire between each pair of computers. Instead, a LAN consists of a single, shared medium to which many computers attach. The computers take turns using the medium to send data.

Although LAN technologies require computers to divide data into small packets called frames, only one packet can be transmitted on a LAN at any time. That is, while transmitting, a computer has exclusive use of the LAN. To make access fair, each computer is permitted to hold the shared medium for the transmission of one frame before allowing another computer to proceed. Thus, after it gains control, a computer sends a frame and then relinquishes control to another computer.

Each computer network can be classified into one of a few basic categories, depending on its topology. A bus topology consists of a single, shared cable to which many computers attach. When it uses a bus, a computer transmits a signal that all other computers attached to the bus receive. A ring topology consists of computers connected in a closed loop. The first computer connects to the second, the second connects to the third, and so on, until the last computer connects back to the first. Finally, a star topology resembles a wheel with the network itself corresponding to a central hub, and the links to individual computers corresponding to spokes. Each topology has advantages and disadvantages; no topology is best for all purposes.

LAN technologies exist that use each topology. An Ethernet LAN uses a bus topology, as does LocalTalk. To access an Ethernet, stations obey Carrier Sense Multiple Access with Collision Detect (CSMA/CD). That is, a station waits for the ether to be idle, and then attempts to send. If two stations transmit at the same time, a collision results, causing them to wait a random time before trying again. Successive collisions cause exponential backoff in which each station doubles its delay.

Wireless LANs such as WaveLAN, RangeLAN, or AirLAN use Carrier Sense Multiple Access With Collision Avoidance (CSMA/CA). Before transmitting a data frame, a sender transmits a small control message to which the receiver responds. The exchange of control messages notifies all stations within range of the receiver that a data transmission is about to occur. Other stations then remain silent while the transmission takes place (i.e., avoid a collision), even if they do not receive a copy of the signal.

Stations attached to a token passing ring network also share the medium. While one station transmits a frame, all other stations pass the bits around the ring, which allows the sender to verify that the bits were transmitted correctly. To coordinate use of the ring and guarantee fairness, stations on a token ring send a special message called a token. A station waits for the token to arrive, uses the complete ring to transmit one frame, and then sends the token to the next station. IBM Token Ring and FDDI networks both use token passing. FDDI differs from conventional token passing technologies because it can be configured with an extra ring that is used to recover from catastrophic failures. The extra ring is called counter-rotating because data flows the opposite direction than on the main ring. An FDDI network with a counter-rotating ring is said to be self-healing because it can detect a failure and loop back along the reverse ring to close the path.

LANs that use ATM technology have a star topology. An ATM switch forms the hub of the star to which each computer connects. Because ATM is designed to operate at high speed, the connection between a computer and an ATM switch uses a pair of optical fibers, with one fiber carrying data in each direction.

EXERCISES

8.1 Keep a record of the people with whom you exchange e-mail for one week and the times messages are sent. Does your communication exhibit spatial locality of reference? Does it exhibit temporal locality of reference?

8.2 See if you can find an example of a point-to-point network. Ask the owner why point-to-point connections were chosen.

8.3 Classify the topology of each network at your site. Which topology is used the most? Which is used the least?

8.4 An Ethernet cable must have a terminator on each end of the cable to prevent reflections. Consult an electrical engineering source to find out what type of component is used in a terminator.

8.5 What data values in an Ethernet packet result in the maximum number of voltage transitions when the packet is transmitted using the Manchester Encoding?

8.6 Assume a one megabyte file must be transferred across a network. Ignoring delays caused by waiting for access and other overhead (i.e., counting only the data transferred), how long would it take to send the file across an Ethernet? Across a LocalTalk network? Across a Fast Ethernet or an FDDI network?

8.7 The Ethernet standard specifies a minimum frame size as well as a maximum. Talk to an electrical engineer to find out why a minimum size is needed. (Hint: how does a 1-bit message appear to hardware?)

Chapter Contents

9

Hardware Addressing And Frame Type Identification

9.1 Introduction

The previous chapter describes Local Area Network (LAN) technologies used to provide communication across short distances. Most LANs are shared networks in which all computers attach to a medium over which they transfer data. One advantage of shared networks arises from their ability to provide universal connectivity: because all computers share the medium, a transmitted signal reaches all computers.

Although a shared LAN provides a physical path from one computer to all others, complete physical connectivity does not solve the communication problem. Indeed, most communication involves only a pair of computers. This chapter considers transmission across a shared LAN in more detail, and explains how a single pair of computers communicate across a LAN without forcing other computers to receive and process a copy of each message. In particular, the chapter describes hardware addressing, and shows how a sending computer uses a hardware address to identify which computer or computers should receive a copy of a given frame. The chapter also explains how network interface hardware uses such addresses to filter incoming packets.

In addition to discussing addressing, this chapter examines a mechanism that allows a sender to identify the type of the data in each frame. It explains the conceptual purpose of frame type identifiers, and uses Ethernet frame types as an example to illustrate the concept.

9.2 Specifying A Recipient

Physically, any signal sent across a shared network reaches all attached stations†. Thus, when a frame is transmitted across an Ethernet or around a token ring network, the electrical signals carrying the bits reach all stations. At a given station, the network interface hardware detects the electrical signal and extracts a copy of the frame. Despite the physical arrangement of a shared network, however, communication does not usually involve all stations. Instead, most communication occurs because an application program on one computer sends data directly to an application program on another.

How can two computers communicate directly across a shared medium in which all attached stations receive a copy of all signals? Most LAN technologies use an *addressing scheme* to provide direct communication. Each station on the LAN is assigned a unique numeric value called a *physical address*, *hardware address*, or *media access address* (*MAC address*). When a sender transmits a frame across the LAN, the sender includes the hardware address of the intended recipient. Although sharing allows all stations to receive a copy of the bits, the LAN hardware on each station checks the address of each incoming frame to determine whether it should accept the frame.

In fact, each frame transmitted across a shared LAN includes two addresses — one that specifies the intended recipient and another that specifies the sender. Each frame begins with a fixed *header* that contains space for the two addresses. Locations in the header reserved for the addresses are known generically as *fields*. Before transmitting a frame, the sender must place the recipient's physical address in the *destination address field* and its own address in the *source address field*. Including the sender's address in each frame makes it easy for a recipient to generate a reply. The network interface hardware is designed to examine address fields in frames that pass across the network, and to accept only those frames in which the destination address matches the station's address.

To summarize:

> *Each computer attached to a LAN is assigned a number known as its* physical address. *A frame sent across a LAN contains the address of the sending computer, called a* source address, *and the address of the intended recipient, called the* destination address.

9.3 How LAN Hardware Uses Addresses To Filter Packets

To appreciate how LAN systems use addresses to provide direct communication, it is necessary to understand the basic organization of LAN hardware. As Figure 9.1 illustrates, we can think of the LAN hardware in a computer as completely separate from the computer's CPU and memory.

---

†The term *station* denotes a conventional computer or a computer-controlled device that is attached to a network.

The LAN interface hardware handles all the details of sending and receiving frames on the shared medium. For example, the hardware checks the length of an incoming frame to ensure that it lies between the minimum and maximum sizes in the standard, checks the CRC to ensure that the bits arrived intact, and discards frames that contain errors. More important, the LAN interface hardware can perform the functions of sending and receiving frames without using the computer's CPU. Thus, after it passes data to the LAN interface and requests transmission, the CPU can continue executing an application program while the LAN interface waits for access to the shared medium and transmits the frame†.

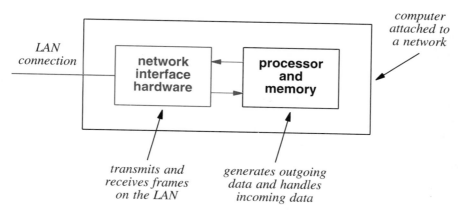

Figure 9.1 Organization of the hardware in a computer attached to a LAN. Because it is powerful and independent, the network interface hardware does not use the CPU when transmitting or receiving bits of a frame.

The hardware organization in Figure 9.1 explains why physical addresses are important. Conceptually, the LAN interface hardware, which operates independent of the computer's processor, uses physical addressing to prevent the computer from receiving all packets that travel across the LAN. Recall that as a frame travels across the shared medium, a copy of the signal passes to each station. Once it has captured a complete frame, the interface hardware compares the destination address in the frame to the station's physical address. If the destination address matches the station's physical address, the hardware accepts the frame and passes it to the operating system. If the destination address in the frame does not match the station's physical address, the hardware discards the frame and waits for the next frame to appear; a frame addressed to a nonexistent station is ignored. Because the LAN interface hardware functions without using the computer's central processor, the capture and address comparisons do not interfere with normal computing. Thus, a computer on a shared LAN remains isolated from most activity on the network — from the computer's point of view, a LAN interface only makes a copy of frames that are destined to the computer.

---

†In fact, LAN interface hardware often contains a small CPU, ROM, and RAM.

To summarize:

> *A shared network system uses physical addresses to filter incoming frames. The network interface hardware, which handles all the details of frame transmission and reception, compares the destination address on each incoming frame to the station's physical address, and discards frames not destined for the station. Because a network interface operates without using a station's CPU, a frame can be transferred across a shared LAN from one computer to another without interfering with processing on the computers.*

9.4 Format Of A Physical Address

Several questions remain unanswered. What numeric values are used for physical addresses, and how are such addresses assigned? Where are the destination address and source addresses located in a frame? The answers to these questions depend on the particular LAN technology being used. For example, Ethernet uses one form of addressing while FDDI uses another. The various address forms can be grouped into three broad categories:

Static   A *static addressing scheme* relies on the hardware manufacturer to assign a unique physical address to each network interface. A static physical address does not change unless the hardware is replaced.

Configurable A *configurable addressing scheme* provides a mechanism that a customer can use to set a physical address. The mechanism can be manual (e.g., switches that must be set when the interface is first installed) or electronic (e.g., a nonvolatile memory such as an EPROM that can be downloaded from a computer). Most hardware needs to be configured only once — configuration is usually done when the hardware is first installed.

Dynamic   A *dynamic addressing scheme* provides a mechanism that automatically assigns a physical address to a station when the station first boots. Most dynamic addressing schemes require a station to try random numbers until it finds a value that no other computer is using as an address. For example, a station might choose the current time of day as an initial value. For each random number it generates, the station sends a message over the network to the specified address. If another computer is already using the address, the computer responds to the message. If no other station responds to a given address, the sender can use that address as its physical address. Thus, the address a computer selects depends on which addresses other computers are using when it boots — a computer might obtain a different address each time it restarts.

The chief advantages of static addressing are ease of use and permanence. The scheme is easy to use because hardware vendors assign addresses and ensure that each hardware device has a physical address that is unique throughout the world. Hardware devices from multiple manufacturers can be connected to a single physical network without address conflicts. Static addressing is permanent because a computer's address does not change each time the computer is rebooted.

Dynamic addressing has two advantages: it eliminates the need for hardware manufacturers to coordinate in assigning addresses, and it allows each address to be smaller. The reason an address can be smaller arises because uniqueness is only important within a single LAN. A dynamic addressing scheme allows stations on one LAN to choose the same addresses as stations on another. The chief disadvantages of dynamic addressing are lack of permanence and potential conflict. Each time a computer boots, it obtains a new address; other computers must learn the new address before they can communicate. Furthermore, if the network is temporarily disconnected when a computer boots, two computers may choose the same physical address.

Configurable addresses provide a compromise between the static and dynamic schemes. Like static addresses, configurable addresses are permanent — a computer's address remains the same across reboots. Like dynamic addresses, configurable addresses do not need to be large because the address is unique only on a given network. In practice, most network administrators choose to assign configurable addresses sequential values. The first computer added to a network is assigned address *1*, the second is assigned address *2*, and so on. One of the advantages of a configurable addressing scheme becomes apparent when network interface hardware fails and must be replaced: unlike hardware that uses a static assignment, a configurable interface can be replaced without changing the computer's physical address.

9.5 Broadcasting

Many applications that use a network rely on a technique known as *broadcasting*. The term, which was originally applied to radio and television transmissions, refers to transmissions that are available to a large audience. When an application broadcasts data, it makes a copy of the data available to all other computers on the network.

Broadcast has many uses. For example, suppose a computer needs to find one of the printers on the network. The computer can form a message that specifies a printer (e.g., by giving the name of the printer) and then broadcast the message to all stations on the network. Although each station receives the broadcast, only the named printer would respond.

Because most Local Area Network technologies employ shared media, they can make broadcasting extremely efficient. In fact, no additional hardware is needed for broadcast on a LAN because all stations connect directly to the shared medium. Thus, all stations receive a copy of the signal each time a frame is transmitted across the network. All that is needed to make efficient broadcast possible is a mechanism that causes all stations to extract and process a copy of the frame.

The physical addressing described above may seem to make broadcasting impossible. In particular, although all stations receive a copy of each frame, the interface hardware on each station uses the frame's destination address to determine whether to keep a copy. If the destination address field in the frame contains the address of a specific computer, C, only the network interface hardware on computer C will accept the frame; all other network interfaces will reject it.

To make broadcasting efficient, most LAN technologies extend the addressing scheme. In addition to assigning each computer an address, the network designers define a special, reserved address known as a *broadcast address*. The hardware interface on a computer is built to recognize the special broadcast address as well as the station's physical address†. If a frame arrives with either of the two addresses in its destination address field, the interface accepts the frame and delivers a copy to the computer's operating system. To summarize:

> *The network interface hardware in a computer makes a copy of every frame that passes across the shared network. The interface accepts the frame and delivers a copy to the operating system if the destination address in the frame is the reserved broadcast address or matches the computer's physical address. Thus, when a frame is sent to the broadcast address, each computer on the network receives a copy.*

9.6 Multicasting

In theory, broadcasting could be used for a variety of applications. Take a network printer, for example. Suppose that each time an application needed to use a printer, the application used the network to broadcast frames containing the data to be printed. Because broadcast frames reach all stations on the network, a copy would reach the printer. Other stations on the network that receive a copy of frames containing data to be printed can be configured to discard such frames, making the whole scheme function correctly.

Despite the apparent feasibility of using broadcast, few network applications have been designed to use it as described above. The reason is simple — broadcasting is extremely inefficient. Although each station on a network can be configured to discard unneeded frames, processing and discarding a frame requires computational resources. When a frame arrives, the network interface hardware places the contents in memory,

---

†Because it denotes a single station, the conventional physical address is classified as a *unicast* address.

interrupts the CPU, and allows system software to determine whether the frame should be ignored. Thus, discarding frames involves using the CPU to make a decision. If a pair of stations on a network broadcast frames instead of sending them directly, other computers on the network must waste CPU time processing and discarding the broadcasts.

How can computers on a shared Local Area Network take advantage of the broadcast capability without wasting CPU resources on other computers? The answer lies in a restricted form of broadcasting known as *multicasting*. At the lowest level, multicasting operates much like broadcasting. A single copy of the frame travels across the network, and the network interfaces on all stations receive a copy. Unlike the way it handles a broadcast frame, however, a network interface does not automatically forward multicast frames to the CPU. Instead, the interface hardware must be programmed with specifications of which multicast frames to accept and which to reject. The interface hardware makes the decision and only accepts those frames that match the specification.

9.7 Multicast Addressing

How is a network interface programmed to accept some multicast packets and reject others? The mechanism is an extension of the basic addressing scheme. Recall that a conventional network interface must examine the destination address of each frame that is sent over the network. If the destination address in a frame matches the computer's address, or if the destination address matches the special broadcast address, the interface passes a copy of the frame to the local system for processing. Otherwise, the interface discards the frame without using the computer's CPU.

Multicasting extends the addressing scheme by reserving some addresses for multicast, and extends the network interface hardware by allowing an interface to recognize an additional set of addresses. When the computer boots, the interface is programmed to recognize only the computer's address and the broadcast address. If an application on the computer wishes to receive multicast frames, the application must inform the network interface which multicast address to use. The interface adds the address to the set it will recognize, and begins accepting frames sent to that address.

As an example, suppose two application programs have been built to send audio over a network. One application accepts and digitizes an audio input stream, and then sends the resulting frames across the network to the other application. The second application receives the digitized audio from the network, converts it back to an audio signal, and plays the result over a speaker. Now suppose that others on the same network wish to listen to the audio. Unless the two applications use broadcast to send frames, no other computers on the network will receive a copy of the frames. However, broadcasting has the disadvantage of consuming CPU resources on all computers even if they are not listening to the audio.

Multicasting provides an excellent solution to the problem of allowing some computers to participate in an audio transmission, while not bothering others. Multicasting offers the advantages of only sending a single copy of each frame across the network and allowing arbitrary computers to receive the transmission. To use multicasting, a multicast address must be chosen for the audio application. Then the audio software must be configured to use the address. The sending program must arrange to place the address in the destination field of each outgoing frame, and the receiving program must be configured to use the address for incoming frames. More specifically, when the receiving application starts, it passes the multicast address to the network interface. The interface adds the address to the set it recognizes, and begins accepting packets sent to that address. Because the network interface checks the address, computers that do not run the audio application will not waste CPU time discarding frames.

9.8 Identifying Packet Contents

Although the addressing schemes described above allow a sender to identify the intended recipient of a packet, the address does not specify what the packet contains. More important, because many data items use the same representation, a receiver cannot use data in the packet to determine what the packet contains. For example, packets that carry e-mail messages, text files, and web pages all use ASCII to represent data. To inform the receiver about its contents, each frame contains additional information that specifies the type of the contents. Two methods are used to identify the contents of a frame:

- Explicit frame type. In this method, the network hardware designers specify how type information is included in the frame and the values used to identify various frame types. The bits of a frame used to identify the contents are called the *frame type field*, and the frame is called *self-identifying*.

- Implicit frame type. In this method, the network hardware does not include a type field in each frame. Instead, the frame carries only data. Thus, the sender and receiver must agree on the contents of a frame or agree to use part of the data portion of the frame as a type field.

9.9 Frame Headers And Frame Format

Each LAN technology defines the exact frame format used with the technology. Although the details vary, most LAN technologies define a frame to consist of two parts, a *frame header* that contains information such as the source and destination addresses, followed by a larger *payload* or *data area* that contains the information being sent. Figure 9.2 illustrates the general format.

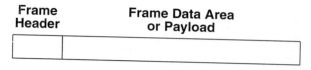

Figure 9.2 The general format of a frame sent across a LAN. The header contains information such as the addresses of the sender and the recipient.

In most LAN technologies, each field in the frame header has a fixed size and location. As a result, all frames used with the technology have the same header size. In contrast, the data area of a frame does not have a fixed size — the amount of data to be sent determines the size of the data area†. To summarize:

Each LAN technology defines a frame format. Most technologies have frames that each consist of a header followed by a data area. Because the size and format of the header is fixed, all frames used with a given technology have the same header format. The size of the data area is determined by the data being sent in the frame.

9.10 An Example Frame Format

An example will clarify the concept of a frame format, and show how address and type fields appear in a frame header when the frame is transmitted. Figure 9.3 illustrates the frame format used with Ethernet. As the figure shows, an Ethernet frame begins with a header that contains three fields. The 64-bit *preamble*, that precedes the frame contains alternating *1*s and *0*s that allow the receiver's hardware to synchronize with the incoming signal. The first two fields of the header contain physical addresses. Ethernet uses a 48-bit static addressing scheme in which each device is assigned a unique address by the manufacturer. The field labeled *Dest. Address* contains the physical address of the station to which the frame is being sent. The field labeled *Source Address* contains the physical address of the station that sent the frame. The third field of the header consists of a 16-bit Ethernet *frame type*.

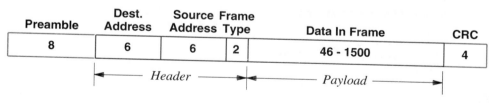

Figure 9.3 Illustration of the frame format used with Ethernet. The number in each field gives the size of the field measured in 8-bit octets.

---

†The hardware sometimes enforces a minimum as well as a maximum frame size. If the sender has less than the minimum amount of data to send, the data can be extended with zeroes.

The Digital-Intel-Xerox Ethernet standard specifies the values that can be used in the header fields and their meanings. For example, the standard specifies that the address with all 48 bits set to *1* is reserved for broadcast, other addresses that start with a *1* bit are used for multicast, and the hexadecimal value *8137* in the *Frame Type* field specifies that data in the frame follows a Novell Corporation protocol known as *IPX*. Hundreds of Ethernet type values have been assigned; the table in Figure 9.4 contains a few examples.

Value	Meaning
0000-05DC	Reserved for use with IEEE LLC/SNAP
0800	Internet IP Version 4
0805	CCITT X.25
0900	Ungermann-Bass Corporation network debugger
0BAD	Banyan Systems Corporation VINES
1000-100F	Berkeley UNIX Trailer encapsulation
6004	Digital Equipment Corporation LAT
6559	Frame Relay
8005	Hewlett Packard Corporation network probe
8008	AT&T Corporation
8014	Silicon Graphics Corporation network games
8035	Internet Reverse ARP
8038	Digital Equipment Corporation LANBridge
805C	Stanford University V Kernel
809B	Apple Computer Corporation AppleTalk
80C4-80C5	Banyan Systems Corporation
80D5	IBM Corporation SNA
80FF-8103	Wellfleet Communications
8137-8138	Novell Corporation IPX
818D	Motorola Corporation
FFFF	Reserved

Figure 9.4 Examples of frame types used with Ethernet (type values are given in hexadecimal). The table lists only a few examples; many other types have been assigned.

As the figure shows, Ethernet types have been assigned for use with systems built by individual companies as well as for use with software that follows international standards such as X.25. Having standardized type assignments ensures that all Ethernet products use the same value for a given frame type. Thus, Ethernet products built by two or more vendors will interoperate. In addition, Section 9.12 describes how standardized frame types can be used to analyze a network.

9.11 Using Networks That Do Not Have Self-Identifying Frames

Some network technologies do not include a type field in the frame header. That is, the frames are not self-identifying. How can computers connected to such networks know the type of data in each frame? There are two possible approaches:

- Before any data is sent, the sender and receiver agree to use a single format for data. Software in the sending computer is programmed to place outgoing data in the chosen format, and software in the receiving computer is programmed to expect data in the chosen format.

- Before any data is sent, the sender and receiver agree to use the first few octets of the data field to store type information. Software on the sending computer adds type information to the beginning of the data before placing the data in an outgoing frame. Software in the receiving computer extracts the type information and uses the type to determine how to process the remainder of the data.

The first technique is seldom used because it limits a pair of computers to exactly one form of data. Thus, the owners of the two computers cannot install new application software unless the applications use the data format that has been selected. More important, if the network supports broadcast, all computers attached to the network must agree to use a single data format.

Figure 9.5 illustrates how the second technique uses part of the data area to store type information.

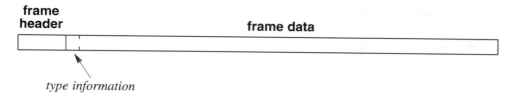

**frame
header**   **frame data**

type information

Figure 9.5 Illustration of how type information can be included in a frame's data area if the frame header does not include a type field.

Using part of the data area to carry a frame type raises two questions. First, exactly what size should the type information be? Second, who should specify values that are allowed in the type field and their meaning? For networks that include a type field in the frame header, such decisions are made by the group that designs the hardware technology. However, if the hardware does not include a frame type field, software is free to choose how to interpret type information. Unfortunately, allowing each application programmer to choose values for the type field does not work well because two programmers might accidentally select the same value for different types. The problem is especially severe if the applications broadcast frames.

To ensure that all software agrees on values used to specify types, standards organizations have defined the meaning of each value. Unfortunately, multiple standards organizations make such assignments, and the organizations do not always coordinate their efforts. As a result, two organizations might accidentally choose to assign the same value to two different types. To solve the problem of multiple standards organizations assigning types, IEEE has defined a standard that includes a field to identify the standards organization as well as a field to identify a type as defined by that organization. Part of IEEE's *802.2* standard, the specification is known as a *Logical Link Control (LLC) SubNetwork Attachment Point (SNAP)* header. The IEEE LLC/SNAP header is widely accepted.

Figure 9.6 shows an example LLC/SNAP header that contains eight octets. The first three octets comprise the *LLC* portion, which specifies that a type field follows.

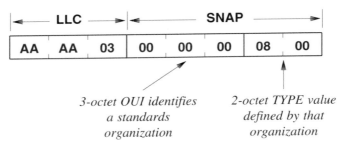

Figure 9.6 An example of the 8-octet IEEE LLC/SNAP header, which is used to specify the type of data. The SNAP portion specifies an organization and a type defined by that organization.

As the figure shows, the SNAP portion of the header is divided into two fields. The first field is called an *Organizationally Unique Identifier (OUI)*, which is used to identify a particular standards organization. The second contains a *type* value defined by that organization. For example, the OUI value of all zeroes shown in Figure 9.6 is assigned to the organization that specifies Ethernet types. Thus, the hexadecimal value *0800* shown in the *TYPE* field of the example is interpreted according to the standard for Ethernet types.

Like a type encoded in a frame header, the LLC/SNAP type field makes it possible for all computers on a shared network to broadcast frames. When a frame arrives at a given computer, the computer looks for LLC/SNAP information at the beginning of the frame data area. If the receiver does not recognize the OUI or does not have software to handle the type of data being sent, the receiver discards the frame. Thus, if only three computers on a network understand a given type, a broadcast frame carrying data of that type will be ignored by all computers except those three.

9.12 Network Analyzers, Physical Addresses, Frame Types

A *network analyzer* or *network monitor* is a device used to determine how well a network system is performing†. Most analyzers are portable, allowing them to be moved easily. After it has been attached to a network, an analyzer can monitor specific events and can report statistics such as the average number of frames per second or the average frame size. For example, an analyzer designed for a CSMA/CD network (e.g., an Ethernet) might report the number of collisions that occur. An analyzer designed to be used with a token ring network might report the average delay until the token arrives or the number of stations that transmit in a given cycle of the token. More important, most analyzers are flexible — a manager can configure the analyzer to observe the frames sent by a specified machine, observe traffic of a specific type, or compute the percentage of frames of each type.

How does a network analyzer work? The hardware needed for an analyzer is surprisingly simple — many analyzers consist of a standard portable computer (e.g., a notebook PC) with a standard LAN interface. While being used as an analyzer, the computer is completely dedicated to the analysis task. The software needed is also straightforward. The analyzer program begins by allowing a user to configure parameters, and then uses the parameters to analyze packets.

To read packets, analyzer software places the computer's network interface hardware into *promiscuous mode*, which overrides the conventional address recognition. That is, software on the computer configures the computer's network interface to accept *all* frames. Once in promiscuous mode, the interface does not check the destination address, nor does it reject any frames. Instead, the interface simply places a copy of each frame in the computer's memory and interrupts the CPU to inform it that a frame has arrived.

Users who are not informed may assume that a special interface card is required for promiscuous mode. Surprisingly, this is not the case. Almost all commercially-available network interface hardware supports promiscuous reading. Furthermore, switching an interface into promiscuous mode is usually trivial — only a handful of CPU instructions need to be executed. As a consequence, any user with a computer attached to a LAN can read all packets that travel across the LAN. That is, any computer attached to a LAN can eavesdrop on all communication; messages sent over a LAN are *not* guaranteed to be private.

---

†Informally, a network analyzer is sometimes called a *network sniffer* after the popular product by Network General Corporation.

To understand what is possible, consider how a network analyzer works. Each time a frame travels across the network, the network interface hardware makes a copy and delivers the copy to the analyzer program. The analyzer can examine fields in the frame header to determine the sender, intended recipient, type, or can look at the data area.

A network analyzer is configurable; the exact configuration that a user selects determines what fields the analyzer examines and what information it keeps. For example, suppose a network administrator is trying to debug a network problem in which a computer appears to be emitting incorrect packets. If the user knows the computer's physical address, P, the user can configure an analyzer to examine all frames that originate from the computer in question. To make such a request, the administrator specifies that the analyzer should display frames with source address equal to P. As it receives each frame, the analyzer will compare the source address field in the frame header to P. When it finds a match, the analyzer displays the frame. Otherwise, the analyzer ignores the frame and goes on to the next one. Similarly, if an administrator suspects a problem with broadcast traffic, the administrator might configure an analyzer to report all broadcast frames.

As an alternative, an administrator might specify that the analyzer should gather general traffic statistics. To provide a continuously updated summary of such information, an analyzer keeps a data structure that contains counters for each possible frame type. The counters begin at zero. When a frame arrives, the analyzer extracts the value from the frame type field in the header, and uses the value to determine which counter should be incremented. Periodically, the analyzer program updates the display for the user. It computes the percentage of total frames of each type, and displays the result in a convenient form (e.g., a pie chart). The analyzer also continues to accumulate counts. Usually, the update time interval is chosen to be small (e.g., one second or less) to give the screen the appearance of being updated continuously.

> *A network analyzer is a device that can be configured to count or display frames as they pass across a shared network. An analyzer obtains a copy of each frame, and then uses header fields such as the physical source address, physical destination address, or type information to determine how to process the frame.*

9.13 Summary

Although computer networks can be shared by many computers, an addressing scheme makes it possible to send a packet to a specific computer. To use a physical or hardware addressing scheme, each computer attached to the shared network is assigned a unique number, which is known as the computer's physical address. When sending a frame, a computer must place the physical address of the destination computer in a field of the frame header. The sender then waits for access to the shared medium, and transmits the frame. As the sender transmits bits of the frame, all attached computers receive a copy of the electrical signals which propagate across the shared medium.

Network interface hardware makes physical addressing efficient. In addition to the usual hardware components, each computer attached to a LAN contains a network interface that handles the details of transmitting and receiving frames. After it collects the bits together into a frame, an interface compares the destination address in the frame header to the computer's physical address and the broadcast address. If the frame is destined for another computer, the network interface discards the copy and begins listening for the next frame. If the destination address in the frame matches the computer's physical address or the broadcast address, the interface hardware interrupts the CPU and passes the incoming frame to the computer for processing. Because the network interface hardware operates independent of the computer's CPU, the computer can continue normal processing while the interface accepts frames and performs the comparison.

Broadcasting is efficient on a shared Local Area Network because a broadcast packet only needs to be transmitted once; all computers receive a copy of the transmission. The chief disadvantage of broadcasting is that all computers not interested in receiving a broadcast frame must spend CPU time to examine the incoming frame and discard it.

Multicasting is a limited form of broadcast that has the advantage of using the network interface hardware to examine frames. To use multicast, an application must be assigned a unique multicast address. The interface hardware on each computer that wishes to participate in the multicast must be configured to receive the specified multicast address. All computers that are configured to accept a given multicast address will receive a copy of any frame sent to that address; other computers will not receive a copy.

The exact details of physical addresses depend on the technology. Some technologies use static addressing in which the vendor that manufactures interface hardware assigns each unit a unique address. Some technologies use configurable addresses in which a system administrator must choose a unique address for each computer added to the network. The network hardware in the computer can then be configured (e.g., using small switches or flash memory) to recognize the address. Finally, some technologies use dynamic addressing in which a computer chooses a sequence of physical addresses at random until it finds an address that is currently unused.

Besides a destination address, the frame header in many network technologies includes a field used to specify the frame type. A unique type must be assigned for each possible use of the network. The sender places the correct value in the type field to specify the type of data in the frame. A receiver examines the contents of the type field to determine how to handle the frame. If it does not recognize the type value in an incoming frame, a receiver discards the frame.

Some network technologies do not have a type field in the frame header. All computers on such a network must agree on how they will represent type information. One technique places an LLC/SNAP header in the first few octets of the frame data area. The sender places type information in the SNAP portion of the header, and the receiver extracts the information from each incoming frame.

A network analyzer is a device that can be used to debug problems on a network. An analyzer consists of a small computer with conventional network interface hardware and analyzer software. The software places the interface in promiscuous mode, which allows the analyzer to receive a copy of each frame that passes across the shared network. After it receives a frame, the analyzer software consults a configuration to determine how to process the frame. If the user has configured the analyzer to display frames emitted by a particular station, the analyzer examines the source address. Similarly, if the user has configured the analyzer to display frames sent to a particular station, the analyzer examines the destination address. Finally, if the technology uses self-identifying frames, an analyzer can be configured to display frames of a given type. In such cases, the analyzer uses the contents of the frame type field to determine whether to display the frame.

9.14 Ethernet Address Assignment

The IEEE assigns 48-bit Ethernet physical addresses to vendors who manufacture Ethernet hardware devices. The address is:

> IEEE Registration Authority
> IEEE Standards Department
> 445 Hoes Lane, P.O. Box 1331
> Piscataway, NJ 08855-1331

EXERCISES

9.1   Find a comprehensive list of all Ethernet frame types. Hint: there is a list in an RFC document on the CD-ROM included with this text.

9.2   Errors sometimes lead to a situation in which two stations on a network are assigned the same hardware address. Who is responsible for such errors on a network that uses: configurable addresses? dynamic addresses? static addresses?

9.3   Explain what might happen if two stations are accidentally assigned the same hardware address.

9.4   In most technologies, a sending station can choose the amount of data in a frame, but the frame header is a fixed size. Calculate the percentage of bits in a frame devoted to the header for the largest and smallest Ethernet frames.

9.5   Use a network analyzer to observe activity on your local network and answer the following questions: What percentage of the time is the network in use? If the network uses CSMA/CD, how many collisions occur per second? What is the distribution of frame sizes? What is the distribution of frame types? Does your network use self-identifying frames (e.g., a DIX type) or another type encoding (e.g., LLC/SNAP)?

9.6 If your site has an Ethernet, find out whether the type field in the header is used or if an LLC/SNAP header is included in the data portion of the frame.

9.7 Determine if any applications at your site use multicasting.

9.8 Why are DIX Ethernet type values *0* through *5DC* reserved for use with an IEEE LLC/SNAP header? Hint: how long is an Ethernet frame?

9.9 Use a network analyzer to find the physical addresses of computers on a LAN.

9.10 If you have a network analyzer, how can you use it to find the physical address of your computer?

Chapter Contents

10

LAN Wiring, Physical Topology, And Interface Hardware

10.1 Introduction

This chapter continues the discussion of Local Area Networks by examining the hardware wiring schemes in more detail. The chapter begins by considering network interface cards that connect a computer to a network and handle the details of transmitting and receiving packets. It discusses the motivation for having a dedicated interface card, describes how a card plugs into a computer like other I/O devices, and explains how a card uses a transceiver to interact with the network medium.

After discussing interfaces, the chapter describes LAN wiring and identifies the major hardware components used in various wiring schemes, including a description of hubs. Finally, it discusses the difference between logical topology and physical topology, and shows how the concepts discussed in Chapter 8 are implemented in practice.

10.2 Speeds Of LANs And Computers

Each network technology specifies a rate at which data must be sent. Surprisingly, many local area networks operate at a rate so fast that a computer's Central Processing Unit (CPU) cannot process bits at network speed. For example, Chapter 8 reports that an FDDI network operates at 100 Megabits per second. By current standards a conventional CPU uses a hardware clock that runs at 800 MegaHertz†. Even if it can execute one instruction in each clock cycle, a CPU running at 800 MHz cannot handle data as fast as it arrives from an FDDI network because many instructions are required for each bit.

The difference between the speed of a CPU and the speed of a network is a fundamental problem. It does not make sense to operate a network at a speed suitable for the slowest CPU, because doing so also slows data transfer between a pair of high-speed computers. Furthermore, it does not make sense to specify that all computers attached to a network must operate at the same speed because designers continue to invent new processors. The continual improvement in the speed of available processors means that whenever a site replaces an old computer, the replacement will be significantly faster than the original. As a result, the computers attached to a typical network do not all operate at the same speed.

Despite the difference between processor and network speeds, networks are designed to operate at the highest rate hardware can support. Furthermore, the speed at which a network operates is usually fixed in the design — the speed does not depend on the CPU rates of the attached computers.

10.3 Network Interface Hardware

How can a computer attach to a network that sends and receives bits faster than the computer's CPU can handle them? The answer is simple: the CPU does not handle the transmission or reception of individual bits. Instead, a special-purpose hardware component connects a computer to a network, and handles all the details of packet transmission and reception. Physically, the special-purpose hardware usually consists of a printed circuit board that contains electronic components. Known as a *network adapter card* or *network interface card* (*NIC*), the printed circuit board plugs into the computer's bus, and a cable connects it to the network medium. Figure 10.1 illustrates how the sockets used for interface cards might be positioned in a computer.

As the figure illustrates, the sockets for interface boards are usually located near the rear of the cabinet. Each NIC is installed vertically in a socket, with one side of the NIC exposed through a slot in the back of the cabinet. The exposed side of the NIC contains a connector — a cable attaches the connector to the network. Figure 10.2 illustrates how the connection on the back of a NIC might appear.

A NIC understands the electrical signals used on a network, the rate at which data must be sent or received, and the details of the network frame format. For example, a NIC designed to be used with Ethernet cannot be used with a Token Ring network, and a NIC designed to be used with a Token Ring cannot be used with an FDDI ring.

---

†Abbreviated MHz, MegaHertz means millions of cycles per second.

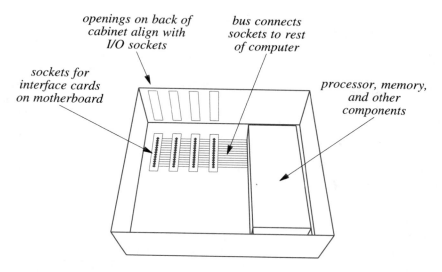

Figure 10.1 The location of I/O sockets inside a typical computer. Each socket aligns with an opening in the back of the cabinet, and the computer's bus connects the socket to other major components such as the processor and memory.

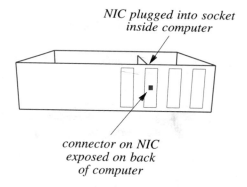

Figure 10.2 The back of a computer with a NIC installed in one of the sockets. A cable attaches the exposed connector to the network.

Most NICs contain *Direct Memory Access* (*DMA*) circuitry that allows the NIC to operate independent of the CPU — the NIC can transmit or receive bits from memory without using the computer's CPU†. From the CPU's point of view, a NIC appears to operate like any I/O device (e.g., like a disk). To transmit on the network, the CPU forms a packet in memory and then instructs the NIC to begin transmission. The CPU can continue other tasks while the NIC handles the details of accessing the medium and transmitting bits (just as the CPU can continue other tasks while a disk interface writes

---

†Less expensive NICs do not support DMA transfers; they rely instead on the CPU.

data to a disk). When it finishes transmitting a packet, a NIC uses the computer's interrupt mechanism to inform the CPU.

Similarly, a NIC can receive an incoming packet without requiring use of the CPU. To receive a packet, the CPU allocates buffer space in memory and then instructs the NIC to read the next incoming packet into the buffer. The NIC waits for a frame to cross the network, makes a copy of the frame, verifies the frame checksum, and checks the destination address. If the destination address matches the computer's address, the broadcast address, or a specified multicast address, the NIC stores a copy of the frame in memory and interrupts the CPU. Otherwise, the NIC discards the frame and waits for another one. Thus, the NIC only interrupts the CPU when a frame arrives that the computer must handle. To summarize:

> *Most computer networks transfer data across a medium at a fixed rate, often faster than the speed at which computers can process individual bits. To accommodate the mismatch in speeds, each computer attached to a network contains special-purpose hardware known as a network interface card (NIC). The NIC functions like an I/O device: it is built for a specific network technology, and handles the details of frame transmission or reception without requiring the CPU to process each bit.*

10.4 The Connection Between A NIC And A Network

The type of connection used between a NIC and a network depends on the network technology. In some technologies, the NIC contains most of the necessary hardware, and attaches directly to the network medium using a single cable or optical fiber. In many other technologies, the NIC does not contain all the electronic circuitry needed to attach directly to the network. Instead, the cable from a NIC attaches to an additional electronic component that then attaches to the network.

Surprisingly, the exact details of the connection between a NIC and a network are not determined by the technology — a given network technology can support multiple wiring schemes. To understand the concept, we will examine a single technology that supports three wiring schemes: Ethernet. We will see that although the underlying Ethernet technology is always the same, the wiring schemes differ dramatically.

10.5 Original Thick Ethernet Wiring

The original Ethernet wiring scheme is informally called *thick wire Ethernet* or *Thicknet* because the communication medium consists of a large coaxial cable; the formal term for the scheme is *10Base5*†. Hardware used with Thicknet is divided into two major parts. The NIC contains circuitry that handles the digital aspects of communica-

---

†Most companies have switched to a more modern wiring scheme.

tion, including error detection and address recognition. For example, the NIC generates the CRC on each outgoing frame, and verifies the CRC on an incoming frame. The NIC also checks the destination address on a frame, and only passes a frame to the CPU if the frame is destined for the computer. Finally, the NIC handles all communication with the computer system (i.e., the NIC uses the bus to transfer data to or from memory, and uses the interrupt mechanism to inform the CPU that an operation has completed).

A NIC used with Thicknet does not include analog hardware, and does not handle analog signals. For example, the NIC does not detect a carrier, convert bits into appropriate voltages for transmission, or convert incoming signals to bits. Instead, analog hardware that handles such chores is placed in a separate electronic device called a *transceiver*. One transceiver is required for each computer. Physically, the transceiver attaches directly to the Ethernet cable, and a separate cable connects the transceiver to the NIC in a computer. Thus, a transceiver is usually remote from a computer. For example, in an office building, transceivers might attach to an Ethernet in a hallway ceiling.

The cable connecting a NIC to a transceiver is known as an *Attachment Unit Interface (AUI)* cable, and the connectors on the NIC and transceiver are known as AUI connectors. Figure 10.3 illustrates how an AUI cable connects a computer to a transceiver.

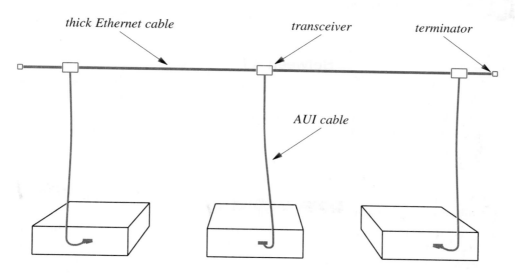

Figure 10.3 Three computers connected to a thick Ethernet. An AUI cable connects the NIC in each computer to its corresponding transceiver.

An AUI cable contains many wires. Of course, two wires are needed to carry outgoing data from the NIC to the transceiver and incoming data from the transceiver to the NIC. In addition, an AUI cable contains separate wires that allow the NIC to control the transceiver and wires that carry electrical power to the transceiver.

Figure 10.3 shows another detail of network wiring required by many wiring technologies — cable termination. Each end of the coaxial cable that forms an Ethernet must have a small, inexpensive termination device installed. A *terminator* consists of a resistor that connects the center wire in the cable to the shield. Essentially, when an electrical signal reaches the terminator, the signal is discarded. Interestingly, termination is essential to correct operation of a network because the end of an unterminated cable reflects electrical signals like a mirror reflects light. If a station attempts to send a signal across an unterminated cable, the signal will reflect back from the unterminated end. When the reflected signal reaches the sending station, it will cause interference. The sender will assume that the interference is caused by another station, and will invoke the Ethernet backoff algorithm normally used to handle a collision. Thus, an unterminated cable cannot be used.

To summarize:

> *In the original Ethernet wiring scheme, the shared medium consists of a thick coaxial cable. Each computer connected to the network requires a hardware device known as a* transceiver *which attaches to the shared cable and connects through an AUI cable to the network interface in the computer.*

10.6 Connection Multiplexing

Thick Ethernet wiring can be inconvenient. For example, consider the case of a laboratory at a university, where many computers occupy a single room. If the Ethernet cable is located in a hallway ceiling outside the room, the university must install an AUI cable between each computer and the corresponding transceiver in the hall. Furthermore, because the Ethernet standard specifies a minimum distance separation between two transceivers, individual transceivers must be spaced along the Ethernet cable.

To solve the problem of multiple computers in a single room, engineers have developed devices known as *connection multiplexors*. A connection multiplexor allows multiple computers to attach to a single transceiver. Figure 10.4 illustrates the idea.

As the figure illustrates, the wiring for a connection multiplexor is straightforward. Each computer has a conventional NIC installed and a conventional AUI cable attached. However, the AUI cables do not attach to individual transceivers. Instead, the cable from each computer connects to a port on the multiplexor. Finally, a single AUI cable connects the multiplexor to the Ethernet (presumably, other computers not shown in the diagram also connect to the same network).

A connection multiplexor is an electronic device designed to provide exactly the same signals as a conventional transceiver. For example, if two computers attempt to transmit at the same time, the multiplexor reports that a collision occurred exactly the same way a transceiver reports a collision on the network. Similarly, if a carrier signal is present on the network, the multiplexor reports the carrier to all attached stations. Thus, a computer does not need to know whether it connects directly to a conventional transceiver or to a multiplexor. To summarize:

A connection multiplexor is an electronic device that allows multiple computers to attach to a network through a single transceiver. Because the multiplexor delivers exactly the same electrical signals as a transceiver, a computer does not know whether it is attached to a transceiver or a multiplexor.

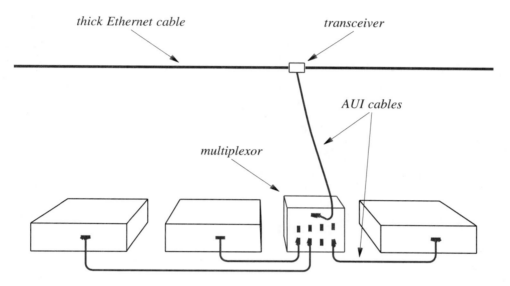

Figure 10.4 A connection multiplexor. Although the multiplexor attaches to a single transceiver, multiple computers can connect to the multiplexor. Each computer operates as if it connects directly to a transceiver.

10.7 Thin Ethernet Wiring

Hardware is also available that allows Ethernet to use a thinner, more flexible coaxial cable than the original thick wiring. Formally named *10Base2* and informally known as *thin wire Ethernet* or *Thinnet*, the wiring scheme differs from Thicknet wiring in three important ways. First, Thinnet generally costs less to install and operate than Thicknet. Second, because hardware that performs the transceiver function is built into the NIC, no external transceivers are needed. Third, Thinnet does not use an AUI cable to attach the NIC to the communication medium. Instead, Thinnet attaches directly to the back of each computer using a *BNC connector*.

In a Thinnet installation, a coaxial cable stretches between each pair of machines. The cable does not need to follow a straight line — it may lie loosely on the tabletop between computers, run under the floor, or run in a conduit. Figure 10.5 illustrates Thinnet wiring.

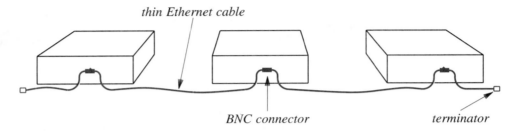

Figure 10.5 Three computers connected on a thin wire Ethernet. The medium is a flexible cable that connects from the NIC on one computer directly to the NIC on another computer.

Although the wiring for a thin Ethernet appears to be completely different than the wiring for a thick Ethernet, the two schemes share several important properties. Both thick and thin cables are coaxial, meaning that they shield signals from outside interference. Both thick and thin cables require termination, and both use the bus topology. Most important, because the two wiring systems have similar electrical characteristics (i.e. resistance and capacitance), signals propagate along the cables in the same way. We can summarize:

> *The Thinnet wiring scheme for Ethernet uses a flexible coaxial cable that attaches directly to each computer without a separate transceiver. Although they differ physically, the thick and thin Ethernet cables have similar electrical characteristics.*

10.8 Twisted Pair Ethernet

A third style of Ethernet wiring illustrates how vendors have invented wiring schemes that lead to an unexpected physical topology. The third style differs dramatically from both thick and thin Ethernet. Formally called *10BaseT*, the scheme is popularly known as *twisted pair Ethernet* or simply *TP Ethernet*. 10BaseT, which has become the standard for Ethernet, does not use a coaxial cable at all. In fact, a 10BaseT Ethernet does not have a shared physical medium like the other wiring schemes. Instead, 10BaseT extends the idea used with connection multiplexing: an electronic device serves as the center of the network. The electronic device is called an *Ethernet hub*.

Like the other wiring schemes, 10BaseT requires each computer to have a network interface card and a direct connection from the NIC to the network. The connection uses twisted pair wiring with *RJ-45* connectors which are larger versions of the modular connectors used with telephones. The connector on one end of a twisted pair plugs into the network interface on a computer, and the connector on the other end plugs into the hub. Thus, each computer has a dedicated connection to the hub device; there is no coaxial cable. Figure 10.6 illustrates 10BaseT wiring.

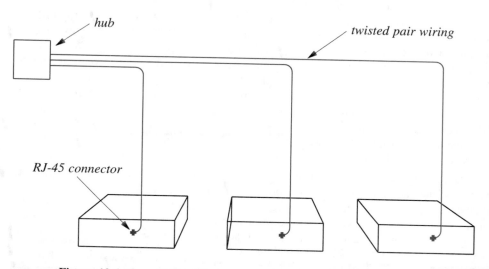

Figure 10.6 Three computers connected to an Ethernet hub using 10BaseT wiring. Each computer has a dedicated connection.

Hub technology is an extension of the connection multiplexor concept. Electronic components in a hub simulate a physical cable, making the entire system operate like a conventional Ethernet. For example, a computer attached to a hub must have a physical Ethernet address; each computer must use CSMA/CD to access the network and the standard Ethernet frame format. In fact, software does not distinguish between thick Ethernet, thin Ethernet, and 10BaseT — the network interface handles the details and hides any differences.

Although all hubs can accommodate multiple computers, hubs come in a variety of sizes. A typical small hub has four or five *ports* that each accept one connection. Thus, one hub is sufficient to connect all the computers in a small group (e.g., in a single department). Larger hubs can accommodate hundreds of connections.

The 10BaseT Ethernet wiring scheme uses an electronic device known as a hub in place of a shared cable. The connection between a computer and the hub uses twisted pair wiring.

10.9 Advantages And Disadvantages Of Wiring Schemes

Each of the three wiring schemes has advantages and disadvantages. Wiring that uses a separate transceiver per connection allows the computer to be changed without disrupting the network. When a transceiver cable is unplugged, the transceiver loses power, but other transceivers continue to operate. Having separate transceivers does have disadvantages. Transceivers often are located in a remote location that is difficult to reach (e.g., a hallway ceiling in an office building). If a transceiver fails, finding, testing, or replacing it can be tedious. In contrast, although it does not have the disadvantage of remote transceivers, a scheme in which the shared medium connects directly to each computer is susceptible to disconnection — unplugging the main cable leaves the segments unterminated, which disrupts the entire network. Furthermore such disruption is likely because, unlike AUI connectors, no tools are required to disconnect the BNC connectors used with Thinnet. Hub wiring makes the network more immune to accidental disconnection because each twisted pair affects only one machine. Thus, if a single wire is accidentally cut, only one machine is disconnected from the hub.

Despite the advantages and disadvantages mentioned above, one factor seems to dominate the choice of wiring technology: cost. Thin Ethernet became popular because it costs less per connection than the original thick Ethernet. 10BaseT wiring is now popular because it costs less per connection than thin Ethernet. Of course, our statements are generalizations — actual costs are not always easy to compare. The total cost depends on the number of computers, the distance between them, the physical placement of walls and conduits, the cost of the interface hardware and wiring, the cost of diagnosing and repairing problems, and how frequently new computers will be added or existing computers moved. Because most organizations use a single wiring scheme to attach computers to a given network, interfaces must be available at reasonable cost for all brands of computers to be connected. Thus, no single wiring scheme is best for all situations. More important, because all wiring schemes use the same standard for frame formats and network access, it is possible to mix wiring technologies on a single network. For example, it is possible to have some computers connected to a network using Thicknet, while others are connected to the same network using Thinnet.

To visualize some of the differences in cost, imagine an entire set of offices with one or more computers in each office. Figure 10.7 illustrates how the three Ethernet wiring schemes might appear in a set of eight offices separated by a common hallway.

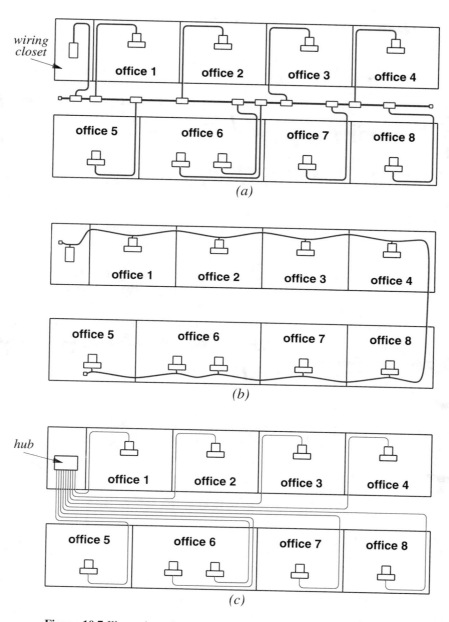

Figure 10.7 Illustration of computers in eight offices wired with (a) thick, (b) thin, and (c) 10BaseT (twisted pair) Ethernet. Wires can run above the ceiling or under a raised floor. A wiring closet may contain a hub or equipment used for network monitoring, control, or debugging.

10.10 The Topology Paradox

An observant reader will have noticed an apparent contradiction in our description of Ethernet technology. Chapter 8 states that Ethernet uses a bus topology. In this chapter, the statement does not always seem to hold. The bus is apparent in thick or thin wiring because the shared bus is the coaxial cable. However, an Ethernet using twisted pair wiring does not resemble a bus. In fact, according to the definitions in Chapter 8, the 10BaseT wiring forms a star topology with the hub as the center of the star.

Is Ethernet a bus topology, or does the topology depend on the wiring? The answer is both! Obviously, a twisted pair Ethernet forms a classic star in which each computer has a dedicated connection to the central hub. Despite its appearance, however, a twisted pair Ethernet functions like a bus. All computers share a single communication medium. Computers must contend for access to the medium, and at most one computer can transmit at a given time. As in conventional Ethernet, the network interfaces in all computers receive a copy of each packet that is transmitted, and the network interface is responsible for filtering packets exactly the same way the interface filters packets that arrive from a thick or thin Ethernet. As a result, when a computer sends a frame to the broadcast address, all other computers receive a copy of the frame.

To solve the apparent paradox and understand network technologies, we must distinguish between physical and logical topologies. Physically, twisted pair Ethernet uses a star topology. Logically, twisted pair Ethernet functions like a bus. Thus a 10BaseT Ethernet is often called a *star-shaped bus†*. To summarize:

> *A given network technology can use a variety of wiring schemes. The technology determines the logical topology, and the wiring scheme determines the physical topology. It is possible for the physical topology to differ from the logical topology.*

10.11 Network Interface Cards And Wiring Schemes

Because it contains circuitry to handle the electrical details of communication, a network interface must support a wiring scheme as well as a network technology. For example, an interface for twisted pair Ethernet must have an RJ-45 connector, and must generate signals according to the 10BaseT specification. However, an interface used with thin Ethernet must have a BNC connector, and must generate signals appropriate for Thinnet. To make it possible to change wiring schemes without changing interface hardware, many network interfaces support multiple wiring schemes. For example, a single Ethernet NIC often has three connectors as Figure 10.8 shows.

---

†Informally, twisted pair Ethernet is called a "bus in a box," or a "network in a box."

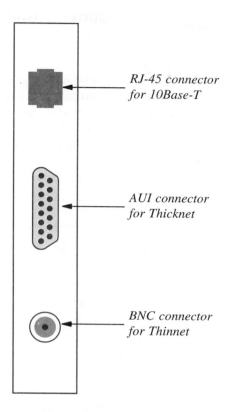

RJ-45 connector
for 10Base-T

AUI connector
for Thicknet

BNC connector
for Thinnet

Figure 10.8 Illustration of the part of an Ethernet interface card exposed
when the card is installed in a computer. The interface can be
used with one of the three basic wiring schemes. Each wiring
scheme uses a different style connector.

Although multiple connectors remain in place at all times, a given interface can use
only one wiring scheme at a time. Software in the computer must activate one of the
connectors; the others are not used. The chief advantage of having multiple wiring
schemes supported by a single NIC is flexibility — a site can choose a wiring scheme
or change to different wiring without replacing interface hardware. More important, because the physical address of a computer is assigned to the NIC, the computer's physical address remains constant when moving to a new wiring scheme.

10.12 Wiring Schemes And Other Network Technologies

We have examined Ethernet wiring schemes in detail and used them to illustrate the important distinction between physical and logical topologies. Other network technologies accommodate a variety of wiring techniques, some of which are variations of the schemes examined here. For example, like thick Ethernet, the original LocalTalk wiring scheme uses transceivers. However, LocalTalk transceivers do not attach to a single cable. Instead, LocalTalk wiring keeps each transceiver close to a computer, and then connects the transceivers in a chain using a point-to-point connection between each pair (similar to the wiring used with thin Ethernet). Figure 10.9 illustrates the concept.

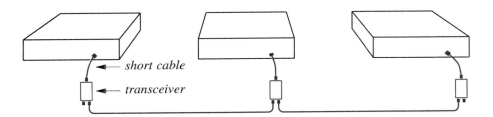

Figure 10.9 Three Macintosh computers connected with LocalTalk wiring. Each computer attaches to a transceiver with a short LocalTalk cable, and LocalTalk cables connect the transceivers. A Local-Talk transceiver with only one connection acts as a terminator for the bus.

Although LocalTalk is a bus technology, wiring is not limited to the scheme that Figure 10.9 illustrates. In particular, an alternative LocalTalk wiring scheme is available that uses hub technology. Like a twisted pair Ethernet hub, a LocalTalk hub is an electronic device that simulates a cable. The hub is placed in a central location, and each computer has a dedicated connection to the hub.

Alternative wiring schemes are not limited to bus networks — almost any network technology can support multiple wiring schemes, and the logical topology may differ from the physical topology. For example, hub wiring is often used with an IBM Token Ring. The hub is an electronic device to which each computer attaches. Logically, the hub manages a ring, including the details of token passing, exactly as if the computer were connected to conventional ring wiring. Thus, using hub wiring with a Token Ring network results in a network with two topologies: a physical star and a logical ring. Consequently, Token Ring hubs are sometimes referred to as a *ring in a box*.

One of the advantages of a hub is that failures can be managed electronically. For example, if the connection between a computer and the hub accidentally breaks, circuitry in the hub can detect the failure, remove the disconnected station from the ring, and allow the remaining computers to communicate.

10.13 Summary

Because networks are designed to operate at high speeds, a computer requires special interface hardware that handles such details as access of the communication medium, frame transmission and reception, and address filtering without using the computer's CPU. Such hardware is usually designed as a separate printed circuit board that plugs into the computer's I/O bus. The unit is known as a *network adapter* or *network interface card* (NIC).

Because no single wiring scheme is best for all situations, many wiring schemes exist for computer networks. Although a given network technology can support more than one wiring scheme, all computers attached to a particular network must use the same scheme.

Ethernet provides an example of the dramatic differences among wiring schemes for the same network technology. The original thick Ethernet wiring uses a single coaxial cable. Computers do not attach directly to the cable. Instead, each computer requires a separate hardware device called a *transceiver* that attaches to the Ethernet itself. An AUI cable connects the transceiver to the network interface in the computer. In the thin Ethernet wiring scheme, computers are connected point-to-point by a flexible coaxial cable that attaches directly to the computer's network interface. Twisted pair Ethernet wiring uses a separate connection from each computer to an electronic device called a *hub*. The hub simulates a shared cable.

An important principle arises from the example wiring schemes: the network's physical topology may differ from the network's logical topology. For example, a wiring scheme that uses a hub is a physical star. However, electronic circuits in the hub can simulate a different logical topology (e.g., a bus or a ring). Such a network is known as a *star-shaped bus* or a *star-shaped ring*.

To accommodate multiple wiring schemes, a network interface often comes with multiple connectors. Only one connector can be active at a time — software in the computer must choose which connector to use.

EXERCISES

10.1   What type of wiring does your organization use? Find out why the choice was made.

10.2   How large is a NIC? See if you can find an Ethernet NIC manufactured several years ago. Compare it to a NIC that fits on a PCMCIA card.

10.3   In a thin wire Ethernet, two cables are plugged into a connector on the back of each computer. What happens if a user unplugs the BNC connector from his or her computer? What happens if a user unplugs one of the two cables?

10.4   Read about commercial hub products. How many computers can connect to a small hub? A large hub?

Chapter Contents

11

Extending LANs: Fiber Modems, Repeaters, Bridges, and Switches

11.1 Introduction

Previous chapters describe basic LAN technologies and associated wiring schemes. Each LAN technology is designed for a specific combination of speed, distance, and cost. The designer specifies a maximum distance that the LAN can span, with typical LANs designed to span a few hundred meters. As a result, LAN technology works best to connect computers within a single building.

Unfortunately, people who interact electronically do not always occupy offices located within a few hundred meters. This chapter discusses mechanisms that can extend a LAN across longer distances, and uses fiber modems, repeaters, and bridges to illustrate some of the possibilities.

11.2 Distance Limitation And LAN Design

Distance limitation is a fundamental part of LAN designs. When designing a network technology, engineers choose a combination of capacity, maximum delay, and distance that can be achieved at a given cost. To help save expense, LAN technologies usually use a shared communication medium such as a shared bus or a ring. As a consequence of using a shared medium, a LAN design must include a mechanism that guarantees each station fair access to the shared medium. For example, some bus technologies use CSMA/CD, while ring technologies use token passing.

The need for a fair access mechanism provides one of the main motivations to limit the length of a LAN. The two most popular access mechanisms, CSMA/CD and token passing, each take time proportional to the size of the network. To ensure that delays do not become significant, a LAN technology is designed to work with a fixed maximum cable length.

Another limitation arises because hardware is engineered to emit a fixed amount of electrical power. Unfortunately, because an electrical signal gradually becomes weaker as it travels along a copper wire, the signal cannot reach arbitrarily far. To ensure that all stations attached to a LAN receive a sufficiently strong signal, designers calculate the maximum length of wire allowed. Thus,

> *A maximum length specification is a fundamental part of LAN technology. LAN hardware is engineered for a fixed maximum length cable, and the hardware will not work correctly over wires that exceed the bound.*

11.3 Fiber Optic Extensions

Engineers have developed a variety of ways to extend LAN connectivity. In general, the mechanisms do not increase the strength of electrical signals generated by interface hardware nor do they merely add wire to extend cables beyond the maximum bounds. Instead, most extension mechanisms use standard interface hardware and insert additional hardware components that can relay signals across longer distances.

The simplest LAN extension mechanism inserts optical fibers and a pair of *fiber modems* between a computer and a transceiver. Because fiber has low delay and high bandwidth, such a mechanism can allow a computer to connect to a transceiver that is attached to a remote network. The computer sends standard signals to control the transceiver, and the transceiver receives standard signals. Thus, the extension can work with standard network interface hardware. Figure 11.1 illustrates fiber modems used to extend an Ethernet connection.

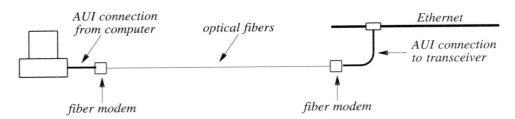

Figure 11.1 Optical fibers and fiber modems used to provide a connection between a computer and a distant Ethernet. The computer and transceiver both use conventional AUI signals.

As the figure shows, one fiber modem resides at each end of the connection and optical fiber connects them. The computer uses a network interface that generates conventional AUI signals to control a transceiver, and sends the signals to the local fiber modem over an AUI cable. Similarly, the remote fiber modem generates standard AUI signals and sends them over an AUI cable to the transceiver.

Each of the fiber modems contains hardware to perform two chores: electronic circuitry in the fiber modem converts between AUI signals and digital representation, and optical driver hardware translates between the digital representation and pulses of light which travel along the fiber. Of course, the circuitry must provide communication in both directions to allow the computer to send and receive frames†. For example, the circuitry in the fiber modem near the computer must accept digital data that arrives over the fiber and convert it into signals that are sent to the computer, as well as accept signals from the computer and convert them into digital data destined for the transceiver.

The chief advantage of fiber modems arises from their ability to provide a connection to a remote LAN without changing the original LAN or the computer. Because delays across fiber are low and bandwidth is high, the mechanism will operate correctly across distances of several kilometers. The most common use involves connecting a computer in one building to a LAN in another building.

To summarize:

> A pair of fiber modems and optical fibers can be used to provide a connection between a computer and a remote LAN. The mechanism is inserted between the network interface on a computer and a remote transceiver.

11.4 Repeaters

Recall that one distance limitation in LANs arises because an electrical signal becomes weaker as it travels along a wire. To overcome such limitations, some LAN technologies allow two cables to be joined together with a device known as a *repeater*. A repeater is usually an analog electronic device that continuously monitors electrical signals on each cable. When it senses a signal on one cable, the repeater transmits an amplified copy on the other cable. Figure 11.2 illustrates how a repeater can double the effective size of an Ethernet network.

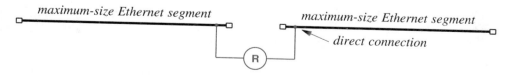

Figure 11.2 A repeater *R* connecting two Ethernets. The repeater connects directly to the cable; it does not use a transceiver.

---

†Many implementations use a pair of fibers to allow simultaneous transmission in both directions.

As the figure shows, a repeater connects two Ethernet cables called *segments*, each of which has the usual termination. Repeaters do not understand the frame format, nor do they have physical addresses. Instead, the repeater attaches directly to the Ethernet cables and sends copies of electrical signals from one to the other without waiting for a complete frame.

The maximum size of an Ethernet segment is 500 meters†. Figure 11.2 shows that a repeater can double the effective length of an Ethernet to 1000 meters by connecting two maximum-sized segments. A pair of repeaters can be used to connect three Ethernet segments to make a network 1500 meters long. Because repeaters propagate all signals between two segments, a computer connected to one segment can communicate with a computer connected to the other segment. In fact, when using repeaters, the source and destination computers cannot determine whether they connect to the same segment or to different segments. To summarize:

> *A repeater is a hardware device used to extend a LAN. The repeater, which connects two cable segments, amplifies and sends all electrical signals that occur on one segment to the other segment. Any pair of computers on the extended LAN can communicate; the computers do not know whether a repeater separates them.*

Can the length of an Ethernet be increased to many segments of 500 meters each merely by adding a repeater to connect each additional segment? The answer is no. Although such an arrangement does guarantee sufficient signal strength, each repeater and segment along the path increase the delay. The Ethernet CSMA/CD scheme is designed for low delay. If the delay becomes too large, the scheme fails. In fact, repeaters are a part of the current Ethernet standard, which specifies that the network will not operate correctly if more than four repeaters separate any pair of stations‡.

The limit of four repeaters in an Ethernet arose from a careful plan. The inventors envisioned using Ethernet in an office building, where multiple offices occupy each floor of the building. To connect computers in such a building, two Ethernet segments can be placed on each floor, and an additional vertical segment can connect floors. Figure 11.3 illustrates the architecture. Although the configuration uses two repeaters per floor, no two stations are separated by more than four repeaters.

Repeaters were originally designed to connect two Ethernet segments that were in close physical proximity (e.g., in a building); the connection can be extended over a long distance by using fiber modems. Known as *Fiber Optic Intra-Repeater Link (FOIRL)*, the technology consists of two devices connected by optical fibers. Each device attaches to a segment exactly like a repeater, and the two then use the fiber to communicate. Each side senses the signal on the LAN like a repeater, and encodes the signal for transmission across the fiber. The remote side receives the encoded form, and recreates the signal on the remote LAN. Because fiber has low delay, a FOIRL can connect segments in two separate buildings.

---

†Thinnet and 10BaseT wiring have smaller limits.
‡An Ethernet hub used with 10BaseT wiring counts as a repeater.

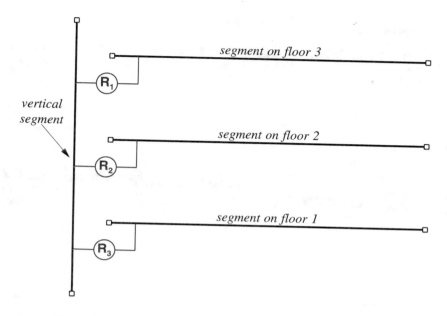

Figure 11.3 Repeaters used to connect Ethernet segments on three floors of an office building. Each floor has one segment, and one segment is placed vertically in the building.

Repeaters have several drawbacks. The most important drawback arises because repeaters do not understand complete frames. As it proceeds to receive electrical signals on one segment and transmit them on another, a repeater does not distinguish between the signals that correspond to a valid frame and other electrical signals. Therefore, when a collision occurs on one segment, a repeater recreates the signals on the other segment, including a copy of the overlapping signals that correspond to the collision. Similarly, when interference (e.g., lightning) generates unwanted electrical noise on a segment, repeaters transmit a copy of the electrical noise on the other segments. The important point is:

> *In addition to propagating copies of valid transmissions from one segment to another, a repeater propagates a copy of other electrical signals. Consequently, if a collision or electrical interference occurs on one segment, repeaters cause the same problem to occur on all other segments.*

11.5 Bridges

Like a repeater, a *bridge* is an electronic device that connects two LAN segments. Unlike a repeater, however, a bridge handles complete frames and uses the same network interface as a conventional computer. The bridge listens to traffic on each segment in promiscuous mode. When it receives a frame from one segment, the bridge verifies that the frame arrived intact (e.g., there was no electrical interference on the LAN during transmission), and then forwards a copy of the frame to the other segment if necessary. Thus, two LAN segments connected by a bridge behave like a single LAN. A computer connected to either segment can send a frame to any of the other computers connected to the two segments. Because each segment supports standard network connections and uses the standard frame format, computers do not know whether they are connected to a LAN or a bridged LAN. Figure 11.4 illustrates the concept.

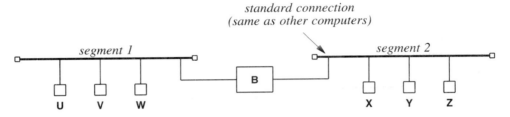

Figure 11.4 Six computers connected to a pair of bridged LAN segments. The bridge, which uses the same type of connection as a computer, always sends and receives complete frames.

Bridges have become more popular than repeaters because they help isolate problems. If two segments are connected by a repeater and lightning causes electrical interference on one of them, the repeater will propagate the interference to the other segment. In contrast, if interference occurs on one of two segments connected by a bridge, the bridge will receive an incorrectly-formed frame, which the bridge simply discards the same way a conventional computer discards a frame that contains an error. Similarly, a bridge will not forward a collision from one segment to another. Thus, the bridge keeps problems on one segment from affecting the other. We can summarize:

> *A bridge is a hardware device used to extend a LAN. A bridge, which connects two cable segments, forwards complete, correct frames from one segment to another; a bridge does not forward interference or other problems. Any pair of computers on the extended LAN can communicate; the computers do not know whether a bridge separates them.*

11.6 Frame Filtering

Most bridges do more than forward a copy of each frame from one LAN to another. In fact, a typical bridge consists of a conventional computer with a CPU, memory, and two network interfaces. A bridge is dedicated to a single task, and does not run application software. Instead, the CPU executes code from ROM. The most valuable function a bridge performs is *frame filtering* — a bridge does not forward a frame unless necessary. In particular, if a computer attached to one segment sends a frame to a computer on the same segment, the bridge does not need to forward a copy of the frame to the other segment. Of course, if the LAN supports broadcast or multicast, the bridge must forward a copy of each broadcast or multicast frame to make the extended LAN operate like a single, large LAN.

To determine whether to forward a frame, a bridge uses the physical address found in the frame's header. The bridge knows the location of each computer attached to the LANs it connects. When a frame arrives on a segment, the bridge extracts and checks the destination address. If the destination computer is attached to the segment over which the frame arrived, the destination and bridge receive the same transmission, and the bridge discards the frame without forwarding a copy. If the destination does not lie on the segment over which the frame arrived, the bridge sends a copy of the frame on the other segment.

How can a bridge know which computers are attached to which segments? Most bridges are called *adaptive* or *learning* bridges because they learn the locations of computers automatically. To do so, a bridge listens in promiscuous mode on the segments to which it attaches, and forms a list of computers attached to each. When a frame arrives, the bridge performs two computations. First, the bridge extracts the physical source address from the frame header, and adds the address to its list of computers attached to the segment. Second, the bridge extracts the physical destination address from the frame, and uses the address to determine whether to forward the frame. Thus, all bridges attached to a segment learn that a computer is present as soon as the computer transmits a frame. Figure 11.5 illustrates how a bridge can learn the locations of computers.

Event	Segment 1 List	Segment 2 List
Bridge boots	–	–
U sends to V	U	–
V sends to U	U, V	–
Z broadcasts	U, V	Z
Y sends to V	U, V	Z, Y
Y sends to X	U, V	Z, Y
X sends to W	U, V	Z, Y, X
W sends to Z	U, V, W	Z, Y, X

Figure 11.5 A sequence of events for the example network shown in Figure 11.4 and the locations of computers that the bridge has learned.

We can summarize:

> *An adaptive bridge examines physical addresses in the header of each frame it receives. The bridge uses the source address to automatically determine the location of the computer that sent a frame, and uses the destination address to determine whether to forward a frame.*

11.7 Startup And Steady State Behavior Of Bridged Networks

After each computer attached to bridged LAN segments has sent a frame, bridges connecting the segments learn the location of the computers and use the information to filter frames. As a result, the behavior of a bridged network that has been running for a long time restricts frames to the fewest segments necessary.

> *Propagation principle for bridged networks: in the steady state, a bridge forwards each frame only as far as necessary.*

Of course, when it first boots, a bridge does not know which computers attach to which LAN segment. Thus, a bridge will forward frames destined for a computer until it determines the location of the computer. In fact, if a computer did not send any frames, a bridge could not detect its location, and would forward frames unnecessarily. Fortunately, computers do not usually remain silent. A computer system that includes network software usually emits at least one frame when the system first boots. Furthermore, computer communication is usually bidirectional — a computer that receives a frame usually sends a reply. Therefore, bridges usually learn locations quickly.

11.8 Planning A Bridged Network

The propagation principle does more than summarize how a bridge behaves — it provides the basis for planning a bridged network. To understand how restricting propagation influences design, one must know an additional fact: bridge hardware is engineered to permit communication on separate segments at the same time. Thus, the key concept underlying the design of a bridged network is parallelism: after bridges learn the locations of all computers, communication can proceed on each segment at the same time. For example, consider the bridged network that Figure 11.4 illustrates. Because the two segments can be used simultaneously, computer U can send a frame to computer W at the same time that computer X sends a frame to computer Y. Although the bridge will receive a copy of each transmission, the bridge will examine the location of the destinations and discard each of the incoming frames without forwarding it.

Knowing that a bridge permits simultaneous use of each segment suggests how network designers arrange a bridged LAN to optimize performance. A set of computers that interact frequently should be attached to the same segment. In Figure 11.4, the division into segments might have resulted from expected interactions among the computers. For example, suppose computer U contains a database that is accessed frequently by computers V and W, and computer X has a printer that is used frequently by computers Y and Z. Separating the two segments by a bridge improves performance: although only one pair of computers can communicate at a time if their communication spans both segments, communication among pairs on separate segments can proceed in parallel. Thus, computer V or W can access the database on computer U at the same time computer Y or Z sends a document to the printer on computer X.

When architects plan a network, they assess expected patterns of interaction among computers, and use the information to group computers onto segments. More important, because computers that communicate frequently are often physically close, it may be possible to improve the performance of an existing LAN by dividing the LAN into two segments and adding a bridge between them. We can summarize:

Because a bridge follows the propagation principle and permits simultaneous activity on attached segments, computers on one segment can communicate at the same time as computers on another segment. As a consequence, performance of a bridged network can be maximized by attaching a set of computers that interact frequently to the same segment.

11.9 Bridging Between Buildings

We have described reasons to use bridges in a local environment. Like repeaters, bridges can also be used to span longer distances. For example, a corporation may need a network that allows computers in one building to communicate with computers in another. If the two buildings are separated by a significant distance or if the buildings are large, a single LAN will not suffice to reach both buildings. More important, using pairs of fiber modems to attach all computers to a single LAN may result in high cost or suboptimal performance.

Because a bridge connects to a LAN the same way a computer connects to a LAN, the simplest way to extend a bridged LAN across a long distance uses a technique described earlier in this chapter. An optical fiber and a pair of fiber modems are used to extend one of the connections between a bridge and a LAN segment, allowing the segment to be located remote from the bridge. Figure 11.6 illustrates how fiber modems can be used to bridge LAN segments in two buildings.

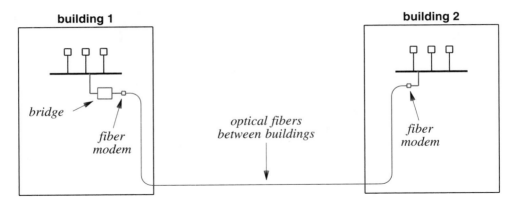

Figure 11.6 A bridge connecting LAN segments in two buildings. An optical
fiber is used to connect the bridge to a remote LAN segment.

The use of a bridge in such situations has three primary advantages. First, because
it requires only a single fiber connection, the bridge solution is less expensive than using a separate fiber connection for each individual computer. Second, because the connection between buildings attaches to the bridge, individual computers can be added or
removed from the segments without installing or changing the wiring between buildings. Third, because a bridge allows simultaneous communication on the two segments,
using a bridge instead of a repeater means communication among computers in one
building does not impact communication among computers in the other building.

11.10 Bridging Across Longer Distances

In most countries, laws prevent an organization from connecting sites with optical
fiber unless the organization owns all the property between the sites and the fiber does
not need to cross a public street. More important, organizations often find that most
computer communication occurs within each site, and that communication between sites
is infrequent. A bridged LAN provides a general solution for such situations: the organization places a LAN segment at each site, and uses a pair of bridges to connect the
segments.

How can a bridged network span long distances? Two methods are popular. Each
involves a long-distance point-to-point connection and special bridge hardware. The
first uses a leased serial line to connect the sites, and the second uses a leased satellite
channel. Use of a leased serial line is more common because it is less expensive.
However, a satellite connection is interesting because it permits communication across
an arbitrary distance. Figure 11.7 illustrates how a bridge can use a satellite connection.

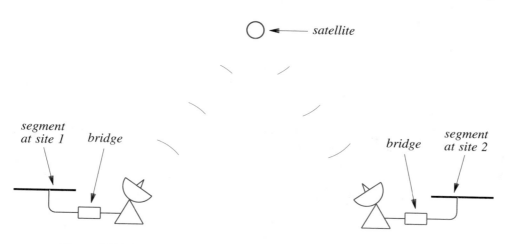

Figure 11.7 A bridge using a leased satellite channel to connect LAN segments at two sites. A satellite bridge can span arbitrary distance.

As the figure shows, the hardware used with a long-distance bridge differs slightly from that used for a local connection. In addition to a LAN segment and the ground station used for satellite communication, each site has bridge hardware. The bridge hardware learns the addresses of local computers at the site and avoids forwarding frames destined for local computers.

The motivation for filtering at both sites arises from bandwidth constraints. Unlike the optical fiber connection used between buildings, bridged LANs connected by leased circuits often use low-bandwidth connections to save cost. Consequently, a typical satellite channel used for bridging operates with much less capacity than a LAN segment†. As a result, the satellite channel does not have sufficient bandwidth to transport all frames from one LAN segment to the other site for filtering. Instead, the bridge hardware at each end of the channel learns the addresses of computers at its site, and does not forward frames unless necessary.

In addition to filtering, bridge hardware used with long-distance connections must perform *buffering* because frames can arrive from the local network faster than they can be sent across the satellite. Buffering means saving a copy of the frame in memory until it can be sent. In essence, the bridge maintains a list of frames awaiting transmission. After it receives a frame from the local network and determines that the frame should be forwarded to the other site, the bridge adds the frame to the list in memory. If the satellite transmitter is idle, the bridge starts sending the frame. If the satellite is already busy, the bridge allows transmission to proceed. When the satellite hardware finishes sending one frame, it automatically begins sending the next one on the list.

Of course, buffering does not solve the problem completely — if frames continue to arrive from the LAN faster than the satellite can send them, the bridge will run out of

---

†A satellite channel operating at 56 Kbps offers less than one percent of the capacity of a typical LAN; a leased serial line that uses telephone standard T1 has approximately 15% of the capacity of a typical LAN.

memory and begin to discard frames. However, most communication software waits for a response after it sends a few frames. In such cases, the bridge allows a computer to send a small set of frames at the speed the LAN permits.

11.11 A Cycle Of Bridges

Because a bridge sends and receives frames, a bridged network can span many segments. For example, Figure 11.8 shows eight LAN segments connected by bridges.

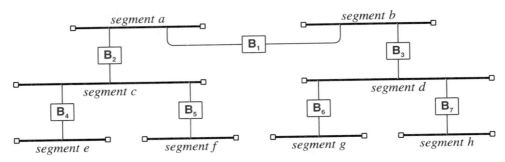

Figure 11.8 A bridged network that consists of eight segments connected by seven bridges. Computers can be attached to any of the segments.

As the figure shows, one bridge is needed to connect each segment to the rest of the bridged network. Although each bridge introduces a small delay, the network will correctly forward a frame from a computer on any segment to a computer on any other segment. For example, suppose a computer on segment g sends a frame to a computer on segment e. Bridge B_6 will forward a copy of the original transmission to segment d. Bridge B_3 will forward a copy to segment b, and so on until a copy reaches segment e.

Broadcast works in a bridged environment because a bridge always forwards a copy of a frame sent to the broadcast address. For example, if a computer on segment g broadcasts a frame, bridge B_6 will forward the broadcast to segment d. Both bridges B_3 and B_7 will receive the copy on segment d, and will forward copies to segments b and h. The copy on segment b will reach B_1, and will eventually be propagated to all remaining segments.

Not all bridges can be allowed to forward broadcast frames, or a cycle of bridges introduces a problem. To see why, consider Figure 11.9, which shows four segments interconnected by four bridges. Consider what happens if a computer on segment a sends a broadcast frame. Bridge B_1 forwards a copy to segment b, while bridge B_2 forwards a copy to segment c. When it receives the copy sent by B_2, bridge B_4 forwards that copy to segment d. Similarly, when it receives the copy sent by bridge B_1, B_3 forwards another copy to segment *d*. Thus, computers attached to segment *d* receive multiple copies. More important, when the copy from B_4 travels across segment *d*, B_3 forwards that copy to segment *b*. Similarly, when the copy from B_3 travels across segment *d*, B_4 forwards it to segment *c*. In fact, unless some bridge is prevented from forwarding broadcasts, copies continue to flow around the cycle forever, with computers on all segments receiving an infinite number of copies.

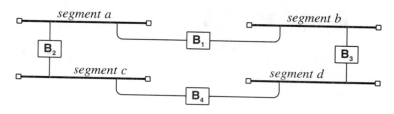

Figure 11.9 An example of bridges connected in a cycle. A problem occurs if all bridges forward broadcast frames.

11.12 Distributed Spanning Tree

To prevent the problem of infinite loops, a bridged network must not allow both of the following conditions to occur simultaneously:

- All bridges forward all frames.
- The bridged network contains a cycle of bridged segments.

In practice, it can be difficult to prevent accidental cycles from being introduced in a large bridged network that spans an organization. Furthermore, organizations sometimes choose to place extra bridges in a network to make the network more immune to failure. To prevent loops, some of the bridges in a bridged network must agree not to forward frames.

The scheme used to prevent loops in a bridged network is interesting because it is automated. A site can connect bridges in an arbitrary configuration and allow them to operate without manually configuring which bridges will forward broadcasts — the bridges configure themselves automatically.

How can a bridge know whether to forward frames? When a bridge first boots, it communicates with other bridges on the segments to which it connects†. The bridges perform a computation known as the *distributed spanning tree (DST)* algorithm to decide which bridges will not forward frames. DST allows a bridge to determine whether forwarding will introduce a cycle. In essence, a bridge does not forward frames if the bridge finds that each segment to which it attaches already contains a bridge that has agreed to forward frames. After the DST algorithm completes, the bridges that agree to forward frames form a graph that does not contain any cycles (i.e., a *tree*).

---

†In most technologies, a special hardware address is reserved for bridges. For example, Ethernet bridges communicate using a multicast address reserved exclusively for bridges.

11.13 Switching

The concept of bridging helps explain a mechanism that is popular, *switching*. In general, a network technology is called *switched* if the hardware includes an electronic device that connects to one or more computers and allows them to send and receive data. More specifically, a *switched LAN* consists of a single electronic device that transfers frames among many computers.

Physically, a switch resembles a hub — the hub consists of a single box with multiple *ports* that each attach to a single computer. The difference between a hub and a switch arises from the way the devices operate: a hub simulates a single shared medium, while a switch simulates a bridged LAN with one computer per segment. Figure 11.10 illustrates the conceptual connections inside a switch†.

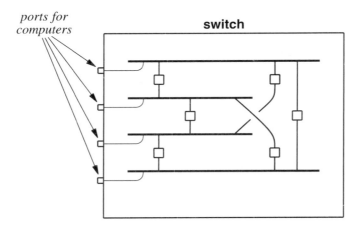

Figure 11.10 The concept underlying a switched LAN. Electronic circuits in the switch provide each computer with the illusion of a separate LAN segment connected to other segments by bridges.

Not surprisingly, the chief advantage of using a switched LAN instead of a hub is the same as the chief advantage of using a bridged LAN instead of a single segment: parallelism. Because a hub simulates a single segment shared by all computers, at most two computers can communicate through a hub at a given time. Thus, the maximum possible throughput of a hub system is R, the rate a single computer can send data across a LAN segment. In a switched LAN, however, each computer has a simulated LAN segment to itself — the segment is busy only when a frame is being transferred to or from the computer. As a result, as many as one-half of the computers connected to a switch can send data at the same time (if they each send to one of the computers that is not busy sending). Thus, the maximum possible throughput of a switch is $RN/2$, where

---

†In practice, a switch is not constructed from independent bridges. Instead, a switch contains processors and a central interconnect (e.g., an electronic cross-bar). A processor looks up the address in an incoming frame, and then uses the interconnect to transfer the frame to the correct output port.

R is the rate at which a given computer can transmit data, and N is the total number of computers connected to the switch.

11.14 Combining Switches And Hubs

Because switching provides higher aggregate data rates than a hub, a switch usually costs more per connection than a hub. To reduce cost, some organizations choose a compromise between the two: instead of connecting one computer to each port on a switch, the organization connects a hub to each port, and then connects each computer to one of the hubs. The result is closer to a conventional bridged LAN: each hub appears to be a single LAN segment, and the switch makes it appear that bridges connect all segments. The system also performs like a conventional bridged LAN: although a computer must share bandwidth with other computers connected to the same hub, communication can occur in parallel between a pair of computers attached to one hub and a pair of computers attached to another.

11.15 Bridging And Switching With Other Technologies

Although the examples in this chapter concentrate on bus technology, the general techniques of fiber modems, bridges, and switches can be used with other technologies as well. In particular, the technique of using fiber modems to connect a computer to a distant LAN has been used with most LAN technologies; commercial products exist for Token Ring, FDDI, and so on.

Hubs are especially important because they can enhance functionality. For example, Chapter 8 describes an FDDI configuration that uses counter-rotating rings to allow the network to continue to operate after a cable is broken. The counter-rotating ring configuration is most often associated with an *FDDI hub*. The hub is an electronic device that contains the circuitry necessary to detect a broken link and reconfigure the network. Each computer has a connection to the hub; circuits inside the hub form the logical ring connections. Thus, although an FDDI network has a logical ring topology, it has a physical star topology.

Switches are also available for a variety of technologies. For example, switches exist that use FDDI technology. Like an Ethernet switch, an FDDI switch consists of an electronic device to which multiple computers connect. The switch provides each computer with the illusion of being connected to a private FDDI ring with bridges connecting to each of the other rings.

11.16 Summary

Although distance limitation is a fundamental aspect of LAN technology, several mechanisms exist that allow LANs to be extended. An optical fiber can be used to extend the connection between a computer and a LAN. The technique uses a pair of fiber modems, with one at each end of the fiber. At the end near the computer, a cable connects the computer's network interface to a fiber modem. At the remote end of the fiber, a cable connects the fiber modem to the LAN. Because optical fiber has low delay, both the computer and the remote LAN operate exactly the same as with a local connection.

A repeater is a hardware device that extends the shared medium itself. Each repeater connects two segments. The repeater senses all electrical signals on one cable and transmits a copy on the other, and vice versa. Repeaters have the disadvantage of propagating electrical interference as well as valid signals.

A bridge is a hardware device that expands the size of a LAN by allowing several LANs to be concatenated. Each bridge connects two segments and arranges to transmit a copy of each frame that arrives from one segment to the other, and vice versa. A bridge attaches to a LAN exactly like a computer. The bridge listens to each segment in promiscuous mode, which guarantees that the bridge will receive a copy of each frame that passes across the segment. The bridge can then send a copy of the frame on the other segment. Bridge systems can use copper cable, optical fibers, leased serial lines, or leased satellite channels to connect LAN segments across short or long distances.

Bridges examine physical addresses in the header of each frame that arrives. A bridge uses the source address to determine which computers connect to which segments, and uses the destination address to determine whether to forward a copy of the frame. Because bridges do not forward frames farther than necessary, a bridged network permits communication between two computers on one segment to occur at the same time as communication between computers on another segment. As a result, the performance of a bridged LAN among a set of computers can exceed the performance of a single, shared LAN among the same computers.

Conceptually, a switched LAN functions like a set of LAN segments connected by bridges. Each computer connected to a switch appears to attach to a private LAN segment. Switches are available for a variety of LAN technologies. The chief advantage of a switched or bridged network lies in its ability to provide maximal performance: the switch permits a given pair of computers to send data at the same time as other pairs of computers.

EXERCISES

11.1   If your organization uses bridges to connect LANs, how many computers are attached to each segment? Did the designers choose to place computers that communicate frequently on the same segment?

11.2   Consider a packet sent across a bridged LAN to a nonexistent address. How far will bridges forward the packet?

11.3   Suppose a bridged network contains three Ethernet segments connected by two bridges, and that each segment contains one computer. If two computers send to a third, what is the maximum data rate that can be achieved between each pair? The minimum?

11.4   Write a computer program that implements a spanning tree algorithm to break cycles in a graph.

11.5   Use a network analyzer to observe traffic on a bridged Ethernet. What do you observe after a bridge reboots?

11.6   Figure 11.6 shows a single bridge connected to a remote building, but Figure 11.7 shows two bridges used with a satellite connection. Why does a satellite require two bridges?

11.7   Organizations that can afford the best network equipment usually choose switches instead of hubs. Why?

11.8   Write a computer program that simulates a bridge function. Let two files of data simulate frames transmitted on two LAN segments to which the bridge is connected. To simulate frame transmission, read a frame from the first file, then a frame from the second file, and so on. For each frame, show whether a bridge will forward a copy of the frame to the other LAN segment.

11.9   Extend the program in the previous exercise to simulate a switch. Have the program begin by reading configuration information that specifies a set of hosts and a set of virtual segments to which they should be attached. Let each host be represented by a file. Read frames from the two input files, one at a time, and show how the frame is forwarded to its destination.

11.10 Figure 11.10 illustrates that a switch with four ports simulates six bridges. Extend Figure 11.10 to have five ports.

11.11 In the previous exercise, write an equation that gives the number of simulated bridges needed as a function of the number of ports.

11.12 Can a bridge connect a Token Ring network to an Ethernet? Can a switch? Why or why not?

Chapter Contents

12

Long-Distance Digital Connection Technologies

12.1 Introduction

Previous chapters describe LAN technologies that provide network communication among a small set of computers. The fundamental limitation of LAN technologies is scale: a single LAN cannot handle an arbitrary number of computers nor can a LAN connect computers at arbitrarily distant sites.

This chapter begins a discussion of networks that overcome the size and distance limitations of LANs. The chapter focuses on two fundamental building blocks: point-to-point digital communication circuits that form the basic long-distance connections in a large network and technologies that provide high-speed digital access to individual homes and businesses. The next chapter continues the discussion by showing how these building blocks can be used to form a large packet-switching network system.

12.2 Digital Telephony

Long before computer networks became important, telephone companies were using digital communication†. The motivation for studying digital communication came from a desire to handle a large quantity of high-quality voice connections that each spanned long distances. Analog signals, the mechanism used in early telephone systems, had problems in a long-distance environment. Because electrical signals degrade as they pass over copper wires, amplifiers are required to boost the signal. Unfortunately, each amplifier along a path distorts the signal slightly and introduces noise. Digital

---

†Digital voice circuits were first used in Chicago, Illinois in 1962.

173

communication avoids the problem of noise by encoding the original audio signal into digital form, sending the digital version across the network, and then recreating the audio at the other end. The digital version of an analog audio signal is called *digital audio*, and the process of converting an analog signal to digital form is called *digitization*.

The hardware to perform digitization is an *analog-to-digital converter (A-to-D converter)*†. An A-to-D converter takes an analog signal as input, samples the signal regularly, and computes a number that gives the current level of the signal (i.e., voltage) at the time of the sample. Thus, digitization converts an analog signal into a continuous stream of numbers. Figure 12.1 illustrates the concept.

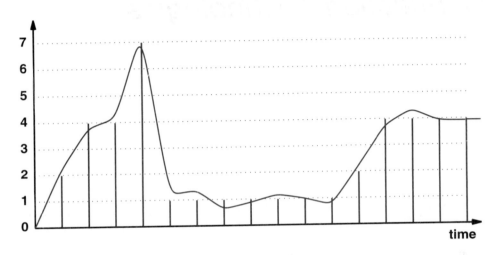

Figure 12.1 An illustration of digitization using eight values. Each vertical line represents an integer value chosen for one sample.

In the figure, vertical lines represent samples, and dotted horizontal lines represent the possible integer values. At each sample, the A-to-D conversion chooses the closest integer to the signal. Thus, the digital form for the example consists of the sequence: *0, 2, 4, 4, 7, 1, 1, 1, 1, 1, 1, 1, 2, 4, 4, 4, 4.*

Researchers, who investigated digital audio, found that reproducing a human voice required a system that reproduces frequencies up to 4000 Hz. Nyquist's *sampling theorem* states that if a continuous signal is sampled at a rate greater than twice the highest significant frequency, the original signal can be reconstructed from the samples. Thus, digitized voice needs samples taken *8000* times per second. That is, an analog-to-digital converter inside the telephone system must sample the signal from a microphone once every *125* μ seconds‡. We will see that the sampling time constant is important throughout digital telephony.

---

†The hardware to recreate an analog signal from a digital representation is called a *digital-to-analog converter (D-to-A converter)*.

‡One *microsecond*, written μ second, equals *10⁻⁶* seconds.

In addition to choosing a sampling rate, someone designing a digital encoding must choose a range of integer values to be used. The tradeoff is between accuracy and data size: a large range of values allows the signal to be reproduced more accurately, but requires the transmission of more bits. Researchers selected the range *0* to *255* for digitized voice. The sampling scheme, part of the world-wide standards for digital telephony, is known as *Pulse Code Modulation* (*PCM*). The integer values produced by PCM are sent across long-distance circuits to the destination, where they are converted back to audio†. We can summarize:

> *Pulse Code Modulation is the standard for digital encoding of audio used in the telephone system. PCM samples a signal once every 125 μseconds and converts each sample into an integer between 0 and 255.*

12.3 Synchronous Communication

Chapter 6 described analog lines that can be leased from the telephone companies and modems that make it possible to send digital data across such lines. However, analog lines are not the most important facilities that the telephone system offers for data networking. In addition to simple modems, the telephone industry has devised complex digital communication systems designed to transport digitized information across long distances. The facilities used for digitized voice differ from the systems used for data because voice systems use *synchronous* or *clocked* technology, while most data networks use *asynchronous* technology. A synchronous network (sometimes called a *synchronized network* or an *isochronous network*) consists of a system designed to move data at a precise rate. In particular, the network does not slow down as the traffic increases, and data emerges from the network at exactly the same rate it enters. To see why clocked transmission is important, consider what might happen to a digitized voice signal when it is transferred across an unsynchronized network. As more traffic enters such a network, the transmission of a given signal can experience increased delay. Thus, a stream of data moving across the network might slow down temporarily when other traffic enters the network, and then speed up again when the traffic subsides. If audio from a digitized phone call is delayed, however, the human listening to the call will hear the delay as annoying interference or noise. More important, there is no easy way to recover if the stream speeds up after a temporary slowdown. Once a receiver starts to play digitized samples that arrive late, the receiver cannot "speed up" the playback to catch up with the rest of the stream. So, to avoid such problems, the telephone system is carefully designed to transmit additional information along with the digitized data and to ensure continuous transmission. Receiving equipment uses the additional information to synchronize its clock and ensure that data leaves the network at exactly the same rate as it entered.

---

†A variant known as *Adaptive Pulse Code Modulation* (*APCM*) achieves a more dynamic range by sending a sequence of differences rather than absolute values.

12.4 Digital Circuits And DSU/CSUs

Despite being designed to carry voice traffic, digital facilities in the telephone system have been used for data traffic. In fact, since the earliest days of computer networking, digital telephone facilities have formed the basic long-distance connections in large computer networks. Telephone companies lease the circuits for a monthly fee; it is possible to lease a *point-to-point digital circuit* (i.e., a circuit that extends between two buildings, across a large city, or from a building in one city to a building in another). The fee depends on the capacity of the circuit as well as the distance spanned. We can summarize:

> *Digital circuits leased from common carriers form the fundamental building blocks for long-distance computer networks. Each circuit extends between two specified points; the fee depends on the circuit capacity and distance.*

Of course, to use a leased digital circuit, one must agree to follow the rules of the telephone system, including adhering to the standards that were designed for transmitting digitized voice. It may seem that following standards for digitized information would be trivial because computers are digital as well. However, because the computer industry and the telephone industry developed independently, the standards for telephone system digital circuits differ from those used in the computer industry. Thus, a special piece of hardware is needed to interface a computer to a digital circuit provided by a telephone company. Known as a *Data Service Unit/Channel Service Unit* (*DSU/CSU*), the device contains two functional parts, usually combined into a single chassis.

A DSU/CSU is required at each end of a leased digital circuit as Figure 12.2 illustrates.

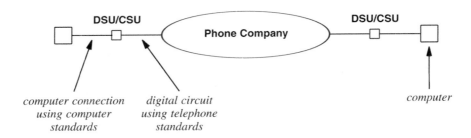

Figure 12.2 Illustration of a digital circuit with a DSU/CSU on each end. The DSU/CSU converts between the digital standards used in the telephone system and those used by computer vendors.

The CSU portion of the DSU/CSU device handles line termination and diagnostics. For example, the CSU contains circuitry to accommodate current surges that are generated by lightning or other electro-magnetic interference. It also contains diagnostic circuitry that can test whether the line has been disconnected and whether the DSU/CSU on the other end is functioning correctly. Finally, the CSU provides a *loopback* capability used when installing and testing circuits. When loopback is enabled, the CSU sends back a copy of all data that arrives across the circuit without passing it through.

A CSU also provides a service that computer engineers find surprising — it prohibits excessive consecutive *1* bits. The need to prevent excessive *1*s arises from the electrical signals used. In particular, because the telephone company originally designed their digital circuits to work over copper cables, engineers were concerned that having too many contiguous *1* bits would mean excessive current on the cable. To prevent problems, a CSU can either use bit stuffing or use a balanced encoding scheme. For example, some digital circuits use zero voltage to represent a *0* bit and nonzero to represent a *1* bit, with successive *1* bits alternating between +3 volts and -3 volts.

The DSU portion of a DSU/CSU handles the data. It translates data between the digital format used on the carrier's circuit and the digital format required by the customer's computer equipment. The interface standard used on the computer side depends on the rate that the circuit operates. If the data rate is less than 56 Kbps, the computer can use RS-232. For rates above 56 Kbps, the computer must use interface hardware that supports higher speeds (e.g., hardware that uses the *RS-449* or *V.35* standards). To summarize:

> *A digital circuit needs a device known as a DSU/CSU at each end. In addition to terminating the line, the DSU/CSU translates between the digital representation used by phone companies and the digital representation used by the computer industry.*

12.5 Telephone Standards

On the connection to a leased circuit, a DSU must accommodate the digital transmission standards used by the phone company. In the U.S., standards for digital telephone circuits were given names that consist of the letter *T* followed by a number. Engineers refer to them collectively as the *T-series standards*. One of the most popular is known as T1; many companies use a T1 circuit for data†.

Unfortunately, T-standards are not universal. Japan adopted a modified version of the T-series standards, and Europe chose a slightly different scheme. (European standards can be distinguished because they use the letter *E*.) Figure 12.3 lists the data rates of three digital circuit standards.

---

†In addition to using copper or optical fiber for land segments, a T1 circuit that crosses an ocean may pass through a satellite.

Name	Bit Rate	Voice Circuits	Location
–	0.064 Mbps	1	
T1	1.544 Mbps	24	North America
T2	6.312 Mbps	96	North America
T3	44.736 Mbps	672	North America
E1	2.048 Mbps	30	Europe
E2	8.448 Mbps	120	Europe
E3	34.368 Mbps	480	Europe

Figure 12.3 Data rates of popular digital circuit standards used in North America and Europe.

12.6 DS Terminology And Data Rates

Although the bit rates in Figure 12.3 may seem to be random numbers, they are easily explained. Recall that the phone companies designed the digital circuits to carry voice. A single voice channel requires 64 Kbps (8000 8-bit samples per second). The data rate of the *T1* standard was chosen to allow the circuit to carry *24* independent voice calls (plus a small amount of overhead). A device is used to multiplex the calls at one end of a T1 circuit, and another device is used to demultiplex calls at the other end. For example, imagine two telephone offices in a city with a single T1 circuit between them. When a call must be directed to the other office, a telephone switch selects one of the currently unused channels in the T1 circuit, and sends the call over that channel.

Note that the capacity of circuits does not increase linearly with their numbers. For example, the T3 standard defines a circuit with much more than three times the capacity of T1. Although the rates have been chosen to permit aggregation of phone calls, the larger capacities were not selected as arbitrary multiples of individual calls. Instead, the upper rates represent integral multiples of lower rates. For example, the T3 rate is equal to *28* T1 circuits. Thus, it is possible to multiplex 28 T1 circuits over a single T3 circuit.

To understand the motivation for multiplexing, imagine a phone company that needs multiple T1 circuits between two cities. The company can choose to install a single T3 circuit and multiplex up to 28 T1 circuits over it.

To be technically precise, one must distinguish between the T-standards, which define the underlying carrier system, and the standards that specify how to multiplex multiple phone calls onto a single connection. The latter are known as *Digital Signal Level standards* or *DS standards*. The names are written as the letters *DS* followed by a number. For example, DS1 denotes a service that can multiplex 24 phone calls onto a single circuit. Furthermore, because DS1 defines the effective data rate, it is technically more accurate to say, ''a circuit running at DS1 speed'' than to refer to ''T1 speed.''

Despite the minor technical distinctions, the terms T1 and DS1 are often interchanged. In fact, few engineers bother to distinguish between them. Thus, one is likely to hear someone cite a circuit as T1 or refer to T1-speed. We can summarize:

> *Digital circuits are classified according to a set of telephone standards. Two of the most popular circuit types in North America are T1 and T3.*

12.7 Lower Capacity Circuits

Currently, T1 circuits are among the most popular. However, a T1 circuit is too expensive for private individuals or small businesses (thousands of dollars per month). Furthermore, many companies do not need the capacity of a T1 circuit. In such cases, it is possible to lease a lower-capacity circuit, which is known as *fractional T1*. Fractional T1 circuits are available with capacity much less than 1.544 Mbps (e.g., 64 Kbps, 128 Kbps, 9.6 Kbps, and 4.8 Kbps). One of the most popular fractional T1 rates consists of a circuit that delivers *56 Kbps*.

The phone company uses the term *Time Division Multiplexing (TDM)*† to refer to the concept of subdividing a T1 circuit. To summarize:

> *A company that does not need T1 capacity can save money by leasing a* fractional T1 *digital circuit. The phone company uses the term* Time Division Multiplexing *for the technology used to subdivide a T1 circuit. One of the most popular fractional T1 capacities is 56 Kbps.*

12.8 Intermediate Capacity Digital Circuits

What if a company needs a circuit with slightly more than T1 capacity, but only T3 circuits are available? Because a T3 circuit has 28 times the capacity of a T1 circuit, T3 costs substantially more than T1. Thus, it does not make sense to lease a T3 circuit and only use a small fraction of the capacity. Technology called *inverse multiplexing* has been developed to handle intermediate capacity circuits. The technology allows one to lease multiple T1 circuits between two points, and use them like a single higher-capacity circuit. An electronic device known as an *inverse multiplexor (inverse mux)* is needed at each end of the lines. On one side, the inverse mux connects to a computer. On the other side, it connects to two or more digital circuits. The inverse mux accepts a stream of data from the computer, and sends part of the data over each of the digital circuits. Similarly, the mux accepts data streams coming over the digital circuits, and recombines them into a single stream. Figure 12.4 illustrates the concept.

---

†When used to refer to phone company circuits, *Time Division Multiplexing* is written in upper case to distinguish it from the generic concept.

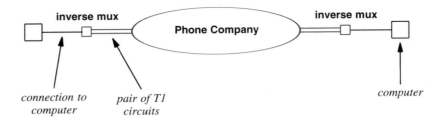

Figure 12.4 An inverse mux using two T1 circuits to provide a connection with twice the capacity. Inverse multiplexing is attractive economically for intermediate capacities because two T1 circuits are much less expensive than a T3 circuit.

In practice, a DSU/CSU is required at the ends of each T1 circuit. Depending on the model used, an inverse mux device may have DSU/CSU functionality built in, or may require separate units.

12.9 Highest Capacity Circuits

Telephone companies use the term *trunk* to denote a high-capacity circuit. As the amount of digital telephony grew, phone companies realized that higher capacity digital circuits would be needed to serve as the major trunk connections across the country or between countries. Consequently, a series of standards was defined for high-capacity digital circuits. Known as the *Synchronous Transport Signal* (*STS*) standards, they specify the details of high speed connections. Figure 12.5 summarizes the data rates associated with various STS standards. All data rates in the table are given in Mbps, making it easy to compare. It should be noted, however, that data rates for STS-24 and above are greater than 1 Gbps.

Standard Name	Optical Name	Bit Rate	Voice Circuits
STS-1	OC-1	51.840 Mbps	810
STS-3	OC-3	155.520 Mbps	2430
STS-12	OC-12	622.080 Mbps	9720
STS-24	OC-24	1,244.160 Mbps	19440
STS-48	OC-48	2,488.320 Mbps	38880

Figure 12.5 Data rates of digital circuits according to the STS hierarchy of standards.

12.10 Optical Carrier Standards

When engineers discuss the STS hierarchy, they often use the terms shown in the second column. *OC* is an abbreviation for *Optical Carrier*. The terminology arises because higher data rates associated with the STS standards require optical fiber. To be precise, one should observe a distinction between the STS and OC terminology: the STS standards refer to the electrical signals used in the digital circuit interface (i.e., over copper), while the OC standards refer to the optical signals that propagate across the fiber. As with other network terminology, however, few people make the distinction. Thus, one often hears networking professionals use the term *OC-3* to refer to both the optical fiber in a circuit and the interface.

12.11 The C Suffix

The Synchronous Transport Signal and Optical Carrier terminology described above has one additional feature not shown in Figure 12.5: an optional suffix of the letter *C*, which stands for *concatenated*. The presence of the suffix denotes a circuit with no inverse multiplexing. That is, an OC-3 circuit consists of three OC-1 circuits operating at 51.840 Mbps each, and is intended to be used as three circuits. An OC-3C (STS-3C) circuit, however, is a single circuit operating at 155.520 Mbps.

The easiest way to think about the multiplexing is to imagine that a circuit either consists of a single fiber running at the specified bit rate, or it consists of several fibers, each running at a slower rate. In fact, most circuits are not formed from separate fibers. Instead, the equipment multiplexes multiple circuits over the underlying infrastructure.

Is a single circuit operating at full speed better than multiple circuits operating at lower rates? The answer depends on how the circuit is being used. In general, having a single circuit operating at full capacity provides more flexibility and eliminates the need for inverse multiplexing equipment. More to the point, data networks are unlike voice networks. In a voice system, high-capacity circuits are used as a way of aggregating smaller voice streams. In a data network, however, there is a single stream of packet traffic. Thus, if given a choice, most network designers prefer an OC-3C circuit over an OC-3 circuit.

12.12 Synchronous Optical NETwork (SONET)

In addition to the STS and OC standards described above, the phone companies have defined a broad set of standards for digital transmission. In North America, the standards use the term *Synchronous Optical NETwork (SONET)*, while in Europe they are known as the *Synchronous Digital Hierarchy (SDH)*. SONET specifies details such as how data is framed, how lower-capacity circuits are multiplexed into a high-capacity circuit, and how synchronous clock information is sent along with data. Because car-

riers use SONET extensively, when someone leases an STS-1 circuit, the carrier is likely to require them to use SONET encoding on the circuit. For example, Figure 12.6
shows the SONET frame format used on an STS-1 circuit. Each frame is *810* octets
long. According to SONET terminology, octets in the frame are divided into *9*
"rows", with *90* "columns" in each row.

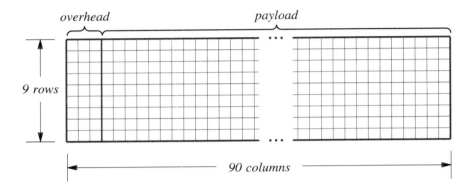

Figure 12.6 Illustration of an STS-1 SONET frame with 810 octets divided
into 9 rows of 90 columns. Octets at the beginning of each row
provide clock synchronization and maintenance information.

Interestingly, the size of a SONET frame depends on the bit rate of the underlying
circuit. As Figure 12.6 shows, a SONET frame on an STS-1 circuit contains *810* octets.
When SONET is used on an STS-3 circuit, however, each frame holds *2430* octets.
How do the numbers arise? To understand the difference, recall that 125 μ seconds is a
fundamental constant for digitized voice because PCM requires taking an *8*-bit sample
every *125* μ seconds. SONET uses the time to define frame size. At the STS-1
transmission rate of *51.840* Mbps, exactly *6480* bits are transferred in 125 μ seconds,
which means that a frame consists of *810* 8-bit octets. Similarly, at the STS-3 rate,
2430 octets can be transmitted in 125 μ seconds. The chief advantage of making the
frame size depend on the bit rate of the circuit is that it makes synchronous multiplexing possible — retaining synchronization while combining three STS-1 SONET streams
into one STS-3 SONET stream is straightforward.

Although most data networks use SONET as an encoding scheme on a single
point-to-point circuit, the standard provides more possibilities. In particular, it is possible to build a high-capacity counter rotating ring network using SONET technology that
handles failures similar to an FDDI ring. Each station on the ring uses a device known
as an *add/drop mux*. In addition to passing received data around the ring, the
add/drop mux can be configured to accept additional data from a local circuit and add
it to frames passing across the ring, or to extract data and deliver it to a local computer.
If the ring is broken, the hardware detects the loss of framing information and uses the
counter rotating ring to reconnect. To summarize:

Although the SONET standard defines a technology that can be used to build a high-capacity ring network with multiple data circuits multiplexed across the fibers that constitute the ring, most data networks only use SONET to define framing and encoding on a leased circuit.

12.13 The Local Subscriber Loop

Although leased data circuits provide the ability to send data across long distances, another problem must be solved before computer networks can become ubiquitous: higher-speed connections are needed that extend to individual residences and businesses. Telephone companies use the term *local loop* or *local subscriber line* to refer to the connection between the phone company *Central Office* (*CO*) and an individual subscriber's residence or place of business; the term has been adopted to refer to the connections from a network provider to individual subscribers. Currently, most local loops use analog signals because they were designed for conventional analog telephone service†. Indeed, most subscribers currently obtain access to networks by using a telephone to dial a local service provider.

Although dialup modems have improved over the years, the voice bandwidth and signal-to-noise ratio of telephone lines limit the rate at which bits can be sent. Fortunately, a variety of technologies have been invented that can provide high throughput digital connections to subscribers.

12.14 ISDN

One of the first efforts to provide large-scale digital services to subscribers was launched by telephone companies under the name *Integrated Services Digital Network* (*ISDN*). ISDN provides digitized voice and data to subscribers over conventional local loop wiring. That is, ISDN uses the same type of twisted pair copper wiring as the analog telephone system.

From a subscriber's point of view, ISDN offers three separate digital channels, designated *B*, *B*, and *D* (usually written *2B + D*). The two *B* channels, which each operate at a speed of 64 Kbps, are intended to carry digitized voice, data, or compressed video; the *D* channel, which operates at 16 Kbps, is intended as a control channel‡. In general, a subscriber uses the *D* channel to request services which are then supplied over the *B* channels (e.g., make a phone call that uses digital voice). The subscriber also uses the *D* channel to manage a session that is in progress or to terminate a session. Finally, both of the *B* channels can be combined or *bonded* to produce a single channel with an effective data rate of 128 Kbps.

The 2B + D channels are known as the ISDN *Basic Rate Interface* (*BRI*). In fact, ISDN uses a form of time division multiplexing to provide the illusion of multiple channels of data traveling over a single pair of wires.

---

†Analog phone service is often referred to as *POTS*, which stands for *Plain Old Telephone Service.*

‡Although the user has a total of 144 Kbps available, the underlying system operates at 160 Kbps; the remaining 16 Kbps are consumed by synchronization and framing.

When the phone companies first defined ISDN many years ago, 64 Kbps seemed fast compared to dialup modems, which operated at less than 10 Kbps. Phone companies hoped that customers would use ISDN for both local and long distance digital communication analogous to the way they use the voice telephone system. As the years passed, however, dialup modems improved, and alternative technologies were invented that provided high data rates across the local loop at lower cost. Consequently, ISDN now is an expensive alternative that offers little throughput.

12.15 Asymmetric Digital Subscriber Line Technology

One of the most exciting types of technology for providing digital services across the local loop goes by the name *Digital Subscriber Line (DSL)*. In fact, there are several variants. Because the names differ by the first word, the set is collectively referred to by the acronym *xDSL*.

Perhaps the most interesting xDSL technology is known as *Asymmetric Digital Subscriber Line (ADSL)*. From a subscriber's point of view, ADSL provides the ability to send and receive digital information at high speed. As the name implies, however, the service is asymmetric. In the case of ADSL, the asymmetry arises from the bit rate — the available bandwidth is divided to make the bit rate in one direction much higher than in the other.

To understand the motivation for asymmetry, think of how an average person uses the Internet. Most of the traffic is generated when the person browses the Web or downloads files. In each case, the traffic that the individual sends out to the Internet consists of short requests (e.g., a few bytes of data). However, the traffic that flows back from the Internet to the user can contain millions of bytes of data (e.g., digitized images). To distinguish the two directions, professionals use the term *downstream* to refer to data flowing out to the user, and *upstream* to refer to data flowing from the user. The subscriber loop can be optimized for asymmetric traffic by allocating the bandwidth to provide a higher bit rate in the downstream direction. We can summarize:

> *ADSL is a local loop technology that is optimized for typical users who receive much more information than they send. To accommodate such use, ADSL provides a higher bit rate downstream (i.e., to the subscriber) than upstream (i.e., from the subscriber to the provider).*

From the user's viewpoint, the optimization offers the advantage of allowing Web pages to be displayed more quickly than a symmetric solution would allow. Of course, the asymmetry makes ADSL inappropriate for connections that send more data than they receive. For example, a business that has an online catalog available to customers would not benefit from ADSL because the business would tend to send more data than it receives.

How fast can ADSL operate? The maximum downstream rate is an astounding *6.144 Mbps*, and the maximum upstream rate is *640 Kbps*. Because there is a mandatory network control channel that requires *64 Kbps*, the effective upstream rate for user data is *576 Kbps*.

Although the data rates are surprisingly high, the most astonishing aspect of ADSL arises from the physical wiring over which it achieves those data rates and the way it uses the wiring. ADSL does not require any changes in local loop wiring because it is designed to run over the same twisted pair wiring that was originally installed for analog telephone service. Furthermore, ADSL does not preempt the local loop — it can run simultaneously over the same wires as the standard phone service! Thus, ADSL has an obvious economic advantage: phone companies can use it to supply high-speed digital service without rewiring the local loop. Figure 12.7 illustrates how ADSL modems attach to standard telephone wiring in parallel with existing analog telephone equipment. Because the service is asymmetric, the modems used at the two ends of a line differ slightly.

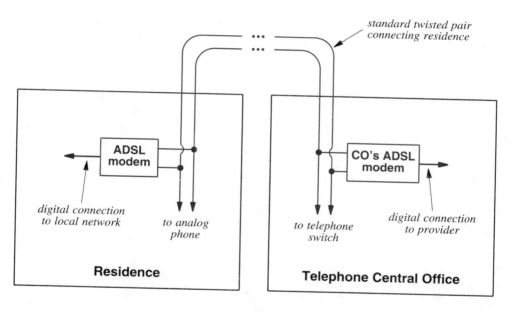

Figure 12.7 ADSL modems connected to existing local loop wiring. The modems can use a pair of wires simultaneously with analog telephone service.

How does ADSL achieve high data rates over twisted pair? Researchers first observed that a scheme like ADSL might be possible because many local loops accommodate signals at frequencies higher than those used by the telephone system. The ADSL solution is complex because no two local loops have identical electrical characteristics. Instead, the ability to carry signals depends on the distance, gauge of wiring used, and level of electrical interference. Thus, the designers could not pick a particular set of carrier frequencies or modulation techniques that would work in all cases. For example, consider two subscribers who live in different parts of a town. If the telephone line leading to the first subscriber passes near a commercial radio station, the station's signal will cause interference at the frequency the station uses. If the second subscriber does not live near the same radio station, the frequency the radio station uses may work well for data on that subscriber's line. However, the second line can experience interference on another frequency.

To accommodate differences in local loop characteristics, ADSL is *adaptive*. That is, when ADSL modems are powered on, they probe the line between them to find its characteristics, and then agree to communicate using techniques that are optimal for the line. In particular, ADSL uses a scheme known as *Discrete Multi Tone modulation* (*DMT*), which combines frequency division multiplexing and inverse multiplexing techniques.

The frequency division multiplexing in DMT is implemented by dividing the bandwidth into *286* separate frequencies or *subchannels†*, with *255* frequencies used for downstream data transmission and *31* used for upstream data transmission, with *2* taken for control information. Conceptually, there is a separate ''modem'' running on each subchannel, which has its own modulated carrier. The carriers are spaced at *4.1325 KHz* intervals to keep the signals from interfering with one another. Furthermore, to guarantee that its transmissions do not interfere with analog phone signals, ADSL avoids using the bandwidth below 4 KHz. When ADSL starts, both ends probe the available frequencies to determine which signals get through and which experience interference. In addition to selecting frequencies, the two ends assess the signal quality at each frequency, and use the quality to select a modulation scheme. If a particular frequency has a high signal-to-noise ratio, ADSL selects a modulation scheme that encodes many bits per baud; if the quality on a given frequency is low, ADSL selects a modulation scheme that encodes fewer bits per baud. We can summarize:

> *To achieve high bit rates over conventional twisted pair wiring, ADSL uses an adaptive technology in which a pair of modems probe many frequencies on the line between them, and select frequencies and modulation techniques that give optimal results on that line.*

The result of adaptation is a robust technology that can adapt to various line conditions automatically. From a user's point of view, adaptation has an interesting property: ADSL does not guarantee a data rate. Instead, ADSL can only guarantee to do as well as line conditions allow its techniques to operate. Thus, the downstream rate varies from *32 Kbps* to *6.4 Mbps*, and the upstream rate varies from *32* to *640 Kbps*.

---

†The terminology arises because the capacity of an ADSL connection can be divided into 1.544 Mbps ''channels'' that each connect to a T1 circuit.

12.16 Other DSL Technologies

In addition to ADSL, other DSL technologies have been developed. Each uses the bandwidth to achieve a slightly different goal. Thus, each has advantages for some applications. For example, *Symmetric Digital Subscriber Line* (*SDSL*) provides symmetric bit rates in both directions. As described above, most individuals who use computer networks follow an asymmetric pattern of use. Many small business users follow the same pattern — they generally use the network to obtain information. However, businesses that provide information to others tend to have exactly the opposite asymmetry — they export more data than they import. Unfortunately, few phone companies offer ADSL with the direction of asymmetry reversed. Thus, businesses that export information may prefer SDSL. Furthermore, because SDSL uses a different encoding scheme than ADSL, it can operate over local loops for which ADSL is inappropriate. Thus, some phone companies choose to offer SDSL service instead of ADSL.

Another DSL service is known as *High-Rate Digital Subscriber Line* (*HDSL*). HDSL provides a DS1 bit rate (i.e., 1.544 Mbps) in two directions. One of the disadvantages of HDSL is a short distance limitation on local loops. Another disadvantage arises from the wiring requirements. Unlike ADSL, which uses a single twisted pair, HDSL requires two independent twisted pairs. To overcome the wiring disadvantage, a variant known as *HDSL2* has been proposed that runs over two wires†.

One of the advantages of HDSL arises from its tolerance of local loop modifications made for the telephone system. In particular, HDSL can be used on a loop that includes a telephone *bridge tap* (some DSL technologies cannot). Furthermore, because its bit rate is compatible with a T1 circuit, moving data between a T1 circuit and HDSL is straightforward.

Another advantage of HDSL arises from its ability to tolerate failure gracefully. The technology is designed so that if one of the two twisted pairs fails, the modems do not fail completely, but instead continue to operate at one half the maximum bit rate. The graceful failure mode especially appeals to businesses because it is often better to have a slow connection than no connection at all.

Another DSL variant has been studied that can provide even higher throughput. Known as *Very-high bit rate Digital Subscriber Line* (*VDSL*), the technology can achieve a data rate of up to *52 Mbps*. Alternatives have also been pursued that offer *13 Mbps* and *26 Mbps*.

Although such high rates can be achieved over copper twisted pair, VDSL cannot be used on existing wiring between the telephone Central Office and subscribers because the distances are too long. So, VDSL requires intermediate concentration points (e.g., one in each neighborhood), with optical fiber connecting the concentration points back to the CO. In VDSL terminology, a concentration point is called an *Optical Network Unit* (*ONU*). Because versions of VDSL with lower data rates run over longer distances of copper, they do not require concentration points to be as close to the subscriber. Thus, lower data rates require fewer concentration points to cover a given geographic area.

---

†Because the upstream and downstream traffic shares a single pair of wires, HDSL2 is sometimes called *SHDSL*.

12.17 Cable Modem Technology

The previous sections examined technologies that deliver digital information over the twisted pair wiring that forms the local loop of the analog telephone system. This section considers use of an alternative wiring scheme that can deliver even higher bit rates.

The primary motivation for considering alternatives to the telephone local loop arises from inherent limitations. The chief problem lies in the electrical characteristics of twisted pair wiring. Although technologies like ADSL can achieve much higher bit rates than dialup modems, the wiring places an upper bound on how fast data can be transferred. Furthermore, the lack of shielding makes the wiring susceptible to interference, which can substantially degrade performance for some subscribers.

In an effort to overcome the limitations of twisted pair wiring, researchers have investigated both wireless and wired technologies for use in the local loop. One alternative technology stands out as particularly attractive because it offers higher speed than telephone wiring, is less susceptible to electromagnetic interference, and does not require completely new infrastructure: *cable television†*. In addition, many residential areas already have cable TV wiring in place.

A CATV system has almost all the facilities needed to send digital information downstream at high-speed. The media consists of coaxial cable, which has high capacity and is immune to electromagnetic interference, and the cable system hardware uses broadband signaling (i.e., frequency division multiplexing) to deliver multiple television channels simultaneously. More important, because cable systems are designed to carry many more television signals than are currently available, the hardware has unused bandwidth (i.e. channels) that can be used to send data. The advantages have been sufficient to stimulate research. The point is:

> *Engineers have devised ways to use the existing cable TV infrastructure as a local loop technology that delivers digital data to subscribers.*

In theory, it is possible to extend a cable system to send digital information downstream by using frequency division multiplexing. To do so, one pair of *cable modems* is needed for each subscriber. One modem resides in the CATV center, and the other at a subscriber's site. Both modems in a pair must be tuned to the same carrier frequency, which is multiplexed onto the cable along with television signals. Data passed to the modem at the CATV center is encoded on the carrier, which is then broadcast across the cable to all subscribers. A matching modem at the subscriber's location picks out the carrier signal, extracts the encoded digital information, and passes the resulting stream to the subscriber's computer.

In practice, however, even the large bandwidth available in CATV systems is not sufficient to handle a frequency division multiplexing scheme that extends to each user.

---

†Formally, the technology is known as *Community Antenna TeleVision (CATV)*.

To understand why, remember that the carrier frequencies must be separated from one another to avoid interference and consider the number of subscribers. In a large metropolitan area, a single cable supplier can have millions of subscribers, making it impossible to allocate a separate carrier frequency to each. As a result, the frequency division multiplexing scheme does not scale.

Engineers have explored several ways to handle the problem of multiplexing downstream signals. One solution is a form of time division multiplexing. Instead of assigning a unique frequency to each subscriber, the cable company uses one frequency for a set of subscribers (typically, everyone in a neighborhood). In addition, each subscriber is assigned an address. A subscriber's modem listens to the assigned frequency for incoming packets. Before accepting a packet, the device verifies that the destination address matches the address assigned to the subscriber. In essence, the data portion of the cable hardware system resembles a set of shared LANs rather than a set of point-to-point links.

From a subscriber's point of view, sharing the bandwidth with other subscribers can be a disadvantage. Although cable modems can deliver up to *36* Mbps, the effective data rate available to each individual station varies over time. If *N* subscribers share a single frequency, the amount of capacity available to an individual subscriber can be as little as *1/N*.

12.18 Upstream Communication

The original CATV infrastructure has another serious disadvantage as a local loop technology: the entire design was optimized to carry signals in the downstream direction only. There was absolutely no provision in a conventional cable system for upstream propagation. The problem is serious because in addition to wires, the cable distribution system contains electronic equipment such as broadband amplifiers that only operate in one direction. The point is:

> *Because the original cable infrastructure only provided downstream delivery, the original system could not be used to provide two-way digital communication.*

How can a cable system be modified to provide upstream communication? One of the earliest attempts focused on a *dual path* approach that is possible because of the asymmetric traffic patterns mentioned above. Instead of sending all data over the cable infrastructure, the cable system handles only downstream traffic, while upstream traffic travels across a dialup telephone connection. To implement the scheme, a subscriber needs a hardware interface device that connects to two modems, a cable modem and a standard dialup telephone modem. To use the service, a subscriber first requests a dialup connection to the service provider. Once the dialup connection is in place, the hardware uses it to send packets. All data that the computer transmits is sent over the dialup connection. All data that the computer receives arrives at higher bit rates from the cable modem. The chief advantage of a dual-path scheme lies in its low cost for cable providers — the existing cable system does not need to change. The chief disadvantage lies in the clumsy interface.

More recent work on using the cable system as a local loop technology has focused on modifications to the basic infrastructure that permit two-way communication across the cable. Of course, the addition of an upstream data path requires significant changes to the cable system, which will incur substantial cost. To help justify costs, cable companies are investigating uses for an upstream path beyond computer network connections. For example, an upstream path can also be used to provide *video on demand* or *interactive TV*, services that permit a customer to select a video for viewing at any time and make changes during the presentation.

12.19 Hybrid Fiber Coax

One of the most promising technologies that provide two-way communication across a cable system is *Hybrid Fiber Coax* (*HFC*). As the name implies, the system uses a combination of optical fibers and coaxial cables, with fiber used for the central facilities and coax used for the connections to individual subscribers. In essence, HFC is hierarchical. It uses fiber optics for the portion of the network that requires the highest bandwidth, and uses coax for parts that can tolerate lower capacities.

To use HFC, cable companies will need to replace much of the existing cable wiring and amplifiers. The industry uses the term *trunk* to refer to the high-capacity connections between the cable office and each neighborhood area, and the term *feeder circuit* to refer to the connection to an individual subscriber†. Although HFC uses existing coax feeder circuits to connect to individual subscribers, it requires the cable company to replace trunk circuits with optical fiber. In addition, new equipment must be added that interfaces the fiber to coax. To permit upstream communication, the company must also replace all amplifiers with bi-directional devices. Finally, before they can take advantage of HFC, each subscriber needs a bidirectional cable modem.

As with other cable technologies, HFC uses a combination of frequency division multiplexing and time division multiplexing. Bandwidth between *50* and *450* MHz is used for analog television (with *6* MHz devoted to each TV channel), and bandwidth from *450* MHz to *750* MHz is reserved for downstream digital communication. Finally, the bandwidth from *5* through *50* MHz is used for upstream communication.

Time division multiplexing operates within a group of one or more subscribers that are assigned to share the bandwidth. Usually, a group is chosen on the basis of geographic proximity (e.g., in a neighborhood). The group shares one carrier frequency, with only one subscriber in the group able to receive a packet at any time. The higher bandwidth of fiber makes it possible to multiplex several independent groups across the trunk lines.

---

†Trunk connections can be up to *15* miles long; feeder circuits are usually less than a mile.

Like ADSL, cable modems are designed to provide higher rates downstream than upstream. The data rate for upstream delivery can be as high as *1.5 to 2.0 Mbps*. However, because the data from multiple subscribers must be multiplexed into a *6 MHz* bandwidth, the effective rate declines when many users transmit data simultaneously.

To summarize:

> *To use Hybrid Fiber Coax, cable companies must change much of the central infrastructure. Trunk lines must be replaced with optical fiber, and all amplifiers must be modified to operate in both directions. However, the system can use existing coax feeder circuits to reach individual subscribers.*

12.20 Fiber To The Curb

In addition to HFC, cable companies have explored other technologies. One alternative is known as *Fiber To The Curb (FTTC)*. As the name implies, FTTC is similar to HFC because it uses optical fiber for high capacity trunks. The idea is to run optical fiber close to the end subscriber, and then use copper for the feeder circuits.

FTTC differs from HFC because it uses two media in each feeder circuit to allow the cable system to provide an additional service. That is, the cable company must run an additional wire to each house to use HFC. The first circuit uses existing coaxial cable to deliver interactive video. The second circuit uses twisted pair, which can be used to carry voice.

12.21 Alternatives For Special Cases

Although technologies such as ADSL or HFC can deliver digital services to most subscribers, they do not handle all circumstances. The primary problems arise in remote and rural areas. For example, imagine a farm many miles from the nearest city or imagine a remote village. The twisted pair wiring used to deliver telephone service to such locations exceeds the maximum distance for technologies like ADSL. In addition, rural areas are least likely to have cable television service.

Technologies like ADSL have further technical restrictions on the type of line they can use. For example, it may be impossible to use high frequencies on telephone lines that contain loading coils, taps, or repeaters. Furthermore, the copper wiring must have sufficient gauge or signals will be attenuated. Thus, even in areas where a local loop technology works for most subscribers, it may not work on all lines.

12.22 Broadcast Satellite Systems

To handle special cases, a variety of alternative local loop technologies have been explored. For example, it is possible to use wireless technologies similar to digital cellular services. Another alternative employs digital communication satellites. Initially, such satellites were deployed by telecommunication companies, primarily as an alternative to terrestrial lines. Thus, they were deployed in situations where terrestrial lines were either expensive or infeasible such as across oceans or in mountainous areas. More important, early satellites provided point-to-point communication (e.g., from a ground station in the United States to a ground station in Europe). When it became obvious that commercial companies could build, deploy, and operate communication satellites, the questions arose: could satellites be used as a local loop technology? If so, are they only appropriate for special cases, or could they provide a general-purpose infrastructure?

On one hand, satellites offer advantages: a satellite system has more bandwidth than a dialup connection, and can reach an arbitrary geographic location. On the other hand, the high orbit of a geosynchronous satellite means long delays. More important, the ground station equipment required to transmit a signal to a satellite (known as an *uplink*) is both expensive and large, making it inappropriate for individuals or small businesses — only large corporations can afford such facilities.

To devise a low-cost local loop system that uses satellites, two innovations were needed:

- Instead of treating satellites as point-to-point communication systems, a *broadcast* mechanism was devised.

- Instead of a large, expensive ground station, an alternative uplink transmission path was used.

The satellite broadcast mechanism uses the same principle described in Chapter 9: a satellite broadcasts each packet, and all stations tuned to the satellite's transmission receive a copy. To ensure that packets only arrive at their intended destination, each station is assigned a unique *address*, and the station filters incoming packets in the same way a LAN interface card filters packets. That is, although the satellite channel is shared, a given station only accepts packets sent to the station's address; other packets are discarded.

Of course, satellite transmission is more complicated than transmission across a LAN. In particular, a satellite can contain multiple transmitters, each operating on a separate channel (i.e., frequency). Thus, a broadcast satellite can use frequency division multiplexing to achieve higher bandwidth, and then use time division multiplexing to allow multiple receivers to share the bandwidth. For our purposes, however, it is sufficient to think of the satellite as offering a single shared channel.

To solve the uplink problem, satellite vendors focused on the asymmetric communication requirements described previously. They observed that a satellite can be used for a high-capacity downstream path, while a lower-capacity path can be used for upstream traffic. In particular, vendors that offer Internet connectivity via broadcast satellites rely on conventional dialup connections for upstream traffic. The important point is:

> *Broadcast satellite technology extends the notion of asymmetric delivery to use two different underlying mechanisms. Although a broadcast satellite is used for downstream traffic; upstream traffic travels over a lower-capacity network such as a conventional dialup telephone connection.*

Thus, to use broadcast satellite technology, each subscriber must have a telephone connection as well as an antenna (i.e. a receiving "dish") and a computer. The satellite vendor supplies a hardware device that interconnects the antenna, computer, and telephone line. The device accepts packets from the antenna, and delivers them to the computer. It also accepts packets from the computer and sends them over the dialup line. To do so, the device has a dialup modem, and is configured to know how to dial and send outgoing packets. To make the entire system work, routing is arranged carefully to ensure that traffic sent to any of the satellite subscribers is forwarded to the satellite vendor, which then transmits the packet over the satellite.

12.23 Summary

Telephone companies pioneered long-distance digital communication to provide high-quality, long-distance voice connections between cities. It is possible to lease point-to-point digital circuits from telephone companies for private use; the cost depends on the capacity and distance spanned. Most Wide Area Networks use such leased digital circuits to provide long-distance communication.

Common carriers have set standards for the representation and data rates of digital circuits; most of the standards were designed to accommodate multiple streams of digitized voice traffic. A DSU/CSU device must be attached to each end of a digital circuit to translate between the digital representation computers use and the representation used by the telephone company.

In North America, many computer networks use T1 or T3 digital circuits. A T1 circuit has a data rate of 1.544 Mbps, and a T3 circuit has a data rate of 44.736 Mbps. Higher capacity circuits are also available that use the Synchronous Transport Signal (STS) standards. Because the high data rates require the use of optical fiber as a media, a parallel set of Optical Carrier standards (OC) define the optical signals used. For example, an OC-3 circuit operates at 155.520 Mbps.

In addition to point-to-point circuits that span long distances, mechanisms are needed that deliver data to individual businesses or residences. Telephone companies, which use the term *local loop* to describe the connections between a central office and subscriber, have investigated several technologies for the local loop. In particular,

Asymmetric Digital Subscriber Line (ADSL) stands out because it provides high-speed digital communication over the existing twisted pair wiring used for analog telephone service. ADSL is especially attractive because it allows conventional telephone service to operate on the line simultaneously.

Companies that offer cable television service have also investigated technologies to deliver digital information to subscribers. One of the chief obstacles arises from the existing cable infrastructure, which is only designed to carry information in one direction. Thus, cable companies must replace significant pieces of their infrastructure before two-way communication will be possible.

Cable companies developed Hybrid Fiber Coax (HFC) technology to provide two-way communication. Although HFC uses optical fiber in place of current trunk lines, it can use existing coaxial cable for connections to individual subscribers. An alternative technology known as Fiber To The Curb (FTTC) requires cable companies to replace trunk lines with fiber and to add twisted pair wiring to each subscriber.

Satellite vendors offer a local loop mechanism that extends asymmetric delivery to use asymmetric hardware. Although a satellite is used for downstream traffic, the upstream traffic travels over another path, usually a dialup connection.

EXERCISES

12.1 Find out if your institution leases digital circuits. If so, to what locations do they connect?

12.2 Contact a common carrier to find the monthly lease rates for a T1 line, a T3 line, and an OC-3 line from your city to a city across the country.

12.3 Read more about ISDN. Why is it called a *switched* technology?

12.4 Consider a Web page that contains a total of 6 megabytes of images. How long will it take to send the data across a T1 circuit, a T3 circuit, an OC-3 circuit, an OC-12 circuit, and an OC-48 circuit? (Ignore all protocol overhead.)

12.5 Read about direct broadcast satellite technology. What is the chief disadvantage of digital service obtained over satellite?

12.6 In addition to the signals sent by another ADSL modem, ADSL must tolerate the signals sent by the analog telephone system. In particular, the modem must tolerate the electrical current used to ring a telephone. Read about analog telephone service to find out what voltage is used.

12.7 Read about Adaptive Pulse Code Modulation (APCM). What is the chief advantage of APCM over PCM?

12.8 Suppose you were given two digital circuits and told that one of them uses a satellite and one of them uses only optical fiber. What experiment could you run to determine which uses fiber?

12.9 In the previous question, will your method work even if the two circuits have different bit rates (e.g., a T1 circuit and an OC-3 circuit)?

Chapter Contents

13

WAN Technologies And Routing

13.1 Introduction

The previous chapter describes technologies that provide digital communication across long distances and technologies that deliver digital communication across a local loop to subscribers. This chapter considers how those basic technologies can be used to build a network that spans a large area. The chapter describes the basic components used to build a packet switching system that can span a large area. As part of the discussion, the chapter explains the fundamental concept of routing and shows how routing is used in such networks; a later chapter extends the discussion of routing to the Internet.

13.2 Large Networks And Wide Areas

In general, a network technology is classified into one of three broad categories, depending on the size of networks that can be created:

- A *Local Area Network* (*LAN*) can span a single building or campus.
- A *Metropolitan Area Network* (*MAN*) can span a single city†.
- A *Wide Area Network* (*WAN*)‡ can span sites in multiple cities, countries, or continents.

---

†Few technologies fall into this category.
‡Wide Area Networks were once called *long-haul networks*.

To appreciate the distinction, it is important to understand how the size of a network is measured. We have seen that although LAN technologies are designed to be used at a single site, techniques exist that can extend the distance spanned. In particular, a satellite bridge can connect two segments of a LAN over an arbitrary distance. However, a bridged LAN is not considered a Wide Area technology because bandwidth limitations prevent a bridged LAN from serving arbitrarily many computers at arbitrarily many sites.

The key issue that separates WAN technologies from LAN technologies is *scalability* — a WAN must be able to grow as needed to connect many sites spread across large geographic distances, with many computers at each site. For example, a WAN should be able to connect all the computers in a large corporation that has offices or factories at dozens of locations spread across thousands of square miles. Furthermore, a technology is not classified as a WAN unless it can deliver reasonable performance for large size networks. That is, a WAN does not merely connect to many computers at many sites — it must provide sufficient capacity to permit the computers to communicate simultaneously.

13.3 Packet Switches

How can a WAN scale to handle many computers? The network itself must be able to grow. Instead of using a point-to-point leased data circuit that connects one computer directly to another, a WAN is constructed from many switches to which individual computers connect. The initial size of a WAN is determined by the number of sites and the number of computers connected. Additional switches can be added as needed to connect additional sites or additional computers.

The basic electronic switch used in a WAN is called a *packet switch* because it moves complete packets from one connection to another. Conceptually, each packet switch is a small computer that has a processor and memory as well as I/O devices used to send and receive packets. The packet switches used in modern, high-speed WANs consist of special-purpose hardware; the packet switches in early WANs were constructed from conventional minicomputers dedicated to the task of packet switching.

Figure 13.1 illustrates that a packet switch contains two types of I/O connectors.

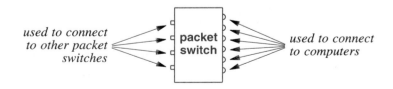

Figure 13.1 A packet switch with two types of I/O connectors: one type is used to connect to other packet switches, and the other is used to connect to computers.

The first type of I/O device, which operates at high-speed, is used to connect the switch to a digital circuit that leads to another packet switch. The second type of I/O device, which operates at a lower speed, is used to connect the switch to an individual computer. The exact details of the hardware depend on the WAN technology and the speed desired. Almost every form of point-to-point communication has been used to build a WAN, including leased data circuits, optical fibers, microwaves, and satellite channels. Many WAN designs allow a customer to choose the interconnection scheme.

13.4 Forming A WAN

A set of packet switches are interconnected to form a Wide Area Network. A switch usually has multiple I/O connectors, making it possible to form many different topologies and to connect multiple computers. For example, Figure 13.2 illustrates one possible way to form a WAN by interconnecting four packet switches and eight computers.

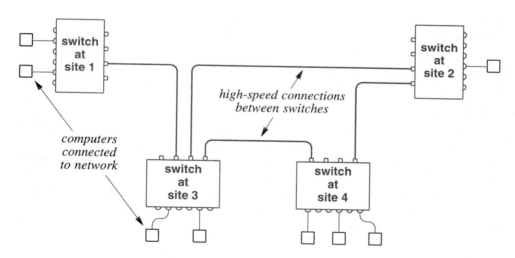

Figure 13.2 A small WAN formed by interconnecting packet switches. Connections between packet switches usually operate at a higher speed than connections to individual computers.

As the figure shows, a WAN need not be symmetric — the interconnections among switches and the capacity of each connection is chosen to accommodate the expected traffic and provide redundancy in case of failure. In the example above, the switch at site *1* connects two computers and has one external connection (e.g., a T1 line) to another switch. In contrast, the switch at site *2* connects to only one computer and has two external connections to switches at other sites.

We can summarize:

> *A packet switch is the basic building block of Wide Area Networks. A WAN is formed by interconnecting a set of packet switches, and then connecting computers. Additional switches or interconnections can be added as needed to increase the capacity of the WAN.*

13.5 Store And Forward

Unlike a shared LAN that allows only one pair of computers to exchange a frame at a given time, a WAN permits many computers to send packets simultaneously. The fundamental paradigm used with wide area packet switching systems is *store and forward* switching. To perform store and forward switching, a packet switch must buffer packets in memory. The *store* operation occurs when a packet arrives: the I/O hardware inside the packet switch places a copy of the packet in the switch's memory and informs the processor a packet has arrived (e.g., using the interrupt mechanism). The *forward* operation occurs next. The processor examines the packet, determines over which interface it should be sent, and starts the output hardware device to send the packet.

A system that uses the store and forward paradigm can move packets through the network as fast as the hardware capacity allows. More important, if multiple packets must be sent to the same output device, the packet switch can hold packets in memory until the output device is ready. For example, consider packet transmission on the network that Figure 13.2 illustrates. Suppose the two computers at site *1* each generate a packet destined for a computer at site *3* at approximately the same time. The computers each send their packet to the packet switch. As each packet arrives, I/O hardware on the switch places the packet in memory and informs the switch processor. The processor examines each packet's destination and determines that the packets should be sent to site *3*. If the output that leads to site *3* is idle when a packet arrives, the processor can start transmission immediately. If the output device is busy, the processor places the outgoing packet in a queue associated with the device. As soon as it finishes sending a packet, the device extracts and begins sending the next packet in the queue.

The concept can be summarized:

> *Wide Area packet switching systems use the store-and-forward technique in which packets arriving at a switch are placed in a queue until the switch can forward them on toward their destination. The technique allows a packet switch to buffer a short burst of packets that arrive simultaneously.*

13.6 Physical Addressing In A WAN

From the view of an attached computer, a WAN network operates similar to a LAN. Each WAN technology defines the exact frame format a computer uses when sending and receiving data. Furthermore, each computer connected to a WAN is assigned a physical address. When sending a frame to another computer, the sender must supply the destination's address.

Many WANs use a *hierarchical addressing scheme* that makes forwarding more efficient. Hierarchical addressing divides an address into multiple parts. The simplest hierarchical scheme partitions an address into two parts: the first part identifies a packet switch, and the second part identifies a computer attached to that packet switch. For example, Figure 13.3 shows two-part hierarchical addresses assigned to computers connected to a pair of packet switches.

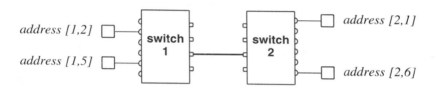

Figure 13.3 Example of hierarchical addresses in a WAN. Each address consists of two parts: the first part identifies a packet switch, and the second part identifies a computer connected to the switch.

The figure shows each address as a pair of decimal integers. A computer connected to port *6* on packet switch *2* is assigned address *[2,6]*. In practice, an address is represented as a single binary value, with some bits of the binary value used to represent the first part of the address and other bits used to represent the second part. Because each address is represented as a single binary value, users and application programs can treat the address as a single integer — they do not need to know that addresses are assigned hierarchically.

13.7 Next-Hop Forwarding

A packet switch must choose an outgoing path over which to forward each packet. If the packet is destined for one of the computers attached directly, the switch forwards the packet to the computer. If the packet is destined for a computer attached to another packet switch, the packet must be forwarded over one of the high-speed connections that leads to the switch. To make the choice, a packet switch uses the destination address stored in the packet.

A packet switch does not keep complete information about how to reach all possible destinations. Instead, a given switch has information about the next place (*hop*) to send a packet so the packet will eventually reach its destination. Called *next-hop forwarding*, the concept is analogous to the way airlines list flights. Suppose an airline passenger traveling from San Francisco to Miami finds that the only available itinerary involves three flights: the first from San Francisco to Dallas, the second from Dallas to Atlanta, and the third from Atlanta to Miami. The ultimate destination remains the same throughout the trip: Miami. However, the next hop changes at each airport. When the passenger is in San Francisco, the next hop is Dallas. When the passenger is in Dallas, the next hop is Atlanta, and when the passenger is in Atlanta, the next hop is Miami. Figure 13.4 illustrates next-hop forwarding in a packet switched network.

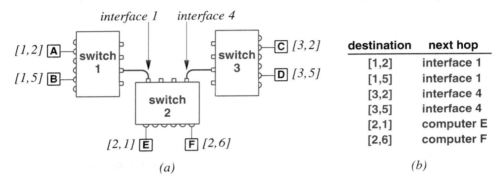

destination	next hop
[1,2]	interface 1
[1,5]	interface 1
[3,2]	interface 4
[3,5]	interface 4
[2,1]	computer E
[2,6]	computer F

(a)   (b)

Figure 13.4 (a) A network consisting of three packet switches and (b) the next-hop forwarding information found in switch 2. Each switch has different next-hop information.

As the figure shows, next-hop information can be organized into a table. Each entry in the table lists a destination and the next hop used to reach that destination. When forwarding a packet, the switch extracts the packet's destination, searches the table for an entry that matches the destination, and then sends the packet to the next hop specified in the entry. The example table shows how packet switch 2 forwards packets. When it encounters a packet destined for address [3,5], the switch forwards the packet to interface 4†, which leads to switch 3. When it finds a packet destined for address [2,1], the switch forwards the packet directly to computer E.

---

†Software inside a packet switch usually assigns each interface a small integer; the value has no meaning outside the switch, and does not appear in packets. The interfaces on switch 2 in the figure are numbered left to right.

13.8 Source Independence

Note that next-hop forwarding does not depend on the packet's original source or on the path the packet has taken before it arrives at a particular packet switch. Instead, the next hop to which a packet is sent depends only on the packet's destination. The concept, which is known as *source independence*, is a fundamental idea in networking, and will be implicit in most of our discussions about forwarding packets.

Many examples of next-hop forwarding that one encounters in everyday life exhibit source independence. In general, forwarding in an airport is source independent because the set of outgoing flights does not depend on the city from which a passenger arrived at the airport. That is, if two passengers traveling to Miami arrive in Atlanta from San Francisco and Boston, both will be directed to the same outgoing flight. More important, a local resident of Atlanta who arrives at the airport by car will see the same list of outgoing flights as passengers who arrive on airplanes.

Source independence allows the forwarding mechanism in a computer network to be compact and efficient. Because all packets follow the same path, only one table is required. Because forwarding does not use source information, only the destination address needs to be extracted from a packet. Furthermore, a single mechanism handles forwarding uniformly — packets that originate on directly connected computers and packets that arrive from other packet switches use the same mechanism.

13.9 Relationship Of Hierarchical Addresses To Routing

The table used to store next-hop information is commonly called a *routing table*, and the process of forwarding a packet to its next hop is known as *routing*. The advantage of two-part hierarchical addressing should be apparent from the routing table in Figure 13.4. Observe that more than one entry contains the same next-hop value. Further examination reveals a pattern: all destination addresses that have an identical first part will be forwarded to the same packet switch. Thus, when forwarding a packet, a packet switch only needs to examine the first part of a hierarchical address.

Using only one part of a two-part hierarchical address to forward a packet has two practical consequences. First, the computation time required to forward a packet can be reduced because the routing table can be organized as an array that uses indexing instead of searching. Second, the entire routing table can be shortened to contain one entry per destination packet switch instead of one entry per destination computer. The reduction in table size can be substantial for a large WAN in which many computers attach to a given packet switch. In fact, if K computers attach to each packet switch, an abbreviated routing table will be a factor of K smaller than a full table. Figure 13.5 illustrates an abbreviated table for the example network.

Destination	Next Hop
(1, anything)	interface 1
(3, anything)	interface 4
(2, anything)	local computer

Figure 13.5 An abbreviated version of the routing table in Figure 13.4b made possible by hierarchical addressing. When forwarding to a local computer, the switch uses the second part of the address to select a specific computer.

In essence, a two-part hierarchical addressing scheme allows all except the final packet switch to use only the first part of the destination address when forwarding a packet. When the packet reaches the switch to which the destination computer attaches, the switch examines the second part of the address and selects the appropriate computer. The algorithm can be summarized:

> *To forward a packet when using two-part hierarchical addresses, begin by extracting the part of the packet's destination address that corresponds to a packet switch, p. If p matches the number assigned to the local packet switch, use the second part of the address to locate an attached computer. Otherwise, use p to select a next hop for the packet from the routing table.*

13.10 Routing In A WAN

The capacity of a WAN must be increased as additional computers are connected to the network. To handle a few additional computers, the capacity of an individual switch can be increased by adding I/O interface hardware or a faster CPU. Such changes can accommodate small increases in the size of the network; large increases require new packet switches. The fundamental concept that makes it possible to build a WAN with large capacity arises because the switching capacity can be increased without adding individual computers. In particular, packet switches can be added to the interior of a network to handle load; such switches do not need to have computers attached. We will call such packet switches *interior switches*, and call packet switches to which computers attach directly *exterior switches*.

For a WAN to work correctly, both interior and exterior packet switches must have a routing table and both types must forward packets. Furthermore, values in the routing table must guarantee the following:

- Universal routing. The routing table in a switch must contain a next-hop route for each possible destination.
- Optimal Routes. In a switch, the next-hop value in the routing table for a given destination must point to the shortest path to the destination.

The easiest way to think about routing in a WAN is to imagine a graph that models the network. Each *node* in the graph corresponds to a packet switch in the network. If the network contains a direct connection between a pair of packet switches, the graph contains an *edge* or *link* between the corresponding nodes†. For example, Figure 13.6 shows an example WAN and the corresponding graph.

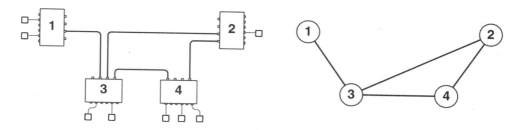

Figure 13.6 The network from Figure 13.2 and the corresponding graph. Each node in the graph corresponds to a packet switch, and each edge between two nodes represents a connection between the corresponding packet switches.

A graph representation of a network is useful. Because a graph represents packet switches without attached computers, a graph shows the essence of a network. In addition, a graph can be used to compute and understand next-hop routes. Figure 13.7 shows the routing tables that correspond to the graph in Figure 13.6.

destin-ation	next hop	destin-ation	next hop	destin-ation	next hop	destin-ation	next hop
1	-	1	(2,3)	1	(3,1)	1	(4,3)
2	(1,3)	2	-	2	(3,2)	2	(4,2)
3	(1,3)	3	(2,3)	3	-	3	(4,3)
4	(1,3)	4	(2,4)	4	(3,4)	4	-
node 1		*node 2*		*node 3*		*node 4*	

Figure 13.7 The routing table for each node in the graph of Figure 13.6. The next-hop field in an entry contains a pair (u, v) to denote the edge in the graph from node u to node v.

---

†Because the relationship between graph theory and computer networking is strong, a machine attached to a network is often called a *network node*, and a serial data circuit connecting two machines is often called a *link*.

13.11 Use Of Default Routes

The routing table for node *1* in Figure 13.7 illustrates an important idea: although hierarchical addressing reduces the size of the routing table by removing duplicate routes for individual computers, the abbreviated routing table still contains many entries with the same next hop. To understand why such duplicates exist, consider the network that Figure 13.6 represents. The packet switch that corresponds to node *1* has only one connection to other packet switches; all outgoing traffic must be sent across that connection. Consequently, except for the entry that corresponds to the node itself, all entries in node *1*'s routing table have a next hop that points to the link from node *1* to node *3*.

In small examples, the list of duplicate entries in a routing table is short. However, a graph that represents a large WAN may contain hundreds of duplicate entries. In such cases, examining the list of routes can be tedious. Furthermore, the situation is common — switches often have duplicate routing table entries.

Most WAN systems include a mechanism that can be used to eliminate the common case of duplication routing. Called a *default route* or a *default routing table entry*, the mechanism allows a single entry in a routing table to replace a long list of entries that have the same next-hop value. Only one default entry is allowed in any routing table, and the entry has lower priority than other entries. If the forwarding mechanism does not find an explicit entry for a given destination, it uses the default entry. Figure 13.8 shows how the routing tables in Figure 13.7 might be revised to use a default route.

destination	next hop	destination	next hop	destination	next hop	destination	next hop
1	-	2	-	1	(3,1)	2	(4,2)
*	(1,3)	4	(2,4)	2	(3,2)	4	-
		*	(2,3)	3	-	*	(4,3)
				4	(3,4)		

node 1	*node 2*	*node 3*	*node 4*

Figure 13.8 Revised version of the routing tables in Figure 13.7. An asterisk in the column labeled *destination* denotes a default route.

Default routing is optional — a default entry is present only if more than one destination has the same next-hop value. For example, the routing table for node *3* does not need a default route because each entry has a unique next hop. However, the routing table for node *1* benefits from a default route because all destinations except node *1* have the same next hop.

13.12 Routing Table Computation

How is a routing table constructed? Although manual computation suffices for trivial examples, such methods are impractical in large networks. Consequently, software is used to compute routing table entries. There are two basic approaches.

- *Static routing.* A program computes and installs routes when a packet switch boots; the routes do not change.

- *Dynamic routing.* A program builds an initial routing table when a packet switch boots; the program then alters the table as conditions in the network change.

Each type of routing has advantages and disadvantages. The chief advantages of static routing are simplicity and low network overhead. The chief disadvantage is inflexibility — static routes cannot be changed easily. Most networks use dynamic routing because it allows the network to handle problems automatically. For example, programs can monitor traffic in the network as well as the status of the network hardware. The programs can then modify routes to accommodate failure. Because large networks are designed with redundant connections to handle occasional hardware failures, most large networks use a form of dynamic routing.

13.13 Shortest Path Computation In A Graph

The software to compute the entries for a routing table represents the network as a graph. The computation then uses a method known as *Dijkstra's Algorithm*†, which finds the distance along a shortest path from a single source node to each of the other nodes in the graph; a next-hop routing table is constructed during the computation of shortest paths. The algorithm must be run once for each routing table. To compute the routing table for packet switch P, the node that corresponds to P is designated as the source node.

Dijkstra's algorithm is popular because it can be used with various definitions of *shortest path*. In particular, the algorithm does not require edges in the graph to represent geographic distance. Instead, the algorithm allows each edge to be assigned a nonnegative value called a *weight*, and defines the distance between two nodes to be the sum of the weights along a path between the nodes. The important point is:

> *Dijkstra's algorithm computes shortest paths in a graph by using weights on edges as a measure of distance. A path with the fewest number of edges may not be the path with least weight.*

---

†The algorithm is named for its inventor, E. Dijkstra.

Figure 13.9 illustrates the concept by showing a least-weight path in an example graph.

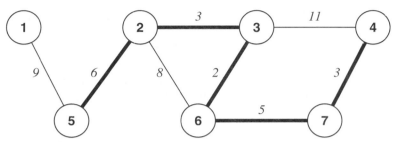

Figure 13.9 A graph with weights assigned to edges. The shortest path between nodes *4* and *5* is shown darkened. The distance along the path is *19*, the sum of the weights on the edges.

Although the fine details of Dijkstra's algorithm are beyond the scope of this text, the basic method is not complex. The algorithm maintains a set of nodes, *S*, for which the minimum distance and next hop have not been computed. The set is initialized to all nodes except the source. The algorithm then iterates. On each iteration, the algorithm selects and deletes a node from *S* that has the least distance from the source. As it deletes node *u*, the algorithm examines the current distance from the source to each neighbor of *u* that remains in the set. If a path from the source through *u* has less weight than the current path, the algorithm updates the distance to the neighbor. After all nodes have been deleted from *S*, the algorithm will have computed the minimum distance to each node and a correct next-hop routing table for all possible paths.

Implementation of Dijkstra's algorithm is straightforward. In addition to the data structure used to store information about the graph, Dijkstra's algorithm needs three data structures to store: the current distance to each node, the next hop for the shortest path, and information about the remaining set of nodes. Nodes can be numbered from *1* to *n* as Figure 13.9 demonstrates. Doing so makes the implementation efficient because it allows a node number to be used as an index into a data structure. In particular, our version of the algorithm uses two arrays, *D* and *R*, that each have one entry per node which can be indexed by the node number. The ith entry in array *D* stores a current value of the minimum distance from the source to node *i*. The ith entry in array *R* stores the next hop used to reach each node *i* along the path being computed. The set *S* can be maintained as a doubly linked list of node numbers, which facilitates searching the entire set or deleting an entry.

The algorithm below uses *weight(i, j)* as a function that returns the weight of the edge from node *i* to node *j*. Function *weight* is assumed to return a reserved value *infinity* if no edge exists from node *i* to node *j*. In practice, any value can be used to represent infinity provided the value is larger than the sum of weights along any path in the graph. One way to generate a value *infinity* consists of adding one to the sum of all weights on all edges.

Allowing arbitrary weights to be assigned to edges of a graph means one algorithm can be used with different measures of distance. For example, some WAN technologies measure distance by counting the number of packet switches along a path. To use the algorithm for such technologies, each edge in the graph is assigned a weight of *1*. In other WAN technologies, weights are assigned to reflect the capacity of the underlying connections. Finally, some WAN technologies assign weights to implement administrative policies.

13.14 Distributed Route Computation

Algorithm 13.1 shows how a routing table can be computed after information about a network is encoded in a graph. The alternative technique is a *distributed route computation* in which each packet switch computes its routing table locally, and then sends messages across the network to neighboring packet switches to inform them of the result.

Networks that use distributed route computation arrange for each packet switch to send its routing information to neighbors periodically (e.g., every few seconds). After an initial startup period, each packet switch learns the shortest paths to all destinations — a distributed algorithm produces the same next-hop routing tables as Algorithm 13.1. The continuous periodic messages allow the network to adapt if an individual packet switch or an individual communication link fails. After a failure, a packet switch stops receiving updates from the hardware that failed. The switch continues receiving updates from working neighbors, and if an alternative path exists, the switch can modify its routing table to avoid the failed hardware.

13.15 Distance Vector Routing

One of the best-known algorithms for distributed route computation is the *distance-vector* algorithm†. As in Algorithm 13.1, each link in the network is assigned a weight, and the *distance* to a destination is defined to be the sum of weights along the path to the destination. Because the distance values needed for the computation must be stored, an additional field is added to each entry of the routing table. The additional field contains the distance to the entry's *destination* along the path that corresponds to the entry's *next hop*.

A packet switch periodically sends routing information across the network to neighbors. Each message contains pairs of (*destination, distance*). When a message arrives at a packet switch from neighbor *N*, the packet switch examines each item in the message, and changes its routing table if the neighbor has a shorter path to some destination than the path the packet switch has been using. Algorithm 13.2 specifies precisely how routes are updated.

---

†The name arises because messages sent from one packet switch to another contain pairs of values that each specify a destination and a distance to that destination.

Algorithm 13.1

Given:

a graph with a nonnegative weight assigned to each edge
and a designated source node

Compute:

the shortest distance from the source node to each other
node and a next-hop routing table

Method:

Initialize set S to contain all nodes except the source node;
Initialize array D so that D[v] is the weight of the edge from the
    source to v if such an edge exists, and *infinity* otherwise;
Initialize entries of R so that R[v] is assigned *v* if an
    edge exists from the source to v, and zero otherwise;

```
while (set S is not empty) {
    choose a node u from S such that D[u] is minimum;
    if (D[u] is infinity) {
        error: no path exists to nodes in S; quit;
    }
    delete u from set S;
    for each node v such that (u,v) is an edge {
        if (v is still in S) {
            c = D[u] + weight(u,v);
            if (c < D[v]) {
                R[v] = R[u];
                D[v] = c;
            }
        }
    }
}
```

Algorithm 13.1 A variant of Dijkstra's algorithm that computes *R*, a next-hop
       routing table, and *D*, the distance to each node from the
       specified source node.

Algorithm 13.2

Given:

   a local routing table, a weight for each link that connects to
   another switch, and an incoming routing message

Compute:

   an updated routing table

Method:

   Maintain a *distance* field in each routing table entry;
   Initialize routing table with a single entry that has the
      destination equal to the local packet switch, the
      next-hop unused, and the *distance* set to zero;

   Repeat forever {
      wait for the next routing message to arrive over the network
         from a neighbor; Let the sender be switch *N*;
      for each entry in the message {
         Let *V* be the destination in the entry and let *D*
            be the distance;
         Compute *C* as *D* plus the weight assigned to the
            link over which the message arrived;
         Examine and update the local routing table:
         if (no route exists to *V*) {
            add an entry to the local routing table for destination
               V with next-hop *N* and distance *C*;
         } else if (a route exists that has next-hop *N*) {
            replace the distance in existing route with *C*;
         } else if (a route exists with distance greater than *C*) {
            change the next-hop to *N* and distance to *C*;
         }
      }
   }

Algorithm 13.2 Distance-vector algorithm for route computation used by
            each packet switch in a WAN. Each switch periodically
            sends the list of (destination, distance) pairs from its routing
            table to all neighbors.

13.16 Link-State Routing (SPF)

An alternative form of distributed route computation exists that uses a version of Algorithm 13.1 instead of a distance-vector algorithm. Formally, the alternative algorithm is known as *link-state routing* or *link-status routing*. Informally, the scheme has become known as *Shortest Path First*† or *SPF* routing.

Although packet switches that use SPF send messages across the network, the messages do not contain information from routing tables. Instead, each message carries the status of a link between two packet switches (e.g., the link between switch *5* and switch *9* is up), and the message is broadcast to all switches. Each switch collects incoming status messages and uses them to build a graph of the network. The switch then uses Algorithm 13.1 to produce a routing table with itself as the source.

Like a distance-vector algorithm, an SPF algorithm can adapt to hardware failures. In addition, SPF has the advantage that all computations can be carried out simultaneously — after the status of a link changes, all packet switches receive a status message, and each switch begins computing its routing table. In contrast, a distance-vector algorithm requires a packet switch to update its routing table before sending a message to another packet switch.

13.17 Example WAN Technologies

Many technologies have been created for experimental and production use in Wide Area Networks. This section presents a few example technologies that illustrate some of the diversity; the next chapter continues the discussion by examining fundamental communication paradigms and showing which paradigm each technology follows.

13.17.1 ARPANET

Packet switched WANs are less than forty years old. In the late 1960s, the *Advanced Research Projects Agency* (*ARPA*) funded research on networking for the U.S. Department of Defense. A major ARPA research project developed a Wide Area Network to determine whether packet switching technology could be used in battlefield conditions. Known as the *ARPANET*, the network was one of the first packet switched WANs. Although by current standards ARPANET was slow (leased serial data lines connecting packet switches operated at only 56 Kbps), the project left a legacy of concepts, algorithms, and terminology that are still in use‡.

13.17.2 X.25

The organization that sets international telephone standards, the International Telecommunications Union (*ITU*), developed an early standard for WAN technology,

---

†The name is somewhat misleading because all routing algorithms find shortest paths.

‡The original ARPANET term *Interface Message Processor* (*IMP*) is still sometimes used as a synonym for *packet switch*.

and public carriers such as telephone companies have offered the service for many years. The ITU was formerly known as the *Consultative Committee for International Telephone and Telegraph (CCITT)*, and the standard is still known as the *CCITT X.25* standard.

X.25 networks are more popular in Europe than in the United States. Each X.25 network consists of two or more X.25 packet switches interconnected by leased lines. Computers connected to the packet switches can send and receive packets.

Because X.25 was invented before personal computers became popular, many early X.25 networks were engineered to connect ASCII terminals to remote timesharing computers. The network provides two-way communication. As a user enters data on the keyboard, an X.25 network interface captures keystrokes, places them in X.25 packets, and transmits each packet across the network. When a program running on the computer displays output, the computer passes the output to the X.25 interface, which places the information in an X.25 packet for transmission back to the user's screen. Although X.25 can be used for communication between computers, the technology is expensive for the performance it delivers, and has limits on the speed at which it can deliver data.

13.17.3 Frame Relay

Long-distance carriers provide several high-speed wide area network services. One such service, *Frame Relay*, is designed to accept and deliver blocks of data, where each block can contain up to 8K octets of data. Part of the motivation for the large data size (and for the name) arises because the inventors designed Frame Relay service for use in bridging LAN segments. An organization with offices in two cities can obtain a Frame Relay connection for each office, and then use the connection to forward packets from a LAN segment at one site to a LAN segment at the other.

To handle data from a LAN segment, a Frame Relay connection must operate at high data rates. Thus, the designers envisioned Frame Relay running at speeds between *4* and *100* Mbps. In practice, however, many Frame Relay subscribers choose to use *1.5* Mbps or 56 Kbps connections.

13.17.4 SMDS

Switched Multi-megabit Data Service (SMDS) is another high-speed wide area data service offered by long-distance carriers. Instead of voice traffic, SMDS is designed to carry data. More important, SMDS is optimized to operate at the highest speeds. For example, header information in packets can require a significant amount of the available bandwidth. To minimize header overhead, SMDS uses a small header and allows each packet to contain up to 9188 octets of data. SMDS also defines a special hardware interface used to connect computers to the network. The special interface makes it possible to deliver data as fast as a computer can handle it.

In fact, as the name implies, SMDS networks often operate at speeds faster than Frame Relay. However, the two services differ in the way they can be used. Chapter

15 describes connection paradigms and discusses the difference between the paradigms used by Frame Relay and SMDS.

13.17.5 ATM

Asynchronous Transfer Mode (ATM), provides another example of a wide area network technology. ATM also came from the telecommunications industry. Unlike other technologies, ATM had ambitious goals — it was designed to handle conventional telephone voice traffic as well as data traffic, and to serve as a local area technology as well as a wide area technology. The next chapter describes ATM in more detail.

13.18 Summary

A Wide Area Network technology can be used to form networks that span an arbitrarily long distance and connect arbitrarily many computers. A typical WAN consists of electronic devices called packet switches interconnected by communication lines. A packet switch is implemented with a special-purpose computer that is dedicated to the task of providing communication. Although an individual computer connects to a single switch, the system is configured to allow a computer to transfer packets to or from any other computer on the network.

Packet switching networks use a store-and-forward approach in which an arriving packet is placed in the memory of a packet switch until the processor can forward the packet to its destination. Under normal circumstances, a packet does not remain in memory long. However, if multiple computers attempt to send packets at the same time, delays increase.

Forwarding relies on a data structure known as a routing table. The table contains an entry for each destination, and specifies the next hop used to reach that destination. To save space, a routing table usually lists packet switches as destinations instead of individual computers.

A WAN can be represented as a graph in which each node corresponds to a packet switch and each edge corresponds to a communication line. The graph representation is useful because it eliminates details, permits analysis of the network, and can be used to compute routing tables. A modified version of Dijkstra's shortest path algorithm can be used to compute a routing table from a network graph.

Many WAN technologies have been created, including ARPANET, X.25, Frame Relay, SMDS, and ATM. Currently, many phone companies use Frame Relay to provide high-speed WAN services.

EXERCISES

13.1   If your organization uses a Wide Area Network, find out the distance the network spans and the number of computers that attach.

13.2   Figure 13.3 shows how addresses can be assigned to computers that connect to a packet switch. Suppose the hardware for one of the interfaces on a switch fails, and a network administrator moves a computer's connection to an unused interface. Will the new configuration work correctly? Why or why not?

13.3   Write a computer program that reads a routing table, and then reads packets from four files that simulate four computer interfaces. Forward each packet according to the routing table. Remember to handle packets that have an incorrect address.

13.4   Default routing helps simplify routing tables. For example, suppose a WAN consists of two packet switches. Each switch can have a routing table entry for each local address (i.e., the address of each computer that attaches to the switch) plus a default route that points to the other switch. Under what circumstances does the scheme fail?

13.5   Write a computer program that implements Dijkstra's algorithm for finding shortest paths in a graph.

13.6   Read Algorithm 13.2. When computer programs running on two packet switches exchange distance-vector information, the programs must agree on a message format. Design an unambiguous message format.

13.7   Extend the previous exercise by implementing a computer program that uses the specified message format. Have another student implement a program from the same specification, and see if they interoperate correctly.

13.8   Contact a commercial network provider to find out how much it costs per year to lease a Frame Relay connection, an ATM connection, and a digital circuit between New York and San Francisco. Why is the difference in cost so great?

13.9   Can one network technology be used for both WAN and LAN connections? (Hint: read the next chapter.)

13.10   Find out if your site uses ATM technology as a WAN or as a LAN.

Chapter Contents

14

Connection-Oriented Networking And ATM

14.1 Introduction

Previous chapters describe both Local Area Network technologies and Wide Area Network technologies. This chapter explores a single technology that was designed to fill both roles. It presents a technical overview and explains the underlying motivation. More important, the chapter introduces the connection-oriented packet switching paradigm in which computers first establish communication, then send data, and finally terminate communication.

14.2 A Single, Global Network

By the mid 1980s, three types of communication networks had evolved; each carried information worldwide. The telephone network carried voice calls; television networks carried video transmissions; and newly emerging computer networks carried data. Telephone companies realized that voice communication was becoming a commodity service and that the profit margin would decrease over time. They also realized that data communication was increasing. As a result, the telecommunication industry decided to expand its business by developing networks to carry traffic other than voice. Telecom companies began exploring ways to create new network infrastructures. Their goals were extremely ambitious:

- *Universal Service.* The new network should serve all subscribers around the world, and any pair of subscribers should be able to communicate.

- *Support For All Uses.* The new network should offer subscribers voice, video, and data services. Moreover, the infrastructure should be sufficiently general to handle other uses that might arise.

- *Single, Unified Infrastructure.* The new network should not be formed from multiple technologies. Instead, it should consist of a single underlying infrastructure that includes support for all services. In particular, the network should be capable of serving as a LAN or as a WAN.

- *Service Guarantees.* The new network should perform with the same reliability and efficiency as existing networks. More important, it should offer the same delivery guarantees that voice and video networks offer.

- *Support For Low-Cost Devices.* The new network should allow users to connect small, low cost devices such as ATM telephones. Because they have minimal processing power and memory, such devices depend on the network to deliver data in order and without loss or delay.

14.3 ISDN And ATM

One of the first attempts to satisfy the network goals was a system called *Integrated Services Digital Network (ISDN)*. Unfortunately, as the planning, standardization, development, and deployment of ISDN proceeded, data networking changed rapidly and dialup modem technology advanced. Consequently, when ISDN finally emerged, it was relatively expensive for the moderate data speeds it offered. Although still available, ISDN has not gained universal acceptance.

After ISDN, the telecom industry developed a second, more comprehensive technology to satisfy its goals. Known as *Asynchronous Transfer Mode (ATM)*, the technology handles much higher speeds and offers many more services.

14.4 ATM Design And Cells

ATM designers faced a difficult challenge because the three intended uses (voice, video, and data) have different sets of requirements. For example, both voice and video require low delay and low *jitter* (i.e., low variance in delay) that make it possible to deliver audio and video smoothly without gaps or delays in the output. Video requires a substantially higher data rate than audio.

Unfortunately, most data networks introduce jitter as they handle packets. To understand why, consider an application sending data across a Local Area Network. As we have seen, the outgoing packet cannot be transmitted until the sending station obtains access to the medium; the delay depends on the number of stations that are attempting to send and the length of the packets each station sends. Furthermore, delay varies over time, rising when many stations contend for access, and falling again when fewer stations contend. Consequently, even if a sending application generates data at a constant rate (zero jitter), packets arrive at the receiving application with varying delay (nonzero jitter).

In addition to its effect on jitter, packet size is a key issue in designing a general purpose network technology. Data achieves maximal throughput when packet sizes are large because the overhead from headers is minimized by carrying a maximum payload with each header. Thus, networks designed to optimize data transport have packet sizes of 4 Kbytes or larger. Unfortunately, voice transmission cannot use such large packets for two reasons. First, the digital voice standard used by the phone companies, PCM, produces an 8-bit audio sample every 125 μ seconds. If the underlying network uses a packet size greater than 4000 octets, a sender must delay for more than half a second while accumulating enough samples to fill the packet; users find such delays intolerable. Second, users are also intolerant of *echo*, a problem that occurs when telephone signals traveling in one direction are inadvertently amplified and transmitted back to the sender. Telephone systems employ *echo cancellation* to avoid having a person hear their own voice played back. Unfortunately, echo cancellation only works when delays are low. If a digital telephone network uses large packets, the delay introduced by waiting to fill a packet makes echo cancellation difficult.

To allow packet switches to operate at high speeds and to achieve low delay, low jitter, and echo cancellation, ATM technology divides all data into small, fixed-size packets called *cells*. Each ATM cell contains exactly 53-octets: 5 octets of header information and 48 octets of data. Figure 14.1 illustrates the format of an ATM cell.

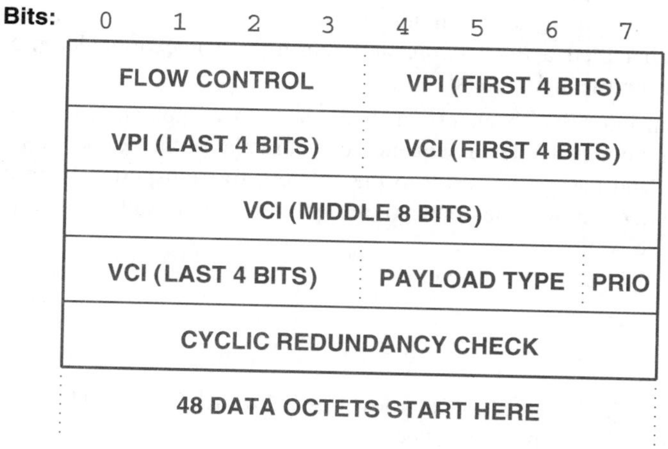

Figure 14.1 Fields in the 5-octet header found in an ATM cell. Each line in the diagram represents one octet.

As the figure shows, the majority of bits in the header are devoted to two fields labeled *VPI* and *VCI*†. We will see that these two fields together identify the cell's destination. Other fields specify a payload type and give an 8-bit CRC used to verify that the cell was not damaged in transit. The field labeled *PRIO* is a Cell Loss Priority bit that identifies if a packet can be discarded when the network becomes congested.

Recall that ATM was designed to be completely general and that the cell size was chosen as a compromise between large cells, which are optimal for data, and small cells, which are optimal for voice. Proponents argue that such a compromise is necessary if a single technology must handle all possible communication. Critics suggest that the choice means that ATM is neither optimal for voice nor for data.

Critics of ATM also criticize the relative size of the header, especially for data transmission. When ATM was designed, the designers decided to limit the header to ten percent of the payload area. Thus, once a payload size of 48 octets was chosen, the header was fixed at 5 octets.

For data networks, ATM's ten percent header overhead is especially high. Compare the cost to Ethernet, for example, in which a packet can be up to 1500 octets with only 14 octets of header (i.e. the header is approximately one percent of the data). Engineers who are critical of ATM's overhead refer to it as a *cell tax*.

14.5 Connection-Oriented Service

Like other network technologies developed by the telephone industry, ATM uses a *connection-oriented service paradigm*. Before two computers can communicate, they must establish a "connection" through the network. One of the computers requests a connection to the other (analogous to dialing a telephone number), and the second computer must agree to accept the connection (analogous to answering the telephone). After both computers agree to communicate, the underlying network hardware establishes a data path called a *connection*, and returns a connection identifier (a binary value) to each of the two computers.

Once a connection has been established, the two computers can exchange data. The sending computer generates a sequence of cells, places the connection identifier in each cell header, and passes the result to the network for transport. When it receives a cell, an ATM switch extracts the connection identifier and consults a table to determine how to forward the cell.

14.6 VPI/VCI

Formally, an ATM connection is known as a *Virtual Channel* (*VC*). We will see that the term *virtual* is appropriate because ATM connections are formed by storing values in memory rather than by attaching physical wires. The term *channel* is less

---

†The format shown is the User Network Interface (UNI) format; the Network Network Interface (NNI) format has a slightly larger *VPI* field.

descriptive. In fact, many professionals expand the acronym *VC* to the more descriptive term *Virtual Circuit.*

ATM assigns each VC a 24-bit identifier that is divided into two parts to produce a hierarchy. The first part, a *Virtual Path Identifier (VPI)*, specifies the path the VC follows through the network. As Figure 14.1 shows, a VPI is 8 bits long. The second part, a *Virtual Channel Identifier (VCI)*, specifies a single VC within the path. A VCI is 16 bits long. Although the network hardware can use the hierarchy to group multiple virtual channels together, a computer using ATM does not interpret the two fields. Instead, the computer views the two parts as a single, 24-bit binary value that gives the connection identifier. Because a computer refers to both parts together, the identifier is known as a *VPI/VCI.*

14.7 Labels And Label Switching

An ATM network is formed from one or more hardware devices known as *ATM switches.* Each ATM switch has multiple physical attachment points; an attachment point can connect to a user's computer or to another switch. Informally, the attachement points are known as *ports.* Thus, the simplest ATM network consists of a single ATM switch with multiple computers attached†.

Surprisingly, an ATM switch changes the VPI/VCI in each cell it handles. Inside each switch is a *forwarding table* that specifies how the hardware will forward cells. Each entry in the table corresponds to a possible VPI/VCI for a given port; the switch uses the VPI/VCI in an incoming cell to locate an entry in its forwarding table. In addition to the number of the physical port over which the cell will be sent, the table entry contains a replacement VPI/VCI. The switch rewrites the VPI/VCI in the cell header with the replacement, and forwards the cell. Thus, unlike the addresses we discussed earlier, a VPI/VCI in a cell does not remain the same as the cell traverses the network. Changing the VPI/VCI is known as *label rewriting* or *label switching*, and ATM is characterized as a *label switching system.*

To understand the consequences of label switching, consider an ATM network that consists of one switch and two computers as Figure 14.2 illustrates.

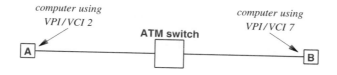

Figure 14.2 Illustration of an ATM VC between two computers.

---

†For an illustration, see Figure 8.11 on page 116.

In the figure, computers *A* and *B* have formed a Virtual Channel between them. When the VC was formed, the switch assigned VPI/VCI 2 to computer *A* and VPI/VCI 7 to *B*. When it assigned the two VPI/VCI values, the switch initialized entries in its forwarding table to map between them. Thus, when it receives a cell from *A* with VPI/VCI 2, the switch changes the VPI/VCI to 7 before forwarding the cell to *B*, and vice versa. Each computer knows the VPI/VCI it must use for the connection, but neither knows the VPI/VCI the other computer is using. To summarize:

> *An ATM switch uses* label switching *to rewrite the connection identifier (VPI/VCI) in each cell it forwards. Two computers using a given VC usually have different VPI/VCI values.*

14.8 An Example Trip Through An ATM Network

Consider how label switching extends to a large ATM network. The forwarding tables in a series of switches must be coordinated to create a "path" through the network. For example, Figure 14.3 illustrates a set of three ATM switches, and shows the values in the forwarding tables that correspond to a single VC between two computers.

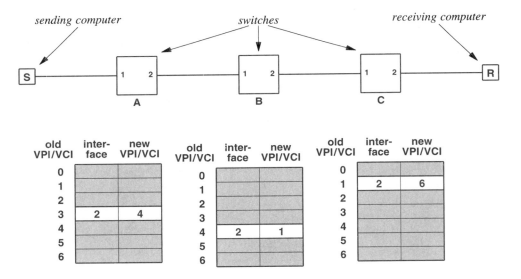

Figure 14.3 An illustration of three ATM switches and the forwarding table in each switch that allows a single VC to span the network. Only those table entries that correspond to the VC are shown.

The figure shows table entries for a single VC from the computer labeled S (sender) to the computer labeled R (receiver). When they send and receive cells across the VC, computer S uses VPI/VCI 3 and computer R uses VPI/VCI 6. That is, computer S places 3 in the header of an outgoing cell and transfers the cell to switch A. Switch A extracts the VPI/VCI from the incoming cell, and looks up entry 3 in its forwarding table. The forwarding table specifies that the VPI/VCI be changed to 4, which A does before forwarding the cell out interface 2 to switch B. Switch B looks up the incoming cell VPI/VCI, and changes the value to 1 before forwarding the cell. Switch C looks up 1 in its table, and changes the value to 6 before forwarding the cell to computer R. As a result, when a cell passes across the VC from S to R, it takes on the following sequence of VPI/VCI values: $3, 4, 1, 6$. The point is:

> As a cell pass through an ATM network, the identifier changes at each switch. The forwarding tables in all switches must be coordinated to define meaningful "paths" through the network from one computer to another.

14.9 Permanent Virtual Circuits

How and when are entries in an ATM forwarding table filled in? How are entries coordinated across a large number of switches to ensure that they are correct? This section answers each of these questions.

Because ATM is designed to provide all networking services, the design must include mechanisms that correspond to existing network technologies. For example, to interconnect two distant sites, a customer specifies exactly which two points should be connected, and then pays a monthly fee to lease a digital circuit from the phone company. The phone company keeps the circuit in place as long as the customer pays the fee. More important, a digital circuit survives computer crashes and even power failures — the circuit can be used again immediately after power has been restored.

ATM offers a facility that is analogous to a leased digital circuit: a subscriber can request an ATM network provider to establish a *permanent virtual channel* (*PVC*). The customer specifies which two computers should be interconnected, and the network provider establishes a VC between them. The analogy between an ATM PVC and a digital circuit is strong. Like a conventional digital circuit, a PVC remains ready to use at all times. A PVC survives power failures as well as computer reboots — a computer can use the PVC to transfer data as soon as power has been restored.

To establish a PVC, the network manager configures entries in the forwarding tables manually. The technical term used by telephone companies (and ATM) for such configuration is *provisioning*; once a PVC has been established, it is said to have been "provisioned".

Correct provisioning requires two steps. First, the network manager determines a complete path (i.e., a sequence of ATM switches) through the network from one computer to another. Second, the manager must choose a VPI/VCI to be used for each step along the path, and must configure each adjacent pair of switches so that the outgoing VPI/VCI at one switch corresponds to the incoming VPI/VCI at the next.

The ability of ATM to swap labels at each switch makes provisioning easy because an ATM cell does not need to contain the same VPI/VCI globally. Instead, a manager who configures a PVC only needs to consider one pair of switches at a given time. To extend the PVC from switch *S* to an adjacent switch *T*, the manager only needs to choose a VPI/VCI that is not currently used on *T*. After reserving the table entry in *T*, the manager can fill in *S*'s forwarding table entry.

14.10 Switched Virtual Circuits

PVCs provide service analogous to a digital circuit between two fixed points that persists for months or years. Most networks offer more dynamic interaction — a computer can choose to communicate with an arbitrary computer, and the interaction between the two can last for an arbitrarily short or long amount of time. To handle dynamic interaction, ATM includes a facility that allows VCs to be established and terminated as needed. A VC created dynamically is a *Switched Virtual Channel* (*SVC*); the terminology comes from telecom jargon, where the term *switching system* refers to the mechanisms used to establish a telephone call.

To create an SVC, a computer interacts with the ATM switch to which it attaches. The computer sends a connection request to the switch. Software on the switch automatically finds a path through the ATM network to the destination, and sends the request along the path. Each pair of ATM switches along the path communicate to choose a VPI/VCI to use for the VC and initialize their tables. The receiver must reserve a slot in its table, and the sender must configure its forwarding table to use the chosen identifier. Once all switches along the path and the destination computer agree to provide the SVC, a message propagates back through the network to the computer that originated the request and the SVC is ready to use. If any switch along the path does not agree to provide the VC, an error message is sent back and the request is denied.

How does a computer interact with an ATM switch to request an SVC? The process, which is known as *signaling*, requires the transmission of network control messages. Like data, control messages are sent in cells, which means they must be sent across a connection. ATM reserves a small set of VPI/VCI values for connection requests and network control traffic. The reserved values can only be used across one connection, and like PVCs, are established in advance. Thus, there is no confusion between data traffic and control traffic.

14.11 Quality Of Service

To satisfy the needs of audio and video users, ATM has facilities that allow a subscriber to specify the *quality of service* (*QoS*) requirements for each communication. We say that ATM uses *fine-grain* quality of service because it allows a subscriber to specify quantitative values. For example, someone using PCM encoding for a telephone call might specify that the throughput required is at least 64Kbps and that the delay must be less than 500 ms. A user sending compressed video might require a throughput of 2 Mbps.

QoS specifications are given when the connection is established, and stay in effect until the connection is terminated. Furthermore, once a request has been approved, the switches must reserve capacity as promised. In particular, an ATM network cannot behave like a shared channel — an established connection does not ''slow down'' simply because other computers generate more traffic. Of course, if a switch along the path cannot meet the QoS requirements when a request is made, it does not approve the request. Instead, an error message is generated, and the connection request is denied.

ATM has several basic ways to specify QoS requirements. Both uncompressed audio and video, for example, generate traffic at a fixed rate. ATM defines a *Constant Bit Rate* (*CBR*) service to handle such traffic. For applications like compressed audio or video, the transmission rate depends on the amount of change in the input during each sample. For applications that know in advance they will vary the rate of traffic, ATM defines a *Variable Bit Rate* (*VBR*) service. In contrast, applications that send data may not know in advance the rate at which they will generate data. More important, the transmission may be bursty, with short periods of intense communication, separated by long periods of silence. For such applications, ATM defines an *Available Bit Rate* (*ABR*). Traffic on an ABR connection can use whatever bandwidth is available at a given time.

14.12 The Motivation For Cells And Label Switching

Several questions arise. Why did ATM designers choose fixed-size cells instead of variable-size packets? What is the chief advantage of label switching, and why did ATM adopt it? The answers are the same: to achieve maximum data rates and satisfy QoS requirements.

14.12.1 Cells vs. Packets.

Research in the 1980s showed that network hardware could be optimized if all packets were exactly the same size and had exactly the same header format. First, variable-size packets can cause memory fragmentation; fixed-size cells do not. Second, variable-size packets require the hardware to accommodate the largest possible incoming packet and to detect the end of the packet; the hardware can simply count the bits of a fixed-size cell. Third, because the time required to transmit a variable-size packet depends on the length, interface hardware that transmits variable-size packets must interact with the switch. Usually, the switch starts output and waits for the interface to interrupt. Finally, variable-size packets make it difficult to guarantee QoS, especially low jitter. The problem arises because once transmission of a packet begins, the transmission cannot be interrupted. Thus, if a small packet arrives on a channel that requires low jitter after a large packet transmission begins, the small packet must wait, violating the QoS requirement.

Speed is most critical in the center of a network; to fulfill its dream, ATM requires more speed than any other network technology. In particular, ATM was designed to accommodate arbitrary numbers of users worldwide, each of whom might be willing to pay for high throughput. Thus, the designers chose fixed-size cells rather than variable-size packets for efficiency.

To achieve the highest bit rates, ATM is designed to work across optical fiber. A typical port on an ATM switch operates at OC-3 speed (155 Mbps) or higher, with the largest and most expensive switches handling much higher capacities. For example, ATM switches exist that can handle data at gigabit speeds; even higher data rates are expected.

14.12.2 Label Switching Vs. Routing

Label switching is another technology that increases hardware speed and capacity. The hardware has little to do when a cell arrives: extraction of the VPI / VCI and table lookup can both be implemented directly in hardware; no CPU is required. As a result, the raw capacity of an ATM switch is usually quite high. For example, a typical ATM switch, designed as a LAN replacement, has an aggregate throughput capacity of 2.4 Gbps.

14.13 ATM Data Transmission And AAL5

Although the ATM service described above is tailored to applications such as voice telephone, applications such as file transfer have been optimized to use large packets. To accommodate a variety of applications, ATM defines a set of *adaptation protocols*, which can be thought of as a set of Application Program Interfaces (APIs). Although five adaptation protocols have been defined, only *ATM Adaptation Layer 5* (*AAL5*) is used to send data. On the sending side, AAL5 accepts a block of data (up to 64K octets), divides the block into cells, and transfers the cells across the ATM network as usual. On the receiving side, AAL5 accepts incoming cells, extracts the data, and delivers the original block. The process is known as *segmentation* and *reassembly†*.

Thus, applications that send and receive data remain unaware that the data has been divided into cells. More important, AAL5 does not require all blocks to be the same size. As a result, an application that uses AAL5 to transfer data can view ATM as

---

†We will learn later that the concept comes from the Internet Protocol, which performs *fragmentation and reassembly*.

using variable-size packets with a maximum size much larger than typical LANs. To summarize:

> *ATM uses a protocol known as ATM Adaptation Layer 5 to send and receive data. AAL5 accepts and delivers variable-size blocks of data, where each block can be up to 64K octets long.*

14.14 Critique Of ATM

Although the goals of ATM are lofty, the technology has several drawbacks.

Expense. Because ATM technology provides a comprehensive list of services, even a moderate ATM switch costs orders of magnitude more than inexpensive LAN hardware. In addition, the network interface card needed to connect a computer to an ATM network is significantly more expensive than a corresponding Ethernet NIC.

Connection Setup Latency. ATM's connection-oriented paradigm introduces significant delay for distant communication. For example, consider an application that needs to send a single packet request to a computer on the other side of the world and receive a single packet reply. The time required to set up and tear down the ATM VC is significantly longer than the time required to use it.

Cell Tax. As we pointed out, ATM cell headers impose a 10% tax on all data transfers. An application that runs over the underlying physical media without using ATM gains 10% in throughput because it avoids the cell tax.

Specification Of Service Requirements. All communication requires a computer to choose service parameters when establishing a connection. An application may not know what to specify, and can err by choosing requirements that are too weak or too strong. For example, imagine an interactive file transfer application using ATM. When it forms a connection to the file server, the application does not know how much data will be transferred or the throughput capability of the server. Suppose the server can only generate X Kbps, but the application specifies $2X$ Kbps. If the ATM network is idle, the request for twice as much throughput will be approved; however, if the network is heavily loaded, the request will be denied unnecessarily.

Lack Of Efficient Broadcast. Connection-oriented networks like ATM are sometimes called *Non Broadcast Multiple Access* (*NBMA*) networks because, unlike most shared-media Local Area Networks, the hardware does not support broadcast or multicast†. On an ATM network, broadcast to a set of computers is "simulated" by arranging for an application program to pass a copy of the data to each computer in the set. As a result, broadcast is inefficient.

---

†The ATM specification does include a *point-to-multipoint* virtual circuit to aid applications in simulating broadcast; one of the exercises asks the reader to investigate the topic further.

Complexity Of QoS. Although the ATM standard allows a computer to specify QoS parameters when establishing a connection, enforcing the limits is non-trivial because accurate enforcement requires the switch hardware to compute statistical averages for each connection. In particular, a switch cannot merely compute the average number of bits sent per unit time. Instead, ATM specifies that data can be sent in bursts, with a mean data rate and mean maximum burst duration. The complexity of the specification makes implementation cumbersome and difficult; many implementations do not support the full standard. More important, many experts argue that fine-grained QoS is not needed — it does not solve the problem when insufficient capacity exists, and it is unnecessary when capacity is abundant.

Assumption Of Homogeneity. ATM is designed to be a single, universal networking system. There is minimal provision for interoperating with other technologies. The lesson we have learned from the Internet is that no single technology suffices; differences in cost and functionality means multiple technologies will exist.

For these and other reasons, ATM has not become the universal network. Phone companies still use ATM in their backbone networks, and large corporations often have one or more ATM networks. Only a few institutions have attempted to use ATM as a universal network, and even they appear to be reconsidering the choice. One of the most significant impacts on ATM came when engineers announced that Gigabit Ethernet was viable, making it possible for companies to upgrade existing Ethernet networks rather than replacing them with more expensive ATM technology. Another impact came when engineers announced that they had succeeded in sending Internet Protocol (IP) traffic directly over SONET†. ATM often uses SONET as an underlying transport, so the ability to send IP directly over SONET means that the ATM cell tax can be eliminated.

14.15 Summary

The phone companies created Integrated Services Digital Network (ISDN) and Asynchronous Transfer Mode (ATM). ATM is intended as a universal networking technology that handles voice, video, and data transmission. ATM uses a connection-oriented paradigm in which an application first creates a Virtual Channel (VC), uses the channel for communication, and then terminates it. The connection is implemented by one or more ATM switches; each places an entry for the VC in its forwarding table.

There are two types of ATM VCs: a PVC is created manually and survives power failures, and an SVC is created on demand. When creating a VC, a computer must specify quality of service (QoS) requirements; the ATM hardware either reserves the requested resources or denies the request.

---

†Chapter 12 discusses SONET.

ATM has not been widely accepted. Although some phone companies still use it in their backbone networks, the expense, complexity and lack of interoperability with other technologies have prevented ATM from becoming more prevalent.

EXERCISES

14.1   The *PRIO* bit in a cell header specifies whether an ATM switch can discard the cell if the switch cannot keep all cells. How can an application use the *PRIO* bit?

14.2   The separation of VPI and VCI means ATM can use a forwarding hierarchy. Describe the details of the algorithm a switch must use to honor such a hierarchy.

14.3   Examine the ATM standard. What is the difference between Available Bit Rate (ABR) and Unspecified Bit Rate (UBR) service?

14.4   Read more about ATM's point-to-multipoint VCs. If a set of *N* applications need to participate in a multicast group, how many point-to-multipoint VCs are needed?

14.5   Devise a scheme that arranges for a set of *N* application programs to participate in multicast over an ATM network without using point-to-multipoint. How many VCs need to be established?

14.6   Read about LAN Emulation (LANE), an effort to provide Ethernet connectivity over an ATM infrastructure. Is LANE sensible? Why or why not?

14.7   Consider implementing a remote database access application. If you had a choice of using ATM or a conventional LAN technology such as Ethernet, which would you prefer? Why?

14.8   Are there any data applications that will work better over ATM than conventional packet networks? If so, describe them and tell why. If not, explain why not.

14.9   If you could replace the entire Internet with an ATM network, would you choose to do so? Why or why not?

Chapter Contents

15

Network Characteristics: Ownership, Service Paradigm, And Performance

15.1 Introduction

Many previous chapters have discussed the primary characteristic of computer network technologies: size. Each technology is classified into one of three categories: LAN, MAN, or WAN, with most technologies classified as LAN or WAN. Such classifications are useful because they help compare network architectures.

This chapter continues the discussion by considering in more detail three additional characteristics of networks: network ownership, the type of service (both the service that the network provides to attached computers and the service it uses internally), and the performance of the resulting system. For each characteristic, the chapter explains the basic concept and uses examples of network technologies to illustrate how such facilities are implemented in real networks. These additional characteristics permit more accurate comparisons among technologies because they provide detail about similarities and differences.

Later chapters use and expand the concepts presented here. In particular, although this chapter discusses service paradigms in the context of network hardware, later chapters explain how Internet protocol software uses the same concepts.

15.2 Network Ownership

Network hardware and software can be owned by a company or individual, or it can be owned by a communication company. A network owned and used by a single company or an individual is said to be *private*, and networks owned by common carriers are called *public* networks.

15.2.1 Private Networks

Local Area Network technologies comprise the most common form of private network. In fact, of all networks in the world, most are private because most are LANs. Even small corporations are likely to have one or more private LANs that connect the computers within a single building or a single site; large corporations have hundreds of private LANs. To run a private network, a corporation hires employees who create and operate the network. The necessary hardware and software are purchased outright, and employees install the wiring, connect computers, and manage the resulting system.

A large corporation may also use private Wide Area Network technologies to connect computers at multiple sites. The corporation purchases WAN hardware such as packet switches, and hires employees to operate the network. The employees design network interconnections, attach computers to the network, assign addresses, and control routing.

Of course, a private corporation can install cables only on property that the corporation owns. To form a private WAN, a corporation must lease connections between its sites from public carriers such as telephone companies. The WAN is still considered private because the leased connections carry data directly between the corporation's sites — no other corporations have access to the wires or the data.

To summarize:

> *A network is said to be* private *if use of the network is restricted to the corporate or individual owner. Although a private Local Area Network can be owned outright, only the basic packet switching hardware for a private Wide Area Network can be owned outright; digital circuits in a private network are leased from a common carrier.*

15.2.2 Public Networks

In contrast to a private network, a public network is analogous to a telephone system — the network is run as a service available to subscribers. That is, any individual or corporation can subscribe to the service and obtain a connection to their computer. Once connected, a computer can use the public network to communicate. One of the features of a public network is universal communication — a given subscriber's computer can communicate with any other subscriber's computer.

Although it is possible to have a small public network, most are large, Wide Area Networks. To see why, consider a potential subscriber. The cost of connecting to the public network is justified if the new subscriber expects to communicate with existing sites on the network. Thus, a public network that is available to many subscribers in many locations is more attractive than one that only serves a small geographic area. Consequently, almost all public networks are WANs.

We can summarize:

> *A public network is owned and operated by a service provider similar to a telephone service. Any subscriber can use a public network to communicate with any other subscriber.*

15.3 Privacy And Public Networks

When applied to a network, the term *public* refers to availability of the service, not the data transferred. In particular, most public networks provide *private* communication (i.e., when a computer sends a message across a public network, only the intended recipient receives a copy).

Some public networks permit a group of computers to communicate analogous to a telephone conference call. However, the public network does not use broadcast technology. That is, the public network does not have a broadcast address, nor does it forward broadcast packets. Thus, networks are *public* only in the same sense as a telephone system — anyone who can afford the service is allowed to subscribe.

15.4 Advantages And Disadvantages

The chief advantage of a private network is that the owner has complete control over both the technical decisions and policies. For example, the owner chooses the brand of hardware to use, the capacity, redundancy, and backup systems. In addition, the owner sets policies that determine how and when the network can be used as well as which computers are allowed to connect. Furthermore, an owner can guarantee that the network is isolated from computers outside the organization and that a computer never accidentally contacts a computer at another organization. Isolation helps enforce security by keeping the organization's data protected and preventing outsiders from interfering with the corporation's computers or communication.

Of course, the advantages of a private network are not free — a large private network can be expensive to install and maintain. In addition to purchasing the network hardware, a corporation must hire and train a staff to install, manage, and operate the network. Special tools and maintenance equipment may also be needed. More important, network technologies continue to change rapidly; keeping up with rapid change can be expensive. The network staff must take training courses to learn about new technologies, and must then devise plans that adapt innovations to the company's networking needs.

The chief advantages of a public network are flexibility and the ability to use state-of-the-art networking without maintaining technical expertise. A public network is flexible because an arbitrary subscriber at an arbitrary location can connect to the network at any time. Furthermore, connections between a computer owned by one organization and a computer owned by another can be made or broken the same way a public telephone system allows voice connections to be made or broken.

15.5 Virtual Private Networks

Because both public and private networks have advantages, a new technology has emerged that combines the advantages of both. Known as a *Virtual Private Network* (*VPN*), the technology allows a company with multiple sites to have a private network, but use a public network as a carrier. In particular, although the company can use the public network as a link between its sites, VPN technology restricts traffic so that packets can travel only between the company's sites. Furthermore, even if an outsider accidentally receives a copy of a packet, VPN technology ensures that they cannot understand the contents.

To build a VPN, a company buys a special hardware and software system for each of its sites. The system is placed between the company's private (i.e., internal) networks and the public network. Each VPN system must be configured with the addresses of the VPN systems at other sites. Once such a configuration has been entered, the VPN system restricts packets. First, the VPN system at each site restricts incoming packets — no packet can enter the site unless the packet came from one of the company's other sites. Second, the VPN system at each site restricts outgoing packets — no packet can leave the site unless it is traveling to another one of the company's sites. As a result, once VPN software has been configured, the company's sites can only communicate with one another; they are cut off from the rest of the network.

To make a VPN work, the network manager must configure routing within each of the company's sites. When two computers within a given site communicate, packets travel from one computer to the other as usual. However, when a computer at one of the company's sites sends a packet to a computer at another of the sites, routing takes the packet to the local VPN system. The VPN system examines the destination, and sends the packet across the public network to the destination site. When the packet arrives, the receiving VPN system verifies that it came from a valid peer site, and then forwards the packet to its destination.

To summarize:

A Virtual Private Network *combines the advantages of private and public networks by allowing a company with multiple sites to have the illusion of a completely private network and to use a public network to carry traffic between sites.*

15.6 Guaranteeing Absolute Privacy

Although public networks do not forward copies of packets to all customers, some corporations are unwilling to send sensitive data across a public network. They worry, for example, that some employee of the public network might see the contents of the packets. To satisfy the need for absolute privacy†, VPN systems have been built guarantee that an outsider cannot understand the contents of packets, even if the outsider manages to obtain a copy. The technology used is encryption: the VPN system encrypts each packet before sending the packet across the public network. The receiving VPN system decrypts each incoming packet before sending it on to the destination computer. Thus, the packet remains encrypted during its trip across the public Internet.

We can summarize:

In addition to restricting packets, VPN systems use encryption to guarantee absolute privacy. Even if an outsider does manage to obtain a copy of a packet, the outsider will be unable to interpret the contents.

15.7 Service Paradigm

Network systems offer a variety of services to attached computers. Of course, at the lowest level, most networks transfer individual packets of data, and the network requires each packet to follow an exact format dictated by the hardware. Some networks only provide a packet interface to attached computers — the network accepts and delivers raw packets. Other network systems offer additional facilities that hide many of the details of packets. The goal is to provide computers with a higher-level interface that allows the computer to specify a remote destination or to transfer data without worrying about packets. Although the exact details of interface mechanisms vary among networks, the general type of interface is known as an *interface paradigm* or a *service paradigm*.

To help explain the similarities and differences among the services they offer, networks are placed in one of two broad categories:

- *Connection-oriented* (*CO*) service
- *Connectionless* (*CL*) service

---

†Although the term *privacy* generally refers to preserving individual anonymity, the term *private network* refers to networks that preserve the confidentiality of data being transferred.

We will see that the terms can be applied to both the interface that the network presents as well as to the way the network operates internally.

15.8 Connection-Oriented Service Paradigm

The previous chapter explains that connection-oriented service is analogous to telephone communication: a ''connection'' must be established between two computers before any data can be transferred. Once a connection is in place, data can be sent across the connection. Finally, when communication is complete, the connection must be terminated.

The term *connection-oriented* is generic — it applies broadly to a class of technologies. The class encompasses many technologies; the designs and details differ. The following sections provide examples.

15.8.1 Continuous And Bursty Traffic

Connection-oriented networks designed to handle voice or video are engineered to accept and deliver continuous data at a fixed rate. Other connection-oriented networks are designed to handle burst traffic that is typical of computer communication. That is, a computer can send data for a while, stop sending data temporarily (e.g., to perform a computation), and then resume sending. The connection does not disappear because no data is being sent. Instead the connection remains in place until the computers decide it is no longer needed.

15.8.2 Simplex And Full Duplex Connections

Some connection-oriented technologies provide *full duplex* connections, which means that each connection allows two-way communication. Other connection-oriented technologies provide *simplex* connections in which traffic on the connection can only flow in a single direction. To communicate using a simplex design, a pair of computers must establish two connections: one from computer *A* to computer *B* and another from computer *B* to computer *A*.

15.8.3 Connection Duration And Persistence

Some connection-oriented networks are designed to use *permanent* connections that persist over months or years. Other connection-oriented technologies permit *switched* connections that can be established or terminated quickly and automatically.

15.8.4 Service Guarantees

Some connection-oriented networks provide guarantees about the service that computers will receive. For example, the network may guarantee a throughput rate or a maximum packet loss rate. Other connection-oriented technologies do not provide guarantees. For example, ATM provides statistical guarantees about performance, but does not absolutely guarantee delivery (i.e., cells can be lost).

15.8.5 Stream Or Message Interface

Some connection-oriented networks provide a *stream interface* to an attached computer. Once the connection is open, the computer can send a stream of data octets that are delivered to the other end. With a stream interface, no boundaries are recorded; the receiver may receive a single block of 60 characters even though the sender generates three blocks of 20 characters. Other connection-oriented technologies provide a *message interface* in which the network guarantees to deliver data in the same size chunks that the sender transmitted.

15.9 Connectionless Service Paradigm

Connectionless networks operate analogous to the postal mail system. Whenever it has data to send, a computer must place the data in the appropriate frame format, attach the address of the computer to which the data should be delivered (analogous to placing the data in an envelope and writing an address on the envelope), and then pass the frame to the network for delivery (analogous to mailing a letter). The connectionless network system transports the frame to the prescribed destination and delivers it.

As in the case of connection-oriented technologies, details differ among connectionless technologies. For example, each technology defines an *addressing scheme* that specifies the length of an address as well as the method by which the address is assigned. Each technology also imposes an upper bound on the size of a frame. Finally, some connectionless technologies (e.g., Ethernet) impose a minimum packet size.

15.10 Interior And Exterior Service Paradigms

We have discussed the concept of connection-oriented and connectionless service from the point of view of computers connected to a network. In fact, a network that provides one service paradigm to attached computers can use an entirely different service paradigm internally. For example, although it provided connectionless service to attached computers, the ARPANET used a connection-oriented paradigm internally. We will see another example of mixed paradigms when we examine the TCP/IP protocols.

15.11 Comparison Of Service Paradigms

Each service paradigm has advantages and disadvantages. The chief advantages of the connection-oriented paradigm lie in the ease of accounting and the ability to inform communicating computers immediately when a connection breaks (e.g., when hardware fails). Public networks that charge customers for network use favor connection-oriented services because less effort is required to charge for the length of time a connection is open than for the number of packets sent. Learning about network failure immediately can help applications that are using the network. Although an application is unable to overcome a failure, the application can inform managers or users. In contrast, a failure in a connectionless system may go unnoticed and unreported — a computer can continue to send packets after a failure occurs.

The chief advantage of the connectionless service paradigm is less initial overhead — a connectionless network allows a computer to send data immediately, without waiting for a connection. Although most networks can form a connection in a few milliseconds, it may take longer to establish and terminate a connection than to send data. Furthermore, some applications do not engage in a continuous dialogue. Instead, the application sends a single packet, receives a reply, and then waits for an extended period before sending another packet, possibly to a different destination. In such cases, a connectionless paradigm works better than a connection-oriented paradigm.

The concept of service paradigm can be summarized:

A network either provides connection-oriented (CO) or connectionless (CL) service to computers using the network. The network itself can use a connection-oriented or connectionless paradigm internally.

15.12 Examples Of Service Paradigms

Basic LAN technologies such as Ethernet, Token Ring, and FDDI use a connectionless service paradigm. Although a computer needs to wait for access to a shared medium before sending a packet, the computer does not need to establish a connection. In fact, the service paradigm does not depend on the wiring scheme — all forms of LAN technologies, including hubs, bridged networks, and switched LANs are connectionless.

Both connection-oriented and connectionless service paradigms are used in public WANs. For example, Frame Relay uses a connection-oriented paradigm. Before a computer can communicate across a Frame Relay network, a connection must be established. Like ATM, Frame Relay supports both switched and permanent virtual circuits (*SVCs*) and (*PVCs*).

Like Frame Relay and ATM, *Switched Multi-megabit Data Service* (*SMDS*) is also used in public WANs. Unlike Frame Relay and ATM, however, SMDS offers a connectionless paradigm. A computer connected to an SMDS network can send a packet to any destination at any time. Each SMDS frame has a header that contains the destination address; no connection is needed.

Although most LAN technologies follow the connectionless paradigm, some LANs take a connection-oriented approach. For example, *ATM* was designed for both WANs and LANs. In all cases, ATM uses a connection-oriented service paradigm.

Figure 15.1 summarizes the service paradigms offered by popular technologies.

Technology	Connection-Oriented	Connectionless	used for LAN	used for WAN
Ethernet		●	●	
Token Ring		●	●	
FDDI		●	●	
Frame Relay	●			●
SMDS		●		●
ATM	●		●	●
LocalTalk		●	●	

Figure 15.1 Summary of major characteristics for example technologies. The technologies suitable for WANs are used in public networks.

15.13 Addresses And Connection Identifiers

In a connectionless network, each packet must contain the address of the intended recipient. However, a connection-oriented service often uses abbreviations. When a computer first requests a new connection, the computer sends a message to the network specifying the address of a remote destination. After it establishes a connection, the network responds with a message that verifies the connection and specifies a *connection identifier* to be used. Usually, a connection identifier is a small integer, much shorter than the full destination address. When sending or receiving data, the computer uses the connection identifier instead of a destination address.

Using connection identifiers reduces overhead because it makes the header of data packets smaller. For example, the previous chapter considered ATM. When establishing an ATM connection, a computer must specify the address of a remote computer. One format ATM uses for such addresses consists of 160 bits. Because ATM is a connection-oriented technology, however, individual ATM cells do not need to contain the full address. Instead, each time a connection is created, the ATM network specifies a 24-bit connection identifier to use. The destination address is not used once a connection has been established — a computer places the 24-bit connection identifier in each outgoing cell, and cells arriving from the network over that connection also contain the same 24-bit identifier.

The point is:

In a connectionless network, each packet must contain the address of the remote destination. In a connection-oriented network, however, the destination address is only used when creating a new connection; packets flowing over the connection contain a connection identifier that is smaller than a full address.

15.14 Network Performance Characteristics

Informally, networks can be classified as *low speed* or *high speed*. However, such definitions are inadequate because network technologies change so rapidly that a network classified as ''high speed'' may become medium or low speed in as little as three or four years. Thus, when scientists or engineers need to specify network speeds precisely, they do not use informal, qualitative terms. Instead, they use quantitative metrics. Although beginners may have difficulty understanding quantitative measures and often prefer informal descriptions, quantitative measures are important because they make it possible to compare any two networks. This section defines the two fundamental quantitative measures of a network, and explains how they relate to capacity.

15.14.1 Delay

The first important property of networks that can be measured quantitatively is *delay*. The delay of a network specifies how long it takes for a bit of data to travel across the network from one computer to another; delay is measured in seconds or fractions of seconds. Delays may differ slightly, depending on the location of the specific pair of computers that communicate. Although users only care about the total delay of a network, engineers need to make more precise measurements. Thus, engineers usually report both the maximum and average delay, and they divide the delay into several parts.

Some delay in a network arises because a signal requires a small amount of time to travel across a wire or optical fiber. Such delays are known as *propagation delays*, and are generally proportional to the distance spanned. For example a typical LAN used within a single building has a delay of a millisecond. Although such delays seem irrelevant to a human, a modern computer can execute over one hundred thousand instructions in a millisecond. Thus, a millisecond delay is significant to a computer. A network that uses a satellite orbiting the earth to relay data from one continent to another has much higher delay — even at the speed of light, it takes over a hundred milliseconds for a bit to travel to the satellite and back to earth.

Electronic devices in a network (e.g., hubs, bridges, or packet switches) introduce another source of delay known as *switching delay*. An electronic device waits until all bits of a packet have arrived, and then takes a small amount of time to choose the next hop before sending a packet. Fast CPUs and special-purpose hardware have made switching delays among the least significant.

Because most LANs use shared media, computers must delay until the medium is available. For example, we have seen that an Ethernet uses CSMA/CD and that a Token Ring network requires a sender to wait for a token. Such delays, which are not usually large, are known as *access delays*.

A final form of delay occurs in a packet switched WAN. Recall that each packet switch enqueues incoming packets as part of the store-and-forward process. If the queue already contains packets, the new packet may need to wait while the CPU forwards packets that arrived earlier. Such delays are known as *queueing delays*.

15.14.2 Throughput

The second fundamental property of networks that can be measured quantitatively is *throughput*. Throughput is a measure of the rate at which data can be sent through the network, and is usually specified in *bits per second (bps)*. Most networks have a throughput of several million bits per second (*Mbps*). However, older communication systems offered throughputs as low as 300 or 1200 bits per second, and networks exist with throughputs as high as several *gigabits per second (Gbps†)*.

Because throughput can be measured several ways, one must be careful to specify exactly what has been measured. For example, in Chapter 5 we learned that the throughput capability of the underlying hardware is called *bandwidth*. In fact, the term *bandwidth* is sometimes used as a synonym for throughput. However, programmers and users do not care about the capability of the underlying hardware — they are interested in the rate at which data can be sent through a network. In particular, in most technologies each frame contains a header, which means that the *effective throughput* (i.e., the rate at which a computer can send data) is less than the hardware bandwidth. Nevertheless, the hardware bandwidth is often used as an approximation of the network's throughput because the bandwidth gives an upper bound on throughput — it is impossible for a user to send data faster than the rate at which the hardware can transfer bits.

Networking professionals often use the term *speed* as a synonym for throughput. For example, one might hear, ''The network has a speed of ten megabits per second.'' Although such statements are common, they can be confusing because delay and throughput are separate ideas. In fact, throughput is a measure of capacity, not speed. To understand the relationship, imagine a network to be a road between two places and packets traveling across the network to be analogous to cars traveling down the road. The throughput rate determines how many cars can enter the road each second, but the delay determines how long it takes a single car to travel the entire road from one town to another. For example, a road that can accept one car every five seconds has a throughput of *0.2* cars per second. If a car requires *30* seconds to traverse the entire

---

†One gigabit per second is 1000 Mbps bits per second.

road, the road has a delay of *30* seconds. Now consider what happens if a second lane is opened on the road (i.e., the capacity doubles). It will be possible for two cars to enter every five seconds, so the throughput has doubled to *0.4* cars per second. Of course, the *30* second delay will remain unchanged because each car must still traverse the entire distance. Thus, when thinking about measures of networks, remember that:

> *Network delay, which is measured in seconds, specifies how long a single bit remains in transit in a network. Network throughput, which is measured in bits per second, specifies how many bits can enter the network per unit time. Throughput is a measure of the network capacity.*

15.14.3 The Relationship Between Delay And Throughput

In theory, the delay and throughput of a network are independent. In practice, however, they can be related. To understand why, think of the road analogy discussed above. If cars enter the road at even time intervals, the cars traveling along the road at uniform speed are spaced at uniform intervals. If a car slows down for any reason (e.g., at an intersection), others behind it will slow down as well, causing temporary traffic congestion. Cars that enter the road when congestion is occurring will experience longer delays than cars traveling on an uncongested road. A similar situation occurs in networks. If a packet switch has a queue of packets waiting when a new packet arrives, the new packet will be placed on the tail of the queue and will need to wait while the switch forwards the previous packets. Analogous to heavy traffic on a road, excessive traffic in a network is called *congestion*. Clearly, data entering a congested network will experience longer delays than data entering an idle network.

Computer scientists have studied the relationship between delay and congestion, and have found that in many cases, the expected delay can be estimated from the current percentage of the network capacity being used. If D_0 denotes the delay when the network is idle, and U is a value between *0* and *1* that denotes the current *utilization*, the effective delay, D, is given by a simple formula:

$$D = \frac{D_0}{(1 - U)}$$

When a network is completely idle, U is zero, and the effective delay is D_0. When a network operates at 1/2 its capacity, the effective delay doubles. As traffic approaches the network capacity (i.e., as U becomes close to *1*), the delay approaches infinity. Although the formula only provides an estimate of what can happen, we can conclude:

> *Throughput and delay are not completely independent. As traffic in a computer network increases, delays increase; a network that operates at close to 100% of its throughput capacity experiences severe delay.*

In practice, network managers understand that extremely high utilization can produce disastrous delay. Thus, most managers work to keep utilization low, and measure the traffic on each network constantly. When the average or peak utilization begins to climb above a preset threshold, the manager increases the capacity of the network. For example, if utilization becomes high on a 10BaseT network, the manager might choose to replace it with a 100BaseT network. Alternatively, the manager might choose to divide a network in two, placing half the computers on one network and half the computers on the other.

How high should the utilization threshold be? There is no simple answer; many managers choose a conservative value. For example, one major ISP that runs a large backbone network keeps utilization on all its digital circuits under 50%. Some others set thresholds at 80% to save money. In any case, managers generally agree that a network should not be operated above 90% of capacity.

15.14.4 Delay-Throughput Product

Once a network's delay and throughput are known, it is also possible to compute another interesting quantity, the *delay-throughput product*†. To understand the meaning of the delay-throughput product, think of the road analogy: when cars are entering a road at a fixed rate of T cars per second and it takes a car D seconds to traverse the road, then $T \times D$ additional cars will enter the road by the time the first car has made a complete trip. Thus, there can be a total of $T \times D$ cars on the road at any time.

In terms of networks:

> *The product of delay and throughput measures the volume of data that can be present on the network. A network with throughput T and delay D has a total of $T \times D$ bits in transit at any time.*

The delay-throughput product is important for any network with especially long delay or especially large throughput because it means a computer sending data on that network can generate a large volume of data before the destination receives the first bit.

---

†When used as a measure of the underlying hardware, the delay-throughput product is often called the *delay-bandwidth product.*

15.15 Jitter

One last measure of networks is becoming important as networks are used for transmission of real-time voice and video. The measure, which is known as the network's *jitter*, represents the variance in delay. To understand why such variations are important, consider sending voice over a network. On the sending side, the analog signal is digitized, and digital samples are emitted every 125 μ seconds. The samples are collected into packets or cells, which are then transferred across the network. At the receiving side, the digital values are extracted and converted back to analog output. If the network has zero jitter (i.e., each packet takes exactly the same time to transit the network), the audio output will exactly match the original input. Otherwise, the output will be flawed. The telephone system and data networks handle jitter in two different ways, as the next sections describe.

15.15.1 Isochronous Networks

To ensure that digitized telephone calls are transmitted and played back correctly, the telephone network is designed so that all transmissions have exactly the same delay. For example, if digitized data from a phone call is transmitted over two paths, the hardware is configured so that both paths have exactly the same delay. We use the term *isochronous*† to characterize such networks, and say that an isochronous network has a jitter of zero.

15.15.2 Asynchronous Networks

The alternative to isochronous networks is a network in which delay among packets can vary. We classify such networks as *asynchronous*. Most data networks are asynchronous. Although isochronous networks work well for voice, they are more expensive than asynchronous networks. Consequently, many systems now use asynchronous networks to carry audio and video. Although audio and video work best when jitter is low, additional protocols have been designed to ensure correct playback even if packets experience variations in delay.

15.16 Summary

In addition to classifying a network technology as a LAN, MAN, or WAN, other characteristics can be used to further distinguish technologies. For example, a network can be private or public. A private network is owned by the individual or corporation that uses the network; a public network is offered to any subscribers who can afford to connect. Because they are available to many organizations over long distances, public networks are WANs.

---

†Isochronous is pronounced ''eye-sock-re-nus''.

A network either provides connection-oriented or connectionless service. The former requires computers to establish a connection before sending data. The latter allows a computer to send data to any destination at any time without first creating a connection or otherwise informing the network.

The primary measures of network performance are delay, the time required to send a bit from one computer to another, and throughput, the number of bits per second that can be transmitted across the network. Although throughput is commonly called speed, throughput is a measure of the network capacity. The delay-throughput product measures the amount of data that is in transit at a given instant. Delay and throughput are not independent — as throughput approaches 100% of capacity, delays increase rapidly.

Jitter, a measure of variance in delay, is becoming important in data networks. Isochronous networks, which have low jitter, can easily accommodate the transmission of real-time audio and video; additional protocol support is needed to compensate for jitter when audio and video are transmitted across an asynchronous data network.

EXERCISES

15.1 Investigate networks your organization uses. Are any public?

15.2 Consider application programs that communicate over a network. Would such programs be easier to write if the network supplied connection-oriented or connectionless service? Why?

15.3 Why are Ethernet and Token Ring inappropriate for use in a WAN?

15.4 Would you expect queueing delays, access delays, and propagation delays to be longer on a LAN or on a WAN? Explain.

15.5 Professionals sometimes refer to a "knee" in the delay curve. To understand what they mean, plot the effective delay for values of utilization between *0* and *0.95*. Can you find a value of utilization for which the curve appears to increase sharply?

15.6 How much data can be present on an original Ethernet segment at one time? To find out, compute the delay-throughput product. The original Ethernet operated at 10 megabits per second, and a segment was limited to 500 meters. Assume the signals propagate down the cable at 66 percent of the speed of light.

15.7 How much data can be "in flight" between a sending ground station, a satellite, and a receiving station? To find out, compute the delay-throughput product for a satellite network that operates at 3 megabits per second. Assume that the satellite orbits at 20,000 miles above the earth, and that radio transmissions propagate at the speed of light.

Chapter Contents

16

Protocols And Layering

16.1 Introduction

Previous chapters discuss basic network hardware and describe the components used to produce LAN and WAN systems. This chapter examines the structure of the software used with network systems. The chapter explains why hardware alone does not solve all communication problems, and shows why protocol software is also needed. It discusses the problems that network protocol software must handle, and the techniques used to solve the problems. More important, the chapter describes the concept of layering that provides a conceptual basis for understanding how a complete set of protocols work together with hardware to provide a powerful communication system.

Later chapters build on the concepts presented here. The next chapter explains how the basic ideas have been extended to an internet environment. Succeeding chapters explore a complete set of protocols, and show how individual protocols in the set handle each of the problems discussed. Chapters that follow the discussion of protocols illustrate how application programs use protocol software to communicate over a network.

16.2 The Need For Protocols

Basic communication hardware consists of mechanisms that can transfer bits from one point to another. However, using raw hardware to communicate is analogous to programming by entering *1*s and *0*s — it is cumbersome and inconvenient. To aid programmers, computers attached to a network use complex software that provides a convenient, high-level interface for applications. The software handles most low-level communication details and problems automatically, making it possible for applications to communicate easily. Thus, most application programs rely on network software to communicate; they do not interact with network hardware directly.

All parties involved in a communication must agree on a set of rules to be used when exchanging messages (e.g., the language to be used and the rules for when messages can be sent). Diplomats call such an agreement a *protocol*. The term is applied to computer communication as well: a set of rules that specify the format of messages and the appropriate actions required for each message is known as a *network protocol* or a *computer communication protocol*. The software that implements such rules is called *protocol software*. An individual network protocol can be simple (e.g., an agreement to use ASCII when transferring a text file), or complex (e.g., an agreement to use a complicated mathematical function to encrypt data). To summarize:

> *An agreement that specifies the format and meaning of messages computers exchange is known as a* communication protocol. *Application programs that use a network do not interact directly with the network hardware. Instead, an application interacts with protocol software that follows the rules of a given protocol when communicating.*

16.3 Protocol Suites

Instead of having a single, giant protocol that specifies complete details for all possible forms of communication, designers have chosen to divide the communication problem into subpieces and to design a separate protocol for each subpiece. Doing so makes each protocol easier to design, analyze, implement, and test. As we will see, dividing communication software into multiple protocols increases flexibility because it allows subsets of protocols to be used as needed.

The division into separate protocols must be chosen carefully to ensure the resulting communication system is efficient and effective. To avoid duplication of effort, each protocol should handle part of the communication problem not handled by other protocols. To make efficient implementation possible, protocols should be designed so they can share data structures and information. Finally, the combination of protocols should handle all possible hardware failures or other exceptional conditions.

How can one guarantee that protocols will work well together? The answer lies in an overall design plan: instead of developing each protocol in isolation, protocols are designed and developed in complete, cooperative sets called *suites* or *families*. Each protocol in a suite solves one part of the communication problem; together, they solve the entire communication problem. Furthermore, the entire suite is designed to make interactions among protocols efficient.

16.4 A Plan For Protocol Design

Several tools have been developed to help protocol designers understand subparts of the communication problem and plan an entire protocol suite. One of the most important tools is called a *layering model*. In essence, a layering model describes one way the communication problem can be divided into subpieces, called *layers*. A protocol suite can be designed by specifying a protocol that corresponds to each layer. For example, early in the history of networking the *International Organization for Standardization (ISO)* defined a *7-layer Reference Model*. Figure 16.1 illustrates the ISO layering model and shows that each layer is numbered.

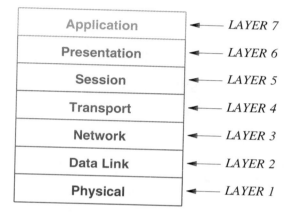

Figure 16.1 The historic ISO 7-Layer Reference Model. A layering model is a tool to help protocol designers construct a suite of protocols that solves all communication problems.

16.5 The Seven Layers

Although ideas about protocol design have changed in the twenty years since the ISO model was developed and many modern protocols do not fit the old model, much of the ISO terminology still persists. In particular, when networking professionals refer to *Layer 1*, they usually mean ISO's layer 1†. We will see in the next chapter how the Internet reference model has replaced the ISO model and changed the way protocols are designed.

Layering models provide a simple explanation of the relationships among the complex hardware and protocol components of a network. In the ISO model, the lowest layer corresponds to hardware, and successive layers correspond to firmware or software that uses the hardware. This section summarizes the purpose of each layer in the ISO model.

---

†The terminology is used informally, and is often stretched when applied to modern internet protocols.

Layer 1: Physical

Layer *1* corresponds to basic network hardware. For example, the specification of RS-232 described in Chapter 5 belongs in Layer *1*, and gives the detailed specification of LAN hardware.

Layer 2: Data Link

Layer *2* protocols specify how to organize data into frames and how to transmit frames over a network. For example, the discussions of frame format, bit or byte stuffing, and checksum computation in Chapter 7 are classified as Layer 2.

Layer 3: Network

Layer *3* protocols specify how addresses are assigned and how packets are forwarded from one end of the network to another. The specification of addressing covered in Chapter 9 and the details of forwarding in Chapter 13 are both found in Layer *3*.

Layer 4: Transport

Layer *4* protocols, which specify how to handle details of reliable transfer, are among the most complex protocols. This chapter discusses the basic transport problems, and later chapters show an example of a transport protocol.

Layer 5: Session

Layer *5* protocols specify how to establish a communication session with a remote system (e.g., how to login to a remote timesharing computer). Specifications for security details such as authentication using passwords belong in Layer *5*.

Layer 6: Presentation

Layer *6* protocols specify how to represent data. Such protocols are needed because different brands of computers use different internal representations for integers and characters. Thus, Layer *6* protocols are needed to translate from the representation on one computer to the representation on another.

Layer 7: Application

Each Layer 7 protocol specifies how one particular application uses a network. For example, the specification for an application that transfers files from one computer to another belongs in Layer 7. The protocol specifies the details of how an application program on one machine makes a request (e.g., how to specify the name of the desired file) and how the application on another machine responds.

16.6 Stacks: Layered Software

When protocols are designed according to a layering model, the resulting protocol software follows the layered organization. The protocol software on each computer is divided into modules, with one module corresponding to each layer. More important, layering determines the interactions among modules: in theory when protocol software sends or receives data, each module only communicates with the module for the next highest layer and the module for the next lowest. Thus, outgoing data passes down through each layer, and incoming data passes up through each layer. Figure 16.2 illustrates the concept.

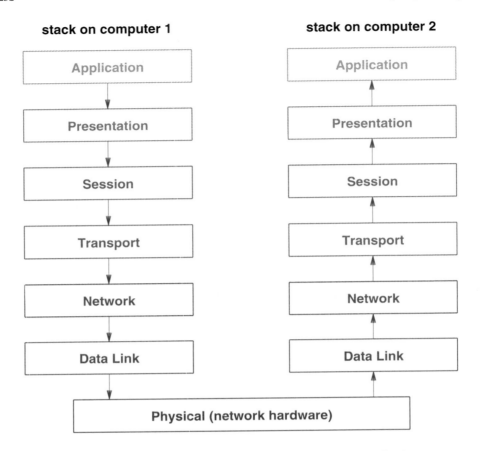

Figure 16.2 The conceptual path of data as it travels from an application on one computer across a network to an application on another computer.

As the figure shows, each computer contains software for an entire suite of protocols. Vendors use the term *stack* to refer to such software because the layering model from which the software is built is often pictured with a set of rectangles as in Figures 16.1 and 16.2. Thus, the question, "Which stack is your computer running?" usually refers to network protocols, not to a stack data structure.

Several stacks are available commercially. The table in Figure 16.3 lists six different protocol stacks.

Vendor	Stack
Novell Corporation	Netware
Banyan System Corporation	VINES
Apple Computer Corporation	AppleTalk
Digital Equipment Corporation	DECNET
IBM	SNA
(many vendors)	TCP/IP

Figure 16.3 Examples of protocol stacks that have been built. Although the stacks share many general concepts, the details differ, making them incompatible.

Because each stack has been designed independently, protocols from a given stack cannot interact with protocols from another. Thus, if one decides to use Novell Corporation's *Netware* stack on a computer, that computer can only communicate with other computers that use the Netware stack. Similarly, if one chooses to use Apple Computer Corporation's *AppleTalk* stack on a computer, that computer can only communicate with other computers that use the AppleTalk stack.

If necessary, a computer can run more than one stack at the same time. For example, a computer can have software for both a Netware stack and a VINES stack. Two stacks can run on the same computer and can transmit across a single physical network without interference because the type field in each frame identifies which stack should handle the message.

16.7 How Layered Software Works

We said that each layer of protocol software solves one part of the communication problem. To do so, software in a given layer on the sending computer adds information to the outgoing data, and software in the same layer on the receiving computer uses the additional information to process incoming data. For example, if two computers have agreed on a frame format that includes a checksum, software in the *Data Link* layer on the two machines perform the checksum computation. In Figure 16.2, whenever an outgoing frame arrives at the *Data Link* software on computer *1*, software adds a checksum before transmitting the frame over the network. Whenever an incoming frame arrives at the *Data Link* software on computer *2*, the software verifies and removes the checksum before passing the frame to the *Network* layer.

16.8 Multiple, Nested Headers

Usually, each layer places additional information in a header before sending data to a lower layer. Thus, a frame traveling across a network contains a series of nested headers as Figure 16.4 illustrates.

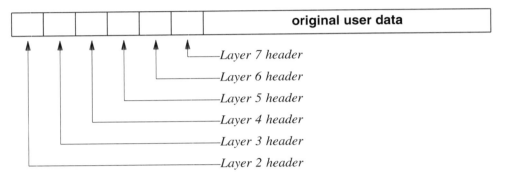

Figure 16.4 The nested protocol headers that appear in a frame as the frame travels across a network. Each layer of protocol software adds a header to an outgoing frame.

As the figure shows, the header corresponding to the lowest-level protocol occurs first. In fact, the header for layer 2, the data link protocol, occurs first. Although Layer 1 specifies the electrical or optical signals used to transmit a frame, Layer 1 does not add a header in the same way that other layers do.

Figure 16.4 illustrates a general concept, but does not show all possibilities. In particular, some protocol software does more than prepend a header to outgoing data. For example, Chapter 7 shows that a data link protocol might prepend one special character to mark the beginning of a frame, append another special character to mark the end of the frame, and insert additional characters in the middle to escape occurrences of special characters. Similarly, some protocols specify that all additional information should be appended to the frame instead of being prepended.

16.9 The Scientific Basis For Layering

The significance of layering arises from a straightforward scientific principle known as the *layering principle*:

> *Layer N software on the destination computer must receive the exact message sent by layer N software on the sending computer.*

In other words, whatever transformation a protocol applies before sending a frame must be completely reversed when the frame is received†. If a particular layer on the sending computer prepends a header to a frame, the corresponding layer on the receiver must remove the header. If one of the layers encrypts a frame before sending, the corresponding layer on the receiving computer must decrypt the frame.

Layering is a powerful idea because it simplifies protocol design and testing. Layering prevents the protocol software in one layer from introducing changes that are visible to other layers. As a result, the sending and receiving software for each layer can be designed, implemented, and tested independent of other layers. Figure 16.5 illustrates how the layering principle applies at various points in the protocol stack.

16.10 Techniques Protocols Use

We have already seen examples of problems that arise in communication systems and the ways protocols solve some of those problems. For example, Chapter 4 discusses how bits can be corrupted during transmission. To detect such errors, data link protocols use a variety of techniques including: a *parity bit*, *frame checksum*, or a *cyclic redundancy check* (*CRC*). The exact technique chosen depends on the design of the entire protocol suite.

Some protocols do more than detect errors — they make an effort to repair or circumvent problems. In particular, transport protocols use a variety of tools to handle some of the most complicated communication problems. This section reviews a set of problems that can arise and discusses techniques protocols use to solve them. As with the data link techniques discussed earlier, the exact details depend on the design of the entire protocol suite.

16.10.1 Sequencing For Out-Of-Order Delivery

A connectionless network system that can change routes may deliver packets out of order. To understand why, consider a sequence of packets being sent, and recall that networks attempt to use the shortest available path at any time. If a shorter path becomes available immediately after the ith packet in the sequence has been sent, the network may send packet $i+1$ along the shorter path, causing it to arrive before packet i.

To handle out-of-order deliveries, transport protocols use *sequencing*. The sending side attaches a sequence number to each packet. The receiving side stores both the sequence number of the last packet received in order as well as a list of additional packets that arrived out of order. When a packet arrives, the receiver examines the sequence number to determine how the packet should be handled. If the packet is the next one expected (i.e., has arrived in order), the protocol software delivers the packet to the next

---

†Mathematically, if the sender applies a transformation T, the receiver must apply the inverse, T^{-1}.

highest layer, and checks its list to see whether additional packets can also be delivered. If the packet has arrived out of order, the protocol software adds the packet to the list.

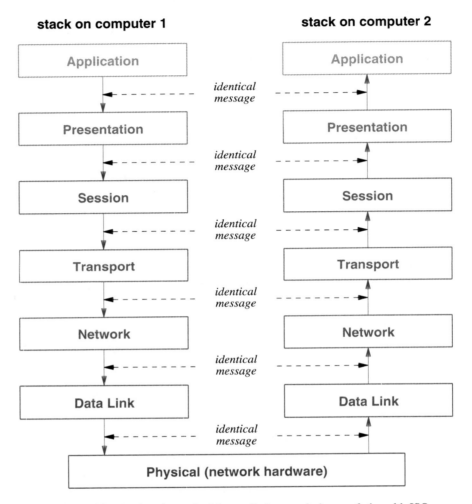

Figure 16.5 The layering principle applied at each layer of the old ISO model. If protocol software on the sending computer changes the message, the change must be reversed by the corresponding protocol software on the receiver.

16.10.2 Sequencing To Eliminate Duplicate Packets

Malfunctioning hardware can cause packets to be duplicated. Duplication often arises in WANs, but can also occur in LANs. For example, a transceiver malfunction in a LAN that uses CSMA/CD can cause the receiver to sense a valid transmission while the sender senses a collision. As a result, the sender will back off from the collision and retransmit, causing two copies of the frame to reach the receiver†.

Sequencing solves the problem of duplication. The receiving software checks for duplicates when it examines the sequence number of an arriving packet. If the sequence has already been delivered or the sequence matches one of the packets waiting on the list, the software discards the new copy.

16.10.3 Retransmitting Lost Packets

Packet loss is a fundamental problem in computer networks because transmission errors can corrupt bits, making the frame invalid. When a receiver detects such problems, the receiver discards the frame.

To guarantee *reliable* transfer (i.e., transfer without loss), protocols use *positive acknowledgement with retransmission*. Whenever a frame arrives intact, the receiving protocol software sends a small message back that reports successful reception. The message is known as an *acknowledgement* (*ACK*). The sender takes responsibility for ensuring that each packet is transferred successfully. Whenever it sends a packet, the sending-side protocol software starts a timer. If an acknowledgement arrives before the timer expires, the software cancels the timer. If the timer expires before an acknowledgement arrives, the software sends another copy of the packet and starts the timer again. The action of sending a second copy is known as *retransmitting*, and the copy is commonly called a *retransmission*.

Retransmission cannot succeed if a hardware failure has permanently disconnected the network or if the receiving computer has crashed. Therefore, protocols that retransmit messages usually bound the maximum number of retransmissions. When the bound has been reached, the protocol stops retransmitting and declares that communication is impossible.

Note that retransmission can introduce duplicate packets. Because a sender cannot distinguish between a packet that has been lost and a packet that experiences long delay, the sender may decide to retransmit too soon. Eventually, both copies of the packet may be delivered. Thus, protocols that use retransmissions to provide reliability must also handle the problem of duplicate packets.

---

†The author experienced such a situation first-hand.

16.10.4 Avoiding Replay Caused By Excessive Delay

One source of delay in a packet switching system arises from the store-and-forward approach. When a packet arrives at a packet switch, the packet is placed in a queue. If packets have arrived faster than the switch can forward them, the queue of waiting packets will be large and delay can be excessive. Extraordinary delays can lead to *replay errors*. Replay means that an old, delayed packet affects later communication. For example, consider the following sequence of events.

- Two computers agree to communicate at *1* PM.
- One computer sends a sequence of ten packets to the other.
- A hardware problem causes packet *3* to be delayed.
- Routes change to avoid the hardware problem.
- Protocol software on the sending computer retransmits packet *3*, and the remaining packets are transmitted without error.
- At 1:05 PM the two computers agree to communicate again.
- After the second packet arrives, the delayed copy of packet *3* arrives from the earlier conversation.
- Packet *3* arrives from the second conversation.

Unfortunately, unless the protocol is designed carefully, a packet from an old conversation might be accepted in a later conversation and the correct packet discarded as a duplicate.

Replay can also happen with control packets. For example, protocols often send a special control packet to terminate a conversation. If a copy of a termination request arrives from a previous conversation, it can cause protocol software to terminate a session prematurely.

To prevent replay, protocols mark each session with a unique ID (e.g., the time the session was established), and require the unique ID to be present in each packet. The protocol software discards any arriving packet that contains an incorrect ID. To avoid replay, an ID must not be reused until a reasonable time has passed (e.g., hours).

16.10.5 Flow Control To Prevent Data Overrun

Computers do not all operate at the same speed. Data overrun occurs when a computer sends data across a network faster than the destination can absorb it. Consequently, data is lost.

Several techniques are available to handle data overrun. Collectively, the techniques are known as *flow control* mechanisms. The simplest form of flow control is a *stop-and-go* system in which a sender waits after transmitting each packet. When the receiver is ready for another packet, the receiver sends a control message, usually a form of acknowledgement.

Although stop-and-go protocols prevent overrun, they can cause extremely inefficient use of network capacity. To understand why, consider what happens on a network
that has a packet size of 1000 octets, a throughput capacity of 2 Mbps, and a delay of
50 milliseconds. The network hardware can transport 2 Mbps from one computer to
another. However, after transmitting a packet, the sender must wait 100 msec before
sending another packet (i.e., 50 msec for the packet to reach the receiver and 50 msec
for an acknowledgement to travel back). Thus, the maximum rate at which data can be
sent using stop-and-go is one packet every 100 milliseconds. When expressed as a bit
rate, the maximum rate that stop-and-go can achieve is 80,000 bps, which is only 4% of
the hardware capacity.

To obtain high throughput rates, protocols use a flow control technique known as
sliding window. The sender and receiver are programmed to use a fixed *window size*,
which is the maximum amount of data that can be sent before an acknowledgement arrives. For example, the sender and receiver might agree on a window size of four packets. The sender begins with the data to be sent, extracts data to fill the first window,
and transmits copies. If reliability is needed, the sender retains a copy in case retransmission is needed. The receiver must have buffer space ready to receive the entire
window. When a packet arrives in sequence, the receiver passes the packet to the receiving application and transmits an acknowledgement to the sender. When an acknowledgement arrives, the sender discards its copy of the acknowledged packet and
transmits the next packet. Figure 16.6 illustrates why the mechanism is known as a
sliding window.

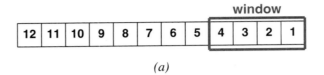

(a)

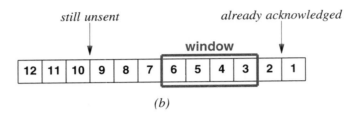

(b)

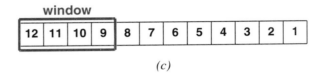

(c)

Figure 16.6 A 4-packet window sliding through outgoing data. The window
is shown (a) when transmission begins, (b) after two packets
have been acknowledged, and (c) after eight packets have been
acknowledged. The sender can transmit all packets in the window.

Sliding window can increase throughput dramatically. To understand why, consider the sequence of transmissions with a stop-and-go scheme and a sliding window
scheme. Figure 16.7 contains a comparison for a 4-packet transmission.

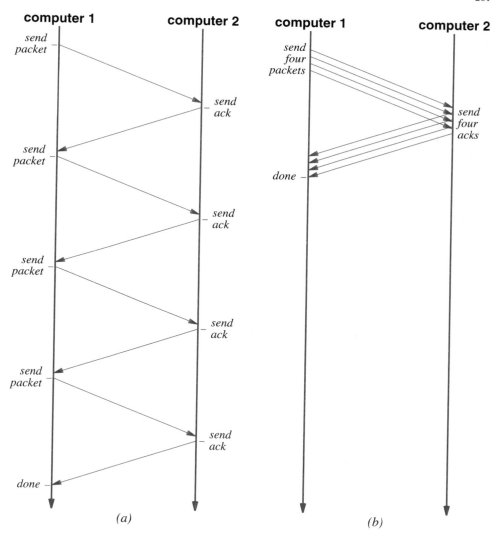

Figure 16.7 Messages required to send a sequence of four packets using (a) stop-and-go flow control, and (b) a 4-packet sliding window. Time proceeds down the page, and each arrow shows one message sent from one computer to the other.

Figure 16.7a shows the sequence of transmissions for a stop-and-go protocol. After sending a packet, the protocol waits for an acknowledgement before sending another packet. If the delay required to send a single packet on one trip through the network is N, the total time required to send four packets is $8N$.

Figure 16.7b shows the sequence of transmissions when using a sliding window. The protocol sends all packets in the window before it waits. To be realistic, the figure shows a small delay between successive packet transmissions. Although the delay may be smaller than shown, transmission is never instantaneous — a short time (usually a few microseconds) is required for the hardware to complete transmission of a packet, interrupt the CPU, and begin to transmit the next packet. Thus, the total time required to send four packets is $2N + \varepsilon$, where ε denotes the small delay.

To understand the significance of sliding window, imagine an extended communication that involves many packets. In such cases, the total time required for transmission is so large that ε can be ignored. To appreciate the benefits of sliding window, consider a network with high throughput and large delay (e.g., a satellite channel). For such networks, a sliding window protocol can increase performance by a factor much greater than *1*. In fact, the potential improvement is:

$$T_w = T_g \times W$$

where T_w is the throughput that can be achieved with a sliding window protocol, T_g is the throughput that can be achieved with a stop-and-go protocol, and W is the window size. The equation explains why the sliding window protocol illustrated in Figure 16.7b has approximately four times the throughput of the stop-and-go protocol in Figure 16.7a. Of course, throughput cannot be made arbitrarily large merely by increasing the window size. The bandwidth of the underlying network imposes an upper bound — bits cannot be sent faster than the hardware can carry them. Thus, the equation can be rewritten:

$$T_w = min(B, T_g \times W)$$

where B is the underlying hardware bandwidth.

16.10.6 Mechanisms To Avoid Network Congestion

Congestion is a fundamental problem in packet switching systems. To understand why, consider a network represented by the graph in Figure 16.8.

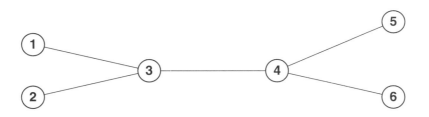

Figure 16.8 A graph that represents a network of six packet switches. Such networks can experience congestion.

Assume each connection in the underlying network has a throughput of 1.5 Mbps, and consider how traffic flows from one side to another across the link in the middle. For example, suppose a computer attached to node *1* sends a sequence of packets to a computer attached to node *5*. Packets can travel between nodes *1* and *3* at 1.5 Mbps, and between nodes *3* and *4* at 1.5 Mbps.

If only one computer is sending packets, the network operates well. However, any additional traffic across the middle link will cause congestion. For example, if a computer attached to node *2* begins sending packets to a destination attached to node *6*, the packets must also travel across the link in the middle. With both nodes *1* and *2* sending packets, data arrives at node *3* twice as fast as it can be sent over the link to node *4*. The packet switch that corresponds to node *3* places incoming packets from nodes *1* and *2* in a queue until they can be sent. Because more packets arrive than can be sent, the queue grows and the effective delay increases†. The situation is known as *congestion*.

If congestion persists, a packet switch will run out of memory and begin discarding packets. Although retransmission can be used to recover lost packets, retransmission takes time. Furthermore, if the situation persists, the entire network can become unusable. The condition is known as *congestion collapse*. Protocols attempt to avoid congestion collapse by monitoring the network and reacting quickly once congestion starts. There are two approaches:

- Arrange for packet switches to inform senders when congestion occurs.
- Use packet loss as an estimate of congestion.

The former scheme is implemented either by having packet switches send a special message to the source of packets when congestion occurs or by having packet switches set a bit in the header of each packet that experiences delay caused by congestion. If the bit in the header is set, the computer that receives the packet includes information in the acknowledgement to inform the original sender‡.

Using packet loss to estimate congestion is reasonable in modern networks because:

> *Modern network hardware works well; most packet loss results from congestion, not hardware failure.*

Thus, a sender that assumes all loss occurs because the network is congested makes a valid assumption most of the time. Packet loss can be measured easily if the sender uses a timeout and retransmission strategy. Each retransmission event means congestion has occurred.

The appropriate response to congestion consists of reducing the rate at which packets are being transmitted. Some protocols use a *rate control* mechanism that monitors how frequently packets are being produced and then reduces the packet rate temporarily when congestion occurs. Sliding window protocols can achieve the same effect by temporarily reducing the window size.

---

†In theory, the delay can grow arbitrarily large as Chapter 15 describes. In practice, the queue in a packet switch is finite.

‡A long delay can occur between the time congestion occurs and the time computers sending packets learn about the congestion.

16.11 The Art Of Protocol Design

Although the techniques needed to solve specific problems are well-known, protocol design is nontrivial for two reasons. First, to make communication efficient, details must be chosen carefully — small design errors can result in incorrect operation, unnecessary packets, or delays. For example, sequence numbers usually are stored in a fixed field in a packet header. The field must be large enough so sequence numbers are not reused frequently, but small enough to avoid wasting unnecessary bandwidth. Similarly, a higher-level protocol can cause excessive overhead if the protocol chooses a nonoptimal message size (e.g., one octet more than the maximum size of a packet). Second, protocol mechanisms can interact in unexpected ways. For example, consider the interaction between flow control and congestion control mechanisms. A sliding window scheme aggressively uses more of the underlying network bandwidth to improve throughput. A congestion control mechanism does the opposite by reducing the number of packets being inserted to prevent the network from collapsing.

The balance between sliding window and congestion control can be tricky, and a design that does both well is difficult. A protocol that is too aggressive about using bandwidth can congest the underlying network; a protocol that is too conservative can result in lower throughput than necessary. More important, designs that attempt to switch from aggressive to conservative whenever congestion occurs tend to oscillate — they slowly increase their use of bandwidth until the network begins to experience congestion, decrease use until the network becomes stable, and then begin to increase again.

16.12 Summary

In addition to hardware, network systems have complex protocol software that controls communication. Instead of interacting directly with network hardware, most application programs and users interact with protocol software.

Layering is a fundamental tool that helps designers master the complexity of protocol software. Layering divides the complex communication problem into distinct pieces, and allows a designer to focus on one piece at a time. This chapter describes the old 7-layer reference model that is still sometimes cited in informal discussions. The model is insufficient for Internet protocols; the next chapter describes the Internet reference model.

A scientific principle known as the *layering principle* provides the basis for layered designs. The layering principle states that the Nth layer at the destination applies the inverse of the transformations applied in the Nth layer at the source.

The organization of protocol software follows the layering model with which it was designed. A software module corresponds to each layer, and vendors call the collection of modules a *stack*. In theory, outgoing data passes down through the layers of the stack on the sending machine and up through the layers of the stack on the receiving machine.

Protocols use several basic techniques to solve communication problems: sequencing to handle out-of-order and duplicate packets, acknowledgement and retransmission to handle packet loss, unique session IDs to prevent replay, a stop-and-go or sliding window mechanism to control the flow of data, and rate reduction to handle network congestion. The chief advantage of sliding window is performance — a sliding window mechanism, which prevents a sender from overrunning a receiver, can be tuned to allow computers to use the available hardware bandwidth.

Although the general techniques that protocols use to handle problems are well-known, designing protocols is nontrivial. Details are important and protocols can interact in unexpected ways.

EXERCISES

16.1   Design a protocol that prevents replay. Have someone else try to find a sequence of crashes and delayed packets that causes your protocol to fail.

16.2   Design a sliding window protocol that allows transmission of up to eight packets before an acknowledgement arrives. To ensure the receiver understands packets that arrive out of order, sliding window protocols include a counter in the header. What size counter is needed? Why?

16.3   Why does a stop-and-go protocol have especially low throughput over a satellite channel that operates at two megabits per second?

16.4   What happens to throughput if a protocol waits too long to retransmit? If a protocol does not wait long enough to retransmit?

16.5   Extend the diagram in Figure 16.7b to show the transmission of 16 packets. (Assume all packets arrive in sequence.)

16.6   Show an example of a network where damage to a single packet can result in congestion. Hint: can retransmission cause congestion?

Internetworking

Internet architecture, addressing, binding, encapsulation, reliable transport, and the TCP/IP protocol suite

Chapter Contents

17

Internetworking: Concepts, Architecture, and Protocols

17.1 Introduction

Previous chapters describe basic networking, including the hardware components used in LAN and WAN networks as well as general concepts such as addressing and routing. This chapter begins an examination of another fundamental idea in computer communication — an internetworking technology that can be used to connect multiple physical networks into a large, uniform communication system. The chapter discusses the motivation for internetworking, introduces the hardware components used, describes the architecture in which those components are connected, and discusses the significance of the concept. The remaining chapters in this section expand the internetworking concept and provide additional details about the technology. They examine individual protocols and explain how each uses techniques from Chapter 16 to achieve reliable, error-free communication. The next section describes applications that use internetworking technology.

17.2 The Motivation For Internetworking

Each network technology is designed to fit a specific set of constraints. For example, LAN technologies are designed to provide high speed communication across short distances, while WAN technologies are designed to provide communication across large areas. Consequently,

No single networking technology is best for all needs.

A large organization with diverse networking requirements needs multiple physical networks. More important, if the organization chooses the type network that is best for each task, the organization will have several types of networks. For example, a LAN technology like Ethernet might be the best solution for connecting computers in an office, but a Frame Relay service might be used to interconnect computers in one city with computers in another.

17.3 The Concept Of Universal Service

The chief problem with multiple networks should be obvious: a computer attached to a given network can only communicate with other computers attached to the same network. The problem became evident in the 1970s as large organizations began to acquire multiple networks. Each network in the organization formed an island. In many early installations, each computer attached to a single network and employees had to choose a computer appropriate for each task. That is, an employee was given access to multiple screens and keyboards, and the employee was forced to move from one computer to another to send a message across the appropriate network.

Users are neither satisfied nor productive when they must use a separate computer for each network. Consequently, most modern computer communication systems allow communication between any two computers analogous to the way a telephone system provides communication between any two telephones. Known as *universal service*, the concept is a fundamental part of networking†. With universal service, a user on any computer in any part of an organization can send messages or data to any other user. Furthermore, a user does not need to change computer systems when changing tasks — all information is available to all computers. As a result, users are more productive. To summarize:

> *A communication system that supplies universal service allows arbitrary pairs of computers to communicate. Universal service is desirable because it increases individual productivity.*

17.4 Universal Service In A Heterogeneous World

Does universal service mean an organization needs to adopt a single network technology, or is it possible to have universal service across multiple networks that use multiple technologies? In Chapter 11 we learned that electrical incompatibilities make it impossible to form a large network merely by interconnecting the wires from two networks. Furthermore, extension techniques such as bridging cannot be used with heterogeneous network technologies because different technologies use incompatible packet

---

†Many technologies have attempted to provide universal service; *Asynchronous Transfer Mode* (ATM) is a recent example.

formats and addressing schemes. Thus, a frame created for one network technology cannot be transmitted on a network that uses a different technology. The point can be summarized:

> *Although universal service is highly desirable, incompatibilities among network hardware and physical addressing prevent an organization from building a bridged network that includes arbitrary technologies.*

17.5 Internetworking

Despite the incompatibilities among network technologies, researchers have devised a scheme that provides universal service among heterogeneous networks. Called *internetworking*, the scheme uses both hardware and software. Additional hardware systems are used to interconnect a set of physical networks. Software on all the attached computers then provides universal service. The resulting system of connected physical networks is known as an *internetwork* or *internet*.

Internetworking is quite general. In particular, an internet is not restricted in size — internets exist that contain a few networks and internets exist that contain thousands of networks. Similarly, the number of computers attached to each network in an internet can vary — some networks have no computers attached, while others have hundreds.

17.6 Physical Network Connection With Routers

The basic hardware component used to connect heterogeneous networks is a *router*. Physically, routers resemble bridges — each router is a special-purpose computer dedicated to the task of interconnecting networks. Like a bridge, a router has a conventional processor and memory as well as a separate I/O interface for each network to which it connects. The network treats a connection to a router the same as a connection to any other computer. Figure 17.1 illustrates that the physical connection of networks with a router is straightforward.

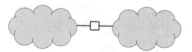

Figure 17.1 Two physical networks connected by a router, which has a separate interface for each network connection. Computers can attach to each network.

The figure uses a cloud to depict each network instead of a line or a circle because router connections are not restricted to a given network technology. A router can connect two LANs, a LAN and a WAN, or two WANs. Furthermore, when a router connects two networks in the same general category, the networks do not need to use the same technology. For example, a router can connect an Ethernet LAN to an FDDI LAN. Thus, each cloud represents an arbitrary network technology.

To summarize:

> *A router is a special-purpose computer dedicated to the task of interconnecting networks. A router can interconnect networks that use different technologies, including different media, physical addressing schemes, or frame formats.*

17.7 Internet Architecture

Routers make it possible for an organization to choose network technologies appropriate for each need, and to use routers to connect all networks into a single internet. For example, Figure 17.2 illustrates how three routers can be used to connect four arbitrary physical networks into an internet.

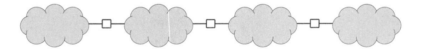

Figure 17.2 An internet formed by using three routers to interconnect four physical networks. Each network can be a LAN or a WAN.

Although the figure shows each router with exactly two connections, commercial routers can connect more than two networks. Thus, a single router could connect all four networks in our example. However, an organization seldom uses a single router to connect all of its networks. There are two reasons:

- Because the CPU and memory in a router are used to process each packet, the processor in one router is insufficient to handle the traffic passing among an arbitrary number of networks.

- Redundancy improves internet reliability. Protocol software continuously monitors internet connections, and instructs the routers to send traffic along alternative paths when a network or router fails.

Thus, when planning an internet, an organization must choose a design that meets the organization's need for reliability, capacity, and cost. In particular, the exact details of internet topology often depend on the bandwidth of the physical networks, the expected traffic, the organization's reliability requirements, and the cost of available router hardware.

> *An internet consists of a set of networks interconnected by routers. The internet scheme allows each organization to choose the number and type of networks, the number of routers to use to interconnect them, and the exact interconnection topology.*

17.8 Achieving Universal Service

The goal of internetworking is universal service across heterogeneous networks. To provide universal service among all computers on an internet, routers must agree to forward information from a source on one network to a specified destination on another. The task is complex because frame formats and addressing schemes used by the underlying networks can differ. As a result, protocol software is needed on computers and routers to make universal service possible.

Later chapters describe internet protocol software in detail. They show how internet protocols overcome differences in frame formats and physical addresses to make communication possible among networks that use different technologies. Before considering how internet protocols work, it is important to understand the effect that an internet system presents to attached computers.

17.9 A Virtual Network

In general, internet software provides the appearance of a single, seamless communication system to which many computers attach. The system offers universal service: each computer is assigned an address, and any computer can send a packet to any other computer. Furthermore, internet protocol software hides the details of physical network connections, physical addresses, and routing information — neither users nor application programs are aware of the underlying physical networks or the routers that connect them.

We say that an internet is a *virtual network* system because the communication system is an abstraction. That is, although a combination of hardware and software provides the illusion of a uniform network system, no such network exists. Figure 17.3 illustrates the virtual network concept as well as a corresponding physical structure.

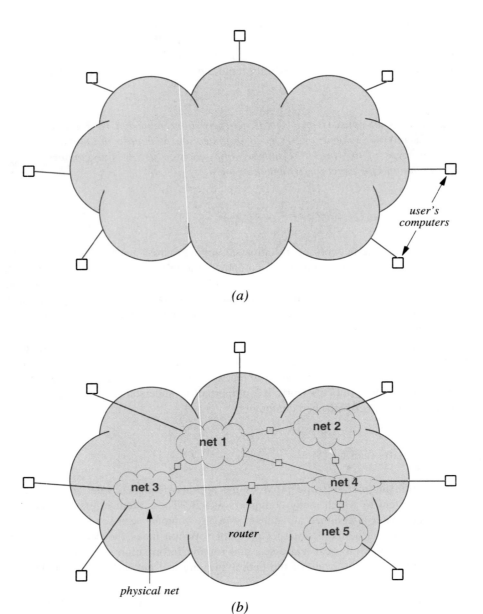

(a)

(b)

Figure 17.3 The internet concept. (a) The illusion of a single network that
TCP/IP software provides to users and applications, and (b) the
underlying physical structure in which a computer attaches to
one physical network, and routers interconnect the networks.

17.10 Protocols For Internetworking

Although many protocols have been adapted for use in an internet, one suite stands out as the most widely used for internetworking. The suite is formally known as *The TCP/IP Internet Protocols*; most networking professionals simply refer to them as *TCP/IP†*.

TCP/IP was the first set of protocols developed for use in an internet. Indeed, researchers who devised TCP/IP also developed the internet architecture described earlier in this chapter. Work on TCP/IP began in the 1970s, approximately the same time that Local Area Networks were being developed. The U.S. military funded much of the research on TCP/IP and internetworking through the *Advanced Research Projects Agency (ARPA)*. The military was among the first organizations to have multiple physical networks. Consequently, the military was among the first to realize the need for universal service. By the mid-1980s, the *National Science Foundation* and other U.S. government agencies were funding development of TCP/IP and a large internet that was used to test the protocols.

17.11 Significance Of Internetworking And TCP/IP

Research on internetworking and TCP/IP protocols has produced dramatic results. Internetworking has become one of the most important ideas in modern networking. In fact, internet technology has revolutionized computer communication. Most large organizations already use internetworking as the primary computer communication mechanism. Smaller organizations and individuals are beginning to do so as well. More important, in addition to private internets, the TCP/IP technology has made possible a global Internet‡ that reaches over *82* million computers in schools, commercial organizations, and government and military sites in more than *210* countries around the world.

The worldwide demand for internetworking products has affected most companies that sell networking technologies. Competition has increased because new companies have been formed to sell the hardware and software needed for internetworking. In addition, many companies have modified their protocol designs to accommodate internetworking. In particular, most network protocols were originally designed to work with one network technology and one physical network at a time. To provide internetworking capabilities, companies have extended the designs in two ways: the protocols have been adapted to work with many network technologies, and new features have been added that allow the protocols to transfer data across an internet.

---

†TCP and IP are acronyms for two of the most important protocols in the suite; the name is pronounced by spelling out T-C-P-I-P.

‡When written with an uppercase *I*, the term *Internet* refers to the *global Internet*, which is also called the *public Internet*.

17.12 Layering And TCP/IP Protocols

The 7-layer reference model described in Chapter 16 was devised before internet-working was invented. Consequently, the model does not contain a layer for internet protocols. Furthermore, the 7-layer reference model devotes an entire layer to *session* protocols, which have become much less important as computer systems have changed from large timesharing systems to private workstations. As a result, researchers who developed TCP/IP invented a new layering model. This section describes the new layering model briefly. Later chapters discuss details of the protocols found in each layer.

The *TCP/IP layering model*, which is also called the *Internet Layering Model* or the *Internet Reference Model*, contains five layers as Figure 17.4 illustrates.

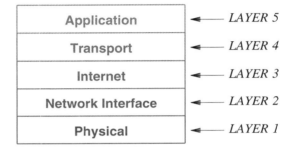

Figure 17.4 The five layers of the TCP/IP reference model.

Four of the layers in the TCP/IP reference model correspond to one or more layers in the ISO reference model. However, the ISO model has no Internet Layer. This section summarizes the purpose of each layer.

Layer 1: Physical

Layer *1* corresponds to basic network hardware just as Layer *1* in the ISO 7-layer reference model.

Layer 2: Network Interface

Layer *2* protocols specify how to organize data into frames and how a computer transmits frames over a network, similar to Layer *2* protocols in the ISO reference model.

Layer 3: Internet

Layer *3* protocols specify the format of packets sent across an internet as well as the mechanisms used to forward packets from a computer through one or more routers to a final destination.

Layer 4: Transport

Layer *4* protocols, like layer *4* in the ISO model, specify how to ensure reliable transfer.

Layer 5: Application

Layer *5* corresponds to layers *6* and *7* in the ISO model. Each Layer *5* protocol specifies how one application uses an internet.

To summarize:

> *TCP/IP protocols are organized into five conceptual layers. Although some layers of the TCP/IP reference model correspond to layers of the ISO reference model, the ISO layering scheme does not have a layer that corresponds to TCP/IP's Internet Layer.*

17.13 Host Computers, Routers, And Protocol Layers

TCP/IP defines the term *host computer* to refer to any computer system that connects to an internet and runs applications. A host can be as small as a personal computer or as large as a mainframe†. Furthermore, a host's CPU can be slow or fast, the memory can be large or small, and the network to which a host connects can operate at high or low speed. TCP/IP protocols make it possible for any pair of hosts to communicate, despite hardware differences.

Both hosts and routers need TCP/IP protocol software. However, routers do not use protocols from all layers. In particular, a router does not need Layer *5* protocols for applications like file transfer because routers do not run such applications‡. The next chapters discuss TCP/IP protocol software in more detail, and explain layering in an internet.

---

†The same terminology does not always apply outside TCP/IP — in some protocol suites the term *host* refers only to large, mainframe systems.

‡Some routers do run applications that permit a manager to administer the router remotely (e.g., change the configuration or correct problems).

17.14 Summary

Physically, an internet is a collection of networks interconnected by devices called *routers*. Each router is a special-purpose computer that connects to two or more networks. Although it has a memory and a processor, a router is dedicated to the task of moving data among the networks to which it attaches.

Conventional computers that connect to an internet are called *hosts*. A host may be a large computer (e.g., a supercomputer) or a small computer (e.g., a personal computer). Each host attaches to one of the physical networks in an internet.

Logically, an internet appears to be a single, seamless communication system. An arbitrary pair of computers connected to an internet can communicate as if they were attached to a single network. That is, a computer can send a packet to any other computer that is attached to the internet.

The illusion of a single communication system is provided by internet protocol software. Each host or router in the internet must run the software, which allows application programs to exchange packets. The protocol software hides the details of the underlying physical connections, and takes care of sending each packet through zero or more routers to its destination.

The most important protocols developed for internetworking are known as the *TCP/IP Internet Protocols*, usually abbreviated as *TCP/IP*. TCP/IP protocol software works well and handles large internets. In addition to being used on many private internets, TCP/IP is used on the global Internet that reaches over 82 million computers in 210 countries.

EXERCISES

17.1   What bandwidth is the connection from your organization to the Internet? What is the approximate utilization?

17.2   If your organization has an internal internet, find out how many physical networks are connected and how many routers are used.

17.3   If a given router can connect to at most K networks, how many routers, R, are required to connect N networks? Write an equation that gives R in terms of N and K.

17.4   Show that universal service is possible without using a universal packet delivery scheme. (Think of application programs running on conventional computers that forward e-mail messages.)

17.5   In the previous exercise, what is the chief disadvantage of using conventional computers to provide universal service?

17.6   Assume that 5 million new computers are added to the Internet in a nine month period. If computers are added at a uniform rate, how much time elapses between two additions?

17.7   Draw a TCP/IP internet that consists of two networks connected by a router. Show a computer attached to each network. Show the protocol stack used on the computers and the stack used on the router.

17.8   Describe how layers in the ISO reference model correspond to layers in the TCP/IP reference model.

Chapter Contents

18

IP: Internet Protocol Addresses

18.1 Introduction

The previous chapter explains the physical architecture of an internet in which routers interconnect physical networks. This chapter begins a description of protocol software that makes an internet appear to be a single, seamless communication system. The chapter introduces the addressing scheme used by the Internet Protocol (IP), and explains how the original IP addressing scheme divided addresses into classes. It then discusses subnet addressing and classless addressing, two additions to the IP addressing scheme.

The next three chapters expand the description of IP. They each consider one aspect of the protocol in detail. Taken as a group, Chapters 18 through 21 define the IP protocol and explain how IP software allows computers to exchange packets across an internet.

18.2 Addresses For The Virtual Internet

Recall from Chapter 17 that the goal of internetworking is to provide a seamless communication system. To achieve the goal, internet protocol software must hide the details of physical networks and offer the facilities of a large virtual network. The virtual internet operates much like any network, allowing computers to send and receive packets of information. The chief difference between an internet and a physical network is that an internet is merely an abstraction imagined by its designers and created entirely by software. The designers are free to choose addresses, packet formats, and delivery techniques independent of the details of the physical hardware.

Addressing is a critical component of the internet abstraction. To give the appearance of a single, uniform system, all host computers must use a uniform addressing scheme, and each address must be unique. Unfortunately, physical network addresses do not suffice because an internet can include multiple network technologies and each technology defines its own address format. Thus, the addresses used by two technologies may be incompatible because they are different sizes or have different formats.

To guarantee uniform addressing for all hosts, protocol software defines an addressing scheme that is independent of the underlying physical addresses. Although an internet addressing scheme is an abstraction created by software, protocol addresses are used as destinations for the virtual internet analogous to the way hardware addresses are used as destinations on a physical network. To send a packet across an internet, the sender places the destination's protocol address in the packet and passes the packet to protocol software for delivery. The software uses the destination protocol address when it forwards the packet across the internet to the destination computer.

Uniform addressing helps create the illusion of a large, seamless network because it hides the details of underlying physical network addresses. Two application programs can communicate without knowing either hardware address. The illusion is so complete that some users are surprised to learn that protocol addresses are supplied by software and are not part of the computer system†. Interestingly, we will learn that many layers of protocol software also use protocol addresses. We can summarize:

> To provide uniform addressing in an internet, protocol software defines an abstract addressing scheme that assigns each host a unique protocol address. Users, application programs, and higher layers of protocol software use the abstract protocol addresses to communicate.

18.3 The IP Addressing Scheme

In the TCP/IP protocol stack, addressing is specified by the *Internet Protocol* (*IP*). The IP standard specifies that each host is assigned a unique 32-bit number known as the host's *Internet Protocol address*, which is often abbreviated *IP address*, or *Internet address*‡. Each packet sent across an internet contains the 32-bit IP address of the sender (source) as well as the intended recipient (destination). Thus, to transmit information across a TCP/IP internet, a computer must know the IP address of the remote computer to which the information is being sent.

To summarize:

---

†Most users do not use protocol addresses; they supply the name of a computer and allow software to map the name into an equivalent address. Chapter 29 describes how such mapping occurs.

‡The three terms are used as synonyms throughout the literature and this text.

An Internet Address (IP address) is a unique 32-bit binary number assigned to a host and used for all communication with the host.

18.4 The IP Address Hierarchy

Conceptually, each 32-bit IP address is divided into two parts: a prefix and suffix; the two-level hierarchy is designed to make routing efficient†. The address prefix identifies the physical network to which the computer is attached, while the suffix identifies an individual computer on that network. That is, each physical network in an internet is assigned a unique value known as a *network number*. The network number appears as a prefix in the address of each computer attached to the network. Furthermore, each computer on a given physical network is assigned a unique address suffix.

Although no two networks can be assigned the same network number and no two computers on the same network can be assigned the same suffix, a suffix value can be used on more than one network. For example, if an internet contains three networks, they might be assigned network numbers *1*, *2*, and *3*. Three computers attached to network *1* can be assigned suffixes *1*, *3*, and *5*, while three computers attached to network *2* can be assigned suffixes *1*, *2*, and *3*.

The IP address hierarchy guarantees two important properties:

- Each computer is assigned a unique address (i.e., a single address is never assigned to more than one computer).

- Although network number assignments must be coordinated globally, suffixes can be assigned locally without global coordination.

The first property is guaranteed because a full address contains both a prefix and suffix, which are assigned to ensure uniqueness. If two computers are attached to different physical networks, their addresses have different prefixes. If two computers are attached to the same physical network, their addresses have different suffixes.

18.5 Original Classes Of IP Addresses

Once they chose a size for IP addresses and decided to divide each address into two parts, the designers of IP had to determine how many bits to place in each part. The prefix needs sufficient bits to allow a unique network number to be assigned to each physical network in an internet. The suffix needs sufficient bits to permit each computer attached to a network to be assigned a unique suffix. No simple choice was possible because adding bits to one part means subtracting bits from the other. Choosing a large prefix accommodates many networks, but limits the size of each network; choosing a large suffix means each physical network can contain many computers, but limits the total number of networks.

---

†This section describes the hierarchy, and the next section shows how an address is divided into two parts. Chapter 20 explains how IP software uses the two parts of an address to forward and deliver packets.

Because an internet can include arbitrary network technologies, one internet might be constructed from a few large physical networks, while another might consist of many small networks. More important, a single internet can contain a mixture of large and small networks. Consequently, the designers chose a compromise addressing scheme that can accommodate a combination of large and small networks. The original scheme, which is known as *classful IP addressing*, divides the IP address space into three primary *classes*, where each class has a different size prefix and suffix.

The first four bits of an address determine the class to which the address belongs, and specify how the remainder of the address is divided into prefix and suffix. Figure 18.1 illustrates the five address classes, the leading bits used to identify each class, and the division into prefix and suffix. The figure follows the convention used in TCP/IP protocols of numbering bits from left to right and using zero for the first bit.

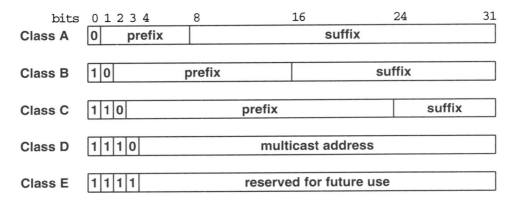

Figure 18.1 The five classes of IP addresses in the classful scheme. The address assigned to a host is either class *A*, *B*, or *C*; the *prefix* identifies a network, and the suffix is unique to a host on that network.

Classes *A*, *B*, and *C* are called the *primary classes* because they are used for host addresses. Class *D* is used for multicasting, which allows delivery to a set of computers†. To use IP multicasting, a set of hosts must agree to share a multicast address. Once the multicast group has been established, a copy of any packet sent to the multicast address will be delivered to each host in the set.

As the figure shows, the primary classes use octet boundaries to partition an address into prefix and suffix. Class *A* places the boundary between the first and second octets. Class *B* places the boundary between the second and third octets, and class *C* places the boundary between the third and fourth octets.

To summarize:

---

†IP multicasting is analogous to hardware multicasting. In both cases, multicast addresses are optional, and even when it participates in multicast, a computer always retains its individual address.

> *The original IP addressing scheme divides host addresses into three primary classes. The class of an address determines the boundary between the network prefix and host suffix.*

18.6 Computing The Class of An Address

Whenever it handles a packet, IP software needs to separate the destination address into a prefix and suffix. Classful IP addresses were called *self identifying* because the class of the address can be computed from the address itself.

Part of the motivation for using leading bits to denote an address class instead of using a range of values arises from computational considerations: using bits can decrease computation time. In particular, some computers can examine bits faster than they can compare integers. For example, on a computer that includes instructions for Boolean *and*, shift, and indexed lookup, four bits of the address can be extracted and used as an index into a table to determine the address class. Figure 18.2 illustrates the contents of the table used in the computation.

First Four Bits Of Address	Table Index (in decimal)	Class of Address
0000	0	A
0001	1	A
0010	2	A
0011	3	A
0100	4	A
0101	5	A
0110	6	A
0111	7	A
1000	8	B
1001	9	B
1010	10	B
1011	11	B
1100	12	C
1101	13	C
1110	14	D
1111	15	E

Figure 18.2 A table that can be used to compute the class of an address. The first four bits of an address are extracted and used as an index into the table.

As the figure shows, the eight combinations that begin with a *0* bit correspond to class *A*. The four combinations that begin with *10* correspond to class *B*, and the two combinations that begin with *110* correspond to class *C*. An address that begins with *111* belongs to class *D*. Finally, an address that begins with *1111* belongs to a reserved class that is not currently used.

18.7 Dotted Decimal Notation

Although IP addresses are 32-bit numbers, users seldom enter or read the values in binary. Instead, when interacting with a user, the software uses a notation that is more convenient for humans to understand. Called *dotted decimal notation*, the form expresses each 8-bit section of a 32-bit number as a decimal value and uses periods to separate the sections. Figure 18.3 illustrates examples of binary numbers and the equivalent dotted decimal forms.

32-bit Binary Number	Equivalent Dotted Decimal
10000001 00110100 00000110 00000000	129 . 52 . 6 . 0
11000000 00000101 00110000 00000011	192 . 5 . 48 . 3
00001010 00000010 00000000 00100101	10 . 2 . 0 . 37
10000000 00001010 00000010 00000011	128 . 10 . 2 . 3
10000000 10000000 11111111 00000000	128 . 128 . 255 . 0

Figure 18.3 Examples of 32-bit binary numbers and their equivalent in dotted decimal notation. Each octet is written in decimal with periods (dots) used to separate octets.

Dotted decimal treats each octet as an unsigned binary integer. As the final example in the figure shows, the smallest possible value, *0*, occurs when all bits of an octet are zero, and the largest possible value, *255*, occurs when all bits of an octet are one. Thus, dotted decimal addresses range from *0.0.0.0* through *255.255.255.255*.

To summarize:

> *Dotted decimal notation is a syntactic form that IP software uses to express 32-bit binary values when interacting with humans. Dotted decimal represents each octet in decimal and uses a dot to separate octets.*

18.8 Classes And Dotted Decimal Notation

Dotted decimal worked well with classful IP addresses because IP uses octet boundaries to separate an address into a prefix and suffix. In a class *A* address, the last three octets correspond to a host suffix. Similarly, class *B* addresses have two octets of host suffix, and class *C* addresses have one octet.

Unfortunately, because dotted decimal notation does not make individual bits of an address visible, the class must be recognized from the decimal value of the first octet. Figure 18.4 shows the decimal range of values for each class.

Class	Range of Values
A	0 through 127
B	128 through 191
C	192 through 223
D	224 through 239
E	240 through 255

Figure 18.4 The range of decimal values found in the first octet of each address class.

18.9 Division Of The Address Space

The IP class scheme does not divide the 32-bit address space into equal size classes, and the classes do not contain the same number of networks. For example, half of all IP addresses (i.e., those addresses in which the first bit is zero) lie in class *A*. Surprisingly, class *A* can contain only 128 networks because the first bit of a class *A* address must be zero and the prefix occupies one octet. Thus, only seven bits remain to use for numbering class *A* networks. Figure 18.5 summarizes the maximum number of networks available in each class and the maximum number of hosts per network.

Address Class	Bits In Prefix	Maximum Number of Networks	Bits In Suffix	Maximum Number Of Hosts Per Network
A	7	128	24	16777216
B	14	16384	16	65536
C	21	2097152	8	256

Figure 18.5 The number of networks and hosts per network in each of the three primary IP address classes.

As the figure shows, the number of bits allocated to a prefix or suffix determines how many unique numbers can be assigned. For example, a prefix of *n* bits allows 2^n

unique network numbers, while a suffix of n bits allows 2^n host numbers to be assigned on a given network.

18.10 Authority For Addresses

Throughout an internet, each network prefix must be unique. For networks connected to the global Internet, an organization obtains network numbers from the communication company that supplies Internet connections. Such companies are called *Internet Service Providers (ISPs)*. Internet service providers coordinate with a central organization, the *Internet Assigned Number Authority*, to ensure that each network prefix is unique throughout the entire Internet.

For a private internet, the choice of network prefix can be made by the organization. To ensure that each prefix is unique, a group that builds a private internet must decide how to coordinate network number assignments. Often, a single network administrator assigns prefixes to all networks in the company's internet to ensure that numbers are not duplicated†.

18.11 A Classful Addressing Example

An example will clarify the ideas and explain how addresses are assigned in practice. Consider an organization that chooses to form a private TCP/IP internet which consists of four physical networks. The organization must purchase routers to interconnect the four networks, and then must assign IP addresses. To begin, the organization chooses a unique prefix for each network.

When assigning a network prefix, a number must be chosen from class *A*, *B*, or *C*; the choice depends on the size of the physical network. Usually, networks are assigned class *C* addresses unless a class *B* is needed; class *A* is seldom justified because few networks contain more than 65,536 hosts. For networks connected to the global Internet, a service provider makes the choice. For networks in a private internet, the local network administrator selects the class.

Consider the example of a private internet described above. The network administrator estimates the ultimate size of each physical network, and uses that size to choose a prefix. If the organization expects one small network, two medium networks, and one extremely large network, the administrator might choose to assign a class *C* prefix (e.g., *192.5.48*), two class *B* prefixes (e.g., *128.10* and *128.211*), and a class *A* prefix (e.g., *10*). Figure 18.6 illustrates an internet with four physical networks that have been assigned these prefixes, and shows examples of IP addresses assigned to hosts.

As the figure shows, the IP address assigned to a host always begins with the prefix that has been assigned to the host's physical network. Suffixes, which are assigned by the local network administrator, can be arbitrary numbers. In the example, the two hosts attached to the network with prefix *128.10* have been assigned suffixes *1* and *2*.

---

†To help an organization choose addresses, RFC 1597 recommends class A, B, and C addresses that can be used in private internets.

Although many administrators choose to assign suffixes sequentially, IP does not require an administrator to do so. The example assignments in the figure show that suffixes can be arbitrary values such as *37* or *85*.

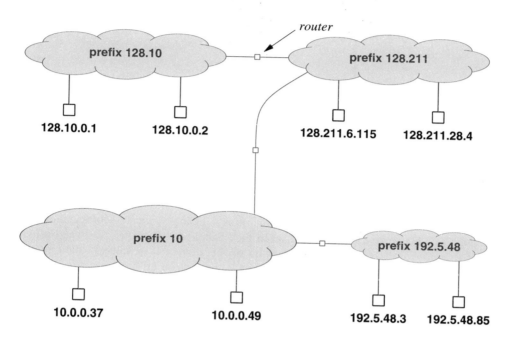

Figure 18.6 An example private internet with IP addresses assigned to hosts. The size of the cloud used to denote a physical network corresponds to the number of hosts expected on the network; the size of a network determines the class of address assigned.

18.12 Subnet And Classless Addressing

As the Internet grew, the original classful addressing scheme became a limitation. On one hand, the IP address space was being exhausted. On the other hand, because all networks had to choose one of three possible sizes, many addresses were unused. Two new mechanisms were invented to overcome the limitations. Known as *subnet addressing* and *classless addressing*, the two are so closely related that they can be considered to be part of a single abstraction. The generalization is straightforward: instead of having three distinct address classes, allow the division between prefix and suffix to occur on an arbitrary bit boundary.

To see why classless addressing helps, consider a network that contains 9 hosts, only four bits of host suffix are needed to represent all possible host values. However, a class C address, which has the fewest hosts possible, devotes eight bits to the host suffix. With classless addressing, it is possible to subdivide a single class C address into sixteen addresses that each have a 28-bit prefix and a 4-bit suffix. Thus, classless addressing allows the creation of sixteen networks that each have up to 14 hosts.

18.13 Address Masks

How can an IP address be divided at an arbitrary boundary? Unlike classful addressing, which uses bits of the address, classless and subnet addressing requires an additional piece of information to be stored with each address. The additional information specifies the exact boundary between the network prefix and the host suffix. Thus, to use classless or subnet addressing, tables inside hosts and routers that contain addresses must keep two pieces of information with each address: the 32-bit address itself and another 32-bit value that specifies the boundary between the network prefix and the suffix. Known as an *address mask* or *subnet mask*†, the second item is also stored as a 32-bit binary value; 1 bits mark the network prefix and zero bits mark the host portion.

Why store the boundary size as a bit mask? Doing so makes computation efficient. In particular, we will see that when they handle an IP packet, hosts and routers need to compare the network prefix portion of the address to a value in their routing tables. The bit-mask representation makes such comparison efficient because it can be performed in two machine instructions. To see how, suppose a router is given a destination address, *D*, and a pair *(A, M)* that represents a 32-bit IP address and a 32-bit address mask. To make a comparison, the router tests the condition:

$$A == (D \ \& \ M)$$

That is, the router uses the mask with a ''logical and'' operation to set the host bits of address *D* to zero, and then compares the result with the network prefix *A*.

As an example, consider the following 32-bit mask:

11111111   11111111   00000000   00000000

which can be denoted in dotted decimal as *255.255.0.0*, and the 32-bit network prefix:

10000000   00001010   00000000   00000000

which has the dotted decimal value *128.10.0.0*. Now consider a 32-bit destination address *128.10.2.3*, which has a binary equivalent of:

10000000   00001010   00000010   00000011

A logical ''and'' between the destination address and the address mask produces the binary result:

10000000   00001010   00000000   00000000

which is indeed equal to the prefix *128.10.0.0*.

---

†The term *subnet mask* still persists because subnet addressing was in use for a decade before the idea was extended to classless addressing.

18.14 CIDR Notation

Inside a computer, each address mask is stored as a 32-bit value. When they enter a prefix and an address mask, however, humans do not use binary representation. Instead, they either use dotted decimal or a new syntactic form that was invented for CIDR addressing. Known as *CIDR notation*, the new form specifies the mask associated with an address by appending a slash and the size of the mask in decimal†. For example, in the original classful scheme, the address 128.10.0.0 consists of a 16-bit network prefix and a 16-bit host suffix. In CIDR notation, the address can be written:

128.10.0.0 / 16

18.15 A CIDR Address Block Example

As an example of how CIDR adds flexibility, consider the difference between a classful and a CIDR world. For the classful case, suppose an ISP begins with a single class B prefix (e.g., *128.211.0.0*). Because classful addressing interprets the prefix as corresponding to a single network, the ISP can only assign the prefix to one customer. That one customer can assign up to 2^{16} host addresses. Thus, the classful interpretation of the address only works if the ISP has a customer with many computers. If the ISP has two customers with only twelve computers each, the classful prefix cannot be used.

Now consider the same situation under CIDR. If it needs to assign the entire prefix to a single organization, the ISP can choose a 16-bit CIDR mask, which is denoted:

128.211.0.0 / 16

That is, by making the CIDR mask correspond exactly to the old classful interpretation, the ISP can choose to follow the classful interpretation and assign the prefix to a single organization. However, if it does have two customers with only twelve computers each, the ISP can use CIDR to partition the address into three pieces: two of them each big enough for one of the customers and the remainder available for future customers. For example, one customer can be assigned:

128.211.0.16 / 28

and the other customer can be assigned:

128.211.0.32 / 28

Although both customers have the same mask size (28 bits), the prefixes differ. Thus, there is no ambiguity — each customer has a unique prefix. More important, the ISP retains most of the original address, which it can allocate to other customers.

---

†Appendix 3 contains a chart of the possible CIDR masks and the equivalent dotted decimal value.

18.16 CIDR Host Addresses

Once an ISP assigns a customer a CIDR prefix, the customer can assign host addresses. For example, suppose an organization is assigned *128.211.0.16/28* as described above. Figure 18.7 illustrates that the organization will have four bits to use as a host address field.

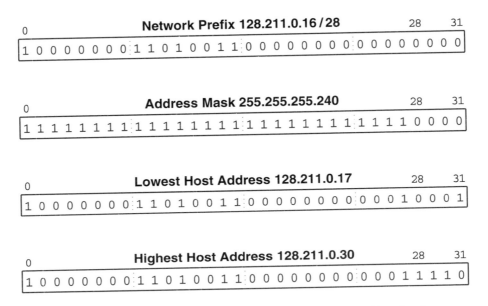

Figure 18.7 Illustration of CIDR addressing for a /28 prefix. Note that because bits are numbered starting at zero, the prefix covers bits 0 through 27. Thus, bits 28 through 31 correspond to the host suffix.

As the figure shows, the CIDR mask */28* corresponds to a dotted decimal value of *255.255.255.240*. Thus, the host suffix consists of four bits, which are labeled *28* through *31* in the figure. We will learn in the next section that the all-zeroes and all-ones host suffixes are reserved. As a result, instead of assigning all possible 4-bit values as host suffixes, the values that can be assigned are limited to decimal values 1 through 14.

Figure 18.7 also illustrates a disadvantage of CIDR and subnet addressing — because the host suffix can start on an arbitrary boundary, values are not easy to read in dotted decimal. For example, when combined with the network prefix, the fourteen possible host suffixes result in dotted decimal values from *128.211.0.17* through *128.211.0.30*.

18.17 Special IP Addresses

In addition to assigning an address to each computer, it is convenient to have addresses that can be used to denote networks or sets of computers. IP defines a set of special address forms that are *reserved*. That is, special addresses are never assigned to hosts. This section describes both the syntax and semantics of each special address form.

18.17.1 Network Address

One of the motivations for defining special address forms can be seen in Figure 18.6 — it is convenient to have an address that can be used to denote the prefix assigned to a given network. IP reserves host address zero, and uses it to denote a *network*. Thus, the address *128.211.0.0/16* denotes a network that has been assigned the prefix *128.211*.

The network address refers to the network itself and not to the host computers attached to that network. Thus, the network address should never appear as the destination address in a packet†.

18.17.2 Directed Broadcast Address

Sometimes, it is convenient to send a copy of a packet to all hosts on a physical network. To make broadcasting easy, IP defines a *directed broadcast address* for each physical network. When a packet is sent to a network's directed broadcast address, a single copy of the packet travels across the internet until it reaches the specified network. The packet is then delivered to all hosts on the network.

The directed broadcast address for a network is formed by adding a suffix that consists of all *1* bits to the network prefix. To ensure that each network can have directed broadcast, IP reserves the host address that contains all *1* bits. An administrator must not assign the all-ones host address to a specific computer or the software may malfunction.

If a network hardware supports broadcast, a directed broadcast will be delivered using the hardware broadcast capability. In such cases, transmission of the packet will reach all computers on the network. When a directed broadcast is sent to a network that does not have hardware support for broadcast, software must send a separate copy of the packet to each host on the network.

18.17.3 Limited Broadcast Address

The term *limited broadcast* refers to a broadcast on a local physical network; informally, we say that the broadcast is limited to a "single wire." Limited broadcast is used during system startup by a computer that does not yet know the network number.

---

†Refer to section 18.19 on Berkeley broadcast for a (nonstandard) exception.

IP reserves the address consisting of all *1* bits to refer to limited broadcast. Thus, IP will broadcast any packet sent to the all-ones address across the local network.

18.17.4 This Computer Address

A computer needs to know its IP address to send or receive internet packets because each packet contains the address of the source and the destination. The TCP/IP protocol suite contains protocols a computer can use to obtain its IP address automatically when the computer boots. Interestingly, the startup protocols use IP to communicate. When using such startup protocols, a computer cannot supply a correct IP source address. To handle such cases, IP reserves the address that consists of all zeroes to mean *this computer*.

18.17.5 Loopback Address

IP defines a *loopback address* used to test network applications. Programmers often use loopback testing for preliminary debugging after a network application has been created. To perform a loopback test, a programmer must have two application programs that are intended to communicate across a network. Each application includes the code needed to interact with TCP/IP protocol software. Instead of executing each program on a separate computer, the programmer runs both programs on a single computer and instructs them to use a loopback IP address when communicating. When one application sends data to another, data travels down the protocol stack to the IP software, which forwards it back up through the protocol stack to the second program. Thus, the programmer can test the program logic quickly without needing two computers and without sending packets across a network.

IP reserves the network prefix *127/8* for use with loopback. The host address used with *127* is irrelevant — all host addresses are treated the same. By convention, programmers often use host number *1*, making *127.0.0.1* the most popular form of loopback.

During loopback testing no packets ever leave a computer — the IP software forwards packets from one application program to another. Consequently, the loopback address never appears in a packet traveling across a network.

18.18 Summary Of Special IP Addresses

The table in Figure 18.8 summarizes the special IP address forms.

Prefix	Suffix	Type Of Address	Purpose
all-0s	all-0s	this computer	used during bootstrap
network	all-0s	network	identifies a network
network	all-1s	directed broadcast	broadcast on specified net
all-1s	all-1s	limited broadcast	broadcast on local net
127	any	loopback	testing

Figure 18.8 Summary of the special IP address forms.

We said that special addresses are reserved and should never be assigned to host computers. Furthermore, each special address is restricted to certain uses. For example, a broadcast address must never appear as a source address, and the all-*0s* address must not be used after a host completes the startup procedure and has obtained an IP address.

18.19 The Berkeley Broadcast Address Form

The University of California at Berkeley developed and distributed an early implementation of TCP/IP protocols as part of BSD UNIX†. The BSD implementation contained a nonstandard feature that has affected many subsequent implementations. Instead of using a host suffix of all ones to represent a directed broadcast address, the Berkeley implementation used a host suffix that contained all zeroes. The address form is known informally as *Berkeley broadcast*.

Unfortunately, many computer manufacturers derived their early TCP/IP software from the Berkeley implementation, and a few sites still use Berkeley broadcast. Some TCP/IP implementations include a configuration parameter that can select between the TCP/IP standard and the Berkeley form; many implementations are built to accept both standard and Berkeley broadcast address forms.

18.20 Routers And The IP Addressing Principle

In addition to assigning an internet address to each host, the Internet Protocol specifies that routers should be assigned IP addresses as well. In fact, each router is assigned two or more IP addresses. To understand why, recall two facts:

- A router has connections to multiple physical networks.

- Each IP address contains a prefix that specifies a physical network.

Thus, a single IP address does not suffice for a router because each router connects to multiple networks. The IP scheme can be explained by a fundamental principle:

---

†BSD stands for the *Berkeley Software Distribution*.

An IP address does not identify a specific computer. Instead, each IP address identifies a connection between a computer and a network. A computer with multiple network connections (e.g., a router) must be assigned one IP address for each connection.

Figure 18.9 illustrates the idea with an example that shows IP addresses assigned to two routers that connect three networks.

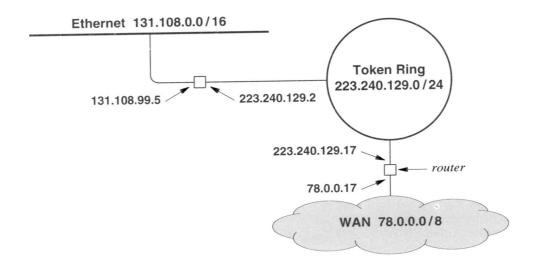

Figure 18.9 An example of IP addresses assigned to two routers. Each interface is assigned an address that contains the prefix of the network to which the interface connects.

IP does not require that the same suffix be assigned to all interfaces of a router. In the figure, for example, the router connecting the Ethernet and Token Ring has suffixes *99.5* (connection to the Ethernet) and *2* (connection to the Token Ring). However, IP does not prevent using the same suffix for all connections. Thus, the example shows that the administrator has chosen to use the same suffix, *17*, for both interfaces of the router that connects the Token Ring network to the WAN. As a practical matter, using the same suffix can help humans who manage the internet because a single number is easier to remember.

18.21 Multi-Homed Hosts

Can a host have multiple network connections? Yes. A host computer that connects to multiple networks is called *multi-homed*. Multi-homing is sometimes used to increase reliability — if one network fails, the host can still reach the internet through the second connection. Alternatively, multi-homing is used to increase performance — connections to multiple networks can make it possible to send traffic directly and avoid routers, which are sometimes congested. Like a router, a multi-homed host has multiple protocol addresses, one for each network connection.

18.22 Summary

To give the appearance of a large, seamless network, an internet uses a uniform addressing scheme. Each computer is assigned a protocol address; users, application programs, and most protocols use the protocol address when communicating.

In TCP/IP, the Internet Protocol specifies addressing. IP divides each internet address into a two-level hierarchy: the prefix of an address identifies the network to which the computer attaches, and the suffix identifies a specific computer on the network. To ensure that addresses remain unique throughout a given internet, a central authority must assign network prefixes. Once a prefix has been assigned, a local network administrator can assign each host on the network a unique suffix.

An IP address is a 32 bit number. Originally, an address was placed in one of five classes, where the class of an address can be determined by the values of the first four bits. A physical network that contains between *257* and *65,536* hosts was assigned a class *B* prefix; smaller networks were assigned a class *C* prefix, and larger networks were each assigned a class *A* prefix.

In addition to the three primary classes used for host addresses, IP defined a class for multicast addressing and a set of reserved addresses that have special meaning. Special addresses can be used to specify loopback (used for testing), the address of a network, broadcast on the local physical network, and broadcast on a remote network.

The original IP address scheme was extended to allow the division between prefix and suffix to occur on an arbitrary bit boundary. To do so, subnet and classless addressing (CIDR) stores a 32-bit mask along with each address. The mask has value *1* for each bit in the prefix, and value *0* for each bit in the suffix.

Although it is convenient to think of an IP address as specifying a computer, each IP address identifies a connection between a computer and a network. Routers and multi-homed hosts, which have connections to multiple physical networks, must have multiple IP addresses.

EXERCISES

18.1 Sketch the TCP/IP internet at your organization and label each network with its IP prefix.

18.2 Extend the diagram in the previous exercise to show the addresses of routers that connect networks.

18.3 Could IP be redesigned to use hardware addresses instead of the 32-bit addresses it currently uses? Why or why not?

18.4 Could IP be redesigned to eliminate address classes completely if each address occupied *64* bits instead of *32* bits? Explain.

18.5 Write a computer program that can translate between 32-bit numbers and dotted decimal form.

18.6 Write a computer program that reads an IP address in dotted decimal form, determines whether the address is class *A*, *B*, or *C*, and prints the network and host portions.

18.7 Extend the program in the previous exercise to handle class *D* and *E* addresses.

18.8 Extend the program in the previous two exercises to recognize and identify special IP addresses such as the limited broadcast address, a directed broadcast address, and so on.

18.9 Write a computer program that translates between CIDR slash notation and an equivalent dotted decimal value.

18.10 Read more about the subnet addressing scheme used with IP. What does subnetting allow that conventional addressing does not?

18.11 What is the chief advantage of CIDR over the original classful addressing scheme? What is the chief advantage of classful addressing over CIDR?

18.12 Instead of assigning one address per network connection, some protocols assign each computer a single address. What is the chief advantage of having a single address for a router? What is the chief disadvantage?

18.13 Devise an internet addressing scheme that divides each address into two parts: a prefix that identifies a router and a suffix that identifies a host associated with that router. Assume that the first part of the address is used to route a packet to the correct router, which then uses the second part to deliver the packet to the destination host. What extra step is required in your design when a computer sends a packet to another computer on the same network?

18.14 Write a computer program that reads an address in CIDR slash notation and determines whether the specified mask is shorter, longer, or exactly the same as the classful interpretation of the address (i.e., whether the address is a CIDR address, a subnet address, or a classful address).

18.15 Write a computer program that reads an address in CIDR notation and prints the resulting address and mask in binary.

Chapter Contents

19

Binding Protocol Addresses (ARP)

19.1 Introduction

The previous chapter describes the IP addressing scheme used to assign high-level protocol addresses to hosts and routers. IP addresses are virtual because they are maintained by software. Neither local nor wide area network hardware understands the relationship between an IP address prefix and a network or the relationship between an IP address suffix and a particular computer. More important, a frame transmitted across a physical network must contain the hardware address† of the destination. Thus, before protocol software can send a packet across a physical network, the software must translate the IP address of the destination computer into an equivalent hardware address.

This chapter describes three general mechanisms that are used to perform address mapping, and uses IP address translation to illustrate each method. The first mechanism, used primarily with WAN hardware, relies on a table that contains address translation information. The second mechanism uses a mathematical function to perform the translation. The third mechanism is the most interesting because it uses a distributed computation in which two computers exchange messages across a network.

---

†Recall that *hardware address* is a synonym for *physical address*.

19.2 Protocol Addresses And Packet Delivery

When an application program generates data to be sent across an internet, software places the data in a packet, which contains the protocol address of the destination. Software in each host or router uses the protocol destination address to select a next hop for the packet. Once a next hop has been selected, software transfers the packet across one physical network to the selected host or router.

To provide the illusion of a single, large network, software works with IP addresses when forwarding packets. Both the next-hop address and the packet's destination address are IP addresses. Unfortunately, protocol addresses cannot be used when transmitting frames across physical network hardware because the hardware does not understand IP addressing. Instead, a frame sent across a given physical network must use the hardware's frame format, and all addresses in the frame must be hardware addresses. Consequently, the protocol address of a next hop must be translated to an equivalent hardware address before a frame can be sent.

To summarize:

> *Protocol addresses are abstractions provided by software; physical network hardware does not know how to locate a computer from its protocol address. The protocol address of the next hop must be translated to an equivalent hardware address before a packet can be sent.*

19.3 Address Resolution

Translation from a computer's protocol address to an equivalent hardware address is known as *address resolution*, and a protocol address is said to be *resolved* to the correct hardware address. Address resolution is local to a network. One computer can resolve the address of another computer only if both computers attach to the same physical network — a computer never resolves the address of a computer on a remote network. For example, consider the simple internet that Figure 19.1 illustrates.

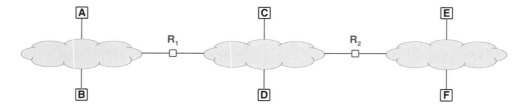

Figure 19.1 A simple internet with routers R_1 and R_2 connecting three physical networks; each network has two host computers attached. A computer can only resolve the address of a computer attached to the same physical network.

In the figure, hosts *A* and *B* attach to the same physical network. If an application on host *A* sends data to an application on host *B*, the application uses *B*'s IP address as the destination. Protocol software on *A* resolves *B*'s IP address to *B*'s hardware address, and uses the hardware address to send the frame directly.

We said the address resolution is always restricted to a single network. In the figure, if an application on host *A* sends a message to an application on host *F*, which lies on a remote network, software on host *A* does not resolve *F*'s address. Instead, the software on *A* first determines that the packet must travel through router R_1. The software on *A* then resolves the address of R_1, and sends the packet to the router. Software on R_1 determines that the packet must reach R_2, resolves the address of R_2, and sends the packet. Finally, R_2 receives the packet, determines that destination *F* is attached to the rightmost physical network, resolves the address of *F*, and delivers the packet. As the example demonstrates, each computer that handles a packet resolves a next-hop address before sending.

To summarize:

> *Mapping between a protocol address and a hardware address is called* address resolution. *A host or router uses address resolution when it needs to send a packet to another computer on the same physical network. A computer never resolves the address of a computer that attaches to a remote network.*

19.4 Address Resolution Techniques

What algorithm does software use to translate a protocol address into a hardware address? The answer depends on the protocol and hardware addressing schemes. For example, the method used to resolve an IP address to an Ethernet address differs from the method used to resolve an IP address to an ATM address because the Ethernet addressing scheme differs from the ATM addressing scheme. More important, because a router or multi-homed host can connect to multiple types of physical networks, such a computer may use more than one type of address resolution. Thus, a computer that attaches to multiple networks may need more than one address translation module.

Address resolution algorithms can be grouped into three basic categories:

- *Table lookup.* Bindings or mappings are stored in a table in memory, which the software searches when it needs to resolve an address.

- *Closed-form computation.* The protocol address assigned to a computer is chosen carefully so the computer's hardware address can be computed from the protocol address using basic Boolean and arithmetic operations.

- *Message exchange.* Computers exchange messages across a network to resolve an address. One computer sends a message that requests an address binding (i.e., translation), and another computer sends a reply that contains the requested information.

The next sections explain the three basic methods and describe the type of hardware with which the method is used.

19.5 Address Resolution With Table Lookup

The table lookup approach to address resolution requires a data structure that contains information about address bindings. The table consists of an array. Each entry in the array contains a pair (P,H), where P is a protocol address and H is the equivalent hardware address. Figure 19.2 shows an example address binding table for the Internet Protocol:

IP Address	Hardware Address
197.15.3.2	0A:07:4B:12:82:36
197.15.3.3	0A:9C:28:71:32:8D
197.15.3.4	0A:11:C3:68:01:99
197.15.3.5	0A:74:59:32:CC:1F
197.15.3.6	0A:04:BC:00:03:28
197.15.3.7	0A:77:81:0E:52:FA

Figure 19.2 An example address binding table. Each entry in the table contains a protocol address and the equivalent hardware address.

In the figure, each entry corresponds to one station on the network. The entry contains two fields that specify the station's IP and hardware addresses.

A separate address binding table is used for each physical network. Consequently, all IP addresses in a given table have the same prefix. For example, the address binding table in Figure 19.2 corresponds to a network with prefix *197.15.3.0/24*. Therefore, each IP address in the table will begin with the 24-bit prefix *197.15.3*. Implementations can save space by omitting the prefix from table entries.

The chief advantage of the table lookup approach is generality — a table can store the address bindings for an arbitrary set of computers on a given network. In particular, a protocol address can map to an arbitrary hardware address. Furthermore, the table lookup algorithm for address resolution is straightforward and among the easiest to program. Given a next-hop IP address, N, the software searches the table until it finds an entry where the IP address matches N. The software then extracts the hardware address from the entry.

For a network that contains less than a dozen hosts, a sequential search can suffice — the resolution software begins at the first entry and searches each entry in sequence until a match is found. For large networks, however, a sequential search requires excessive CPU time. In such cases, software can use one of two standard implementations to improve computational efficiency: hashing or direct indexing.

Hashing is a general purpose data structure technique that is well-known to most programmers. Direct indexing is a slightly more efficient, but less general technique. In particular, direct indexing is possible only in cases where protocol addresses are assigned from a compact range†. For example, direct indexing can be used with the IP addresses in Figure 19.2 because the addresses are sequential values that begin with *197.15.3.2*. To use direct indexing with such values, the software maintains a one-dimensional array of hardware addresses, and uses the host suffix from an IP address as an index into the array. Figure 19.3 illustrates the technique.

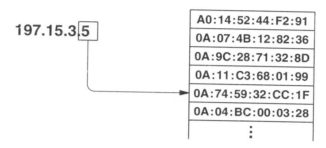

Figure 19.3 An example of direct lookup for a class *C* network. The host portion of an address is used as an array index.

The figure shows how direct mapping is used to translate the IP address *197.15.3.5*. Software extracts the host suffix *5*, and uses it as an index into the array to obtain the hardware address *0A:74:59:32:CC:1F*. In practice, to prevent an illegal IP address from causing a subscript error, the software must check to ensure the suffix is in range.

19.6 Address Resolution With Closed-Form Computation

Recall that although many network technologies use static physical addresses, some technologies use configurable addressing in which a network interface can be assigned a specific hardware address. For such networks, it is possible to choose addresses that make closed-form address resolution possible. A resolver that uses a closed-form method computes a mathematical function that maps an IP address to a hardware address. If the relationship between an IP address and the corresponding hardware address is straightforward, the computation requires only a few arithmetic operations.

To understand why closed-form computation can be especially efficient for a network with configurable addresses, remember that both the hardware and IP addresses can be changed. Thus, values can be chosen to optimize the translation. In fact, the host portion of a computer's IP address can be chosen to be identical to the computer's hardware address, making the translation trivial.

---

†Some administrators choose nonsequential numbers for IP addresses to help identify the purpose of a computer (e.g., hosts are assigned suffixes less than *200*, while routers are assigned suffixes greater than *200*).

As an example, suppose a configurable network has been assigned the network number *220.123.5.0/24*. As computers are added to the network, each computer is assigned an IP address suffix and a matching hardware address. The first host is assigned IP address *220.123.5.1* and hardware address *1*. The second host is assigned IP address *220.123.5.2* and hardware address *2*. The suffixes need not be sequential: if a router attached to the network is assigned IP address *220.123.5.101*, the router is assigned hardware address *101*. Given the IP address of any computer on the network, the computer's hardware address can be computed by a single Boolean *and* operation:

$$\text{hardware\_address} = \text{ip\_address} \ \& \ 0xff$$

It should be obvious from the example why closed-form resolution is often used with configurable networks. The computation is trivial to program, does not require a table of values to be maintained, and is computationally efficient.

To summarize:

> When a computer connects to a network that uses configurable addressing, the local network administrator must choose a hardware address as well as an IP address. The two values can be chosen to make address resolution trivial.

19.7 Address Resolution With Message Exchange

The address resolution mechanisms described above can be computed using a single computer at each step: the instructions and data needed for the computation are kept in the computer's operating system. The alternative to local computation is a distributed approach in which a computer that needs to resolve an address sends a message across a network and receives a reply. The message carries a request that specifies the protocol address, and the reply carries the corresponding hardware address.

Where should an address resolution request be sent? Most protocol systems choose one of two possible designs. In the first design, a network includes one or more servers† that are assigned the task of answering address resolution requests. Whenever address resolution is needed, a message must be sent to one of the servers, which will send a reply. In some protocol suites, each computer is given the address of one or more servers that can be used — the computer sends a message to each of them in sequence until it finds an active server and receives a reply. In other protocol suites, a computer simply broadcasts its request to all servers simultaneously.

In the second design, no special address resolution servers are needed. Instead, each computer on the network participates in address resolution by agreeing to answer resolution requests for its address. When a computer needs to resolve an address, it broadcasts a request on the network. All machines receive the request and examine the requested address. If an incoming request matches a computer's address, the computer responds.

---

†Later chapters describe servers in detail and provide examples. For now, it is sufficient to think of a server as a computer program that is capable of communicating over a network.

The chief advantages of the first scheme arise from centralization. Because a few address resolution servers handle all address resolution tasks on the network, address resolution is easier to configure, manage, and control. The chief advantages of the second scheme arise from distributed computation. Address resolution servers can be expensive. In addition to the expense of additional hardware (e.g., extra memory), servers are expensive to maintain because address binding information stored in servers must be updated whenever new computers are added to the network or hardware addresses change. Furthermore, address resolution servers can become a bottleneck on a large, busy network. Requiring each computer to resolve its own address eliminates servers completely.

The table in Figure 19.4 summarizes features of the three methods.

Feature	Type Of Resolution
Useful with any hardware	T
Address change affects all hosts	T
Protocol address independent of hardware address	T, D
Hardware address must be smaller than protocol address	C
Protocol address determined by hardware address	C
Requires hardware broadcast	D
Adds traffic to a network	D
Produces resolution with minimum delay	T, C
Implementation is more difficult	D

Figure 19.4 Comparison of address resolution using a table lookup (*T*), closed-form computation (*C*), and dynamic message exchange (*D*).

19.8 Address Resolution Protocol

TCP/IP can use any of the three address resolution methods; the method chosen for a particular network depends on the addressing scheme used by the underlying hardware. Table lookup is usually employed to resolve IP addresses across a WAN, closed-form computation is used with configurable networks, and message exchange is used on LAN hardware that has static addressing.

To guarantee that all computers agree on the exact format and meaning of messages used to resolve addresses, the TCP/IP protocol suite includes an *Address Resolution Protocol* (*ARP*). The ARP standard defines two basic message types: a request and a response. A request message contains an IP address and requests the corresponding hardware address; a reply contains both the IP address, sent in the request, and the hardware address.

19.9 ARP Message Delivery

The ARP standard specifies exactly how ARP messages should be sent across a network. In particular, the protocol specifies that an ARP request message should be placed in a hardware frame and broadcast to all computers on the network. Each computer receives the request and examines the IP address. The computer mentioned in the request sends a response; all other computers process and discard the request without sending a response.

When a computer sends an ARP response, the response is not broadcast. Instead, the response is placed in a frame and sent directly back to the computer that issued the request. Figure 19.5 illustrates an ARP exchange by computers on an Ethernet.

The figure shows that although the ARP request message reaches all computers, the reply does not. We will see that the protocol supplies information in the broadcast request, and that all computers receive the information when they process the request.

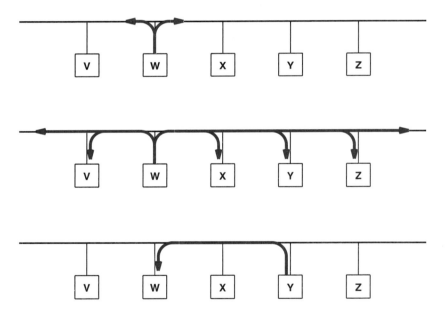

Figure 19.5 An ARP message exchange. (a) computer *W* begins to broadcast an ARP request that contains computer *Y*'s IP address. (b) all computers receive the request, and (c) computer *Y* sends a response directly to *W*.

19.10 ARP Message Format

Although the Address Resolution Protocol contains an exact specification of the ARP message format, the standard does not give a fixed format that must be used for all communication. Instead, the ARP standard describes the general form for ARP messages, and specifies how to determine the details for each type of network hardware. The motivation for adapting ARP messages to the hardware arises because an ARP message contains fields for hardware addresses. The ARP designers realized that they could not choose a fixed size for hardware address fields because new network technologies might be invented that have addresses larger than the size chosen. Consequently, the designers included a fixed-size field at the beginning of an ARP message to specify the size of the hardware addresses being used. For example, when ARP is used with an Ethernet, the hardware address length is set to 6 octets because an Ethernet address is 48 bits long.

To increase the generality of ARP, the designers included an address length field for protocol addresses as well as for hardware addresses. Thus, ARP is not restricted to IP addresses or specific hardware addresses — in theory, the protocol can be used to bind an arbitrary high-level address to an arbitrary hardware address. In practice, the generality of ARP is seldom used: most implementations of ARP are used to bind IP addresses to Ethernet addresses. To summarize:

> *Although the ARP message format is sufficiently general to allow arbitrary protocol and hardware addresses, ARP is almost always used to bind a 32-bit IP address to a 48-bit Ethernet address.*

Figure 19.6 illustrates the format of an ARP message when the protocol is used with IP protocol addresses (4 octets) and Ethernet hardware addresses (6 octets).

0	8	16	24	31
HARDWARE ADDRESS TYPE		PROTOCOL ADDRESS TYPE		
HADDR LEN	PADDR LEN	OPERATION		
SENDER HADDR (first 4 octets)				
SENDER HADDR (last 2 octets)		SENDER PADDR (first 2 octets)		
SENDER PADDR (last 2 octets)		TARGET HADDR (first 2 octets)		
TARGET HADDR (last 4 octets)				
TARGET PADDR (all 4 octets)				

Figure 19.6 The format for an ARP message when used to bind Internet protocol addresses to Ethernet hardware addresses.

Each line of the figure corresponds to 32 bits of an ARP message. The first two 16-bit fields contain values that specify the type of hardware and protocol addresses being used. For example, field *HARDWARE ADDRESS TYPE* contains *1* when ARP is used with Ethernet, and field *PROTOCOL ADDRESS TYPE* contains *0x0800* when ARP is used with IP. The second pair of fields, *HADDR LEN* and *PADDR LEN* specify the number of octets in a hardware address and a protocol address. Field *OPERATION* specifies whether the message is a request (value *1*) or a response (value *2*).

Interestingly, each ARP message contains fields for two address bindings. One binding corresponds to the sender, while the other corresponds to the intended recipient, which ARP calls the *target*. When a request is sent, the sender does not know the target's hardware address (that is the information being requested). Therefore, field *TARGET HADDR* in an ARP request can be filled with zeroes because the contents are not used. In a response, the target binding refers to the initial computer that sent the request. Thus, the target information in a response serves no purpose — it has survived from an early version of the protocol.

19.11 Sending An ARP Message

When one computer sends an ARP message to another, the message travels inside a hardware frame. The ARP message is treated as data being transported — the network hardware does not know about the ARP message format and does not examine the contents of individual fields.

Technically, placing a message inside a frame for transport is called *encapsulation*; ARP is encapsulated directly in a hardware frame. Figure 19.7 illustrates the concept.

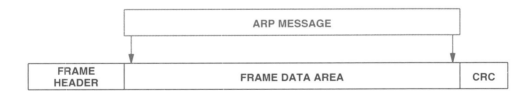

Figure 19.7 Illustration of an ARP message encapsulated in an Ethernet frame. The entire ARP message travels in the data area of the frame; the network hardware neither interprets nor modifies contents of the ARP message.

19.12 Identifying ARP Frames

How does a computer know whether an incoming frame contains an ARP message? The *type field* in the frame header specifies that the frame contains an ARP message. A sender must assign the appropriate value to the type field before transmitting the frame, and a receiver must examine the type field in each incoming frame. For example, the Ethernet standard specifies that the type field in an Ethernet frame carrying an ARP message must contain the hexadecimal value *0x806*. Figure 19.8 illustrates the concept.

Dest. Address	Source Address	Frame Type	Data In Frame
		806	complete ARP message

Figure 19.8 Illustration of the type field in an Ethernet header used to specify the frame contents. A value of *0x806* informs the receiver that the frame contains an ARP message.

Because Ethernet assigns a single type value to ARP, an Ethernet frame that contains an ARP request message will have the same type as an Ethernet frame that carries an ARP response. Thus, the frame type does not distinguish between multiple types of ARP messages — a receiver must examine the *OPERATION* field in the message to determine whether an incoming message is a request or a response.

19.13 Caching ARP Responses

Although message exchange can be used to bind addresses, sending a request for each binding is hopelessly inefficient. To see why, consider the network traffic ARP generates. When computer *W* has a packet to deliver to computer *Y*, *W* first broadcasts an ARP request to find *Y*'s hardware address. After *Y* sends a reply, *W* can deliver the original packet to *Y*. Thus, three packets traverse the network for each ARP transmission. More important, because most computer communication involves a sequence of packets, *W* is likely to repeat the exchange many times.

To reduce network traffic, ARP software extracts and saves the information from a response so it can be used for subsequent packets. The software does not place the information in permanent storage, nor does it attempt to save the bindings forever. Instead, ARP maintains a small table of bindings in memory. ARP manages the table as a *cache* — an entry is replaced whenever a response arrives, and the oldest entry is removed whenever the table runs out of space or after an entry has not been updated for a long period of time (e.g., 20 minutes).

Whenever ARP performs address binding, it searches the cache before using the network. If the binding is present, ARP uses the binding without transmitting a request. If the binding is not present in the cache, ARP broadcasts a request, waits for a response, updates the cache, and then proceeds to use the binding. The next section describes the algorithm in more detail.

19.14 Processing An Incoming ARP Message

When an ARP message arrives, the protocol specifies that the receiver must perform two basic steps. In the first step, the receiver extracts the sender's address binding and checks to see if the sender's address is present in the cache. If so, the receiver uses the binding in the incoming ARP message to replace the previously stored binding. Updating a stored binding is an optimization that is especially useful in cases where the sender's hardware address has changed. In the second step, the receiver examines the *OPERATION* field of the message to determine whether the message is a request or a response. If the message is a response, the receiver must have previously issued a request, and is waiting for the binding. If the message is a request, the receiver compares field *TARGET PADDR* with the local protocol address. If the two are identical, the computer is the target of the request, and must send an ARP response. To form the response, the computer begins with the incoming message, reverses the sender's and target's bindings, inserts its hardware address in field *SENDER HADDR*, and changes the *OPERATION* field to *2*.

ARP contains a further optimization: after a computer replies to an ARP request, the computer extracts the sender's address binding from the request and adds the binding to its cache for later use. To understand the optimization, it is necessary to know two facts:

- Most computer communication involves two-way traffic — if a message travels from one computer to another, probability is high that a reply will travel back.

- Because each address binding requires memory, a computer cannot store an arbitrary number of address bindings.

The first fact explains why extracting the sender's address binding optimizes ARP performance. To understand the optimization, recall that a computer only sends an ARP request for a given target when it has a packet to deliver to that target. Thus, when computer W sends an ARP request for computer Y, W must have a message to deliver to Y. It is likely that once the packet has been delivered, a packet will be sent back from Y to W. If Y does not have an address binding for W, Y will need to broadcast an ARP request (and W will need to reply). Arranging for Y to extract W's binding from the incoming ARP request eliminates the need for a later ARP request from Y to W.

The second fact explains why the optimization is only performed by the computer that is the target of an ARP request. Because all computers on the net receive each ARP broadcast, it would be possible for all computers to extract the sender's binding and store it locally. However, doing so wastes CPU time and memory because it is unlikely that all pairs of computers will need to communicate. Thus, ARP has been optimized so it prerecords only those address bindings that are likely to be needed.

19.15 Layering, Address Resolution, Protocol Addresses

Recall that the lowest layer of the TCP/IP layering model corresponds to the physical network hardware, and the next layer corresponds to the network interface software used to transmit and receive packets. Address resolution is an example of a function associated with the network interface layer. Address resolution software hides the details of physical addressing, allowing software in higher layers to use protocol addressing. Thus, there is an important conceptual boundary imposed between the network interface layer and all higher layers: applications as well as higher-layers of protocol software are built to use protocol addresses only.

The next chapters will explain the advantages of using protocol addresses for functions such as routing. For now, it is sufficient to understand where the details of physical addressing are hidden. Figure 19.9 illustrates the addressing boundary.

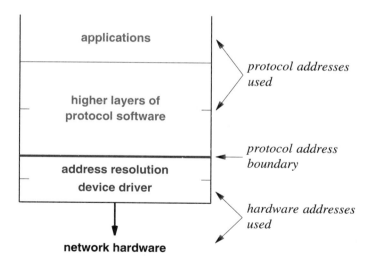

Figure 19.9 Layered protocol software in a computer and the conceptual boundary between the network interface layer and higher layers. Software above the boundary uses protocol addresses; software below the boundary translates each protocol address to an equivalent hardware address.

19.16 Summary

To provide the illusion of a single, seamless internet, each computer is assigned a high-level protocol address. Because network hardware does not understand protocol addresses, a network cannot locate a computer from its protocol address. Instead, software must translate the protocol address to an equivalent hardware address before sending a packet; the translation is called *address resolution*.

Three general methods are used for address resolution; the method used depends on the underlying hardware. Table lookup is most often used with wide area networks, closed form computation is used with configurable networks, and message exchange is used with LANs that have static addressing.

The TCP/IP suite contains a standard Address Resolution Protocol (ARP). ARP defines the format of messages that computers exchange as well as the rules for handling ARP messages. The standard specifies that a computer should broadcast an ARP request message, but that a response should be directed. Although the ARP message format is sufficiently general to be used with arbitrary protocol and hardware addresses, the protocol is used most often to resolve an IP address into an Ethernet address.

EXERCISES

19.1 Which type or types of address resolution do computers at your site use?

19.2 Can dynamic address resolution be used on a point-to-point network? on a token ring network? on a network that does not provide broadcast? Why or why not?

19.3 How does a computer know whether an arriving frame contains an IP datagram or an ARP message?

19.4 How many responses does a computer expect to receive when it broadcasts an ARP request? Why?

19.5 Suppose a computer receives two ARP replies for a single request. The first reply claims that the hardware address is H_1, and the second reply claims that the hardware address is H_2. How does ARP software handle the replies?

19.6 How can a computer use ARP to break security? Hint: think about the previous exercise.

19.7 ARP only permits address resolution to occur on a single network. Could ARP send a request to a remote server in an IP datagram? Why or why not?

Chapter Contents

20

IP Datagrams And Datagram Forwarding

20.1 Introduction

Previous chapters describe the architecture of an internet, Internet addressing, and address resolution software used to bind Internet addresses to hardware addresses. This chapter discusses the fundamental communication service in an internet. It describes the format of packets that are sent across an internet, and discusses how routers process and forward such packets. Later chapters extend the discussion by considering how routers use the underlying hardware to transmit packets.

20.2 Connectionless Service

The goal of internetworking is to provide a packet communication system that allows a program running on one computer to send data to a program running on another computer. In a well-designed internet, application programs remain unaware of the underlying physical networks — they can send and receive data without knowing the details of the local network to which a computer connects, the remote network to which the destination connects, or the interconnection between the two.

Designers must decide what communication services an internet protocol will offer and how to deliver those services efficiently. In particular, designers must decide whether to offer programs a *connection-oriented* service, a *connectionless* service, or both.

TCP/IP designers chose to include protocols for both connectionless and connection-oriented services. They chose to make the fundamental delivery service connectionless, and to add a reliable connection-oriented service that uses the underlying connectionless service. The design was successful, and is often emulated by other protocols.

20.3 Virtual Packets

Connectionless internet service is an extension of packet-switching — the service allows a sender to transmit individual packets of data across an internet. Each packet travels independently, and contains information that identifies the intended recipient.

How does a packet pass across an internet? In general, the answer is that a router forwards each packet from one network to another. A source host creates a packet, places the destination address in the packet header, and then sends the packet to a nearby router. When a router receives a packet, the router uses the destination address to select the next router on the path to the destination, and then transmits the packet. Eventually, the packet reaches a router that can deliver the packet to its final destination.

What format is used for an internet packet? Unfortunately, conventional hardware frame formats cannot be used for internet packets. To understand why, recall that a router can connect heterogeneous networks. The router cannot transfer a copy of a frame from one type of network to another because the frame formats differ. More important, the router cannot simply reformat the frame header because the two networks may use incompatible address formats (e.g., the addresses in an incoming frame may make no sense on another network).

To overcome heterogeneity, internet protocol software defines an internet packet format that is independent of the underlying hardware. The result is a *universal, virtual* packet that can be transferred across the underlying hardware intact†. As the term *virtual* implies, protocol software creates and handles internet packets — the underlying hardware does not understand or recognize the internet packet format. As the term *universal* implies, each host or router in an internet contains protocol software that understands internet packets. We can summarize:

> *Because it can connect heterogeneous networks, a router cannot transmit a copy of a frame that arrives on one network across another. To accommodate heterogeneity, an internet must define a hardware-independent packet format.*

---

†The next chapter describes in detail how an internet packet travels across a physical network.

20.4 The IP Datagram

TCP/IP protocols use the name *IP datagram* to refer to an internet packet. Surprisingly, an IP datagram has the same general format as a hardware frame: the datagram begins with a header followed by a data area. Figure 20.1 illustrates the datagram format.

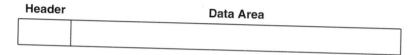

Figure 20.1 The general form of an IP datagram with a header followed by data. The header contains information that controls where and how the datagram is to be sent.

The amount of data carried in a datagram is not fixed. The sender chooses an amount of data that is appropriate to a particular purpose†. For example, an application that transmits keystrokes across a network can place each keystroke in a separate datagram, while an application that transfers large files can send large datagrams. The point is:

> *The size of a datagram is determined by the application that sends data. Allowing the size of datagrams to vary makes IP adaptable to a variety of applications.*

In the current version of IP (version 4), a datagram can contain as little as a single octet of data or at most 64K octets, including the header. In most datagrams, the header is much smaller than the data area. To understand why, it is necessary to examine the cost of transmitting data. Like a frame header used with a physical network, a datagram header represents overhead — while it is occupied transferring header octets, a network cannot transfer a user's data. Because the size of the datagram header is fixed, sending large datagrams results in more data octets transmitted per unit of time (i.e., higher throughput).

Similar to a frame header, a datagram header contains information to route the datagram across the internet. For example, the header contains the address of the computer that sent the datagram as well as the address of the computer to which the datagram is destined. The addresses that appear in a datagram header differ from the addresses used in a frame header — a datagram contains IP addresses, while a frame contains hardware addresses.

---

†In extreme cases, a datagram may carry no data.

To summarize:

> *A packet sent across a TCP/IP internet is called an IP datagram.*
> *Each datagram consists of a header followed by data. Source and*
> *destination addresses in the datagram header are IP addresses.*

20.5 Forwarding An IP Datagram

We said that datagrams traverse an internet by following a path from their initial source through routers to the final destination. Each router along the path receives the datagram, extracts the destination address from the header, and uses the destination address to determine a next hop to which the datagram should be sent. The router then forwards the datagram to the next hop, either the final destination or another router.

To make the selection of a next hop efficient and to make it possible for humans to understand the computation, each IP router keeps information in a *routing table*. A routing table must be initialized when the router boots, and must be updated if the topology changes or hardware fails.

Conceptually, the routing table contains a set of entries that each specify a destination and the next hop used to reach that destination. Figure 20.2 shows the contents of a routing table in one of three routers that are used to interconnect four networks in a small internet.

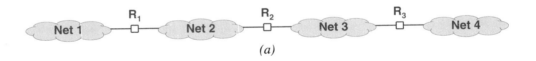

(a)

Destination	Next Hop
net 1	R_1
net 2	deliver direct
net 3	deliver direct
net 4	R_3

(b)

Figure 20.2 (a) An example internet with three routers connecting four physical networks, and (b) the conceptual routing table found in router R_2. Each entry in the table lists a destination network and the next hop along a route to that network.

As the figure shows, router R_2 connects directly to the networks labeled *Net 2* and *Net 3*. Therefore, R_2 can deliver a datagram to any destination attached to those networks. When a datagram is destined for network *4*, R_2 sends the datagram to router R_3.

Each destination listed in a routing table is a network, not an individual host. The distinction is important because an internet can contain over *1000* times as many hosts as networks. Thus, using networks as destinations keeps routing tables small. To summarize:

> *Because each destination in a routing table corresponds to a network, the number of entries in a routing table is proportional to the number of networks in an internet.*

20.6 IP Addresses And Routing Table Entries

In practice, an IP routing table is slightly more complex than Figure 20.2 illustrates. First, the *Destination* field in each entry contains the network prefix of the destination network. Second, an additional field in each entry contains an *address mask* that specifies which bits of the destination correspond to the network prefix. Third, an IP address is used when the *Next Hop* field denotes a router. Figure 20.3 illustrates how the routing table from Figure 20.2 might appear†.

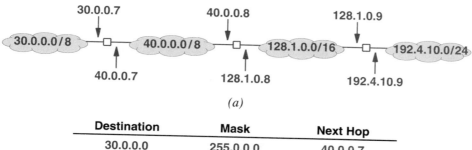

(a)

Destination	Mask	Next Hop
30.0.0.0	255.0.0.0	40.0.0.7
40.0.0.0	255.0.0.0	deliver direct
128.1.0.0	255.255.0.0	deliver direct
192.4.10.0	255.255.255.0	128.1.0.9

(b)

Figure 20.3 (a) An internet of four networks and three routers with an IP address assigned to each router interface, and (b) the routing table found in the center router. Each entry in the table lists a destination, a mask, and the next hop used to reach the destination.

---

†In practice, most internets connect more than four networks, and a typical routing table contains a *default route* (i.e., a single entry that corresponds to all destinations not explicitly mentioned).

The first two networks in Figure 20.3 each have a class *A* prefix, the third network has a class *B* prefix, and the fourth network has a class *C* prefix. Each router has been assigned two IP addresses, one for each interface. For example, the router that connects net *30.0.0.0/8* to net *40.0.0.0/8* has been assigned addresses *30.0.0.7* and *40.0.0.7*. Although the same host suffix has been assigned to both interfaces on the router, IP does not require uniformity — a network administrator is free to assign different values to each interface.

20.7 The Mask Field And Datagram Forwarding

The process of using a routing table to select a next hop for a given datagram is called *routing* or *forwarding*. Recall from Chapter 18 that the *Mask* field in a routing table entry is used to extract the network part of an address during lookup. To understand the mask, imagine that the routing software is given a datagram to forward. Also assume that the datagram contains a destination IP address *D*. The routing software must find an entry in the routing table that specifies a next hop for *D*. To do so, the software examines each entry in the table by using the mask in the entry to extract a prefix of address *D* and comparing the result to the *Destination* field of the entry. If the two are equal, the datagram will be forwarded to the *Next Hop* in the entry.

A bit mask representation makes extraction efficient — software computes the Boolean *and* of the mask and the datagram destination address, *D*. Thus, the computation to examine the ith entry in the table can be expressed as:

if ((Mask[i] & D) == Destination[i]) forward to NextHop[i];

As an example, consider a datagram destined for address *192.4.10.3*, and assume the datagram arrives at a router that contains the routing table Figure 20.3 illustrates. Further assume software searches entries of the table in order. The first entry fails because *255.0.0.0 & 192.4.10.3* is not equal to *30.0.0.0*. After rejecting the second and third entries in the table, the routing software eventually chooses next hop *128.1.0.9* because

255.255.255.0 & 192.4.10.3 == 192.4.10.0

20.8 Destination And Next-Hop Addresses

What is the relationship between the destination address in a datagram header and the address of the next hop to which the datagram is forwarded? The *DESTINATION IP ADDRESS* field in a datagram contains the address of the ultimate destination. When a router receives a datagram, the router extracts the destination address, *D*, and uses it to compute the address of the next router to which the datagram should be sent, *N*. Although the datagram is sent directly to address *N*, the header in the datagram retains destination address *D*. In other words:

The destination address in a datagram header always refers to the ultimate destination. When a router forwards the datagram to another router, the address of the next hop does not appear in the datagram header.

All routes are computed using IP addresses. After computing the address of a next hop, N, IP software uses the address binding described in Chapter 19 to translate N to an equivalent hardware address for transmission. In the next chapter, we will learn how the datagram is sent across a physical network.

20.9 Best-Effort Delivery

In addition to defining the format of internet datagrams, the Internet Protocol defines the semantics of communication, and uses the term *best-effort* to describe the service it offers. In essence, the standard specifies that although IP makes a best-effort attempt to deliver each datagram, IP does not guarantee that it will handle the problems of:

- Datagram duplication
- Delayed or out-of-order delivery
- Corruption of data
- Datagram loss

Additional layers of protocol software are needed to handle each of these errors.

It may seem strange for IP to specify that these errors can occur. However, there is an important reason: each layer of protocol software is responsible for certain aspects of communication, and IP does not handle these problems. Furthermore, because underlying physical networks can cause such problems, any software that uses IP must take responsibility for solving them.

To summarize:

Because IP is designed to operate over all types of network hardware, the underlying hardware may misbehave. As a result, IP datagrams may be lost, duplicated, delayed, delivered out of order, or delivered with corrupted data. Higher layers of protocol software are required to handle each of these errors.

20.10 The IP Datagram Header Format

Figure 20.4 shows the fields of an IP datagram header, including the *SOURCE IP ADDRESS*, which contains the Internet address of the sender, the *DESTINATION IP ADDRESS*, which contains the Internet address of the intended recipient, and the *TYPE* field, which specifies the type of the data.

0	4	8		16	19	24		31
VERS	H. LEN	SERVICE TYPE		TOTAL LENGTH				
IDENTIFICATION			FLAGS		FRAGMENT OFFSET			
TIME TO LIVE		TYPE		HEADER CHECKSUM				
SOURCE IP ADDRESS								
DESTINATION IP ADDRESS								
IP OPTIONS (MAY BE OMITTED)						PADDING		
BEGINNING OF DATA								

Figure 20.4 Fields in the IP datagram header. Both the source and destination addresses are Internet addresses.

Each field in an IP datagram header has a fixed size. The datagram begins with a 4-bit protocol version number (the current version is *4*) and a 4-bit header length that specifies the number of 32-bit quantities in the header. The *SERVICE TYPE* field contains a value that specifies whether the sender prefers the datagram to travel over a route with minimal delay or a route with maximal throughput; a router that knows multiple routes to the destination can use the value to choose a route. The *TOTAL LENGTH* field contains a 16-bit integer that specifies the total number of octets in the datagram, including both the header and the data. Chapter 21 explains the *IDENTIFICATION*, *FLAGS*, and *FRAGMENT OFFSET* fields.

The *TIME TO LIVE* field is used to prevent a datagram from traveling forever around a path that contains a loop; such paths can arise when software malfunctions or when a manager misconfigures routes. The sender initializes the *TIME TO LIVE* field to a positive integer between *1* and *255*. Each router that handles the datagram decrements *TIME TO LIVE* by *1*. If the counter reaches zero, the datagram is discarded and an error message is sent back to the source.

The *HEADER CHECKSUM* field ensures that bits of the header are not changed in transit. A sender computes the 1's-complement sum of all 16-bit quantities in the header excluding the checksum field itself, and then stores the 1's-complement of the sum in the *HEADER CHECKSUM* field. A receiver computes the same 16-bit sum of values in the header, including the checksum field. If the checksum is correct, the result is zero†.

---

†Mathematically, the 1's-complement is an additive inverse. Thus, adding a value to its complement produces zero.

To keep the headers of most datagrams small, IP defines a set of *options* that can be present, if needed. When an IP datagram does not carry options, the header length field (labeled *H. LEN*) contains 5, and the header ends after the *DESTINATION IP AD-DRESS* field. Because the header length is specified in 32-bit multiples, if options do not end on a 32-bit boundary, *PADDING* that contains zero bits is added to make the header a multiple of 32 bits.

20.11 Summary

The Internet protocol defines an IP datagram to be the basic unit of transfer across a TCP/IP internet. Each datagram resembles a hardware frame because the datagram contains a header followed by a data area. Like a hardware frame, the header contains information used to transfer the datagram to a specific destination. Unlike a hardware frame, a datagram header contains IP addresses.

IP software in routers uses a table of routes to determine the next hop to which the datagram should be sent. Each entry in a routing table corresponds to one destination network, making the size of a routing table proportional to the number of networks in an internet. When selecting a route, IP compares the network prefix of a destination address to each entry in the table.

Although IP selects a next hop to which a datagram must be sent, the address of the next hop does not appear in the datagram header. Instead, the header always specifies the address of the ultimate destination.

EXERCISES

20.1   What is the chief advantage of using virtual packets instead of frames?

20.2   Write a computer program that takes as input an IP routing table as in Figure 20.3b, and a sequence of destination addresses. For each destination address, search the table sequentially to find the correct next hop, and output the results.

20.3   Revise the program in the previous exercise to use a search tree instead of sequential search, and compare the speed of the two programs.

20.4   Write a computer program to extract the source and destination addresses from an IP datagram and print them in dotted decimal notation.

20.5   Write a computer program to compute a header checksum. Use the program to check headers on datagrams captured from a network. How often does the checksum fail?

20.6   Write a program to extract all fields from an IP datagram header. Print the values in hexadecimal or dotted decimal as appropriate.

20.7   If a datagram contains one 8-bit option and one 8-bit data value, what values will be found in header fields *H. LEN* and *TOTAL LENGTH*?

20.8   Assume two routers are misconfigured to form a routing loop for some destination, *D*. Explain why a datagram destined for *D* will not go around the loop forever.

20.9   A set of RFC documents describe exactly how to encapsulate an IP datagram in the frames of various hardware technologies. Examine the RFC documents found on the CD-ROM that accompanies this text. Which RFC defines Ethernet encapsulation?

20.10   Regarding the previous exercise, read RFCs 1149 and 1217. Are they serious network standards? (Hint: consider the date.)

Chapter Contents

21

IP Encapsulation, Fragmentation, And Reassembly

21.1 Introduction

The previous chapter describes the IP datagram format and discusses how information in a routing table is used to select the next hop at each step along a path to the datagram's destination. This chapter concludes the discussion of IP by describing datagram transmission in detail. It shows how a host or router sends a datagram across a physical network, and how routers handle the problem of sending large datagrams.

21.2 Datagram Transmission And Frames

When a host or router handles a datagram, IP software first selects the next hop to which the datagram should be sent, N, and then transmits the datagram across a physical network to N. Unfortunately, network hardware does not understand datagram format or Internet addressing. Instead, each hardware technology defines a frame format and a physical addressing scheme; the hardware only accepts and delivers packets that adhere to the specified frame format and use the specified hardware addressing scheme. More important, because an internet can contain heterogeneous network technology, the frame format needed to cross a network may differ from the frame format needed to cross the previous network.

21.3 Encapsulation

How can a datagram be transmitted across a physical network that does not under-stand the datagram format? The answer lies in a technique known as *encapsulation*†. When an IP datagram is encapsulated in a frame, the entire datagram is placed in the data area of a frame. The network hardware treats a frame that contains a datagram ex-actly like any other frame. In fact, the hardware does not examine or change the con-tents of the frame data area. Figure 21.1 illustrates the concept.

Figure 21.1 An IP datagram encapsulated in a hardware frame. The entire
datagram resides in the frame data area. In practice, the frame
format used with some technologies includes a frame trailer as
well as a frame header.

How does a receiver know whether the data area in an incoming frame contains an IP datagram or other data? The sender and receiver must agree on the value used in the frame type field. When it places a datagram in a frame, the sender assigns the frame type field the special value that is reserved for *IP*. When a frame arrives with the spe-cial value in its type field, the receiver knows that the data area contains an IP da-tagram.

A frame that carries an IP datagram must have a destination address as usual. Therefore, in addition to placing a datagram in the data area of a frame, encapsulation requires the sender to supply the physical address of the next computer to which the da-tagram should be sent. To compute the appropriate address, software on the sending computer must perform address binding as described in Chapter 19. The binding translates the IP address of the next hop into an equivalent hardware address, which is then used as the destination address in the frame header.

To summarize:

> *A datagram is encapsulated in a frame for transmission across a phy-sical network. The destination address in the frame is the address of the next hop to which the datagram should be sent; the address is ob-tained by translating the IP address of the next hop to an equivalent hardware address.*

---

†IP encapsulation is similar to the encapsulation of ARP messages covered in Chapter 19.

21.4 Transmission Across An Internet

Encapsulation applies to one transmission at a time. After the sender selects a next hop, the sender encapsulates the datagram in a frame and transmits the result across the physical network to the next hop. When the frame reaches the next hop, the receiving software removes the IP datagram and discards the frame. If the datagram must be forwarded across another network, a new frame is created. Figure 21.2 illustrates how a datagram appears as it is encapsulated and unencapsulated as it travels from a source host to a destination host through three networks and two routers. Each network can use a different hardware technology than the others, meaning that the frame formats can differ.

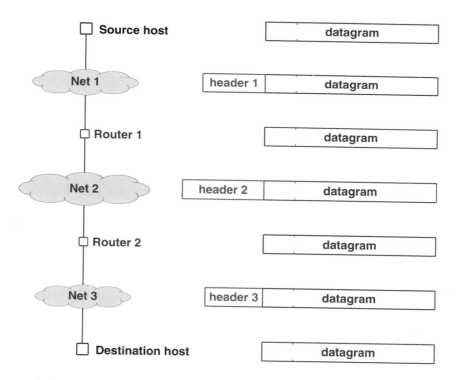

Figure 21.2 An IP datagram as it appears at each step during a trip across an internet. Whenever it travels across a physical network, the datagram is encapsulated in a frame appropriate to the network.

As the figure shows, hosts and routers store a datagram in memory with no additional header. When the datagram passes across a physical network, the datagram is encapsulated in a frame suitable for the network. The size of the frame header that appears before the datagram depends on the network technology. For example, if Network *1* is an Ethernet, the header in frame *1* is an Ethernet header. Similarly, if Network *2* is an FDDI ring, the header in frame *2* is an FDDI header.

It is important to observe that frame headers do not accumulate during a trip through the internet. Before a datagram is transmitted across a given network, the datagram is encapsulated, which usually means a frame header is prepended. When the frame arrives at the next hop, the datagram is removed from the incoming frame before being routed and encapsulated in an outgoing frame. Thus, when the datagram reaches its final destination, the frame that carried the datagram is discarded and the datagram appears exactly the same size as when it was originally sent. The point is:

> *When a datagram arrives in a network frame, the receiver extracts the datagram from the frame data area and discards the frame header.*

21.5 MTU, Datagram Size, And Encapsulation

Each hardware technology specifies the maximum amount of data that a frame can carry. The limit is known as a *maximum transmission unit* (*MTU*). There is no exception to the MTU limit — the network hardware is not designed to accept or transfer frames that carry more data than the MTU allows. Thus, a datagram must be smaller or equal to the network MTU or it cannot be encapsulated for transmission.

In an internet that contains heterogeneous networks, MTU restrictions can cause a problem. In particular, because a router can connect networks with different MTU values, the router can receive a datagram over one network that cannot be sent over another. For example, Figure 21.3 illustrates a router that interconnects two networks with MTU values of *1500* and *1000*.

Figure 21.3 An example of a router that connects two networks with different MTU values. A frame that travels across Network *1* can contain *1500* octets of data, while a frame that travels across network *2* can contain at most *1000* octets of data.

In the figure, host H_2 attaches to a network that has an MTU of *1000*. Therefore, each datagram that H_2 transmits must be *1000* octets or less. However, because host H_1 attaches to a network that has an MTU of *1500* octets, H_1 can transmit datagrams that contain up to *1500* octets. If H_1 sends a *1500*-octet datagram to H_2, router R will receive the datagram, but will not be able to send it across Network *2*.

An IP router uses a technique known as *fragmentation* to solve the problem of heterogeneous MTUs. When a datagram is larger than the MTU of the network over which it must be sent, the router divides the datagram into smaller pieces called *fragments*, and sends each fragment independently.

Surprisingly, a fragment has the same format as other datagrams — a bit in the *FLAGS* field of the header indicates whether a datagram is a fragment or a complete datagram†. Other fields in the header are assigned information that is used to reassemble the fragments to reproduce the original datagram. In particular, the *FRAGMENT OFFSET* field in the header of a fragment specifies where in the original datagram the fragment belongs.

To fragment a datagram for transmission across a network, a router uses the network MTU and the datagram header size to calculate the maximum amount of data that can be sent in each fragment and the number of fragments that will be needed. The router then creates the fragments. It begins by starting each fragment with a copy of the original header, and then modifies individual header fields. For example, the router sets the appropriate bit in the *FLAGS* field to indicate that the datagram is a fragment. Finally, the router copies the appropriate data from the original datagram into the fragment, and transmits the result. Figure 21.4 illustrates the process.

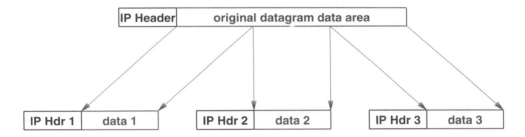

Figure 21.4 An IP datagram divided into three fragments. Each fragment carries some data from the original datagram, and has an IP header similar to the original datagram.

To summarize:

> *A datagram cannot be larger than the MTU of a network over which it is sent. When a router receives a datagram that is larger than the MTU of the network over which it is to be sent, the router divides the datagram into smaller pieces called* fragments. *Each fragment uses the IP datagram format, but carries only part of the data.*

---

†The datagram header format can be found in Figure 20.4 on page 324.

21.6 Reassembly

The process of creating a copy of the original datagram from fragments is called *reassembly*. Because each fragment begins with a copy of the original datagram header, all fragments have the same destination address as the original datagram from which they were derived. Furthermore, the fragment that carries the final piece of data has an additional bit set in the header. Thus, a receiver performing reassembly can tell whether all fragments have arrived successfully.

Interestingly, the Internet Protocol specifies that the ultimate destination host should reassemble fragments. For example, consider the internet that Figure 21.5 illustrates.

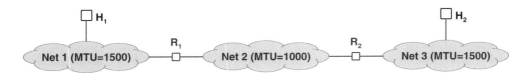

Figure 21.5 An example internet in which hosts can generate datagrams that require fragmentation. Once a datagram has been fragmented, the fragments are forwarded to the final destination, which reassembles them.

In the figure, if host H_1 sends a *1500*-octet datagram to host H_2, router R_1 will divide the datagram into two fragments, which it will forward to R_2. Router R_2 does not reassemble the fragments. Instead R_2 uses the destination address from each fragment to forward the fragment. The final destination host, H_2, collects the fragments and reassembles them to produce the original datagram.

Requiring the ultimate destination to reassemble fragments has two main advantages. First, it reduces the amount of state information in routers. When forwarding a datagram, a router does not need to know whether the datagram is a fragment. Second, it allows routes to change dynamically. If an intermediate router reassembles fragments, all fragments would need to reach that router. By postponing reassembly until the ultimate destination, IP is free to pass some fragments from a datagram along a different route than other fragments.

21.7 Identifying A Datagram

Recall that IP does not guarantee delivery. Thus, individual fragments can be lost or arrive out of order. More important, if a source sends multiple datagrams to a given destination, the fragments from the datagrams can arrive in arbitrary order.

How does IP software reassemble fragments that arrive out of order? A sender places a unique identification number in the *IDENTIFICATION* field of each outgoing datagram. When a router fragments the datagram, the router copies the identification number into each fragment. A receiver uses the identification number and IP source address in an incoming fragment to determine the datagram to which the fragment belongs. In addition, the *FRAGMENT OFFSET* field tells a receiver how to order fragments within a given datagram.

21.8 Fragment Loss

Recall that IP does not guarantee datagram delivery — if an underlying network drops packets, an encapsulated datagram or fragment can be lost. When all fragments from a datagram arrive, the datagram can be reassembled. However, a problem arises when one or more fragments from a datagram arrive, and some fragments are delayed or lost. Although the datagram cannot be reassembled, the receiver must save the fragments in case missing fragments are only delayed.

A receiver cannot hold fragments an arbitrarily long time because fragments occupy space in the receiver's memory. To avoid exhausting memory, IP specifies a maximum time to hold fragments. When the first fragment arrives from a given datagram, the receiver starts a timer. If all fragments of a datagram arrive before the timer expires, the receiver cancels the timer and reassembles the datagram. However, if the timer expires before all fragments arrive, the receiver discards those fragments that have arrived.

The result of IP's reassembly timer is all-or-nothing: either all fragments arrive and IP reassembles the datagram, or IP discards the complete datagram. In particular, there is no mechanism for a receiver to tell the sender which fragments have arrived. The design makes sense because the sender does not know about fragmentation. Furthermore, if the sender did retransmit the datagram, routes may be different, which means a retransmission would not necessarily traverse the same routers. Hence, there is no guarantee that a retransmitted datagram would be fragmented in the same way as the original.

21.9 Fragmenting A Fragment

After performing fragmentation, a router forwards each fragment on to its destination. What happens if a fragment eventually reaches another network that has a smaller MTU? The fragmentation scheme has been planned carefully to make it possible to further fragment a fragment. Another router along the path divides the fragment into smaller fragments. In a poorly designed internet where networks are arranged in a sequence of decreasing MTUs, each router along the path must further fragment each fragment.

IP does not distinguish between original fragments and subfragments. In particular, a receiver cannot know whether an incoming fragment was the result of one router fragmenting a datagram or multiple routers fragmenting fragments. The advantage of making all fragments the same is that a receiver can perform reassembly of the original datagram without first reassembling subfragments. Doing so saves CPU time, and reduces the amount of information needed in the headers of each fragment.

21.10 Summary

An IP datagram is encapsulated in a network frame for transmission across a hardware network. To encapsulate a datagram, the sender places the entire datagram in the data area of a network frame. The sender must also resolve the next-hop address to a physical address, which it places in the destination field of the frame header. Encapsulation occurs on one network at a time — a router removes a datagram from an incoming frame before encapsulating the datagram in an outgoing frame.

Each network technology defines the maximum amount of data that can be transmitted in a packet; the limit is known as the network's maximum transmission unit (MTU). When a router receives a datagram that is larger than the network MTU over which the datagram must be sent, the router divides the datagram into smaller datagrams called *fragments*. Each fragment travels to the ultimate destination, which is responsible for reassembling fragments into the original datagram.

EXERCISES

21.1 Why is fragmentation needed on an internet but not on a typical Wide Area Network?

21.2 Suppose a datagram passes through N routers on a trip across an internet. How many times is the datagram encapsulated?

21.3 Although a sender can avoid fragmentation by using small datagrams, senders seldom do. Explain why.

21.4 What is the maximum number of fragments that can result from a single datagram? Explain.

21.5 IP specifies that any datagram can be delayed, meaning that datagrams can arrive in a different order than they were sent. If a fragment from one datagram arrives at a destination before all the fragments from a previous datagram arrive, how does the destination know to which datagram the fragments belong?

21.6 Write a computer program that takes as input an IP datagram and an MTU size. Have the program create fragments for the datagram so that each fragment fits into the specified MTU.

21.7 Write a computer program that implements reassembly. Have the program accept a sequence of fragments and reassemble them into a complete datagram. Test the program by giving it fragments out of order. Hint: look up the meaning of the *MORE FRAGMENTS* bit in the *FLAGS* field.

21.8   A *path MTU* is defined to be the minimum MTU along a path from a source to a destination. The current IP standards recommend that a host discover the path MTU before choosing an initial datagram size. Read about path MTU discovery. What technique discussed in this chapter is similar to the technique used for discovering a path MTU?

21.9   In the previous exercise, what is the chief advantage of knowing a path MTU?

21.10   Do you expect fragmentation to occur when datagrams pass from a WAN through a router to a LAN or when they pass from a LAN through a router to a WAN? Why or why not?

Chapter Contents

22

The Future IP (IPv6)

22.1 Introduction

Previous chapters discuss the current version of the Internet Protocol. The chapters describe an IP datagram as a header followed by data. The header contains information such as a destination address that IP software uses to deliver the datagram; each header field has a fixed size to make processing efficient. Chapter 21 describes how an IP datagram is encapsulated in a network frame as it travels across a physical network.

This chapter concentrates on the future of the Internet Protocol. The chapter begins by assessing the strengths and limitations of the current version of IP, and then considers an entirely new version of IP that the IETF is developing to replace the current version. The chapter explains features of the new version, and shows how they overcome some of the limitations in the current version.

22.2 The Success Of IP

The current version of IP has been extremely successful. IP has made it possible for the Internet to handle heterogeneous networks, dramatic changes in hardware technology, and extreme increases in scale. To handle heterogeneity, IP defines a uniform packet format (the IP datagram) and a packet transfer mechanism. IP datagrams are the fundamental unit of communication in the Internet — when an application transfers data across the Internet from one computer to another, the data travels in an IP datagram. IP also defines a set of addresses that allow applications and higher layer protocols to communicate across heterogeneous networks without knowing the differences in hardware addresses used by the underlying network systems. The demonstration of scalability is evident because the current Internet includes millions of users around the world.

The current version of IP has also accommodated changes in hardware technology. Although the protocol was defined before local area network technologies became popular, the original design has continued to work well through several generations of hardware technologies. IP is now used over networks that operate several orders of magnitude faster than the networks that were in use when IP was designed. Furthermore, some modern networks offer frame sizes that are much larger than the frame sizes available when IP was defined. More important, IP works efficiently over such networks because it can take advantage of the increased frame size.

To summarize:

> *The success of the current version of IP is incredible — the protocol has accommodated changes in hardware technologies, heterogeneous networks, and extremely large scale.*

22.3 The Motivation For Change

If IP works so well, why change? The primary motivation for change arises from the limited address space. When IP was defined, only a few computer networks existed. The designers decided to use 32 bits for an IP address because doing so allowed the Internet to include over a million networks. However, the global Internet is growing exponentially, with the size doubling in less than a year. At the current growth rate, each of the possible network prefixes will soon be assigned, and no further growth will be possible. Thus, the primary motivation for defining a new version of IP arose from the address space limitation — larger addresses are necessary to accommodate continued growth of the Internet.

Secondary motivations for changes in IP have arisen from new Internet applications. For example, applications that deliver audio and video need to deliver data at regular intervals. To keep such information flowing through the Internet without disruption, IP must avoid changing routes frequently. Although the current IP datagram header includes a field that can be used to request a type of service, the protocol did not define a type of service that can be used for real-time delivery of audio and video.

New applications are being developed that require more complex addressing and routing capabilities. For example, interest has increased in *collaboration technologies* that provide communication among a group of colleagues analogous to a telephone conference call. To make collaboration effective, an internet needs a mechanism that allows groups to be created or changed and provides a way to send a copy of a packet to each participant in a given group. In addition to groups that must each receive a copy of a packet, some applications use groups to handle load sharing. That is, several identical copies of a service exist, and a packet sent to the group is routed to the copy of the service that is closest to the sender. Thus, a new version of IP needs to include mechanisms that make such addressing and routing possible.

22.4 A Name And A Version Number

When researchers began working on a new version of IP, they needed a temporary name for the work. Borrowing from a popular television show, they said they were working on *IP — The Next Generation*, and many early reports referred to *IPng*. Unfortunately, many competing proposals were made for IPng, and the name became ambiguous.

When a specific protocol was defined, the group doing the work needed to distinguish the protocol from all other proposals. They decided to use an official version number in the header of the final standardized protocol. In fact, the version number was a surprise. Because the current IP version number is *4*, most researchers expected the next official version of IP to be *5*. However, version number *5* had been assigned to an experimental protocol known as *ST*. Consequently, the new version of IP received *6* as its official version number, and the protocol became known as *IPv6†*.

22.5 IPv6 Features

IPv6 retains many of the design features that have made IPv4 so successful. Like IPv4, IPv6 is connectionless — each datagram contains a destination address, and each datagram is routed independently. Like IPv4, the header in a datagram contains a maximum number of hops the datagram can take before being discarded. More important, IPv6 retains most of the general facilities provided by the IPv4 options.

Despite retaining the basic concepts from the current version, IPv6 changes all the details. For example, IPv6 uses larger addresses and an entirely new datagram header format. Finally, IPv6 uses a series of fixed-length headers to handle header information. Thus, unlike IPv4, which places key information in fixed fields of the header and only appends variable-length options for less important information, the IPv6 header is always variable size.

The new features in IPv6 can be grouped into five broad categories:

- *Address Size.* Instead of 32 bits, each IPv6 address contains 128 bits. The resulting address space is large enough to accommodate continued growth of the world-wide Internet for many decades.

- *Header Format.* The IPv6 datagram header is completely different than the IPv4 header. Almost every field in the header has been changed; some have been replaced.

- *Extension Headers.* Unlike IPv4, which uses a single header format for all datagrams, IPv6 encodes information into separate headers. A datagram consists of the base IPv6 header followed by zero or more extension headers, followed by data.

- *Support for audio and video.* IPv6 includes a mechanism that allows a sender and receiver to establish a high-quality path through the underlying network and to asso-

---

†To distinguish the current IP protocol from the new version, the current protocol is called *IPv4*.

ciate datagrams with that path. Although the mechanism is intended for use with audio and video applications that require high performance guarantees, the mechanism can also be used to associate datagrams with low-cost paths.

- *Extensible Protocol.* Unlike IPv4, IPv6 does not specify all possible protocol features. Instead, the designers have provided a scheme that allows a sender to add additional information to a datagram. The extension scheme makes IPv6 more flexible than IPv4, and means that new features can be added to the design as needed.

22.6 IPv6 Datagram Format

As Figure 22.1 illustrates, an IPv6 datagram begins with a *base header*, which is followed by zero or more *extension headers*, followed by data.

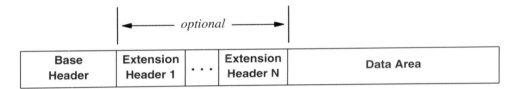

Figure 22.1 The general form of an IPv6 datagram. Extension headers are optional — the minimum datagram has a base header followed by data.

Although it illustrates the general datagram structure, fields in the figure are not drawn to scale. In particular, some extension headers are larger than the base header, while others can be smaller. Furthermore, in many datagrams, the size of the data area is much larger than the size of the headers.

22.7 IPv6 Base Header Format

Although it is twice as large as an IPv4 header, the IPv6 base header contains less information. Figure 22.2 illustrates the format. As the figure shows, most of the space in the header is devoted to two fields that identify the sender and the recipient. As in IPv4, the *SOURCE ADDRESS* field identifies the sender, and the *DESTINATION ADDRESS* field identifies the intended recipient. Each address occupies sixteen octets, four times more than an IPv4 address.

In addition to the source and destination addresses, the base header contains six fields. The *VERS* field identifies the protocol as version *6*. The *TRAFFIC CLASS* field specifies the *traffic class*, which is used to choose a route. The traffic class specifies general characteristics that the datagram needs. For example, to send interactive traffic (e.g., keystrokes and mouse movements), one might specify a general traffic class for low delay. To send real-time audio across an internet, however, a sender might request the underlying network hardware to establish a path that has delay less than 100 milliseconds. The *PAYLOAD LENGTH* field corresponds to IPv4's datagram length field. Unlike IPv4, the *PAYLOAD LENGTH* specifies only the size of the data being carried (i.e., the payload); the size of the header is excluded. The *HOP LIMIT* corresponds to the IPv4 *TIME-TO-LIVE* field. IPv6 interprets the *HOP LIMIT* strictly — the datagram will be discarded if the *HOP LIMIT* counts down to zero before the datagram arrives at its destination.

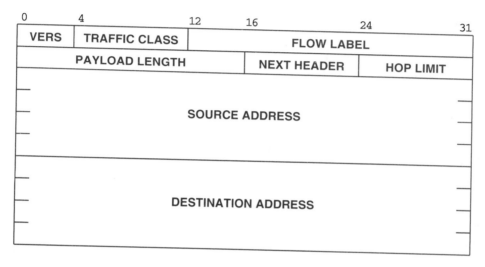

Figure 22.2 The format of an IPv6 base header. The header contains fewer fields than the IPv4 datagram header.

Remaining fields in the header require further explanation. Field *FLOW LABEL* is intended for use with new applications that require performance guarantees. The label can be used to associate a datagram with a particular underlying network path. Originally, the flow label occupied 28 bits, but it has been partitioned into a *TRAFFIC CLASS* field and a separate *FLOW LABEL* field used to identify a specific path through the network. When a path has been established that meets the traffic class requirements, the network system returns an identifier that the sender places in each datagram to be sent along the path. Routers use the value in the *FLOW LABEL* field to route the datagram along the prearranged path.

The *NEXT HEADER* field is used to specify the type of information that follows the current header. For example, if the datagram includes an extension header, the *NEXT HEADER* field specifies the type of the extension header. If no extension header exists, the *NEXT HEADER* field specifies the type of data being carried in the datagram. Figure 22.3 illustrates the concept.

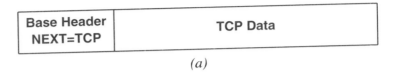

(a)

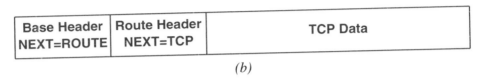

(b)

Figure 22.3 Two IPv6 datagrams in which (a) contains a base header plus data, and (b) contains a base header, route header, and data. The *NEXT HEADER* field in each header specifies the type of the item that follows†.

22.8 How IPv6 Handles Multiple Headers

Because the standard specifies a unique value for each possible header type, there is never ambiguity about the interpretation of the *NEXT HEADER* field. A receiver uses the *NEXT HEADER* field in each header to determine what follows. If the value in the field corresponds to a type used for data, the receiver passes the datagram to a software module that handles the data. If the value in the *NEXT HEADER* field corresponds to another header, IP software parses the header and interprets its contents. Once it finishes with a header, IP uses the *NEXT HEADER* field to determine whether data or another header follows.

How does IPv6 software know where a particular header ends and the next item begins? Some header types have a fixed size. For example, a base header has a fixed size of exactly forty octets. To move to the item following a base header, IPv6 software simply adds *40* to the address of the base header.

Some extension headers do not have a fixed size. In such cases, the header must contain sufficient information to allow IPv6 to determine where the header ends. For example, Figure 22.4 illustrates the general form of an IPv6 *options header* that carries information similar to the options in an IPv4 datagram.

The options extension header illustrates one way IPv6 handles headers that do not have a fixed size. When composing a datagram, the sender stores the length of the options header in field *HEADER LEN*. When a receiver encounters an options extension header, it uses the *HEADER LEN* field to determine the location of the next item, and the *NEXT HEADER* field to determine the type.

---

†Chapter 24 explains the TCP protocol that is used for data.

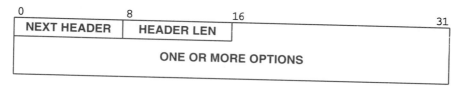

Figure 22.4 The IPv6 options extension header. Because the size of the options header can vary from one datagram to another, the *HEADER LEN* field specifies the exact length.

22.9 Fragmentation, Reassembly, And Path MTU

Although IPv6 fragmentation resembles IPv4 fragmentation, the details differ. Like IPv4, a prefix of the original datagram is copied into each fragment, and the payload length is modified to be the length of the fragment. Unlike IPv4, however, IPv6 does not include fields for fragmentation information in the base header. Instead, IPv6 places them in a separate fragment extension header; the presence of the header identifies the datagram as a fragment. Figure 22.5 illustrates IPv6 fragmentation.

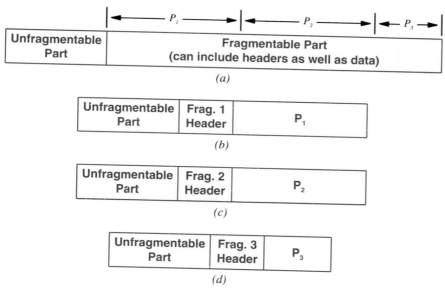

Figure 22.5 Illustration of fragmentation in IPv6. The fragmentable part of the original datagram (*a*), is placed in the payload area of fragments (*b, c,* and *d*). Each fragment begins with a copy of the unfragmentable part and a fragment extension header.

As the figure illustrates, each fragment is smaller than the original datagram. As with IPv4, the fragment size is chosen to be the maximum transmission unit (MTU) size of the underlying network over which the fragments must be sent. Thus, the final fragment may be smaller than the others because it represents the amount remaining after MTU-size pieces have been extracted from the original datagram.

Fragmentation in IPv6 differs dramatically from fragmentation in IPv4. Recall that in IPv4, a router performs fragmentation when the router receives a datagram too large for the network over which the datagram must be sent. In IPv6, a sending host is responsible for fragmentation. That is, hosts are expected to choose a datagram size that will not require fragmentation; routers along the path that receive a large datagram will not fragment the datagram.

How can a host choose a datagram size that will not result in fragmentation? The host must learn the MTU of each network along the path to the destination, and must choose a datagram size to fit the smallest. The minimum MTU along a path from a source to a destination is known as the *path MTU*, and the process of learning the path MTU is known as *path MTU discovery*. In general, path MTU discovery is an iterative procedure. A host sends a sequence of various-size datagrams to the destination to see if they arrive without error†. Once a datagram is small enough to pass through without fragmentation, the host chooses a datagram size equal to the path MTU.

22.10 The Purpose Of Multiple Headers

Why does IPv6 use separate extension headers? There are two reasons: economy and extensibility. Economy is easiest to understand: partitioning the datagram functionality into separate headers is economical because it saves space. To understand why, one must realize that although the IPv6 protocol includes many facilities, designers expect a given datagram to use only a small subset. Having separate headers in IPv6 makes it possible to define a large set of features without requiring each datagram header to have at least one field for each feature. For example, although many IPv4 datagrams are not fragmented, the IPv4 header has fields used to hold fragmentation information. In contrast, IPv6 does not waste space on fields for fragmentation unless the datagram is fragmented. Because most datagrams only need a few headers, avoiding unnecessary header fields can save considerable space. Smaller datagrams also take less time to transmit. Thus, reducing datagram size also reduces the bandwidth consumed.

To understand extensibility, consider adding a new feature to a protocol. A protocol like IPv4 that uses a fixed header format requires a complete change — the header must be redesigned to accommodate fields needed to support the new feature. In IPv6, however, existing protocol headers can remain unchanged. A new *NEXT HEADER* type is defined as well as a new header format.

The chief advantage of placing new functionality in a new header lies in the ability to experiment with a new feature before changing all computers in the Internet. For ex-

---

†The next chapter discusses the error reporting mechanism that IPv4 uses; IPv6 includes a similar error reporting mechanism.

ample, suppose the owners of two computers wish to test a new datagram encryption technique. The two must agree on the details of an experimental encryption header. The sender adds the new header to a datagram, and the receiver interprets the header in incoming datagrams. As long as the new header appears after the headers used for routing, routers in the internet between the sender and receiver can pass the datagram without understanding the experimental header†. Once an experimental feature proves useful, it can be incorporated in the standard.

22.11 IPv6 Addressing

Like IPv4, IPv6 assigns a unique address for each connection between a computer and a physical network. Thus, if a computer (e.g., a router) connects to three physical networks, the computer is assigned three addresses. Also like IPv4, IPv6 separates each such address into a prefix that identifies the network and a suffix that identifies a particular computer on the network.

Despite adopting the same approach for assigning computer addresses, IPv6 addressing differs from IPv4 addressing in significant ways. First, all address details are completely different. Like CIDR addresses, the division between prefix and suffix can occur on an arbitrary boundary. Unlike IPv4, IPv6 includes addresses with a multi-level hierarchy. Although the address assignments are not fixed, one can imagine that the highest level corresponds to an ISP, the next level corresponds to an organization (e.g., a company), the next to a site, and so on. Second, IPv6 defines a set of special addresses that differ dramatically from IPv4 special addresses. In particular, IPv6 does not include a special address for broadcasting on a given network. Instead, each IPv6 address is one of three basic types:

unicast   The address corresponds to a single computer. A datagram sent to the address is routed along a shortest path to the computer.

multicast The address corresponds to a set of computers, possibly at many locations; membership in the set can change at any time. When a datagram is sent to the address, IPv6 delivers one copy of the datagram to each member of the set.

anycast   The address corresponds to a set of computers that share a common address prefix (e.g., all reside in a single location). A datagram sent to the address is routed along a shortest path and then delivered to exactly one of the computers (e.g., the computer closest to the sender).

Anycast addressing was originally known as *cluster* addressing. The motivation for such addressing arises from a desire to allow replication of services. For example, a corporation that offers a service over the network assigns an anycast address to several computers that all provide the service. When a user sends a datagram to the anycast ad-

---

†If an experimental header is incorrectly placed before routing headers, a router will discard the datagram.

dress, IPv6 routes the datagram to one of the computers in the set (i.e., in the "cluster"). If a user from another location sends a datagram to the anycast address, IPv6 can choose to route the datagram to a different member of the set, allowing both computers to process requests at the same time.

22.12 IPv6 Colon Hexadecimal Notation

Although an address that occupies 128 bits can accommodate Internet growth, writing such numbers can be unwieldy. For example, consider a 128-bit number written in dotted decimal notation:

105.220.136.100.255.255.255.255.0.0.18.128.140.10.255.255

To help reduce the number of characters used to write an address, the designers of IPv6 propose using a more compact syntactic form known as *colon hexadecimal notation*† in which each group of 16 bits is written in hexadecimal with a colon separating groups. For example, when the above number is written in colon hex, it becomes:

69DC:8864:FFFF:FFFF:0:1280:8C0A:FFFF

As the example illustrates, colon hex notation requires fewer characters to express an address. An additional optimization known as *zero compression* further reduces the size. Zero compression replaces sequences of zeroes with two colons. For example, the address:

FF0C:0:0:0:0:0:0:B1

can be written as:

FF0C::B1

The large IPv6 address space and the proposed address allocation scheme make zero compression especially important because the designers expect many IPv6 addresses to contain strings of zeroes. In particular, to help ease the transition to the new protocol, the designers mapped existing IPv4 addresses into the IPv6 address space. Any IPv6 address that begins with *96* zero bits contains an IPv4 address in the low-order *32* bits.

---

†The name is commonly abbreviated to *colon hex*.

22.13 Summary

Although the current version of IP has worked well for many years, exponential growth of the Internet means that the 32-bit address space will be exhausted within 20 years. The IETF has designed a new version of IP that uses 128 bits to represent each address. The new address space is so large that it will not be exhausted for many decades.

To distinguish the new version of IP from the current version, the two protocols are named using their version number. The current version of IP is IPv4, and the new version is IPv6.

IPv6 retains many of the concepts from IPv4, but changes all the details. For example, like IPv4, IPv6 provides a connectionless service in which two computers exchange short messages called datagrams. However, unlike an IPv4 datagram in which the header contains fields for each function, IPv6 defines separate headers for each function. Each IPv6 datagram consists of a base header followed by zero or more extension headers, followed by data.

Like IPv4, IPv6 defines an address for each network connection. Thus, as in IPv4, a computer that connects to multiple physical networks (e.g., a router) has multiple addresses. However, special addresses are completely changed in IPv6. Instead of IPv4's notion of network broadcast, IPv6 defines multicast and anycast (cluster) addresses, both of which correspond to a set of computers. A multicast address corresponds to a set of computers at multiple sites that are treated as a single entity — each computer in the set will receive a copy of any datagram sent to the set. A cluster permits replication of services — a datagram sent to a cluster address will be delivered to exactly one member of the cluster (e.g., the member that is closest to the sender).

To make IPv6 addresses easier for people to use, the designers propose using colon hexadecimal notation. Colon hex notation expresses groups of *16* bits in hexadecimal, with a colon separating groups. The resulting notation is more compact than the dotted decimal form used in IPv4.

EXERCISES

22.1   How many octets does the smallest possible IPv6 datagram contain? The largest?

22.2   Write a computer program that reads a 128-bit binary number and prints the number in colon hex notation.

22.3   Extend the program in the previous exercise to implement zero compression.

22.4   Write a computer program that extracts and prints the fields in an IPv6 datagram base header.

22.5   What is the maximum number of fragments that can result from one IPv6 datagram that contains only a base header? If it contains a base header plus a TCP header?

Chapter Contents

23

An Error Reporting
Mechanism (ICMP)

23.1 Introduction

The previous chapters describe the connectionless datagram delivery service that the Internet Protocol provides. They define the IP datagram format, explain how routing tables are used to select a next hop to which a datagram is forwarded, and show how datagrams are encapsulated for transmission. This chapter examines an error reporting protocol that is integrated with IP. It reviews the basic errors that can be reported, and explains how and where such messages are sent.

Although it was originally intended to provide a way for a source to learn why datagrams could not be delivered, researchers have found creative ways to use the control message system. In particular, tools have been created that gather information about an internet by sending datagrams that generate error messages. The chapter reviews some of the tools and techniques that use error messages to probe for information.

23.2 Best-Effort Semantics And Error Detection

We said that IP defines a best-effort communication service in which datagrams can be lost, duplicated, delayed, or delivered out of order. It may seem that a best-effort service does not need any error detection. However, it is important to realize that a best-effort service is not careless — IP attempts to avoid errors and to report problems when they occur.

We have already seen one example of error detection in IP: a header checksum that is used to detect transmission errors. When a host creates an IP datagram, the host includes a checksum that covers the entire header. Whenever a datagram is received, the checksum is verified to ensure that the header arrived intact. To verify the checksum, the receiver recomputes the checksum including the value in the checksum field. If a bit in the IP header is damaged during transmission across a physical network, the receiver will find that the checksum does not result in zero. After changing fields in the header (e.g., after decrementing the *TIME TO LIVE* field), a router must recompute the checksum before forwarding the datagram to its next hop†.

The action taken in response to a checksum error is straightforward: the datagram must be discarded immediately without further processing. The receiver cannot trust any fields in the datagram header because the receiver cannot know which bits were altered. In particular, the receiver cannot send an error message back to the computer that sent the datagram because the receiver cannot trust the source address in the header. Likewise, the receiver cannot forward the damaged datagram because the receiver cannot trust the destination address in the header. Thus, the receiver has no option but to discard the damaged datagram.

23.3 Internet Control Message Protocol

Problems that are less severe than transmission errors result in error conditions that can be reported. For example, suppose some of the physical paths in an internet fail, causing the internet to be partitioned into two sets of networks with no path between the sets. A datagram sent from a host in one set to a host in the other cannot be delivered.

The TCP/IP suite includes a protocol that IP uses to send error messages when conditions such as the one described above arise: the *Internet Control Message Protocol* (*ICMP*). The protocol is required for a standard implementation of IP. We will see that the two protocols are co-dependent. IP uses ICMP when it sends an error message, and ICMP uses IP to transport messages.

Figure 23.1 lists the ICMP messages, which include both error and informational messages. After reviewing a few examples, we will see how they can be used.

---

†An exercise suggests that instead of recomputing the entire checksum, a router can achieve higher performance by incrementally changing the checksum if the only change in the header is a decrement of the *TTL*.

Type	Name
0	Echo Reply
1	Unassigned
2	Unassigned
3	Destination Unreachable
4	Source Quench
5	Redirect
6	Alternate Host Address
7	Unassigned
8	Echo
9	Router Advertisement
10	Router Selection
11	Time Exceeded
12	Parameter Problem
13	Timestamp
14	Timestamp Reply
15	Information Request
16	Information Reply
17	Address Mask Request
18	Address Mask Reply
19	Reserved (for Security)
20-29	Reserved (for Robustness Experiment)
30	Traceroute
31	Datagram Conversion Error
32	Mobile Host Redirect
33	IPv6 Where-Are-You
34	IPv6 I-Am-Here
35	Mobile Registration Request
36	Mobile Registration Reply
37-255	Reserved

Figure 23.1 A list of ICMP messages. Each message is identified by an 8-bit
type field.

Examples of ICMP error messages include:

- *Source Quench.* A router sends a source quench whenever it has
  received so many datagrams that it has no more buffer space available. A router that has temporarily run out of buffer space must
  discard incoming datagrams. When it discards a datagram, the
  router sends a source quench message to the host that created the
  datagram. When it receives a source quench, a host is required to
  reduce the rate at which it is transmitting.

- *Time Exceeded.* A time exceeded message is sent in two cases. Whenever a router reduces the *TIME TO LIVE* field in a datagram to zero, the router discards the datagram and sends a time exceeded message. In addition, a time exceeded message is sent by a host if the reassembly timer expires before all fragments from a given datagram arrive.

- *Destination Unreachable.* Whenever a router determines that a datagram cannot be delivered to its final destination, the router sends a destination unreachable message to the host that created the datagram. The message specifies whether the specific destination host is unreachable or the network to which the destination attaches is unreachable. In other words, the error message distinguishes between a situation in which an entire network is temporarily disconnected from an internet (e.g., because a router has failed) and the case where a particular host is temporarily offline (e.g., because the host is powered down).

- *Redirect.* When a host creates a datagram destined for a remote network, the host sends the datagram to a router, which forwards the datagram to its destination. If a router determines that a host has incorrectly sent a datagram that should be sent to a different router, the router uses a redirect message to cause the host to change its route. A redirect message can specify either a change for a specific host or a change for a network; the latter is more common.

- *Parameter Problem.* One of the parameters specified in a datagram is incorrect.

In addition to error messages, ICMP defines informational messages that include:

- *Echo Request/Reply.* An echo request message can be sent to the ICMP software on any computer. In response to an incoming echo request message, ICMP software is required to send an ICMP echo reply message. The reply carries the same data as the request.

- *Address Mask Request/Reply.* A host broadcasts an address mask request when it boots, and routers that receive the request send an address mask reply that contains the correct 32-bit subnet mask being used on the network.

23.4 ICMP Message Transport

ICMP uses IP to transport each error message. When a router has an ICMP message to send, it creates an IP datagram and encapsulates the ICMP message in the datagram. That is, the ICMP message is placed in the data area of the IP datagram. The datagram is then forwarded as usual, with the complete datagram being encapsulated in a frame for transmission. Figure 23.2 illustrates the two levels of encapsulation.

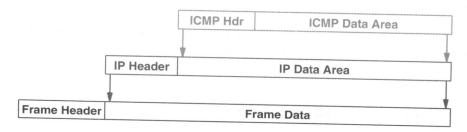

Figure 23.2 Two levels of encapsulation that occur when an ICMP message is sent. The ICMP message is encapsulated in a datagram, which is encapsulated in a frame for transmission across a physical network.

Where should an ICMP message be sent? ICMP messages are always created in response to a datagram. Either the datagram has encountered a problem (e.g., a router finds that the destination specified in the datagram is unreachable), or the datagram carries an ICMP request message to which the destination replies. In either case, an ICMP error message or an ICMP reply is sent back to the source.

Sending a message back to the source is straightforward because each datagram carries the IP address of its source in the header. A router extracts the source address from the header of the incoming datagram and places the address in the *DESTINATION* field of the header of the datagram that carries the ICMP message.

Datagrams carrying ICMP messages do not have special priority — they are forwarded like any other datagram, with one minor exception. If a datagram carrying an ICMP error message causes an error, no error message is sent. The reason should be clear: the designers wanted to avoid an internet becoming congested carrying error messages about error messages. We can summarize:

The Internet Control Message Protocol includes both messages about errors and informational messages. ICMP is integrated with IP: ICMP encapsulates messages in IP for transmission and IP uses ICMP to report problems.

23.5 Using ICMP Messages To Test Reachability

Chapter 2 described the *ping* program that tests to see if a given destination can be reached. Now that we have seen ICMP, we can understand exactly how ping operates. Ping uses the ICMP echo request and echo reply messages. When invoked, ping sends an IP datagram that contains an ICMP echo request message to the specified destination. After sending the request, it waits a short time for the reply. If no reply arrives, ping retransmits the request. If no reply arrives for the retransmissions (or if an ICMP destination unreachable message arrives), ping declares that the remote machine is not reachable.

ICMP software on a remote machines replies to the echo request message. According to the protocol, whenever an echo request arrives, the ICMP software must send an echo reply.

23.6 Using ICMP To Trace A Route

We said that the *TIME TO LIVE* field in a datagram header is used to recover from routing errors. To prevent a datagram from following a cycle of routes forever, each router that handles a datagram decrements the *TIME TO LIVE* counter in the header. If a counter reaches zero, the router discards the datagram and sends an ICMP time exceeded error back to the source.

ICMP messages are used by the *traceroute* tool described in Chapter 2 when it constructs a list of all routers along a path to a given destination. Traceroute simply sends a series of datagrams and waits for a response to each. Traceroute sets the *TIME TO LIVE* value in the first datagram to *1* before sending the datagram. The first router that receives the datagram decrements the time to live, discards the datagram, and sends back an ICMP time exceeded message. Because the ICMP message travels in an IP datagram, traceroute can extract the IP source address and announce the address of the first router along the path to the destination.

After it discovers the address of the first router, traceroute sends a datagram with *TIME TO LIVE* set to *2*. The first router decrements the counter and forwards the datagram; the second router discards the datagram and sends an error message. Similarly, once it has received an error message from a router that is distance *2*, traceroute sends a datagram with *TIME TO LIVE* set to *3*, then *4*, and so on.

Several details remain that traceroute must handle. Because IP uses best-effort delivery, datagrams can be lost, duplicated, or delivered out of order. Thus, traceroute must be prepared to handle duplicate responses and to retransmit datagrams that are lost. Choosing a retransmission timeout can be difficult because traceroute cannot know how long to wait for a response — traceroute allows the user to decide how long to wait.

Traceroute faces another problem: routes can change dynamically. If routes change between two probes, the second probe may take a longer or shorter path than the first. More important, the sequence of routers that traceroute finds may not correspond to a valid path through the internet. Thus, traceroute is most useful in an internet where routes are relatively stable.

23.7 The Last Address Printed By Traceroute

Traceroute continues to increment the *TIME TO LIVE* until the value is large enough for the datagram to reach its final destination. What happens when the TTL is sufficiently large for the datagram to reach its destination? To ensure that it receives a reply, traceroute sends a datagram to which the destination host is required to respond. There are two possibilities in widespread use:

- Send an ICMP *echo request* message; the destination host will generate an ICMP *echo reply*.

- Send a datagram to a nonexistent application; the destination host will generate an ICMP *destination unreachable* message.

The Microsoft implementation of traceroute (*tracert*) implements the first approach by sending an ICMP echo request message. Thus, each time it transmits a datagram, tracert either receives an ICMP time exceeded message from a router along the path or an ICMP *echo reply* message from the destination computer. Most Unix versions of traceroute use the second approach. They send a *User Datagram Protocol* (*UDP*), message because UDP messages are delivered to application programs. Traceroute sends the UDP message to a nonexistent program on the destination machine. When a UDP message arrives for a nonexistent program, ICMP sends an ICMP *destination unreachable* message. Thus, each time it transmits a datagram, traceroute either receives an ICMP time exceeded message from a router along the path or an ICMP destination unreachable message from the ultimate destination computer.

The two implementations of traceroute can produce different results when the destination is a router or a host with multiple network interfaces†. To understand why, one must know two additional details about ICMP. When an *echo request* arrives at the destination computer, ICMP generates a reply with the source address equal to the IP address to which the request was sent. However, when a datagram arrives and no application program is waiting, ICMP uses the address of the interface over which the error message is sent.

Suppose a user specifies traceroute to one particular address of a router. The Unix version of traceroute will print information about the actual interface of the router over which the datagram arrived. However, the Microsoft version, will always list the same information the user supplied on the command line. The difference is only important to network managers who use traceroute to check routing — they need to know exact details about the route, not merely that the datagram arrived.

---

†In addition to the functional difference discussed in this chapter, some implementations of traceroute insert a delay between each probe, meaning that the program is noticeably slower than other versions.

We can summarize:

> *The traceroute program uses ICMP error messages to find intermediate routers along a path to a given destination. Two implementations exist that can produce different addresses for the final destination in cases where the final destination has multiple network interfaces.*

23.8 Using ICMP For Path MTU Discovery

In a router, IP software fragments any datagram that is larger than the MTU of the network over which the datagram is being transmitted. Although fragmentation solves the problem of heterogeneous networks, fragmentation often impacts performance. A router uses memory and CPU time to construct fragments. Similarly, a destination host uses memory and CPU time to collect incoming fragments and reassemble them into a complete datagram. In some applications, fragmentation can be avoided if the original sender chooses a smaller datagram size. For example, a file transfer application can send an arbitrary amount of data in each datagram. If the application chooses a datagram size less than or equal to the smallest network MTU along the path to the destination, no router will need to fragment the datagram.

Technically, the smallest MTU along a path from a source to a destination is known as the *path MTU*. Of course, if routes change (i.e., the path changes), the path MTU can change as well. However, in many parts of the Internet, routes tend to remain stable for days or weeks. In such cases, it makes sense for a computer to find the path MTU, and create datagrams that are small enough.

What mechanism can a host use to determine the path MTU? The answer lies in an ICMP error message and a probe that will cause the error message to be sent. The error message consists of an ICMP message that reports fragmentation was required but not permitted, and the technique for requesting it is a bit in the *FLAGS* field of the IP header that specifies the datagram should not be fragmented. When a router determines that a datagram must be fragmented, the router examines the bit in the header to verify that fragmentation is allowed. If the bit is set, the router does not perform fragmentation. Instead, the router sends an ICMP error message back to the source, and discards the datagram.

To determine the path MTU, IP software on a host sends a sequence of probes, where each probe consists of a datagram that has the header bit set to prevent fragmentation. If a datagram is larger than the MTU of a network along the path, the router connected to that network will discard the datagram and send the appropriate ICMP message to the host. The host can then send a smaller probe until one succeeds. As with traceroute, a host must be prepared to retransmit probes for which no response is received.

23.9 Summary

Although IP uses best-effort delivery semantics, IP includes error detection and reporting mechanisms. In addition to a header checksum that is used to detect transmission errors, IP implementations include an error reporting system known as the Internet Control Message Protocol (ICMP). ICMP includes informational messages as well as messages used to report errors. Routers send ICMP error messages to the original source of a datagram that causes a problem.

ICMP error messages can be used to test an internet to obtain information. The ping program uses ICMP echo request and reply messages to determine whether a destination is reachable. The traceroute program uses ICMP time exceeded messages to find a sequence of routers at distance *1*, *2*, *3*, etc. along a path to a given destination. Finally, a host can use ICMP messages to determine the path MTU for a given destination.

EXERCISES

23.1   Suppose a router decrements the *TIME TO LIVE* field in a datagram header by *1*, but makes no other changes to the header. Find a way to incrementally produce a new value for the checksum that takes less CPU time than recomputing the entire checksum. Hint: the checksum is computed by treating the header as a sequence of 16-bit integers and taking the complement of the sum that results from using 1's-complement arithmetic to add the integers.

23.2   Suppose a user specified a directed broadcast address as a destination for ping. What results are possible? Explain.

23.3   To determine whether routes remain stable in your organization, use the traceroute program to find a route to each network in your organization. Repeat the test once each day for five consecutive days. Do routes change?

23.4   Choose ten distant locations on the Internet and run the experiment in the previous exercise to determine how often routes change. Do the results surprise you?

23.5   Experiment with the version of traceroute that you have available to determine whether it sends ICMP *echo request* messages or UDP messages. (Do not look at the contents of packets.)

Chapter Contents

24

TCP: Reliable Transport Service

24.1 Introduction

Previous chapters describe the connectionless packet delivery service provided by IP and the companion protocol used to report errors. This chapter examines TCP, the major transport protocol in the TCP/IP suite, and explains how the protocol provides reliable delivery.

TCP achieves a seemingly impossible task: it uses the unreliable datagram service offered by IP when sending data to another computer, but provides a reliable data delivery service to application programs. TCP must compensate for loss or delay in an internet to provide efficient data transfer, and it must do so without overloading the underlying networks and routers. After reviewing the service that TCP provides to applications, this chapter examines the techniques TCP uses to achieve reliability.

24.2 The Need For Reliable Transport

Programmers are trained to think that reliability is fundamental in a computer system. For example, a programmer might be asked to build an application that sends data to an I/O device such as a printer. The application writes data to the device, but does not need to verify that data arrives intact. Instead, the application relies on the underlying computer system to ensure reliable transfer; the system guarantees that data will not be lost, duplicated, or delivered out of order.

To allow programmers to follow conventional techniques when creating applications that use an internet, software in the internet must provide the same semantics as a conventional computer system. That is, software must guarantee prompt, reliable communication. The data must be delivered in exactly the same order that the data was sent, and there must be no loss or duplication.

24.3 The Transmission Control Protocol

Reliability is the responsibility of a transport protocol; applications interact with a transport service to send and receive data. In the TCP/IP suite, the *Transmission Control Protocol (TCP)* provides reliable transport service. TCP is remarkable because it solves a difficult problem well — although other protocols have been created, no general-purpose transport protocol has proved to work better. Consequently, most internet applications are built to use TCP.

To summarize:

> *Transport protocols provide reliability, which is fundamental for many applications. The Transmission Control Protocol (TCP) is the transport level protocol that provides reliability in the TCP/IP protocol suite.*

24.4 The Service TCP Provides To Applications

From an application program's point of view, the service offered by TCP has seven major features:

- *Connection Orientation.* TCP provides connection-oriented service in which an application must first request a connection to a destination, and then use the connection to transfer data.

- *Point-To-Point Communication.* Each TCP connection has exactly two endpoints.

- *Complete Reliability.* TCP guarantees that the data sent across a connection will be delivered exactly as sent, with no data missing or out of order.

- *Full Duplex Communication.* A TCP connection allows data to flow in either direction, and allows either application program to send data at any time. TCP can buffer outgoing and incoming data in both directions, making it possible for an application to send data and then to continue computation while the data is being transferred.

- *Stream Interface.* We say that TCP provides a stream interface in which an application sends a continuous sequence of octets across a connection. That is, TCP does not provide a notion of records, and does not guarantee that data will be delivered to the receiving application in the same size pieces that it was transferred by the sending application.

- *Reliable Connection Startup.* TCP requires that when two applications create a connection, both must agree to the new connection; duplicate packets used in previous connections will not appear to be valid responses or otherwise interfere with the new connection.

- *Graceful Connection Shutdown.* An application program can open a connection, send arbitrary amounts of data, and then request that the connection be shut down. TCP guarantees to deliver all the data reliably before closing the connection.

To summarize:

TCP provides a completely reliable (no data duplication or loss), connection-oriented, full-duplex stream transport service that allows two application programs to form a connection, send data in either direction, and then terminate the connection. Each TCP connection is started reliably and terminated gracefully, with all data being delivered before the termination occurs.

24.5 End-To-End Service And Datagrams

TCP is called an *end-to-end* protocol because it provides a connection directly from an application on one computer to an application on a remote computer. The applications can request that TCP form a connection, send and receive data, and close the connection.

The connections provided by TCP are called *virtual connections* because they are achieved in software. Indeed, the underlying internet system does not provide hardware or software support for connections. Instead, the TCP software modules on two machines exchange messages to achieve the illusion of a connection.

TCP uses IP to carry messages. Each TCP message is encapsulated in an IP datagram and sent across the internet. When the datagram arrives on the destination host, IP passes the contents to TCP. Note that although TCP uses IP to carry messages, IP does not read or interpret the messages. Thus, TCP treats IP as a packet communication system that connects hosts at two endpoints of a connection, and IP treats each TCP message as data to be transferred.

Figure 24.1 contains an example internet with two hosts and a router that illustrates the relationship between TCP and IP software.

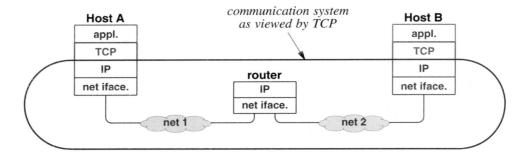

Figure 24.1 An example internet that illustrates why TCP is an end-to-end transport protocol. TCP views IP as a mechanism that allows TCP software on a host to exchange messages with TCP software on a remote host.

As the figure shows, TCP software is needed at each end of a virtual connection, but not on intermediate routers. From TCP's point of view, the entire internet is a communication system that can accept and deliver messages without changing or interpreting their contents.

24.6 Achieving Reliability

A transport protocol like TCP must be carefully designed to achieve reliability. The major problems are: unreliable delivery by the underlying communication system and computer reboot. To understand the scope of the problem, consider a situation in which two application programs form a TCP connection, communicate, close the connection, and then form a new connection. Because any message can be lost, duplicated, delayed, or delivered out of order, messages from the first connection can be duplicated and a copy delayed long enough for the second connection to be established. Messages must be unambiguous, or the protocol will accept duplicate messages from the old connection and allow them to interfere with the new connection.

Computer system reboot poses another serious challenge to TCP protocol designers. Imagine a situation where two application programs establish a connection and then one of the computers is rebooted. Although the protocol software on the computer that reboots has no knowledge of the connection, protocol software on the computer that did not reboot considers the connection valid. More important, duplicate packets that are delayed pose an especially difficult challenge because a protocol must be able to reject packets from a previous reboot (i.e., the packets must be rejected even if the protocol software has no record of the previous connection).

24.7 Packet Loss And Retransmission

How does TCP achieve reliability? The answer is complex because TCP uses a variety of techniques to handle parts of the problem. One of the most important techniques is *retransmission*. When TCP sends data, the sender compensates for packet loss by implementing a retransmission scheme. Both sides of a communication participate. When TCP receives data, it sends an *acknowledgement* back to the sender. Whenever it sends data, TCP starts a timer. If the timer expires before an acknowledgement arrives, the sender retransmits the data. Figure 24.2 illustrates retransmission.

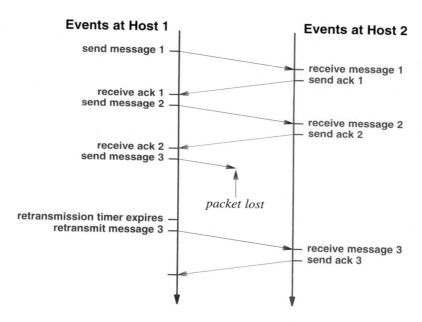

Figure 24.2 Example of retransmission. Items on the left correspond to events in a computer sending data, items on the right correspond to events in a computer receiving data, and time goes down the figure. The sender retransmits lost data.

TCP's retransmission scheme is the key to its success because it handles communication across an arbitrary internet and allows multiple application programs to communicate concurrently. For example, one application can send data across a satellite channel to a computer in another country, while another application sends data across a local area network to a computer in the next room. TCP must be ready to retransmit any message that is lost on either connection. The question is: how long should TCP wait before retransmitting? Acknowledgements from a computer on a local area network are expected to arrive within a few milliseconds. Waiting too long for such an acknowledgement leaves the network idle and does not maximize throughput. Thus, on a local area network, TCP should not wait a long time before retransmitting. However, retransmitting after a few milliseconds does not work well on a long-distance satellite connection because the unnecessary traffic consumes network bandwidth and lowers throughput.

TCP faces a more difficult challenge than distinguishing between local and remote destinations: bursts of datagrams can cause congestion, which causes transmission delays along a given path to change rapidly. In fact, the total time required to send a message and receive an acknowledgement can increase or decrease by an order of magnitude in a few milliseconds. To summarize:

> *The delay required for data to reach a destination and an acknowledgement to return depends on traffic in the internet as well as the distance to the destination. Because TCP allows multiple application programs to communicate with multiple destinations concurrently and because traffic conditions affect delay, TCP must handle a variety of delays that can change rapidly.*

24.8 Adaptive Retransmission

Before TCP was invented, transport protocols used a fixed value for retransmission delay — the protocol designer or network manager chose a value that was large enough for the expected delay. Designers working on TCP realized that a fixed timeout would not operate well for an internet. Thus, they chose to make TCP's retransmission *adaptive*. That is, TCP monitors current delay on each connection, and adapts (i.e., changes) the retransmission timer to accommodate changing conditions.

How can TCP monitor internet delays? In fact, TCP cannot know the exact delays for all parts of an internet at all times. Instead, TCP estimates *round-trip delay* for each active connection by measuring the time needed to receive a response. Whenever it sends a message to which it expects a response, TCP records the time at which the message was sent. When a response arrives, TCP subtracts the time the message was sent from the current time to produce a new estimate of the round-trip delay for that connection. As it sends data packets and receives acknowledgements, TCP generates a sequence of round-trip estimates and uses a statistical function to produce a weighted average. In addition to a weighted average, TCP keeps an estimate of the variance, and uses a linear combination of the estimated mean and variance as a value for retransmission.

Experience has shown that TCP adaptive retransmission works well. Using the variance helps TCP react quickly when delay increases following a burst of packets. Using a weighted average helps TCP reset the retransmission timer if the delay returns to a lower value after a temporary burst. When the delay remains constant, TCP adjusts the retransmission timeout to a value that is slightly longer than the mean round-trip delay. When delays start to vary, TCP adjusts the retransmission timeout to a value greater than the mean to accommodate peaks.

24.9 Comparison Of Retransmission Times

To understand how adaptive retransmission helps TCP maximize throughput on each connection, consider a case of packet loss on two connections that have different round-trip delays. For example, Figure 24.3 illustrates traffic on two such connections.

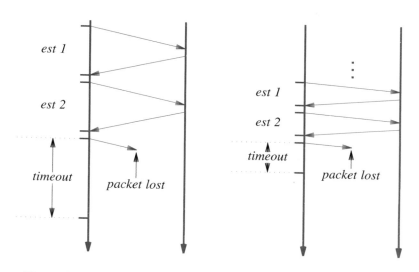

Figure 24.3 Timeout and retransmission on two connections that have different round-trip delays. TCP optimizes throughput by using a round-trip estimate to compute a retransmission timer.

As the figure shows, TCP sets the retransmission timeout to be slightly longer than the mean round-trip delay. If the delay is large, TCP uses a large retransmission timeout; if the delay is small, TCP uses a small timeout. The goal is to wait long enough to determine that a packet was lost, without waiting longer than necessary.

24.10 Buffers, Flow Control, And Windows

TCP uses a *window* mechanism to control the flow of data. When a connection is established, each end of the connection allocates a buffer to hold incoming data, and sends the size of the buffer to the other end. As data arrives, the receiver sends acknowledgements, which also specify the remaining buffer size. The amount of buffer space available at any time is called the *window*, and a notification that specifies the size is called a *window advertisement*. A receiver sends a window advertisement with each acknowledgement.

If the receiving application can read data as quickly as it arrives, a receiver will send a positive window advertisement along with each acknowledgement. However, if the sending side operates faster than the receiving side (e.g., because the CPU is faster), incoming data will eventually fill the receiver's buffer, causing the receiver to advertise a *zero window*. A sender that receives a zero window advertisement must stop sending until the receiver again advertises a positive window. Figure 24.4 illustrates window advertisements.

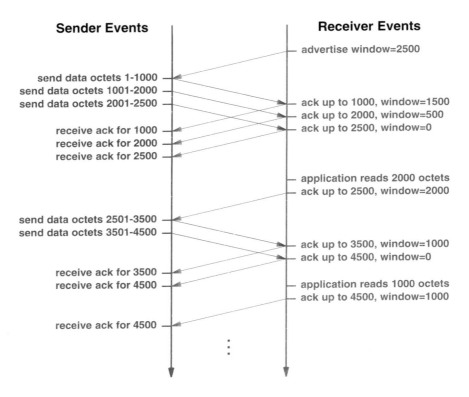

Figure 24.4 A sequence of messages that illustrates TCP flow control when the maximum segment size is *1000* octets. A sender can transmit enough data to fill the currently advertised window.

In the figure, the sender uses a maximum segment size of *1000* octets. Transfer begins when the receiver advertises an initial window size of *2500* octets. The sender immediately transmits three segments, two that contain *1000* octets of data and one that contains *500* octets. As the segments arrive, the receiver generates an acknowledgement with the window size reduced by the amount of data that has arrived.

In this example, the first three segments fill the receiver's buffer faster than the receiving application can consume data. Thus, the advertised window reaches zero, and the sender cannot transmit additional data. After the receiving application consumes *2000* octets of the data, the receiving TCP sends an additional acknowledgement that advertises a window of *2000* octets. The window size is always measured beyond the data being acknowledged, so the receiver is advertising that it can accept *2000* octets beyond the *2500* it has already received. The sender responds by transmitting two additional segments. As each segment arrives, the receiver sends an acknowledgement with the window size reduced by *1000* octets (i.e., the amount of data that has arrived).

Once again, the window reaches zero, causing the sender to stop transmission. Eventually, the receiving application consumes some of the data, and the receiving TCP transmits an acknowledgement with a positive window size. If the sender had more data waiting to be sent, the sender could proceed to transmit another segment.

24.11 Three-Way Handshake

To guarantee that connections are established or terminated reliably, TCP uses a *3-way handshake* in which three messages are exchanged†. Scientists have proved that a 3-way exchange is necessary and sufficient to ensure unambiguous agreement despite packet loss, duplication, and delay.

TCP uses the term *synchronization segment* (*SYN segment*) to describe messages in a 3-way handshake used to create a connection, and the term *FIN segment* (short for *finish*) to describe messages in a 3-way handshake used to close a connection. Figure 24.5 illustrates the 3-way handshake used to close a connection.

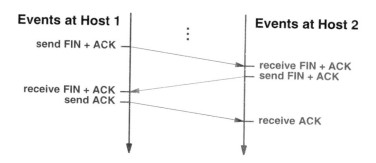

Figure 24.5 The 3-way handshake used to close a connection. Acknowledgements sent in each direction are used to guarantee that all data has arrived before the connection is terminated.

---

†During the 3-way handshake, each end of the connection includes an initial window advertisement in the message that carries the SYN.

Like other messages, TCP retransmits lost SYN or FIN segments. Furthermore, the handshake guarantees that TCP will not open or close a connection until both ends have interacted.

Part of the 3-way handshake used to create a connection requires each end to generate a random 32-bit sequence number. If an application attempts to establish a new TCP connection after a computer reboots, TCP chooses a new random number. Because each new connection receives a new random sequence, a pair of application programs can use TCP to communicate, close the connection, and then establish a new connection without interference from duplicate or delayed packets.

24.12 Congestion Control

One of the most interesting aspects of TCP is a mechanism for *congestion control*. In most modern internets, packet loss (or extremely long delay) is more likely to be caused by congestion than a hardware failure. Interestingly, transport protocols that retransmit can exacerbate the problem of congestion by injecting additional copies of a message. If congestion triggers excessive retransmission, the entire system can reach a state of *congestion collapse*, analogous to a traffic jam on a highway. To avoid the problem, TCP always uses packet loss as a measure of congestion, and responds by reducing the rate at which it retransmits data.

Whenever a message is lost, TCP begins congestion control. Instead of retransmitting enough data to fill the receiver's buffer (i.e., the receiver's window size), TCP begins by sending a single message containing data. If the acknowledgement arrives without additional loss, TCP doubles the amount of data being sent, and sends two additional messages. If acknowledgements arrive for those two, TCP sends four more, and so on. The exponential increase continues until TCP is sending half of the receiver's advertised window, at which time TCP slows down the rate of increase.

TCP's congestion control scheme responds well to increased traffic in an internet. By backing off quickly, TCP is able to alleviate congestion. More important, because it avoids adding retransmissions to a congested internet, TCP's congestion control scheme helps prevent congestion collapse.

24.13 TCP Segment Format

TCP uses a single format for all messages, including messages that carry data, those that carry acknowledgements, and messages that are part of the 3-way handshake used to create or terminate a connection. TCP uses the term *segment* to refer to a message; Figure 24.6 illustrates the segment format.

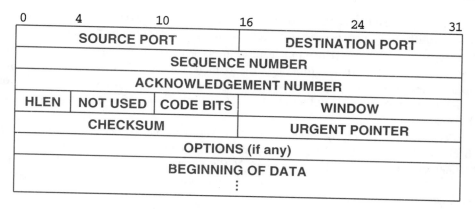

Figure 24.6 The TCP segment format. Each message sent from TCP on one machine to TCP on another uses this format, including data and acknowledgements.

To understand the segment format, it is necessary to remember that a TCP connection contains two streams of data, one flowing in each direction. If the applications at each end are sending data simultaneously, TCP can send a single segment that carries the acknowledgement for incoming data, a window advertisement that specifies the amount of additional buffer space available for incoming data, and outgoing data. Thus, some of the fields in the segment refer to the data stream traveling in the forward direction, while other fields refer to the data stream traveling in the reverse direction.

When a computer sends a segment, the *ACKNOWLEDGMENT NUMBER* and *WINDOW* fields refer to incoming data: the *ACKNOWLEDGMENT NUMBER* specifies the sequence number of the data that has been received, and the *WINDOW* specifies how much additional buffer space is available for more data. The *SEQUENCE NUMBER* field refers to outgoing data. It gives the sequence number for the data being carried in the segment. The receiver uses the sequence number to reorder segments that arrive out of order and to compute an acknowledgement number. Field *DESTINATION PORT* identifies which application program on the receiving computer should receive the data, while field *SOURCE PORT* identifies the application program that sent the data. Finally, the *CHECKSUM* field contains a checksum that covers the TCP segment header and the data.

24.14 Summary

The Transmission Control Protocol (TCP) is the major transport protocol in the TCP/IP protocol suite. TCP provides application programs with a reliable, flow-controlled, full-duplex, stream transport service. After requesting TCP to establish a connection, an application program can use the connection to send or receive data; TCP guarantees to deliver the data in order without duplication. Finally, when the two applications finish using a connection, they request that the connection be terminated.

TCP on one computer communicates with TCP on another computer by exchanging messages. All messages from one TCP to another use the TCP segment format, including messages that carry data, acknowledgements, and window advertisements, or messages used to establish and terminate a connection. Each TCP segment travels in an IP datagram.

TCP uses a variety of mechanisms to ensure reliable service. In addition to a checksum in each segment, TCP retransmits any message that is lost. To be useful in an internet where delays vary over time, TCP's retransmission timeout must be adaptive. An adaptive retransmission scheme measures the current round-trip delay separately for each connection, and uses the round-trip time to choose a timeout for retransmission.

EXERCISES

24.1   Write two computer programs that communicate reliably. To test your programs, simulate packet loss by discarding messages periodically.

24.2   Assume that messages sent between two programs can be lost, duplicated, delayed, or delivered out of order. Design a protocol that reliably allows the two programs to agree to communicate. Give your design to someone, and see if they can find a sequence of failures that make the protocol fail.

24.3   Suppose two programs use TCP to establish a connection, communicate, terminate the connection, and then open a new connection. Further suppose a *FIN* message sent to shut down the first connection is duplicated and delayed until the second connection has been established. If a copy of the old *FIN* is delivered, will TCP terminate the new connection?

24.4   Write a computer program to extract and print fields in a TCP segment header.

24.5   Figure 24.4 illustrates how data flows on a TCP connection. In reality, TCP uses *slow start* when it first starts sending data. Use a network analyzer to watch TCP transmissions and ACKs. What happens during slow start after each ACK arrives?

24.6   Is the TCP checksum necessary or could TCP allow IP to checksum the data?

24.7   Could TCP be used directly over a network (e.g. an Ethernet) without using IP? Why or why not?

24.8   Before it knows the mean round-trip time, TCP must be prepared to retransmit the initial segment (the one used to open a connection). How long does TCP wait before retransmitting the segment? How many times does TCP retry before declaring that it cannot open the connection? To find out, attempt to open a connection to a nonexistent address, and use a network analyzer to watch the resulting TCP traffic.

Chapter Contents

25

Internet Routing

25.1 Introduction

Previous chapters describe the fundamental concept of datagram forwarding, and explain how IP uses a routing table to forward datagrams. This chapter explores an important aspect of internetworking technology: the propagation of routing information that is used to create and update routing tables. The chapter discusses how routing tables are built initially, and explains how routing software updates the tables as needed.

The chapter focuses on the propagation of routing information in the global Internet. It explains the general concept of routing information exchange, and then describes several routing update protocols used in the Internet.

25.2 Static Vs. Dynamic Routing

IP routing can be partitioned into two broad categories: *static routing* and *dynamic routing*. Routes are called *static* if they do not change. Thus, a static routing table is loaded with values when the system starts, and the routes do not change unless an error is detected. In contrast, *dynamic routing* refers to a system that can change routing table information over time. Ironically, dynamic routing begins exactly like static routing by loading an initial set of routes into a routing table when the system boots. The system also starts *route propagation software*, which is also called *routing software*, when it boots. The routing software on one computer interacts with routing software on other computers to learn about optimal routes to each location. The software then updates the local routing table to ensure that datagrams follow optimal routes.

25.3 Static Routing In Hosts And A Default Route

Static routing is straightforward, easy to specify, and does not require extra routing software. It does not consume bandwidth, and no CPU cycles are required to propagate routing information. However, static routing is relatively inflexible; it cannot accommodate network failures or changes in topology.

Where is static routing used? Most hosts use static routing, especially in cases where the host has one network connection and a single router connects the network to the rest of the Internet. For example, consider the architecture that Figure 25.1 illustrates. Four hosts are attached to an Ethernet, which connects to the rest of the Internet through router R_1.

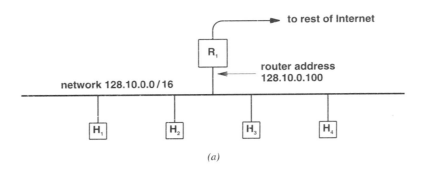

(a)

Net	Mask	Next hop
128.10.0.0	255.255.0.0	direct
default	0.0.0.0	128.10.0.100

(b)

Figure 25.1 (a) An architecture where static routing is used, and (b) a static routing table used in a host.

As the figure shows, a static routing table can be extremely small. In the example, two entries suffice — one for the directly connected network and the other for a *default route* that is followed for all other destinations. When an application generates a datagram for a computer on the local net, the first entry in the routing table directs IP to deliver the datagram directly to its destination. When a datagram is destined for any other network, the second entry in the table directs IP to send the datagram to the router.

Is static routing used in the Internet? Yes. In fact, most PCs on the Internet use static routing. When configuring IP software on a PC, a user enters a network prefix, a subnet mask, and the address of a default IP router. The three items comprise the information needed to create the static routing table illustrated in Figure 25.1. When a PC boots, the operating system reads the three values from a configuration file and uses them to construct a routing table.

To summarize:

> *Most hosts use static routing. The host's routing table contains two entries: one for the network to which the host attaches and a default entry that directs all other traffic to a specific router.*

25.4 Dynamic Routing And Routers

Can a router in the global Internet use static routing the same way a host does? If so, how large is the routing table in a router? The answers to these questions are complex. Although cases exist where a router uses static routing, most routers use dynamic routing.

To understand an exceptional case where static routing does suffice for a router, look at Figure 25.1 again. We can imagine that the figure corresponds to a small organization that is a customer of an ISP. All traffic leaving the customer's site through router R_1 must travel to the ISP (e.g., across a DSL connection). Because routes never change, the routing table in router R_1 can be static. Furthermore, the routing table in R_1 can use a default route just as the routing table in a host does.

Despite a few exceptions, static routing and default routes do not suffice for most routers; the use is limited to configurations like the one that Figure 25.1 depicts. When two ISPs interconnect, both need to exchange routing information dynamically. To see why, consider three networks interconnected by two routers as Figure 25.2 illustrates.

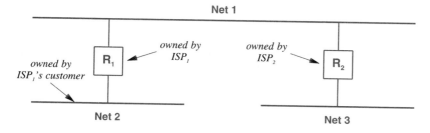

Figure 25.2 Three networks connected by two routers. In such situations, dynamic routing can be used to propagate information about remote networks.

In the figure, each of the two routers belong to a separate ISP. The network labeled *Net 2* belongs to a corporate customer of ISP_1, and the network labeled *Net 3* belongs to a corporate customer of ISP_2. Both routers know about the network labeled *Net 1*, of course, because that is the network that interconnects them. However, router R_1 does not know about *Net 3* because there is no direct connection. Similarly, router R_2 does know about *Net 2*.

How can a router in one ISP have routes to networks owned by customers of another ISP? Because the example in Figure 25.2 has only three networks, static routing seems to make sense. However, because static routing requires manual installation of routes, the scheme does not scale to ISPs that have hundreds or thousands of customers. Each time an ISP adds a new customer's network, the information must be passed to a person at the other ISP, who then updates the routing table. More important, the manual process is far too slow to accommodate network failures or congestion. For example, if a network interface card fails or someone accidentally unplugs a router, routing software needs to detect the disconnection and find an alternative route quickly (within milliseconds).

To ensure that all routers maintain information about how to reach each possible destination, each router runs software that uses a route propagation protocol to exchange information with other routers. When it learns about changes in routes, the routing software updates the local routing table. Furthermore, because routers exchange information periodically, the local routing table is updated continuously.

As an example, assume that routers R_1 and R_2 in Figure 25.2 each run routing software; the software uses a route propagation protocol to exchange routing information across *Net 1*. As a result, software running on R_2 installs a route to *Net 2*. Similarly, software running on R_1 installs a route to *Net 3*. If router R_2 crashes, the route propagation software in R_1 will detect that *Net 3* is no longer reachable, and will remove the route from R_1's table. Later, when R_2 comes back on line, the routing software in R_1 will determine that *Net 3* is reachable again, and will reinstall the route.

To summarize:

> *Each router runs routing software that learns about destinations other routers can reach, and informs other routers about destinations that it can reach. The routing software uses incoming information to update the local routing table continuously.*

25.5 Routing In The Global Internet

So far, we have described routing for the most trivial connectivity (i.e., situations that involve only a few routers). This section begins to look at a broader issue: routing in the global Internet. The section considers general principles; later sections explain specific route propagation protocols.

We said that a route propagation protocol allows one router to exchange routing information with another. However, such a scheme cannot scale to the entire Internet — if all routers attempted to exchange routing information, the resulting traffic would overwhelm the backbone networks. To limit routing traffic, the Internet uses a two-level routing hierarchy. Routers and networks in the Internet are divided into groups. All routers within a group exchange routing information. Then, at least one router (possibly more) in each group summarizes the information before passing it to other groups.

How large is a group? What protocol do routers use within a group? How is routing information represented? What protocol do routers use between groups? The designers of the Internet routing system did not dictate an exact size nor did they specify an exact data representation or protocol. Instead, the designers purposefully kept the architecture flexible enough to handle a wide variety of organizations. For example, to accommodate organizations of various size, the designers avoided specifying a minimum or maximum size for a group. To accommodate arbitrary routing protocols, the designers decided to permit each organization to choose a routing protocol independently.

25.6 Autonomous System Concept

To capture the concept of groups of routers, we use the term *Autonomous System* (*AS*). Intuitively, one can think of an autonomous system as a contiguous set of networks and routers all under control of one administrative authority. There is no exact meaning for *administrative authority* — the term is sufficiently flexible to accommodate many possibilities. For example, an autonomous system can correspond to an entire corporation or to an entire university. Alternatively, a large organization with multiple sites may choose to define one autonomous system for each site. In particular, each ISP is usually a single autonomous system, but it is possible for a large ISP to divide itself into multiple autonomous systems.

The choice of autonomous system size can be made for economic, technical, or administrative reasons. For example, consider a large corporation with multiple physical sites. It may be less expensive for the corporation to divide into multiple autonomous systems, each of which has a connection to an ISP than to act as a single autonomous system with one connection to the rest of the Internet. More important, the selection of a routing protocol may determine whether an organization chooses to use multiple autonomous systems — the protocol may bound the maximum size of the network or may generate excessive routing traffic when used on a large number of routers (i.e., the routing traffic may grow as the square of the number of routers).

To summarize:

> *Routers in the global Internet are divided into groups, where each group is known as an* autonomous system. *The routers within an autonomous system exchange routing information, which is then summarized before being passed to another group.*

25.7 The Two Types Of Internet Routing Protocols

Now that we understand the autonomous system concept, Internet routing can be defined more precisely. All Internet routing protocols fall into one of two categories. After defining the two categories, we examine specific protocols in each category.

25.7.1 Interior Gateway Protocols (IGPs)

The routers within an autonomous system use an *Interior Gateway Protocol* (*IGP*) to exchange routing information. There are several IGPs available; each autonomous system is free to choose its own IGP. Usually, an IGP is easy to install and operate, but an IGP may limit the size or routing complexity of an autonomous system.

25.7.2 Exterior Gateway Protocols (EGPs)

A router in one autonomous system uses an *Exterior Gateway Protocol* (*EGP*) to exchange routing information with a router in another autonomous system. EGPs are usually more complex to install and operate than IGPs, but EGPs offer more flexibility and lower overhead (i.e., less traffic). To save traffic, an EGP summarizes routing information from the autonomous system before passing it to another autonomous system. More important, an EGP implements *policy constraints* that allow a system manager to determine exactly what information is released outside the organization.

25.7.3 When EGPs And IGPs Are Used

Figure 25.3 illustrates the two-level routing hierarchy used in the global Internet.

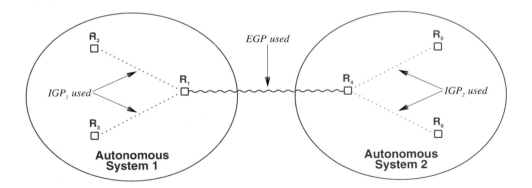

Figure 25.3 The Internet routing architecture. Each autonomous system chooses an IGP to use internally; an EGP is used to communicate between autonomous systems.

In the figure, Autonomous System 1 (AS_1) has chosen IGP_1 to use internally, and Autonomous System 2 (AS_2) has chosen IGP_2. All routers in AS_1 communicate using IGP_1 and all routers in AS_2 communicate using IGP_2. Routers R_1 and R_4 use an EGP to communicate between the two autonomous systems. That is, R_1 must summarize information from its autonomous system and send the summary to R_4. In addition, R_1 accepts a summary from R_4, and uses IGP_1 to propagate the information to routers in AS_1. R_4 performs the same service for AS_2.

25.7.4 Optimal Routes, Routing Metrics, and IGPs

It may seem that instead of merely discovering one path to each destination, routing software should find all possible paths and then choose one that is optimal. Although the global Internet usually does have multiple paths between any source and destination, there is no universal agreement about which path is optimal. To understand why, consider the requirements of various applications. For an interactive login application, a path with least delay is optimal. For a browser downloading a large graphics file, a path with maximum throughput is optimal. For an audio webcast application that receives real-time audio, a path with least jitter is optimal.

We use the term *routing metric* to refer to a measure of the path that routing software uses when choosing a route. Although it is possible to use throughput, delay, or jitter as a routing metric, most Internet routing software does not. Instead, typical Internet routing uses a combination of two metrics: *administrative cost* and *hop count*. In Internet routing, a hop corresponds to an intermediate network (or router). Thus, the hop count for a destination gives the number of intermediate networks on the path to the destination. Administrative costs are assigned manually, often to control which paths traffic can use. For example, suppose in a corporation two paths connect the accounting department to the payroll department: a 2-hop path that includes a network designated to be used for customer traffic and a 3-hop path that includes networks for internal corporate traffic. That is, the shortest path violates the corporate policy by traversing a network designated to serve customers. In such cases, a network administrator can override the actual cost of the 2-hop path by assigning the path an administrate cost of 4 hops (i.e. the manager replaces the actual cost with an administrative value to achieve the desired effect). Routing software will choose the path with the lower cost (i.e., the path with a metric of 3 hops). Thus, traffic will follow the corporate policy.

IGPs and EGPs differ in an important way with respect to routing metrics: IGPs use routing metrics, but EGPs do not. That is, each autonomous system chooses a routing metric and arranges internal routing software to send the metric with each route so receiving software can use the metric to choose optimal paths. Outside an autonomous system, however, an EGP does not attempt to choose an optimal path. Instead, the EGP merely finds a path. The reason is simple: because each autonomous system is free to choose a routing metric, an EGP cannot make meaningful comparisons. For example suppose one autonomous system reports the number of hops along a path to destination D and another autonomous system reports the throughput along a different path to D.

An EGP that receives the two reports cannot choose which of the two paths has less cost because there is no way to convert from hops to throughput. Thus, an EGP can only report the existence of a path and not its cost. We can summarize:

> *Within an autonomous system, IGP software uses a routing metric to choose an optimal path to each destination. EGP software finds a path to each destination, but cannot find an optimal path because it cannot compare routing metrics from multiple autonomous systems.*

25.8 Routes And Data Traffic

An aphorism in networking suggests that the response to a routing advertisement is data. The concept is straightforward: data traffic for a given destination flows in exactly the opposite direction of routing traffic. For example, suppose an autonomous system owned by ISP_1 contains network N. Before traffic can arrive destined for N, ISP_1 must advertise a route to N. That is, when the routing advertisement flows out, data will begin to flow in. Figure 25.4 illustrates the flow.

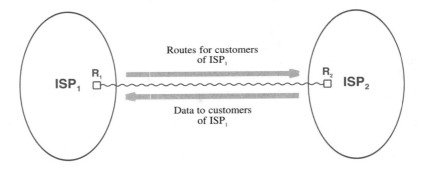

Figure 25.4 The flow of routes and data illustrated with ISPs. After a router in ISP_1 advertises routes to customers, data can arrive for those customers.

25.9 The Border Gateway Protocol (BGP)

One protocol has emerged as the most popular Exterior Gateway Protocol in the Internet. Known as the *Border Gateway Protocol* (*BGP*), the protocol has survived three major revisions. Version 4 is the current standard, and the abbreviation *BGP-4* is often used.

BGP has the following characteristics:

- *Routing Among Autonomous Systems.* Because it is intended for use as an Exterior Gateway Protocol, BGP provides routing information at the autonomous system level. That is, all routes are given as a path of autonomous systems. For example, the path to a given destination may consist of autonomous systems *17, 2, 56*, and *12*. There is no use of routing metrics, and no way for BGP to provide details about the routers within each autonomous system on the path.

- *Provision For Policies.* BGP allows the sender and receiver to enforce policies. In particular, a manager can configure BGP to restrict which routes BGP advertises to outsiders.

- *Facilities For Transit Routing.* BGP classifies each autonomous system as a *transit* system if it agrees to pass traffic through to another autonomous system, or as a *stub* system if it does not. Similarly, traffic passing through on its way to another AS is classified as transit traffic. The classification allows BGP to distinguish between ISPs and other autonomous systems. More important, BGP allows a corporation to classify itself as a stub even if it is *multi-homed* (i.e., a corporation with multiple external connections can refuse to accept transit traffic).

- *Reliable Transport.* BGP uses TCP for all communication. That is, a BGP program on a router in one autonomous system forms a TCP connection to a BGP program on a router in another autonomous system, and then sends data across the connection. TCP ensures that the data arrives in the correct order and that no data is missing.

BGP is especially important in the global Internet because all major ISPs use BGP to exchange routing information. In addition, a central database of routing information is maintained to ensure that routing remains consistent. Known as the *routing arbiter system*, the scheme keeps a distributed database of all possible destinations in the Internet, with information about the ISP that owns each destination. Each copy of the authoritative database runs on a separate *route server*. Within the Internet, major ISPs use BGP to communicate with one of the route servers to obtain routing information that has been verified. To summarize:

> *Version 4 of the Border Gateway Protocol (BGP-4) is the Exterior Gateway Protocol used to exchange routing information among autonomous systems in the global Internet. ISPs use BGP-4 to obtain routing information from each other and from an authoritative route server. Because all ISPs participate, a datagram from an arbitrary computer to an arbitrary destination will be forwarded correctly.*

25.10 The Routing Information Protocol (RIP)

Although BGP-4 provides for routing exchange among autonomous systems, additional Interior Gateway Protocol support is needed to allow routers to pass such information within an autonomous system. We examine two such protocols. This section examines the *Routing Information Protocol* (*RIP*); the next section examines *OSPF*.

RIP was among the first routing protocols used with IP. The protocol is implemented by the program *routed*† that comes with most Unix systems. RIP has the following characteristics.

- *Routing Within An Autonomous System.* RIP is designed as an Interior Gateway Protocol used to pass information among routers within an autonomous system.

- *Hop Count Metric.* RIP measures distance in network *hops*, where each network between the source and destination counts as a single hop. Furthermore, RIP uses origin-one counting, meaning that a directly connected network is 1 hop away, not zero.

- *Unreliable Transport.* RIP uses UDP for all message transmission.

- *Broadcast Or Multicast Delivery.* RIP is intended for use over Local Area Network technologies that support broadcast or multicast (e.g., Ethernet). Version 1 of RIP uses hardware broadcast when sending messages between routers; version 2 allows delivery via multicast.

- *Support For Default Route Propagation.* In addition to specifying explicit destinations, RIP allows a router to advertise a *default route*. Thus, an organization can use RIP to install a default route in each router such that the default routes all forward traffic to the organization's ISP.

- *Distance Vector Algorithm.* RIP uses the *distance-vector* approach to routing defined in Algorithm 13.2‡.

- *Passive Version For Hosts.* Although only a router can propagate routing information, RIP allows a host to listen passively and update its routing table. Passive RIP is useful on networks that have multiple routers attached — a host running passive RIP will learn which destinations lie beyond each router.

To understand how RIP propagates routes, recall how distance vector routing works. Each outgoing message contains an advertisement that lists the networks the sender can reach. When it receives an advertisement, RIP software on the receiving router uses the list of destinations to update the routing table. Each entry in the advertisement consists of a pair:

(destination network, distance)

---

†The program name is pronounced "route dee".
‡Algorithm 13.2 can be found on page 211.

where *distance* is the number of Internet *hops* to the destination. When a message arrives, if the receiver does not have a route to an advertised destination or if an advertised distance is shorter than the distance of the current route, the receiver replaces its route with a route to the sender.

The chief advantage of RIP is simplicity. RIP requires little configuration — a manager merely starts RIP running on each router in the organization and allows the routers to broadcast messages to one another. After a short time, all routers in the organization will have routes to all destinations.

RIP also handles the propagation of a default route. The organization merely needs to configure one of its routers to have a default; the organization usually chooses the router that connects to an ISP. RIP propagates the default route to all other routers in the organization. Thus, any datagram sent to a destination outside the organization will be forwarded to the ISP.

25.11 RIP Packet Format

The RIP message format will help illustrate how a distance vector protocol operates. Figure 25.5 illustrates a RIP update message.

0	8	16	24	31
COMMAND (1-5)	VERSION (2)	MUST BE ZERO		
FAMILY OF NET 1		ROUTE TAG FOR NET 1		
IP ADDRESS OF NET 1				
SUBNET MASK FOR NET 1				
NEXT HOP FOR NET 1				
DISTANCE TO NET 1				
FAMILY OF NET 2		ROUTE TAG FOR NET 2		
IP ADDRESS OF NET 2				
SUBNET MASK FOR NET 2				
NEXT HOP FOR NET 2				
DISTANCE TO NET 2				
. . .				

Figure 25.5 The format of a RIP version 2 update message. The message contains a list of destinations and a distance to each. RIP measures distance in hops.

Although an update message consists of a list of entries, a few details complicate the format. As expected, each entry contains the IP address of a destination and a distance to that destination. In addition, to permit RIP to be used with CIDR or subnet addressing, an entry contains a 32-bit subnet mask. Each entry also has a next hop address, and two 16-bit fields that identify the entry as an IP address and provide a tag used to group entries together. In all, each entry contains twenty octets.

To summarize:

> *RIP is an Interior Gateway Protocol that uses a distance vector algorithm to propagate routing information. A router running RIP advertises the destinations it can reach along with a distance to each destination; adjacent routers receive the information and update their routing tables.*

25.12 The Open Shortest Path First Protocol (OSPF)

RIP illustrates some of the disadvantages of a distance vector protocol. Because each message contains a complete list of destinations and distances, messages are large. Because the receiving router must compare each entry in the incoming message to the current route for the destination, processing a message consumes CPU cycles and introduces delay. The delay means that route changes propagate slowly, one router at a time. Thus, although RIP works well among a few routers, it does not scale to a large internet.

As the Internet grew in size, so did organizations. In particular, large ISPs appeared. To satisfy demand for a routing protocol that can scale to large organizations, the IETF devised an IGP known as the *Open Shortest Path First Protocol (OSPF)*†. OSPF has the following characteristics:

- *Routing Within An Autonomous System.* OSPF is designed as an Interior Gateway Protocol used to pass routing information among routers within an autonomous system.

- *Full CIDR And Subnet Support.* OSPF includes a 32-bit address mask with each address, which allows the address to be classful, classless, or subnetted.

- *Authenticated Message Exchange.* A pair of routers using OSPF can authenticate each message to ensure that messages are only accepted from a trusted source.

- *Imported Routes.* OSPF allows a router to introduce routes learned from another means (e.g., from BGP).

---

†The name is derived from the use of Dijkstra's SPF algorithm which computes shortest paths.

- *Link-State Algorithm.* OSPF uses *link-state routing* described in Section 13.16.

- *Support For Multi-access Networks.* Traditional link state routing is inefficient across a multi-access network, such as an Ethernet, because all routers attached to the network broadcast link status. OSPF optimizes by designating a single router to broadcast on the network.

To summarize:

> *OSPF is an Interior Gateway Protocol that uses a link-status algorithm to propagate routing information. Each router participating in OSPF must periodically probe adjacent routers and then broadcast a link-status message; routers that receive the message use Dijkstra's SPF algorithm to compute shortest paths.*

25.13 An Example OSPF Graph

Recall from Chapter 13 that link-state routing uses a graph-theoretic abstraction. Although OSPF allows a complex relationship between networks and a graph, a simple example will help explain the basic concept. Consider the network and associated graph illustrated in Figure 25.6.

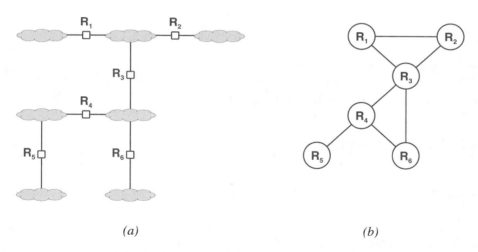

(a)   *(b)*

Figure 25.6 (a) An internet consisting of seven networks interconnected by routers, and (b) a corresponding OSPF graph. In the simplest case, each router corresponds to a node in the graph.

The figure shows a typical OSPF graph in which each node corresponds to a router. An edge in the graph corresponds to a connection between a pair of routers (i.e., a network). Routers running OSPF follow the link-status algorithm — each pair of routers connected by a network periodically probe one another and then broadcast a link-status message to other routers. All routers receive the broadcast message; each uses the message to update its local copy of the graph, and recomputes shortest paths when the status changes.

25.14 OSPF Areas

One particular feature that makes OSPF more complex than other routing protocols also makes it more powerful: hierarchical routing. To achieve a hierarchy, OSPF allows an autonomous system to be partitioned for routing purposes. That is, a manager can divide routers and networks in an autonomous system into subsets that OSPF calls *areas*. Each router is configured to know the area boundary (i.e., exactly which other routers are in its area). When OSPF runs, routers within a given area exchange link-status messages periodically.

In addition to exchanging information within an area, OSPF allows communication between areas. One router in each area is configured to communicate with a router in one or more other area(s). The two routers summarize routing information they have learned from other routers within their respective area, and then exchange the summary. Thus, instead of broadcasting to all routers in the autonomous system, OSPF limits link-status broadcasts to routers within an area. As a result of the hierarchy, OSPF can scale to handle much larger internets than other routing protocols.

The point is:

> *Because it allows a manager to partition the routers and networks in an autonomous system into multiple* areas, *OSPF can scale to handle a larger number of routers than other IGPs.*

25.15 Multicast Routing

25.15.1 IP Multicast Semantics

So far, we have discussed unicast routing. That is, we have considered routing protocols that propagate information about destinations that each have a static address and a location that does not change. One of the design goals for unicast route propagation is *stability* — continual changes in routes are undesirable because they lead to higher jitter and datagrams arriving out of order. Thus, once a unicast routing protocol finds a shortest path, it usually retains the route until a failure makes the path unusable.

Propagating *multicast routing* information differs dramatically from unicast route propagation. The difference arises because Internet multicast allows dynamic group membership and anonymous senders. Dynamic group membership means that an application can choose to participate in a group at any time and remain a participant for an arbitrary duration. That is, the IP multicast abstraction allows an application running on an arbitrary computer to:

- Join a multicast group at any time and begin receiving a copy of all packets sent to the group. When an application decides to join a group, the computer on which the application is running informs a nearby router. If multiple applications on the same computer decide to join a group, the computer receives one copy of each datagram sent to the group and makes a local copy for each application.

- Leave a multicast group at any time. While one or more applications on a computer remain a member of a group, the computer periodically sends membership messages to the local router. Once the last application on the computer leaves the group, the computer informs the local router that it is no longer participating in the group.

An IP multicast group is anonymous in two ways. First, neither a sender nor a receiver knows (or can find out) the identity or the number of group members. Second, routers and hosts do not know which applications will send a datagram to a group because an arbitrary application can send a datagram to any multicast group at any time. That is, membership in a multicast group only defines a set of receivers — a sender does not need to join a multicast group before sending a message to the group.

To summarize:

> *Membership in an IP multicast group is dynamic: a computer can join or leave a group at any time. Group membership defines a set of receivers; an arbitrary application can send a datagram to the group, even if the application is not a group member.*

25.15.2 IGMP

How does a host join or leave a group? A standard protocol exists that allows a host to inform a nearby router whenever the host needs to join or leave a particular multicast group. Known as the *Internet Group Multicast Protocol* (*IGMP*), the protocol is used only on the network between a host and a router. Furthermore, the protocol defines the computer, not the application, to be a group member. If multiple applications on a given computer join a multicast group, the computer must make copies of each datagram it receives for the group. Only when the last application on the computer leaves a group does the computer uses IGMP to inform the local router that it is no longer a member of the group.

25.15.3 Forwarding And Discovery Techniques

When a router learns that a host on one of its networks has joined a multicast group, the router must establish a path to that group and propagate datagrams it receives for the group to the host. Thus, routers, not hosts, have responsibility for the propagation of multicast routing information.

Dynamic group membership and support for anonymous senders makes general-purpose multicast routing extremely difficult. Moreover, the size and topology of groups vary considerably among applications. For example, teleconferencing often creates small groups (e.g., between two and five members) who may be geographically dispersed or in the same organization. An application, such as webcasting, can create a large group that spans the globe.

To accommodate dynamic membership, multicast routing protocols must be able to change routing quickly and continually. For example, if a user in France joins a multicast group that has members in the U.S. and Japan, multicast routing software must first find other members of the group, and then create an optimal forwarding structure. More important, because an arbitrary user can send a datagram to the group, routing must extend beyond group members. In practice, multicast protocols have followed three different approaches for datagram forwarding:

- *Flood-And-Prune.* Flood-and-prune is ideal in a situation where the group is small and all members are attached to contiguous Local Area Networks (e.g., a group within a corporation). Initially, routers forward each datagram to all networks. That is, when a multicast datagram arrives, a router transmits the datagram on all directly attached LANs via hardware multicast. To avoid routing loops, flood-and-prune protocols use a technique known as *Reverse Path Broadcasting* (*RPB*) that breaks cycles. While the flooding stage proceeds, routers exchange information about group membership. If a router learns that no computers on a given network are members of the group, the router stops forwarding multicast to that network (i.e. ''prunes'' the network from the set).

- *Configuration-And-Tunneling.* Configuration-and-tunneling is ideal in a situation where the group is geographically dispersed (i.e., has a few members at each site, with sites separated by long distances). A router at each site is configured to know about other sites. When a multicast datagram arrives, the router at a site transmits the datagram on all directly attached LANs via hardware multicast. The router then consults its configuration table to determine which other sites should receive a copy. The router uses IP-in-IP tunneling to transfer a copy of the multicast datagram to other sites.

- *Core-Based Discovery.* Although flood-and-prune and configuration-and-tunneling each handle extreme cases well, a technique is needed that allows multicast to scale gracefully from a small group in one area to a large group with members at arbitrary locations. To provide smooth growth, some multicast routing protocols designate a *core* unicast address for each multicast group. Whenever a router R_1 needs to reach a group, R_1 sends a datagram to the group's core address. As the datagram travels through the Internet, each router examines the contents. When the datagram reaches a router R_2 that participates in the group, R_2 removes and processes the message. If the message contains a multicast datagram with a destination address equal to the group's address, R_2 forwards the datagram to members of the group. If the message contains a request to join the group, R_2 adds the information to its routes, and then uses IP-in-IP to forward a copy of each multicast datagram to R_1. Thus, the set of routers participating in a multicast group grows from the core outward. In graph theoretic terms, the set forms a *tree*.

25.15.4 Multicast Protocols

Although many multicast routing protocols have been proposed; no Internet-wide multicast routing currently exists. Some of the proposed protocols are:

Distance Vector Multicast Routing Protocol (DVMRP). A protocol used by the Unix program *mrouted* and the Internet *Multicast backBONE (MBONE)*†. DVMRP performs local multicast and uses IP-in-IP encapsulation to send multicast datagrams from one site on the Internet to another.

Core Based Trees (CBT). A multicast routing scheme in which the protocol software builds a delivery tree from a central point. When a user joins a group, routers send a message toward the central point (i.e., the core) to search for the nearest participating router.

Protocol Independent Multicast – Sparse Mode (PIM-SM). A protocol that uses the same approach as CBT to form a multicast routing tree. The designers chose the term *protocol independent* to emphasize that although unicast datagrams are used to contact remote destinations when establishing multicast forwarding, PIM-SM does not depend on any particular unicast routing protocol.

Protocol Independent Multicast – Dense Mode (PIM-DM). A protocol designed for use within an organization. Routers that use PIM-DM broadcast (i.e. flood) multicast packets to all locations within the organization. Each router that has no member of a particular group sends back a message to *prune* the multicast routing tree (i.e., a request to stop the flow of packets). The scheme works well for short-lived multicast sessions (e.g., a few minutes) because it does not require setup before transmission begins.

Multicast extensions to the Open Shortest Path First protocol (MOSPF). A protocol designed for use within an organization, MOSPF builds on OSPF and reuses many of the same basic concepts and facilities.

---

†The URL http://www.lbl.gov/Web/MBONE.html contains information about the MBONE.

To summarize:

> *The dynamic characteristics of Internet multicast make the problem of multicast route propagation difficult. Although many protocols have been proposed, the Internet does not currently have an Internet-wide multicast routing facility.*

25.16 Summary

Both hosts and routers contain an IP routing table. Most hosts use static routing in which the routing table is initialized at system startup; routers and some hosts use dynamic routing in which the routing table is initialized and then route propagation software updates the table continuously.

The Internet is divided into a set of autonomous systems. Protocols used to pass routes between autonomous systems are known as Exterior Gateway Protocols (EGPs); routers use Interior Gateway Protocols (IGPs) to exchange routing information within an autonomous system. The Border Gateway Protocol (BGP) is the primary EGP in the Internet. Popular IGPs include RIP and OSPF.

Because Internet multicast allows dynamic group membership and an arbitrary source can send to a multicast group without being a member, the problem of multicast route propagation is difficult. Although several multicast routing protocols have been proposed, no Internet-wide multicast technology exists.

EXERCISES

25.1   Examine the TCP/IP configuration file on your local computer. What entries do you expect to find in the routing table? Give the destination, address mask, and next hop for each entry.

25.2   Ask the network administrator at your site to provide you with a list of all routes contained in the routing table of the router that connects your site to the Internet. What next hop is associated with the default route?

25.3   How large is the autonomous system for your organization?

25.4   What routing protocols are used within your organization?

25.5   Under what circumstances does BGP fail to provide optimal routes? Hint: what happens if some autonomous systems are several orders of magnitude larger than others?

25.6   Suppose that all routers in the Internet contain a default route; show that a routing loop must exist.

25.7   Write a computer program that reads a RIP update message and prints the contents of each field.

25.8 RIP limits distance values to a maximum of 16 hops. Devise an example corporate intranet that has more that 16 routers and more than 16 networks but can still use RIP.

25.9 Find a sequence of events that allow two routers running a distance vector protocol to form a routing loop. Hint: imagine that the only path to a particular destination, D, lies beyond Router 1; Router 1 has told Router 2 about the path; and the path suddenly becomes unusable.

25.10 In version 1 of RIP, routers connected by an Ethernet broadcast all messages to one another; version 2 allows the routers to use Ethernet multicast. What is the chief disadvantage of broadcast? What is the chief advantage?

25.11 Suppose you and two friends at distant colleges want to participate in a 3-way teleconference using IP multicast. Which multicast routing protocols would work best? Why?

25.12 Although each IP multicast group needs a unique IP multicast address, using a central server to allocate unique addresses creates a central bottleneck. Devise a scheme that allows a set of computers to choose a multicast address at random, and resolve a conflict, if one should arise.

25.13 The traffic generated by flood-and-prune limits the size of an intranet over which it can be used. Estimate the total traffic on one network if G multicast groups each generate traffic at a rate of P packets per second, each packet contains B bits, N networks comprise the intranet, and each network contains at least one listener for each group.

Network Applications

**How application programs
use protocol software
to communicate across
networks and internets**

Chapter Contents

26

Client-Server Interaction

26.1 Introduction

This chapter begins a new section of the text that focuses on network applications. Previous sections provide a general background needed to understand the underlying facilities that applications use. They explain the hardware employed in LANs and WANs, show how heterogeneous networks can be interconnected, and examine protocol software used to achieve reliable transport across the resulting internet. The combination of networking hardware and protocol software results in a general-purpose communication infrastructure that allows application programs on an arbitrary pair of computers to communicate. Throughout the remainder of this text, we will assume that such an infrastructure is in place. In particular, we will assume that protocol software and necessary routing information is available on all computers (i.e., all computers are connected to a functioning internet†).

Chapters in this section focus on high-level services available on an internet and the application software that provides such services. The text explains principles, techniques, and the programming interface used to construct network applications as well as the structure of the software. Several chapters contain examples of popular applications. In addition to characterizing the service that the application provides, each chapter describes the structure of the software and shows how the application uses network communication.

This chapter extends the brief introduction found in Chapter 3. It focuses on client-server interaction, the fundamental concept that forms the basis for all network applications. The chapter explains the basic client-server model and describes how the need for client-server interaction arises from the way network protocols operate. Successive chapters expand the discussion by showing how example applications use the client-server paradigm.

---

†Our use of the term *internet* does not preclude individual networks; a single network is merely a special case of a more general internet.

26.2 The Functionality Application Software Provides

Although underlying physical network connections and communication protocols are required for communication across an internet, the most interesting and useful functionality is provided by application software. Applications supply the high-level services that users access, and determine how users perceive the capabilities of the underlying internet. For example, application software makes it possible to send or receive electronic mail, to browse information archives, or to transfer a copy of a file from one computer to another.

Applications determine the format in which information is displayed and the mechanisms users have to select or access information. Most important, applications define symbolic names used to identify both the physical and abstract resources available on an internet. For example, application software defines names for computers and I/O devices such as printers as well as names for abstract items such as files, electronic mailboxes, and databases. High-level, symbolic names make it possible for users to specify or locate information or services without understanding or remembering the low-level addresses used by the underlying protocol software. Indeed, most Internet users access remote computers by name — a user never needs to know or enter a computer's IP address. Similarly, a user can access a service by name without knowing the internal number protocol software uses to identify the service. Application software handles the details of translating symbolic names to equivalent numeric values automatically†.

26.3 The Functionality An Internet Provides

Internets provide a general communication infrastructure without specifying which services will be offered, which computers will run those services, how the availability of services will become known, or how services will be used — such issues are left to application software and users. In fact, an internet is much like a telephone system. Although it provides the ability to communicate, the internet does not specify which computers interact or what those computers do with the communication service.

An internet is like a telephone system in another significant way — the network hardware and associated protocol software do not know when to initiate contact with, or when to accept incoming communication from, a remote computer. Instead, like a telephone service, communication across an internet requires a pair of application programs to cooperate. An application on one computer attempts to communicate with an application on another (the analog of placing a telephone call), and an application on the other computer answers the incoming request (the analog of answering a telephone call). The point is:

---

†Chapter 29 examines the mapping from computer names to IP addresses in detail.

Although an internet system provides a basic communication service, the protocol software cannot initiate contact with, or accept contact from, a remote computer. Instead, two application programs must participate in any communication: one application initiates communication and the other accepts it.

26.4 Making Contact

Despite the similarities between internet communication and telephone calls, there is one important difference between the way two applications use an internet and the way two people use a telephone system. The difference arises because protocol software does not have a mechanism analogous to a telephone bell — there is no way for protocol software to inform an application that communication has arrived, and no way for an application to agree to accept arbitrary incoming messages.

If no signal is given, how can an application know when communication has arrived? The answer lies in a method of interaction that differs from the telephone model. Instead of waiting for an arbitrary message to arrive, an application that expects communication must interact with protocol software before an external source attempts to communicate. The application informs local protocol software that a specific type of message is expected, and then the application waits. When an incoming message matches exactly what the application has specified, protocol software passes the message to the application. Of course, two applications involved in a communication cannot both wait for a message to arrive — one application must actively initiate interaction, while the other application passively waits.

26.5 The Client-Server Paradigm

The paradigm of arranging for one application program to wait passively for another application to initiate communication pervades so much of distributed computing that it has been given a name: the *client-server paradigm of interaction*.

The terms *client* and *server* refer to the two applications involved in a communication. The application that actively initiates contact is called a *client*, while the application that passively waits for contact is called a *server*. To summarize:

Network applications use a form of communication known as the client-server paradigm. A server application waits passively for contact, while a client application initiates communication actively.

26.6 Characteristics Of Clients And Servers

Although minor variations exist, most instances of client-server interaction have the same general characteristics. In general, client software:

- is an arbitrary application program that becomes a client temporarily when remote access is needed, but also performs other computation locally.
- is invoked directly by a user, and executes only for one session.
- runs locally on a user's personal computer.
- actively initiates contact with a server.
- can access multiple services as needed, but actively contacts one remote server at a time.
- does not require special hardware or a sophisticated operating system.

In contrast, server software:

- is a special-purpose, privileged program dedicated to providing one service, but can handle multiple remote clients at the same time.
- is invoked automatically when a system boots, and continues to execute through many sessions.
- runs on a shared computer (i.e., not on a user's personal computer).
- waits passively for contact from arbitrary remote clients.
- accepts contact from arbitrary clients, but offers a single service.
- requires powerful hardware and a sophisticated operating system.

26.7 Server Programs And Server-Class Computers

Confusion sometimes arises over the term *server*. Formally, the term refers to a program that waits passively for communication, and not to the computer on which it executes. However, when a computer is dedicated to running one or more server programs, the computer itself is sometimes (incorrectly) called a *server*. Hardware vendors contribute to the confusion because they classify computers that have fast CPUs, large memories, and powerful operating systems as *server* machines.

We adhere to scientifically accurate terminology and use the term *server* to refer to the running program and not the computer. The term *server-class computer* refers to a powerful computer used to run server software.

26.8 Requests, Responses, And Direction Of Data Flow

Information can pass in either or both directions between a client and a server. Typically, a client sends a request to a server, and the server returns a response to the client. In some cases, a client sends a series of requests and the server issues a series of responses (e.g., a database client might allow a user to look up more than one item at a time). In other cases, the server provides continuous output without any request — as soon as the client contacts the server, the server begins sending data (e.g., a local weather server might send continuous weather reports with updated temperature and barometric pressure).

It is important to understand that servers can accept incoming information as well as deliver outgoing information. For example, most file servers are configured to export a set of files to clients. That is, a client sends a request that contains a file name, and the server responds by sending a copy of the file. However, a file server can also be configured to import files (i.e., to allow a client to send a copy of a file which the server accepts and stores on disk). The concept can be summarized:

Information can flow in either or both directions between a client and server. Although many services arrange for the client to send one or more requests and the server to return responses, other interactions are possible.

26.9 Transport Protocols and Client-Server Interaction

Like most application programs, a client and server use a transport protocol to communicate. For example, Figure 26.1 illustrates a client and server using the TCP/IP stack.

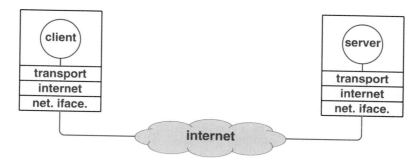

Figure 26.1 A client and server using TCP/IP protocols to communicate across an internet. The client and server each interact with a protocol in the transport layer.

As the figure shows, a client or server application interacts directly with a transport-layer protocol to establish communication and to send or receive information. The transport protocol then uses lower layer protocols to send and receive individual messages. Thus, a computer needs a complete stack of protocols to run either a client or a server.

26.10 Multiple Services On One Computer

A sufficiently powerful computer system can run multiple clients and servers at the same time. Two capabilities are required. First, the computer must have sufficient hardware resources (e.g., a fast processor and large memory). Second, the computer must have an operating system that allows multiple application programs to execute concurrently (e.g., UNIX or Windows). On such systems, one server program runs for each service being offered. For example, a single computer might run a file server as well as a World Wide Web server. Figure 26.2 illustrates one possible arrangement.

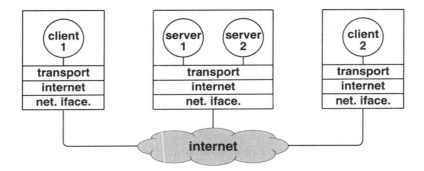

Figure 26.2 Two servers on a single computer accessed by clients on two other computers. Client *1* can access server *1*, while client *2* accesses server *2*.

The figure illustrates clients on two computers accessing two servers on a third computer. Although a computer can operate multiple servers, the computer needs only a single physical connection to the internet.

Allowing a computer to operate multiple servers is useful because the hardware can be shared by multiple services. Consolidating servers onto a large, server-class computer also helps reduce the overhead of system administration because it results in fewer computer systems to administer. More important, experience has shown that the demand for a server is often sporadic — a server can remain idle for long periods of time. An idle server does not use the CPU while waiting for a request to arrive. Thus, if demand for services is low, consolidating servers on a single computer can dramatically reduce cost without significantly reducing performance†. To summarize:

---

†Of course, the highest performance is achieved by running a single server or a single client on each computer.

A single, server-class computer can offer multiple services at the same time; a separate server program is needed for each service. Running many servers on a single computer is practical because a server does not consume computational resources while waiting for a request.

26.11 Identifying A Particular Service

Transport protocols provide a mechanism that allows a client to specify unambiguously which service is desired. The mechanism assigns each service a unique identifier, and requires both the server and client to use the identifier. When a server begins execution, it registers with the local protocol software by specifying the identifier for the service it offers. When a client contacts a remote server, the client specifies the identifier for the desired service. Transport protocol software on the client's machine sends the identifier to the server's machine when making a request. Transport protocol software on the server's machine uses the identifier to determine which server program should handle the request.

As an example of service identification, consider the Transmission Control Protocol (TCP) described in Chapter 24. TCP uses 16-bit integer values known as *protocol port numbers* to identify services, and assigns a unique protocol port number to each service. A server specifies the protocol port number for the service it offers, and then waits passively for communication. A client specifies the protocol port number of the desired service when sending a request. Conceptually, TCP software on the server's computer uses the protocol port number in an incoming message to determine which server should receive the request.

To summarize:

Transport protocols assign each service a unique identifier. Both clients and servers specify the service identifier; protocol software uses the identifier to direct each incoming request to the correct server.

26.12 Multiple Copies Of A Server For A Single Service

Technically, a computer system that permits multiple application programs to execute at the same time is said to support *concurrency*, and a program that has more than one thread of control† is called a *concurrent* program. Concurrency is fundamental to the client-server model of interaction because a concurrent server offers service to multiple clients at the same time, without requiring each client to wait for previous clients to finish.

---

†Some systems use the term *process* or *task* for a thread of control.

To understand why simultaneous service is important, consider what happens if a service requires significant time to satisfy each request. For example, a file transfer service allows a client to obtain a copy of a remote file: the client sends the name of a file in a request, and the server returns a copy of the file. If a client requests a small file, the server can send the entire file in a few milliseconds. However, a server may require several minutes to transfer a file that contains a series of high-resolution digital images.

If a file server handles one request at a time, all clients must wait while the server transfers a file to one of them. In contrast, a concurrent file server can handle multiple clients simultaneously. When a request arrives, the server assigns the request to a thread of control that can execute concurrently with existing threads. In essence, a separate copy of the server handles each request. Thus, short requests can be satisfied quickly, without waiting for long requests to complete.

26.13 Dynamic Server Creation

Most concurrent servers operate dynamically. The server creates a new thread for each request that arrives. In fact, the server program is constructed in two parts: one that accepts requests and creates a new thread for the request, and another that consists of the code to handle an individual request. When a concurrent server starts executing, only the first part runs. That is, the main server thread waits for a request to arrive. When a request arrives, the main thread creates a new service thread to handle the request. The service thread handles one request and then terminates. Meanwhile, the main thread keeps the server alive — after creating a thread to handle a request, the main thread waits for another request to arrive.

If N clients are using a given service on a single computer, there are $N+1$ threads providing the service: the main thread is waiting for additional requests, and N service threads are each interacting with a single client. We can summarize:

> *Concurrent execution is fundamental to servers because concurrency permits multiple clients to obtain a given service without having to wait for the server to finish previous requests. In a concurrent server, the main server thread creates a new service thread to handle each client.*

26.14 Transport Protocols And Unambiguous Communication

If multiple copies of a server exist, how can a client interact with the correct copy? More to the point, how can an incoming request be passed to the correct copy of a server? The answer to these questions lies in the method transport protocols use to identify a server. We said that each service is assigned a unique identifier and that each request from a client includes the service identifier, making it possible for transport protocol software on the server's computer to associate the incoming request with the correct server. In practice, most transport protocols assign each client a unique identifier, and require the client to include its identifier when making a request. Transport protocol software on the server's computer uses both the client and server identifiers to choose the copy of the server that has been created to handle the client.

As an example, consider the identifiers used on a TCP connection. TCP requires each client to choose a local protocol port number that is not assigned to any service. When it sends a TCP segment, a client must place its local protocol port number in the *SOURCE PORT* field and the protocol port number of the server in the *DESTINATION PORT* field. On the server's computer, TCP uses the combination of source and destination protocol port numbers (as well as client and server IP addresses) to identify a particular communication. Thus, messages can arrive from two or more clients for the same service without causing a problem. TCP passes each incoming segment to the copy of the server that has agreed to handle the client. To summarize:

> *Transport protocols assign an identifier to each client as well as to each service. Protocol software on the server's machine uses the combination of client and server identifiers to choose the correct copy of a concurrent server.*

26.15 Connection-Oriented And Connectionless Transport

Transport protocols support two basic forms of communication: connection-oriented or connectionless. To use a connection-oriented transport protocol, two applications must establish a connection, and then send data across the connection. For example, TCP provides a connection-oriented interface to applications. When it uses TCP, an application must first request TCP to open a connection to another application. Once the connection is in place, the two applications can exchange data. When the applications finish communicating, the connection must be closed.

The alternative to connection-oriented communication is a connectionless interface that permits an application to send a message to any destination at any time. When using a connectionless transport protocol, the sending application must specify a destination with each message it sends. For example, in the TCP/IP protocol suite, the *User Datagram Protocol* (UDP) provides connectionless transport. An application using UDP can send a sequence of messages, where each message is sent to a different destination.

Clients and servers can use either connection-oriented or connectionless transport protocols to communicate. When using a connection-oriented transport, a client first forms a connection to a specific server. The connection then stays in place while the client sends requests and receives responses. When it finishes using the service, the client closes the connection†.

---

†The exact details depend on the service; in some designs, the client requests the server to close the connection.

Clients and servers that use connectionless protocols exchange individual messages. For example, many services that use connectionless transport require a client to send each request, and the server to return each response, in a single message.

26.16 A Service Reachable Through Multiple Protocols

Servers need not choose between connectionless and connection-oriented transport; it is possible to offer both. That is, the same service can be made available over two or more transport protocols, with the choice of transport left to the client. Allowing the use of multiple transport protocols increases flexibility by making the service available to clients that may not have access to a particular transport protocol.

There are two possible implementations of a multiprotocol server. The first implementation is straightforward: two servers exist for the same service. One server uses connectionless transport, while the other uses connection-oriented transport. The second implementation is more complex: a single server program interacts with two or more transport protocols at the same time. The server accepts requests that arrive from either protocol, and uses the protocol in which the request arrived when sending a response.

26.17 Complex Client-Server Interactions

Some of the most interesting and useful functionality of client-server computing arises from arbitrary interactions among clients and servers. In particular, it should be noted that:

- A client application is not restricted to accessing a single service. An application can first become a client of one service, and then become a client of another. The client contacts a different server (perhaps on a different computer) for each service.

- A client application is not restricted to accessing a single server for a given service. In some services, each server provides different information than servers running on other computers. For example, a date server might provide the current time and date for the computer on which it runs. A server on a computer in a different time zone gives a different answer. In other services, all servers provide the same information. In such cases, a client might send a request to multiple servers to improve performance — the client uses the information sent by the server that responds first.

- A server is not restricted from performing further client-server interactions — a server for one service can become a client of another. For example, a file server that needs to record the time that a file was accessed might become a client of a time server. That is, while it is handling a request for a file, the file server sends a request to a time server, waits for the response, then continues handling the file request.

26.18 Interactions And Circular Dependencies

Of course, servers must be planned carefully to avoid circular dependencies. To understand how problems can arise, consider a file server that uses a time server to obtain the current time whenever a file is accessed. A circular dependency can result if the time server also uses the file server. For example, suppose a programmer is asked to modify the time server so it keeps a record of each request. If the programmer chooses to have the time server become a client of the file server, a cycle can result: the file server becomes a client of the time server which becomes a client of the file server, and so on. The result is a disaster analogous to an infinite loop in a program.

Although dependencies among a pair of servers are easy to spot and avoid, a larger set of dependencies may not be obvious. Imagine a dependency cycle that includes a dozen servers, each operating on a separate computer. If each server is maintained by a separate programmer, the dependencies among them may be difficult to identify.

26.19 Summary

Application programs that communicate across a network or internet all use a single form of interaction. The interaction is called the client-server paradigm. A program that passively waits for contact is called a *server*, and a program that actively initiates contact with a server is called a *client*.

A client program is often invoked by a user, and usually executes on the user's private computer. Server programs usually run on large, server-class computers that have sophisticated operating systems. Many server-class computers are powerful enough to run servers for multiple services concurrently.

Clients and servers use transport protocols to communicate. Because transport protocols use lower-layer protocols, a full protocol stack is needed on a computer that runs a client or a server.

To permit servers for multiple services to operate on a given computer, each service is assigned a unique identifier. A client includes the identifier for the desired service when sending a request; transport protocol software on the receiving computer uses the identifier to determine which server should receive an incoming request.

Concurrency is fundamental in client-server interaction. Most servers are concurrent programs that create an independent thread of control for each request. Using concurrent threads of control permits a server to handle requests from multiple clients at the same time, without requiring a client to wait for previous requests to be handled.

Client-server interaction can be complex. A single client can access more than one service, a client can access servers on multiple machines, and a server for one service can become a client for other services. Designers and programmers must be careful to avoid circular dependencies among servers.

EXERCISES

26.1 Conduct a survey of networking professionals at your institution. What percentage can give an accurate definition of *server*?

26.2 Examine the most powerful computer at your organization. How many servers does it run simultaneously?

26.3 Write a program to analyze network packets and print a pie chart of services to which they are directed.

26.4 Examine commercial software used for the World Wide Web. Which costs more, client or server software? Explain.

Chapter Contents

27

The Socket Interface

27.1 Introduction

The previous chapter describes client-server interaction, the fundamental paradigm that application programs use when they communicate across an internet. The chapter presents the motivation for using client-server, discusses concepts such as concurrency, and shows how clients and servers use transport protocols to communicate.

This chapter provides additional details about client-server interaction by explaining the interface between an application and protocol software. The chapter considers how an application uses protocol software to communicate, and explains an example set of procedures that an application uses to become a client or a server, to contact a remote destination, or to transfer data.

The next chapter continues the discussion by illustrating how the interface procedures are used in practice. The chapter shows complete programs for both an example client and server.

27.2 Application Program Interface

We said that client and server applications use transport protocols to communicate. When it interacts with protocol software, an application must specify details such as whether it is a server or a client (i.e., whether it will wait passively or actively initiate communication). In addition, applications that communicate must specify further details (e.g., the sender must specify the data to be sent, and the receiver must specify where incoming data should be placed).

411

Recall from Chapter 3 that the interface an application uses when it interacts with transport protocol software is known as an *Application Program Interface* (*API*). Because an API defines a set of operations that an application can perform when interacting with protocol software, the API determines the functionality that is available. In addition, details, such as the arguments required, determine the difficulty of creating a program to use the functionality.

Most programming systems define an API similar to the example in Chapter 3. The definition lists a set of procedures available to applications, the arguments that each procedure expects, and the data types. Usually, an API contains a separate procedure for each logical function. For example, an API might contain one procedure that is used to establish communication and another procedure that is used to send data.

27.3 The Socket API

Communication protocol standards do not usually specify an API that applications use to interact with the protocols. Instead, the protocols specify the general operations that should be provided, and allow each operating system to define the specific API an application uses to perform the operations. Thus, a protocol standard might suggest an operation is needed to allow an application to send data, and the API specifies the exact name of the function and the type of each argument.

Although protocol standards allow operating system designers to choose an API, many have adopted the *socket API†*. The socket API is available for many operating systems, including systems used on personal computers (e.g., Microsoft's Windows systems) as well as various UNIX systems (e.g., Sun Microsystems' Solaris).

The socket API originated as part of the BSD UNIX operating system. The work was supported by a government grant, under which the University of California at Berkeley developed and distributed a version of UNIX that contained TCP/IP internetworking protocols. Many computer vendors ported the BSD system to their hardware, and used it as the basis of commercial operating system products. Thus, the socket API became the *de facto* standard in the industry. To summarize:

> *The interface between an application program and the communication protocols in an operating system is known as the* Application Program Interface *or API. The socket API is a* de facto *standard.*

27.4 Sockets And Socket Libraries

In BSD UNIX and the systems derived from it, socket functions are part of the operating system itself. As sockets became more widely used, vendors of other systems decided to add a socket API to their systems. In many cases, instead of modifying their basic operating system, vendors created a *socket library* that provides the socket API. That is, the vendor created a library of procedures that each have the same name and arguments as one of the socket functions.

---

†The phrase *socket API* is sometimes abbreviated *sockets*.

From an application programmer's point of view, a socket library provides the same semantics as an implementation of sockets in the operating system. The program calls socket procedures, which are either supplied by operating system procedures or library routines. Thus, an application that uses sockets can be copied to a new computer, compiled, loaded along with the socket library on the computer, and then executed — the source code does not need to change when porting the program from one computer system to another†.

Despite apparent similarities, socket libraries have a completely different implementation than a native socket API supplied by an operating system. Unlike native socket routines, which are part of the operating system, the code for socket library procedures is linked into the application program and resides in the application's address space. When an application calls a procedure from the socket library, control passes to the library routine which, in turn, makes one or more calls to the underlying operating system functions to achieve the desired effect. Interestingly, functions supplied by the underlying operating system need not resemble the socket API at all — routines in the socket library hide the native operating system from the application and present only a socket interface. To summarize:

> *A socket library can provide applications with a socket API on a computer system that does not provide native sockets. When an application calls one of the socket procedures, control passes to a library routine that makes one or more calls to the underlying operating system to implement the socket function.*

27.5 Socket Communication And UNIX I/O

Because they were originally developed as part of the UNIX operating system, sockets employ many concepts found in other parts of UNIX. In particular, sockets are integrated with I/O — an application communicates through a socket similar to the way the application transfers data to or from a file. Thus, understanding sockets requires one to understand UNIX I/O facilities.

UNIX uses an *open-read-write-close* paradigm for all I/O; the name is derived from the basic I/O operations that apply to both devices and files. For example, an application must first call *open* to prepare a file for access. The application then calls *read* or *write* to retrieve data from the file or store data in the file. Finally, the application calls *close* to specify that it has finished using the file.

When an application opens a file or device, the call to *open* returns a *descriptor*, a small integer that identifies the file; the application must specify the descriptor when requesting data transfer (i.e., the descriptor is an argument to the *read* or *write* procedure). For example, if an application calls *open* to access a file named *foobar*, the open procedure might return descriptor *4*. A subsequent call to *write* that specifies descriptor *4* will cause data to be written to file *foobar*; the file name does not appear in the call to *write*.

---

† In practice, socket libraries are seldom perfect, and minor differences sometimes occur between the standard implementation of a socket API and a socket library (e.g., in the way errors are handled).

27.6 Sockets, Descriptors, And Network I/O

Socket communication also uses the descriptor approach. Before an application can use protocols to communicate, the application must request the operating system to create a *socket* that will be used for communication. The system returns a small integer descriptor that identifies the socket. The application then passes the descriptor as an argument when it calls procedures to transfer data across the network; the application does not need to specify details about the remote destination each time it transfers data.

In a UNIX implementation, sockets are completely integrated with other I/O. The operating system provides a single set of descriptors for files, devices, interprocess communication†, and network communication. As a result, procedures like *read* and *write* are quite general — an application can use the same procedure to send data to another program, a file, or across a network. In current terminology, the descriptor represents an object, and the *write* procedure represents a method applied to that object. The underlying object determines how the method is applied.

The chief advantage of an integrated system lies in its flexibility: a single application can be written that transfers data to an arbitrary location. If the application is given a descriptor that corresponds to a device, the application sends data to the device. If the application is given a descriptor that corresponds to a file, the application stores data in the file. If the application is given a descriptor that corresponds to a socket, the application sends data across an internet to a remote machine. To summarize:

> *When an application creates a socket, the application is given a small integer descriptor used to reference the socket. If a system uses the same descriptor space for sockets and other I/O, a single application can be used for network communication as well as for local data transfer.*

27.7 Parameters And The Socket API

Socket programming differs from conventional I/O because an application must specify many details to use a socket. For example, an application must choose a particular transport protocol, provide the protocol address of a remote machine, and specify whether the application is a client or a server. To accommodate all the details, each socket has many parameters and options — an application can supply values for each.

How should options and parameters be represented in an API? To avoid having a single socket function with separate parameters for each option, designers of the socket API chose to define many functions. In essence, an application creates a socket and then invokes functions to specify in detail how the socket will be used. The advantage of the socket approach is that most functions have three or fewer parameters; the disadvantage is that a programmer must remember to call multiple functions when using sockets. The next sections illustrate the concept.

_____

†UNIX provides a *pipe* mechanism for interprocess communication.

27.8 Procedures That Implement The Socket API

27.8.1 The Socket Procedure

The *socket* procedure creates a socket and returns an integer descriptor:

descriptor = socket(protofamily, type, protocol)

Argument *protofamily* specifies the protocol family to be used with the socket. The identifier *PF_INET* which specifies the TCP/IP protocol suite is by far the most common choice.

Argument *type* specifies the type of communication the socket will use. The two most common types are a connection-oriented stream transfer (specified with the value *SOCK_STREAM*) and a connectionless message-oriented transfer (specified with the value *SOCK_DGRAM*).

Argument *protocol* specifies a particular transport protocol used with the socket. Having a *protocol* argument in addition to a *type* argument, permits a single protocol suite to include two or more protocols that provide the same service. Of course, the values that can be used with the *protocol* argument depend on the protocol family. For example, although the TCP/IP protocol suite includes the protocol TCP, the AppleTalk suite does not.

27.8.2 The Close Procedure

The *close* procedure tells the system to terminate use of a socket†. It has the form:

close(socket)

where *socket* is the descriptor for a socket being closed. If the socket is using a connection-oriented transport protocol, *close* terminates the connection before closing the socket. Closing a socket immediately terminates use — the descriptor is released, preventing the application from sending more data, and the transport protocol stops accepting incoming messages directed to the socket, preventing the application from receiving more data‡.

27.8.3 The Bind Procedure

When created, a socket has neither a local address nor a remote address. A server uses the *bind* procedure to supply a protocol port number at which the server will wait for contact. *Bind* takes three arguments:

bind(socket, localaddr, addrlen)

---

†Microsoft *Windows Sockets* interface uses the name *closesocket* instead of close.
‡A later section discusses how *close* works in a concurrent program.

Argument *socket* is the descriptor of a socket that has been created but not previously bound; the call is a request that the socket be assigned a particular protocol port number. Argument *localaddr* is a structure that specifies the local address to be assigned to the socket, and argument *addrlen* is an integer that specifies the length of the address. Because sockets can be used with arbitrary protocols, the format of an address depends on the protocol being used. The socket API defines a generic form used to represent addresses, and then requires each protocol family to specify how their protocol addresses use the generic form.

The generic format for representing an address is defined to be a *sockaddr* structure. Although several versions have been released, the latest Berkeley code defines a sockaddr structure to have three fields:

```
struct sockaddr {
        u_char   sa_len;            /* total length of the address */
        u_char   sa_family;         /* family of the address       */
        char     sa_data[14];       /* the address itself          */
};
```

Field *sa_len* consists of a single octet that specifies the length of the address. Field *sa_family* specifies the family to which an address belongs (the symbolic constant *AF_INET* is used for TCP/IP addresses). Finally, field *sa_data* contains the address.

Each protocol family defines the exact format of addresses used with the *sa_data* field of a *sockaddr* structure. For example, TCP/IP protocols use structure *sockaddr_in* to define an address:

```
struct sockaddr_in {
        u_char   sin_len;           /* total length of the address */
        u_char   sin_family;        /* family of the address       */
        u_short  sin_port;          /* protocol port number        */
        struct   in_addr sin_addr;/* IP address of computer      */
        char     sin_zero[8];       /* not used (set to zero)      */
};
```

The first two fields of structure *sockaddr_in* correspond exactly to the first two fields of the generic *sockaddr* structure. The last three fields define the exact form of address that TCP/IP protocols expect. There are two points to notice. First, each address identifies both a computer and a particular application on that computer. Field *sin_addr* contains the IP address of the computer, and field *sin_port* contains the protocol port number of an application. Second, although TCP/IP needs only six octets to store a complete address, the generic *sockaddr* structure reserves fourteen octets. Thus, the final field in structure *sockaddr_in* defines an 8-octet field of zeroes, which pad the structure to the same size as *sockaddr*.

We said that a server calls *bind* to specify the protocol port number at which the server will accept contact. However, in addition to a protocol port number, structure *sockaddr_in* contains a field for an IP address. Although a server can choose to fill in the IP address when specifying an address, doing so causes problems when a host is multi-homed because it means the server only accepts requests sent to one specific address. To allow a server to operate on a multi-homed host, the socket API includes a special symbolic constant, *INADDR_ANY*, that allows a server to use a specific port at any of the computer's IP addresses. To summarize:

> *Structure* sockaddr_in *defines the format TCP/IP uses to represent an address. Although the structure contains fields for both an IP address and a protocol port number, the socket API includes a symbolic constant that allows a server to specify a protocol port at any of the computer's IP addresses.*

27.8.4 The Listen Procedure

After specifying a protocol port, a server must instruct the operating system to place a socket in passive mode so it can be used to wait for contact from clients. To do so, a server calls the *listen* procedure, which takes two arguments:

listen(socket, queuesize)

Argument *socket* is the descriptor of a socket that has been created and bound to a local address, and argument *queuesize* specifies a length for the socket's request queue.

The operating system builds a separate request queue for each socket. Initially, the queue is empty. As requests arrive from clients, each is placed in the queue; when the server asks to retrieve an incoming request from the socket, the system returns the next request from the queue. If the queue is full when a request arrives, the system rejects the request. Having a queue of requests allows the system to hold new requests that arrive while the server is busy handling a previous request. The parameter allows each server to choose a maximum queue size that is appropriate for the expected service.

27.8.5 The Accept Procedure

All servers begin by calling *socket* to create a socket and *bind* to specify a protocol port number. After executing the two calls, a server that uses a connectionless transport protocol is ready to accept messages. However, a server that uses a connection-oriented transport protocol requires additional steps before it can receive messages: the server must call *listen* to place the socket in passive mode, and must then accept a connection request. Once a connection has been accepted, the server can use the connection to communicate with a client. After it finishes communication, the server closes the connection.

A server that uses connection-oriented transport must call procedure *accept* to accept the next connection request. If a request is present in the queue, *accept* returns immediately; if no requests have arrived, the system blocks the server until a client forms a connection. The *accept* call has the form:

newsock = accept(socket, caddress, caddresslen)

Argument *socket* is the descriptor of a socket the server has created and bound to a specific protocol port. Argument *caddress* is the address of a structure of type *sockaddr*, and *caddresslen* is a pointer to an integer. *Accept* fills in fields of argument *caddress* with the address of the client that formed the connection, and sets *caddresslen* to the length of the address. Finally, *accept* creates a new socket for the connection, and returns the descriptor of the new socket to the caller. The server uses the new socket to communicate with the client, and then closes the socket when finished. Meanwhile, the server's original socket remains unchanged — after it finishes communicating with a client, the server uses the original socket to accept the next connection from a client.

27.8.6 The Connect Procedure

Clients use procedure *connect* to establish connection with a specific server. The form is:

connect(socket, saddress, saddresslen)

Argument *socket* is the descriptor of a socket on the client's computer to use for the connection. Argument *saddress* is a *sockaddr* structure that specifies the server's address and protocol port number†. Argument *saddresslen* specifies the length of the server's address measured in octets.

When used with a connection-oriented transport protocol such as TCP, *connect* initiates a transport-level connection to the specified server. In essence, *connect* is the procedure a client uses to contact a server that has called *accept*.

Interestingly, a client that uses a connectionless transport protocol can also call *connect*. However, doing so does not initiate a connection or cause packets to cross the internet. Instead, *connect* merely marks the socket *connected*, and records the address of the server.

To understand why it makes sense to connect a socket that uses connectionless transport, recall that connectionless protocols require the sender to specify a destination address with each message. In many applications, however, a client always contacts a single server. Thus, all messages go to the same destination. In such cases, a connected socket provides a shorthand — the client can specify the server's address once instead of specifying the address with each message. The point is:

---

†The combination of an IP address and a protocol port number is sometimes called an *endpoint address*.

> *The* connect *procedure, which is called by clients, has two uses. When used with connection-oriented transport,* connect *establishes a transport connection to a specified server. When used with connectionless transport,* connect *records the server's address in the socket, allowing the client to send many messages to the same server without requiring the client to specify the destination address with each message.*

27.8.7 The Send, Sendto, And Sendmsg Procedures

Both clients and servers need to send information. Usually, a client sends a request, and a server sends a response. If the socket is connected, procedure *send* can be used to transfer data. *Send* has four arguments:

> send(socket, data, length, flags)

Argument *socket* is the descriptor of a socket to use, argument *data* is the address in memory of the data to send, argument *length* is an integer that specifies the number of octets of data, and argument *flags* contains bits that request special options†.

Procedures *sendto* and *sendmsg* allow a client or server to send a message using an unconnected socket; both require the caller to specify a destination. *Sendto*, takes the destination address as an argument. It has the form:

> sendto(socket, data, length, flags, destaddress, addresslen)

The first four arguments correspond to the four arguments of the *send* procedure. The final two arguments specify the address of a destination and the length of that address. The form of the address in argument *destaddress* is the *sockaddr* structure (specifically, structure *sockaddr_in* when used with TCP/IP).

The *sendmsg* procedure performs the same operation as *sendto*, but abbreviates the arguments by defining a structure. The shorter argument list can make programs that use *sendmsg* easier to read:

> sendmsg(socket, msgstruct, flags)

Argument *msgstruct* is a structure that contains information about the destination address, the length of the address, the message to be sent, and the length of the message:

```
struct  msgstruct {                      /* structure used by sendmsg  */
        struct sockaddr *m_saddr;  /* ptr to destination address */
        struct datavec  *m_dvec;   /* ptr to message (vector)    */
        int     m_dvlength;        /* num. of items in vector    */
        struct access   *m_rights; /* ptr to access rights list  */
        int     m_alength;         /* num. of items in list      */
};
```

---

†Many options are intended for system debugging, and are not available to conventional client and server programs.

The details of the message structure are unimportant — it should be viewed as a way to combine many arguments into a single structure. Most applications use only the first three fields, which specify a destination protocol address and a list of data items that comprise the message.

27.8.8 The Recv, Recvfrom, And Recvmsg Procedures

A client and a server each need to receive data sent by the other. The socket API provides several procedures that can be used. For example, an application can call *recv* to receive data from a connected socket. The procedure has the form:

recv(socket, buffer, length, flags)

Argument *socket* is the descriptor of a socket from which data is to be received. Argument *buffer* specifies the address in memory in which the incoming message should be placed, and argument *length* specifies the size of the buffer. Finally, argument *flags* allows the caller to control details (e.g., to allow an application to extract a copy of an incoming message without removing the message from the socket).

If a socket is not connected, it can be used to receive messages from an arbitrary set of clients. In such cases, the system returns the address of the sender along with each incoming message. Applications use procedure *recvfrom* to receive both a message and the address of the sender:

recvfrom(socket, buffer, length, flags, sndraddr, saddrlen)

The first four arguments correspond to the arguments of *recv*; the two additional arguments, *sndraddr* and *saddrlen*, are used to record the sender's IP address. Argument *sndraddr* is a pointer to a *sockaddr* structure into which the system writes the sender's address, and argument *saddrlen* is a pointer to an integer that the system uses to record the length of the address. *Recvfrom* records the sender's address in exactly the same form that *sendto* expects. Thus, if an application uses *recvfrom* to receive an incoming message, sending a reply is easy — the application simply uses the recorded address as a destination for the reply.

The socket API includes an input procedure analogous to the *sendmsg* output procedure. Procedure *recvmsg* operates like *recvfrom*, but requires fewer arguments. It has the form:

recvmsg(socket, msgstruct, flags)

where argument *msgstruct* gives the address of a structure that holds the address for an incoming message as well as locations for the sender's IP address. The *msgstruct* recorded by *recvmsg* uses exactly the same format as the structure required by *sendmsg*. Thus, the two procedures work well for receiving a message and sending a reply.

27.9 Read And Write With Sockets

We said the socket API was originally designed to be part of UNIX, which uses *read* and *write* for I/O. Consequently, sockets also allow applications to use *read* and *write* to transfer data. Like *send* and *recv*, *read* and *write* do not have arguments that permit the caller to specify a destination. Instead, *read* and *write* each have three arguments: a socket descriptor, the location of a buffer in memory used to store the data, and the length of the memory buffer. Thus, *read* and *write* must be used with connected sockets.

The chief advantage of using *read* and *write* is generality — an application program can be created that transfers data to or from a descriptor without knowing whether the descriptor corresponds to a file or a socket. Thus, a programmer can use a file on a local disk to test a client or server before attempting to communicate across a network. The chief disadvantage of using *read* and *write* is that a socket library implementation may introduce additional overhead in the file I/O of any application that also uses sockets.

27.10 Other Socket Procedures

The socket API contains other useful procedures. For example, after a server calls procedure *accept* to accept an incoming connection request, the server can call procedure *getpeername* to obtain the complete address of the remote client that initiated the connection. A client or server can also call *gethostname* to obtain information about the computer on which it is running.

We said that a socket has many parameters and options. Two general-purpose procedures are used to set socket options or obtain a list of current values. An application calls procedure *setsockopt* to store values in socket options, and procedure *getsockopt* to obtain current option values. Options are used mainly to handle special cases (e.g., to increase performance by changing the internal buffer size the protocol software uses).

Two procedures are used to translate between IP addresses and computer names†. Procedure *gethostbyname* returns the IP address for a computer given the computer's name. Clients often use *gethostbyname* to translate a name entered by a user into a corresponding IP address needed by the protocol software.

Procedure *gethostbyaddr* provides an inverse mapping — given an IP address for a computer, it returns the computer's name. Clients and servers can use *gethostbyaddr* when displaying information for a person to read.

---

†Chapter 29 describes computer names in detail.

27.11 Sockets, Threads, And Inheritance

Because many servers are concurrent, the socket API is designed to work with concurrent programs. Although the details depend on the underlying operating system, implementations of the socket API adhere to the following principle:

> *Each new thread that is created inherits a copy of all open sockets from the thread that created it.*

To understand how servers use socket inheritance, it is important to know that sockets use a *reference count* mechanism. When a socket is first created, the system sets the socket's reference count to *1*; the socket exists as long as the reference count remains positive. When a program creates an additional thread, the system provides the thread with a list of all the sockets that the program owns, and increments the reference count of each by *1*. When a thread calls *close* for a socket, the system decrements the reference count on the socket by *1* and removes the socket from the thread's list†.

The main thread of a concurrent server creates a socket that the server uses to accept incoming connections. When a connection request arrives, the system creates a new socket for the new connection. Immediately after the main thread creates a service thread to handle the new connection, both threads have access to the new and old sockets, and the reference count of each socket has the value *2*. However, the main thread will not use the new socket, and the service thread will not use the original socket. Therefore, the main thread calls *close* for the new socket, and the service thread calls *close* for the original socket, reducing the reference count of each to *1*.

After a service thread finishes, it calls *close* on the new socket, reducing the reference count to zero and causing the socket to be deleted. Thus, the lifetime of sockets in a concurrent server can be summarized:

> *The socket that a concurrent server uses to accept connections exists as long as the main server thread executes; a socket used for a specific connection exists only as long as the thread exists to handle that connection.*

27.12 Summary

An Application Program Interface specifies the details of how an application program interacts with protocol software. The Socket API is a *de facto* standard. Although it was originally developed by U. C. Berkeley as part of their version of the UNIX operating system, many vendors sell a library of procedures that allow a program to use the socket API on a non-UNIX system.

---

†If a thread exits before closing sockets, the system automatically calls *close* on each of the sockets the thread had open.

A program views the socket API as an input-output (I/O) mechanism. Sockets follow the open-read-write-close paradigm used for most I/O; a socket must be created, used, and then destroyed. Because sockets have many more functions and parameters than conventional I/O, additional procedures are needed to manipulate a socket. When creating a socket, an application must specify the protocol family to be used as well as the type of service desired (connection-oriented or connectionless). After a server creates a socket, the server specifies a local address for the socket and the size of the request queue. After a client creates a socket, the client specifies the address of a remote server.

Once a socket has been established, applications can transfer information. The basic procedure used to transmit information is *send*. Several variants of *send* exist, with the appropriate procedure being determined by the type of service required. The basic procedure used to receive information is *recv*; a variant of *recv* exists that corresponds to each variant of *send*. Socket I/O is integrated with conventional I/O because the socket API also allows an application to use *read* or *write* procedures when transferring data.

Because many servers are concurrent, sockets are designed to work with concurrent applications. When a new thread is created, the new thread inherits access to all sockets that the creating thread owned. A concurrent server first opens a socket used to accept requests. The system then creates a new socket when a connection request arrives. After the main thread in a server creates a service thread to handle the incoming connection, the main thread calls *close* on the new socket and the service thread calls *close* on the original socket.

EXERCISES

27.1   The software in some computer systems numbers socket descriptors independently from other I/O descriptors, which means that a given number may be assigned to both an I/O connection and a socket. Determine whether the computer system you are using coordinates socket descriptors and I/O descriptors or assigns them independently.

27.2   Although the socket API defines many functions, the same functionality can be provided by a single function, sometimes called a *universal function*. Design a universal function for the socket API.

27.3   From a computer vendor's point of view, what is the chief advantage of including a library of procedures that implements the socket API with every computer system sold?

27.4   Write a computer program to test whether it is possible to bind a socket to an address, use the address, and then bind the socket to a new address.

27.5   In the previous question, is there any reason the API should permit an application to change the binding? If so, what is the reason? If not, should the binding be a parameter of the *socket* procedure?

Chapter Contents

28

Example Of A Client And A Server

28.1 Introduction

Chapter 3 presents examples of clients and servers using a simplistic, nonstandard API. The previous chapter explains the procedures that comprise the socket API used in most Internet applications. This chapter continues and expands the explanation of sockets by examining a client and server that use sockets to communicate. Although it does not illustrate all possible client and server designs, the example code will clarify the purpose of major socket procedures, and will show how socket programming differs from programs written using the API in Chapter 3. The example code illustrates a sequence of socket procedure calls, and allows the reader to compare the sequence of calls used in a client and the sequence of calls used in a server.

28.2 Connection-Oriented Communication

A client and server must select a transport protocol that supports connectionless service or one that supports connection-oriented service. Connectionless service allows an application to send a message to an arbitrary destination at any time; the destination does not need to agree that it will accept the message before transmission occurs. In contrast, a connection-oriented service requires two applications to establish a transport connection before data can be sent. To establish a connection, the applications each interact with transport protocol software on their local computer, and the two transport protocol modules exchange messages across the network. After both sides agree that a connection has been established, the applications can send data.

28.3 An Example Service

An example client and server will help clarify many of the details of connection-oriented interaction, and show how software for a connection-oriented service uses sockets. To keep the size of the programs small and focus on the socket calls, we have chosen a trivial service: the server keeps a count of the number of clients that have accessed the service, and reports the count whenever a client contacts the server.

To simplify implementation and debugging, the service is designed to use ASCII. A client forms a connection to a server and waits for output. Whenever a connection request arrives, a server creates a message in printable ASCII form, sends the message over the connection, and then closes the connection. The client displays the data it receives and then exits.

For example, the tenth time a client connects to the server, the client receives and prints the following:

`This server has been contacted 10 times.`

28.4 Command-Line Arguments For The Example Programs

The example server takes one command-line argument, a protocol port number at which to accept requests. The argument is optional; if no port number is specified, the code uses port *5193*†.

The example client has two command-line arguments: the name of a host on which to contact a server and a protocol port number to use. Both arguments are optional. If no protocol port number is specified, the client uses *5193*. If neither argument is specified, the client uses the default port and the host name *localhost*, which is usually an alias that maps to the computer on which the client is running. In most cases, a user will specify a host name because contacting a server on the local machine is uninteresting. However, allowing the client to contact a server on the local machine is useful for debugging.

28.5 Sequence Of Socket Procedure Calls

Figure 28.1 illustrates the sequences of socket procedures that the example client and server call.

---

†The particular port number used in the code has no significance; a value was chosen that did not conflict with existing services on the author's computer.

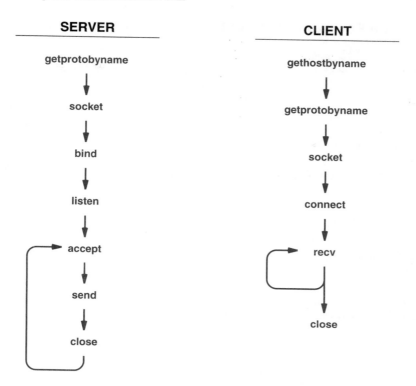

Figure 28.1 The sequence of socket procedure calls in the example client and server. The server must call *listen* before a client calls *connect*.

As the figure shows, the server calls seven socket procedures and the client calls six. The client begins by calling library procedures *gethostbyname* to convert the name of a computer to an IP address and *getprotobyname* to convert the name of a protocol to the internal binary form used by the socket procedure. The client then calls *socket* to create a socket and *connect* to connect the socket to a server. Once the connection is in place, the client repeatedly calls *recv* to receive the data that the server sends. Finally, after all data has been received, the client calls *close* to close the socket.

The server also calls *getprotobyname* to generate the internal binary identifier for the protocol before calling *socket* to create a socket. Once a socket has been created, the server calls *bind* to specify a local protocol port for the socket and *listen* to place the socket in passive mode. The server then enters an infinite loop in which it calls *accept* to accept the next incoming connection request, *send* to send a message to the client, and *close* to close the new connection. After closing a connection, the server calls *accept* to extract the next incoming connection.

28.6 Code For Example Client†

```
/* client.c - code for example client program that uses TCP */

#ifndef unix
#define WIN32
#include <windows.h>
#include <winsock.h>
#else
#define closesocket close
#include <sys/types.h>
#include <sys/socket.h>
#include <netinet/in.h>
#include <arpa/inet.h>
#include <netdb.h>
#endif

#include <stdio.h>
#include <string.h>

#define PROTOPORT       5193            /* default protocol port number */

extern  int             errno;
char    localhost[] =   "localhost";    /* default host name            */
/*------------------------------------------------------------------------
 * Program:   client
 *
 * Purpose:   allocate a socket, connect to a server, and print all output
 *
 * Syntax:    client [ host [port] ]
 *
 *                   host - name of a computer on which server is executing
 *                   port - protocol port number server is using
 *
 * Note:      Both arguments are optional.  If no host name is specified,
 *            the client uses "localhost"; if no protocol port is
 *            specified, the client uses the default given by PROTOPORT.
 *
 *------------------------------------------------------------------------
 */
main(argc, argv)
int     argc;
char    *argv[];
{
```

---

†The example code was compiled and tested under BSD UNIX, Solaris, and Windows NT, with *#ifdef* constructs used to make minor changes in the code (e.g., Windows Sockets uses *closesocket* instead of *close*).

```
        struct  hostent *ptrh;   /* pointer to a host table entry      */
        struct  protoent *ptrp;  /* pointer to a protocol table entry  */
        struct  sockaddr_in sad; /* structure to hold an IP address    */
        int     sd;              /* socket descriptor                  */
        int     port;            /* protocol port number               */
        char    *host;           /* pointer to host name               */
        int     n;               /* number of characters read          */
        char    buf[1000];       /* buffer for data from the server    */
#ifdef WIN32
        WSADATA wsaData;
        WSAStartup(0x0101, &wsaData);
#endif
        memset((char *)&sad,0,sizeof(sad)); /* clear sockaddr structure */
        sad.sin_family = AF_INET;          /* set family to Internet    */

        /* Check command-line argument for protocol port and extract   */
        /* port number if one is specified.  Otherwise, use the default */
        /* port value given by constant PROTOPORT                       */

        if (argc > 2) {                    /* if protocol port specified */
                port = atoi(argv[2]);      /* convert to binary          */
        } else {
                port = PROTOPORT;          /* use default port number    */
        }
        if (port > 0)                      /* test for legal value       */
                sad.sin_port = htons((u_short)port);
        else {                             /* print error message and exit */
                fprintf(stderr,"bad port number %s\n",argv[2]);
                exit(1);
        }

        /* Check host argument and assign host name. */

        if (argc > 1) {
                host = argv[1];            /* if host argument specified  */
        } else {
                host = localhost;
        }

        /* Convert host name to equivalent IP address and copy to sad. */

        ptrh = gethostbyname(host);
        if ( ((char *)ptrh) == NULL ) {
                fprintf(stderr,"invalid host: %s\n", host);
```

```
        exit(1);
}
memcpy(&sad.sin_addr, ptrh->h_addr, ptrh->h_length);

/* Map TCP transport protocol name to protocol number. */

if ( ((int)(ptrp = getprotobyname("tcp"))) == 0) {
        fprintf(stderr, "cannot map \"tcp\" to protocol number");
        exit(1);
}

/* Create a socket. */

sd = socket(PF_INET, SOCK_STREAM, ptrp->p_proto);
if (sd < 0) {
        fprintf(stderr, "socket creation failed\n");
        exit(1);
}

/* Connect the socket to the specified server. */

if (connect(sd, (struct sockaddr *)&sad, sizeof(sad)) < 0) {
        fprintf(stderr,"connect failed\n");
        exit(1);
}

/* Repeatedly read data from socket and write to user's screen. */

n = recv(sd, buf, sizeof(buf), 0);
while (n > 0) {
        write(1,buf,n);
        n = recv(sd, buf, sizeof(buf), 0);
}

/* Close the socket. */

closesocket(sd);

/* Terminate the client program gracefully. */

exit(0);
}
```

28.7 Code For Example Server

```
/* server.c - code for example server program that uses TCP */
#ifndef unix
#define WIN32
#include <windows.h>
#include <winsock.h>
#else
#define closesocket close
#include <sys/types.h>
#include <sys/socket.h>
#include <netinet/in.h>
#include <netdb.h>
#endif

#include <stdio.h>
#include <string.h>

#define PROTOPORT        5193           /* default protocol port number */
#define QLEN             6              /* size of request queue        */

int     visits    =    0;              /* counts client connections    */
/*------------------------------------------------------------------------
 * Program:    server
 *
 * Purpose:    allocate a socket and then repeatedly execute the following:
 *                (1) wait for the next connection from a client
 *                (2) send a short message to the client
 *                (3) close the connection
 *                (4) go back to step (1)
 *
 * Syntax:     server [ port ]
 *
 *                 port  - protocol port number to use
 *
 * Note:       The port argument is optional.  If no port is specified,
 *             the server uses the default given by PROTOPORT.
 *
 *------------------------------------------------------------------------
 */
main(argc, argv)
int     argc;
char    *argv[];
{
```

```
        struct  hostent  *ptrh;   /* pointer to a host table entry        */
        struct  protoent *ptrp;   /* pointer to a protocol table entry    */
        struct  sockaddr_in sad;  /* structure to hold server's address   */
        struct  sockaddr_in cad;  /* structure to hold client's address   */
        int     sd, sd2;          /* socket descriptors                   */
        int     port;             /* protocol port number                 */
        int     alen;             /* length of address                    */
        char    buf[1000];        /* buffer for string the server sends   */

#ifdef WIN32
        WSADATA wsaData;
        WSAStartup(0x0101, &wsaData);
#endif
        memset((char *)&sad,0,sizeof(sad)); /* clear sockaddr structure */
        sad.sin_family = AF_INET;          /* set family to Internet    */
        sad.sin_addr.s_addr = INADDR_ANY; /* set the local IP address   */

        /* Check command-line argument for protocol port and extract   */
        /* port number if one is specified.  Otherwise, use the default */
        /* port value given by constant PROTOPORT                       */

        if (argc > 1) {                   /* if argument specified      */
                port = atoi(argv[1]);     /* convert argument to binary */
        } else {
                port = PROTOPORT;         /* use default port number    */
        }
        if (port > 0)                     /* test for illegal value     */
                sad.sin_port = htons((u_short)port);
        else {                            /* print error message and exit */
                fprintf(stderr,"bad port number %s\n",argv[1]);
                exit(1);
        }

        /* Map TCP transport protocol name to protocol number */

        if ( ((int)(ptrp = getprotobyname("tcp"))) == 0) {
                fprintf(stderr, "cannot map \"tcp\" to protocol number");
                exit(1);
        }

        /* Create a socket */

        sd = socket(PF_INET, SOCK_STREAM, ptrp->p_proto);
        if (sd < 0) {
```

```
                fprintf(stderr, "socket creation failed\n");
                exit(1);
        }


        /* Bind a local address to the socket */

        if (bind(sd, (struct sockaddr *)&sad, sizeof(sad)) < 0) {
                fprintf(stderr,"bind failed\n");
                exit(1);
        }


        /* Specify size of request queue */

        if (listen(sd, QLEN) < 0) {
                fprintf(stderr,"listen failed\n");
                exit(1);
        }


        /* Main server loop - accept and handle requests */

        while (1) {
                alen = sizeof(cad);
                if ( (sd2=accept(sd, (struct sockaddr *)&cad, &alen)) < 0) {
                        fprintf(stderr, "accept failed\n");
                        exit(1);
                }
                visits++;
                sprintf(buf,"This server has been contacted %d time%s\n",
                        visits,visits==1?".":"s.");
                send(sd2,buf,strlen(buf),0);
                closesocket(sd2);
        }
}
```

28.8 Stream Service And Multiple Recv Calls

Although the server makes only one call to *send* to transmit data, the client code iterates to receive data. During each iteration, the client calls *recv* to obtain data; the iteration stops when the client obtains an end-of-file condition (i.e., a count of zero).

In most cases, TCP on the server's computer will place the entire message in a single TCP segment, and then transmit the segment across a TCP/IP internet in an IP datagram. However, TCP does not guarantee that the data will be sent in a single segment, nor does it guarantee that each call to *recv* will return exactly the same amount of data that the server transferred in a call to *send*. Instead, TCP merely asserts that data will be delivered in order, with each call of *recv* returning one or more octets of data. Consequently, a program that calls *recv* must be prepared to make repeated calls until all data has been extracted.

28.9 Socket Procedures And Blocking

Most procedures in the socket API are *synchronous* or *blocking* in the same way as most I/O calls. That is, when a program calls a socket procedure, the program is suspended until the procedure completes†. There is no time limit for suspension — the operation may take arbitrarily long.

To understand how clients and servers use blocking procedures, first consider the server. After creating a socket, binding a protocol port, and placing the socket in passive mode, the server calls *accept*. If a client has already requested a connection before the server calls *accept*, the call returns immediately. If the server reaches the *accept* call before any client requests a connection, the server will be suspended until a request arrives. In fact, the server spends most of its time suspended at the *accept* call.

Calls to socket procedures in the client code can also block. For example, some implementations of the library procedure *gethostbyname* send a message across a network to a server and wait for a reply. In such cases, the client remains suspended until the reply is received. Similarly, the call to *connect* blocks until TCP can perform the 3-way handshake to establish a connection.

Perhaps the most important suspension occurs during data transmission. After the connection has been established, the client calls *recv*. If no data has been received on the connection, the call blocks. Thus, if the server has a queue of connection requests, a client will remain blocked until the server sends data.

28.10 Size Of The Code And Error Reporting

Although each of the example programs is large, much of the size can be attributed to comments. For example, removing blank lines and comments reduces the code size by over forty percent.

Many lines of code check for errors. In addition to checking values specified by command-line arguments, the code checks the return value from each procedure call to ensure that the operation was successful. Errors are not expected, so when an error does occur, the programmer has arranged for the program to print a short error message and terminate. Fifteen percent of the code is devoted to error checking.

---

†While suspended, a program does not use the CPU.

28.11 Using The Example Client With Another Service

Although the example service may seem trivial, both the client and server can be used with other services. Using the example client with another service provides an easy way to debug the client before the server has been written. For example, TCP/IP defines a *DAYTIME* service that prints the date and time of day. The DAYTIME service uses the same interaction paradigm as our example — a client forms a connection to a DAYTIME server and then prints the information the server sends.

To use the example client with the DAYTIME service, the client program must be invoked with two arguments that specify a host on which a DAYTIME server is running and the protocol port number for the DAYTIME service, *13*. For example, if the client code is compiled and the result placed in an executable file named *client*, it can be used to contact the DAYTIME service on computers around the Internet:

```
$ client localhost 13
Fri Oct 27 08:32:32 2000
$ client www.prenhall.com 13
Fri Oct 27 09:32:38 2000
$ client stanford.edu 13
Fri Oct 27 06:32:37 2000
```

The example output shows the time from three computers; the output was generated by running the client three times in rapid succession. The first output comes from the computer on which the client is running; the computer is located at Purdue University in West Lafayette, Indiana. The second output comes from a computer located in New Jersey, and the third comes from a computer located at Stanford University in California. Each computer reports the local time, so one expects differences in the hour. If the clocks on all computers were accurate, one would expect the times to differ by at most the one or two seconds that elapse while the commands run. The time on the local computer is known to be accurate† and agrees with the time reported by Stanford. However, the clock at prenhall.com is a few seconds ahead (perhaps the clock was set by hand).

28.12 Using Another Client To Test The Server

The example server can be tested separately from the client. To do so, one can use the *telnet* client program to contact the server. The *telnet* program requires two arguments: the name of a computer on which the server runs and the protocol port number of the server. For example, the following output shows the result of using *telnet* to connect to the example server.

---

†The time is obtained from the WWV time standard.

```
$ telnet xx.yy.nonexist.com 5193
Trying...
Connected to xx.yy.nonexist.com 5193
Escape character is '^]'.
This server has been contacted 4 times.
Connection closed by foreign host.
```

Although the output contains five lines, only the fourth was emitted by the server; the others came from the *telnet* client program.

28.13 Summary

We have examined the code for an example client and server that use a connection-oriented transport protocol to communicate. To keep the example easy to understand, we chose a trivial service in which the server transmits a single string each time a client connects. After it calls *socket* to create a socket, *bind* to specify a protocol port number, *listen* to place the socket in passive mode, and *accept* to accept a connection, the server calls *send* to transmit data, and *close*† to terminate the connection. After it calls *socket* to create a socket, the client calls *connect* to establish a connection to a server, *recv* to receive data, and *close* to terminate use of the socket.

Although the example client and server are trivial, they can interoperate with clients and servers for standard services. The *telnet* client can be used to contact the example server, and the example client can be used to contact the *DAYTIME* service on protocol port *13*.

EXERCISES

28.1 Try using the example client to contact DAYTIME servers on computers at your site. Do the reported times agree? Why or why not?

28.2 Use the example client to contact DAYTIME servers on computers in foreign countries. Do all computers display the time and date in the same format?

28.3 Use the example client to contact the *CHARGEN* service (protocol port number *19*). How could the CHARGEN service be used?

28.4 Write a computer program that takes the name of a protocol port and prints the port number.

28.5 Write a computer program that takes the name of a computer and prints the computer's IP address in dotted decimal notation.

---

†Note that for Windows systems, *close* is defined to be *closesocket*.

28.6 Experiment to see if TCP at your site handles the request queue correctly. To do so, modify the example server to delay for thirty seconds before responding to a request. Arrange to have *N* copies of the example client contact the server within a thirty second period. What happens if *N* is greater than *QLEN*?

28.7 What is the advantage or disadvantage of using *INADDR_ANY* instead of the IP address of the computer running the server?

28.8 Modify the example server to keep a log of all the clients that contact it. Hint: look up the socket procedure *getpeername*.

28.9 Can a client and a server both use protocol port *5193* on the same computer at the same time? Explain.

28.10 Modify the example server to make two calls to *send* to transmit two lines of output. Modify the example client to show how many calls to *recv* occur.

28.11 Extend the above exercise to have the server place two lines of output in a buffer and transmit the buffer using a single call to *send*. How many times does the client call *recv* to obtain the data? Can you explain the results?

28.12 Modify the example client and server to provide file transport by having the client send a file name and having the server send a copy of the file.

28.13 Use the socket API to implement the five functions in the high-level API given in Chapter 3 (omit *send* and *recv*). Approximately how many lines of code are required for each function?

Chapter Contents

29

Naming With The Domain Name System

29.1 Introduction

Previous chapters describe how each computer is assigned an Internet Protocol address that appears in each IP datagram sent to the computer. Although IP addresses are fundamental in TCP/IP, anyone who has used the Internet knows that users do not need to remember or enter IP addresses. Instead, computers are also assigned symbolic names; application software allows a user to enter one of the symbolic names when identifying a specific computer. For example, when specifying a destination for an electronic mail message, a user enters a string that identifies the recipient to whom the message should be delivered and the name of the recipient's computer. Similarly, a computer name is embedded in a string that a user enters to specify a site on the World Wide Web.

Although symbolic names are convenient for humans, they are inconvenient for computers. Because it is more compact than a symbolic name, the binary form of an IP address requires less computation to manipulate (e.g., to compare). Furthermore an address occupies less memory and requires less time to transmit across a network than a name. Thus, although application software permits users to enter symbolic names, the underlying network protocols require addresses — an application must translate each name into an equivalent IP address before using it for communication. In most cases, the translation is performed automatically, and the results are not revealed to the user — the IP address is kept in memory and only used to send or receive datagrams.

The software that translates computer names into equivalent Internet addresses provides an interesting example of client-server interaction. The database of names is not kept on a single computer. Instead, the naming information is distributed among a potentially large set of servers located at sites across the Internet. Whenever an application program needs to translate a name, the application becomes a client of the naming system. The client sends a request message to a name server, which finds the corresponding address and sends a reply message. If it cannot answer a request, a name server temporarily becomes the client of another name server, until a server is found that can answer the request.

This chapter describes the naming hierarchy, the organization of name servers, and the details of client-server interaction among them. The chapter also explains how caching improves efficiency of the naming system, and makes it possible for a large-scale distributed system to function.

29.2 Structure Of Computer Names

The naming scheme used in the Internet is called the *Domain Name System* (*DNS*). Syntactically, each computer name consists of a sequence of alpha-numeric segments separated by periods. For example, a computer in the Computer Science Department at Purdue University has the domain name:

mordred.cs.purdue.edu

and a computer in the College of Engineering at Bucknell University has the domain name:

www.eg.bucknell.edu

Domain names are hierarchical, with the most significant part of the name on the right. The left-most segment of a name (*mordred* and *www* in the examples) is the name of an individual computer. Other segments in a domain name identify the group that owns the name. For example, the segments *purdue* and *bucknell* each give the name of a university.

How many segments does a name have, and how are they assigned? The answer is that beyond specifying how the most significant segments are chosen, the domain name system does not specify an exact number of segments in each name nor does it specify what those segments represent. Instead, each organization can choose how many segments to use for computers inside the organization and what those segments represent.

The domain name system does specify values for the most significant segment, which is called the *top-level* of the DNS. The table in Figure 29.1 lists the top-level domains:

Domain Name	Assigned To
com	Commercial organization
edu	Educational institution
gov	Government organization
mil	Military group
net	Major network support center
org	Organization other than those above
arpa	Temporary ARPA domain (still used)
int	International organization
country code	A country

Figure 29.1 Values for the most significant segment of a domain name. DNS does not distinguish between names in upper or lower case.

Proposals have been made to add new top-level domains, but none has been successful. At the time of this writing, the *Internet Corporation for Assigned Names and Numbers (ICANN)*, the organization responsible for domain names, is once again soliciting proposals for new top-level domains. Thus, a change appears imminent.

Top-level domains are important because each organization that chooses to participate in the domain name system must apply for a name under one of the existing top-level domains. Most corporations choose to register under the *com* domain. For example, a corporation named *Foobar* might request to be assigned domain *foobar* under the top-level domain *com*. If the request is approved, Foobar Corporation will be assigned the domain:

foobar.com

Once an organization has been assigned a domain, the suffix is reserved for the organization — no other organization will be assigned the same name suffix. For example, once *foobar.com* has been assigned, another organization named Foobar could apply for *foobar.edu* or *foobar.org*, but not *foobar.com*. To summarize:

> To obtain a domain, an organization must register with the Internet authority. A unique domain suffix is assigned to each organization.

29.3 Geographic Structure

In addition to the familiar organizational structure, the DNS allows organizations to use a geographic registration. For example, the Corporation For National Research Initiatives registered the domain:

cnri.reston.va.us

because the corporation is located in the town of Reston, Virginia in the United States. Thus, names of computers at the corporation end in *.us* instead of *.com*.

Some foreign countries have adopted a combination of geographic and organizational domain names. For example, universities in the United Kingdom register under the domain:

ac.uk

where *ac* is an abbreviation for *academic*, and *uk* is the official country code for the United Kingdom.

29.4 Domain Names Within An Organization

Once an organization owns a particular domain, the organization can decide whether to introduce additional hierarchical structure. A small corporation can choose no additional hierarchy, while a large organization can choose many levels. For example, if the Foobar Corporation is small, it might decide that all names have the form:

computer.foobar.com

where *computer* denotes the name assigned to a single computer. However, if Foobar is large enough to have multiple locations, one level of the domain hierarchy can be used to denote location, resulting in domain names of the form:

computer.*location*.foobar.com

Finally, if Foobar has many divisions at each location, one level of the domain name hierarchy could be used to distinguish among divisions, resulting in names of the form:

computer.*division*.*location*.foobar.com

Because domain names are logical concepts, they do not need to conform to physical locations. For example, Foobar might own plants in five locations, with each location containing computers from two divisions. Foobar might choose to assign domain names by division instead of by location. As a result, a name would not encode the location of the computer:

computer.division.foobar.com

    Freedom to choose a naming hierarchy extends to groups within an organization. Consequently, two computers in a given organization can have a different number of segments in their domain names. For example, suppose a large division of Foobar corporation makes candy bars, while a small division makes soap. Because it is small, the soap-making division might choose to assign domain names of the form:

computer.soap.foobar.com

The candy-making division might choose to add one level to the domain hierarchy to distinguish among the various subdivisions that make each candy bar:

computer.*subdivision*.candy.foobar.com

For example, Figure 29.2 uses a graphical representation to illustrate the Foobar DNS hierarchy if the company has three subdivisions for *peanut*, *almond*, and *walnut* candy.

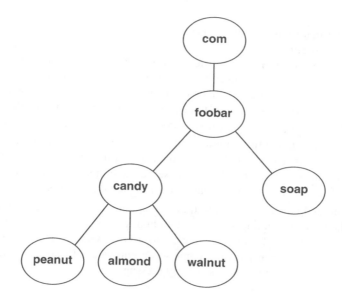

Figure 29.2 A graphical representation that illustrates one way a DNS hierarchy might be structured in a corporation. Names for individual computers can be added to the diagram as well.

As the figure shows, the hierarchy corresponds directly to the syntax of names. For example, computers in the *walnut* subdivision have names that end with the suffix:

walnut.candy.foobar.com

In terms of the diagram, the naming suffix corresponds exactly to the sequence of labels found along a path going upward in the hierarchy from the item labeled *walnut*.

We can summarize:

> *The number of segments in a domain name corresponds to the naming hierarchy. There is no universal standard because each organization can choose how to structure names in its hierarchy. Furthermore, names within an organization do not need to follow a uniform pattern because individual groups within the organization can choose a hierarchical structure that is appropriate for the group.*

29.5 The DNS Client-Server Model

One of the main features of the Domain Naming System is autonomy — the system is designed to allow each organization to assign names to computers or to change those names without informing a central authority. The naming hierarchy helps achieve autonomy by allowing an organization to control all names with a particular suffix. Thus, Purdue University is free to create or change any name that ends with *purdue.edu*, while IBM Corporation is free to create or change names that end with *ibm.com*.

In addition to hierarchical names, the DNS uses client-server interaction to aid autonomy. In essence, the entire naming system operates as a large, distributed database. Most organizations that have an Internet connection run a domain name server. Each server contains information that links the server to other domain name servers; the resulting set of servers functions as a large, coordinated database of names.

Whenever an application needs to translate a name to an IP address, the application becomes a client of the naming system. The client places the name to be translated in a DNS request message, and sends the request to a DNS server. The server extracts the name from the request, translates the name to an equivalent IP address, and returns the resulting address to the application in a reply message.

29.6 The DNS Server Hierarchy

DNS servers are arranged in a hierarchy that matches the naming hierarchy, with each being the *authority* for part of the naming hierarchy. A *root server* occupies the top of the hierarchy, and is an authority for the top-level domains (e.g., *.com*). Although it does not contain all possible domain names, a root server contains information about how to reach other servers. For example, although it does not know the names of computers at IBM Corporation, a root server knows how to reach a server that handles requests for *ibm.com*. Similarly, a root server knows how to reach the server that handles requests for *purdue.edu*.

Although the hierarchy of DNS servers follows the naming hierarchy, the structure is not identical. A corporation can choose to place all its domain names in a single server, or can choose to run several servers. For example, Figure 29.3 illustrates two ways Foobar corporation might choose to allocate its naming hierarchy to two servers. In *(a)*, the server for *foobar.com* also includes the *soap* division, while in *(b)*, the server for *foobar.com* includes everything except the *walnut* subdivision.

As the figure illustrates, a server is not restricted to a single level in the domain naming hierarchy, nor is it required to contain multiple levels. For example, although the server for *foobar.com* in Figure 29.3b contains names at three different levels of the hierarchy, the server for the *walnut* subdivision contains names at a single level. Figure 29.3 also illustrates that a given level in the hierarchy can be partitioned into multiple servers. In Figure 29.3a, separate servers are authorities for *soap* and *candy*, which both reside at the same level of the hierarchy. In Figure 29.3b, the authority for *walnut* differs from the authority for *almond* and *peanut*, although all three domains occur at the same level in the hierarchy under *candy*.

29.7 Server Architectures

How should a domain name server architecture be chosen? In particular, when does an organization need more than one server? In general, an architecture in which an organization uses a single server is the simplest — a small organization can minimize cost by placing all its domain information in a single server†.

Larger organizations usually find that a single, centralized server does not suffice for two reasons. First, a single server and the computer on which it runs cannot handle arbitrary requests at high speed. Second, large organizations often find it difficult to administer a central database. The problem is especially severe because most DNS software does not provide automated update — a human must enter changes and additions in the server's database. Thus, the group of people who are responsible for administering an organization's centralized server must coordinate to ensure that only one manager attempts to make changes at a given time. If the organization runs multiple servers, each group can manage a server that is an authority for the group's computers. More important, each group can make changes to its server database without centralized coordination.

---

†The smallest organizations do not run a server themselves. Instead, the organization contracts with an Internet Service Provider that runs a domain name server on behalf of its customers.

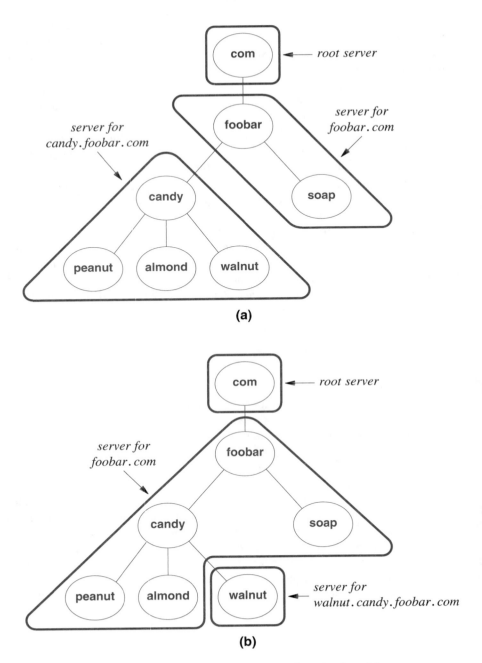

Figure 29.3 Two examples of ways the domain name hierarchy from Figure 29.2 can be divided among three servers. Each organization chooses how to divide names among its servers.

29.8 Locality Of Reference And Multiple Servers

The *locality of reference principle* discussed in Chapter 8 applies to the domain name system, and helps explain why multiple servers work well. The domain name system follows the locality of reference principle in two ways. First, a user tends to look up the names of local computers more often than the names of remote computers. Second, a user tends to look up the same set of domain names repeatedly.

Having multiple servers within an organization works well because a server can be placed within each group. The local server is an authority for names of computers in the group. Because the DNS obeys the locality principle, the local server can handle most requests. Thus, in addition to being easier to administer, multiple servers help balance the load, and thereby reduce the problems of contention a centralized server may cause.

29.9 Links Among Servers

Although the DNS allows the freedom to use multiple servers, a domain hierarchy cannot be split into servers arbitrarily. The rule is: a single server must be responsible for all computers that have a given suffix. In terms of the graphical representation, subtrees can be moved to a separate server, but a given node cannot be split.

Servers in the domain name system are linked together, making it possible for a client to find the correct server by following links. In particular, each server is configured to know the locations of servers of subparts of the hierarchy. For example, in either server arrangement illustrated in Figure 29.3, the server for *.com* must be configured to know the location of the server for *foobar.com*. Furthermore, the server for *foobar.com* must be configured to know the location of other servers. For example, in Figure 29.3b the server for *foobar.com* would be configured to know the location of the server for *walnut.candy.foobar.com*. Finally, each DNS server is configured to know the location of a root server. To summarize:

> *All domain name servers are linked together to form a unified system. Each server knows how to reach a root server and how to reach servers that are authorities for names further down the hierarchy.*

29.10 Resolving A Name

The translation of a domain name into an equivalent IP address is called *name resolution*, and the name is said to be *resolved* to an address. Software to perform the translation is known as *name resolver* (or simply *resolver*) software.

Many operating systems provide name resolver software as a library routine that an application can call. For example, on UNIX systems, an application can call library routine *gethostbyname* to resolve a name. *Gethostbyname* takes a single argument and returns a structure. The argument is a character string that contains the domain name to be looked up. If it succeeds, *gethostbyname* returns a structure that contains a list of one or more IP addresses that correspond to the specified name. If it fails to resolve the name, *gethostbyname* returns a *NULL* pointer instead of a structure.

How does resolver software work? Each resolver is configured with the address of a local domain name server†. To become a client of the DNS server, the resolver places the specified name in a *DNS request* message, and sends the message to the local server. The resolver then waits for the server to send a *DNS reply* message that contains the answer. Although a client can choose to use either UDP or TCP when communicating with a DNS server, most resolvers are configured to use UDP because it requires less overhead for a single request.

When an incoming request specifies a name for which a server is an authority, the server answers the request directly. That is, the server looks up the name in its local database, and sends a reply to the resolver. However, when a request arrives for a name outside the set for which the server is an authority, further client-server interaction results. The server temporarily becomes a client of another name server. When the second server returns an answer, the original server sends a copy of the answer back to the resolver from which the request arrived.

How does a DNS server know which other DNS server is the authority for a given name? It does not. However, each server knows the address of a root server. Knowing the location of a root server is sufficient because the name can be resolved from there. For example, suppose the servers for Foobar Corporation are organized as in Figure 29.3b, and a resolver at a remote site (e.g., at a university) sends a request to its local server, *L*, for the name:

venus.walnut.candy.foobar.com

Server *L* is not an authority for the name, so it proceeds to act as a client of other servers. In the first step, *L* sends a request to the root server. The root server is not an authority for the name, but the response from the root server gives the location of a server for *foobar.com*.

When it receives the response from the root server, server *L* contacts the server for *foobar.com*. Although it is not the authority for names in the *walnut* subdivision, the main server at Foobar knows the location of the server for *walnut*. Thus, it returns a response to inform *L*. Finally, *L* contacts the server that is the authority for names of the form:

computer.walnut.candy.foobar.com

That server returns an *authoritative answer* to *L*, either the IP address for the name or an indication that no such name exists.

---

†Some resolvers are configured with a list of servers, allowing the resolver to try alternatives in case a server is temporarily unavailable.

Stepping through the hierarchy of servers to find the server that is an authority for a name is called *iterative query resolution*, and is used only when a server needs to resolve a name. The resolvers that applications call always request *recursive query resolution*. That is, they request complete resolution — the reply to a recursive request is either the IP address being sought or an authoritative statement that no such name exists. To summarize:

> *The resolver software in a host always requests recursive resolution in which a name is resolved to an equivalent address. When it becomes a client of another server, a server can request iterative resolution to step through the server hierarchy one level at a time.*

29.11 Optimization Of DNS Performance

Measurements have shown that the domain name system as described above is hopelessly inefficient. Without optimizations, traffic at a root server would be intolerable because the root server would receive a request each time someone mentioned the name of a remote computer. Furthermore, the principle of locality suggests that a given computer will emit the same requests repeatedly — if a user enters the name of a remote computer, the user is likely to specify the same name again.

There are two primary optimizations used in the DNS: replication and caching. Each root server is replicated; many copies of the server exist around the world. When a new site joins the Internet, the site configures its local DNS server with a list of root servers. The site's server uses whichever root server is most responsive at a given time. In practice, the geographically closest server usually responds best. Thus, a site in Europe will tend to use a root server in Europe, while a site in the state of California will choose to use a root server on the west coast of the United States.

DNS caching is more important than replication because caching affects most of the system. Each server maintains a cache of names. Whenever it looks up a new name, the server places a copy of the binding in its cache. Before contacting another server to request a binding, the server checks its cache. If the cache contains the answer, the server uses the cached answer to generate a reply.

Caching works well because name resolution shows a strong tendency toward temporal locality of reference. That is, on a given day, a user is likely to look up the same name repeatedly. For example, if a user sends e-mail to an address, the user is likely to receive a reply to which the user will send a reply, and so on. When an application looks up a name for the first time, the local DNS server caches the binding. The server can then answer subsequent requests by returning the binding from its cache instead of contacting the authoritative server again.

29.12 Types Of DNS Entries

Each entry in a DNS database consists of three items: a domain name, a record type, and a value. The record type specifies how the value is to be interpreted. More important, a query sent to a DNS server specifies both a domain name and a type; the server only returns a binding that matches the type of the query.

We have discussed the type used for a binding between a domain name and an equivalent IP address. DNS classifies such bindings as type *A* (the *A* stands for *address type*). Type *A* bindings are common because they are used by most applications. For example, when a user supplies a computer name to an application program such as *FTP*, *ping*, or a World Wide Web browser, the application requests a binding that matches type *A*.

In addition to type *A*, DNS supports several other types. One popular type is *MX* (an abbreviation for *Mail eXchanger*), which is used to map the computer name found in an e-mail address to an IP address. E-mail software specifies type *MX* when it sends a request to a DNS server. The answer that the server returns matches the requested type. Thus, an e-mail system will receive an answer that matches type *MX*. To summarize:

> *The domain name system stores a type with each entry. When a resolver looks up a name, the resolver must specify the type that is desired; a DNS server returns only entries that match the specified type.*

29.13 Aliases Using The CNAME Type

Another type, *CNAME*, is especially useful. *CNAME* entries are analogous to a symbolic link in a file system — the entry provides an alias for another DNS entry. To understand how aliases can be useful, suppose Foobar Corporation has two computers named *hobbes.foobar.com* and *calvin.foobar.com*. Further suppose that Foobar decides to run a Web server, and wants to follow the convention of using the name *www* for the computer that runs the organization's Web server. Although the organization could choose to rename one of their computers (e.g., *hobbes*), a much easier solution exists: the organization can create a *CNAME* entry for *www.foobar.com* that points to *hobbes*. Whenever a resolver sends a request for *www.foobar.com*, the server returns the address of computer *hobbes*.

The use of aliases is especially convenient because it permits an organization to change the computer used for a particular service without changing the names or addresses of the computers. For example, Foobar Corporation can move its Web service from computer *hobbes* to computer *calvin* by moving the server and changing the *CNAME* record in the DNS server — the two computers retain their original names and IP addresses.

29.14 An Important Consequence Of Multiple Types

The type system in the DNS is convenient because it permits a manager to use a single name for multiple purposes (e.g., to direct Web traffic to one computer, while sending e-mail to a different computer). However, users are sometimes surprised at the consequence of having specific types in DNS requests — a name that works with one application may not work with another. For example, it may be possible to send e-mail to a computer, while an attempt to communicate with the computer using a program like *ping* or *traceroute* results in a message that no such computer exists. The apparent inconsistency arises because the DNS type requested by e-mail differs from the type requested by other applications. If the domain database contains a type *MX* record for the name, a request from the e-mail system will succeed. However, if the database does not also contain a type *A* record, a request from programs like *ping* will result in a negative reply.

The type system that the DNS uses can produce unexpected results because some applications are configured to use multiple types. For example, the resolvers used in some e-mail systems try two types when resolving a name. The resolver begins by sending the server a type *MX* request. If the server responds negatively, the resolver then tries a type *A* request. The scheme can help in situations where an organization specifies a type *A* record in their domain database for a given name, but fails to specify a type *MX* entry for the name as well.

29.15 Abbreviations And The DNS

Because users tend to enter names for local computers more often than they enter names for remote computers, abbreviations for local names are convenient. For example, Foobar Corporation might choose to allow users to omit the suffix *foobar.com* when entering a domain name. With such an abbreviation in effect, a user could enter the name *venus.walnut.candy* to refer to computer *venus* in the *walnut* subdivision of the *candy* division.

Domain name servers do not understand abbreviations — a server only responds to a full name. To handle abbreviations, resolvers are programmed to try a set of suffixes. For example, each resolver at Foobar Corporation might be programmed to look up a name twice: once with no change and once with the suffix *foobar.com* appended. The suffix scheme allows both local and remote names to be handled the same way. Given the valid name of a remote computer, a DNS server will return a valid answer, which the resolver uses. However, given an abbreviated local name, a DNS server will return an error message (because no such name exists). The resolver can then try appending each of the suffixes.

Usually, each computer contains resolver software that all applications on that computer use. Because abbreviations are handled by a resolver, the set of abbreviations allowed on each computer can differ. For example, a resolver on a computer in the candy division might try appending the suffix *candy.foobar.com* to a name before appending *foobar.com*. As a result, a user in the *candy* division could reference any computer in the division without entering the suffix. Similarly, resolvers on computers in the *soap* division might append the suffix *soap.foobar.com* before appending *foobar.com*. If each division follows the pattern, a user can abbreviate the name of any computer in his or her division.

29.16 Summary

The domain name system provides automated mapping between computer names and equivalent IP addresses. Each name is a character string that consists of a sequence of alpha-numeric segments separated by periods. Names are allocated hierarchically, and segments in the name correspond to levels in the hierarchy.

There is no standard for the number of segments in a name because each organization is free to choose how to assign levels of the hierarchy. In fact, two groups within a given organization may use two different levels of hierarchy.

A set of online servers provides answers to resolution requests. Each organization chooses how to allocate its names to a server, and the servers are linked together to form a unified system. An application program that calls a resolver becomes a client of the domain name system. The client sends a request to its local server, which either answers the request directly, or contacts other servers to find the answer.

DNS servers use two performance optimization techniques: replication and caching. Root servers are replicated to reduce the load on a given server. More important, because name resolution obeys the principle of locality, all DNS servers place a copy of resolved bindings in their cache for later use.

EXERCISES

29.1 Most companies prefer to use the organizational structure for domain names instead of the geographic structure. What is the chief advantage of the organizational structure?

29.2 Sketch the domain hierarchy at your organization, and show how it has been divided into servers.

29.3 Use a network analyzer to watch traffic to the Internet as a host requests a domain name. How many datagrams travel to and from remote servers?

29.4 Repeat the experiment in the previous exercise five times. What do you observe?

29.5 Write a computer program that accepts a domain name as input, and prints the IP address of the computer in dotted decimal form. Hint: use *gethostbyname*.

29.6 Can you use the program described in the previous exercise to obtain the IP address of a root server? If so how, and if not, why not?

29.7   Does it make sense for two domain servers to contain exactly the same set of names? Why or why not?

29.8   Can a host be a domain name server? To find out configure program *nslookup* to use a host at your organization as a domain name server, and then ask *nslookup* to resolve a domain name. Try several hosts.

29.9   Use program *nslookup* with *type=PTR*, and look up *1.2.10.128.in-addr.arpa*. Compare the results to looking up *arthur.cs.purdue.edu*. What is the relationship between the two names?

29.10 Read about the special domain *in-addr.arpa* used in the previous exercise. Which server stores the data for the special domain?

29.11 Does the *in-addr.arpa* domain work for computers at your site?

29.12 Use a program like *nslookup* to test the IP addresses of computers in your organization with various DNS types. Try computer names like *www*.

29.13 Program *nslookup* allows a user to specify the type of a query when making a DNS request. Try multiple query types with names of computers at your site to see if your organization has a domain name that resolves to a different IP address when the query type is changed.

29.14 Does limiting the number of levels in a DNS hierarchy result in faster name resolution? For example, if an organization limits all names to three segments each instead of allowing ten segments, will name resolution be faster? Why or why not?

29.15 If your organization has two computer names with different numbers of segments, run an experiment to validate your answer to the previous question. Write a computer program that resolves a name repeatedly (e.g., one hundred times), test with each name, and determine the running time of the program for each. Can you explain the results?

Chapter Contents

30

Electronic Mail Representation And Transfer

30.1 Introduction

Chapters in this section define the client-server model of interaction, which forms the basis for all distributed computing. They discuss fundamental concepts as well as the socket API that client and server programs use to interact. The previous chapter examines the domain name system, a large, distributed application that uses client-server interaction to resolve a name.

This chapter continues the discussion of client-server programming by examining one of the most widely-used network applications: electronic mail. The chapter focuses on the interactions between clients and servers that occur when electronic mail is transferred across an internet. The chapter describes the basic mail transport service, mail forwarding, and mailbox access.

30.2 The Electronic Mail Paradigm

Originally, *electronic mail* (*e-mail*) was designed as a straightforward extension of the traditional office memo. That is, the original e-mail systems were built to allow a person to communicate with other people; an individual created a message and specified other individuals as recipients. The e-mail software transmitted a copy of the message to each recipient.

Electronic mail systems have evolved from the original design, and are automated to permit more complex interactions. In particular, because a computer program can answer an e-mail message and send a reply, e-mail can be used in a variety of ways. For example, a company can establish a computer program that responds automatically to requests for information that arrive in mail messages. A user sends an e-mail request to the program, and receives the desired information in a reply.

30.3 Electronic Mailboxes And Addresses

An e-mail system uses many of the terms and concepts from a traditional office environment. Before e-mail can be sent to an individual, the person must be assigned an *electronic mailbox*. The mailbox consists of a passive storage area (e.g., a file on disk). Like a conventional mailbox, an electronic mailbox is private — the permissions are set to allow the mail software to add an incoming message to an arbitrary mailbox, but to deny anyone except the owner the right to examine or remove messages. In most cases, an electronic mailbox is associated with a computer account. Thus, a person who has multiple computer accounts can have multiple mailboxes.

Each electronic mailbox is assigned a unique *electronic mail address* (*e-mail address*); when someone sends a memo, they use an electronic mail address to specify a recipient. A full e-mail address contains two parts, the second specifies a computer and the first specifies a mailbox on that computer. In the most widely used format, an ''at sign'' separates the two components:

mailbox @ computer

where *mailbox* is a string that denotes a user's mailbox, and *computer* is a string that denotes the computer on which the mailbox is located (i.e., a domain name).

The division of an e-mail address into two parts is important because it achieves two goals. First, the division allows each computer system to assign mailbox identifiers independently. Thus, two computers can use different mailbox identification schemes or they can both choose to use the same mailbox names. Second, the division permits users on arbitrary computer systems to exchange e-mail messages. E-mail software on the sender's computer uses the second part to determine which computer to contact, and e-mail software on the recipient's computer uses the first part of the address to select a particular mailbox into which the message should be placed. Thus, the first part of an address is interpreted locally; the string may not have meaning outside of a single computer system. To summarize:

> *Each electronic mailbox has a unique address, which is divided into two parts: the first identifies a user's mailbox, and the second identifies a computer on which the mailbox resides. E-mail software on the sender's computer uses the second part to select a destination; e-mail software on the recipient's computer uses the first part to select a particular mailbox.*

What format is used for the *mailbox* portion of an address? The answer depends on the e-mail software available on a computer as well as on the operating system being used. Some software systems allow the system administrator to choose mailbox names, while other systems require a user's mailbox identifier to be the same as the user's login identifier. Administrators often create a mailbox identifier by concatenating a user's first name, middle initial, and last name, with underscores to separate the three items. For example, the e-mail address for employee John Quiggley Public at Foobar Corporation might be:

John_Q_Public@foobar.com

On systems that require a user's login identifier to be used as a mailbox identifier, the resulting e-mail address is not nearly as readable. For example, if login accounts on a computer at Nonexistent Corporation consist of two six-digit numbers separated by a period, an individual's e-mail address on that computer might be:

912743.253843@nonexist.com

Obviously, a mnemonic form makes the *mailbox* portion of an e-mail address easier to remember and enter correctly.

30.4 Electronic Mail Message Format

An electronic mail message has a simple format. The message consists of ASCII text that is separated into two parts by a blank line. Called a *header*, the first part contains information about the message: the sender, intended recipients, date the message was sent, and the format of the contents. The second part is known as the *body*; it contains the text of the message.

Although the body of a message can contain arbitrary text, the header follows a standard form that e-mail software uses when it sends or receives a message. Each header line begins with a *keyword* followed by a colon and additional information. The keyword tells e-mail software how to interpret the remainder of the line.

Some keywords are required in each e-mail header; others are optional. For example, each header must contain a line that begins with the keyword *To* and specifies a list of recipients. The remainder of the header line following *To:* contains a list of one or more e-mail addresses, where each address corresponds to one recipient. E-mail software places a line that begins with the keyword *From* followed by the e-mail address of the sender in the header of each message. Figure 30.1 contains an example e-mail message that shows how lines in the header appear.

```
From: John_Q_Public@foobar.com
To: 912743.253843@nonexist.com
Date: Wed, 15 Nov 00 10:21:32 EST
Subject: lunch with me?

Bob,

    Can we get together for lunch when you visit next
week?  I'm free on Tuesday or Wednesday -- just let me
know which day you would prefer.

John
```

Figure 30.1 An example e-mail message. Lines of the header begin with a keyword and a colon; a blank line separates the header from the body .

The figure shows two additional header lines that contain the date the message was sent and the subject of the message. Both are optional; the sender's e-mail software chooses whether to include them.

If e-mail software does not understand a header line, the software passes it through unchanged. Thus, application programs that use e-mail messages to communicate can add additional lines to the message header to control processing. More important, a vendor can build e-mail software that uses header lines to add functionality — if an incoming message contains a special header line, the software knows that the message was created by the company's product. Finally, some companies add header lines to advertise a product (e.g., the brand name of the software that was used to create the message). Figure 30.2 lists some of the keywords commonly found in Internet mail, and describes the purpose of each.

Keyword	Meaning
From	Sender's address
To	Recipients' addresses
Cc	Addresses for carbon copies
Date	Date on which message was sent
Subject	Topic of the message
Reply-To	Address to which reply should go
X-Charset	Character set used (usually ASCII)
X-Mailer	Mail software used to send the message
X-Sender	Duplicate of sender's address
X-Face	Encoded image of the sender's face

Figure 30.2 Examples of keywords found in Internet mail.

30.5 Carbon Copies

The list of keywords in Figure 30.2 reveals that electronic mail has borrowed a concept and terminology from office memos: an electronic mail header can contain a line that specifies recipients who should receive a copy of the message. Like conventional office memos, electronic mail uses the keyword *Cc* to denote a carbon copy. A list of e-mail addresses follows on the *Cc:* line; each address listed is sent a copy of the message.

Conventional office etiquette requires the sender of a memo to inform the recipient when copies are sent to others. Sometimes a sender wishes to give a copy of a memo to someone without revealing that a copy was sent. Some electronic mail systems provide such an option. Those that do follow conventional office terminology and use the term *blind carbon copy*. The user who creates a message specifies one or more blind copies by giving a list of e-mail addresses following the *Bcc* keyword. Although the *Bcc* line appears to the sender, the mail system removes it from the message when transmitting a copy. A recipient can examine the *To* and *Cc* lines in the header to determine whether the message was sent directly or as a blind copy†; other recipients cannot determine the identity of users who received a blind copy.

We can summarize:

> *Electronic mail uses a format and terminology taken from conventional office memos. A header contains information about the message, and the body contains the text of the message. Lines in an e-mail header specify the sender, recipients, date, topic, and the list of people who should receive a copy.*

30.6 Multipurpose Internet Mail Extensions

The original Internet e-mail system was designed to handle only text. The body of an e-mail message was restricted to printable ASCII characters and could not contain arbitrary bytes. In particular, one could not transfer a binary file directly as the body of a mail message.

Researchers who found e-mail useful, devised schemes to allow e-mail to be used to transfer arbitrary data (e.g., a binary program or a graphics image). In general, all the schemes *encode* the data in a textual form, which can then be sent in a mail message. Once it arrives, the body of the message must be extracted and converted back to binary form. For example, one method uses a hexadecimal representation. The binary data is divided into four-bit units, with each unit encoded as one of the sixteen characters *0* through *9* and *A* through *F*. The sequence of hexadecimal characters is then sent in an e-mail message; the receiver must translate the characters back to binary.

---

†Some mail system add information to the body of a message that informs the recipient that the message is a blind copy.

To help coordinate and unify the various schemes that have been invented for encoding binary data, the IETF invented *MIME*, the *Multipurpose Internet Mail Extensions*. MIME does not dictate a single standard for encoding binary data. Instead, MIME permits a sender and receiver to choose an encoding that is convenient. When using MIME, the sender includes additional lines in the header to specify the message follows MIME format as well as additional lines in the body to specify the type of the data and the encoding. Besides providing a way for the sender and receiver to agree on an encoding, MIME allows a sender to divide a message into several parts and to specify the encoding for each part independently. Thus, with MIME, a user can send a plain text message and attach a graphics image. When the recipient views the message, the e-mail system displays the text message, and then asks the user how to handle the attached image (e.g., save a copy on the disk or display a copy on the screen). When the user decides how to handle the attachment, the MIME software decodes the attached data automatically.

To achieve transparent encoding and decoding, MIME adds two lines to an e-mail header: one to declare that MIME was used to create the message, and another to specify how MIME information is included in the body. For example, the header lines:

```
MIME-Version: 1.0
Content-Type: Multipart/Mixed; Boundary=Mime_separator
```

specify that the message was composed using version *1.0* of MIME, and that a line containing *Mime_separator* will appear in the body before each part of the message. When MIME is used to send a standard text message, the second line becomes:

```
Content-Type: text/plain
```

The chief advantage of MIME lies in its flexibility — the standard does not specify a single encoding scheme that all senders and receivers must use. Instead, MIME allows new encodings to be invented at any time. A sender and receiver can use a conventional e-mail system to communicate, provided they agree on the encoding scheme and a unique name for it. Furthermore, MIME does not specify a value to be used to separate parts of the message or a way to name the encoding scheme used. The sender can choose any separator that does not appear in the body; the receiver uses information in the header to determine how to decode the message.

MIME is compatible with older e-mail systems. In particular, an e-mail system that transfers the message does not need to understand the encoding used for the body or the MIME header line — the message can be treated exactly like any other e-mail message. The mail system transfers header lines without interpreting them, and treats the body as a single block of text. To summarize:

> *Although Internet e-mail only transfers text, MIME can be used to transport binary data by encoding it in printed characters. A MIME mail message includes additional information that a receiving application uses to decode the message.*

30.7 E-mail And Application Programs

Because computer programs can process e-mail, distribution and processing of electronic mail differs from that of traditional office memos. In particular, it is possible to configure an e-mail address to correspond to a program instead of a mailbox on disk. When e-mail arrives destined for such an address, the mail system sends a copy to the specified program instead of placing a copy on disk.

Allowing a computer program to send or receive mail makes it possible to invent interesting ways to interact. For example, consider an application that permits a user to obtain information from a database. The user places a request (e.g., a database query) in an e-mail message, and sends the message to the program. The program extracts the request from the incoming message, looks up the answer in the database, and then uses e-mail to send a reply to whoever sent the request.

30.8 Mail Transfer

After a user composes an e-mail message and specifies recipients, e-mail software transfers a copy of the message to each recipient. In most systems, two separate pieces of software are required. A user interacts with an *e-mail interface* program when composing or reading messages. The underlying e-mail system contains a *mail transfer* program that handles the details of sending a copy of a message to a remote computer. When a user finishes composing an outgoing message, the e-mail interface places the message in a queue that the mail transfer program handles.

The mail transfer program waits for a message to be placed on its queue, and then transfers a copy of the message to each recipient. Sending a copy of a message to a recipient on the local computer is trivial because the transfer program can append the message to the user's mailbox. Sending a copy to a remote user is more complex. The mail transfer program becomes a client that contacts a server on the remote machine. The client sends the message to the server, which places a copy of the message in the recipient's mailbox. Figure 30.3 illustrates the interaction.

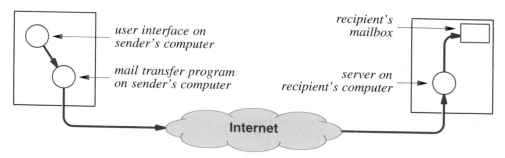

Figure 30.3 The path of an e-mail message. The mail transfer program on the sender's computer becomes a client of the remote mail server.

30.9 The Simple Mail Transfer Protocol

When a mail transfer program contacts a server on a remote machine, it forms a TCP connection over which it communicates. Once the connection is in place, the two programs follow the *Simple Mail Transfer Protocol* (*SMTP*) that allows the sender to identify itself, specify a recipient, and transfer an e-mail message.

Although mail transfer may seem simple, the SMTP protocol handles many details. For example, SMTP requires reliable delivery — the sender must keep a copy of the message until the receiver has stored a copy in nonvolatile memory (e.g., on disk). Furthermore, SMTP allows the sender to ask whether a given mailbox exists on the remote computer.

30.10 Optimizing For Multiple Recipients On A Computer

Although Figure 30.3 shows an e-mail message being transferred to a single mailbox on a remote computer, most mail transfer programs are optimized to handle all recipients on a given remote computer at the same time. For example, suppose a user on computer *nonexist.com* sends a message to three users at *foobar.com*. The mail transfer program on *nonexist.com* does not need to establish three separate connections to the server on *foobar.com*. Instead, the transfer program forms a single connection to the server, specifies all three recipients, and transfers a single copy of the message. The server accepts the message, and then delivers a copy to each of the three recipients.

Optimizing for multiple recipients is important for two reasons. First, it dramatically reduces the network bandwidth required to transfer e-mail. For example, if a user sends to three recipients on a given computer, the optimization reduces the network load by a factor of three. Second, optimization reduces the delay required for all users to receive a copy of a message — recipients who have their mailbox on a given computer will receive a copy of the message at approximately the same time. More important, if the internet between the sender and receiver fails, either all recipients receive a copy of the message or none do.

30.11 Mail Exploders, Lists, And Forwarders

Because they can process e-mail messages, computer programs can be used to manipulate and forward messages. For example, many mail systems include a *mail exploder* or *mail forwarder*, a program that can forward copies of a message. The exploder uses a database to determine how to handle a message. Commonly called a *mailing list*, each entry in the database is a set of e-mail addresses. Furthermore, each entry in the database is assigned its own e-mail address.

When an e-mail message arrives, the mail exploder examines the destination address. If the destination address corresponds to a list in its database, the exploder forwards a copy of the message to each address on the list. For example, Figure 30.4 shows an example mail exploder database.

List	Contents
friends	Joe@foobar.com, Jill@bar.gov, Tim@StateU.edu, Mary@acollege.edu, Hank@nonexist.com,
customers	george@xyz.com, VP_Marketing@news.com
bball-interest	Hank@nonexist.com, Linda_S_Smith@there.com, John_Q_Public@foobar.com, Connie@foo.edu,

Figure 30.4 An example database used by a mail exploder. Each entry is assigned a name and contains a list of e-mail addresses.

The example database contains three mailing lists. The first list, which has the name *friends*, specifies five recipients (*Joe*, *Jill*, *Tim*, *Mary*, and *Hank*), each at a different location. The second list, *customers*, specifies two recipients, while the third, *bball-interest*, specifies four.

The example database specifies only the local part of a list's address. To complete the address, one must append the name of the computer on which the exploder operates to the name that is given. For example, if the exploder runs on computer *wit.com*, the first mailing list has the full address:

$$friends@wit.com$$

If someone sends a message to *friends@wit.com*, the exploder will forward a copy to each of the five recipients.

Mail exploders make it possible for a large group to communicate via e-mail without requiring senders to specify all recipients explicitly. To send mail to the group, a message is sent to the list address. The exploder receives the message and forwards a copy to each member of the list. To receive mail sent to the group, an individual must request that their e-mail address be added to the list.

30.12 Mail Gateways

Although a mail exploder can operate on any computer, forwarding an e-mail message to a large mailing list can require significant processing time. Thus, many organizations do not permit exploders or large mailing lists on conventional computers. Instead, the organization selects a small set of computers to run exploders and forward e-mail. A computer dedicated to processing electronic mail is often called a *mail gateway*, *e-mail gateway*, or *e-mail relay*.

The mailing lists maintained on most mail gateways are *public*. That is, anyone is allowed to join the list, and anyone can send a message to the list. Thus, a message often arrives at the gateway from a remote computer. Figure 30.5 illustrates how programs interact when an arbitrary user sends a message to a mailing list on a mail gateway machine.

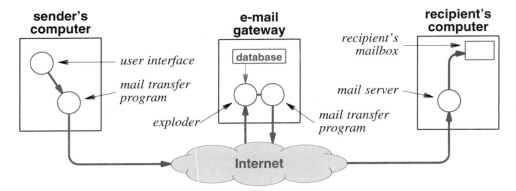

Figure 30.5 The path of a message as it passes from a sender's interface through a mail gateway. On the gateway computer, an exploder handles incoming e-mail, and a conventional mail transfer program sends a copy to each recipient.

As the figure shows, a message passes across the Internet at least twice. Initially, a single copy passes from the sender's computer to the mail gateway. After it consults the database of mailing lists, the exploder generates a request to send copies of the message. A conventional mail transfer program on the gateway computer sends each copy across the Internet to the recipient's computer, where a server stores it in the recipient's mailbox. Although the figure shows a single transfer from the gateway machine to a recipient, one transfer occurs for each destination on the mailing list. We can summarize:

> *A mail gateway or relay is a computer dedicated to the task of forwarding e-mail. Inside a mail gateway, an exploder program accepts a message sent to a mailing list, and forwards a copy to each recipient on the list.*

30.13 Automated Mailing Lists

Because computer programs can be created to send and receive e-mail messages, it is possible to build programs that handle routine chores without human intervention. One especially useful form of automated program is used in conjunction with an e-mail exploder. The special program, called a *list manager*, automatically maintains the exploder's database of mailing lists. A user who wants to create a new mailing list, add their address to a list, or remove their address from a list sends an e-mail message to the list manager program. For example, one list manager expects incoming e-mail to contain commands such as:

add *mailbox* to *list*

where *mailbox* is an e-mail address and *list* is the name of a mailing list. Other list managers use alternative forms (e.g., *subscribe* instead of *add*).

The advantages of automated list management should be obvious. From the participant's point of view, automated management improves service because it allows a participant to join or leave a list without contacting a human or waiting for a person to enter a change. From the list owner's point of view, automated management reduces the cost of maintaining the list.

30.14 Mail Relays And E-mail Addresses

Because a user's e-mail address includes the name of the user's computer, an organization that has many computers can have a variety of e-mail addresses. For example, consider the names of computers for the hypothetical Foobar Corporation. If each employee's e-mail address includes the name of their computer, the e-mail addresses of two employees will differ:

$$Smith @ venus.walnut.candy.foobar.com$$

and

$$S\_Johnson @ susie.soap.foobar.com$$

Knowing one employee's e-mail address would not help someone guess another employee's e-mail address.

To avoid confusion and make e-mail addresses for all employees uniform, an organization might choose to run a mail gateway, and assign all e-mail addresses relative to the gateway. For example, if Foobar Corporation names their mail gateway computer:

$$foobar.com$$

the corporation can assign each employee an e-mail address of the form:

$$employee @ foobar.com$$

where the string *employee* is chosen to designate a single employee (e.g., the employee's first name, middle initial, and last name separated by underscores).

Because each e-mail address includes the name of the mail gateway, a message sent to an employee at Foobar Corporation will arrive at the gateway computer. The database on the gateway must contain an entry for each employee that specifies the employee's mailbox on a specific machine in the corporation. More important, the da-

tabase on the e-mail gateway allows the external and internal addresses to differ —
external e-mail addresses can be independent of the mailbox identifiers used by particular computer systems. For example, if employee John T. Doe uses computer

bubbles.soap.foobar.com

and has the 7-digit number *8456311* assigned as a mailbox identifier, the entry in the
corporate mail gateway might specify:

List	Contents
John_T_Doe	8456311@bubbles.soap.foobar.com

In essence, the database would contain a mailing list for John's external e-mail identifier with a single recipient. The exploder at the gateway would forward mail sent to
John_T_Doe@foobar.com to John's internal mailbox.

In addition to making e-mail addresses uniform across an entire organization, the
gateway scheme permits flexibility. Because no one outside the corporation knows the
specific computer an employee uses to receive mail or the employee's internal mailbox
identifier, the organization can move an employee or rename a computer without changing the employee's e-mail address.

30.15 Mailbox Access

On which computer should a mailbox be placed? Given a choice, most users
prefer to have their mailbox located on the computer they use most. For example,
someone who has a workstation on their desk might choose to place their electronic
mailbox on the hard disk of the workstation. Similarly, someone who spends most of
the time logged into a timesharing system might choose to place their mailbox on the
system's disk.

Unfortunately, mailboxes cannot be placed on all computer systems. To understand why, consider how e-mail transfer works. As we have seen, a mailbox is merely
a storage location on disk; remote programs do not access the mailbox directly. Instead,
each computer system that has mailboxes must run a mail server program that accepts
incoming e-mail and stores it in the correct mailbox. On powerful computer systems,
mail server programs operate in background, allowing a user to run other applications at
the same time. To permit multiple clients to send e-mail simultaneously, most mail
servers arrange to run multiple copies of the server program at the same time.

A mailbox cannot be placed on a computer unless the computer runs a mail server.
For example, a computer that does not have enough memory, does not have an operating system that allows programs to run in background, or does not have sufficient CPU
capacity, cannot run a server. More important, servers are expected to run continuously
— a computer that remains powered off or disconnected from the Internet for extended

periods of time (e.g., outside working hours) will not suffice as an e-mail receiver. Thus, a personal computer is not usually chosen to run an e-mail server.

Using a separate computer for e-mail can be inconvenient. For example, someone who uses a personal computer on their desktop would find it annoying to move to another computer merely to read e-mail. To avoid the problem, the TCP/IP protocols include a protocol that provides remote access to an electronic mailbox. The protocol allows a user's mailbox to reside on a computer that runs a mail server, and allows the user to access items in the mailbox from another computer.

Known as the *Post Office Protocol* (*POP*), the protocol requires an additional server to run on the computer with the mailbox. The additional server uses the POP protocol. A user runs e-mail software that becomes a client of the POP server to access the contents of the mailbox. Figure 30.6 illustrates one way to use POP.

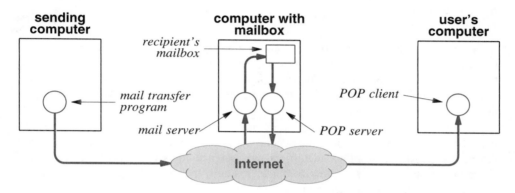

Figure 30.6 The path of e-mail when POP is used to access a mailbox. The mail can arrive from the sender's computer or a mail gateway. To retrieve messages from the mailbox, a user runs a program that becomes a client of the POP server.

As the figure shows, a computer that has a mailbox must run two servers. A conventional mail server accepts incoming e-mail and stores it in the appropriate mailbox. The mail can arrive either directly from the original sender or from a mail gateway. A POP server allows a user on a remote machine to access the mailbox.

Although both the e-mail server and POP server communicate across the Internet, there are several differences. First, the mail server uses the SMTP protocol, while the POP server uses the POP protocol. Second, the mail server accepts a message from an arbitrary sender, while the POP server only allows a user to access the mailbox after the user enters authentication information (e.g., a password). Third, the mail server can transfer only e-mail messages, while a POP server can provide information about the mailbox contents.

30.16 Dialup Connections And POP

Although Figure 30.6 shows a client receiving mail from the POP server across the Internet, POP is especially popular among users who rely on dialup telephone connections. In such cases, a computer with the user's mailbox remains attached to the Internet as shown in the figure. However, the user's computer does not need a permanent Internet connection. Instead, the computer can attach to a modem and use a telephone connection. To receive e-mail, the user forms a dialup connection either to the mailbox computer or to some other computer on the Internet. Once the user connects to a computer on the Internet, the user can run a POP client to contact the server and access e-mail.

30.17 Summary

Electronic mail uses the office memo paradigm in which a message contains a header that specifies the sender, recipients, and subject, followed by a body that contains the text of the message. To participate in e-mail, a person must be assigned a mailbox (a storage area) into which messages can be placed. Each mailbox has an address.

An e-mail address is a string divided into two parts by the @ character. The first part is a mailbox identifier, and the second gives the name of the computer on which the mailbox resides. Mailbox identifiers are assigned locally, and only have significance on one computer. On some computer systems, the mailbox identifier is the same as a user's login account identifier; on other systems, the two are independent. The computer name in an e-mail address is a domain name.

Because e-mail systems use ASCII text to represent messages, binary data cannot be included directly in e-mail. The MIME standard allows a sender to encode non-text data for transmission. MIME does not specify a single standard for encoding. However, MIME does provide a mechanism that the sender can use to inform a recipient about the encoding.

In the simplest case, e-mail transfer occurs directly from the sender's computer to the recipient's. A background program on the sender's computer becomes a client by contacting the e-mail server on the recipient's computer. The two programs use the SMTP protocol to transfer a message, and the server places the message in recipients' mailboxes on the remote computer.

Although it was originally intended to provide communication between pairs of people, computer programs can be used to send, receive, or forward e-mail. A mail exploder program uses a database of mailing lists to provide communication among large groups of participants. When a message is sent to a mailing list, the exploder forwards a copy to each member of the list. It is possible to build a program that automates list management — the program accepts a request to create or change a specified mailing list by adding or removing a participant's address.

A computer dedicated to the task of forwarding mail is called a mail gateway or mail relay. An organization can use a mail gateway to make e-mail addresses of all employees uniform.

Some computers cannot accept e-mail because the computer system is not powerful enough to run an e-mail server, the computer is frequently powered down, or the computer is not permanently attached to the Internet. A user who has such a computer must arrange to keep their mailbox on another machine. In such circumstances, a user runs software that uses the Post Office Protocol (POP) to access the remote mailbox. POP is especially useful for computers that have dialup connections to the Internet.

EXERCISES

30.1   Does a numeric mailbox identifier have any advantages over a mnemonic identifier? Explain.

30.2   Some companies that manufacture e-mail programs add a line to the header of each outgoing mail message that contains the name of the company or the name of the product used to create the message. Does such information have any use beyond advertising? Explain.

30.3   How long would you prefer an outgoing e-mail message to be kept if the mail system cannot form a connection to the destination computer? Why?

30.4   Write two computer programs that use e-mail to send and receive an arbitrary binary file. To translate the file into ASCII, use a hexadecimal dump. Use a special line in the header to identify the contents of the message.

30.5   Write a computer program that reads the header on an e-mail message and deletes all lines except those that begin with *From:*, *To:*, *Subject:*, and *Cc:*.

30.6   If an e-mail message is sent to a mailing list, is every recipient on the list guaranteed to receive a copy? Explain.

30.7   Some mailing list software rewrites the *From:* lines in the header of any message sent to a list to make it appear that the message was sent from the list instead of an individual. The advantage is that if a recipient replies, everyone on the list receives a copy of the reply. What is the danger of rewriting headers? Hint: imagine that one of the addresses on the list contains a typo.

30.8   Some sites run a program called *mailer* that allows a user to create arbitrary aliases for their own e-mail address. The user will receive mail sent to any of the aliases. What is the chief advantage of allowing such aliases? The chief disadvantage?

30.9   Read about SMTP. How is a *HELO* message used?

30.10   Can SMTP be used as the transfer protocol for Web pages? Why or why not?

Chapter Contents

31

File Transfer And Remote File Access

31.1 Introduction

Previous chapters define the client-server paradigm and give an example of a network application. This chapter presents another example: a network application that can transfer copies of a file from one computer to another. In addition to discussing the file transfer interface, the chapter considers file access and explains how the underlying software uses the client-server paradigm.

31.2 Data Transfer And Distributed Computation

Before networks, transferring data from one computer to another required the use of magnetic media such as tapes or disks. Data was written on the magnetic medium by an application on one computer, and the medium was physically moved to another. To cross long distances, media was shipped (e.g., via postal mail). Computer networks reduced the delay substantially, and made possible a new form of computation in which programs on two or more computers cooperate to achieve a solution. Output from one program becomes the input of another program.

The chief disadvantage of direct communication among programs is that it requires coordination of applications on many computers, and such coordination can be difficult. Managers must ensure that the computers are running, and that the applications are ready at the same time. Furthermore, to achieve high throughput, the managers must prevent other programs on the computers from using significant amounts of CPU, memory, or network bandwidth.

A second disadvantage of direct communication arises from its inability to recover from a failure. If any computer or application program crashes, the entire computation must be restarted from the beginning. Because no intermediate results are saved, such failures can be especially costly if they occur late in a long computation (e.g., after many hours of processing).

31.3 Saving Intermediate Results

Programmers and managers observed that a single technique helps overcome both disadvantages of direct communication. Instead of sending data across a network as it is generated, each application stores intermediate results in files on disk. That is, an application reads input from a file on disk, processes the data, and writes output to a file. The data is transferred from an output file on one computer to an input file on another.

The advantages of using intermediate files should be apparent. First, because data is saved at each step of the computation, a manager can recover from a failure that occurs in a later step without re-running all previous steps. Second, because it permits managers to schedule each step of the computation independently, the intermediate file solution eliminates most of the logistic problems that arise when attempting to use multiple computers simultaneously. If all computers connect to a shared network, using intermediate files avoids having all steps of the computation compete for network bandwidth.

31.4 Generalized File Transfer

As network applications began to use intermediate files, programmers wrote code to transfer a complete file from one computer to another. Because the steps required to transfer a file for one application are similar to the steps required to transfer a file for another, programmers were duplicating code, making only minor modifications in file names or the way data was represented. It quickly became apparent that a single, generalized utility could be devised to work with many applications. The problem became known as the *file transfer* problem, and a software system that moved arbitrary data from a file on one computer to a file on another became known as *file transfer* software.

To be useful, file transfer software must be general and flexible. It must allow transfer of an arbitrary file, and must accommodate multiple file types. Because an internet can connect heterogeneous computer systems, file transfer software must accommodate differences among the ways computer systems store files. For example, each computer system has rules about file names — a name that is valid on one computer system may be invalid on another. Furthermore, because most computer systems use login accounts to define file ownership, the owner on one computer system may not have a corresponding login account on another computer. Finally, file transfer software must accommodate other minor differences in file representations, type information, and file protection mechanisms.

31.5 Interactive And Batch Transfer Paradigms

Some early file transfer systems used a *batch* approach similar to the one used for e-mail transfer. A user invoked an interface program which allowed the user to form a request that specified details such as the remote computer to contact and the files to be transferred. The interface program then placed the request in a queue, and started a transfer program. The transfer program contacted a server on the remote machine and transferred the specified files. If the remote machine or the network was unavailable, the transfer program automatically retried the transfer later. When the transfer was complete, the transfer program informed the user.

Batch transfer is most useful when the probability of gaining access to a remote computer is low or the time required for the transfer is large. For example, batch transfer worked well initially because early networks were unreliable; it was not uncommon for a network to be down. Batch transfer also works well when a large file is transferred across a low-capacity connection. In such circumstances, a batch transfer program handles the transfer automatically, without requiring a user to wait. The transfer program periodically attempts to contact the remote machine. When communication succeeds, the program waits for the file transfer to complete and terminates communication gracefully (e.g., closes the network connection).

Batch transfer has disadvantages as well. In situations where networks and computers remain available most of the time, interactive transfer is more convenient. A user receives information continuously as the transfer program contacts a server on the remote computer and transfers the requested file. For example, a user finds out immediately if the remote machine name contains an error. Similarly, a user quickly learns about an incorrect file name or a request that is denied because the remote file protections do not permit transfer. Finally, a user is notified immediately when the transfer completes.

A file transfer service can offer the advantages of both interactive and batch approaches. To do so, the service must provide an interface that permits either a human user or a program to invoke the service. To operate interactively, a human invokes the service, enters a request, and waits for a response. To operate in batch mode, a transfer program manages a queue of requests. When handling a request, the transfer program passes a request to the service and waits for the transfer to complete. To summarize:

> *A file transfer service can move a copy of a file from one computer to another, either interactively or in batch mode. It is possible to build a service that can be used in either mode.*

31.6 The File Transfer Protocol

The most widely-deployed Internet file transfer service uses the *File Transfer Protocol* (*FTP*). A general-purpose protocol, FTP handles many of the concepts discussed above. FTP permits transfer of an arbitrary file, and includes a mechanism that allows files to have ownership and access restrictions. More important, because it hides the details of individual computer systems, FTP accommodates heterogeneity — it can be used to transfer a copy of a file between an arbitrary pair of computers.

FTP is among the oldest application protocols still used in the Internet. Originally defined as part of the ARPANET protocols, FTP predates both TCP and IP. As TCP/IP was created, a new version of FTP was developed that worked with the new Internet protocols.

FTP is among the most heavily-used applications. Early in the history of the Internet, datagrams carrying file transfers accounted for approximately one-third of all Internet traffic; the traffic generated by services such as e-mail and the domain name system did not come close to exceeding that generated by FTP†.

To summarize:

> *The most popular file transfer service in the Internet uses FTP, the File Transfer Protocol. FTP is a general-purpose protocol that can be used to copy an arbitrary file from one computer to another.*

31.7 FTP General Model And User Interface

FTP is designed to permit interactive or batch use. Most users invoke FTP interactively — they run an FTP client that establishes communication with a specified server to transfer files. However, some software systems invoke FTP automatically, without requiring a user to interact with an FTP client. For example, a MIME interface to e-mail can extract and follow an FTP reference. When a program invokes FTP, the program must handle all details. The program interacts with FTP, and then informs the user whether the operation succeeded or failed; the program completely hides the FTP interface from the user.

When a user invokes FTP interactively, the user communicates with a command-driven interface. FTP issues a *prompt* to which the user responds by entering a command. FTP executes the command, and then issues another prompt.

FTP has commands that allow a user to specify a remote computer, provide authorization, find out which remote files are available, and request file transfer of one or more files. Some FTP commands require little or no time to execute, while others can take a significant time. For example, it may take many seconds to transfer a copy of a large file.

---

†In 1995, traffic carrying World Wide Web information surpassed FTP for the first time.

31.8 FTP Commands

Although the FTP protocol standard specifies exactly how FTP software on one computer interacts with FTP software on another, the standard does not specify a user interface. Consequently, the interface available to a user can vary from one implementation of FTP to another. To help maintain similarity among products, many vendors have chosen to adopt the interface that first appeared in an early version of FTP software written for the BSD UNIX system.

The BSD interface for FTP supports over 50 individual commands. Figure 31.1 lists the command names.

!	cr	macdef	proxy	sendport
$	delete	mdelete	put	status
account	debug	mdir	pwd	struct
append	dir	mget	quit	sunique
ascii	disconnect	mkdir	quote	tenex
bell	form	mls	recv	trace
binary	get	mode	remotehelp	type
bye	glob	mput	rename	user
case	hash	nmap	reset	verbose
cd	help	ntrans	rmdir	?
cdup	lcd	open	runique	
close	ls	prompt	send	

Figure 31.1 The names of commands found in the BSD interface for FTP. Many vendors support a variant of the BSD interface.

The list of commands can seem overwhelming to a beginner for two reasons. First, the BSD interface contains options that are seldom implemented (e.g., the *proxy* command that permits simultaneous communication with two remote sites). Second, the interface provides several options to handle obscure details, some of which have become irrelevant. For example, when the interface was defined, a version of FTP already existed on a computer operating system named *TENEX*. However, because the file representation used by TENEX differs from the file representation used by UNIX, a scheme was introduced to translate between the two representations, and the command *tenex* was introduced to invoke the translation. Today, other operating systems have replaced TENEX, making the option meaningless.

Similarly, early computer systems implemented *carriage control* by placing an extra character at the beginning of each line of a text file to specify printer spacing. Multiple standards existed for carriage control. When the BSD interface was designed, options were included to allow a user to specify that a particular file included carriage control. The intent was to have FTP translate between different carriage control standards. Because files are now rarely stored with carriage control, few vendors implement the option.

FTP also accommodates multiple representations of text files. For example, some computer systems use a single *linefeed* character to separate lines of text. Other systems use a two-character sequence that consists of a *carriage return* followed by a *linefeed*. The *cr* command allows a user to specify which representation the remote machine uses, making it possible for FTP to translate between the remote and local representations.

A final form of complexity arises because the BSD interface also includes aliases (i.e., multiple names for a function). For example, either of the commands *close* or *disconnect* can be used to terminate a connection to a remote computer. Similarly, either *bye* or *quit* can be used to exit from the FTP program, and either *help* or *?* can be used to obtain a list of available commands.

31.9 Connections, Authorization, And File Permissions

Fortunately, most users need only a handful of FTP commands to transfer a file. After starting an FTP program, a user must enter the *open* command before any files can be transferred. *Open* requires the user to give the domain name of a remote computer, and then forms a TCP connection to the computer.

Known as a *control connection*, the TCP connection to a remote machine is used to send commands. For example, once a connection has been opened, FTP requests the user to supply authorization to the remote computer. To do so, the user must enter a login name and a password; most versions of FTP prompt for each. The login name, which must correspond to a valid account on the remote computer, determines which files can be accessed. If an FTP user supplies login name *smith*, the user will have the same file access permission as someone who logs in as *smith* on the remote machine.

After a user opens a control connection and obtains authorization, the user can transfer files. The control connection remains in place as long as it is needed. When a user finishes accessing a particular computer, the user enters the *close* command to terminate the control connection. Closing a control connection does not terminate use of the FTP program — the user can choose to open a new control connection to another computer. We can summarize:

> *FTP requires a user to establish a control connection to a remote computer before files can be transferred. To obtain authorization, a user must supply a login and password. The control connection remains in place until the user decides to close it.*

31.10 Anonymous File Access

Although the use of a login name and password can help keep files secure from unauthorized access, such authorization can also be inconvenient. In particular, requiring each user to have a valid login name and password makes it difficult to allow arbitrary access. For example, suppose a corporation finds a bug in one of the programs it sells. The corporation might create a file of changes, and make the file available to anyone.

To permit arbitrary users to access a file, many sites follow the convention of establishing a special computer account used only for FTP. The account, which has the login name *anonymous*, permits an arbitrary user minimal access to files. Early systems used the password *guest* for anonymous access. More recent versions of FTP often request that a user send their e-mail address as a password, making it possible for the remote FTP program to send the user e-mail if problems arise. In either case, the term *anonymous FTP* is used to describe the process of obtaining access with the *anonymous* login name.

31.11 File Transfer In Either Direction

Interestingly, FTP allows file transfer in either direction. After a user establishes a connection to a remote computer, the user can obtain a copy of a remote file or transfer a copy of a local file to the remote machine. Of course, such transfers are subject to access permissions — the remote computer can be configured to prohibit creation of new files or changes to existing files, and the local computer enforces conventional access restrictions on each user.

A user enters either the *get* or *mget* command to retrieve a copy of a remote file. The *get* command, which is used most often, handles a single file transfer at a time. *Get* requires a user to specify the name of the remote file to copy; the user can enter a second name if the local file into which the copy should be placed has a different name than the remote file. If the user does not supply a remote file name on the input line along with the command, FTP prompts the user to request a name. Once it knows the name of a file, FTP performs the transfer and informs the user when it completes. Command *mget* permits a user to request multiple files with a single request. The user specifies a list of remote files, and FTP transfers each file to the user's computer.

To transfer a copy of a file from the local computer to a remote computer, a user enters a *put*, *send*, or *mput* command. *Put* and *send* are two names for the command that transfers a single file. As with *get*, a user must enter the name of the file on the local computer, and can also enter a different file name to use on the remote computer. If no file name is present on the command line, FTP prompts the user. The *mput* command is analogous to *mget* — it permits a user to request multiple file transfers with a single command. The user specifies a list of files, and FTP transfers each.

31.12 Wildcard Expansion In File Names

To make it easy for users to specify a set of file names, FTP allows a remote computer system to perform traditional file name expansion. The user enters an abbreviation, which FTP expands to produce a valid file name. In abbreviations, a *wildcard* character stands for zero or more characters. Many computer systems use the asterisk (*) as a wildcard. On such systems, the abbreviation:

li*

matches all file names that begin with the prefix *li*. Thus, if a remote computer contains the six files:

dark light lonely crab link tuft

FTP will expand the abbreviation *li** to two names: *light* and *link*. File name expansion can be especially useful with commands *mget* or *mput* because expansion makes it possible to specify a large set of files without entering each file name explicitly.

31.13 File Name Translation

Because FTP can be used between heterogeneous computer systems, the software must accommodate differences in file name syntax. For example, some computer systems restrict file names to uppercase letters, while others permit a mixture of lowercase and uppercase. Similarly, some computer systems permit a file name to contain as many as *128* characters, while others restrict names to *8* or fewer characters.

File name differences can be especially important when using an abbreviation (e.g., on an *mget* or *mput* command). In such commands, a user can specify an abbreviation that FTP expands into a list of names. Unfortunately, a file name that is valid on one computer may be illegal on another.

To handle incompatibilities among computer systems, the BSD interface to FTP permits a user to define rules that specify how to translate a file name when moving to a new computer system. Thus, a user can specify that FTP should translate each lowercase letter to its uppercase equivalent.

31.14 Changing Directories And Listing Contents

Many computers have a hierarchical file system that places each file in a *directory*†. The hierarchy arises because a directory can contain other directories as well as files. FTP supports a hierarchical file system by including the concept of a current directory — at any time, the local and remote sides of a control connection are each in a specific directory. All file names are interpreted in the current directory, and all file

---

†Some systems use the term *folder* instead of *directory*; the two are synonymous.

transfers affect the current directory. Command *pwd* can be used to find the name of the remote directory.

Commands *cd* and *cdup* permit a user to control the directory that FTP is using on the remote computer. Command *cd* changes to a specified directory; a valid directory name must be specified on the command line. Command *cdup* changes to the parent directory (i.e., moves up one level in the hierarchy). *Cdup* is convenient because the name needed to reference a parent directory may not be obvious. For example, UNIX systems use the name ''..'' to refer to the parent of the current directory.

To determine the set of files available in the current directory on the remote computer, a user can enter the *ls* command. *Ls* produces a list of file names, but does not tell about the type or contents of each file. Thus, a user cannot determine whether a given name refers to a text file, a graphics image, or another directory.

31.15 File Types And Transfer Modes

Although the file representations used by a pair of computer systems can differ, FTP does not attempt to handle all possible representations. Instead, FTP defines two basic types of transfer that accommodate most files: textual and binary. The user must select a transfer type, and the mode stays in effect for the entire file transfer.

Textual transfer is used for basic text files. A text file contains a sequence of characters separated into lines. Most computer systems use either the *ASCII* or *EBCDIC* character set to represent characters in a text file. A user, who knows the character set used on a remote computer, can use the *ascii* or *ebcdic* command to specify textual transfer and request FTP to translate between the local and remote character sets when copying a file.

The only alternative to text transfer in FTP is binary transfer, which must be used for all non-text files. For example, an audio clip, a graphics image, or a matrix of floating-point numbers must be transferred in binary mode. A user enters the *binary* command to place FTP in binary mode.

FTP does not interpret the contents of a file transferred in binary mode, and does not translate from one representation to another. Instead, binary transfer merely produces a copy — the bits of a file are reproduced without change. Unfortunately, a binary transfer may not produce the expected result. For example, consider a file of 32-bit floating point numbers. In binary mode, FTP will copy the bits of the file from one computer to another without change. However, if the floating point representations used by the computers differ, the computers will interpret the values in the file differently. To summarize:

> *FTP has two basic transfer modes: one used for text files and the other for all non-text files. Although binary mode produces an exact copy of the bits, the resulting copy may be meaningless because FTP does not convert values to the local representation.*

31.16 Example Of Using FTP

An example of an FTP session will make it clear how a user can issue commands to find and retrieve a file. In the example, a user invokes FTP, opens a control connection to remote computer *ftp.cs.purdue.edu*, lists the files in the current directory, lists the files in subdirectory *pub/Xinu*, changes to directory *pub/Xinu* and retrieves a copy of the file named *XINU-SPARC.README*. Finally, the user changes to directory */pub/comer* which contains a README file†, closes the connection, and exits FTP. Commands the user enters are shown in boldface (ftp does not display the password that the user enters).

```
$ ftp
ftp> open
(to) ftp.cs.purdue.edu
Connected to lucan.cs.purdue.edu.
220 lucan.cs.purdue.edu FTP server   Wed Jul 5 15:27:21 EST 2000) ready.
Name (ftp.cs.purdue.edu:comer): anonymous
331 Guest login ok, send your complete e-mail address as password.
Password:
230-
230-                          Purdue University
230-                   Department of Computer Sciences
230-
230-     Access is allowed all day.  Local time is Sun Oct 15 15:39:45 2000.
230-
230-     All transfers are logged with your host name and email address.
230-     If you don't like this policy, disconnect now!
230-
230-     If your FTP client crashes or hangs shortly after login, try using a
230-     dash (-) as the first character of your password.  This will turn off
230-     the informational messages which may be confusing your ftp client.
230-
230-     Report any problems to postmaster@cs.purdue.edu
230-
230 Guest login ok, access restrictions apply.
ftp> pwd
257 "/" is current directory.
ftp> ls
200 PORT command successful.
550 No files found.
ftp> ls pub/Xinu
200 PORT command successful.
150 Opening ASCII mode data connection for file list.
pub/Xinu/CONC.Z
```

---

†FTP displays the contents of the README file in response to the change of directory.

```
pub/Xinu/PURDUE-XINU-LAB-DOCUMENT.ps
pub/Xinu/TCPIP-vol2.dist.tar.Z
pub/Xinu/XINU-68K.README
pub/Xinu/XINU-68K.TAR.Z
pub/Xinu/XINU-MAC.TAR.Z
pub/Xinu/XINU-PDP11.TAR.Z
pub/Xinu/XINU-PDP11.V7.TAR.Z
pub/Xinu/XINU-PENTIUM.TAR.Z
pub/Xinu/XINU-SPARC.README
pub/Xinu/XINU-SPARC.TAR.Z
pub/Xinu/XINU-VAX.README
pub/Xinu/XINU-VAX.TAR.Z
226 Transfer complete.
remote: pub/Xinu
355 bytes received in 0.0025 seconds (139.96 Kbytes/s)
ftp> cd pub/Xinu
250------------------------------------------------------------------------
250-
250-                              **********
250-      If you have questions about files available in this directory,
250-               please direct them to xinu-librarian@cs.purdue.edu.
250-                              **********
250------------------------------------------------------------------------
250-
250 CWD command successful.
ftp> get
(remote-file) XINU-SPARC.README
(local-file) junk
200 PORT command successful.
150 Opening ASCII mode data connection for XINU-SPARC.README (5017 bytes).
226 Transfer complete.
local: junk remote: XINU-SPARC.README
5135 bytes received in 0.044 seconds (112.76 Kbytes/s)
ftp> cd /pub/comer
250-                              **********
250-   If you have questions about the files in this directory that pertain
250-to the code from the Internetworking books,  please direct them to
250-                         dls@sequent.com
250-
250-
250-   Note that there is a version of the software for Volume 2 prepared
250-with Gnu zip in file:
250-                         TCPIP-vol2.dist.tar.gz
250-
```

```
250-
250-   if you have questions about the Pentium version of Xinu, please direct
250-them to:
250-                            micheal@cs.purdue.edu
250-                              **********
250-
250 CWD command successful.
ftp> close
221-You have transferred 5135 bytes in 1 files.
221-Total traffic for this session was 7868 bytes in 2 transfers.
221-Thank you for using the FTP service on lucan.cs.purdue.edu.
221 Goodbye.
ftp> quit
```

31.17 Verbose Output

As the example shows, output from FTP begins with a three-digit number that identifies the message. For example, FTP places *226* at the beginning of a message that informs the user that a transfer has completed. Similarly, the remote FTP places *221* at the beginning of a message that acknowledges a request to close the control connection.

A user can choose whether FTP should issue informational messages (*verbose mode*) or omit such messages and report only the results (*quiet mode*). For example, in verbose mode, FTP calculates and prints the total number of bytes in each transfer, the time required for the transfer, and the number of bytes transferred per second. To control the mode, a user enters the *verbose* command. *Verbose* is a toggle that reverses the mode whenever entered. Thus, entering the verbose command once turns verbose mode off, and entering the command a second time turns verbose mode on again.

31.18 Client-Server Interaction In FTP

Like other network applications, FTP uses the client-server paradigm. A user runs a local FTP application, which interprets commands that the user enters. When a user enters an *open* command and specifies a remote computer, the local application becomes an FTP client that uses TCP to establish a control connection to an FTP server on the specified computer. The client and server use the FTP protocol to communicate across the control connection. That is, the client does not pass the user's keystrokes directly to the server. Instead, when a user enters a command, the client interprets the command. If the command requires interaction with the server, the client forms a request using the FTP protocol, and sends the request to the server. The server uses the FTP protocol when it sends a reply.

31.19 Control And Data Connections

FTP uses a control connection only to send commands and receive responses. When it transfers a file, FTP does not send the data across the control connection. Instead, the client and server establish a separate *data connection* for each file transfer, use it to send one file, and then close the connection. If the user requests another transfer, the client and server establish a new data connection. To avoid conflict between the control and data connections, FTP uses a different protocol port number for each.

Although data connections appear and disappear frequently, the control connection persists for the entire session. Thus, while a transfer is in progress, the client and server have two connections open: a control connection and a data connection for the transfer. Once the transfer completes, the client and server close the data connection, and continue to use the control connection. Figure 31.2 illustrates the concept.

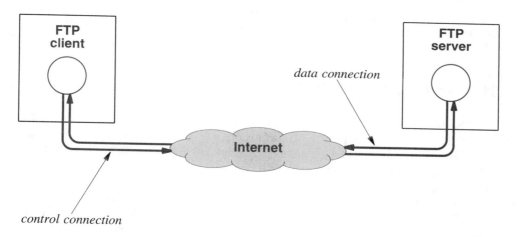

Figure 31.2 TCP connections between an FTP client and server during a file transfer. Although the control connection remains open, the data connection is closed after the transfer completes.

In the figure, arrows on the connections show which side initiated the connection. The arrow on the control connection extends from the client to the server because a client forms the control connection. Interestingly, a data connection is formed in the opposite direction. That is, the roles of client and server are reversed, with the server acting as a client, and the client acting as a server.

31.20 Data Connections And End Of File

Using separate connections for transfer and control has several advantages. First, the scheme keeps the protocols simpler and makes implementation easier — data from a file is never confused with FTP commands. Second, because the control connection remains in place, it can be used during the transfer (e.g., the client can send a request to abort the transfer). Third, an end-of-file condition can be used to inform the other side that all data has been transferred.

Using end-of-file to indicate that a transfer has completed is important because it permits a file to be created dynamically. For example, consider the case where an application is writing to a file on the server's computer while FTP is sending a copy of the file to the client. Because the file is transferred across a separate connection, the server does not need to tell the client the file size in advance. Instead, the server opens a connection, reads data from the file, and sends the data across the connection. When the server reaches the end of the file, the server closes the data connection, causing the client to receive an end-of-file condition. Because the server does not tell the client how much data to expect in advance, the file can grow during the transfer without causing a problem.

31.21 Trivial File Transfer Protocol

The Internet protocols include a second file transfer service known as *TFTP*, the *Trivial File Transfer Protocol*. TFTP differs from FTP in several ways. First, communication between a TFTP client and server uses UDP instead of TCP. Second, TFTP only supports file transfer. That is, TFTP does not support interaction and does not have a large set of commands. Most important, TFTP does not permit a user to list the contents of a directory or interrogate the server to determine the names of files that are available. Third, TFTP does not have authorization. A client does not send a login name or password; a file can be transferred only if the file permissions allow global access.

Although TFTP is less powerful than FTP, TFTP does have two advantages. First, TFTP can be used in environments where UDP is available, but TCP is not. Second, the code for TFTP requires less memory than the code for FTP. Although these advantages are not important in a general-purpose computer, they can be important in a small computer or a special-purpose hardware device.

TFTP is especially useful for bootstrapping a hardware device that does not have a disk on which to store system software. All the device needs is a network connection and a small amount of *Read-Only Memory* (*ROM*) into which TFTP, UDP, and IP are hardwired. When it receives power, the device executes the code in ROM, which broadcasts a TFTP request across the network. A TFTP server on the network is configured to answer the request by sending a file that contains the binary program to be run. The device receives the file, loads it into memory, and begins to execute the program.

Bootstrapping over a network adds flexibility and reduces cost. Because a separate server exists for each network, a server can be configured to supply a version of the software that is configured for the network. Cost is reduced because software can be changed without changing the hardware. For example, the manufacturer can release a new version of software for the device without changing the hardware or installing a new ROM.

31.22 Network File System

Although it is useful, file transfer is not optimal for all data transfers. To understand why, consider an application running on computer A that needs to append a one-line message to a file located on computer B. Before the message can be appended, a file transfer service requires that the entire file be transferred from computer B to computer A. Then, the updated file must be transferred from A back to B. Transferring a large file back and forth introduces long delays and consumes network bandwidth. More important, the transfer is unnecessary because the contents of the file are never used on computer A.

To accommodate applications that only need to read or write part of a file, TCP/IP includes a *file access* service. Unlike a file transfer service, a file access service allows a remote client to copy or change small pieces without copying an entire file.

The file access mechanism used with TCP/IP is known as the *Network File System* (*NFS*). NFS allows an application to open a remote file, move to a specified position in the file, and read or write data starting at that position. For example, to append data to a file using NFS, an application moves to the end of the file and writes the data. The NFS client software sends the data to the server where the file is stored along with a request to write the data to the file. The server updates the file and returns an acknowledgement. Only the data being read or written travels across the network; a small amount of data can be appended to a large file without copying the entire file.

In addition to reducing the load on the network, the file access scheme used by NFS allows shared file access. A file that resides at an NFS server can be accessed by multiple clients. To prevent others from interfering with file updates, NFS allows a client to lock a file. When the client finishes making changes, the client unlocks the file, allowing others access.

The interface to NFS is unlike the interface to FTP. Instead of creating a separate client application, NFS is integrated into a computer's file system. Such integration is possible because NFS provides the conventional file operations such as *open*, *read*, and *write*. To configure NFS, a special directory is created in the computer's file system and associated with a remote computer. Whenever an application program performs an operation on a file in the special directory, NFS client software uses the network to perform the operation on a file in the remote file system. Thus, once NFS is installed and configured, a computer's file system appears to contain directories that correspond to remote file systems — any operation performed on a file in the special directory occurs on the corresponding remote file. The chief advantage of such a scheme is flexibility: any application program can be used with a remote file because the application performs standard file operations.

31.23 Summary

A file transfer service provides the ability to send a copy of an entire file from one computer to another. TCP/IP protocols include two file transfer services: FTP and TFTP. FTP has more functionality because it supports a command-oriented interactive interface that allows the user to list the contents of a directory, set the transfer mode for textual or binary files, control file name translation, and specify character set translation for text files. TFTP provides only basic transfer service: it can be used to send a copy of a file in either direction.

Although both FTP and TFTP use the client-server paradigm, the underlying transport protocols differ: a TFTP client and server use UDP to communicate, while an FTP client and server use TCP. The use of UDP makes TFTP especially attractive as a hardware bootstrap protocol — TFTP, UDP, and IP software can reside in ROM.

An FTP client opens a control connection to a server over which the client sends requests and receives responses. The control connection remains open during the entire session. FTP does not send data across the control connection. Instead, a server forms a separate data connection whenever a file transfer is requested. The data connection is never confused with a control connection because FTP uses two different protocol port numbers.

A file access service permits an application to read or modify parts of a remote file without requiring the client to copy the entire file. A file access service also permits file sharing in which multiple clients can access a file that resides on a server.

The file access mechanism used with TCP/IP is known as NFS, the Network File System. Unlike file transfer clients, NFS is integrated into a computer's file system. The integration allows an arbitrary application program to operate on a remote file: whenever an application performs a file operation, NFS client software communicates with the remote computer to perform the operation.

EXERCISES

31.1   Does a binary transfer take more or less time than a text transfer? To find out, use FTP to transfer a text file twenty times using text mode, and then transfer the same file twenty times using binary mode. Does the average time required to transfer in the two modes differ?

31.2   Look carefully at the example in Section *31.16*. File *XINU-SPARC.README* contains *5015* bytes, but FTP reports that a total of *5135* bytes were transferred. What causes the larger transfer size? Hint: the file contains *118* lines of text.

31.3   Verify your answer to the previous exercise by using a network analyzer to capture frames that contain FTP traffic during a file transfer. What is the exact reason for the larger transfer size?

31.4   Experiment by using FTP to transfer a file that contains arbitrary (nontext) values. Transfer the file in binary mode and then in text mode. Compare the results to the original file. How does text transfer change the file?

31.5   On some computers, a program named *fetch* can be used to transfer files. *Fetch* uses FTP to perform the transfer, but provides an interface that permits a user to request transfer of a complete directory (i.e., folder) instead of specific files. Does a standard FTP server provide sufficient information to allow *fetch* to operate? Explain.

31.6   Extend the previous exercise by using *fetch* to obtain a copy of a directory (i.e., folder). What happens if a folder contains a symbolic link (sometimes called a *shortcut*) to another directory? What happens if a symbolic link points back to the same directory?

31.7   Protocol suites other than TCP/IP include a file transfer protocol. If you have access to a Macintosh computer, use Appleshare to transfer a file that contains a *carriage return* character. How does the copy of the file differ from the original?

31.8   FTP uses port *21* for control connections. Use *telnet* to connect to port *21*. Can you list the contents of a directory or perform a file transfer? Why or why not?

31.9   Experiment with FTP across a LAN by transferring a large file. Compare the throughput achieved by FTP to the bandwidth that the LAN hardware provides. What percentage of the hardware bandwidth is user data?

31.10   In the previous exercise, assume that each datagram occupies a full hardware frame, and that the TCP header is twenty octets and the IP header is twenty octets. Calculate the percentage of the hardware bandwidth that carries protocol headers.

31.11   How much does the speed of the computer system affect the FTP transfer rate? To find out, repeat exercise *31.9* using FTP clients and servers on computers of various speeds. Explain the results.

31.12   If your site has a network file system such as NFS, compare the time required to copy a file using NFS to the time required to transfer the same file using FTP. Which is more efficient for small files? For large files?

Chapter Contents

32

World Wide Web Pages
And Browsing

32.1 Introduction

Previous chapters cover examples of network services, describe the functions of clients and servers, and show how each service uses the client-server paradigm. Chapter 3 introduces basic client and server software that can be used with the World Wide Web. This chapter continues the discussion by considering the World Wide Web and interactive Web browsing.

After describing the hypertext model and the general concept of the Web, the chapter examines the structure of browser software. It shows how a browser reacts to a user's selection by becoming a client, contacting a server to obtain information, and then displaying the information it receives. The chapter also explains how a URL is embedded in a document, and describes how a browser uses a URL to determine which protocol to use and which server to contact.

32.2 Browser Interface

The *World Wide Web* (*WWW*) is a large-scale, online repository of information that users can search using an interactive application program called a *browser*. Most browsers have a *point and click* interface — the browser displays information on the computer's screen and permits a user to navigate using the mouse. The information displayed includes both text and graphics. Furthermore, some of the information on the display is highlighted to indicate that an item is *selectable*. When the user places the cursor over a selectable item and clicks a mouse button, the browser displays new information that corresponds to the selected item. To summarize:

> *A browser is an interactive program that permits a user to view information from the World Wide Web. Selectable items in the information allow the user to view other information.*

32.3 Hypertext And Hypermedia

Technically, the Web is a distributed *hypermedia* system that supports interactive access. A hypermedia system provides a straightforward extension of a traditional *hypertext* system. In either system, information is stored as a set of documents. Besides the basic information, a document can contain pointers to other documents in the set. Each pointer is associated with a selectable item that allows a user to select the item and follow the pointer to a related document. The difference between hypertext and hypermedia arises from document content: hypertext documents contain only textual information, while hypermedia documents can contain additional representations of information, including digitized photographic images or graphics.

The difference between a distributed and nondistributed hypermedia system is significant. In a nondistributed system, information resides within a single computer, usually on a single disk. Because the entire set of documents is available locally, links among them can be checked for consistency. That is, a nondistributed hypermedia system can guarantee that all links are valid and consistent.

In contrast, the Web distributes documents across a large set of computers. Furthermore, a system administrator can choose to add, remove, change, or rename a document on a computer without notifying other sites. Consequently, links among Web documents are not always consistent. For example, suppose document D_1 on computer C_1 contains a link to document D_2 on computer C_2. If the administrator responsible for computer C_2 chooses to remove document D_2, the link on C_1 becomes invalid. We can summarize:

> *Because the computers used to store Web documents are administered independently, links among documents can become invalid.*

32.4 Document Representation

A hypermedia document available on the WEB is called a *page*; the main page for an organization or an individual is known as a *homepage*. Because a page can contain many items, the format must be defined carefully so a browser can interpret the contents. In particular, a browser must be able to distinguish among arbitrary text, graphics, and links to other pages. More important, the author of a page should be able to describe the general document layout (e.g., the order in which items are presented).

Each Web page that contains a hypermedia document uses a standard representation. Known as the *HyperText Markup Language (HTML)*, the standard allows an author to give general guidelines for display and to specify the contents of the page.

HTML is a *markup language* because it does not include detailed formatting instructions. For example, although HTML contains extensions that allow an author to specify the size of text, the font to be used, or the width of a line, most authors choose instead to specify only a level of importance as a number from *1* through *6*. The browser chooses a font and display size appropriate for each level. Similarly, HTML does not specify exactly how a browser marks an item as selectable — some browsers underline selectable items, others display selectable items in a different color, and some do both. To summarize:

> *Web documents use the HyperText Markup Language representation. Instead of specifying a detailed document format, HTML allows a document to contain general guidelines for display, and allows a browser to choose details. Consequently, two browsers may display an HTML document differently.*

32.5 HTML Format And Representation

Each HTML document is divided into two major parts: a *head* followed by a *body*. The head contains details about the document, while the body contains the majority of the information. For example, the head contains a title for the document — most browsers use the title as a label to let a user know which page is being viewed.

Syntactically, each HTML document is represented as a text file that contains *tags* along with other information. As in most programming languages, white space (i.e., extras lines and blank characters) can be inserted in a document to make the source readable; they have no effect on the formatted version that a browser displays.

HTML tags provide structure for the document as well as formatting hints. Some tags specify an action that takes effect immediately (e.g., move to a new line on the display); the tag is placed exactly where the action should occur. Other tags are used to specify a formatting operation that applies to all text following the tag. Such tags occur in pairs, with a leading tag and a trailing tag that start and terminate the action, respectively.

A tag used to specify an immediate action or to start a formatting operation appears as a tag name bracketed by *less-than* and *greater-than* symbols†:

<TAGNAME>

The corresponding tag used to end an operation begins with the two-character sequence *less-than* and *slash*, and ends with a *greater-than* symbol:

---

†Although tag names are not case sensitive, we follow the convention of showing them in uppercase.

```
</TAGNAME>
```

For example, an HTML document starts with the tag <HTML>. The pair of tags <HEAD> and </HEAD> bracket the head, while the pair of tags <BODY> and </BODY> bracket the body. In the head, the tags <TITLE> and </TITLE> bracket the text that forms the document title. Figure 32.1 illustrates the general form of an HTML document.

```
<HTML>

  <HEAD>
      <TITLE>
              text that forms the document title
      </TITLE>
  </HEAD>

  <BODY>
    body of the document appears here
  </BODY>

</HTML>
```

Figure 32.1 The general form of an HTML document. The head contains information about the document; the body contains the document itself.

In the figure each tag appears on a new line, and indentation is used to show the structure. However, such conventions are only important to humans reading the document — a browser ignores all such spacing. Thus, the HTML document in Figure 32.2 is equivalent to the document in Figure 32.1.

```
<HTML><HEAD><TITLE>text that forms
the document
title</TITLE></HEAD><BODY>body of the
document appears here</BODY></HTML>
```

Figure 32.2 The HTML document from Figure 32.1 with some of the unnecessary white space removed. A browser produces the same output for both documents.

32.6 Example HTML Formatting Tags

Because an HTML document is stored in a text file, the document must contain explicit tags that specify how the output should be displayed. For example, the <BR> tag instructs a browser to introduce a line break. That is, when it encounters a <BR> in the input, the browser moves to the beginning of the next line on the display before generating more output. Thus, the following sequence of HTML:

```
Hello there.<BR>This is an example<BR>of HTML.
```

causes a browser to display three lines of output:

> Hello there.
> This is an example
> of HTML.

Two breaks in sequence leave a blank line in the output. Thus,

```
Hello there.<BR><BR>This shows<BR> HTML spacing.
```

results in the following output:

> Hello there.
>
> This shows
> HTML spacing.

32.7 Headings

HTML includes six pairs of tags that can be used to display headings in the output. A tag of the form <Hi> marks the start of a level i heading, and a tag of the form </Hi> marks the end. For example, text for the most important level of heading is bracketed between <H1> and </H1>. Browsers usually display text from a level *1* heading in the largest size, level *2* headings slightly smaller, and so on. Thus, when a browser displays the input:

```
Hello.<BR><H1>This Is A Heading</H1><BR>Back to normal.
```

the browser will choose a large point size for the heading:

> Hello.
>
> # This Is A Heading
> Back to normal.

32.8 Lists

In addition to headings, HTML allows a document to contain lists. The simplest form is an *unordered list*, which requests the browser to display a list of items†. In the HTML specification, the tags `<UL>` and `</UL>` bracket the entire list, and each list item begins with the tag `<LI>`. Usually, a browser places a bullet in front of each item.

In most browsers, for example, the input:

```
Here is a list of 5 names:
<UL>
<LI> Scott
<LI> Sharon
<LI> Jan
<LI> Stacey
<LI> Rebecca
</UL>
This text occurs after the list.
```

produces output with the list indented and a bullet before each item:

Here is a list of 5 names:
- Scott
- Sharon
- Jan
- Stacey
- Rebecca

This text occurs after the list.

32.9 Embedding Graphics Images In A Web Page

If an HTML document is a text file, how can a Web page contain nontextual information? In general, nontextual information such as a graphics image or a digitized photo is not inserted directly in an HTML document. Instead, the data resides in a separate location, and the document contains a reference to the data. When a browser encounters such a reference, the browser goes to the specified location, obtains a copy of the image, and inserts the image in the displayed document.

HTML uses the *IMG* tag to encode a reference to an external image. For example, the tag:

```
<IMG SRC="fred_photo.gif">
```

---

†The term *unordered* means that the browser does not need to sort the list according to a sequence number.

specifies that file *fred_photo.gif* contains an image that the browser should insert in the document.

Files listed in an *IMG* tag differ from files used to store Web pages. Image files are not stored as text files and do not follow HTML format. Instead, each image file contains binary data that corresponds to one image, and the file is stored in *graphics interchange format* (*gif*). Because the image file does not include any formatting information, the *IMG* tag includes additional parameters that can be used to suggest positioning. In particular, when an image appears with other items (i.e., text or other images), the keyword *ALIGN* can be used to specify whether the top, middle, or bottom of the image should be aligned with other items on the line. For example, Figure 32.3 illustrates how given the input:

```
Here is a picture. <IMG SRC="fred_photo.gif" ALIGN=middle>
```

a browser positions the image vertically so the text aligns with the middle of the image.

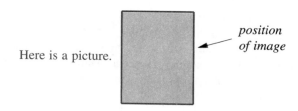

Figure 32.3 Illustration of image alignment. As requested in the tag, text on
the line is positioned in the middle of the image.

32.10 Identifying A Page

When a user invokes a browser, the user must specify an initial page to view. Identifying a page is complicated for several reasons. First, the Web includes many computers, and a page can reside on any of them. Second, a given computer can contain many pages; each must be given a unique name. Third, the Web supports multiple document representations, so a browser must know which representation a page uses (e.g., whether the name refers to an HTML document or to an image stored in binary form). Fourth, because the Web is integrated with other applications, a browser must know which application protocol must be used to access a page.

A syntactic format was invented that incorporates all the information needed to specify a remote item. The syntactic form encodes the information in a character string known as a *Uniform Resource Locator* (*URL*). The general form of a URL is:

protocol://computer_name:port/document_name

where *protocol* is the name of the protocol used to access the document, *computer_name* is the domain name of the computer on which the document resides, *:port* is an optional protocol port number†, and *document_name* is the name of the document on the specified computer. For example, the URL

http://www.netbook.cs.purdue.edu/toc/toc01.htm

specifies protocol *http*, a computer named *www.netbook.cs.purdue.edu*, and a file named *toc/toc01.htm*.

As the example shows, a URL contains the information a browser needs to retrieve a page. The browser uses the separator characters colon and slash to divide the URL into three components: a protocol, a computer name, and a document name. The browser then uses the information to access the specified document.

32.11 Hypertext Links From One Document To Another

Although HTML includes many features used to describe the contents and format of a document, the feature that distinguishes HTML from conventional document formatting languages is its ability to include hypertext references. Each hypertext reference is a passive pointer to another document. Unlike an *IMG* reference which causes a browser to retrieve external information immediately, a hypertext reference does not cause an immediate action. Instead, a browser turns a hypertext reference into a selectable item when displaying the document. If the user selects the item, the browser follows the reference, retrieves the document to which it refers, and replaces the current display with the new document.

HTML allows any item to be designated as a hypertext reference. Thus, a single word, a phrase, an entire paragraph, or an image can refer to another document. If an entire image is designated as a hypertext reference, the user can select the reference by placing the cursor at any position in the image and clicking a mouse button. Similarly, if an entire paragraph is designated as a hypertext reference, clicking on any character in the paragraph causes the browser to follow the reference.

The HTML mechanism for specifying a hypertext reference is known as an *anchor*. To permit arbitrary text and graphics to be included in a single reference, HTML uses tags *<A>* and *</A>* as a bracket for the reference; all items between the two are part of the anchor. Tag *<A>* includes information that specifies a URL; if the user selects the reference, the browser uses the URL to obtain the document. For example, the following input:

```
This book is published by
<A HREF="http://www.prenhall.com">
Prentice Hall, </A> one of
the larger publishers of Computer Science textbooks.
```

---

†Because the optional protocol port number is seldom used, we will omit it from the discussion.

contains an anchor that references the URL *http://www.prenhall.com*. When displayed on a screen, the input produces:

> This book is published by <u>Prentice Hall,</u> one of the larger publishers of Computer Science textbooks.

The example shows a convention that many browsers use to indicate that text is selectable: the anchored text is displayed with an underline. Only the words *Prentice Hall* are underlined because the others are not anchored.

Everything in the input between the tags that start and end an anchor form part of the selectable item. The input inside an anchor can include text, tags that specify formatting, or graphics images. Thus, an HTML document can contain a picture or an icon that corresponds to a hypertext link as easily as a sequence of words.

32.12 Client-Server Interaction

Like other network applications, Web browsing uses the client-server paradigm. When given the URL of a document, a browser becomes a client that contacts a server on the computer specified in the URL to request the document. The browser then displays the document for the user.

Unlike network applications that arrange for a client and server to maintain an established connection, the connection between a Web browser and a server has a short duration. The browser establishes a connection, sends a request, and receives the requested item or a message that no such item exists. As soon as the document or image has been transferred, the connection is closed; the client does not remain connected to a server.

Terminating connections quickly works well in most instances because browsing does not exhibit high locality. A user might access a Web page on one computer, and then immediately follow a link to a Web page on another computer. However, terminating connections too quickly can introduce overhead in cases where a browser must return to the same server for many documents. For example, consider a page that contains references to several images, all of which reside on the same computer as the page. When a user selects the page, the user's browser opens a connection, obtains the page, and closes the connection. When it needs to display an image (i.e., when it encounters an *<IMG>* tag in the page), the browser must open a new connection to the same server to obtain a copy of the image.

32.13 Web Document Transfer And HTTP

When a browser interacts with a Web server, the two programs follow the *Hyper-Text Transfer Protocol* (*HTTP*). In principle, HTTP is straightforward: it allows a browser to request a specific item, which the server then returns. In practice, however, HTTP is complex because a server sends additional status information with each transfer and the protocol allows a browser to send and request information.

As Chapter 3 describes, HTTP requests are sent as text encoded in ASCII. HTTP supports four basic operations that a browser can specify when making a request:

- *GET* requests a specified item from the server. The server returns a heading that contains status information followed by a blank line followed by the item.

- *HEAD* requests status information about an item. The server returns the status without returning a copy of the item itself.

- *POST* sends data to the server. The server appends the data to a specified item (e.g., a message is appended to a list of messages).

- *PUT* sends data to the server. The server uses the data to replace a specified item†.

A browser generates an HTTP request when a user enters a URL or selects a link. In either case, the browser sends a GET request that specifies an item, and the server returns the requested item. A GET request has the following form:

GET *item   version   CRLF*

where *item* gives the URL for the item being requested, *version* specifies a version of HTTP (usually 1.0 or 1.1), and *CRLF* denotes the ASCII *carriage return* and *linefeed* characters.

Each response from the server begins with an ASCII header. The first line of the header contains a status code that tells the browser whether the server handled the request. If the request was incorrectly formed or the requested item was not available, the status code pinpoints the problem. For example, a server returns the well-known status code *404* if the requested item cannot be found. When it honors a request, a server returns status code *200*; additional lines of the header give further information about the item such as its length, when it was last modified, and the content type. Figure 32.4 contains an example HTTP header.

---

†PUT is seldom used; most Web pages that send data use POST instead.

```
HTTP/1.0 200 OK
Date: Mon, 30 Oct 2000 01:22:22 GMT
Server: Apache/1.2.5
Last-Modified: Sat, 28 Oct 2000 01:03:37 GMT
ETag: "130fe-81-3883bbe9"
Content-Length: 129
Accept-Ranges: bytes
Connection: close
Content-Type: text/plain
```

Figure 32.4 Example HTTP header returned by a server. The status code *200* on the first line indicates that the server honored the request; additional lines give further information about the requested item.

32.14 Browser Architecture

Web browsers have a more complex structure than Web servers. A server performs a straightforward task repeatedly: the server waits for a browser to open a connection and request a specific page. The server then sends a copy of the requested item, closes the connection, and waits for the next connection. A browser handles most of the details of document access and display. Consequently, a browser contains several large software components that work together to provide the illusion of a seamless service. In particular, a browser consists of a set of clients, a set of interpreters, and a controller that manages them. The controller forms the central piece of the browser. It interprets both mouse clicks and keyboard input, and calls other components to perform operations specified by the user. For example, when a user enters a URL or clicks on a hypertext reference, the controller calls a client to fetch the requested document from the remote server on which it resides, and an interpreter to display the document for the user.

Each browser must contain an HTML interpreter to display documents. Other interpreters are optional. Input to an HTML interpreter consists of a document that conforms to the HTML syntax; output consists of a formatted version of the document on the user's display. The interpreter handles layout details by translating HTML specifications into commands that are appropriate for the user's display hardware. For example, if it encounters a heading tag in the document, the interpreter changes the size of the text used to display the heading. Similarly, if it encounters a break tag, the interpreter begins a new line of output. Figure 32.5 illustrates the conceptual organization of a browser.

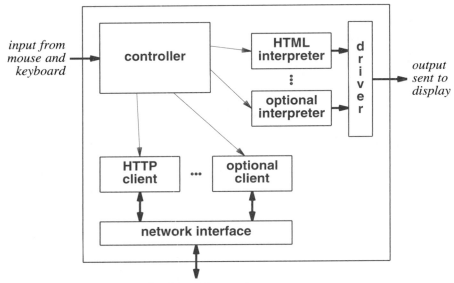

input from mouse and keyboard

output sent to display

communication with remote server

Figure 32.5 Major components of a Web browser. Dark arrows show the flow of data; other arrows show control paths. The data paths from clients to interpreters are not shown.

One of the most important functions in an HTML interpreter involves selectable items. The interpreter must store information about the relationship between positions on the display and anchored items in the HTML document. When the user selects an item with the mouse, the browser uses the current cursor position and the stored position information to determine which item the user has selected.

32.15 Optional Clients

Besides an HTTP client and an HTML interpreter, a browser can contain components that enable the browser to perform additional tasks. For example, many browsers include an FTP client that is used to access the file transfer service. Some browsers also contain e-mail client software that enables the browser to send and receive e-mail messages.

How can a user access a service such as FTP from within a browser? The answer is that a user does not invoke such services explicitly nor does the user interact with conventional client software. Instead, the browser invokes the service automatically, and uses it to perform a task as needed. If the browser is well-designed, it hides details from a user, who may be unaware that an optional service has been invoked. For example, file transfer can be associated with a selectable item on the screen. When the user selects the item, the browser uses its FTP client to obtain a copy of the file.

How can file transfer be specified in a Web page? Recall that the first field in a URL specifies a protocol. The controller uses the field to determine which client to call. For example, if the URL specifies *http*, the controller calls the HTTP client. Similarly, the URL:

ftp://ftp.cs.purdue.edu/pub/comer/netbook/client.c

specifies that the browser should use anonymous FTP to retrieve the file *pub/comer/netbook/client.c* from computer *ftp.cs.purdue.edu*.

A URL that specifies FTP can be embedded in an HTML anchor as easily as a URL that specifies HTTP. For example, the HTML input:

```
Many of the examples in this text are available
online.  Source code from
<A HREF="ftp://ftp.cs.purdue.edu/pub/comer/netbook/client.c">
an example client program
</A>
or code from
<A HREF="ftp://ftp.cs.purdue.edu/pub/comer/netbook/server.c">
an example server program
</A>
are available.
```

causes a browser to display two sentences, a part of each selectable:

Many of the examples in this text are available online. Source code from <u>an example client program</u> or code from <u>an example server program</u> are available.

If the user selects the first underlined segment, the browser uses its FTP client to obtain a copy of the file *client.c*; clicking the second segment causes the browser to retrieve file *server.c*. After it retrieves a copy of the file, the browser checks the contents and attempts to display the results.

32.16 Caching In Web Browsers

The pattern of client-server contact in Web browsing is unlike the pattern in many of the applications described earlier. There are two reasons. First, because users tend to view Web pages outside of their organization, Web browsers tend to reference remote pages more frequently than local pages. Second, because users do not search for the same information repeatedly, they do not tend to repeat accesses day after day.

Because browsing produces a different locality of reference than other applications, the techniques browsers use to optimize performance differ from other applications. In particular, neither browsers nor Web servers are optimized for physical locality. Furthermore, browsers employ unusual techniques to handle temporal locality of reference.

Like other applications, browsers use a *cache* to improve document access. The browser places a copy of each item it retrieves in a cache on the local disk. When a user selects an item, the browser checks the disk cache before retrieving a fresh copy. If the cache contains the item, the browser obtains the copy from the cache — the browser only contacts the *origin server* (i.e., the server that owns the page) if the page cannot be found in the cache.

Keeping items in a cache can improve performance dramatically — a browser can read the item from disk without waiting for network delays. Caching is especially important for large pages or for users who have slow network connections. For example, consider a user who connects to the Internet over a dialup telephone line. At dialup speeds, retrieving a large item over the Internet can take several orders of magnitude longer than retrieving the same item from a local disk cache. In fact, local disk access can seem instantaneous when compared to dialup Internet access.

Despite the large improvement in speed, retaining items in a cache for extended periods is not always desirable. First, a cache can take vast amounts of disk space. For example, suppose a user visits ten pages, each of which contain five large images. The browser will store the page documents plus all fifty images in the cache on the local disk. Second, improvements in performance are only helpful if a user decides to view an item again. Unfortunately, users often browse because they are looking for information; when the information has been found, the user stops browsing. For example, a user who views ten pages may decide that nine of the pages contain nothing of interest. Thus, storing a copy of such pages in a cache will not improve performance because the user will never return to the pages. In fact, in such situations, caching lowers performance because the browser takes time to write items to disk unnecessarily.

To help users control how a browser handles the cache, most browsers allow the user to adjust the cache policy. The user can set a time limit for caching, and the browser removes items from the cache after the time limit expires. Browsers usually maintain a cache during a particular session. A user who does not want items to remain in the cache between sessions can request a cache time of zero. In such cases, a browser removes the cache whenever the user terminates the session.

32.17 HTTP Support For Caching

HTTP has several features that make caching possible. When the server generates an HTTP header, the server can specify a cache timeout for the page. Alternatively, if the page contains information that changes constantly, the server can specify that the page may not be cached. Similarly, a browser can send an HTTP header that specifies the request must not be answered with data from a cache.

The HTTP HEAD operation also helps with cache management because cache timeout values are usually conservative (i.e., a server chooses a small timeout value if there is doubt about when a document will change). To understand how HEAD can be used to optimize document access, consider a browser that has cached a large document. Suppose the user requests the document after the cache timeout has expired. Instead of downloading a fresh copy, the browser can attempt to revalidate the cached version. To do so, the browser sends a HEAD request for the document. If the status information returned by the server confirms that the cached copy is still valid, the browser displays the cached copy. Otherwise, the browser sends a GET request for a new copy.

32.18 Alternative Transfer Protocols

Several groups have proposed extensions and alternatives to HTTP. HTTP version 1.1 introduced the concept of *persistent connections* in which a single TCP connection is used for multiple transfers (i.e., multiple *GET* requests from the browser). The World Wide Web Consortium has also proposed *HTTP-NG* as the Next-Generation of HTTP that uses binary encoding for headers instead of the current ASCII representation. In addition, the *HTTPS* protocol provides for secure HTTP transfers (i.e., it uses encryption to guarantee confidentiality of the data being transferred in an HTTP session).

The *Wireless Access Protocol* (*WAP*) is among the most widely publicized alternative protocols. Designed by a consortium of vendors known as the WAP Forum, the WAP protocol suite is intended to be used with portable, hand-held devices such as cell phones, two-way pagers, and palm-size organizers. WAP is not merely a replacement for HTTP. Instead, it consists of a large suite of protocols, each aimed at a specific problem. For example, WAP defines an application environment, page markup and presentation standards, network transport protocols, a security protocol, voice telephone interface protocols, a transaction protocol, and a scripting language. In short, instead of taking advantage of existing standards, WAP defines an entirely new protocol stack.

Of course, WAP designers want to interface WAP devices with existing web servers. Consequently, the design envisions *WAP Proxys* that provide the connection. When a WAP device requests a web page, a proxy obtains the page from a web server and forwards the page to the requesting device using WAP. In cases where the web page is represented in HTML, the proxy invokes an *HTML filter* to translate the page from HTML to the WAP markup language.

32.19 Other Markup Languages

Although most Web pages currently use HTML, other markup languages have been created for special purposes. For example, the *WAP Markup Language* (*WML*) and the *Hand-held Device Markup Language* (*HDML*) are each designed to accommodate small, hand-held devices. *Voice Extensible Markup Language* (*VoiceXML*) specifies communication in human speech (e.g., for delivery over a cell phone).

Another variation know as the *Extensible Markup Language* (*XML*) has also gained acceptance. Unlike HTML, XML does not specify layout. Instead, XML gives an internal representation that provides names for each field in a data item. Tags in XML are well-balanced — each occurrence of a tag *<X>* must be followed by an occurrence of *</X>*. Furthermore, because XML does not assign any meaning to tags, tag names can be created as needed. In particular, the tag names can be selected to make data easy to parse or access. For example, if two companies agree to exchange corporate telephone directories, they can define an XML format that has data items such as an employee's name, phone number, and office. The companies can choose to further divide a name into a last name and a first name. Figure 32.6 contains an example.

```
<ADDRESS>
    <NAME>
        <FIRST>  John      </FIRST>
        <LAST>   Public    </LAST>
    </NAME>
    <OFFICE> Room 320      </OFFICE>
    <PHONE>  765-555-1234 </PHONE>
</ADDRESS>
```

Figure 32.6 An example of XML for a corporate phone book. Each data item is given a name.

32.20 Summary

The World Wide Web is a distributed hypermedia repository of information that is accessed with an interactive browser. Although several alternatives have been proposed, the majority of Web documents are written in the HyperText Markup Language (HTML). In addition to text, a document contains tags that specify document layout and formatting. Images are not included directly in a document. Instead, a tag is placed in the document to specify the place at which an image should be inserted and the source of the image. The anchor tag is used to specify that items in an HTML document correspond to an external reference. When it displays the document, a browser marks the items as selectable; if the user makes the selection, the browser follows the external reference to obtain a new document.

External references are given in the form of a Uniform Resource Locator (URL). A browser extracts from the URL the protocol used to access the item, the name of the computer on which the item resides, and the name of the item.

A browser consists of a controller, one or more clients used to access documents, and one or more interpreters used to display documents. To make document retrieval efficient, the web uses caching. A copy of each document or image that a user views is placed in a cache; instead of obtaining a new copy from the origin server, the cached copy is used for subsequent requests. The HyperText Transfer Protocol, used to transfer web documents, includes a header that describes the document and specifies how long the document can be cached.

Alternative markup languages have been invented to handle special cases. Markup languages such as WML and HDML are designed for hand-held devices. XML, which does not specify layout or formatting, is used to communicate the structure of the data. Alternatives to HTTP have been designed as well. HTTPS provides secure transfers. WAP defines an entirely new protocol suite designed for portable, hand-held devices such as cell phones and pagers.

EXERCISES

32.1   Suppose a link from one Web document to another contains a typo that causes the reference to contain an invalid computer name. What does a browser report if a user attempts to access the link?

32.2   In the previous question, what does a browser report if an error causes the link to refer to a valid computer that is not running a Web server?

32.3   What is the chief advantage of allowing HTML to choose display details such as the size of items on the display? What is the chief disadvantage?

32.4   Experiment with a browser by resizing the window. Does the browser always redraw the page to fit the new window? Can you identify circumstances in which it introduces scroll bars?

32.5   Create a static document that contains a title. How does a browser use the title?

32.6   A browser maintains a set of *bookmarks* or *favorites* that each correspond to a Web page; at any time, a user can request that the browser save a bookmark for the currently visible page. To return to the page later, a user pulls down the bookmark menu and selects the page. What appears on the pull-down menu to identify a page to the user?

32.7   Should a browser cache a copy of all bookmarked pages? Why or why not?

32.8   What interpreters can a browser contain besides HTML and FTP?

32.9   Use a network analyzer to monitor traffic while a browser fetches a page of textual information. How many TCP connections are formed?

32.10   In the previous question, compute the percentage of packets that contain data.

32.11   What is the average number of segments transmitted for each TCP connection in the traffic monitored in exercise *32.9*? Does the average HTTP transfer trigger congestion control in TCP? Why or why not?

32.12   How large is the cache your browser uses? To find out, conduct an experiment: visit three Web pages, disconnect your computer from the network, and attempt to return to one of the pages you visited. Can your browser cache a dozen pages?

32.13   Can a browser format and display XML? Why or why not?

32.14   Read more about HTTPS. What protocol does it use to encrypt data?

32.15   A browser understands FTP and can retrieve files from an FTP site. What login ID and password does a browser pass to the FTP server?

32.16   Read the HTTP specification. What is a *conditional get* operation? Explain how it can produce a substantial increase in retrieval speed.

32.17   Modify the web server from Chapter 3 to return caching information in the header.

32.18   Use a network analyzer to measure the traffic generated when several users simultaneously fetch pages from Web servers. Do the TCP connections proceed simultaneously or are they serial? Explain.

32.19   How many protocols comprise the WAP suite? To find out, look under *What Is WAP* on the WAP Forum's web site (*www.wapforum.org*).

32.20   The web was originally designed to follow the *end-to-end* model. That is, a browser formed a TCP connection to a server and used HTTP across the connection. WAP replaces the end-to-end model with a proxy model. What are the disadvantages of the proxy model?

Chapter Contents

33

Dynamic Web Document Technologies (CGI, ASP, JSP, PHP, ColdFusion)

33.1 Introduction

The previous chapter describes the World Wide Web and browser software used to access information on the Web. The chapter explains the HTML language that hypermedia documents use, and shows how one document can contain a reference to another. In addition, the chapter shows how a browser displays a document, allows a user to choose a selectable item, and then becomes a client of a Web server to obtain and display the new document that corresponds to the selection. Finally, the chapter explains how a browser's functionality can be extended by adding additional clients.

This chapter continues the discussion of browser software by explaining two alternative forms of Web documents, and then examining one form in detail. Unlike the HTML documents discussed previously, the alternative forms allow computer programs to control the contents of a document dynamically. In one form, a Web server runs an auxiliary program to create a document whenever a request arrives from a browser. In the other form, a server provides the browser with a computer program. The browser then runs the program locally, and allows the program to display information, interact with the user, and become a client of other network services.

This chapter describes the two alternative forms of documents and summarizes the advantages and disadvantages of each. The chapter then concentrates on one of the two alternatives, explaining how a server can use an application program to generate documents dynamically. More important, the chapter discusses the concept of state information, and shows how state information can be encoded in a dynamically created document. The next chapter continues the discussion by explaining details of the second alternative form.

33.2 Three Basic Types of Web Documents

Although the previous chapter describes a Web page as a simple textual document stored in a file, alternative representations exist. In general, all Web documents can be grouped into three broad categories according to the time at which the contents of the document are determined.

- *Static*. A static Web document resides in a file that is associated with a Web server. The author of a static document determines the contents at the time the document is written. Because the contents do not change, each request for a static document results in exactly the same response.

- *Dynamic*. A dynamic Web document does not exist in a predefined form. Instead, a dynamic document is created by a Web server whenever a browser requests the document. When a request arrives, the Web server runs an application program that creates the dynamic document. The server returns the output of the program as a response to the browser that requested the document. Because a fresh document is created for each request, the contents of a dynamic document can vary from one request to another.

- *Active*. An active document is not fully specified by the server. Instead, an active document consists of a computer program that understands how to compute and display values. When a browser requests an active document, the server returns a copy of the program that the browser must run locally. When it runs, the active document program can interact with the user and change the display continuously. Thus, the contents of an active document are never fixed — they can continue to change as long as the user allows the program to run.

33.3 Advantages And Disadvantages Of Each Document Type

The chief advantages of a static document are simplicity, reliability, and performance. Because it contains straightforward formatting specifications, a static document can be created by someone who does not know how to write a computer program. More important, after it has been created and tested thoroughly, a static document remains valid indefinitely. Finally, a browser can display a static document rapidly, and can place a copy in a cache on a local disk to speed future requests for the document.

The chief disadvantage of a static document is inflexibility — the document must be revised whenever information changes. Furthermore, changes are time-consuming because they require a human to edit a file. Thus, a static document is not useful for reporting information that changes frequently.

The chief advantage of a dynamic document lies in its ability to report current information. For example, a dynamic document can be used to report information such as current stock prices, current weather conditions, or the current availability of tickets for a concert. Whenever a browser requests the information, the server runs an application that accesses the needed information and creates a document. The server then sends the document to the browser.

Dynamic documents place the responsibility on the server; a browser uses the same interaction to obtain a dynamic page as to retrieve a static page. In fact, from a browser's point of view, dynamic pages are indistinguishable from static pages. Because both static and dynamic pages use HTML, a browser does not know whether the server extracted the page from a disk file or obtained the page dynamically from a computer program.

The chief disadvantages of a dynamic document approach are increased cost and the inability to display changing information. Like a static document, a dynamic document does not change after a browser retrieves a copy. Thus, information in a dynamic document begins to age as soon as it has been sent to the browser. For example, consider a dynamic document that reports current stock prices. Because stock prices change quickly, the document can become obsolete while a user is browsing through its contents.

A dynamic document is more expensive to create and access than a static document. Personnel costs for creating dynamic documents are higher because the creator of a dynamic Web page must know how to write a computer program. Moreover, the program must be designed carefully and tested extensively to ensure that the output is valid. Verifying the correctness of such a program can be difficult because the input can include multiple data values obtained from several sources.

In addition to the higher cost of creating dynamic documents, hardware costs increase for dynamic documents because a more powerful computer system is needed to operate the server. Finally, a dynamic document takes slightly longer to retrieve than a static document because the server requires additional time to run the application program that creates the document.

Although a dynamic document is created when the document is requested, the information can become stale quickly. The chief advantage of an active document over a dynamic document lies in its ability to update information continuously. For example, only an active document can change the display quickly enough to show an animated image. More important, an active document can access sources of information directly and update the display continuously. For example, an active document that displays stock prices can continue to retrieve stock information and change the display without requiring any action from the user.

The chief disadvantages of active documents arise from the additional costs of creating and running such documents, and from a lack of security. First, active document display requires more sophisticated browser software and a powerful computer system to run the browser. Second, writing active documents that are correct requires more programming skill than other forms, and the resulting documents are more difficult to test. In particular, because an active document must run on an arbitrary computer instead of a server, the program must be written to avoid depending on features available on one computer system that are not available on other systems. Finally, an active document is a potential security risk because the document can export as well as import information.

To summarize:

> *Web documents can be grouped into three categories depending on when the information in the document changes. The information in a* static *document remains unchanged until the author revises the document. The information in a* dynamic *document can change whenever a server receives a request for the document. Information displayed by an* active *document can change after the document has been loaded into a browser.*

33.4 Implementation Of Dynamic Documents

Because the responsibility for creating a dynamic document rests with the Web server that manages the document, changes required to support dynamic documents involve only servers. In practice, the changes involve extensions — a server that manages dynamic documents also contains code to handle static documents.

Three additions are required before a conventional Web server can handle a dynamic document. First, the server program must be extended so it is capable of executing a separate application program that creates a document each time a request arrives. The server must be programmed to capture the output from the application program and return the document to the browser. Second, a separate application program must be written for each dynamic document. Third, the server must be configured so it knows which URLs correspond to dynamic documents and which correspond to static documents. For each dynamic document, the configuration must specify the application program that generates the document.

Each request contains a URL that corresponds to a static or dynamic document. A server uses configuration information and the URL in each incoming request to determine how to proceed. If the configuration information specifies that the URL corresponds to a static document, the server fetches the document from a file as usual. If the URL corresponds to a dynamic document, the server determines the application program that generates the document, executes the program, and uses the output from the program as the document to be returned to the browser.

33.5 The CGI Standard

A widely used technology for building dynamic Web documents is known as the *Common Gateway Interface (CGI)*. Originally developed by the *National Center for Supercomputer Applications (NCSA)* for use with the NCSA Web server, the CGI standard specifies how a server interacts with an application program that implements a dynamic document. The application is called a *CGI program*†.

CGI provides general guidelines, and allows a programmer to choose most details. For example, CGI does not specify a particular programming language. Instead, the standard permits a programmer to choose a language and to use different languages for different dynamic documents. Thus, a programmer can choose an appropriate language for each document. For example, a programmer can use a conventional programming language like FORTRAN, C, or C++ for documents that require intense arithmetic computation, and use a scripting language like Perl, TCL, or the UNIX shell for documents that require only minor text formatting.

33.6 Output From A CGI Program

In practice, output from a CGI program is not restricted to HTML — the standard permits CGI applications to generate arbitrary document types. For example, in addition to HTML, a CGI program can generate plain text or a digital image. To distinguish among various document types, the standard allows a CGI program to place a header on its output. The header consists of text that describes the document type.

Headers generated by a CGI program use the same general format as headers a Web server uses when sending a document to a browser: the header consists of one or more lines of text and a blank line. Each line of the header specifies information about the document and the data representation.

After it runs a CGI program, a server examines the header before returning the document to the browser that issued the request. Thus, a CGI program can use the header to communicate with the server when necessary. For example, a header that consists of the line:

Content-type: text/html

followed by a blank line specifies that the output is an HTML document.

The header in the output from a CGI program can also be used to specify that the document is in a new location. The technique is known as *redirection*. For example, suppose a CGI program associated with the URL:

http://someserver/cgi-bin/foo

needs to refer incoming requests to the document associated with the URL:

---

†Because the original design placed all CGI programs in a directory named *bin*, programmers sometimes use the term *CGI—bin program*.

```
http://someserver/new/bar.txt
```

The CGI program can generate two lines of output:

```
Location: /new/bar.txt
        <blank line>
```

When it detects the *Location:* directive in the header, the server will retrieve the document as if the browser had requested *new/bar.txt* (instead of *cgi—bin/foo*) with the URL:

http://someserver/new/bar.txt

We can summarize:

> *The output from a CGI program can begin with a header that the server interprets. A header can specify the format of the document, or a header can specify that the requested document has been moved to a different URL.*

33.7 An Example CGI Program

Figure 33.1 contains the source code for a trivial CGI program written in the UNIX shell language. When executed, the program creates a plain text document that contains the current date and time.

```
#!/bin/sh

#
# CGI script that prints the date and time at which it was run
#

# Output the document header followed by a blank line

echo Content-type: text/plain
echo

# Output the date

echo This document was created on `date`
```

Figure 33.1 An example CGI program written in UNIX shell language.

Shell scripts can be difficult to understand. In essence, the shell is a command interpreter — a shell script contains commands in the same format a user follows when entering commands on a keyboard. Except for the first line, the shell ignores blank lines or any line that begins with the hash symbol, #. In the example, lines that contain a hash symbol are used for comments. Other lines contain a valid command. The first "word" of a line is the name of the command; subsequent words form arguments to the command.

The only command used in the example script is *echo*. Each invocation of *echo* generates one line of output. When run, the script invokes *echo* three times. Thus, the script will generate exactly three lines of output.

When invoked with no arguments, *echo* creates a blank line of output. Otherwise, *echo* writes an exact copy of its arguments. For example, the command:

```
echo smord hplar
```

generates one line of output that contains two words:

```
smord hplar
```

The only unusual item in the example script is the construction `` `date` ``. The shell interprets the accent grave quotes as a request to execute the date program and substitute its output. Thus, before it invokes *echo* for the third time, the shell replaces the string `` `date` `` with the current date and time. As a result, the third invocation of *echo* generates a line of output that contains the actual date. For example, if the script is run on June 3, 2001 at 37 seconds past 2:19 PM, the script would generate the following output:

```
Content-type: text/plain

This document was created on Sun Jun  3 14:19:37 EST 2001
```

A server that is capable of running CGI programs must be configured before it can invoke the example script. The configuration specifies a URL that the server uses to locate the script. When a browser contacts the server and requests the specified URL, the server runs the program. When the browser receives the document, the browser displays a single line for the user:

```
This document was created on Sun Jun  3 14:19:37 EST 2001
```

Unlike a static document, the contents of the dynamic document change each time the user instructs the browser to reload the document. Because the browser does not cache a dynamic document, a request to reload the document causes the browser to contact the server. The server invokes the CGI program, which creates a new document with the current time and date. Thus, the user sees the contents of the document change after each request to reload.

33.8 Parameters And Environment Variables

The standard permits a CGI program to be parameterized. That is, a server can pass arguments to a CGI program whenever the program is invoked. Parameterization is important because it allows a single CGI program to handle a set of dynamic documents that differ only in minor details. More important, values for parameters can be supplied by the browser. To do so, the browser adds additional information to a URL. When a request arrives, the server divides the URL in the request into two parts: a prefix that specifies a particular document and a suffix that contains additional information. If the prefix of the URL corresponds to a CGI program, the server invokes the program and passes the suffix of the URL as an argument.

Syntactically, a question mark (?) in the URL separates the prefix from the suffix. Everything before a question mark forms a prefix, which must specify a document. The server uses its configuration information to determine how to map the prefix to a particular CGI program. When it invokes the CGI program, a server passes an argument to the program that consists of all characters in the URL following the question mark.

Because it was originally designed for Web servers that run under operating systems like UNIX and Windows, the CGI standard follows an unusual convention for passing arguments to CGI programs. Instead of using the command-line, a server places argument information in *environment variables* and then invokes the CGI program. The CGI program inherits a copy of the environment variables, from which it extracts the values. For example, the server assigns the suffix of the URL to the environment variable *QUERY_STRING*†.

A server also assigns values to other environment variables that the CGI program can use. The table in Figure 33.2 lists examples of CGI environment variables along with their meanings.

Name of Variable	Meaning
SERVER_NAME	The domain name of the computer running the server.
GATEWAY_INTERFACE	The version of the CGI software the server is using.
SCRIPT_NAME	The path in the URL after the server name.
QUERY_STRING	Information following "?" in the URL.
REMOTE_ADDR	The IP address of the computer running the browser that sent the request.

Figure 33.2 Examples of environment variables passed to a CGI program.

---

†In fact, the server encodes the suffix using the standard URL format: each blank is replaced by a plus sign (+), and nonprintable characters are replaced by the percent character (%) followed by two hexadecimal digits that give the numeric value of the special character.

33.9 State Information And Cookies

A server invokes a CGI program each time a request arrives for the associated URL. Furthermore, because a server does not maintain any history of requests, the server cannot tell the CGI program about previous requests from the same user. Nevertheless, a history is useful because it allows a CGI program to participate in a dialog. For example, a history of previous interactions makes it possible to avoid having a user answer questions repeatedly when specifying additional requests. To provide a nonrepetitive dialog, a CGI program must save information between requests.

Information that a program saves between invocations is called *state information*. In practice, the method a dynamic document uses to store state information depends on the length of time the information must be kept as well as the size of the information. A server can give a small amount of information to a browser; the browser stores the state information on its disk, and returns the information to the server in a subsequent request. If a server needs to store large amounts of state information, the server must keep the information on a local disk.

State information is passed to a browser in the form of a *cookie*. Each cookie consists of a pair of strings which are known as a *name/value* pair. The *name* portion contains the name of the Web site, and the *value* portion is a small string that the browser stores. When it contacts the Web site again, the browser inserts the cookie in the request. Thus, from a server's perspective, it appears that the browser can store and return state information.

The chief disadvantage of cookies arises from their limited size — a cookie can contain at most a few hundred bytes of data. Thus, most server software does not store actual data in a cookie. Instead, information that must be kept across invocations of a browser is placed in long-term storage on the server computer (e.g., in a file on disk), and a cookie is used as an index to the information.

Information that is transient can be communicated by a *session cookie* which works like a persistent cookie except that a browser only stores the value in memory and not on disk. Thus, a session cookie is lost as soon as the browser exits. As an alternative to session cookies, a dynamic document can arrange to encode information in URLs that appear in the document. The next sections contain examples that clarify the concepts.

33.10 A CGI Script With Long-Term State Information

The CGI script in Figure 33.3 illustrates two concepts we have discussed. First, the script illustrates how a server uses environment variables to pass arguments to a CGI program. Second, the script shows how a dynamic document program can store long-term state information in a file.

The example script keeps a record of IP addresses of computers from which it has been contacted. When a request arrives, the script examines the browser's IP address and generates a document. The document tells whether the request is the first to arrive from the computer.

```
#!/bin/sh
FILE=ipaddrs

echo Content-type: text/plain
echo

# See if IP address of browser's computer appears in our file

if grep -s $REMOTE_ADDR $FILE >/dev/null 2>&1
then

    echo Computer $REMOTE_ADDR has requested this URL previously.

else

    # Append browser's address to the file

    echo $REMOTE_ADDR >> $FILE
    echo This is the first contact from computer $REMOTE_ADDR

fi
```

Figure 33.3 An example CGI program that stores long-term state information.

Although many syntactic details make the script appear complex, its operation is straightforward. In essence, the script maintains a list of IP addresses in a local file named *ipaddrs*. When invoked, the script searches the file for the browser's IP address. If a match is found, the script reports that it has been contacted from the browser's computer previously. Otherwise, the script appends the browser's IP address to the file, and reports that the contact was the first from the browser's computer.

The script uses environment variable *REMOTE_ADDR* to obtain the IP address of the computer running the browser that issued the request. In the shell language, variables are referenced by placing a dollar sign in front of the variable name. Thus, the string *$REMOTE_ADDR* is replaced by the value of variable *REMOTE_ADDR*.

The main body of the script consists of a single *if-then-else* statement. The statement uses the *grep* command to determine whether the browser's IP address appears in file *ipaddrs*. The result of the search determines whether the script follows the *then* or *else* part of the *if* statement. If the address is found, the script emits a message that reports the request is not the first. If the address is not present, the script appends the address to the file, and then emits a message that acknowledges the first contact.

When run, the script in Figure 33.3 generates three lines of output: two lines of header followed by a single line of text. The line of text contains the IP address of the browser's computer, and tells whether a request has been received from the same computer previously. For example, the first time a user on computer 128.10.2.26 requests the document, the user will receive the following line of output:

> This is the first contact from computer 128.10.2.26

Subsequent requests for the document from the same computer produce the following:

> Computer 128.10.2.26 has requested this URL previously.

We can summarize:

> *A dynamic document program uses files that reside on the server's computer to store long-term state information. Because such files persist between requests, information written in a file while handling a request will remain available when the server handles subsequent requests.*

33.11 A CGI Script With Short-Term State Information

To understand how state information can be encoded in a URL, recall that the text beyond a question mark in a URL is passed to a dynamic document program as an argument. Because a dynamic document program creates a copy of a document on demand, each invocation of the program can produce a document that contains a new set of URLs. In particular, any text that the program places beyond a question mark in a URL will become an argument if the user selects the URL.

As an example, consider the CGI program in Figure 33.4

```sh
#!/bin/sh

echo Content-type: text/html
echo

N=$QUERY_STRING
echo "<HTML>"

case "x$N" in

x)        N=1
          echo "This is the initial page.<BR><BR>"
          ;;

x[0-9]*)  N=`expr $N + 1`
          echo "You have displayed this page $N times.<BR><BR>"
          ;;

*)        echo "The URL you used is invalid.</HTML>"
          exit 0
          ;;

esac
echo "<A HREF=\"http://$SERVER_NAME$SCRIPT_NAME?$N\">"
echo "Click here to refresh the page.</A> </HTML>"
```

Figure 33.4 An example CGI program that maintains short-term state.

The script in Figure 33.4 is more complex than the previous example. First, the script emits an HTML document instead of plain text. Second, the script uses environment variable *QUERY_STRING* to determine whether the server passed an argument to the script. Third, the script concatenates the contents of variables *SERVER_NAME* and *SCRIPT_NAME* to obtain a URL for the script, and appends a question mark and the count from variable *N*. Fourth, the script uses a *case* statement to choose among three possibilities: the argument string is empty, the argument string contains an integer, or the argument string contains something else. In two cases, the script emits appropriate output; in the last case, the script reports that the URL is invalid.

To understand how the script passes state information, assume that the server *www.nonexist.com* has been configured so the script corresponds to path */cgi/ex4*. When a user invokes URL:

http://www.nonexist.com/cgi/ex4

The script generates six lines of output:

```
Content-type: text/html

<HTML>
This is the initial page.<BR><BR>
<A HREF="http://www.nonexist.com/cgi/ex4?1">
Click here to refresh the page.</A> </HTML>
```

Because the header specifies that the document is HTML, a browser will interpret the HTML commands and display three lines of output:

> This is the initial page.
>
> Click here to refresh the page.

Although it does not appear on the user's screen, state information is embedded in a URL in the document. To see the state information, look at the URL in the HTML version of the document carefully. The last two characters, *?1*, encode information about the number of times the page has been refreshed. If the user clicks on the second sentence, the browser will request URL:

http://www.nonexist.com/cgi/ex4?1

When invoked, the script will find that *QUERY_STRING* contains *1*. Thus, the script will generate six lines of output:

```
Content-type: text/html

<HTML>
You have displayed this page 2 times.<BR><BR>
<A HREF="http://www.nonexist.com/cgi/ex4?2">
Click here to refresh the page.</A> </HTML>
```

When a browser displays the document, the screen changes to show the following:

> You have displayed this page 2 times.
>
> Click here to refresh the page.

Notice that the new document has argument ?2 embedded in the URL. Thus, if the user clicks the second sentence again, the browser will report that the page has been displayed *3* times.

It is important to realize that the dynamic document program does not know how many times the page has been refreshed — the program merely reports what the argument specifies. For example, if a user manually enters the URL:

http://www.nonexist.com/cgi/ex4?5693

The script will (incorrectly) report that the page has been displayed *5694* times!

To summarize:

> *When it generates a document, a dynamic document program can embed state information as arguments in URLs. The argument string is passed to the dynamic document program for the URL, enabling a program to pass state information from one invocation to the next.*

33.12 Forms And Interaction

The notion of embedding state information in a URL has been generalized and extended to an HTML *form*. A user must supply values for a set of named items on a form before selecting a link that causes the browser to send the form back to the server. When sending a form, the browser appends an argument string onto the URL that contains the named items and values. Thus, a dynamic program can obtain values that the user provides.

Syntactically, a form is delineated with HTML tags *<FORM>* and *</FORM>*. Within the form, it is possible to have a variety of items, including buttons that the user can click and text areas into which the user can enter text. Each item is given a unique name. When the browser communicates the contents of the form to the server, the browser sends the values for each item as arguments in the URL. For example, suppose a form contains three items named *AA*, *BB*, and *CC*, and suppose the user has supplied values *yes*, *no*, and *maybe*. When it collects the values into a URL, the browser creates a string:

?AA=yes&BB=no&CC=maybe

which the browser appends to the specified URL. To summarize:

> *An HTML form is a document that contains items a user must supply. The information is encoded in a URL for transmission to another document.*

33.13 Server-Side Scripting Technologies

The chief disadvantage of the CGI technology arises from its paradigm — a CGI program must generate an entire page, even if only a few lines of HTML differ for each generation. In many instances, the bulk of a dynamic page remains the same for each occurrence. For example, on a page that contains a stock quote, only the company name and current stock price need to be inserted dynamically; the headings and format information always remain the same.

Dynamic document technologies have been invented to handle the case where only a small portion of a page must be changed. Instead of running a separate program that generates the page, such technologies are closely integrated with server software. The server has a built-in interpreter that can make small modifications to a page as needed. The stored form of the page, which is known as a *template* or *skeleton*, contains a mixture of conventional HTML and scripting information. The interpreter allows conventional HTML to pass through unchanged, and replaces the scripting information with the results of interpreting the script. To make interpretation run at high speed, special syntax is used to bracket the scripting information.

Several server-side scripting technologies exist.

- *ASP* (*Active Server Pages*) is a dynamic page technology from Microsoft. The scripting information is written in the Visual Basic programming language, and the interpreter is closely integrated with Microsoft's web server, *Internet Information Server* (*IIS*).

- *JSP* (*Java Server Pages*) is a dynamic page technology that is intended to be platform-independent. As the name implies, pages contain embedded scripting code written in the Java programming language.

- *PHP* (*Perl Helper Pages*) is a less well-known dynamic page technology that uses the Perl programming language. Proponents claim that it is faster than JSP or ASP; detractors claim that the embedded code is difficult to read.

- *ColdFusion* is a dynamic page technology used to embed SQL database queries in pages. When a server handles such a page, the interpreter sends each SQL query to a database system, converts the result to HTML, and replaces the query. Thus, some items on the resulting page come directly from the company's database.

We can summarize:

Server-side scripting technologies allow a dynamic page to be created from a template or skeleton that contains embedded commands or program scripts. Instead of using a computer program to generate an entire page, an interpreter copies the page and replaces only the scripting commands.

33.14 Summary

Web documents can be grouped into three broad categories: static, dynamic, and active. The contents of a static document do not change until the author revises the document. Because a server creates a fresh copy of a dynamic document each time a browser requests the document, the contents of a dynamic document can change for each request. An active document is a computer program that can change the display continuously.

Responsibility for dynamic documents rests with servers; browsers cannot determine whether a URL refers to a dynamic or static document. An application program must be written for each dynamic document, and a server must be configured to establish the association between a dynamic document program and the URL used to invoke it. When it runs, the application program creates a document as output.

The primary technology used to create dynamic documents is called the *Common Gateway Interface* (*CGI*). The CGI standard specifies how a server invokes a CGI program and how the server interprets the program's output. For example, the standard specifies that a server uses environment variables to pass arguments to the program. Furthermore, the standard specifies that a CGI program must place a header on the output. A CGI program can use the header to identify the format of the output or to communicate with the server (e.g., to direct the server to a new URL).

Server-side dynamic web page technologies have been invented that do not require generation of the entire page. Pages are created that contain a mixture of conventional HTML and scripting commands; the server contains an interpreter that replaces the scripting information each time the page is accessed. Examples of scripting technologies include ASP, JSP, PHP, and ColdFusion.

The term *state information* refers to any information preserved from one invocation of a program to the next. Information that must persist across invocations of a browser can be stored in disk files on the server computer. A browser can store and return a cookie that a server can use as an index to information stored on the local disk. Information that persists while the browser remains active can be embedded in an HTML form or a document URL.

EXERCISES

33.1 Experiment to find out what happens if a CGI program fails to include a *Content-type* header on its output.

33.2 Consider the CGI program in Figure 33.3 carefully. Explain how the program can cause a server to fail.

33.3 Suppose a CGI program requires thirty seconds of CPU time to compute the answer to a request. Explain what happens if two or more clients make a request within thirty seconds.

33.4 Is there a limit on the number or size of parameters that a browser can send to a CGI program? Experiment to find out.

33.5 Most Web servers do not contain an interpreter for CGI programs. Instead, the server uses a standard interpreter (e.g., a shell). What is the chief advantage of keeping the interpreter separate from the server? The chief disadvantage?

33.6 Write a CGI program that keeps a list of computers that have contacted the server along with a count of how many times a browser on each computer has contacted the server.

33.7 Write a CGI program that prompts a user for a name, and keeps a list of the names of users who have contacted the server.

33.8 Write a CGI program and two Web pages that reference the program. Have the program identify the Web page from which the link was followed.

33.9 What does a browser display if a CGI program generates an invalid HTML document? Does it differ from what the browser displays if a static HTML document is invalid? Experiment with a browser to find out.

33.10 Suppose a corporation decides to create a Web site that allows online shopping. What are the advantages of a technology like ColdFusion?

33.11 If you were given a choice, would you choose ASP or JSP? Why?

33.12 A server-side scripting technology known as *Server Side Include* (*SSI*) allows a dynamic page to include the contents of another file, but does not support any additional scripting commands. Why is SSI useful? Hint: consider the contents that one might find on a web page sent by a large web site.

Chapter Contents

34

Technology For Active Web Documents (Java, JavaScript)

34.1 Introduction

The previous two chapters introduce the World Wide Web and describe the interaction between browsers and servers. The first of the two chapters describes hypermedia and the HTML language used to specify document contents. The second extends the discussion by defining and comparing the three basic forms of Web documents. Chapter 33 also examines dynamic Web documents in detail. It explains that a server invokes an application program to create a dynamic document whenever a request arrives for the document's URL. It also explains the concept of state information, and shows how a dynamic document can store state information for a short or long duration. Finally, Chapter 33 explains the CGI technology that servers use to invoke dynamic document programs.

This chapter considers the third form of Web documents: active. It describes the motivation for active documents, explains the basic concepts, and compares the active document approach to an earlier server-based technology used for continuous update. In addition, the chapter describes the translation steps used to prepare and load an active document, and shows how a browser is extended before it can run an active document. Finally, the chapter considers the Java technology that is used to create and run active documents. It characterizes the Java language, and presents a simple example of a Java applet.

34.2 An Early Form Of Continuous Update

As HTTP and Web browsers were being designed, it became apparent that dynamic documents would not suffice for all purposes. In particular, because information contained in a dynamic document is fixed when the document is created, a dynamic document cannot update information on the screen as information changes and cannot change graphic images to provide animation.

Two techniques have been invented to allow continuous update of a user's screen. The first technique places responsibility on the server. Called *server push*, the mechanism requires a server to periodically generate and send new copies of a document. In essence, the server must run the application program associated with a dynamic document continuously. As it runs, the program generates fresh output, which the server forwards to the browser for display. From the user's point of view, the contents of the page continue to change while being viewed.

Although it provides the ability to change information continuously, the server push approach has two disadvantages: it causes excessive server overhead and introduces delay. To understand why the overhead is significant, observe that a server must satisfy many clients. When a user views a page that requires server push, the server must run the dynamic application program associated with the page. If many clients request documents that use server push, the server must run the application programs concurrently. More important, because the contents of a dynamic document can depend on the source of the request, a server must run a separate copy of a dynamic document application for each request.

Delays arise from limits in available CPU and network bandwidth. When N application programs run concurrently on a timesharing computer, each program receives at most $1/N$ of the available CPU power. Thus, the amount of CPU available for server push applications decreases rapidly as the number of requests increases. If many browsers view pushed documents simultaneously, the CPU on the server's computer will become overloaded, and updates will be delayed.

Limited network bandwidth can also introduce delays. Server push requires each browser to maintain an active TCP connection over which the server sends updates continuously. Unfortunately, most computers that run servers have a single Internet connection over which all traffic must pass. If many applications attempt to send data, the network can become a bottleneck. To provide fairness, the operating system requires applications to take turns sending packets. As a result, an individual application is delayed waiting for access to the network. To summarize:

> *The first technique that was developed to provide continuous update of information on a Web page is known as* server push *because a server continuously computes and sends new versions of the document to the browser. A server can become overloaded if many clients attempt to access pushed documents simultaneously.*

34.3 Active Documents And Server Overhead

Active documents, the second technique used to provide continuous update of information, arose as a way to avoid overloading servers. Instead of requiring a server to continuously compute updates for many clients, the active document approach moves computation to the browser. When a browser requests an active document, the server returns a computer program that the browser runs locally. Once it sends a copy of the document, the server has no further responsibility for execution or update — the browser handles all computation locally. Thus, unlike the server push approach, the active document approach does not require a server to use large amounts of CPU time. Furthermore, because it does not require a server to transmit continuous updates, an active document does not use as much network bandwidth as a pushed document.

An active document can introduce less server overhead than a dynamic document. To understand why, it is important to know three things. First, for purposes of transport, a browser and a server treat an active document like a static document. Each active document resides in a file on the server. The contents of an active document do not change unless the programmer revises the document. Thus, unlike a dynamic document, a browser can cache a copy of an active document. Second, an active document does not contain all software — a browser that runs active documents contains support software. Third, an active document can be translated to a compressed representation that can take less space than a dynamic document. Thus, from a server's point of view, storage, access, and transport of active documents can be performed efficiently.

34.4 Active Document Representation And Translation

What representation should be used for an active document? The answer is complex. Because an active document is a program that specifies how to compute and display information, many representations are possible. Furthermore, no single representation is optimal for all purposes — various representations are needed. For example, when a programmer creates a computer program, the programmer needs a form that can be understood and easily manipulated by humans. To achieve highest execution speed, computer hardware requires a program to be stored in binary form. Finally, a compressed representation minimizes the delay and communication bandwidth required to transfer a program across the Internet.

To satisfy all requirements for representation, active document technologies use the same general approach to program representation as a conventional programming language: translation. In particular, most active document systems define multiple representations, where each representation is optimized for one purpose. Software is then created that can automatically translate among the document representations. Thus, a programmer can define and edit a document using one form, while a browser that runs the document can use another form.

Figure 34.1 illustrates three popular active document representations, and shows the translations used to move from one to another.

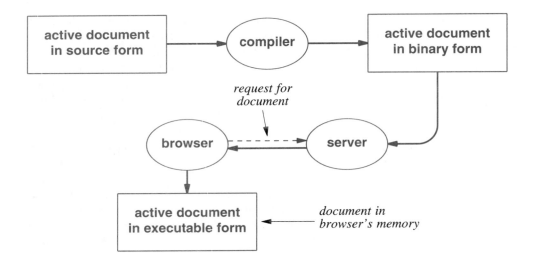

Figure 34.1 Illustration of three active document representations and the programs that translate or transport the document. The darkened arrow shows the direction a document moves.

As the figure shows, an active document begins in a *source representation*. The source representation contains declarations for local data and implementations of algorithms used to compute and display information. In addition, the source representation allows a programmer to insert comments that help humans understand the program. In fact, because the source representation of an active document is similar to the source representation used for conventional computer programs, a programmer can use conventional programming tools such as text editors to create and change the source of an active document.

Although some active document technologies arrange for a browser to accept and interpret a source document, most systems provide an optimization for larger documents: a *compiler* is used to translate a document from the source representation to a *binary representation* similar to the object representation used for a conventional program. In the binary representation, each executable statement is represented in binary form, and identifiers in the program are replaced by binary offsets. Also like a conventional object file, the binary representation includes a symbol table that records the relationships between names in the source representation and locations in the binary representation.

After a browser obtains a copy of an active document in binary form, software in the browser translates the document to the *executable representation*, and loads the resulting program into the browser's memory. The translation is similar to the final steps an operating system performs when loading an object program. The browser must resolve remaining references, and must link the program to library routines and system functions. Once linking is complete, the symbol table is no longer needed — the entire document has been translated to binary values.

34.5 Java Technology

Developed by Sun Microsystems, Incorporated, *Java* is the name of a specific technology used to create and run active documents. Java uses the term *applet*† to describe active document programs and to distinguish active documents from conventional computer programs. The Java technology includes three key components related to applets:

- *Programming Language.* Java includes a new programming language that can be used as the source language for conventional computer programs or for Java applets.

- *Runtime Environment.* The Java system defines a runtime environment that provides the facilities needed to run a Java program.

- *Class Library.* To make applets easier to write, Java provides a large library that contains software to handle many of the chores that an applet performs.

In practice, it can be difficult to distinguish among the components because they are designed to work together. For example, the language contains features that depend on run-time support, and the library contains software that provides an interface to facilities in the runtime environment. The next sections characterize each of the components separately; later sections clarify relationships among them.

34.6 The Java Programming Language

When a programmer creates an active document, the programmer writes the program in a source language. Instead of relying on an existing language, the Java technology defines a new programming language that attempts to make writing and reading source programs for applets convenient. Formally, the language is called the *Java Programming Language*; informally, programmers often use the abbreviation *Java*‡.

---

†The name was chosen to emphasize that in Java, an active document is a small application program.
‡We will follow the informal practice of abbreviating the language name whenever the meaning is unambiguous.

34.6.1 Language Characteristics

The Java language can be characterized as:

- *High Level.* Like most programming languages, Java is classified as a high-level programming language that is designed to hide hardware details and make it easy for a programmer to express computation.

- *General Purpose.* Although it was originally designed as a tool for writing applets, the language has sufficient expressive power to make it useful in other applications. More important, there are no limitations that prevent the Java language from being used for programs other than applets.

- *Similar to C++.* Java descended from the C++ Programming Language. Thus, both syntactic and semantic similarities exist between the two languages.

- *Object Oriented.* As in other object oriented languages, Java requires a programmer to define a set of objects that each contain data as well as *methods* that operate on the data.

- *Dynamic.* An instance of an object is created dynamically at run-time. Furthermore, Java allows some bindings to be delayed until run-time.

- *Strongly Typed.* Java supports strong typing: each data item is declared to have a type, and the language prohibits operations from being applied to data other than the type for which the operation is intended.

- *Statically Type Checked.* In Java, type checking does not occur at run-time. Instead the type compatibility of all items in a program is determined when the program is compiled.

- *Concurrent.* Java allows a program to have multiple threads of control; the threads execute concurrently (i.e., they appear to execute at the same time).

34.6.2 Similarities to C++

Java bears a strong resemblance to C++; the language retains many semantic constructs from C++ as well as much of the syntax. For example, most of the Java statement types are found in C++. In addition, the type mechanism in Java uses a class hierarchy.

The basic differences between Java and C++ occur because the designers wanted to make programming easier and to make programs more reliable. Consequently, Java was crafted to reduce some of the complexity in C++. In particular, Java omits C++ language features that are seldom used, easily misunderstood, or prone to errors. For example, Java does not have operator overloading, multiple inheritance, or extensive automatic data coercions. In some cases, Java retains features from C++, but restricts their use.

34.7 The Java Run-Time Environment

Java technology defines a run-time environment in which Java programs execute. The run-time environment is characterized by:

- *Interpretative Execution.* Although a Java program can be compiled into code for a specific computer, the designers intended the language to be used with an interpreter. That is, unlike a conventional compiler that translates a source program into a binary object program for a specific architecture, a Java compiler translates a Java program into a machine-independent binary representation known as the *Java bytecode representation*. A computer program called an *interpreter* reads the bytecode representation and interprets the instructions.

- *Automatic Garbage Collection.* Memory management in Java differs dramatically from the memory management used with languages like C and C++. Instead of requiring a program to call procedures such as *malloc* and *free* to allocate and release memory, the Java run-time system provides automatic garbage collection. That is, a program can depend on the run-time system to find and reclaim memory that is no longer being used. In essence, when a program discards all references to an object, the garbage collector reclaims the memory allocated to that object.

- *Multithreaded Execution.* The Java run-time system provides support for concurrent thread execution. In essence, the run-time system contains parts of an operating system that handle scheduling and context switching†. By switching the CPU among the set of currently active threads, the run-time system permits all threads to proceed.

- *Internet Access.* The Java run-time system includes a socket library that a program uses to access the Internet. In particular, a Java program can become a client — the Java program can use TCP or UDP to contact a remote server.

- *Graphics Support.* Because an applet needs to control the display, the Java run-time system includes basic mechanisms that allow a Java program to create windows on the screen that contain text or graphics.

34.7.1 Machine Independence And Portability

The Java language and run-time system are designed to make Java independent of computer hardware. For example, the language does not contain any implementation-defined features. Instead, the language reference manual defines the meaning of each operator and statement in the language unambiguously. In addition, the Java bytecode representation is independent of the underlying hardware. Consequently, once a Java program has been compiled into the bytecode representation, the program produces exactly the same output on any computer.

---

†The run-time support for concurrent thread execution is sometimes called a *microkernel*.

Using a machine-independent binary representation and an interpreter makes Java programs portable across computer architectures. Consider a Java program compiled on a computer that has a Pentium processor, stored on a Web server that uses a Sparc processor, and run on a computer that has an Alpha processor. The same bytecode representation will result if the program is compiled by a Java compiler that runs on another architecture. Similarly, the same output will result if the compiled program is run on another computer.

Keeping an applet independent of underlying computer hardware is essential for three reasons. First, in the Internet, users have many types of computers. Machine independence allows a browser running on an arbitrary brand of computer to download and run a copy of the active document. Second, machine independence guarantees that the document will produce correct output on all browsers. Third, machine independence dramatically reduces document creation costs because a programmer can build and test one version of an active document instead of building one version for each type of computer.

34.8 The Java Library

The third component of the Java technology is a library of class definitions. The library is extensive — it contains dozens of class definitions with approximately *2000* individual methods. More important, the library contains classes that span a variety of needs. For example, the library contains classes for:

- *Graphics Manipulation.* Graphics manipulation routines in the library allow a Java program to have precise control over the contents and appearance of the user's display screen (e.g., facilities in the library allow an applet to display text, graphics, images, or dialog boxes).

- *Low-Level Network I/O.* The library contains classes that provide access to the socket-level I/O facilities in the run-time system. A Java program can use low-level network I/O facilities to send and receive UDP datagrams, or can open a TCP connection to send and receive streams of data.

- *Interaction With A Web Server.* An applet may need to access static or dynamic Web documents or other applets. For example, an applet may follow a URL to retrieve and display a static document (e.g., an image). The library contains classes to handle such tasks.

- *Run-Time System Access.* The Java library contains classes that an applet can use to access facilities in the run-time environment. For example, a running program can request the creation of a thread.

- *File I/O.* An applet uses file I/O facilities to manipulate files on the local computer. File I/O is used by programs that save long-term state information.

- *Conventional Data Structures.* The library includes classes that define conventional data structures. For example a program can use a *dictionary* class to create an efficient data structure that stores items for later retrieval.

- *Event Capture.* Events occur when a user depresses or releases a mouse button or key on the keyboard. The library contains classes that allow a Java program to capture and handle such events.

- *Exception Handling.* When an unexpected condition or an error occurs in a Java program, the run-time environment raises an *exception.* The Java library includes a set of classes that make exception handling easier.

To summarize:

> *Java is a technology used to create and run active documents, called* applets. *The Java technology includes a new programming language, an extensive class library, and a run-time environment.*

34.9 A Graphics Toolkit

The Java run-time environment includes facilities that allow an applet to manipulate a user's display, and the Java library contains software that provides a high-level graphics interface. Together, the run-time graphics support and graphics library are known as a *graphics toolkit*; the specific graphics toolkit in Java is known as the *Abstract Window Toolkit (AWT).*† There are two reasons why Java needs a substantial graphics toolkit. First, the central purpose of an applet is complex display — an applet is used whenever a static display is inadequate. Second, a program that controls a graphics display must specify many details. For example, when a Java program needs to display a new item for the user, the program must choose between displaying the item in a subarea of an existing window or creating a new, independent window. If a new window is created, the program must specify a heading for the window, the window size, the colors to use, and details such as where to place the window and whether the window has a scroll bar.

The AWT does not specify a particular style of graphics or level of interaction. Instead, the toolkit includes classes for both low-level and high-level manipulation; a programmer can choose whether to manage the details or invoke toolkit methods to do so. For example, the toolkit does not dictate the form of a window. On one hand, the toolkit includes low-level classes to create a blank rectangular panel on the screen, draw lines or polygons, or capture keystrokes and mouse events that occur in the panel. On the other hand, the toolkit includes high-level classes that provide a window complete with a heading, borders, and vertical and horizontal scroll bars. A programmer can choose whether to use the window style provided or program all details.

---

†At various times, the designers have also expanded AWT to *Alternative Window Toolkit, Advanced Window Toolkit,* and *Applet Widget Toolkit.*

Similarly, a programmer must choose between high-level and low-level facilities for interaction with the user. For example, an applet can use high-level classes from the toolkit to create buttons, pull-down menus, or dialog boxes on the screen. Alternatively, an applet can create such items by using low-level toolkit classes to draw lines, specify shading, and control the font used to display text.

Because an applet may need to interact with static documents, the toolkit includes classes that perform conventional Web browsing operations. For example, given a URL, an applet can use toolkit classes to fetch and display a static HTML document, fetch and display an image, or fetch and play an audio clip.

To summarize:

> *Java includes an extensive graphics toolkit that consists of run-time support for graphics as well as interface software in the library. The toolkit allows a programmer to choose a high-level interface, in which the toolkit handles details, or a low-level interface, in which the applet handles details.*

34.10 Using Java Graphics On A Particular Computer

Because the Abstract Window Toolkit is designed to be independent of a specific vendor's computer hardware and graphics system, Java does not need to use display hardware directly. Instead, Java can run on top of conventional window systems. For example, if a user runs a browser on a computer that uses the X Window System, a Java applet uses *X* to create and manipulate windows on the display. If another user runs a browser with a different window system, an applet will use that window system to create and manipulate the display.

How can a Java applet work with multiple window systems? The answer lies in an important mapping built into the run-time environment and a set of intermediate functions. A Java run-time environment includes an intermediate layer of software. Each function in the intermediate layer uses the computer's window system to implement one specific Java graphics operation. Before an applet executes, the run-time environment establishes a mapping between each Java graphics method and the appropriate intermediate function. When an applet requests an AWT operation, control passes to a method in the Java library. The library method then forwards control to the appropriate intermediate function, which uses the computer's window system to provide the operation. The concept is known as a *factory*.

The advantages of using an intermediate layer of software are portability and generality. Because intermediate functions use the computer's window system, only one version of the AWT library is needed — the library does not contain code related to specific graphics hardware. Because the binding between Java graphics methods and the computer's window system software is established by the run-time system, a Java applet is portable. The chief disadvantage is the imprecision that arises because the intermediate layer of software can interpret operations. As a result, a Java program run on two different computers does not always produce identical results. To summarize:

> *To make Java applets portable across multiple hardware platforms, the Java graphics toolkit does not manipulate display hardware. Instead, the run-time system maps Java graphics methods to equivalent operations that use the computer's window system.*

34.11 Java Interpreters And Browsers

Recall from Chapter 32 that a browser can contain one or more interpreters. A conventional browser contains an HTML interpreter that is used to display static or dynamic documents. A browser that runs Java contains two: an HTML interpreter and an additional interpreter for applets.

A Java interpreter is a complex program. The heart of the interpreter is a simple loop that simulates a computer. The interpreter maintains an *instruction pointer* that is initialized to the beginning of an applet. At each iteration, the interpreter fetches the bytecode found at the address in the instruction pointer. The interpreter then decodes the instruction and performs the specified operation. For example, if the interpreter finds the *add* bytecode and two integer operands, the interpreter adds the two integers, updates the instruction pointer, and continues with the next iteration.

In addition to a basic instruction decoder, a Java interpreter must include support for the Java run-time environment. That is, a Java interpreter must be able to display graphics on the user's screen, access the Internet, and perform I/O. In addition, the interpreter must be designed to allow an applet to use facilities in the browser that retrieve and display static and dynamic documents. Thus, the Java interpreter in a browser must be able to communicate with the browser's HTTP client and HTML interpreter.

34.12 Compiling A Java Program

As Figure 34.1 illustrates, a Java applet must be compiled and stored on a Web server before a browser can download and run the applet. The Java technology includes a compiler that is named *javac*. A programmer runs *javac* to compile a Java source program into the Java bytecode representation.

Input to *javac* is a Java source program. The name of the input file must end with the suffix *.java*. *Javac* verifies that the source program is syntactically correct, translates the program into the bytecode representation, and places the output in a file with the suffix *.class*.

A Java program consists of a sequence of declarations. An item that is declared *public* is exported to make it available to other applets; an item that is declared *private* is not exported and cannot be referenced externally. A source file must contain exactly one *public* class, which must use the same name as the source file prefix. That is, the public class in file *zzz.java* must be named *zzz*. Thus, a file that contains the compiled bytecode for class *zzz* has the name *zzz.class*.

To understand the details, consider an example. Suppose that source file *aaa.java* contains the declarations:

```
public class aaa { ... }
    class bbb { ... }
    class ccc { ... }
```

The program declares class *aaa* to be public, while classes *bbb* and *ccc* are private. When *aaa.java* is compiled, *javac* produces output file *aaa.class*.

34.13 An Example Applet

Figure 34.2 contains a simple applet that illustrates the basic concepts. The applet begins with a sequence of *import* statements. Each import statement directs the compiler to use a set of classes from the Java library.

```
import java.applet.*;
import java.awt.*;

public class clickcount extends Applet {
  int count;
  TextField f;

  public void init() {
    count = 0;
    add(new Button("Click Here"));
    f = new TextField("The button has not been clicked at all.");
    f.setEditable(false);
    add(f);
  }

  public boolean action(Event e, Object arg) {
    if (((Button) e.target).getLabel() == "Click Here") {
      count += 1;
      f.setText("The button has been clicked " + count + " times.");
    }
    return true;
  }
}
```

Figure 34.2 An example applet that counts the number of times a user clicks a button.

An *import* statement contains a pattern that specifies a set of classes to be import-ed. In the pattern, most characters represent a literal match; an asterisk, *, is used to denote a wildcard that matches an arbitrary string. Thus, the statement:

```
import java.applet.*;
```

specifies that the compiler should import all classes with names that begin with the string *java.applet*.

In the example applet, the two *import* statements are used to import the standard Applet and Abstract Window Toolkit classes. As a result, the applet will have access to methods that create the applet environment and methods that manipulate the display.

The example applet defines a subclass of type *Applet* named *clickcount*. In addi-tion to the methods that the class inherits from *Applet*, class *clickcount* redefines two methods: *init* and *action*.

When a browser invokes a reference to the applet, Java creates a new instance of the *clickcount* object. *Clickcount* defines two data items: an integer named *count* and a *TextField* named *f*. As part of the creation, the run-time system invokes the *init* method. *Init* performs several initialization steps. After setting *count* to zero, *init* uses the *new* operation to create an instance of a *Button* object, and calls *add* to add the but-ton to the applet's window. Finally, *init* uses *new* to create an instance of a *TextField* and assign it to variable *f*, method *setEditable* to make the text in *f* read-only, and *add* to associate *f* with the applet's window.

Figure 34.3 illustrates how the display appears after *init* has added two graphical items to the applet's window.

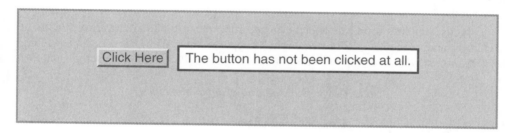

Figure 34.3 Illustration of the display after the applet in Figure 34.2 begins execution.

The heart of the example applet is method *action*. If the button labeled *Click Here* is selected, the applet increments variable *count* and changes the display. To do so, the applet invokes method *setText*, which replaces the message in *f*. Thus, each time a user clicks on the button, the display changes. For example, Figure 34.4 illustrates how the display appears after the user clicks the button once.

Figure 34.4 The display after the user has clicked the button once.

From a user's point of view, the example applet appears to operate similar to the CGI script in Figure 33.4†. From an implementation point of view, the two operate quite differently. Unlike a CGI script, an applet maintains state information locally. Thus, unlike the example CGI script, the example applet does not contact a server before updating the screen.

34.14 Invoking An Applet

Two methods can be used to invoke an applet. First, a user can supply the URL of an applet to a browser that understands Java. When the browser contacts the server specified in the URL, the server will inform the browser that the document is a Java applet. Second, an HTML document can contain an *applet tag* that refers to an applet. When a browser encounters the tag, the browser contacts the server to obtain a copy of the applet.

In its simplest form, an applet tag specifies the location of a *.class* file to be fetched and executed. For example, suppose the Web server on machine *www.nonexist.edu* stores file *bbb.class* in directory *example*. The URL for the applet is:

http://www.nonexist.edu/example/bbb.class

The applet tag that specifies the location contains two items: a *codebase* that specifies the machine and path, and a *code* that gives the name of the class file. For example, the applet tag:

<applet codebase="www.nonexist.edu/example" code="bbb.class">

contains the same information as the URL above. A browser that encounters the tag will contact the server, obtain a copy of the class file, create an instance of class *bbb*, and call its *init* method.

---

†Figure 33.4 can be found on page 520.

34.15 Example Of Interaction With A Browser

An applet can interact with both the HTTP client and HTML interpreter in a browser. An applet uses the browser's HTTP client to retrieve documents and the browser's HTML interpreter to display pages of information. The applet in Figure 34.5 illustrates the concept.

```
import java.applet.*;
import java.net.*;
import java.awt.*;

public class buttons extends Applet {

  public void init() {
    add(new Button("Yin"));
    add(new Button("Yang"));
  }

  public boolean action(Event e, Object arg) {
    if (((Button) e.target).getLabel() == "Yin") {
      try {
        getAppletContext().showDocument(new
        URL("http://www.nonexist.com/yin"));

      }
      catch( Exception ex ) {
      // note: code to handle the exception goes here //
      }
    }
    else if (((Button) e.target).getLabel() == "Yang") {
      try {
        getAppletContext().showDocument(new
        URL("http://www.other.com/yang"));
      }
      catch( Exception ex ) {
      // note: code to handle the exception goes here //
      }
    }
    return true;
  }

}
```

Figure 34.5 An example applet that interacts with the HTTP and HTML facilities in a browser.

As the example shows, Java provides high-level library facilities that simplify interaction between an applet and the browser. To use the facilities, the applet begins with three *import* statements. In addition to the Applet and Abstract Window Toolkit definitions, the applet imports *java.net.**, which contains definitions of classes related to the network.

Operation of the applet is straightforward. When a browser starts the applet, the browser creates an instance of the *buttons* class, and then invokes the *init* method. *Init* creates two *Button* objects, and uses the *add* method to add them to the applet's display. One button is labeled *Yin*, while the other is labeled *Yang*. Once *init* completes, the screen appears as Figure 34.6 illustrates:

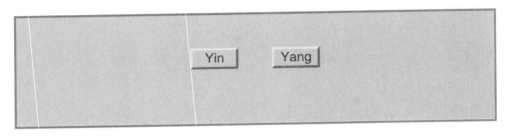

Figure 34.6 Illustration of the display produced by the applet in Figure 34.5.

Code that interacts with the browser can be found in the *action* method. When the user clicks the button labeled *Yin*, the *action* method performs three tasks. First, the *if* statement tests the label on the button to determine which button has been clicked. Second, the applet retrieves the appropriate document. For example, if the user clicks the button labeled *Yin*, the applet invokes:

`new URL("http://www.nonexist.com/yin")`

to request that the browser's HTTP client retrieve a copy of the document associated with URL *http://www.nonexist.com/yin*. The *new* operation creates a local object to hold the document. Third, the Java code:

`getAppletContext().showDocument`

requests the HTML interpreter to display the document on the user's screen. The browser will replace its current display with the new document; the user must click the browser's *back* button to return to the applet.

34.16 Errors And Exception Handling

In Java, all errors produce *exceptions*; an applet is required to handle such exceptions explicitly. For example, the applet in Figure 34.5 uses the *URL* object to request that the HTTP client fetch a document. If the URL is incorrect, the network is down, or the server is unavailable, the invocation will result in an exception.

The example applet uses the *try-catch* construct to handle exceptions. The syntactic form:

$$\texttt{try \{ } S \texttt{ \} catch (} E \texttt{) \{ } H \texttt{ \}}$$

means: if exception *E* occurs while executing *S*, invoke handler *H*. In the example code, *E* is a variable *ex* declared to be of type *Exception*, and the handler is not specified, which means that all exceptions are to be ignored. Thus, the example simply ignores errors, and forces the user to click a button to retry the operation.

34.17 JavaScript Technology

Several alternatives exist to the Java technology. For example, a variation known as *JavaScript*† is used for active pages that do not contain large or complex code. Instead of compiling an applet into the bytecode representation, JavaScript provides a scripting language, and arranges for a browser to read and interpret a script in source form. More important, JavaScript can be integrated with HTML — an HTML page can contain a JavaScript function that provides simple interaction with a user. For example, a JavaScript function can request a user to enter information, and then verify that the information is in an acceptable form before communicating with the server. A JavaScript function can also perform an action such as playing an audio file.

As an example, consider a JavaScript program that solves the same problem as the Java program in Figure 34.2 (i.e., records how many times a button has been clicked). Figure 34.7 contains the code.

---

†There is little relationship between the Java language and JavaScript except for the name; the ECMA organization has standardized a version of JavaScript under the name *ECMA script*.

```
<HTML>
<HEAD>
  <TITLE>JavaScript counter</TITLE>
</HEAD>
<BODY onLoad="return incrementcount(document.demo);">
  <CENTER>
  <SCRIPT>
    var n;
    n = -1;

    function incrementcount(form) {
      n = n + 1;
      if (n==0) {
        s = "  The button has not been clicked at all. ";
      } else {
        s = "   The button has been clicked " + n + " times."
      }
      form.elements["OutputArea"].value = s;
    }
  </SCRIPT>

  <CENTER>
    <FORM NAME="demo">
      <INPUT TYPE="BUTTON" NAME="ButtonClick" value=" Click here "
          onClick="incrementcount(this.form);">
      <TEXTAREA NAME="OutputArea" ROWS=1 COLS=42> </TEXTAREA>
    </FORM>
  </CENTER>

</BODY>
</HTML>
```

Figure 34.7 A JavaScript program that performs the same function as the
Java applet in Figure 34.2. JavaScript is embedded in an HTML
page.

As the figure shows, tags *<SCRIPT>* and *</SCRIPT>* bracket the JavaScript code.
When it encounters the *SCRIPT* tag, the browser invokes the built-in JavaScript interpreter. In the example, the JavaScript code declares *n* to be a variable, assigns *n* the initial value -1, and declares function *incrementcount*. Each time it is invoked, function
incrementcount increments variable *n*, and tests the resulting value to determine which
of two messages to display. The output is placed in a text area associated with the
function argument.

In addition to the JavaScript code that defines the *incrementcount* function, the example document contains an *onLoad* directive in the *<BODY>* tag. The presence of the *onLoad* directive means that the browser invokes function *incrementcount* whenever the document is loaded (or reloaded). When the document is loaded, the interpreter initializes variable *n* to -1 before *incrementcount* is invoked. Thus, the first call to *incrementcount* increments the value of *n* to zero, which causes the following message to appear:

The button has not been clicked at all.

The directive *onClick*, associated with the button, causes the browser to call *incrementcount* each time the user clicks the button. Thus, for each click, the browser invokes *incrementcount*, which increments variable *n* and displays a message that gives the current value. For example, after the third click, the window displays the message:

The button has been clicked 3 times.

The JavaScript language has both advantages and disadvantages. As the example illustrates, the chief advantages are simplicity and ease of use. A small script can be embedded in a web page. Just like an ordinary web page, the script can be tested with a browser; no separate compiler is needed. The chief disadvantages are speed and scalability — because the source representation is less compact than a bytecode representation, transporting a source program takes longer. Furthermore, a script takes longer to interpret than a program that has been translated into a bytecode representation.

34.18 Alternatives

Researchers and companies are exploring many alternatives to Java and JavaScript. For example, variations of active web page technology exist that permit a programmer to write applets in other languages. One group explored an obvious way to incorporate other languages — compile the language into the Java bytecode representation.

Perhaps the most important topic being explored focuses on providing an active page with more direct control of the display. Internally a browser maintains a data structure that describes objects on the screen. Similar to a *display list* in a graphics system, the internal structure in a browser is called a *Document Object Model* (*DOM*). One part of the browser continually scans the DOM and updates the screen, while other parts of the browser modify the DOM (e.g., take active page output and incorporate it into the DOM). Microsoft and others are developing active web page technologies that allow a program to manipulate the DOM directly.

34.19 Summary

Two Web technologies have been invented to update a display continuously. Called *server push*, an early technology places responsibility on a server — a dynamic document program on the server runs continuously to produce new versions of the document. The alternative scheme, *active documents*, places responsibility on the browser — the server returns an active document that the browser runs locally.

The most widely used technology for active documents was produced by Sun Microsystems, Incorporated. Known as *Java*, the technology includes three components: a programming language, a run-time environment, and an extensive library of classes. The Java language is a general-purpose, high-level, object-oriented language descended from C++. The Java run-time environment supports dynamic, multi-threaded execution, and provides programs with access to the user's display as well as to the Internet. Because an active document manipulates the user's display, the Java library and run-time system provide a graphics toolkit to make graphics programming easier. The toolkit includes both low-level and high-level facilities; a programmer can choose to handle details or allow library methods to do so.

In Java, an active document is called an *applet*. A programmer creates an applet by writing a source program in the Java Programming Language. The programmer then uses the Java compiler, *javac*, to translate the source program into a bytecode representation, and places the bytecode representation on a Web server. When a browser requests the URL associated with the applet, the server downloads a copy of the bytecode representation; the Java interpreter in the browser then executes the applet. The interpreter provides the Java run-time environment as well as access to the user's screen and the Internet.

The JavaScript language is an alternative technology used to construct active web pages. Although not as powerful as other technologies, JavaScript is easier to use. Unlike Java, JavaScript programs are not compiled. Instead the source code for a JavaScript program, called a script, is embedded directly in an HTML page. The browser interprets the JavaScript program, allowing it to manipulate items on the display.

EXERCISES

34.1   Read more about the Java language. Make a list of the differences between Java and C++. Which differences are the most significant?

34.2   Can dynamic document technologies provide functionality that cannot be achieved with active document technologies? Explain. Hint: consider the CGI programs in the previous chapter.

34.3   Suppose computers were arbitrarily fast and networks had zero delay. Would an active document technology provide any functionality that could not be achieved with a dynamic document technology? Explain.

34.4   When an applet stores long-term state information in a file, where is the file located?

34.5   Explain how active document technologies pose a security risk.

34.6   Can an applet act as a server? Hint: look at the documentation on socket functions available in the applet run-time library.

34.7   The applet in Figure 34.2 uses a *TextField* object to display the initial message. The size of a box created for the object depends on the length of the message. Does the size of the box change when the *setText* method is called with a longer string? If not, what happens?

34.8   Consider the applet shown in Figure 34.2. The first time a user clicks the button, the applet displays a message that says *The button has been clicked 1 times*. Modify the code to display the message: *The button has been clicked 1 time*. Be sure the code uses the plural when the count is greater than one.

34.9   Extend the JavaScript program in Figure 34.7 to correct the problem discussed in the previous exercise.

34.10 Modify the applet shown in Figure 34.5 to catch the exception that occurs when the applet references an invalid URL. Print an error message for the user.

34.11 Extend the previous exercise to prompt the user when an exception occurs. Have the applet obtain a new URL from the user. Can you prevent a sequence of errors from producing a recursive stack of exceptions?

Chapter Contents

35

RPC and Middleware

35.1 Introduction

Previous chapters describe specific applications that use the client-server model to communicate across a network and mechanisms such as CGI that programmers use to construct client-server systems. This chapter continues the discussion of tools that aid programmers in creating client-server systems.

35.2 Programming Clients And Servers

Any programmer who has built client-server software knows that such programming is difficult. In addition to the usual tasks, programmers who build clients and servers must deal with the complex issues of communication. Although many of the needed functions are supplied by a standard API such as the socket interface, programmers still face a challenge. The socket calls require the programmer to specify many low-level details such as names, addresses, protocols, and ports. More important, small errors in the code that can easily go undetected when the program is tested can cause major problems when the program runs in production.

Programmers who write clients and servers realize that multiple programs often follow the same general structure and repeat many of the same details. That is, most client-server software systems follow a few basic architectural patterns. Furthermore, because implementations tend to use the same standard API (e.g., the socket interface), much of the detailed code found in one program is replicated in others. For example, all client programs that use a connection-oriented transport must create a socket, specify the server's endpoint address, open a connection to the server, send requests, receive responses, and close the connection when interaction is complete.

To avoid writing the same code repeatedly and to produce code that is both correct and efficient, programmers use automated tools to construct clients and servers. A *tool* is software that generates all or part of a computer program. The tool accepts a high-level description of the service to be offered, and produces much of the needed code automatically. The tool cannot eliminate all programming — a programmer must supply code that performs the computation for the particular service. However, a tool can handle the communication details. As a result, the code contains fewer bugs. To summarize:

> *Because writing client and server programs involves many low-level details and because client-server software follows a few basic architectural forms, programmers can use tools to generate much of the code automatically. Tools make the resulting programs more efficient and correct.*

35.3 Remote Procedure Call Paradigm

One of the earliest facilities that was created to help programmers write client-server software is known generically as a *Remote Procedure Call* (*RPC*) mechanism. The idea of RPC arises from the observation that most programmers are familiar with procedure calls as an architectural construct. When programmers build a large program, they begin by dividing the program into major pieces. The most widely-available programming language feature used for such divisions is the *procedure*; a programmer begins by associating a procedure with each major piece of the design.

When implementing a program, the programmer uses procedures to keep the code manageable. Instead of defining a single, large procedure that performs many tasks, the programmer divides the tasks into sets and uses shorter procedures to handle each set. If the resulting tasks require substantial amounts of code, the programmer subdivides the task, and uses a subprocedure to perform each of the subtasks. Thus, the overall form of a program consists of a hierarchy of procedure calls.

The procedural hierarchy of a program can be represented with a directed graph in which each node represents a procedure, and an edge from node X to node Y means that procedure X contains a call to procedure Y. The graphical representation is known as a *procedure call graph*. Figure 35.1 shows an example.

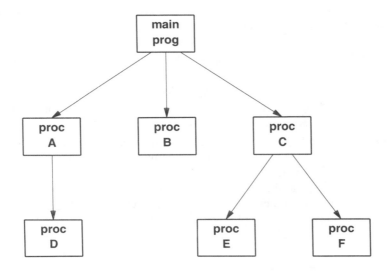

Figure 35.1 An example procedural call graph in a conventional program.
An arrow from one procedure to another means that the first
procedure contains a call to the second.

In the figure, the main program calls three procedures, *A*, *B*, and *C*. Procedure *A*
calls procedure *D*, and procedure *C* calls two other procedures, *E* and *F*.

Another aspect of conventional procedure calls will be important when we consider
remote calls: parameters. To make procedures general and enable a given procedure to
solve a set of related tasks, each procedure is *parameterized* — the definition is given
with a set of *formal parameters*. When the procedure is invoked, the caller supplies *actual arguments* that correspond to the formal parameters.

Because parameterized procedures have worked well as a programming abstraction,
researchers examined ways to use a procedural abstraction to build clients and servers.
The premise of the research is:

> *If a programmer follows the same procedure call paradigm used to
> build conventional programs when building client and server
> software, the programmer will find the task easier and will make
> fewer mistakes.*

To follow the premise, researchers have investigated ways to make client-server
programming as much like conventional programming as possible. Unfortunately, most
programming languages are designed to produce code for a single computer. Neither

the language nor the compiler are designed for a distributed environment — the code that is generated restricts the flow of control and parameter passing to a single address space.

A few researchers have investigated language modifications that embed client-server facilities in the language. For example, *Modula-3* and *Java Remote Method Invocation* (*Java RMI*) both have facilities that allow a program to invoke procedures on other computers. Also, both have facilities that synchronize the computations from separate machines to ensure consistent results.

Most of the research on facilities to support client-server programming has avoided direct modifications to the programming language by taking the approach of defining a set of tools that programmers can use to build distributed programs. In particular, tools are available that accept a high-level program specification, insert the code necessary for network communication, and automatically translate the resulting code to produce client and server programs. The tool-based approach is now widely accepted.

To summarize:

> *Because conventional programming languages do not allow procedure calls to pass from a program on one computer across a network to a program on another, tools are used to help programmers build client-server software using the procedure call abstraction.*

35.4 RPC Paradigm

When using RPC, a programmer's attention is not focused on the computer network or communication protocols. Instead, the programmer is encouraged to think about the problem being solved. That is, a programmer does not begin by thinking about two separate programs. The programmer begins by imagining how the problem would be solved by a conventional program running on a single computer. The programmer designs and builds the program, using procedure calls as the basic architectural feature.

Once a programmer has built a conventional program to solve the problem at hand, the programmer then considers how to divide the program into two pieces. In essence, the programmer must partition the call graph into two parts. The part that contains the main program and the procedures it calls becomes the client, while the remaining procedures become the server. When selecting a set of procedures that comprise the client and a set that comprise the server, a programmer must consider data — the global data that each procedure references must be located on the same computer as the procedure.

The partition in Figure 35.2 illustrates one possible way to divide the program from Figure 35.1 into two parts.

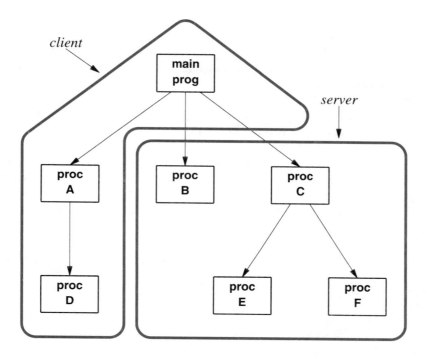

Figure 35.2 The example program from Figure 35.1 divided into a client and a server.

In the figure, the client consists of the main program plus procedures *A* and *D*. The server consists of procedures *B*, *C*, *E*, and *F*. Other divisions of the call graph are possible; we cannot tell from the figure why the programmer made this particular choice. For example, procedures *A* and *D* might be in the client because they handle interaction with the user, or they might be grouped with the main program because they reference global variables in the main program.

RPC extends the procedure call mechanism to allow a procedure in the client to call a procedure across the network in the server. That is, when such a procedure call occurs, the thread of control appears to pass across the network from the client to the server; when the called procedure returns, the thread of control appears to pass back from the server to the client.

After deciding which procedures to place in the server and which to place in the client, the programmer is ready to use an RPC tool. To do so, the programmer creates a specification that describes the set of procedures that will be *remote* (i.e., the set of procedures that form the server). For each remote procedure, the programmer must specify the types of its parameters. The tool creates software that handles the necessary communication.

35.5 Communication Stubs

A thread of control cannot jump from a program on one computer to a procedure on another. Instead, it uses client-server interaction. When a client calls a remote procedure, it uses conventional protocols to send a request message across the network to the server. The request identifies a procedure to invoke. After sending a request, the process on the client side blocks to await a response. When the remote program (i.e. the server) receives a request from a client, it invokes the specified procedure, and then sends the result back to the client.

Obviously, extra software must be added to each part of the program to implement the interaction. The extra software on the client side handles the details of sending a message across the network and waiting for a response. The extra software on the server side handles the details of receiving the incoming message, calling the specified procedure, and sending a response.

Technically, each piece of added software is known as a *communication stub* or *proxy*. The two stubs, one in the client and one in the server, handle all communication details. In addition, the stubs are constructed to fit into the existing program; the rest of the program simply uses procedure calls as if all procedures were local. If a call is made to a procedure that is not local, a communication stub intercepts the procedure call, gathers values for the arguments (known as argument *marshaling*), and sends a message across the network to the communication stub on the server. The communication stub on the server side uses the conventional procedure call mechanism to invoke the specified procedure, and sends the results back to the client stub. When the client stub receives a response, it returns the results to its caller exactly as if a local procedure was returning. Figure 35.3 illustrates how communication stubs are added to the client and server sides of a program.

Figure 35.3a shows the procedure call in the original program before RPC stubs have been added. When the *main* procedure calls procedure *B*, the arguments it passes must agree exactly with the formal parameters of *B*. That is, the call must contain the correct number of arguments, and the type of each argument must match the type declared for the formal parameter.

Figure 35.3b shows the communication stubs that must be added to the program when it is divided into client and server pieces. It is important to understand that the procedural interfaces in part *b* use the same number and type of arguments as the original interface in *a*. Thus, the call from *main* to the client stub and the call from the server stub to procedure *B* use exactly the same interface as the conventional call from *main* to procedure *B*. More important, client stubs can be given the same name as the procedure they replace†. As a result, code from the original program need not be changed. To summarize:

---

†The origin of the term *proxy* should be clear — each client stub acts as an exact replacement for one of the procedures in the original program.

Because the communication stubs inserted between two procedures to implement remote procedure call can use exactly the same name and interface as the original procedure call, neither the calling procedure nor the called procedure need to be changed.

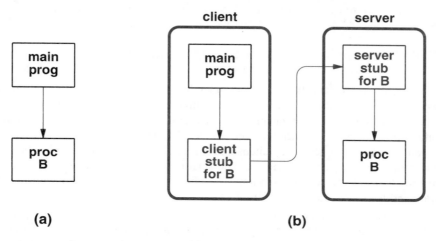

Figure 35.3 (a) The original call in a conventional program, and (b) the remote version of the same call implemented with communication stubs.

35.6 External Data Representation

Computer systems do not all use the same internal data representation. For example, some computers store the most significant byte of an integer at the lowest address, and others store the least significant byte at the lowest address. Thus, when clients and servers send integer values between heterogeneous computers, they must agree on details such as whether the client or server will convert and which representation will be sent across the network.

The term *external data representation* refers to the form of data that is sent across the network. In addition to defining an interface language, a remote procedure call technology defines an external data representation. Some systems negotiate a representation — the client and server stubs exchange messages to determine which representations each will use and which needs to translate. Many systems choose another approach in which the external representation is fixed. In such cases, the sender always converts from the local representation to the external representation, and the receiver always converts from the external representation to the local representation. We can summarize:

> *Because computer systems do not all use the same internal data representation and clients and servers can run on two types of computers, remote procedure call technology must handle the problem of converting from one data representation to another. A widely accepted method defines a standard external representation and requires each side to translate between the external and local representations.*

35.7 Middleware And Object-Oriented Middleware

To review, a tool can help a programmer build a program that uses remote procedure call. The programmer specifies a set of procedures that will be remote by giving the interface details (i.e., number and type of arguments). To do so, the programmer uses the tool's *Interface Definition Language (IDL†)*. The tool reads the IDL specifications and generates the necessary client and server stubs. The programmer then compiles and links two separate programs. The server stubs are combined with the remote procedures to form the server program. The client stubs are combined with the main program and local procedures to form the client program.

A variety of commercial tools have been developed that use the paradigm described above to help programmers construct client-server software. Such tools are generally called *middleware* because they provide software that fits "between" a conventional application program and the network software.

In the 1990s, programming language research shifted focus from the procedure paradigm to the object-oriented paradigm. As a result, most new programming languages are *object-oriented languages*. The basic structuring facility in an object-oriented language is called an *object*, which consists of data items plus a set of operations for those items, which are known as *methods*. The basic control mechanism in an object-oriented language is *method invocation*. In response to the change in languages, designers are creating new middleware systems that extend method invocation across computers in the same way that remote procedure call extended procedure call. Such systems are known as distributed object systems. The next sections briefly describe several widely-used middleware and object-oriented middleware technologies.

35.7.1 ONC RPC

One of the first RPC mechanisms to achieve widespread acceptance was designed by Sun Microsystems, Incorporated. Formally known as *Open Network Computing Remote Procedure Call (ONC RPC)*, the technology is often called *Sun RPC*. In addition to specifying an interface definition language and a message format that the client and server stubs use to communicate, ONC RPC includes a data representation standard known as *eXternal Data Representation (XDR)*. Finally, like most other RPC technologies, ONC RPC uses the TCP/IP protocols, and allows a programmer to choose UDP or TCP transport.

---

†Some technologies expand IDL to *Interface Description Language*.

35.7.2 DCE RPC

The Open Software Foundation† defined the *Distributed Computing Environment* (*DCE*), which is composed of multiple components and tools that are designed to work together. DCE includes its own remote procedure call technology, which is often referred to as *DCE/RPC*, and its own interface definition language (IDL), which differs from others in minor ways. DCE/RPC also permits a client to access more than one server (i.e., some remote procedures can be located on one server, while other remote procedures are located on another). In all cases, DCE/RPC can use TCP/IP protocols, with a programmer choosing between UDP and TCP transport.

35.7.3 MSRPC

Microsoft Corporation defined its own remote procedure call technology, *Microsoft Remote Procedure Call* (*MSRPC*). Because MSRPC was derived from DCE/RPC, it shares the same central concepts and general program structure. However, MSRPC differs in a few details. It defines its own IDL and its own protocol that the client and server stubs use to communicate.

35.7.4 CORBA

Perhaps the best known object-oriented middleware is named *Common Object Request Broker Architecture* (*CORBA*). CORBA permits an entire object to be placed on a server, and extends method invocation using the same general approach as described above. One difference arises because proxies are instantiated at run-time like other objects. When a program receives a reference to a remote object, a local proxy is created that corresponds to the object. When the program invokes a method on the object, control passes to the local proxy. The proxy then sends a message across the network to the server, which invokes the specified method and returns the results. Thus, CORBA makes method invocation for remote and local objects appear identical.

In addition to focusing on objects instead of procedures, CORBA differs from conventional RPC technologies because it is more dynamic. In conventional RPC technologies, the programmer uses a tool to create stub procedures when constructing the program. In CORBA, the software creates a proxy at run-time when it is needed (i.e., when a method is invoked on a remote object for which no proxy exists).

35.7.5 MSRPC2

Microsoft developed a second generation of MSRPC called *MSRPC2*. Microsoft frequently uses the name *Object RPC* (*ORPC*) instead of MSRPC2 because the second version represents a more significant change than a simple revision. It extends the underlying concepts to provide more support for objects. The ideas in MSRPC2 are derived from several sources, including research done at Digital Equipment Corporation using Modula-3.

---

†The organization is now called *The Open Group*.

35.7.6 COM/DCOM

In yet another effort, Microsoft Corporation also produced COM and DCOM, which are object-oriented technologies. The *Component Object Model* (*COM*) is an object-oriented software architecture that was defined in 1994. The standard defines a binary interface between components on a given computer, sometimes referred to as a *packaging scheme*. Within COM, all objects are given globally unique names, and all object references use the global scheme.

Defined in 1998, the *Distributed Component Object Model* (*DCOM*) extends COM by creating an application-level protocol for object-oriented remote procedure calls†. DCOM uses ORPC for transport. Because ORPC was derived from DCE/RPC, DCOM uses exactly the same packet format and semantics for remote invocation as DCE/RPC uses for remote procedure calls.

35.8 Summary

Because it is difficult to create correct client-server application programs and much of the detailed code can be reused, many programmers use automated tools to aid in the construction of distributed software. Called middleware, most of the tools follow the same basic paradigm, which is known generically as the remote procedure call paradigm. The programmer creates a conventional program, and then divides the program into client and server pieces.

To aid in the division, most middleware provides an Interface Definition Language (IDL) that allows the user to specify the types of arguments for each remote procedure. An automated tool then reads the IDL description and generates the necessary proxy software automatically.

The chief advantage of using middleware lies in ease of programming. Programmers can use conventional programming techniques, with which they are familiar, to design and construct distributed programs. Furthermore, a programmer can build and test a conventional version of a program before adding communication stubs that convert it to a distributed version.

Several middleware technologies have been developed. The earliest use the Remote Procedure Call (RPC) abstraction. For example, ONC RPC, DCE RPC, and MSRPC all follow the same pattern: a tool is used to generate client and server stubs that allow a procedure call to pass from a client on one computer to a server on another. Because programming languages have shifted focus from procedural to object-oriented forms, later middleware technologies use the remote object paradigm. For example, CORBA, MSRPC2, and DCOM all support remote objects and remote method invocation.

---

†The combination of COM and DCOM is referred to as *COM+*.

EXERCISES

35.1   Read more about ONC RPC. Does the technology depend on a particular programming language? If so, which one?

35.2   The term *big endian* is used to describe a computer architecture in which the most significant byte of an integer occupies the lowest memory address, and the term *little endian* is used to describe an architecture in which the least significant byte of an integer occupies the lowest memory address. Design a computer program that tests whether it is running on a big endian or little endian architecture.

35.3   The XDR standard for external data representation† specifies a fixed format used for all transfers (i.e., both the client and server must translate to or from the external representation). Some computer manufacturers praise XDR and others condemn it. Why?

35.4   Write a program to translate a *4*-byte integer from the local computer representation to the XDR representation and vice versa. How many integers can your program translate per second?

35.5   Read about the ISO presentation protocol ASN.1 and compare it to XDR. Under what circumstances will one of the standards be superior to the other?

35.6   Read about the middleware available on your local computer system, and use the IDL to declare a remote procedure that has four arguments: an integer, a character, a floating point number, and a string of characters.

35.7   Can an IDL allow arbitrary argument types to be passed to a remote procedure? Why or why not?

35.8   To assess middleware, build two client-server systems. Code one from scratch, and use middleware to build the other. Measure the time required for each. Did the use of middleware decrease or increase the time you spent? Why?

---

†The specification for XDR can be found in RFC *1014* on the CD-ROM that accompanies this text.

Chapter Contents

36

Network Management (SNMP)

36.1 Introduction

Preceding chapters describe a variety of applications that use the Internet. Each chapter examines the structure of software for a single service, and shows how a client and server interact.

This chapter expands our study of network applications by considering application software that managers use to measure or control networks. After explaining why network management is both important and difficult, the chapter describes how network management software operates and the functionality it provides. Finally, the chapter considers a specific example of a network management protocol, and explains how software for the protocol operates.

36.2 Managing An Internet

A *network manager* is a person responsible for monitoring and controlling the hardware and software systems that comprise an internet. A manager works to detect and correct problems that make communication inefficient or impossible and to eliminate conditions that will produce the problem again. Because either hardware or software failures can cause problems, a network manager must monitor both.

Management of a network can be difficult for two reasons. First, most internets are heterogeneous. That is, the internet contains hardware and software components manufactured by multiple companies. Small mistakes by one vendor can make components incompatible. Second, most internets are large. In particular, the global Internet spans many sites in countries around the world. Detecting the cause of a communication problem can be especially difficult if the problem occurs between computers at two sites.

Interestingly, failures that cause the most severe problems are often the simplest to diagnose. For example, if the coaxial cable in an Ethernet is cut or a LAN switch loses power, computers connected to the LAN will be unable to send or receive packets. Because the damage affects all computers on the network, a manager can locate the source of the failure quickly and reliably. Similarly, a manager can also detect catastrophic failures in software such as an invalid route that causes a router to discard all packets for a given destination.

In contrast, intermittent or partial failures often produce a difficult challenge. For example, imagine a network interface device that corrupts bits infrequently, or a router that misroutes a few packets and then routes many correctly. In the case of an intermittent interface failure, the checksum or CRC in a frame may be sufficient to hide the problem — the receiver discards the corrupted frame, and the sender must eventually retransmit it. Thus, from a user's perspective, the network appears to operate correctly because data eventually passes through the system. The point is:

> *Because protocols accommodate packet loss, intermittent hardware or software failures can be difficult to detect and isolate.*

36.3 The Danger Of Hidden Failures

Unfortunately, although they remain hidden, intermittent failures can affect network performance. Each retransmission uses network bandwidth that could be used to send new data. More important, hardware failures often become worse over time because the hardware deteriorates. As the frequency of errors increases, more packets must be retransmitted. Because retransmissions lower throughput and increase delay, overall network performance decreases.

In a shared network, a failure associated with one computer can affect others. For example, suppose the interface begins to fail on a computer attached to an Ethernet. Because the failing hardware corrupts some of the packets the computer sends, the computer will eventually retransmit them. While the network is being used for a retransmission, other computers must wait to send packets. Thus, each retransmission reduces the throughput available for all computers. To summarize:

> *Although network hardware and protocol software contain mechanisms to automatically detect failures and retransmit packets, network managers work to detect and correct underlying problems because retransmissions result in lower performance for all computers that share the network.*

36.4 Network Management Software

How can a network manager find problems and isolate their cause? The answer lies in *network management software* that allows a manager to monitor and control network components. For example, network management software allows a manager to interrogate devices such as host computers, routers, switches, and bridges to determine their status and to obtain statistics about the networks to which they attach. The software also allows a manager to control such devices by changing routes and configuring network interfaces.

36.5 Clients, Servers, Managers, And Agents

Surprisingly, network management is not defined as part of the transport or internet protocols. Instead, the protocols that a network manager uses to monitor and control network devices operate at the application level. That is, when a manager needs to interact with a specific hardware device, the management software follows the conventional client-server model: an application program on the manager's computer acts as a client, and an application program on the network device acts as a server. The client on the manager's computer uses conventional transport protocols (e.g., TCP or UDP) to establish communication with the server. The two then exchange requests and responses according to the management protocol.

To avoid confusion between application programs that users invoke and applications that are reserved for network managers, network management systems avoid the terms *client* and *server*. Instead, the client application that runs on the manager's computer is called a *manager*, and an application that runs on a network device is called an *agent*†.

It may seem odd that conventional networks and conventional transport protocols are used for network management. After all, failures in either the protocols or underlying hardware can prevent packets from traveling to or from a device, making it impossible to control a device while failures are occurring. In practice, however, using an application protocol for network management works well for two reasons. First, in cases where a hardware failure prevents communication, the level of the protocol does not matter — a manager can communicate with those devices that remain operating, and use success or failure to help locate the problem. Second, using conventional transport protocols means a manager's packets will be subject to the same conditions as normal traffic. Thus, if delays are high, a manager will find out immediately.

---

†Although we will follow the convention of using *manager* and *agent*, the reader should keep in mind that they operate like any client and server.

36.6 Simple Network Management Protocol

The standard protocol used to manage an internet is known as the *Simple Network Management Protocol* (*SNMP†*). The SNMP protocol defines exactly how a manager communicates with an agent. For example, SNMP defines the format of requests that a manager sends to an agent and the format of replies that an agent returns. In addition, SNMP defines the exact meaning of each possible request and reply. In particular, SNMP specifies that an SNMP message is encoded using a standard known as *Abstract Syntax Notation.1* (*ASN.1*)‡.

Although the full details of ASN.1 encoding are beyond the scope of this text, a simple example will help explain the encoding: consider sending an integer between an agent and a manager. To accommodate large values without wasting space on every transfer, ASN.1 uses a combination of length and value for each object being transferred. For example, an integer between *0* and *255* can be transferred in a single octet. Integers in the range *256* through *65535* require two octets, while larger integers require three or more octets. To encode an integer, ASN.1 sends a pair of values: a length, *L*, followed by *L* octets that contain the integer. To permit encoding of arbitrarily large integers, ASN.1 also allows the length to occupy more than one octet; extended lengths normally are not needed for the integers used with SNMP. Figure 36.1 illustrates the encoding.

decimal integer	hexadecimal equivalent	length octet	octets of value (in hex)
27	1B	01	1B
792	318	02	03 18
24,567	5FF7	02	5F F7
190,345	2E789	03	02 E7 89

Figure 36.1 An example of ASN.1 encoding for integers. Each integer is preceded by a length field that specifies the number of octets used to encode the integer value.

36.7 Fetch-Store Paradigm

The SNMP protocol does not define a large set of commands. Instead, the protocol uses a *fetch-store paradigm* in which there are two basic operations: *fetch*, used to obtain a value from a device, and *store*, used to set a value in a device. Each object that can be fetched or stored is given a unique name; a command that specifies a fetch or store operation must specify the name of the object.

It should be obvious how fetch operations can be used to monitor a device or obtain its status: a set of status objects must be defined and given names. To obtain status information, a manager fetches the value associated with a given object. For example, an object can be defined that counts the number of frames a device discards because the

---

†Although many sites still used SNMP version 2, written *SNMPv2*; the current standard is, *SNMPv3*.

‡The name is pronounced *abstract syntax notation dot one*, and the abbreviation is pronounced by reading the characters, *A S N dot one*.

frame checksum is incorrect. The software must be programmed to increment the counter whenever a checksum error is detected. A manager can use SNMP to fetch the value associated with the counter to determine whether checksum errors are occurring.

Using the fetch-store paradigm to control a device may not seem obvious; control operations are defined to be the side-effect of storing into an object. For example, SNMP does not include separate commands to *reset* the checksum error counter or to *reboot* the device. In the case of the checksum error counter, storing a zero into the object is intuitive because it resets a counter to zero. For operations like reboot, however, an SNMP agent must be programmed to interpret store requests and to execute the correct sequence of operations to achieve the desired effect. Thus, SNMP might define a reboot object, and specify that storing zero into the object should cause the system to reboot. In practice, however, most systems do not have a reboot counter — software in the agent must explicitly check for a store operation that specifies the reboot object, and must then execute the sequence of steps needed to reboot the system. To summarize:

> *SNMP uses the fetch-store paradigm for interaction between a manager and an agent. A manager fetches values to determine the device status; operations that control the device are defined as the side-effects of storing into objects.*

36.8 The MIB And Object Names

Each object to which SNMP has access must be defined and given a unique name. Furthermore, both the manager and agent programs must agree on the names and the meanings of fetch and store operations. Collectively, the set of all objects SNMP can access is known as a *Management Information Base (MIB)*.

In fact, SNMP does not define a MIB. Instead, the SNMP standard only specifies the message format and describes how messages are encoded; a separate standard specifies MIB variables along with the meaning of fetch and store operations on each variable.

Objects in a MIB are defined with the ASN.1 naming scheme, which assigns each object a long prefix that guarantees the name will be unique. For example, an integer that counts the number of IP datagrams a device has received is named:

iso.org.dod.internet.mgmt.mib.ip.ipInReceives

Furthermore, when the object name is represented in an SNMP message, each part of the name is assigned an integer. Thus, in an SNMP message, the name of *ipInReceives* is:

1.3.6.1.2.1.4.3

36.9 The Variety Of MIB Variables

Because SNMP does not specify a set of MIB variables, the design is flexible. New MIB variables can be defined and standardized as needed, without changing the basic protocol. More important, the separation of the communication protocol from the definition of objects permits groups of people to define MIB variables as needed. For example, when a new protocol is designed, the group who creates the protocol can also define MIB variables that are used to monitor and control the protocol software. Similarly, when a group creates a new hardware device, the group can specify MIB variables used to monitor and control the device.

As the original designers intended, many sets of MIB variables have been created. For example, there are MIB variables that correspond to protocols like UDP, TCP, IP, and ARP, as well as MIB variables for network hardware such as Ethernet, Token Ring, and FDDI. In addition, groups have defined MIBs for hardware devices such as bridges, switches, and printers.

36.10 MIB Variables That Correspond To Arrays

In addition to simple variables such as integers that correspond to counters, a MIB can include variables that correspond to tables or arrays. Such definitions are useful because they correspond to the implementation of information in a computer system. For example, consider an IP routing table. In most implementations, the routing table can be viewed as an array of entries, where each entry contains a destination address and a next-hop used to reach that address.

Unlike a conventional programming language, ASN.1 does not include an index operation. Instead, indexed references are implicit — the sender must know that the object being referenced is a table, and must append the indexing information onto the object name. For example, the MIB variable:

standard MIB prefix.ip.ipRouting Table

corresponds to the IP routing table, each entry of which contains several fields. Conceptually, the table is indexed by the IP address of a destination. To obtain the value of a particular field in an entry, a manager specifies a name of the form:

standard MIB prefix.ip.ipRouting Table.ipRouteEntry.field.IPdestaddr

where *field* corresponds to one of the valid fields of an entry, and *IPdestaddr* is a 4-octet IP address that is used as an index. For example, field *ipRouteNextHop* corresponds to the next-hop in an entry. When converted to the integer representation, the request for a next-hop becomes:

1.3.6.1.2.1.4.21.1.7.destination

where *1.3.6.1.2.1* is the standard MIB prefix, *4* is the code for *ip*, *21* is the code for *ipRoutingTable*, *1* is the code for *ipRouteEntry*, *7* is the code for the field *ipRouteNext-Hop*, and *destination* is the numeric value for the IP address of a destination. To summarize:

Although ASN.1 does not provide a mechanism for indexing, MIB variables can correspond to tables or arrays. To emulate a table or an array with an ASN.1 variable, the index for an entry is encoded by appending it to the variable name; when agent software encounters a name that corresponds to a table, the software extracts and uses the index information to select the correct table entry.

36.11 Summary

A network manager is a person who monitors and controls the hardware and software systems that comprise an internet. Network managers use network management software to help them locate, diagnose, and correct problems.

Because network management software uses the client-server model, the software requires two components. The component that runs on a manager's computer and acts as a client is called a *manager*; the component that runs on a device in the network and acts as a server is called an *agent*.

The *Simple Network Management Protocol* (*SNMP*) is the standard network management protocol used in the Internet. SNMP defines the format and meaning of messages that a manager and agent exchange. Instead of defining many operations, SNMP uses the fetch-store paradigm in which a manager sends requests to fetch values from or store values into variables. All operations are defined as side-effects of store operations.

SNMP does not define the set of variables that can be used. Instead, variables and their meanings are defined in separate standards, making it possible for groups to define a different set of MIB variables for each hardware device or protocol. The names of MIB variables are named using the ASN.1 standard; all MIB variables have long, hierarchical ASN.1 names, which are translated to a more compact numeric representation for transmission. ASN.1 does not include aggregate data types such as tables or arrays, nor does it include a subscript operator. Instead, to make a MIB variable emulate a table or an array, ASN.1 extends the variable name by appending the indexing information.

EXERCISES

36.1   If any device at your site runs an SNMP agent, use an SNMP management station to monitor the device.

36.2   What is the chief advantage of appending index information to a name instead of using a conventional array that is indexed by integers?

36.3   Read about how ASN.1 encodes names and values. Write a computer program to encode and decode ASN.1 names such as the name assigned to *ipInReceives*.

36.4   Write a program that reads an arbitrarily large integer in decimal, encodes the integer as in Figure 36.1, and prints the result.

Chapter Contents

37

Network Security

37.1 Introduction

Previous chapters describe how network hardware and software systems operate, and explain how client and server applications use the underlying network facilities to communicate. This chapter considers the important aspect of network security. The chapter characterizes security problems, describes the levels of security users expect from a network system, and explains basic techniques used to increase network security.

37.2 Secure Networks And Policies

What is a secure network? Can an internet be made secure? Although the concept of a secure network is appealing to most users, networks cannot be classified simply as secure or not secure because the term is not absolute — each organization defines the level of access that is permitted or denied. For example, some organizations store data that is valuable. Such organizations define a secure network to be a system that prevents outsiders from accessing the organization's computers. Other organizations need to make information available to outsiders, but prohibit outsiders from changing the data. Such organizations may define a secure network as one that allows arbitrary access to data, but includes mechanisms that prevent unauthorized changes. Still other groups focus on keeping communication confidential: they define a secure network as one in which no one other than the intended recipient can intercept and read a message. Finally, many large organizations need a complex definition of security that allows access to selected data or services the organization chooses to make public, while preventing access or modification of sensitive data and services that are kept confidential.

Because no absolute definition of *secure network* exists, the first step an organization must take to achieve a secure system is to define the organization's *security policy*. The policy does not specify how to achieve protection. Instead, it states clearly and unambiguously the items that are to be protected.

Defining a network security policy is complex. The primary complexity arises because a network security policy cannot be separated from the security policy for computer systems attached to the network. In particular, defining a policy for data that traverses a network does not guarantee that data will be secure. For example, consider data stored in a file that is readable. Network security cannot prevent unauthorized users who have accounts on the computer from obtaining a copy of the data. Thus, to be effective, a security policy must apply at all times. The policy must hold for the data stored on disk, data communicated over a telephone line with a dialup modem, information printed on paper, data transported on portable media such as a floppy disk, and data communicated over a computer network.

Assessing the costs and benefits of various security policies also adds complexity. In particular, a security policy cannot be defined unless an organization understands the value of its information. In many cases, the value of information is difficult to assess. Consider, for example, a simple payroll database that contains a record for each employee, the hours the employee worked, and the rate of pay. The easiest aspect of value to assess is the replacement cost. That is, one can compute the man-hours required to recreate or verify the contents of the database (e.g., by restoring the data from an archive or by performing the work needed to collect the information). A second aspect of value arises from the liability an organization can incur if the information is incorrect. For example, if an unauthorized person increases the pay rate in a payroll database, the company could incur arbitrary costs because employees would be overpaid. A third aspect of value arises from the indirect costs that can be incurred from security violations. For example, if payroll information becomes public, competitors might choose to hire workers, which results in costs for hiring and training replacements as well as increased salaries needed to retain other employees.

To summarize:

> *Devising a network security policy can be complex because a rational policy requires an organization to assess the value of information. The policy must apply to information stored in computers as well as to information traversing a network.*

37.3 Aspects Of Security

Defining a security policy is also complicated because each organization must decide which aspects of protection are most important, and often must compromise between security and ease of use. For example, an organization can consider:

- *Data Integrity.* Integrity refers to protection from change: is the data that arrives at a receiver exactly the same as the data that was sent?

- *Data Availability.* Availability refers to protection against disruption of service: does data remain accessible for legitimate uses?

- *Data Confidentiality.* Confidentiality refers to protection against unauthorized data access (e.g., via snooping or wiretapping): is data protected against unauthorized access?

- *Privacy.* Privacy refers to the ability of a sender to remain anonymous: is the sender's identity revealed?

37.4 Responsibility And Control

Many organizations discover that they cannot design a security policy because the organization has not specified how responsibility for information is assigned or controlled. The issue of responsibility for information has several aspects to consider:

- *Accountability.* Accountability refers to how an audit trail is kept: which group is responsible for each item of data? How does the group keep records of access and change?

- *Authorization.* Authorization refers to responsibility for each item of information and how such responsibility is delegated to others: who is responsible for where information resides and how does a responsible person approve access and change?

The critical issue underlying both accountability and authorization is *control* — an organization must control access to information analogous to the way the organization controls access to physical resources such as offices, equipment, and supplies.

37.5 Integrity Mechanisms

Chapter 7 discusses techniques used to ensure the integrity of data against accidental damage: *parity bits*, *checksums*, and *cyclic redundancy checks (CRCs)*. To use such techniques, a sender computes a small, integer value as a function of the data in a packet. The receiver recomputes the function from the data that arrives, and compares the result to the value that the sender computed.

A checksum or CRC cannot absolutely guarantee data integrity for two reasons. First, if malfunctioning hardware changes the value of a checksum as well as the value of the data, it is possible for the altered checksum to be valid for the altered data†. Second, if data changes result from a planned attack, the attacker can create a valid checksum for the altered data.

---

†The probability of random changes producing a correct checksum is extremely low, but not zero.

Several mechanisms have been used to guarantee the integrity of messages against intentional change. In general, the methods encode transmitted data with a *message authentication code (MAC)* that an attacker cannot break or forge. Typical encoding schemes use *cryptographic hashing* mechanisms. For example, one cryptographic hashing scheme uses a *secret key* known only to the sender and receiver. When the sender encodes the message, the cryptographic hash function uses the secret key to scramble the position of bytes within the message as well as to encode the data. Only the receiver can unscramble the data; an attacker, who does not have the secret key, cannot decode the message without introducing an error. Thus, the receiver knows that any message that can be decoded correctly is authentic.

37.6 Access Control And Passwords

Many computer systems use a *password* mechanism to control access to resources. Each user has a password, which is kept secret. When the user needs to access a protected resource, the user is asked to enter the password.

A simple password scheme works well for a conventional computer system because the system does not reveal the password to others. In a network, however, a simple password mechanism is susceptible to eavesdropping. If a user at one location sends a password across a network to a computer at another location, anyone who wiretaps the network can obtain a copy of the password. Wiretapping is especially easy when packets travel across a LAN because many LAN technologies permit an attached station to capture a copy of all traffic. In such situations, additional steps must be taken to prevent passwords from being reused.

37.7 Encryption And Confidentiality

To ensure that the content of a message remains confidential despite wiretapping, the message must be *encrypted*. In essence, encryption scrambles bits of the message in such a way that only the intended recipient can unscramble them. Someone who intercepts a copy of the encrypted message will not be able to extract information.

Several technologies exist for encryption. In some technologies, a sender and receiver must both have a copy of an *encryption key*, which is kept secret. The sender uses the key to produce an encrypted message, which is then sent across a network. The receiver uses the key to decode the encrypted message. That is, the *encrypt* function used by the sender takes two arguments: a key, K, and a message to be encrypted, M. The function produces an encrypted version of the message, E.

$$E \ = \ encrypt(K, M)$$

The *decrypt* function reverses the mapping to produce the original message:

$$M = decrypt(K, E)$$

Mathematically, *decrypt* is the inverse of *encrypt*:

$$M = decrypt(K, encrypt(K, M))$$

37.8 Public Key Encryption

In many encryption schemes, the key must be kept secret to avoid compromising security. One particularly interesting encryption technique assigns each user a pair of keys. One of the user's keys, called the *private key*, is kept secret, while the other, called the *public key*, is published along with the name of the user, so everyone knows the value of the key. The encryption function has the mathematical property that a message encrypted with the public key cannot be easily decrypted except with the private key, and a message encrypted with the private key cannot be decrypted except with the public key.

The relationships between encryption and decryption with the two keys can be expressed mathematically. Let M denote a message, *pub-u1* denote user *1*'s public key, and *prv-u1* denote user *1*'s private key. Then

$$M = decrypt(pub\text{-}u1, encrypt(prv\text{-}u1, M))$$

and

$$M = decrypt(prv\text{-}u1, encrypt(pub\text{-}u1, M))$$

Revealing a public key is safe because the functions used for encryption and decryption have a *one way property*. That is, telling someone the public key does not allow the person to forge a message that appears to be encrypted with the private key.

Public key encryption can be used to guarantee confidentiality. A sender who wishes a message to remain confidential uses the receiver's public key to encrypt the message. Obtaining a copy of the message as it passes across the network does not enable someone to read the contents because decryption requires the receiver's private key. Thus, the scheme ensures that data remains confidential because only the receiver can decrypt the message.

37.9 Authentication With Digital Signatures

An encryption mechanism can also be used to authenticate the sender of a message. The technique is known as a *digital signature*. To sign a message, the sender encrypts the message using a key known only to the sender. The recipient uses the inverse function to decrypt the message. The recipient knows who sent the message because only the sender has the key needed to perform the encryption. To ensure that encrypted messages are not copied and resent later, the original message can contain the time and date that the message was created.

Consider how a public key system can be used to provide a digital signature. To sign a message, a user encrypts the message using his or her private key. To verify the signature, the recipient looks up the user's public key and uses it to decrypt the message. Because only the user knows the private key, only the user can encrypt a message that can be decoded with the public key.

Interestingly, two levels of encryption can be used to guarantee that a message is both authentic and confidential. First, the message is signed by using the sender's private key to encrypt it. Second, the encrypted message is encrypted again using the recipient's public key. Mathematically, double encryption can be expressed as:

$$X = encrypt(pub\text{-}u2, encrypt(prv\text{-}u1, M))$$

where M denotes a message to be sent, X denotes the string that results from the double encryption, $prv\text{-}u1$ denotes the sender's private key, and $pub\text{-}u2$ denotes the recipient's public key.

At the receiving end, the decryption process is the reverse of the encryption process. First, the recipient uses his or her private key to decrypt the message. The decryption removes one level of encryption, but leaves the message digitally signed. Second, the recipient uses the sender's public key to decrypt the message again. The process can be expressed as:

$$M = decrypt(pub\text{-}u1, decrypt(prv\text{-}u2, X))$$

where X denotes the encrypted string that was transferred across the network, M denotes the original message, $prv\text{-}u2$ denotes the recipient's private key, and $pub\text{-}u1$ denotes the sender's public key.

If a meaningful message results from the double decryption, it must be true that the message was confidential and authentic. The message must have reached its intended recipient because only the intended recipient has the correct private key needed to remove the outer encryption. The message must have been authentic, because only the sender has the private key needed to encrypt the message so the sender's public key will correctly decrypt it.

37.10 Internet Firewall Concept

Although encryption technology helps solve many security problems, a second technology is also needed. Known as an *Internet firewall*†, the technology helps protect an organization's computers and networks from unwanted Internet traffic. Like a conventional firewall, an Internet firewall is designed to keep problems in the Internet from spreading to an organization's computers.

---

†The term is derived from the fireproof physical boundary placed between two structures to prevent fire from moving between them.

A firewall is placed between an organization and the rest of the Internet; Figure 37.1 illustrates the concept.

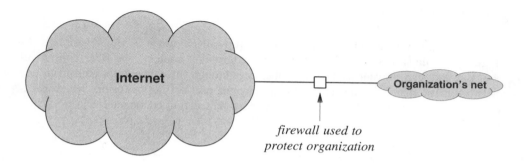

Figure 37.1 Illustration of a firewall that is used to protect an organization against unwanted interaction with the Internet.

If an organization has multiple Internet connections, a firewall must be placed at each, and all the organization's firewalls must be configured to enforce the organization's security policy. Furthermore, the firewall itself must be secure. That is,

- All traffic entering the organization passes through the firewall.
- All traffic leaving the organization passes through the firewall.
- The firewall implements the security policy and rejects any traffic that does not adhere to the policy.
- The firewall itself is immune to security attacks.

Firewalls are the most important security tool used to handle network connections between two organizations that do not trust each other. By placing a firewall on each external network connection, an organization can define a *secure perimeter* that prevents outsiders from interfering with the organization's computers. In particular, by limiting access to a small set of computers, a firewall can prevent outsiders from probing all computers in an organization, flooding the organization's networks with unwanted traffic, or attacking a computer by sending a sequence of IP datagrams that is known to cause the computer system to misbehave (e.g., to crash).

A firewall can lower the cost of providing security. Without a firewall to prevent access, outsiders can send packets to arbitrary computers in an organization†. Consequently, to provide security, an organization must make all of its computers secure. With a firewall, however, a manager can restrict incoming packets to a small set of computers. In the extreme case, the set can contain a single computer. Although computers in the set must be secure, other computers in the organization do not need to be.

---

†An outsider can guess the IP address of the computers in an organization by finding the set of network numbers that the organization has been assigned, and then trying each of the possible hosts on those networks.

Thus, an organization can save money because it is less expensive to install a firewall than to make all computer systems secure.

37.11 Packet Filtering

The primary mechanism used to build a firewall is known as a *packet filter*. As Figure 37.2 illustrates, a packet filter is embedded in a router. The filter consists of software that can prevent packets from passing through the router on a path from one network to another. A manager must configure the packet filter to specify which packets are permitted to pass through the router and which should be blocked†.

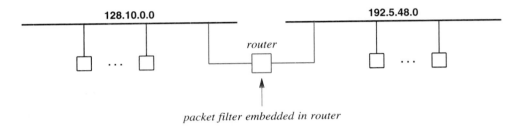

packet filter embedded in router

Figure 37.2 Illustration of the location of a packet filter. The filter software is configured to discard specified packets as they pass from one network to another.

A packet filter operates by examining fields in the header of each packet. The filter can be configured to specify which header fields to examine and how to interpret the values. To control which computers on a network can communicate with computers on another, a manager specifies that the filter should examine the *source* and *destination* fields in each datagram header. In the figure, to prevent a computer with IP address *192.5.48.27* on the right-hand network from communicating with any computers on the left-hand network, a manager specifies that the filter should block all packets with a source address equal to *192.5.48.27*. Similarly, to prevent a computer with address *128.10.0.32* on the left-hand network from receiving any packets from the right-hand network, a manager specifies that the filter should block all packets with a destination address equal to *128.10.0.32*.

In addition to using the source and destination IP addresses, a packet filter can examine the protocol in the packet or the high-level service to which the packet corresponds. The ability to selectively block packets for a particular service means that a manager can prevent traffic to one service, while allowing traffic to another. For example, a manager can configure a packet filter to block all packets that carry World Wide Web communication, while allowing packets that carry e-mail traffic.

---

†Some LAN switches provide a similar form of filtering that allows a manager to configure which frames are permitted to pass from one computer to another and which should be blocked.

A packet filter mechanism allows a manager to specify complex combinations of source and destination addresses, and service. Typically, the packet filter software permits a manager to specify Boolean combinations of source, destination, and service type. Thus, a manager can control access to specific services on specific computers. For example, a manager might choose to block all traffic destined for the FTP service on computer *128.10.2.14*, all World Wide Web traffic leaving computer *192.5.48.33*, and all e-mail from computer *192.5.48.34*. The filter blocks only the specified combinations — the filter passes traffic destined for other computers and traffic for other services on the specified computers.

37.12 Using Packet Filters To Create A Firewall

In practice, an Internet firewall consists of at least three systems. A packet filter restricts datagrams that arrive from the Internet. A separate packet filter restricts datagrams that leave the organization's intranet. Finally, a secure computer system in the firewall runs application software. Figure 37.3 illustrates the architecture.

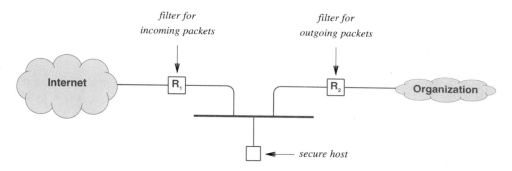

Figure 37.3 The architecture of a firewall with a secure computer bracketed by two packet filters. One filter restricts incoming packets, and the other restricts outgoing packets.

As the figure shows, the secure host is located on the network that also connects to the routers. Logically, the secure host is placed "between" the two packet filters — the packet filters are configured to direct packets to the host. That is, the filter in router R_1 is configured to reject all incoming packets except those to specific applications running on the secure host. Similarly, the filter in router R_2 is configured to reject all outgoing packets except those to applications running on the secure host. Thus, all communication between computers in the organization and the global Internet passes through the secure host.

What software is available on the secure host? A secure host runs special application programs known as *application-layer gateways* or *proxies* that provide secure Internet services. For example, suppose a user inside the organization wants to use FTP to obtain a file. When the user makes a request, client software on the user's computer contacts an FTP proxy on the secure host. When the client sends a request for a file, the proxy verifies that the request is allowed under the organization's security policy, obtains a copy of the file from a server on the Internet, checks the copy for viruses, and then passes the copy back to the user's computer. The application gateway software may also keep a log of all requests for offline auditing purposes.

37.13 Virtual Private Networks

A corporation with multiple geographic sites can use one of two approaches to building a corporate intranet:

- *Private Network Connections.* The corporation leases serial lines to connect its sites. Each leased connection extends from a router at one of the corporation's sites to a router at another site; data passes directly from a router at one site to a router at another site.

- *Public Internet Connections.* Each site contracts with a local ISP for Internet service. Data sent from one corporate site to another passes across the global Internet.

The chief advantage of using leased lines to interconnect sites arises because the resulting network is completely *private†*. No other organization has access to a leased line, so no other organization can read the data that passes from one corporate site to another. The chief advantage of using Internet connections is low cost — instead of paying for lines to connect sites, the corporation only needs to pay for Internet service from each site. Unfortunately, the Internet cannot guarantee confidentiality. As it travels from source to destination, a datagram passes across intermediate networks that may be shared. As a consequence, outsiders may be able to obtain copies of the datagram and examine the contents.

How can an organization's intranet be devised that has the advantage of confidentiality as well as the advantage of low cost? The answer lies in a technology that allows a corporation to create a *Virtual Private Network (VPN)*. The idea is straightforward: use the global Internet to transfer data among corporate sites, but take additional steps to ensure that the data cannot be read by outsiders.

A VPN is implemented in software. First, the organization obtains an Internet connection for each of its sites. Second, the organization chooses a router at each site to run VPN software (usually, the router that connects the site to the Internet). Third, the organization configures the VPN software in each router to know about the VPN routers at each of the other sites. Figure 37.4 illustrates the physical connections between each site and the Internet as well as the logical architecture imposed by the VPN software.

---

†Recall from Chapter 15 that the term *private network* is used for a network that keeps data confidential.

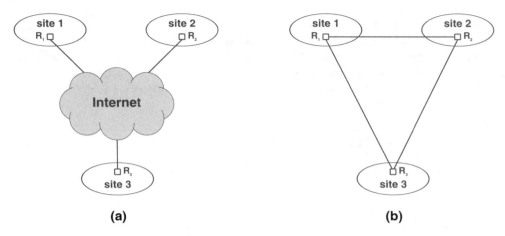

Figure 37.4 (a) The physical Internet connections between routers at three sites of an organization, and (b) the equivalent logical connections created by VPN software running on the routers.

As the figure shows, VPN software in a router at each site gives the appearance of a private network. To achieve the desired effect, VPN software must perform two functions. First, the VPN software operates like a conventional packet filter — the next hop for each outgoing datagram must be a VPN router at another site of the organization. Thus, traffic is restricted to pass directly from one corporate site to another exactly as if the sites had leased lines connecting them. Second, VPN software encrypts each outgoing datagram before transmission. As a result, all communication remains confidential. Even if an outsider does obtain a copy of a datagram, the outsider will not be able to interpret the contents.

37.14 Tunneling

Should the entire datagram be encrypted for transmission? On one hand, if the datagram header is encrypted, routers in the Internet will not be able to interpret header fields they need to use when forwarding the datagram. On the other hand, if the header is not encrypted, outsiders will know the source and destination addresses, and may be able to deduce information. For example, an outsider may be able to observe that shortly after the chief financial officer's computer communicates with the president's computer, the stock price increases.

To keep information completely hidden as datagrams pass across the Internet from one site to another, VPN software uses an *IP-in-IP tunnel*. That is, the sending VPN software encrypts the entire datagram, and places the result inside another datagram for transmission. For example, consider the connections in Figure 37.4 again. Suppose a computer X at site 1 creates a datagram for a computer Y at site 3. The datagram is forwarded through site 1 to router R_1 (i.e., the router that connects site 1 to the Internet). VPN software on R_1 encrypts the original datagram and encapsulates it in a new datagram for transmission to router R_2, the router at site 2. When the encapsulated datagram arrives, VPN software on R_2 decrypts the payload to extract the original datagram, and then forwards it to destination Y. Figure 37.5 illustrates the concept.

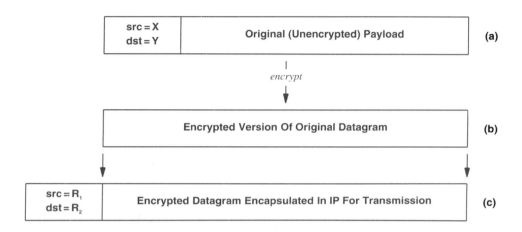

Figure 37.5 IP-in-IP encapsulation used over a VPN. (a) A datagram, (b) the
encrypted version of the datagram, and (c) the encrypted version
encapsulated in another datagram for transmission across the Internet.

As the figure shows, the original datagram header has the source and destination addresses of two computers in the organization. To keep data secure during transmission across the Internet, the entire original datagram, including the header, is encrypted. Thus, all datagrams traveling across the Internet from site 1 to site 2 have a source address of router R_1 and a destination address of router R_2.

37.15 Summary

Although most organizations want secure networks, it is not possible to give a single definition of security that satisfies all needs. Instead, each organization must assess the value of information and then define a security policy that specifies the items to be protected. Devising such a policy is complex because the policy must apply to information stored in arbitrary form or communicated by arbitrary means.

There are several aspects of security that need to be considered when defining a security policy. Data integrity refers to protection against change, data availability refers to protection against disruption of service, and data confidentiality and privacy refer to protection against snooping and discovery. In addition, an organization must consider accountability (i.e., how an audit trail is kept) and authorization (i.e., how responsibility for information is passed from one person to another).

A set of mechanisms have been created to provide various aspects of security. To keep information confidential in an internet environment, two computers can use encryption. The sender uses an algorithm to scramble a message, and the receiver uses the inverse mapping to reconstruct the original message from the scrambled version. One form of encryption and decryption has many uses. Known as *public-key encryption*, the form assigns each user two keys. One key is kept secret, but the other, called *public*, is published along with the owner's name. Public-key encryption is used for digital signatures — a sender uses his or her private key to encrypt a particular document. The receiver uses the sender's public key to decrypt the document. Because only the sender has the private key used to encrypt the document, the receiver knows unambiguously who sent the document.

To ensure that unwanted traffic does not interfere with its computers, an organization places an Internet firewall around the organization's perimeter (i.e., on each external connection). The firewall consists of *packet filters* that run in routers as well as a secure host that runs *application gateways*. The firewall is configured to prevent outsiders from accessing the organization's computers and to prevent computers inside the organization from accessing arbitrary computers on the Internet.

EXERCISES

37.1   If your organization has a firewall, draw a diagram of the architecture and show the packet filter configuration(s).

37.2   What are the security risks inherent in using an active document technology?

37.3   How can two parties use public key encryption to sign a contract that is then sent to a third party?

37.4   Build a client and server that send a file from one computer to another without revealing the contents during transmission.

37.5   In some VPN systems, a sender adds a random number of zero octets to a datagram before encrypting, and the receiver discards the extra octets after the datagram has been decrypted. Thus, the only effect of the random padding is to make the length of the encrypted datagram independent of the length of the unencrypted version. Why is length important? Hint: consider TCP and the direction of data transfer.

37.6   Read about the *Data Encryption Standard (DES)*. What size key should be used for data that is extremely important?

Chapter Contents

38

Initialization (Configuration)

38.1 Introduction

Previous chapters consider how networks and internets operate. They explain how protocol software allows a computer to communicate with other computers, and how packets flow across an internet. Later chapters describe the client-server paradigm, and explain how applications use client-server interaction when they communicate. In each case, the text assumes host computer systems and routers are already running. That is, each computer has been powered on, the operating system has started, protocol software has loaded, and values such as entries in the routing table have been initialized.

This chapter considers a fundamental question: how does the protocol software in a host or router begin operation? In particular, what steps must a computer system take before protocol software is ready to use? The chapter describes the variables that must be initialized, and explains mechanisms that can be used to assign values to those variables. The chapter explains why automatic initialization is needed, and describes a protocol that computers can use to obtain information automatically. Surprisingly, we will see that initialization is another example of application programs that use client-server.

38.2 Bootstrapping

What happens when a computer first begins operation? The process is known as *bootstrapping*†. When a user turns on the computer, the hardware searches permanent storage devices, usually disks, until it finds a device that contains a special program called a *boot program* at location zero. The hardware then copies the boot program into memory and branches to it. When the boot program runs, it accesses the storage device

---

†Sometimes abbreviated *booting*, the term is derived from the phrase ''pulling oneself up by one's own bootstraps.''

to read and load additional software (e.g., the operating system). Finally, after the software has been loaded, the operating system allows a user to run application programs. The operating system software remains resident in memory, making it possible for an application to invoke operating system services at any time.

38.3 Starting Protocol Software

When is protocol software loaded during bootstrapping? There is no single answer. On a computer that uses a dialup telephone modem for communication, protocol software can be embedded in applications. When a user invokes an application that needs to communicate, the application manages the modem; only one application can use the modem at any time. More sophisticated computer systems, especially those with permanent network connections, embed protocol software in the computer's operating system where it is shared by all applications. In such systems, the bootstrap process loads protocol software into memory along with the operating system. Thus, like other operating system functions, the protocol software is ready to use before any application program runs.

The question of how protocol software starts execution is further complicated because some systems use a computer network as part of the bootstrap process. For example, some computer systems use a network to download a copy of the operating system from a remote server. In such cases, a computer must have basic protocol capabilities built into the hardware or a bootstrap program. Later sections in this chapter describe examples of the basic protocols a computer uses to bootstrap.

38.4 Protocol Parameters

Protocol software must understand many details. For example, the software must know such details as the exact packet format, the header size, and the locations of fields in the header. Furthermore, the software must recognize addresses, and must know how to route packets to their destination. More important, the protocol software running on a specific computer must know many details about the computer. For example, the software must know the protocol address that has been assigned to the computer.

To make protocol software general and portable, programmers who implement protocol software do not fix all details in the source code. Instead, they *parameterize* protocol software to make it possible to use a single binary image on many computers. Each detail that differs from one computer to another is encoded in a separate parameter that can be changed. Before the software runs, a value must be supplied for each parameter. For example, most protocol software does not have a computer's address compiled into the code. Instead, the software has an *address parameter* that can be changed. Before the software can send or receive packets, a value must be supplied for the address.

We can summarize:

> *Protocol software is parameterized to allow a compiled binary to run on multiple computers without change. When a copy of the software is started on a given computer, information about the computer must be supplied to the software through parameters.*

38.5 Protocol Configuration

The act of supplying values for parameters in protocol software is known as *protocol configuration*. After a value has been supplied for each parameter, the protocol software is said to be *configured*. Protocol software must be configured before it can be used.

Although the concept of protocol configuration is easy to understand, the implementation can be complicated for three reasons. First, several mechanisms exist for obtaining the needed information. Second, several methods exist for passing the information to the protocol software. Third, a given computer system can choose to use multiple methods — some parameters can be obtained and specified using one method, while other parameters are obtained or specified using other methods. Furthermore, the system may allow some pieces of protocol software to be used before all pieces are configured. The next sections discuss configuration, and show why allowing protocols to operate after partial configuration can be useful.

38.6 Examples Of Items That Need To Be Configured

The configuration information that protocol software needs can be divided into two general classes: internal and external. Internal information pertains to the computer itself (e.g., the computer's protocol address). External information pertains to the environment that surrounds a computer (e.g., the location of printers that can be reached over the network).

The exact details of configuration information depend on the protocol stack. For example, the items TCP/IP protocol software needs to configure include:

- *IP address.* Each computer must have a unique IP address for each interface. Protocol software places the address in the *SOURCE ADDRESS* field in the header of all outgoing datagrams, and uses the address to recognize datagrams sent to the computer.

- *Default router address.* To communicate with computers on remote networks, a computer must know the address of at least one router. Protocol software places the address in its routing table as the next hop for a default route.

- *Subnet mask.* Protocol software must be configured with a subnet mask before the software can know whether IP subnet addressing is being used on the network and, if so, how many bits are used in the subnet portion of an address.

- *DNS server address.* Before application software on a computer can use the domain name system to translate a computer name to an IP address, the underlying protocol software must be configured with the address of a local DNS server.

- *Printer server addresses.* When an application specifies that data should be printed on a remote printer, protocol software must know the address of a server for that printer. One such address must be configured for each remote printer that can be accessed.

- *Other server addresses.* Most client programs specify the computer on which a server runs. However, some services are an integral part of the protocol software. For example, many computer systems expect protocol software to provide access to a *time of day* server that the system software can use to set the computer's clock. Protocol software must be configured with the address of a server for each such service.

38.7 Example Configuration: Using A Disk File

How does protocol software receive configuration information? Many computer systems use a file on the computer's disk. When the computer system begins execution, the protocol software reads the disk file and extracts values for parameters.

To make the configuration file convenient for a human to edit, many systems use a textual representation. For example, a configuration file might contain lines of the form:

```
parameter_name = value
```

where *parameter_name* is the name of a parameter, and *value* is the value to be assigned. The protocol software must convert values from the form used in the configuration file to the form used internally (e.g., numeric values might be converted from ASCII text to binary). Once it has converted the value to internal form, the protocol software stores the value in an appropriate variable in memory.

Configuration from a disk file usually occurs once, when the protocol software begins execution. Thus, changing the contents of the disk file has no effect on software that has started running. To force changes in the configuration file to take effect, the system administrator must notify the protocol software that reconfiguration is needed. Some systems provide a special mechanism for notification (e.g., in UNIX, a *signal* is sent to the protocol software). Other systems require that the operating system be rebooted before the protocol software will read the configuration file and use the new values.

38.8 The Need To Automate Protocol Configuration

The disadvantage of storing protocol configuration information in a disk file becomes obvious when an administrator must handle many computers or when an administrator must manage computers that are moved from one network to another. When a computer is moved, for example, most of the internal configuration information changes, and the external configuration information can change as well. If the configuration information resides in a file, the administrator must manually change the file before the new configuration can be used.

To see why such changes can become significant, consider laptop computers that can be moved easily. For example, imagine a student enrolled in a university carrying a portable computer. The student might attach the computer to a network in his or her dormitory each night, and attach the same computer to networks in one or more laboratories during the day†. Changing a configuration file two or more times a day is tiresome, and someone entering such changes manually can make a mistake. More important, if thousands of students move computers to new networks during the day, the effort required to enter configuration changes is overwhelming. To summarize:

> *Because portable computers can require protocol configuration information to change frequently, administrators who manage networks to which many portable computers attach cannot rely on manual update.*

38.9 Methods For Automated Protocol Configuration

Protocol designers have found ways to automate the configuration process. For example, some computer systems use a computer network as part of the bootstrap process. Instead of searching on local storage devices to find a bootstrap program, the computer hardware is designed to transmit a packet that contains a bootstrap request. A server on the network that is programmed to respond to such requests returns a series of packets that contain the bootstrap program.

Other computer systems are designed to boot the operating system from a local disk and to use the network to obtain protocol configuration information. For example, TCP/IP protocols include the *Reverse Address Resolution Protocol* (*RARP*) that a computer can use to determine its own IP address. The computer sends a *RARP request* to a server. The server returns a *RARP reply* that contains the computer's IP address.

The ICMP protocol described in Chapter 23 provides other examples that show how protocol software can use a network to obtain configuration information. ICMP includes *Address Mask Request* and *Router Discovery* messages. A host broadcasts a Router Discovery message to locate routers on the local network; routers respond by informing the host of their presence. A host sends an Address Mask Request to a router to request information about the address mask that is used on the network. The router receives the request, and sends an *Address Mask Reply* message that specifies the IP subnet mask.

---

†Wireless network technologies are making mobility among networks more common.

38.10 The Address Used To Find An Address

The protocols described above may seem impossible. After all, how can a computer send or receive packets before the protocol software has been configured? And how can a computer communicate with a server before the computer knows the address of the server? In the case of RARP, the answer to the first question is simple: although the computer does not know its IP address when it boots, the computer does know its hardware address. In fact, RARP can only be used on networks, such as an Ethernet, that have each computer's hardware address permanently fixed in the NIC hardware. RARP extracts the computer's hardware address from the NIC, places it in a *RARP request* message, and sends the request to a server. The server extracts the hardware address, consults a database that specifies the binding between a hardware address and an IP address, and returns a *RARP reply* message that contains the computer's IP address. To make it possible for RARP to send and receive frames, the computer system must initialize the network hardware before using RARP to configure IP.

To generalize:

> *In a layered protocol stack, layers are configured from lowest to highest, making it possible for a higher-layer protocol to use lower-layer protocols to obtain configuration information.*

The question of how a computer can communicate with a server before the computer knows the server's address is easy to answer: the computer simply broadcasts a request. For example, when sending a frame that contains a RARP request, a computer uses the hardware broadcast address as a destination address (RARP can only be used on networks that support broadcast). Similarly, a computer does not need to know the address of a router that will answer an *ICMP Address Mask Request*; the computer broadcasts the message and allows any router on the network to answer.

When a network contains multiple servers, broadcasting a request may result in multiple responses. To understand why, consider an example. According to the ICMP protocol standard, any router that receives an *ICMP Address Mask Request* must return an *ICMP Address Mask Reply*. If a computer broadcasts a request on a network to which multiple routers attach, each router will receive a copy, and each will return a response. As a consequence:

> *Any software that uses broadcast to reach a server must be prepared to receive multiple responses.*

Most implementations accept the first response and ignore others. However, because the network might also contain broadcast packets that are unrelated to the configuration request, each protocol must be designed so that a receiver can distinguish a valid response from other traffic on the network. For example, some protocols use the *TYPE* field in a hardware frame. Others place a randomly-generated identification number in a request, and then wait for a response that contains the same value.

38.11 A Sequence Of Protocols Used During Bootstrap

Using a separate protocol to obtain each piece of configuration information results in a sequence of configuration steps. Figure 38.1 illustrates the first few steps that TCP/IP protocol software configuration requires.

Step 1. Broadcast a *RARP Request* message to obtain an IP address.

Step 2. Wait for a *RARP Response* message. If none arrives within T_1 seconds, return to Step *1*.

Step 3. Broadcast an *ICMP Address Mask Request* message.

Step 4. Wait for an *ICMP Address Mask Response* message. If none arrives within T_2 seconds, return to Step *3*.

Step 5. Use *ICMP Gateway Discovery* to find the IP address of a default router, and add a default route to the routing table.

Figure 38.1 The first few steps that TCP/IP protocol software takes to obtain configuration information. T_1 and T_2 denote timeout values.

38.12 Bootstrap Protocol (BOOTP)

The chief advantage of using a separate step to obtain each item of configuration information is flexibility — each computer system can choose which items to obtain from a local file on disk and which to obtain over the network. The chief disadvantage becomes apparent when one considers the network traffic and delay. A given computer issues a series of small request messages. More important, each response returns a small value (e.g., a 4-octet IP address). Because networks enforce a minimum packet size, most of the space in each packet is wasted.

TCP/IP protocol designers observed that many of the configuration steps could be combined into a single step if a server was able to supply more than one item of configuration information. To provide such a service, the designers invented the *BOOTstrap Protocol* (*BOOTP*). To obtain configuration information, protocol software broadcasts a *BOOTP Request* message. A BOOTP server that receives the request looks up several pieces of configuration information for the computer that issued the request, places the information in a single *BOOTP Response* message, and returns the reply to the requesting computer. Thus, in a single step, a computer can obtain information such as the computer's IP address, the server's name and IP address, and the IP address of a default router.

Like other protocols used to obtain configuration information, BOOTP broadcasts each request. Unlike other protocols used for configuration, BOOTP appears to use a protocol that has not been configured: BOOTP uses IP to send a request and receive a response. How can BOOTP send an IP datagram before a computer's IP address has been configured? The answer lies in a careful design that allows IP to broadcast a request and receive a response before all values have been configured. To send a BOOTP datagram, IP uses the all-1's broadcast address as a *DESTINATION ADDRESS*, and uses the all-0's address as a *SOURCE ADDRESS*. If a computer uses the all-0's address to send a request, a BOOTP server either uses broadcast to return the response or uses the hardware address on the incoming frame to send a response via unicast†. Thus, a computer that does not know its IP address can communicate with a BOOTP server.

Figure 38.2 illustrates the BOOTP packet format.

0	8	16	24	31
OP	HTYPE	HLEN	HOPS	
TRANSACTION IDENTIFIER				
SECONDS ELAPSED		UNUSED		
CLIENT IP ADDRESS				
YOUR IP ADDRESS				
SERVER IP ADDRESS				
ROUTER IP ADDRESS				
CLIENT HARDWARE ADDRESS (16 OCTETS) ⋮				
SERVER HOST NAME (64 OCTETS) ⋮				
BOOT FILE NAME (128 OCTETS) ⋮				
VENDOR-SPECIFIC AREA (64 OCTETS) ⋮				

Figure 38.2 The format that BOOTP uses for request and response messages. The message is sent using UDP, which is encapsulated in IP.

Each field in a BOOTP message has a fixed size. The first seven fields contain information used to process the message. The *OP* field specifies whether the message is a *Request* or a *Response*, the *HTYPE* and *HLEN* fields specify the network hardware type and the length of a hardware address. The *HOPS* field specifies how many servers forwarded the request, and the *TRANSACTION IDENTIFIER* field provides a value that a client can use to determine if an incoming response matches its request. The *SECONDS ELAPSED* field specifies how many seconds have elapsed since the computer began to boot. Finally, if a computer knows its IP address (e.g., the address was obtained using RARP), the computer fills in the *CLIENT IP ADDRESS* field in a request.

---

†The server must be careful to avoid using ARP because a client that does not know its IP address cannot answer ARP requests.

Later fields are used in a response message to carry information back to the computer that is booting. If a computer does not know its address, the server uses field *YOUR IP ADDRESS* to supply the value. In addition, the server uses fields *SERVER IP ADDRESS* and *SERVER HOST NAME* to give the computer information about the location of a computer that runs servers. Field *ROUTER IP ADDRESS* contains the IP address of a default router.

In addition to protocol configuration, BOOTP allows a computer to negotiate to find a boot image. To do so, the computer fills in field *BOOT FILE NAME* with a generic request (e.g., the computer can request the UNIX operating system). The BOOTP server does not send an image. Instead, the server determines which file contains the requested image, and uses field *BOOT FILE NAME* to send back the name of the file. Once a BOOTP response arrives, a computer must use a protocol like TFTP to obtain a copy of the image.

38.13 Automatic Address Assignment

Although it simplifies loading parameters into protocol software, BOOTP does not solve the configuration problem completely. When a BOOTP server receives a request, the server looks up the computer in its database of information. Thus, even a computer that uses BOOTP cannot boot on a new network until the administrator manually changes information in the database.

Can protocol software be devised that allows a computer to join a new network without manual intervention? Yes — several such protocols exist. For example, IPX protocols generate a protocol address from the computer's hardware address. To make the IPX scheme work correctly, the hardware address must be unique. Furthermore, if the hardware address and protocol address are not the same size, it must be possible to translate the hardware address into a protocol address that is also unique.

The AppleTalk protocols use a *bidding* scheme to allow a computer to join a new network. When a computer first boots, the computer chooses a random address. For example, suppose computer *C* chooses address *17*. To ensure that no other computer on the network is using the address, *C* broadcasts a request message and starts a timer. If no other computer is using address *17*, no reply will arrive before the timer expires; *C* can begin using address *17*. If another computer is using *17*, the computer replies, causing *C* to choose a different address and begin again.

Choosing an address at random works well for small networks and for computers that run client software. However, the scheme does not work well for servers. To understand why, recall that each server must be located at a well-known address. If a computer chooses an address at random when it boots, clients will not know which address to use when contacting a server on that computer. More important, because the address can change each time a computer boots, the address used to reach a server may not remain the same after a crash and reboot.

A bidding scheme also has the disadvantage that two computers can choose the same network address. In particular, assume that computer B sends a request for an address that another computer (e.g., A) is already using. If A fails to respond to the request for any reason, both computers will attempt to use the same address, with disastrous results. In practice, such failures can occur for a variety of reasons. For example, a piece of network equipment such as a bridge can fail, a computer can be unplugged from the network when the request is sent, or a computer can be temporarily unavailable (e.g., in a hibernation mode designed to conserve power). Finally, a computer can fail to answer if the protocol software or operating system is not functioning correctly.

38.14 Dynamic Host Configuration Protocol (DHCP)

To automate configuration, the IETF devised the *Dynamic Host Configuration Protocol (DHCP)*. Unlike BOOTP, DHCP does not require an administrator to add an entry for each computer to the database that a server uses. Instead, DHCP provides a mechanism that allows a computer to join a new network and obtain an IP address without manual intervention. The concept has been termed *plug-and-play networking*. More important, DHCP accommodates computers that run server software as well as computers that run client software:

- When a computer that runs client software is moved to a new network, the computer can use DHCP to obtain configuration information without manual intervention.

- DHCP allows nonmobile computers that run server software to be assigned a permanent address; the address will not change when the computer reboots.

To accommodate both types of computers, DHCP cannot use a bidding scheme. Instead, it uses a client-server approach. When a computer boots, the computer broadcasts a *DHCP Request* to which a server sends a *DHCP Reply†*. An administrator can configure a DHCP server to have two types of addresses: permanent addresses that are assigned to server computers, and a pool of addresses to be allocated on demand. When a computer boots and sends a request to DHCP, the DHCP server consults its database to find configuration information. If the database contains a specific entry for the computer, the server returns the information from the entry. If no entry exists for the computer, the server chooses the next IP address from the pool, and assigns the address to the computer.

---

†The reply is actually classified as a DHCP *offer* message that contains an address the server is offering to the client.

In fact, addresses assigned on demand are not permanent. Instead, DHCP issues a *lease* on the address for a finite period of time†. When the lease expires, the computer must renegotiate with DHCP to extend the lease. Normally, DHCP will approve a lease extension. However, a site may choose an administrative policy that denies the extension (e.g., a university that has a network in a classroom might choose to deny extensions on leases at the end of a class period to allow the next class to reuse the same addresses). If DHCP denies an extension request, the computer must stop using the address.

38.15 Optimizations In DHCP

If the computers on a network use DHCP to obtain configuration information when they boot, an event that causes all computers to restart at the same time can cause the network or server to be flooded with requests. To avoid the problem, DHCP uses the same technique as BOOTP: each computer waits a random time before transmitting or retransmitting a request.

The DHCP protocol has two steps: one in which a computer broadcasts a *DHCP Discover* message to find a DHCP server, and another in which the computer selects one of the servers that responded to its message and sends a request to that server. To avoid having a computer repeat both steps each time it boots or each time it needs to extend the lease, DHCP uses *caching*. When a computer discovers a DHCP server, the computer saves the server's address in a cache on permanent storage (e.g., a disk file). Similarly, once it obtains an IP address, the computer saves the IP address in a cache. When a computer reboots, it uses the cached information to revalidate its former address. Doing so saves time and reduces network traffic.

38.16 DHCP Message Format

Interestingly, DHCP is designed as an extension of BOOTP. As Figure 38.3 illustrates, DHCP uses a slightly modified version of the BOOTP message format.

---

†When the administrator establishes a pool of addresses for DHCP to assign, the administrator must also specify the length of the lease for each address.

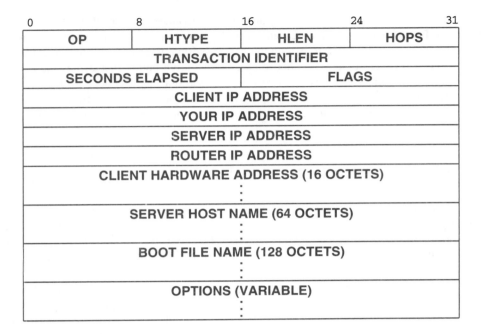

Figure 38.3 The DHCP message format, a slightly modified version of the
BOOTP format.

Most of the fields in a DHCP message have the same meaning as in BOOTP;
DHCP replaces the 16-bit *UNUSED* field with a *FLAGS* field, and uses the *OPTIONS*
field to encode additional information. For example, as in BOOTP, the *OP* field specifies either a *Request* or a *Response*. To distinguish among various messages that a
client uses to discover servers or request an address, or that a server uses to acknowl-
edge or deny a request, DHCP uses a *message type option*. That is, each message contains a code that identifies the message type.

38.17 DHCP And Domain Names

Although DHCP makes it possible for a computer to obtain an IP address without
manual intervention, DHCP does not interact with the Domain Name System. As a
result, a computer cannot keep its name when it changes addresses. Interestingly, the
computer does not need to move to a new network to have its name change. For example, suppose a computer obtains IP address *192.5.48.195* from DHCP, and suppose the
domain name system contains a record that binds the name *x.y.z.com* to the address.
Now consider what happens if the owner turns off the computer and takes a two-month
vacation during which the address lease expires. DHCP may assign the address to

another computer. When the owner returns and turns on the computer, DHCP will deny the request to use the same address. Thus, the computer will obtain a new address. Unfortunately, the DNS continues to map the name *x.y.z.com* to the old address.

For several years, researchers have been considering how DHCP should interact with the DNS. Although a dynamic DNS udpate protocol has been defined, it has not been widely deployed. Thus, sites that use DHCP often do not have a mechanism to udpate a DNS database. From a user's perspective, the lack of communication between DHCP and DNS means that when a computer is assigned a new address, the computer's name changes.

38.18 Summary

To make protocol software portable, the software is parameterized. Parameters correspond to internal values such as the address that is associated with the computer or to external values such as the address of a default router. The chief value of parameterization is that the same compiled binary code can run on many computers.

Values for parameters must be filled in before protocol software can be used; the process is known as *configuration*. Some computer systems read configuration information from a file on permanent storage; others use a network to obtain the information. When using a network, layers of protocol software are configured in order from lowest to highest, making it possible for each layer to use layers beneath it to communicate.

Initially, separate protocols were used to obtain each piece of configuration information for TCP/IP protocols. For example, a computer can send a *RARP Request* to obtain an IP address, and an *ICMP Address Mask Request* to obtain the subnet mask being used on the network. The BOOTstrap Protocol, BOOTP, was invented to consolidate separate requests into a single protocol. A BOOTP response provides information such as the computer's IP address, the address of a default router, and the name of a file that contains a boot image.

The Dynamic Host Configuration Protocol (DHCP) extends BOOTP. In addition to permanent addresses assigned to computers that run a server, DHCP permits completely automated address assignment. That is, DHCP allows a computer to join a new network, obtain a valid IP address, and begin using the address without requiring an administrator to enter information about the computer in a server's database.

When DHCP allocates an address automatically, the DHCP server does not assign the address forever. Instead, the server specifies a lease during which the address may be used. A computer must extend the lease, or stop using the address when the lease expires.

EXERCISES

38.1   If any computers in your organization use a network to boot, find out which protocols they use.

38.2   Make a list of all the information that can be configured when a computer boots.

38.3   Some network applications defer configuration until a service is needed. For example, a computer can wait until a user attempts to print a document before the software searches for available printers. What is the chief advantage of deferred configuration? The chief disadvantage?

38.4   Build a server program and a client program that use deferred configuration as described in the previous exercise. Have the client broadcast to find one or more servers, ask the user to select a particular server, and then contact that server.

38.5   A *RARP* reply contains address binding information about the sender (i.e., the server) as well as the computer that made the request. Does a computer that receives a *RARP* reply save the information about the server, or does the computer ignore the information and use a protocol to obtain the binding again? To find out, use a network analyzer. Look for *RARP* and *ARP* messages. After receiving a *RARP* reply from server *Y*, does a computer send an *ARP* request to find *Y*'s address binding? Can you explain the results?

38.6   Before a computer can use a network to boot, the computer must have some protocol code stored locally. Make a list of protocols that must be available before a computer can use *BOOTP* to boot.

38.7   Compare an address assignment protocol that uses bidding and a protocol that uses a server (e.g., DHCP). Which type of protocol works best on a WAN? on a busy LAN? Why?

38.8   BOOTP and DHCP permit servers to be located on remote networks. If a computer is restricted to using the local hardware broadcast address (e.g., all *1*s) before it obtains an IP address, how can the computer send BOOTP or DHCP messages to a server on another network? (Hint: read about BOOTP or DHCP *relay agents*.)

38.9   Devise a distributed algorithm that implements a bidding scheme. Assume that one copy of the algorithm will run on each computer, and have the algorithm assign each computer a unique address. Should all copies of the algorithm use the same initial value? Why or why not?

38.10   Extend the previous exercise by writing a computer program that implements the algorithm. Run multiple copies of the program, and test to see that each copy is assigned a unique number.

Appendix 1

Glossary Of Networking Terms And Abbreviations

Networking Terminology

Networking terminology can be extremely confusing to beginners because the terminology is neither logical nor consistent. There are three reasons. First, because no single theory explains all of networking, the terminology is not derived from one underlying theoretical framework. Second, because many groups and organizations have developed and standardized networking technologies, there are variations in terminology. Third, practitioners have invented informal terms and abbreviations that are often used in place of formal technical terms.

The glossary in this appendix includes terminology used in practice as well as technical terms found in literature. The definitions are brief — they include neither detailed explanations of terms nor examples. Instead, the definitions are meant to refresh the reader's memory by giving an overview of the general concept associated with each term.

Acronyms and terms are listed in alphabetical order†, with the expansion of an acronym given in parentheses. For example, the acronym *MTU* is followed by the expansion, *(Maximum Transmission Unit)*.

---

†To make items easier to find, the alphabetical order of entries ignores differences between uppercase and lowercase.

Networking Terms and Abbreviations
In Alphabetical Order

10BaseT
The technical name for twisted pair Ethernet.

2-3 swap
A reference to a cable in which the wire used to transmit on one end connects to the wire used to receive on the other, and vice-versa. The numbers *2* and *3* refer to the transmit and receive pins on a DB-25 connector.

2B+D service
An ISDN service that includes two standard telephone connections plus a data connection.

3-way handshake
A technique used by TCP and other transport protocols to reliably start or gracefully terminate communication.

3-wire circuit
A wiring scheme often used with asynchronous serial connections between a pair of computers. The first wire is used to transmit data from one computer to another, the second wire is used to transmit data in the reverse direction, and the third wire is a common electrical ground.

4-wire circuit
A wiring scheme often used with asynchronous serial connections between a pair of computers. One pair of wires is used to carry data in one direction and the other pair is used to carry data in the reverse direction. A 4-wire circuit is usually used to span longer distances than a 3-wire circuit.

7-layer reference model
An early conceptual model devised by the International Organization for Standardization to specify how a set of protocols work together to provide communication services. The 7-layer model did not include an internet protocol layer.

802.2
The IEEE Standard for Logical Link Control. See LLC and SNAP.

802.3
The IEEE standard for Ethernet.

802.5

The IEEE standard for Token Ring.

AAL5 (ATM Adaptation Layer 5)

The protocol an application uses to send data over an ATM network. AAL5, which is part of the ATM stack, accepts and delivers large packets of data (up to 64K bytes).

access delay

The time a network interface waits before it can access a shared network.

acknowledgement

A short message returned to inform a sender that data has arrived at its intended destination.

active document

A World Wide Web document that is a computer program. After downloading an active document, the browser runs the program on the user's computer. The active document can change the display continuously. See dynamic document, static document, and URL.

adaptive retransmission

The ability of a transport protocol to change its retransmission timer continuously to accommodate variations in internet delay. TCP is the best known protocol that uses adaptive retransmission.

address

A unique binary value assigned to a computer; network hardware and software uses the address in a packet to forward the packet to its destination.

address mask

A 32-bit value that specifies the bits of an IP address that correspond to a network and a subnet. Address bits not covered by the mask correspond to the host portion. Also called a subnet mask.

address resolution

The mapping from one address to another, usually from a high-level address (e.g., an IP address) to a low-level address (e.g., an Ethernet address).

ADSL (Asymmetric Digital Subscriber Line)

A technology to deliver digital information at high-speed over the same twisted pair wiring used to deliver telephone service. The downstream bit rate is higher than the upstream rate because most subscribers retrieve much more information than they send. See HDSL.

anonymous FTP

Access to an FTP server using the login name *anonymous* and the password *guest*. Not all FTP servers permit anonymous FTP.

APCM (Adaptive Pulse Code Modulation)

A scheme for digital encoding of audio in which successive values represent differences in the sampled wave instead of absolute values. See PCM.

API (Application Program Interface)

A generic reference to a set of procedures that an application program uses to access a service. A network API consists of procedures a program uses to access protocol software; the most well-known is the socket API.

applet

A computer program that forms the central part of an active World Wide Web document. An applet is written in a programming language such as Java.

AppleTalk

A set of network protocols developed and sold by Apple Computer Corporation.

application-layer gateway

A program that acts as a proxy to provide service indirectly. Application gateways are used in Internet firewalls to allow employees in an organization to access the Internet according to the organization's security policy.

area

An OSPF term for a set of routers that use OSPF to exchange link-status information.

ARP (Address Resolution Protocol)

The protocol a computer uses to map an IP address into a hardware address. A computer that invokes ARP broadcasts a request to which the target computer replies.

AS (Autonomous System)

A group of networks and routers under one administrative authority. For routing purposes, the Internet is divided into Autonomous Systems.

ASCII (American Standard Code for Information Interchange)

A standard that assigns unique values to 128 characters, including upper and lower case letters, digits, punctuation, and control characters. Details can be found in Appendix 2. See EBCDIC.

ASN.1 (Abstract Syntax Notation.1)

A standard for representing data. The SNMP protocol uses ASN.1 to represent object names.

ASP (Active Server Pages)

A dynamic web page technology closely linked to Microsoft's web server. The server interprets Visual Basic code that is embedded in each page whenever the page is requested.

asynchronous

Characteristic of any communication system in which the sender can transmit data without warning. The receiver must be prepared to accept data at any time. See synchronous.

ATM (Asynchronous Transfer Mode)

A connection-oriented technology defined by the ITU and the ATM Forum. At the lowest level, ATM sends data in fixed cells with *48* octets of data per cell.

AUI (Attachment Unit Interface)

The type of connector used with thick wire Ethernet. An AUI connection exists between a computer and an Ethernet transceiver.

AWT (Abstract Window Toolkit)

A library of graphics procedures used with the Java language to manipulate windows on a bit-mapped display. At various times, the designers have expanded AWT to Alternative Window Toolkit and Applet Widget Toolkit.

B channel (Bearer channel)

The term telephone companies use to denote a channel configured to handle a voice telephone circuit. ISDN includes B channel service. See D channel.

bandwidth

A measure of the capacity of a transmission system. Bandwidth is measured in Hertz.

base header

The required header found at the beginning of an IPv6 datagram.

baseband technology

The term used to describe a networking technology that uses a small part of the electromagnetic spectrum and sends only one signal at a time over the underlying medium. Most LANs use baseband signaling (e.g., Ethernet and FDDI). See broadband technology.

baud

The number of changes in a signal per second. Each change can encode one or more bits of information.

best-effort

Characteristic of any network system that makes a best attempt to deliver data, but does not guarantee delivery. Many networks use the best-effort approach.

BGP (Border Gateway Protocol)

The main Exterior Gateway Protocol used in the Internet. BGP provides routing among Autonomous Systems.

bidding

A technique protocols use for dynamic address configuration. A computer selects an address at random, and broadcasts a message to determine whether the address is in use. Alternative schemes use servers to manage addresses. See DHCP.

binary exponential backoff

The scheme used by computers on an Ethernet following a collision. Each computer doubles the time it waits after each successive collision.

BNC connector

The type of connector used with thin wire Ethernet.

BOOTP (BOOTstrap Protocol)

A protocol that a computer uses when it first starts to obtain information needed to configure the protocol software. BOOTP uses IP and UDP to broadcast a request and receive a response before IP has been completely configured.

bps (bits per second)

The rate at which data can be transmitted across a network. The number of bits per second may differ from the baud rate because more than one bit can be encoded in a single baud.

BRI (Basic Rate Interface)

The ISDN service that provides two B channels plus a data channel. BRI is suitable for small businesses. See PRI.

bridge

A hardware device that connects two LAN segments and copies frames from one to the other. Most bridge hardware uses physical addresses to learn which computers attach to which segments so the bridge can avoid copying frames unless needed.

broadband technology

The term used to describe a networking technology that uses a large part of the electromagnetic spectrum to achieve higher throughput rates. Usually broadband systems employ frequency division multiplexing to allow multiple, independent communications to proceed simultaneously over a single underlying medium. See baseband technology.

broadcast

A form of delivery in which one copy of a packet is delivered to each computer on a network. See cluster, multicast, and unicast.

broadcast address

A special address that causes the underlying system to deliver a copy of a packet to all computers on a network.

broadcast satellite

A network system in which a satellite broadcasts all packets and allows individual receivers to discard packets intended for other recipients.

browser

A computer program that accesses and displays information from the World Wide Web. A browser contains multiple application programs, and uses an object's name to determine which application should be used to access the object. See URL.

bus topology

A network architecture in which all computers attach to a shared medium, often a single cable. The bus architecture is mainly used for Local Area Networks.

byte stuffing

A protocol technique in which data is changed by inserting additional bytes to distinguish between data values and packet control values (i.e. headers).

cable modem

A modem used to send digital information over the coaxial cables used for cable television.

carrier

The basic signal transmitted across a network. A carrier is modulated (i.e., changed) to encode data.

category 5 cable

A type of wiring needed for twisted pair Ethernet. The electrical characteristics of category 5 make it less susceptible to electrical interference than lower categories.

CATV (Community Antenna TeleVision)

The name applied to cable television systems. CATV technology uses frequency division multiplexing to propagate multiple television channels over a single cable simultaneously. See cable modem.

CBT (Core Based Trees)

A protocol for propagating multicast routing information.

CCITT (Consultative Committee on International Telephone and Telegraph)

The former name of the ITU.

CDDI (Copper Distributed Data Interconnection)

FDDI technology adapted to run over copper wire.

cell

A small, fixed size packet (e.g., ATM networks send 48-octet cells).

cell tax

A pejorative term used to refer to the 10% header overhead introduced by ATM.

CGI (Common Gateway Interface)

A technology used to create dynamic World Wide Web documents. CGI programs run on the server computer.

chat

An Internet service that allows multiple users to communicate by entering text that is displayed on the screens of other participants.

checksum

A value used to verify that data is not corrupted during transmission. The sender computes a checksum by adding the binary values of the data, and transmits the result in a packet with the data. A receiver computes a checksum over the data received, and compares the value to the checksum in the packet. See CRC.

CIDR (Classless Inter-Domain Routing)

The IP addressing and routing scheme that replaced classful addressing. CIDR uses a 32-bit address mask to denote the boundary between the prefix and suffix of an IP address.

CL (ConnectionLess)

Characteristic of a network in which each transmission is independent. The alternative to connectionless networking is connection-oriented networking.

classful addressing

Characteristic of the original IP addressing scheme in which unicast addresses were divided into three primary classes. The class of an address determines the division between the prefix and suffix in the address. See classless addressing.

classless addressing

Characteristic of the current IP addressing scheme in which a 32-bit address mask is used to determine the division between the prefix and suffix of an IP address. See classful addressing.

client

When two programs communicate over a network, a client is the one that initiates communication, while the program that waits to be contacted is a server. A given program can act as a server for one service and a client for another.

client-server paradigm

The method of interaction used when two application programs communicate over a network. A server application waits at a known address, and a client application contacts the server.

cluster

A form of addressing used by IPv6 in which a set of computers is assigned one address; a datagram sent to the address can be delivered to any one of the computers in the set. See broadcast, multicast, and unicast.

CO (Connection-Oriented)

Characteristic of a network in which a connection must be established before data can be sent, and terminated after all data has been transferred. The alternative to connection-oriented networking is connectionless networking.

coaxial cable

A type of cable used for computer networks as well as for cable television. The name arises from the structure in which a metal shield surrounds a center wire. The shield protects the signal on the inner wire from electrical interference.

ColdFusion

A dynamic web page technology that allows items in a page to come from a conventional database. The server interprets SQL queries embedded in each page whenever the page is requested.

collision

An event that occurs on a CSMA/CD network when two stations attempt to transmit simultaneously. The signals interfere with each other, forcing the two stations to back off and try again.

colon hexadecimal notation

The syntactic notation used to express an IPv6 address.

congestion

A condition in which each packet sent through a network experiences excessive delay because the network is overrun with packets. Unless protocol software detects congestion and reduces the rate at which packets are sent, a network can experience congestion collapse.

connection-oriented

A characteristic of a network system that requires a pair of computers to establish a connection before sending data. Connection-oriented networks are analogous to a telephone system in which a call must be placed and answered before communication can begin. See connectionless.

connectionless

A characteristic of a network system that allows a computer to send data to any other computer at any time. Connectionless networks are analogous to a postal system in which each letter carries the address of the recipient; letters can be sent at any time. See connection-oriented.

cookie

A small value a web server passes to a browser in a reply to help the server identify the user. A browser returns the cookie when sending subsequent requests from the user to the server that issued the cookie.

CRC (Cyclic Redundancy Check)

A value used to verify that data is not corrupted during transmission. The sender computes a CRC and transmits the result in a packet with the data. A receiver computes the CRC over the data received, and compares the value to the CRC in the packet. A CRC is more complex to compute than a checksum, but can detect more transmission errors.

CSMA (Carrier Sense Multiple Access)

The technique used with bus architecture networks in which computers attached to the common bus check for the presence of a carrier before transmitting.

CSMA/CD (Carrier Sense Multiple Access with Collision Detection)

A CSMA network that has the capability to detect errors that result when multiple stations transmit simultaneously. See collision.

D channel

The term telephone companies use to denote a channel configured to handle data. ISDN includes D channel service. See B channel.

DB-25

A 25-pin connector often used with serial lines.

default route

A wild-card entry in a routing table. The routing software follows the default route if the table does not contain an explicit route to the destination.

delay-bandwidth product

A measure of a network that specifies the amount of data that is present in the network between the sender and receiver.

demodulator

A device that accepts a modulated carrier wave and extracts the information used to modulate it. See modem.

demultiplex

A general concept that refers to separating information received over a common communication channel into its original components. Demultiplexing occurs both in hardware (i.e., electrical signals can be demultiplexed) and in software (i.e., protocol software can demultiplex incoming messages and pass each to the correct application program). See multiplex.

denial-of-service

A form of network attack in which a site is flooded with so many fictitious requests or packets that the site cannot respond to legitimate requests.

destination address

An address in a packet that specifies the ultimate destination to which the packet is sent. In a hardware frame, the destination address must be a hardware address. In an IP datagram, the destination address must be an IP address.

DHCP (Dynamic Host Configuration Protocol)

A protocol that computers use to obtain configuration information. DHCP allows a computer to be assigned an IP address without requiring a manager to configure information about the computer in a server's database.

dialup modem

A modem that uses the dialup telephone network to communicate. Dialup modems use an audible tone as a carrier wave, and must be able to dial or answer a telephone call.

digital signature

Data encrypted in such a way that the receiver can verify the identity of the sender.

Dijkstra's algorithm

An algorithm for computing shortest paths in a graph. Routing protocols use Dijkstra's algorithm to compute optimal routes.

directed broadcast

A broadcast to all computers on a remote network achieved by sending a single copy of the packet to the remote network and broadcasting the packet when it arrives. TCP/IP supports directed broadcast.

distance-vector

An algorithm that routers use to compute optimal routes to each destination. Periodically, each router receives routing information from neighboring routers. A router replaces a current route if a lower cost route becomes available. See link-status and SPF.

distributed spanning tree

An algorithm that bridges use when they boot to detect and break cycles.

DIX Ethernet (Digital Intel Xerox Ethernet)

A term used for the original Ethernet because the standard was developed jointly by the three companies.

DNS (Domain Name System)

The automated system used to translate computer names into equivalent IP addresses. A DNS server responds to a query by looking up the name and returning the address. See domain.

domain

A subtree of the computer naming hierarchy used in the Internet. For example, commercial organizations have names registered under the *.com* domain.

dotted decimal notation

The syntactic notation used to express a 32-bit IPv4 address. Each octet is written in decimal with a period separating octets.

downlink

The path of data transmitted from a satellite to an earth station. See uplink.

downstream

The path of data from the Internet to a residential customer. The term is often used with DSL or cable modem technologies. See upstream.

DS-1, DS-3

The designations that telephone companies use for the speeds of popular point-to-point digital circuits. DS-1 denotes 1.544 Mbps and DS-3 denotes 44.736 Mbps. See T1, T3.

DSL (Digital Subscriber Line)

A generic reference to any of the services such as ADSL and HDSL that supply broadband data rates over telephone lines.

DSU/CSU (Data Service Unit / Channel Service Unit)

An electronic device that connects a leased digital data circuit to computer equipment. The DSU/CSU translates between the digital format used by the telephone companies and the format used by the computer industry. See modem.

DV (Distance Vector)

One of two basic algorithms used by routing protocols. The alternative to distance vector routing is link-status routing.

DVMRP (Distance Vector Multicast Routing Protocol)

The multicast routing protocol used on the MBONE. DVMRP sends multicast locally, but uses IP-in-IP tunneling to transfer multicast datagrams among sites.

dynamic document

A computer program, associated with a World Wide Web document, that can generate a document on demand. When a browser requests a dynamic document, the server runs the program and sends the output to the browser. A dynamic document program can generate different output for each request. See active document, static document, and URL.

e-mail (electronic mail)

A popular application in which a user or computer sends a memo to one or more recipients.

EBCDIC (Extended Binary Coded Decimal Interchange Code)

A standard that assigns unique values to 256 characters, including upper and lower case letters, digits, punctuation, and control characters. See ASCII.

echo reply

A message used for testing and debugging. An ICMP echo reply is returned in answer to an ICMP echo request message. The ping program receives echo replies. See echo request.

echo request

A message used for testing and debugging. The ping program sends ICMP echo request messages to elicit echo replies. See echo reply.

EGP (Exterior Gateway Protocol)

Term applied to any route propagation protocol used to transfer routing information among Autonomous Systems. Also see IGP.

encapsulation

The technique in which information to be sent is placed inside the data area of a packet or frame. A packet from one protocol can be encapsulated in another (e.g., ICMP can be encapsulated in IP).

encryption key

The short value used when encrypting data to guarantee confidentiality. In some encryption schemes, the receiver must use the same key to decrypt the data. Other schemes use a pair of keys — one to encrypt and a different key to decrypt.

end-to-end

Characteristic of any protocol or function that operates on the original source and ultimate destination, but not on intermediate computers (e.g., not on routers).

endpoint address

A generic term for any address assigned to a computer that can be used as a destination address. For example, an IP address is one type of endpoint address.

Ethernet

A popular Local Area Network technology that uses a shared bus topology and CSMA/CD access. Basic Ethernet operates at 10 Mbps, Fast Ethernet operates at 100 Mbps, and Gigabit Ethernet operates at 1000 Mbps (i.e., 1 Gbps).

even parity

A parity bit added to a unit of data, usually each character, to make the number of *1* bits even. A receiver checks the parity to determine whether data has been corrupted during transmission. See odd parity.

extension header

An optional header used in the IPv6 protocol.

exterior switch

A switch in a packet switched network to which host computers connect. See interior switch.

Fast Ethernet

A version of Ethernet technology that operates at 100 Mbps.

FDDI (Fiber Distributed Data Interconnect)

A Local Area Network technology that uses fiber optics to interconnect stations in a ring topology.

FDM (Frequency Division Multiplexing)

Characteristic of a mechanism used to share a communication medium among multiple senders in which each sender is assigned a unique frequency or channel. Because they use separate frequencies, the simultaneous transmissions do not interfere with one another. See TDM.

feeder circuit

A term used with cable television that refers to the wiring between a neighborhood concentration point and individual subscribers. A feeder circuit is less than two miles long. See trunk circuit.

fiber

Abbreviation for optical fiber.

fiber modem

A modem that uses modulated light waves to provide digital communication. A fiber modem uses light emitting diodes or lasers to transmit light. See optical fiber.

flow control

A protocol mechanism that allows a receiver to control the rate at which a sender transmits data. Flow control makes it possible for a receiver running on a low-speed computer to accept data from a high-speed computer without being overrun.

forward
See store and forward.

fragment
A small IP datagram produced by fragmentation.

fragmentation
The technique IP uses to divide a large datagram into smaller datagrams called fragments. The ultimate destination reassembles the fragments. See reassembly.

frame
The form of a packet that the underlying hardware accepts and delivers.

Frame Relay
A Wide Area Network technology that provides connection-oriented service.

framing error
An error that occurs on asynchronous serial lines in which the receiver does not detect a valid frame (usually a character). Differences in the sender's and receiver's baud rate can cause framing errors.

frequency division multiplexing
See FDM.

FTP (File Transfer Protocol)
A protocol used to transfer a complete file from one computer to another.

FTTC (Fiber To The Curb)
A technology proposed as a replacement for the existing cable television infrastructure that uses fiber optic trunks and a combination of coaxial cable and twisted pair to each subscriber.

full-duplex transmission
A communication between two computers in which data can flow in both directions at the same time. Full-duplex transmission requires two independent channels, one for data in each direction. See half-duplex transmission.

Gbps (Giga bits per second)
A unit of data transfer equal to *1000* Mbps or 10^9 bps.

GEO (Geostationary Earth Orbit)
A height for communication satellites that causes their orbit to match the rotation of the earth (approximately 36,000 kilometers or 20,000 miles). Also called Geosynchronous Earth Orbit. See LEO.

GIF (Graphics Interchange Format)

A standard format for storing a graphics image. GIF images are especially popular on the World Wide Web.

Gigabit Ethernet

A version of Ethernet technology that operates at 1000 Mbps (i.e., 1 Gbps).

half-duplex transmission

A communication between two computers in which data can flow in only one direction at a given time. Half-duplex transmission requires less hardware than full-duplex transmission because a single, shared physical medium can be used for all communication. See full-duplex transmission.

hardware address

The address assigned to a computer that attaches to a network. A frame sent from one computer to another must contain the recipient's hardware address. A hardware address is also called a physical address or a MAC address.

HDSL (High-rate Digital Subscriber Line)

A technology developed by the phone companies to provide high speed digital service over local loop wiring. See ADSL.

Hertz

A unit of measure equal to an oscillation per second. Hardware bandwidth is measured in multiples of Hertz.

HFC (Hybrid Fiber Coax)

A replacement for the existing cable television infrastructure that uses optical fiber trunks with coaxial cable connections to each subscriber and provides 2-way digital information transfer in addition to television signals. See cable modem.

hierarchical addressing

An addressing scheme in which part of an address gives information about the location. For example, a telephone number is hierarchical because it begins with an area code followed by an exchange.

homepage

A document stored on a World Wide Web server that is the starting point for obtaining information about a particular individual, company, group, or topic. A homepage can contain pointers to additional pages of related information or to homepages for other topics.

hop

A unit of measure used by Internet routing protocols. Each network counts as one hop.

hop count

A number in a protocol header that determines how many intermediate machines a packet visits. Protocols like IP require the sender to specify a maximum hop count; doing so prevents a packet from traveling around a routing loop forever.

hop limit

A synonym for hop count that is used by IPv6.

host

An end-user's computer connected to a network. In an internet, each computer is classified as a host or a router.

HTML (HyperText Markup Language)

The source form used for documents on the World Wide Web. HTML embeds commands that determine formatting along with the text to be displayed (e.g., to move to a new line or indent text).

HTTP (HyperText Transfer Protocol)

The protocol used to transfer a World Wide Web page from one computer to another.

hub

An electronic device that implements a network. Computers connected to a hub can communicate as if they attach to a network.

hypermedia

A set of documents in which a given document can contain text, graphics, video and audio clips as well as embedded references to other documents. World Wide Web pages are hypermedia documents.

hypertext

A set of documents in which a given document can contain text as well as embedded references to other documents. See hypermedia.

IANA (Internet Assigned Number Authority)

The organization responsible for assigning numbers that the TCP/IP protocols use. For example, IANA assigns numeric values used in protocol header fields.

IBM Token Ring
A Local Area Network technology developed by IBM Corporation that uses a ring topology.

ICMP (Internet Control Message Protocol)
The protocol that IP uses to report errors and exceptions. ICMP also includes informational messages used by programs like ping.

IGMP (Internet Group Multicast Protocol)
The protocol a host uses to inform a router when it joins (or leaves) an Internet multicast group. IGMP is only used on a local network; a router must use another multicast routing protocol to inform other routers of group membership.

IGP (Interior Gateway Protocol)
Term applied to any route propagation protocol used to transfer routing information within a single Autonomous Systems. Also see EGP.

interior switch
A switch in a packet switched network that only connects to other packet switches, but not to host computers. See exterior switch.

internet
A set of networks connected by routers that are configured to pass traffic among any computers attached to networks in the set. Most internets use TCP/IP protocols.

Internet
The global internet that uses TCP/IP protocols.

Internet address
See IP address.

ICS (Internet Connection Sharing)
The name of Microsoft's implementation of Network Address Translation. See NAT.

Internet firewall
A security mechanism placed at the connection between networks in an organization and networks outside the organization. The firewall restricts access to the organization's computers and services.

Internet reference model
A 5-layer model that describes the conceptual purpose of protocols in the TCP/IP protocol suite.

intranet

A set of networks and routers at a given organization using TCP/IP protocols to communicate. Usually, an organization's intranet connects to the global Internet.

IP (Internet Protocol)

The protocol that defines both the format of packets used on a TCP/IP Internet and the mechanism for routing a packet to its destination.

IP address

A 32-bit address assigned to a computer that uses TCP/IP protocols. The sender must know the IP address of the destination computer before sending a packet.

IP datagram

The form of a packet sent across a TCP/IP internet. Each datagram contains two pieces: a header that identifies both the sender and receiver and a payload area that contains the data being carried.

IP switching

An effort to combine IP with hardware switching (especially ATM) to achieve higher speed. See layer-3 switching.

IP tunnel

A mechanism used to send a datagram (possibly one that is not routable) across the Internet by encapsulating it in another IP datagram.

IP-in-IP

Term applied to the encapsulation used in an IP tunnel. An IP datagram is encapsulated in the payload area of another IP datagram for transmission.

IPng (Internet Protocol - the Next Generation)

The generic name used during early discussions of a new protocol to succeed IPv4. Researchers proposed several possible protocols for IPng. See IPv6.

IPv4 (Internet Protocol Version 4)

The version of IP currently used in the Internet. IPv4 uses 32-bit addresses.

IPv6 (Internet Protocol Version 6)

A specific protocol that has been chosen by the IETF as a successor to IPv4. IPv6 uses 128-bit addresses.

IPX (Internet Packet eXchange)

A protocol family defined by Novell Corporation. IPX is not related to IP.

ISDN (Integrated Services Digital Network)

A digital communication service defined by the telephone companies. Many experts think that high price and low bit rates make ISDN unattractive.

ISO (International Organization for Standardization)

The standards organization best known for having proposed the 7-layer reference model early in the history of data networking.

isochronous

A network engineered to deliver data with extremely low jitter. The voice telephone network is isochronous; most computer networks are not.

ISP (Internet Service Provider)

A commercial organization that provides its subscribers with access to the Internet.

ITU (International Telecommunications Union)

The organization that controls standards for telephone systems. The ITU also standardizes a few network technologies (e.g., ATM).

Java

A programming language defined by Sun Microsystems used to create active World Wide Web documents. Java programs are compiled into a bytecode representation. After a browser loads a Java program, the program runs locally to control the display.

JavaScript

An interpretive language used for active World Wide Web documents. Because they are kept in source form, JavaScript programs can be integrated with text in a World Wide Web page.

jitter

A term that refers to the amount of variation in delay that a network introduces. A network with zero jitter takes exactly the same amount of time to transfer each packet, while a network with high jitter takes much longer to deliver some packets than others. Jitter is important when sending audio or video, which must arrive at regular intervals.

JSP (Java Server Pages)

A dynamic web page technology intended to be platform-independent. Whenever the page is requested, the server interprets Java code that is embedded in each page.

Kbps (Kilo bits per second)

A unit of data transfer equal to *1000* bits per second.

label switching

A technique used by switching technologies such as ATM in which each switch that handles a cell rewrites the cell's label.

LAN (Local Area Network)

A network that uses technology designed to span a small geographic area. For example, an Ethernet is a LAN technology suitable for use in a single building. LANs have lower propagation delay than WANs. See WAN.

layer-3 switching

An effort to combine IP with hardware switching (especially ATM) to achieve higher speed. See IP switching.

layering model

A conceptual framework used to explain the purpose and interaction among a set of protocols. Layering is primarily beneficial to protocol designers; once implemented, protocols can be used without understanding layering.

LEO (Low Earth Orbit)

A height for communication satellites in which one orbit takes approximately 90 minutes. See GEO.

link-state

Synonym for link-status.

link-status

An algorithm that routers use to compute optimal routes to each destination. Each router receives information about the status of network links, and uses the information in a shortest-path computation. See Dijkstra's algorithm, SPF, and distance-vector.

LLC (Logical Link Control)

Part of the IEEE LLC/SNAP header used to identify the type of a packet. The entire header is 8 octets, with the LLC portion occupying the first three. See SNAP.

local loop

A term that telephone companies use to refer to the wiring between the central office and a subscriber (e.g., an individual business or residence). A variety of technologies have been developed to provide high speed digital services over existing local loop wiring. See ADSL.

locality of reference

A term used to express the idea that communication tends to follow patterns. Spatial locality of reference means that a computer is more likely to communicate with a nearby computer than a distant computer, and temporal locality of reference means that a computer is more likely to communicate with the same computer repeatedly than to communicate with a new computer each time.

LocalTalk

A Local Area Network technology developed by Apple Computer Corporation that uses a bus topology. LocalTalk uses AppleTalk protocols.

long-haul network

Synonym for WAN.

loopback address

A special address that is used for testing or debugging. A packet sent to the loopback address is not transmitted over a network, but is returned by the protocol system as if it arrived over the network.

mail exploder

A program used to forward e-mail messages. A mail exploder consults a database to determine how to handle each message. The name arises because a mail exploder may send copies of a message to multiple recipients if the database specifies many recipients for a given address.

mask

See address mask.

Masquerade

The name of a Linux program that implements Network Address Translation. See NAT.

MBONE (Multicast backBONE)

An experimental system used to send multicast data across the Internet. Although MBONE routers multicast locally, they use an IP tunnel to transfer multicast datagrams across the Internet from one site to another.

Mbps (Mega bits per second)

A unit of data transfer equal to 10^6 bps.

mesh network

A network architecture in which a computer has a point-to-point connection to other computer(s). Full mesh networks, in which each pair of computers is directly connected, offer the highest throughput but are uncommon because they are expensive and difficult to change. See bus topology and ring topology.

MIB (Management Information Base)

A set of named items that an SNMP agent understands. To monitor or control a remote computer, a manager must fetch or store values to MIB variables.

MIME (Multipurpose Internet Mail Extensions)

A mechanism that allows nontext data to be sent in a standard Internet e-mail message. A MIME sender encodes data using printable characters; a MIME reader decodes the message.

modem (MOdulator/DEModulator)

A device that encodes digital information in a carrier wave for transmission across copper wires or a dialup telephone connection. A pair of modems permits two-way communication because each modem contains circuitry to encode outgoing data and decode incoming data. See DSU/CSU.

modulation

The process of changing a carrier wave (usually a sine wave) to encode information. The frequency of the carrier and the modulation technique determine the rate at which data can be sent.

MOSPF (Multicast extensions OSPF)

A multicast routing protocol that extends OSPF to handle multicast.

mrouted (multicast route daemon)

A Unix program that performs multicast routing. Mrouted implements the DVMRP protocol, and is used in the MBONE.

MTU (Maximum Transmission Unit)

The largest amount of data that can be sent across a given network in a single packet. Each network technology defines an MTU (e.g., the MTU of an Ethernet is 1500 octets).

multicast

A form of addressing in which a set of computers is assigned one address; a copy of any datagram sent to the address is delivered to each of the computers in the set. Often used for audio or video conferences. See broadcast, cluster, and unicast.

multihomed

Any host computer that attaches to more than one network. In most protocol systems, a multihomed computer has more than one address.

multiplex

A general concept that refers to combining independent sources of information into a form that can be transmitted over a single communication channel. Multiplexing can occur both in hardware (i.e., electrical signals can be multiplexed) and in software (i.e., protocol software can accept messages sent by multiple application programs and send them over a single network to different destinations). See demultiplex.

NAT (Network Address Translation)

A technology that provides connectivity for many computers at a site through a single valid IP address. NAT rewrites the header of each outgoing and incoming datagram to replace the internal address with the globally valid IP address and vice versa.

Netware

The name of a network system developed and sold by Novell Incorporated that uses the IPX protocol family.

network adapter

Synonym for NIC.

network analyzer

A device that listens to a network, usually a LAN, in promiscuous mode and reports on traffic. Also called a network monitor.

network management

A reference to the job of administering, monitoring, and controlling a network. Protocols like SNMP automate some of the monitoring and control tasks.

network monitor

A synonym for network analyzer.

next header

A field in an IPv6 header that specifies the type of the next item.

next-hop forwarding

The technique used by protocols like IP to forward a packet to its final destination. Although a given router does not contain complete information about the path a datagram will follow, the router does know the next router to which the datagram should be sent.

NFS (Network File System)

A remote file access mechanism originally defined by Sun Microsystems for use with the UNIX operating system. NFS allows applications on one computer to access files on a remote computer.

NIC (Network Interface Card)

A hardware device that plugs into a computer and connects the computer to a network. Often called a network adapter.

node

A term used informally to refer to a router or a computer attached to a network. The term is derived from graph theory.

Nyquist Sampling Theorem

A mathematical result from information theory that specifies the number of samples that must be taken to digitize and then reconstruct a wave. The sampling theorem applies to sending audio over a network.

Nyquist's Intersymbol Interference Theorem

A mathematical result from information theory that specifies an upper bound on the maximum rate at which data can be sent. See Shannon's Theorem.

OC (Optical Carrier)

A set of standards adopted by common carriers for the high-speed transmission of digital information over optical fiber. OC-1 operates at 51.840 Mbps; OC-n runs at n times that bit rate. See STS.

OC-3 (Optical Carrier 3)

A standard for the optical fiber encoding used in popular telephone company digital circuits. An OC-3 circuit operates at 155.520 Mbps. See OC.

odd parity

A parity bit added to a unit of data, usually each character, to make the number of 1 bits odd. A receiver checks the parity to determine whether data has been corrupted during transmission. See even parity.

one-arm router

Term used informally to define a computer that only has one network interface, but has been configured to behave like a router. One-armed routers are often used with Network Address Translation. See router and NAT.

optical fiber

Glass fiber used in computer networks. The chief advantage of optical fiber over copper wire is that fiber supports higher bandwidth. See fiber modem.

optical modem

A synonym for fiber modem.

OSPF (Open Shortest Path First Protocol)

A popular protocol used to propagate routing information within a single Autonomous System.

OUI (Organizationally Unique Identifier)

A field in an LLC header that specifies which organization assigned the numbers used for type information.

packet

A small, self-contained parcel of data sent across a computer network. Each packet contains a header that identifies the sender and recipient, and a payload area that contains the data being sent.

packet filter

A mechanism in a router used to control traffic, typically as part of an Internet firewall. The packet filter discards all packets that do not adhere to the criteria the manager specifies.

packet switching network

Any communication network that accepts and delivers individual packets of information. Most modern networks are packet switching.

PAR (Positive Acknowledgement with Retransmission)

The basic technique protocols use to achieve reliable delivery. The receiving protocol returns an acknowledgement when a packet arrives. After transmitting a packet, the sender starts a timer. If the acknowledgement does not arrive before the timer expires, the sender retransmits the packet.

parity bit

An extra bit added to a unit of data, usually each character, to verify that the data is transferred without corruption. A receiver checks the parity on each incoming unit of data. See even parity and odd parity.

path MTU

The maximum amount of data that can be sent along the path from a source to a destination in one packet. Technically, the path MTU is the minimum MTU of any network along the path.

payload

Generically, the data being carried in a packet. The payload of a frame is the data in the frame; the payload of a datagram is the data area of the datagram.

PCM (Pulse Code Modulation)

The technique used to sample audio and encode it for transmission across a telephone network. PCM uses 8000 samples per second, with each sample encoded in 8 bits.

phase shift

A technique modems use to modulate a carrier. The phase of the carrier wave is shifted to encode data.

PHP (Perl Helper Pages)

A dynamic web page technology that is not widely used. Whenever the page is requested, the server interprets Perl code that is embedded in each page.

physical address

A synonym for hardware address.

PIM-DM (Protocol Independent Multicast - Dense Mode)

A multicast routing protocol designed to be used across a set of networks that have many listeners (e.g., across Local Area Networks within an organization).

PIM-SM (Protocol Independent Multicast - Sparse Mode)

A multicast routing protocol designed to be used in cases where only a few networks contain listeners (e.g., across Wide Area Networks in the Internet).

ping (packet inter-net groper)

A program used to test network connectivity. Ping sends an ICMP Echo Request message to a destination, and reports whether it receives an ICMP Echo Reply as expected.

plug-and-play networking

Characteristic of any network system that allows a new computer to begin communicating without requiring configuration by the network manager. DHCP provides plug-and-play internet connections.

point-to-multipoint

A mechanism used in an ATM network to deliver a copy of data to multiple destinations. A point-to-multipoint circuit in a connection-oriented network provides functionality equivalent to multicasting in connectionless network.

point-to-point network

Any network technology that uses a nonshared technology to connect pairs of computers. Point-to-point technology is more popular in Wide Area Networks than in Local Area Networks.

PRI (Primary Rate Interface)

An ISDN service that has sufficient bandwidth for larger businesses. See BRI.

promiscuous mode

A mode in which a computer connected to a shared network captures all packets, including packets destined for other computers. Promiscuous mode is useful for network monitoring, but presents a security risk for a production network. Many standard interfaces allow promiscuous mode.

propagation delay

The time required to send a signal across a network. The term comes from electrical engineering terminology, and describes an electrical signal propagating down a wire.

protocol

A design that specifies the details of how computers interact, including the format of messages they exchange and how errors are handled. See protocol suite.

protocol address

A number assigned to a computer that is used as the destination address in packets sent to that computer. Each IP address is 32 bits long; other protocol families use other sizes of protocol addresses.

protocol configuration

A step that a computer system must perform to assign values to parameters before protocol software can be used. Usually, protocol configuration requires a system to obtain a protocol address.

protocol port number

A small integer used to identify a specific application program on a remote computer. Transport protocols like TCP assign a unique port number to each service (e.g., e-mail uses port *25*).

protocol suite

A set of protocols that work together to provide a seamless communication system. Each protocol handles a subset of all possible details. The Internet uses the TCP/IP protocol suite. See stack.

provisioned

An adjective used to describe a network facility that is configured manually (e.g., a provisioned circuit is established manually). The term derives from the telecommunications industry.

PVC (Permanent Virtual Circuit)

A connection from one computer to another through a connection-oriented network. A PVC is permanent in the sense that it survives computer reboots or power cycles; a PVC is virtual because it is achieved by placing routes in routing tables, not by establishing physical wires. ATM expands the acronym to Permanent Virtual Channel. See SVC.

QoS (Quality of Service)

Term applied to any mechanism that gives statistical guarantees about the service received. QoS mechanisms achieve guarantees by discarding some of the packets from users who do not purchase high-quality service.

queuing delay

The total amount of time a packet must wait in packet switches as it travels through a packet switching network. The queueing delay is related to the amount of traffic in a network — when no other packets are being sent, the queueing delay is zero.

RARP (Reverse Address Resolution Protocol)

A protocol that a computer system uses during bootstrap to obtain an IP address.

reassembly

The procedure a receiver uses to recreate a copy of an original datagram from the fragments that arrive. See fragmentation.

redirect

An ICMP error message sent from a router to a host. The message specifies that the host has an incorrect route which should be changed, and specifies the destination and a correct next-hop to reach that destination.

replay

A condition in which the arrival of a copy of an old packet confuses communication. For example, if a copy of a packet that requests termination of a communication is delayed until after a new communication has begun, the packet can incorrectly cause termination of the new communication. Protocols must be designed to prevent re-play from causing problems.

retransmission

The retransmission of a packet that has been sent previously. Transport protocols use retransmission to achieve reliability. See PAR.

RF (Radio Frequency)

A range of frequencies used for sending radio signals through the air (e.g., from a commercial radio station). Wireless network technologies use RF.

RF modem

A modem that can send and receive information by modulating a radio frequency carrier. RF modems are used in wireless network technologies.

ring topology

A network architecture in which computers are linked into a cycle with the first con-nected to the second, the second connected to the third, and so on until the last con-nects back to the first. Ring topology is usually used in Local Area Networks.

RIP (Routing Information Protocol)

A protocol that uses the distance-vector approach to propagate routing information within an Autonomous System.

RJ-45

The type of connector used with twisted pair Ethernet.

root server

A domain name server that knows the locations of top-level domains such as *.com* and *.edu*. See DNS and domain.

route propagation

The act of passing routing information from one router to another. See IGP and EGP.

route server

A server that contains complete routing information for the global Internet. All route servers together form the routing arbiter system.

routed

A Unix program that implements the RIP route propagation protocol.

router

The basic building block of an internet. A router is a computer that attaches to two or more networks and forwards packets according to information found in its routing table. Routers in the Internet run the IP protocol. See host.

routing arbiter system

The system of route servers that each contain complete information about all destinations in the global Internet.

routing table

A table used by routing software to determine the next hop for a packet. A routing table is kept in a router's memory.

RS-232

The technical name of the standard used for serial data connections such as those between a keyboard and a computer. The standard defines such details as the voltage used to represent a *1* and a *0*.

secure proxy

An application gateway that is part of a firewall. A secure proxy allows users on one side of the firewall to access a specific service on the other side of the firewall according to the organization's security policy.

segment

A single piece of cable that forms a bus network. Multiple segments can be connected by bridges or routers. A hub simulates a single segment.

segmentation and reassembly

The term ATM uses for the division of a large message into small cells for transmission across an ATM network. On the sending computer, the AAL5 protocol segments the message; on the receiving computer, AAL5 reassembles the message.

self-healing network

A network system that has the ability to automatically detect a hardware failure and route traffic along an alternative path. Self-healing requires redundant paths. FDDI is the best known self-healing network technology.

serial line

A physical wire between two points over which data is sent one bit at a time. RS-232-C is often used with serial lines.

server

When two programs communicate over a network, a client is the one that initiates communication, while a server is the program that waits to be contacted. A given program can act as a server for one service and a client for another.

session cookie

A cookie that a browser holds in memory. Because it is kept in memory instead of on disk, a session cookie only persists while the browser is running.

Shannon's Theorem

An important result that specifies the maximum data rate that can be achieved over a transmission channel that has noise associated with it. See Nyquist's Intersymbol Interference Theorem.

shielded twisted pair

A cable that contains one (or more) twisted pairs of wire surrounded by a heavy metal shield similar to the shield that surrounds a single wire in a coaxial cable. The shield protects the inner pairs of wires from electrical interference.

signal loss

The amount of electrical energy lost as a wave travels down a medium such as a copper wire. A network connection cannot be arbitrarily long because the signal loss eventually makes the wave too weak to detect.

slash notation

A syntactic form used in CIDR addressing and routing. An address is given in dotted decimal followed by a slash and an integer between 0 and 32 that represents the length of the address mask.

sliding window

A technique that a protocol can use to improve throughput by allowing a sender to transmit additional packets before receiving any acknowledgement. A receiver tells a sender how many packets can be sent at one time (called a window size).

SMDS (Switched Multi-megabit Data Service)

A connectionless Wide Area Network technology offered by telephone companies.

SMTP (Simple Mail Transfer Protocol)

The protocol used to transfer e-mail from one computer to another across the Internet. SMTP is part of the TCP/IP protocol suite.

SNAP (SubNetwork Attachment Point)

Part of the IEEE LLC/SNAP header used to identify the type of a packet. The entire header is *8* octets, with the SNAP portion occupying the last five. See LLC.

sniffer

A synonym for network analyzer taken from a popular product.

SNMP (Simple Network Management Protocol)

The protocol that specifies how a network management station communicates with agent software in remote devices such as routers. SNMP defines the format of messages and their meaning. See MIB.

socket API

A set of procedures that an application program can use to communicate across a network. The name arises because the set includes a *socket* procedure that must be called to establish communication. See API.

source address

An address in a packet that specifies the computer that sent the packet. In a hardware frame, the source address must be a hardware address. In an IP datagram, the source address must be an IP address.

SPF (Shortest Path First)

A general link-status algorithm that routers can use to compute routes. See link-status and distance-vector.

spread spectrum

A transmission technique used to avoid interference and achieve higher throughput. Instead of a single carrier frequency, a sender and receiver agree to use a set of frequencies, either at the same time or by changing from one to another. The technique is especially important for wireless networks.

stack

An informal term for an implementation of a protocol suite. The term arises because a protocol layering diagram shows protocols in a vertical ''stack''.

star topology

A network architecture that consists of a central hub to which all computers connect. Star topologies are often used with Local Area Networks (e.g., twisted pair Ethernet). See hub and switch.

stateful server

A server that is designed so the action performed for a given request depends on the prior history of requests. See stateless server.

stateless server

A server that handles each request independently. Most servers are designed to be as stateless as possible. See stateful server.

static document

A page of information available on the World Wide Web. The contents of a static document do not change until the author places new information in the document. See active document, dynamic document, and URL.

statistical multiplexing

A variant of STDM that only services a given source when the source has something to send. The chief advantage of statistical multiplexing arises because it never leaves the communication channel idle while a source has something to send.

store and forward

Characteristic of a network that uses packet switches to forward packets. The name arises because each switch along a path to the destination receives a packet and temporarily stores the packet in memory. Meanwhile the switch continuously selects a packet from the queue in memory, routes the packet, and then transmits the packet to the appropriate next hop.

STDM (Synchronous Time Division Multiplexing)

Also expanded to *Slotted Time Division Multiplexing*. Any time-division multiplexing mechanism that proceeds round-robin among all sources.

STS (Synchronous Transport Signal)

A set of standards adopted by common carriers for high-speed digital circuits. STS-1 operates at 51.840 Mbps; STS-*n* runs at *n* times that bit rate. See OC.

subnet addressing

An extension of the original IP addressing scheme in which an organization uses a single IP prefix for multiple physical networks. See address mask.

subnet mask

A synonym for address mask.

suite

See protocol suite.

SVC (Switched Virtual Circuit)

A connection from one computer to another through a connection-oriented network. An SVC is virtual because it is achieved by placing routes in routing tables, not by establishing physical wires; an SVC is switched because it can be created on demand analogous to a telephone call. ATM expands the acronym to Switched Virtual Channel. See PVC.

switch

An electronic device that forms the center of a star topology network. A switch uses the destination address in a frame to determine which computer should receive the frame.

switched network

Any network that uses switches instead of routers. Usually, switching implies connection-oriented technology. ATM is an example of a technology that uses switching.

switching

A general term used to describe the operation of a switch. Because it is associated with hardware, switching is usually higher speed than routing. Also, switching differs from routing because switching uses the hardware address in a frame.

synchronous

Characteristic of any communication system in which the sender must coordinate (i.e., synchronize) with the receiver before sending data. Synchronization is usually handled by having the sending hardware transmit regular pulses when no data is available. The receiver uses the pulses to extract data from the incoming signal. See asynchronous.

T1, T3

The designations that telephone companies use for popular point-to-point digital circuits. A T1 circuit operates at 1.544 Mbps and a T3 circuit operates at 44.736 Mbps. See DS-1, DS-3.

TCP (Transmission Control Protocol)

The TCP/IP protocol that provides application programs with access to a connection-oriented communication service. TCP offers reliable, flow-controlled delivery. More important TCP accommodates changing conditions in the Internet by adapting its retransmission scheme. See UDP.

TCP/IP

The protocol suite used in the Internet. Although the suite contains many protocols, TCP and IP are two of the most important.

TDM (Time Division Multiplexing)

Characteristic of a mechanism that allows multiple senders to share a communication medium by taking turns. At any time, only one sender transmits across the channel. See FDM.

terminator

A device attached to the end of a wire or a transmission cable to prevent electrical signals from reflecting back. A bus network such as an Ethernet requires each end of the cable to have a terminator.

TFTP (Trivial File Transfer Protocol)

A protocol used to transfer a file from one computer to another. TFTP is simpler than FTP, but does not have as much capability.

thick wire Ethernet

An informal term used for the original DIX Ethernet.

Thicknet

A synonym for thick wire Ethernet.

thin wire Ethernet

An informal term used for the version of Ethernet that uses thinner coaxial cable.

Thinnet

A synonym for thin wire Ethernet.

throughput

A measure of the capacity of a digital network. The value is given as a ratio of bits transmitted per unit time. In informal situations, the term *bandwidth* is often used to refer to throughput.

time division multiplexing

See TDM.

token passing

A technique used in ring topology networks to control transmission. The token consists of a special message sent around the ring. When a station has a packet to send, the station waits for the token to arrive, sends one packet, and then sends the token.

token ring

A ring topology network that uses token passing for access control. The phrase also applies to a specific token passing ring topology defined by IBM Corporation.

topology

A term used to describe the general shape of a network. Common topologies include bus, point-to-point, ring, and star.

TP Ethernet (Twisted Pair Ethernet)

See 10BaseT.

traceroute

A network diagnostic program that finds the address of all routers between the user's computer and a specified destination. Traceroute sends datagrams with successively larger time-to-live values, and uses ICMP error messages to determine routers along the path.

transceiver

An electronic device that connects the Network Interface Card in a computer to a physical medium. Transceivers are used with thick wire Ethernet.

transmission error

Any change introduced as data passes across a network. Transmission errors can be caused by electrical interference or hardware that malfunctions.

trunk circuit

A term with more than one meaning. Telephone companies use the term to refer to large-capacity circuits that form the main interconnect of the phone network (e.g., between cities). Cable television companies use the term to refer to the high-capacity coaxial cables used to connect between the cable company and neighborhood concentration points, which can be up to fifteen miles long. See feeder circuit.

TTL (Time To Live)

A value found in the header of an IP datagram. Each router decrements the TTL value. If the TTL reaches zero, the router discards the datagram and sends an ICMP error message to the source.

tunnel

Any mechanism that encapsulates a packet in a high-level protocol for transmission. See IP tunnel and IP-in-IP.

twisted pair

A form of wiring in which a pair of wires is wrapped around one another again and again. Twisting two wires reduces their susceptibility to electrical interference.

UDP (User Datagram Protocol)

The TCP/IP protocol that provides application programs with connectionless communication service. See TCP.

unicast

A form of packet delivery in which each computer is assigned a unique address. When a packet is sent to a unicast address, exactly one copy of the packet is delivered to the computer to which the address corresponds. Unicast delivery is the most common type. See broadcast, cluster, and multicast.

uplink

The path of data transmitted from an earth station to a satellite. See downlink.

upstream

The path of data from a residential customer to the Internet. The term is often used with DSL or cable modem technologies. See downstream.

URL (Uniform Resource Locator)

A syntactic form used to identify a page of information on the World Wide Web.

VC (virtual circuit)

A connection from one computer to another through a connection-oriented network. The term *virtual* arises because the circuit is achieved by placing routes in routing tables, not by establishing physical wires. Also called a virtual channel.

vector-distance

The original name for distance-vector.

virtual channel

A synonym for virtual circuit. The term virtual channel is used with technologies such as ATM. See VC.

VPI/VCI (Virtual Path Identifier/Virtual Channel Identifier)

A binary value used in an ATM network to identify a particular connection. Each switch along a path rewrites the VPI/VCI.

VPN (Virtual Private Network)

A technology that uses encryption and IP tunneling to allow a multi-site organization to use low-cost Internet connections among sites but still keep data confidential.

WAN (Wide Area Network)

A network that uses technology designed to span a large geographic area. For example, a satellite network is a WAN because a satellite can relay communication across an entire continent. WANs have higher propagation delay than LANs. See LAN.

WAP (Wireless Access Protocol)

A set of protocols designed to deliver and display pages of information on small, portable wireless devices such as portable phones and pagers. The set includes transport and transfer protocols, a scripting language, and a page markup protocol.

Web

A synonym for World Wide Web.

window

An amount of data that a receiver is willing to accept at any time. Window size can be measured in packets or in bytes. See sliding window.

WWW (World Wide Web)

The hypermedia system used on the Internet in which a page of information can contain text, images, audio or video clips, and references to other pages. See active document, dynamic document, static document, URL and browser.

xDSL (-Digital Subscriber Line)

A generic acronym used to refer to any of the local loop technologies such as ADSL, HDSL, etc.

XML (Extensible Markup Language)

A markup language that is used primarily for exchange of data between two computer programs. An XML document contains embedded tags that give names for fields in the data. Unlike HTML, XML does not specify formatting information.

zero compression

A technique IPv6 uses to abbreviate hexadecimal colon notation by replacing a sequence of zeroes with a pair of colons.

Appendix 2

The ASCII Character Set

The American Standard Code for Information Interchange assigns a 7-bit representation to each character available on the computer keyboards used in the United States. The following table lists each hexadecimal value followed by the corresponding character. In cases where the character does not have a printable representation, the table contains an abbreviation of the character's name (e.g., *esc* is an abbreviation for *escape*, and *cr* is an abbreviation for *carriage return*).

00	nul	01	soh	02	stx	03	etx	04	eot	05	enq	06	ack	07	bel
08	bs	09	ht	0A	IF	0B	vt	0C	np	0D	cr	0E	so	0F	si
10	dle	11	dc1	12	dc2	13	dc3	14	dc4	15	nak	16	syn	17	etb
18	can	19	em	1A	sub	1B	esc	1C	fs	1D	gs	1e	rs	1F	us
20	sp	21	!	22	"	23	#	24	$	25	%	26	&	27	'
28	(	29	)	2A	*	2B	+	2C	,	2D	–	2E	.	2F	/
30	0	31	1	32	2	33	3	34	4	35	5	36	6	37	7
38	8	39	9	3A	:	3B	;	3C	<	3D	=	3E	>	3F	?
40	@	41	A	42	B	43	C	44	D	45	E	46	F	47	G
48	H	49	I	4A	J	4B	K	4C	L	4D	M	4E	N	4F	O
50	P	51	Q	52	R	53	S	54	T	55	U	56	V	57	W
58	X	59	Y	5A	Z	5B	[	5C		5D	]	5E	^	5F	_
60	`	61	a	62	b	63	c	64	d	65	e	66	f	67	g
68	h	69	i	6A	j	6B	k	6C	l	6D	m	6E	n	6F	o
70	p	71	q	72	r	73	s	74	t	75	u	76	v	77	w
78	x	79	y	7A	z	7B	{	7C	l	7D	}	7E	~	7F	del

Appendix 3

Address Masks In Dotted Decimal

Classless Inter-Domain Routing (CIDR) and IP subnetting techniques each use a 32-bit *address mask* to denote the boundary between the network prefix and host suffix. Because humans must specify and read them, mask values are not usually specified in binary. Instead, software that interacts with humans either uses the *slash notation* that was developed for CIDR or dotted decimal notation.

The table in this appendix shows equivalents between the thirty-two possible *slash notation* values for an address mask and dotted decimal values.

Length (CIDR)	Address Mask				Notes
/ 0	0	. 0	. 0	. 0	All 0s (equivalent to no mask)
/ 1	128	. 0	. 0	. 0	
/ 2	192	. 0	. 0	. 0	
/ 3	224	. 0	. 0	. 0	
/ 4	240	. 0	. 0	. 0	
/ 5	248	. 0	. 0	. 0	
/ 6	252	. 0	. 0	. 0	
/ 7	254	. 0	. 0	. 0	
/ 8	255	. 0	. 0	. 0	Original Class A mask
/ 9	255	. 128	. 0	. 0	
/ 10	255	. 192	. 0	. 0	
/ 11	255	. 224	. 0	. 0	
/ 12	255	. 240	. 0	. 0	
/ 13	255	. 248	. 0	. 0	
/ 14	255	. 252	. 0	. 0	
/ 15	255	. 254	. 0	. 0	
/ 16	255	. 255	. 0	. 0	Original Class B mask
/ 17	255	. 255	. 128	. 0	
/ 18	255	. 255	. 192	. 0	
/ 19	255	. 255	. 224	. 0	
/ 20	255	. 255	. 240	. 0	
/ 21	255	. 255	. 248	. 0	
/ 22	255	. 255	. 252	. 0	
/ 23	255	. 255	. 254	. 0	
/ 24	255	. 255	. 255	. 0	Original Class C mask
/ 25	255	. 255	. 255	. 128	
/ 26	255	. 255	. 255	. 192	
/ 27	255	. 255	. 255	. 224	
/ 28	255	. 255	. 255	. 240	
/ 28	255	. 255	. 255	. 248	
/ 39	255	. 255	. 255	. 252	
/ 31	255	. 255	. 255	. 254	
/ 32	255	. 255	. 255	. 255	All 1s (host specific mask)

Appendix 4

How To Use The CD-ROM
Included With This Book

Introduction

The CD-ROM included with the text contains a variety of supplemental materials for readers and instructors. The materials are also available on the World Wide Web at:

http://www.netbook.cs.purdue.edu

In addition to materials found on the CD-ROM, the Website contains items added after the text was published, instructional aids, and news about the text. This appendix describes the organization of the supplemental materials, and explains how to access the information on the CD-ROM and the Website.

Software Needed For Browsing

To simplify access, both the Website and CD-ROM can be accessed with a single tool — a World Wide Web browser. The contents of each consist of HTML documents, photos, and multimedia materials that are interconnected with hypermedia links. Furthermore, the CD-ROM is written in a format that can be read by an Apple Macintosh computer, a computer running Microsoft Windows, or a computer running the UNIX operating system.

641

Because many documents on the CD-ROM use conventional HTML, an arbitrary Web browser can be used to view them. However, additional browser facilities are needed to view graphics. In particular, to handle all materials, a browser must be able to display ShockWave or QuickTime movies and in-line photos in GIF format. Although the necessary facilities are not available for all browsers, they are available for version 2.0 or higher of Netscape Navigator. A copy of the latest version of the Netscape browser can be downloaded at no cost from Website:

http://www.netscape.com

Software that extends a browser's functionality to allow it to display an additional document type is known as a *plugin*. Animations on the CD-ROM require the ShockWave plugin, which is available at no cost from Website:

http://www.macromedia.com

If a ShockWave plugin is unavailable†, animations can also be displayed in Quick-Time format. To use QuickTime, a browser must be configured to run a *helper* application. In the Netscape browser, the configuration can be found in the preferences menu. Appropriate helper applications include *Simple Player* for Apple Macintosh, *PLAY32* for Windows, and *xv* for UNIX.

How To Browse The CD-ROM

After browser software has been obtained and configured, using the browser to access the CD-ROM is straightforward:

1. Place the CD-ROM in the CD-ROM drive. Close the drawer to make it ready.

2. Start the browser application (e.g., by double-clicking on the icon). Note: a browser that uses plugins may need to be started from the folder in which the plugins reside.

3. Select the *Open File* item from the *File* menu on the browser. Select file *index.htm* in the CD-ROM folder. The next section describes how to make the file selection on various computers.

4. The screen will display a graphic front page with links to the areas of the CD-ROM. Click on any link to follow a pointer to another page of information exactly as when browsing the World Wide Web.

---

†At the time this appendix is being written, no ShockWave plugin is available for UNIX versions of the Netscape browser.

Selecting File index.htm In The CD-ROM Folder

The third step in the instructions above requires a user to select a file on the CD-ROM. The exact details of the selection depend on the computer system being used. After a user selects the *Open File* item from the *File* menu, a browser will create a window through which it can interact with the user.

- On an Apple Macintosh computer, select the *Desktop* button. The browser will display a list of all available disks. Select the CD-ROM labeled *NET-BOOK*. The browser will display a list of files on the CD-ROM. Select file *index.htm*.

- On a computer running Windows, pull down the menu labeled *Look in:* and select the drive that corresponds to the CD-ROM in your computer. Usually the drive is labeled *Netbook [D:]* or *Netbook [E:]*. The browser will display a list of files available on the CD-ROM. Select file *Index*.

- On a computer running UNIX, enter the full path name of the CD-ROM in the *File Name* dialog box. Some versions of UNIX mount the CD-ROM as */cdrom*, making the full path name: */cdrom/netbook/index.htm*. However, other versions of UNIX mount the CD-ROM under a different name (e.g., */CDROM* or */mnt/cdrom*). Consult the system administrator who configured the computer to determine the correct name.

Alternatively, the name of the file on the CD-ROM can be specified in a URL:

Computer system	URL
Macintosh	file:///NETBOOK/index.htm
Windows	file:///D:/index.htm
	file:///E:/index.htm
UNIX	file:///cdrom/netbook/index.htm

Additional information and hints about using the CD-ROM are available at the Website for this text. The URL for information about the CD-ROM is:

http://www.netbook.cs.purdue.edu/intro.htm

If you have problems...

- Make sure you are using a browser that can interpret JavaScript and display frames. Netscape Navigator version 2.0 or higher has the necessary features.

- Make sure JavaScript is enabled in your browser.

- If you are using Netscape Navigator on a Macintosh, configure your browser to allocate at least 12000K of memory.

- You can select the *About Plugins* menu entry in Netscape Navigator to check that the ShockWave plugin is available and will interpret files with filename extension *.dcr* as ShockWave files.

- If you are not using Netscape Navigator version 3.0 or higher and your browser is not configured with the ShockWave plugin, the browser will display a broken icon or a dialog box every time you access the cover page for one of the animations.

Structure Of Supplemental Materials

The CD-ROM contains a large collection of materials that supplement the text, including figures, animations, digitized photos, and data files. Each item is stored in a separate document to make it possible for the item to be accessed in multiple ways. The next section explains the mechanisms used to access items; this section explains how the items are stored.

An item is represented in a pair of files: a basic file and a presentation file. The basic file for an item contains the item itself, with no explanation, caption, or other descriptive information. For example, the basic file for a photo consists of the digitized photo without surrounding text. Basic files are not intended for normal viewing. Instead, they have been included for instructors who wish to extract underlying items for classroom presentations or to combine multiple items into new Web documents.

The presentation file for an item consists of an HTML document, called a *cover page*, that is intended for human browsing. The cover page for an item includes both the item itself, a title, a brief description of the item, and keywords. Thus, when a browser follows a pointer to a cover page, the user sees both the basic item and the descriptive text.

Because the links on the CD-ROM are intended for humans to use while browsing, each link points to a cover page. For example, when a user searches for supplemental materials relevant to a specific chapter, the resulting list of materials consists of pointers to cover pages for the items. Thus, when a user follows a link, the browser will display a cover page that provides a meaningful description of the item being displayed†.

---

†To reach the basic file for an item, select the item from a cover page.

Indexes On The CD-ROM

The materials can be used in a variety of ways. On one hand, a reader may wish to browse all items associated with a given technology (e.g., Ethernet). On the other hand, both readers and instructors may find it helpful to browse the items associated with a given chapter. For example, pictures of network wiring are especially helpful in understanding the conceptual wiring diagrams in Chapter 10. Instructors will also find that the items from a chapter provide a useful way to enhance and reinforce lectures on topics from the chapter.

To make it possible to access supplemental materials in a variety of ways, the CD-ROM contains several pre-defined indexes and automated search tools. To find index and search information, click on *What's on the CD-ROM* on the first page to view an overview of the CD-ROM. The indexes can be found through the *CD-ROM indexes* link in the CD-ROM overview.

The *chapter index* lists the materials that are relevant to each chapter, including copies of figures, animations of material, and relevant photos. The *media type index* groups materials into five categories: *figure*, *animation*, *photo*, *data*, or *code* file. The *subject index* categorizes the materials according to subject (e.g., listing all the materials associated with LAN technologies, internetworking, and so on). The subject index has two levels — selecting a subject at the top level produces a second index of items relevant to the selection. Selecting a link at the second level displays an individual item.

Keyword Searching

In addition to the indexes described above, the CD-ROM contains mechanisms that use keyword searching to select items. These search tools can be found through the *Search the CD-ROM* link on the CD-ROM overview. In general, the keyword mechanisms prompt a user for one or more keywords; the search mechanism then constructs a list of items that match the specified keywords. Each item is assigned a media type: *figure*, *photo*, *animation*, *data*, or *code* and the type name is matched in the keyword search. Thus, it is possible to limit a search to a specific type such as *figure*.

The CD-ROM includes electronic versions of the glossary, the table of contents, and the index from the text along with mechanisms to perform a search of each. The glossary search mechanism operates similar to the keyword search described above. Given a keyword, the glossary search produces a list of all glossary items that contain the specified keyword in an acronym, term, or definition. Because multiple glossary entries can match a given search, the result of a search is a list of matching entries.

A keyword search mechanism also exists for the table of contents and index. The result of searching the table of contents or index is a list of all entries that match the search; each entry contains the page numbers in the text at which the item can be found.

Appendix 5

Building A Network At Home With NAT

Introduction

Many residences now have high-speed Internet access via DSL, cable modem, or satellite technologies. However, the basic service offered by most ISPs connects only one computer per customer. That is, the ISP only issues one valid IP address to each customer. If a customer has multiple computers that each need an IP address, the ISP levies an additional charge for each address.

This appendix explains a low-cost alternative to multiple addresses — a technology that allows multiple computers on a network to ''share'' a single IP address. The basic mechanism is known as *Network Address Translation* (*NAT*). From the ISP's point of view, NAT completely hides additional computers at the customer's site — to the ISP, the customer appears to have a single computer attached to the Internet. From the customer's point of view, a device that implements NAT appears to function like a default router — when a computer on the local net generates a datagram, the computer forwards the datagram to the NAT device for delivery. Most important, NAT is completely transparent, meaning computers on the local net do not need special software. Instead, each computer can run a standard operating system and standard network software. Thus, NAT combines the advantage of connectivity for multiple computers with the advantage of low cost Internet service.

Basic NAT Architecture

The easiest way to envision a home network using NAT is to imagine inserting a NAT hardware device between an ISP and computers at a residence. The NAT device acts like an IP router, forwarding IP datagrams between the local net at the residence and the Internet. Like a router, a NAT device has two network interfaces: one that connects to the ISP and another that connects to the local network. Figure A5.1 illustrates the idea.

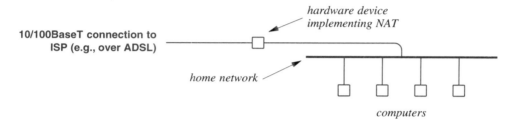

Figure A5.1 The conceptual architecture of a home network with a dedicated hardware device handling NAT. The NAT device connects the ISP and the home network.

NAT Software, Hardware, And Commercial Products

NAT is available commercially. Two forms exist: a dedicated, special-purpose hardware device or software that runs on a conventional PC. When a PC is used to run NAT, the PC needs two Network Interface Cards as Figure A5.1 shows. One interface connects to the ISP and the other connects to the local network. When a dedicated NAT hardware device is used, the device usually incorporates a 4-port Ethernet hub (or Ethernet switch) for the home network, as Figure A5.2 illustrates.

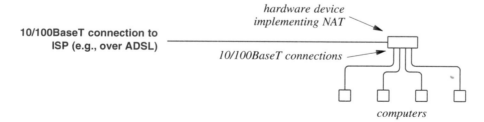

Figure A5.2 NAT implemented by a special-purpose hardware device. The NAT device includes an Ethernet hub for the home network as well as an Ethernet connection for the ISP.

Commercial NAT software is available for most operating systems. For example, the program *Masquerade* implements NAT for the Linux Operating System, and Microsoft's *Internet Connection Sharing* (*ICS*) software implements NAT for Windows systems. Although NAT software offers the same functionality as a dedicated NAT hardware device, the hardware solution has several advantages over a PC running NAT software. First, a dedicated hardware device is physically much smaller than a PC. Second, a dedicated hardware device is easy to install and configure. Third, the cost of buying a dedicated NAT device (a few hundred dollars) is less than the cost of buying a new PC to run NAT software. Of course, the third advantage is mitigated if the customer has an unused PC that can be used for NAT.

How NAT Works

The basic idea behind NAT is straightforward — computers on the local network use arbitrary addresses, and NAT translates any invalid address to the customer's valid IP address before it forwards a datagram to the Internet. That is, the customer chooses an arbitrary prefix for the internal network, and then assigns host addresses using that prefix. For example, the IETF recommends a set of prefixes that include 10.0.0.0/8 and 192.168.0.0/16 because those prefixes will never be assigned on the Internet. Once a prefix has been selected, each host is assigned an address with that prefix. For example, a site that chooses 10.0.0.0/8 will assign computers addresses 10.0.0.1, 10.0.0.2, and so on.

Of course, when a computer on the local network generates a datagram, the source address will be a net 10 address. For example, if a computer with address 10.0.0.5 generates a datagram, the IP source address field in the header will contain 10.0.0.5. When the datagram reaches the NAT device, the source address is translated as Figure A5.3 illustrates.

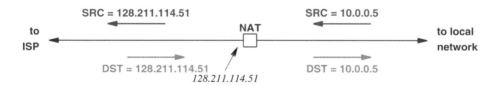

Figure A5.3 An example of NAT address translation for datagrams traveling from local computer 10.0.0.5 to a computer on the Internet and vice versa. Address *128.211.114.51* is the customer's valid IP address.

As the figure shows, NAT must change address fields in the header of both outgoing and incoming datagrams. When it receives an outgoing datagram, NAT replaces the source address with the customer's valid IP address (i.e., the address of the NAT device). NAT also records the translation in a table so it will know how to translate replies. Finally, NAT forwards the datagram toward its destination. When a datagram arrives from the Internet (i.e., a reply), NAT looks up the source in the translation table and replaces the destination address with the appropriate internal address†. Finally, NAT forwards the datagram over the local net to the correct computer.

Configuring NAT Under Windows 98 SE

This section describes the steps required to configure Microsoft's *Internet Connection Sharing* under *Windows 98 Second Edition (SE)*‡. The outline below assumes that the computer has two Network Interface Cards installed. The first steps launch a wizard that performs the installation:

- From the *Start Menu* choose *Settings → Control Panel.*
- Open the *Add/Remove Programs* control panel.
- Select the *Windows Setup* tab.
- Select *Internet Tools* in the list of components.
- Click the *Details* button.
- Check *Internet Connection Sharing* in the list of components.
- Click *OK.*
- Click *OK.*

After the above steps have been completed, Windows will request that the *Windows 98 CD* be inserted in the CD drive. Once the needed files have been installed, a wizard will provide guidance for the remaining setup of ICS. The following lists the steps needed at the screen labeled *Instructions for NIC connection*:

- From the list provided, select the NIC that connects the computer to the Internet. (Note: the choice may be confusing if both NICs use the same model hardware.)
- Click *Next.*
- From the list provided, select the NIC that connects the computer to the private (i.e. ''home'') network.
- Click *Next.*
- Note: it is *not* necessary to create a ''client disk''.
- Click *Finish.*
- Windows requires that you reboot the computer for the changes to take effect.

Windows uses IP prefix 192.168.0.0/24 for the private network, and assigns the ICS computer a host address of 1. Thus, the setting associated with:

---

†In practice, NAT also translates protocol port numbers; for details refer to RFC 2663 and RFC 2766.

‡ICS is not available under the original version of Windows 98. Although Windows ME has ICS and the setup follows essentially the same steps, the interface differs.

TCP/IP (Home) → <Interface Name>

in the *Network Control Panel* will be 192.168.0.1.

Addresses for other computers on the private network are allocated from the range:

192.168.0.2 through 192.168.0.254

An address can be assigned to one of the other computers in one of two ways. Either, the address is manually configured, or the computer uses DHCP to obtain an address automatically at startup. Because many PCs use DHCP to obtain addresses, ICS software automatically starts a DHCP server. That is, a DHCP server will be running and ready to answer any DHCP request that arrives over the private network. Furthermore, the DHCP server will choose an address in the range listed above.

Running Servers

The configuration described above allows a computer on the private network to act as a client, but not as a server. For example, the configuration described above satisfies the main goal of most home users — it allows a computer on the private network to contact an arbitrary web site to obtain a page. Few home users attempt to run servers. For the few users who do, additional steps must be taken. In particular:

- The computer on which the server will run must be configured with a static IP address (i.e., the computer cannot obtain its IP address automatically via DHCP).

- If the server runs on protocol port N, the computer acting as the ICS gateway must be configured to route packets for port N to the computer on which the server runs.

The details of establishing a mapping for a server and an example can be found in Microsoft Article Q231162:

http://support.microsoft.com/support/kb/articles/Q231/1/62.ASP

NAT Under Linux

NAT is also available under Linux. For more information along with installation instructions, see:

http://www.indyramp.com/masq/

Appendix 6

The Undergrad Networking Lab At Purdue

Introduction

A comprehensive appreciation of networking technologies cannot be gained merely by reading a text — deep understanding requires hands-on experimentation and use. This appendix describes the networking lab that the author created to accompany his undergraduate course at Purdue. It shows how a modest amount of equipment makes it possible to conduct a variety of experiments, including building packet analyzer software. Readers with an extremely limited budget should note that a small-scale version of the lab with a single station can be built with older, slower computers for a few hundred dollars; in many cases, experiments do not require powerful computers.

Range Of Experiments

Because the undergraduate CS curriculum at Purdue contains only one networking course, we decided that the lab, like the course, should cover everything from bits to applications. The first week in lab, we show students the facilities, have them plug in an Ethernet, and show them how a Time Domain Reflectometer can calculate where a cable has been cut. The second week lab work begins in earnest. We focus on applications and programming by giving students the code in Chapter 3 that can contact a web server, and asking them to write a program that extracts and prints text from the page returned.

653

Although programming continues throughout the semester, programming labs are intermixed with other labs. For example, when the lectures discuss Ethernet, students use the lab to compare throughput on a 10BaseT network and a 100BaseT network. Similarly, when the lectures cover protocol headers, students use the lab to capture packets and decode headers. That is, the lab facilities allow students to capture arbitrary packets from the local network; the students write a program that decodes packet headers.

Packet capture is exciting because it makes protocols easy to understand. For example, once a packet capture facility is in place, it is possible to watch a TCP connection start, to see packets flow between a browser and a web server, and to watch email being transferred from one computer to another. One particular experiment that seems to enlighten focuses on how protocol port numbers are used to identify a TCP connection.

During the last half of the semester, most of the labs focus on socket programming (the skill that is most important to programmers). As a final project, students construct a web server that correctly answers HTTP requests from a commercial browser. Once the basic web server works, it is extended in two stages. First concurrent execution is added so the server can handle multiple, simultaneous connections. Second, CGI capability is added, which allows the server to generate and deliver dynamic content pages.

Basic Hardware

Only two computers and an Ethernet hub are required to support the programming labs. In fact, except for final testing, a client and server can be built and debugged on a single computer.

For experiments with protocol headers and packet traces, capturing the packets from a live network makes the lab much more exciting than reading a set of packets from a file. Thus, a lab facility should allow one to capture packets from the local network. For a private network (e.g., at home), packet capture is not a problem. In the case of a university, however, the production network in a lab contains packets that should not be made public (e.g., packets that carry passwords as students log in over the net). The challenge is to build a facility that permits monitoring of a live network without allowing access to a production network.

We have used two approaches. In the first version, we created a facility that allowed students to monitor an extra, private network. To do so, we acquired a set of wheeled carts, each of which had two inexpensive computers and an Ethernet hub. We then added an extra Network Interface Card (NIC) to each workstation in the lab. When a student was ready to perform an experiment, the student wheeled one of the equipment carts over to the workstation and connected the extra NIC to the hub on the cart. Figure A6.1 illustrates the configuration.

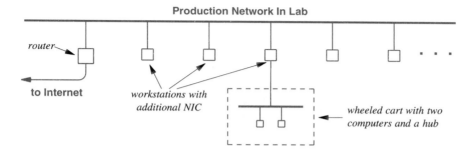

Production Network In Lab

router

to Internet

workstations with additional NIC

wheeled cart with two computers and a hub

Figure A6.1 One possible lab architecture that allows monitoring of a private network, while protecting the production network. The private network consists of two computers plus an Ethernet hub.

Second Generation Lab Architecture

The biggest problem with the lab architecture described above was popularity. When the author taught the course, nearly ninety students enrolled and others were wait listed. To accommodate the demand, we created fifteen carts, held many lab sessions during the week, and scheduled students to work in teams. Because the physical lab space was shared with other courses, however, carts could not be left in the lab. Instead, they were rolled into the lab before the networking students arrived, and rolled back into storage when other classes used the lab.

When the university offered a new, larger lab with more workstations, we accepted. The wheeled carts had to be abandoned because the new area did not have sufficiently large storage space. Thus, we were forced to rethink the equipment. We retained the basic approach, but substituted a hub between pairs of workstations in place of a cart. We lost some flexibility, but there was little choice. Figure A6.2 illustrates the resulting configuration.

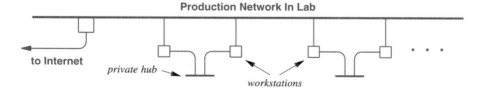

Production Network In Lab

to Internet

private hub

workstations

Figure A6.2 A second lab architecture in which each workstation has an additional network interface card used for packet capture. Each pair of workstations connects to a private network.

Lab Software

Each workstation in our lab runs Solaris, the version of the Unix operating system from Sun Microsystems. To create an environment where students can only monitor the private network, we use two Solaris commands: *snoop* and *sudo*.

Snoop. The *snoop* command provides most of the required functionality. Snoop can place a Network Interface Card in *promiscuous mode* (i.e., a mode that allows it to receive all packets), and can capture and save incoming packets in a file. However, snoop is restricted; only superuser has permission to run it.

Sudo. The *sudo* command grants a user superuser privilege to run a specific command. The system administrator creates a list of users along with the exact commands and arguments that each user is authorized to execute. If the requested command appears on sudo's authorization list, sudo invokes the command as superuser.

Because it controls the arguments a given user can pass to snoop, the sudo authorization list determines whether each user can run snoop on the private or public interface. To ensure that they do not access the production network, the authorization list is set to restrict students to the private interface. Thus, a student cannot monitor the lab network.

As further protection against unauthorized monitoring, the production network in the lab uses an Ethernet switch rather than a hub. Thus, even if someone manages to circumvent access protections, they will not receive copies of unicast packets destined for another workstation.

Snooping On One's Self

The original architecture offers the most flexibility. The two computers on the cart can run arbitrary software, including two different operating systems. Because the packet analyzer runs on a separate computer, it does not interact with the network traffic nor does it use the CPU on the systems being measured.

In the second architecture, snoop runs in one of the two systems that participate in communication. Fortunately, snoop operates independent of the normal packet forwarding and handling, meaning that applications on a workstation can use the network while snoop runs in background. Unfortunately, snoop uses resources, meaning that transfer times differ when snoop runs. For many experiments, the difference is not substantial. In cases where more accurate measurements are required, temporary rewiring is possible. Three workstations can be attached to a private network: two transfer data while the third runs snoop to monitor packets.

Student Reaction

Lab facilities provide excellent motivation — the opportunity to learn about real networks and put the ideas into practice is exciting. A packet analyzer reveals so many interesting features that students sometimes stay after normal lab hours to ''play.'' For example, watching a Telnet session in progress shows how each character occupies one datagram, or watching an email transfer illustrates how SMTP sends ASCII data. Most important, everyone is more enthusiastic about building software when they can experiment with the underlying hardware first-hand. Indeed, having access to a lab helps instill a much deeper understanding of the subject.

Bibliography

ABRAMSON, N. [1970], The ALOHA System — Another Alternative for Computer Communications, *Proceedings of the Fall Joint Computer Conference.*

AHO, A., B. W. KERNIGHAN, and P. J. WEINBERGER [1988], *The AWK Programming Language*, Addison-Wesley, Reading, MA.

ANDREWS, D. W., and G. D. SHULTZ [1982], A Token-Ring Architecture for Local Area Networks: An Update, *Proceedings of Fall 82 COMPCON, IEEE.*

ATALLAH, M., and D. E. COMER [June 1998], Algorithms for Variable Length Subnet Address Assignment, *IEEE Transactions on Computers*, vol. 47:6, 693-699.

BBN [1981], A History of the ARPANET: The First Decade, *Technical Report*, Bolt, Beranek, and Newman, Inc.

BBN [December 1981], Specification for the Interconnection of a Host and an IMP (revised), *Technical Report 1822*, Bolt, Beranek, and Newman, Inc.

BERTSEKAS D., and R. GALLAGER [1991], *Data Networks*, 2nd edition, Prentice-Hall, Upper Saddle River, NJ.

BIAGIONI E., E. COOPER, and R. SANSOM [March 1993], Designing a Practical ATM LAN, *IEEE Network*, 32-39.

BIRRELL, A., and B. NELSON [February 1984], Implementing Remote Procedure Calls, *ACM Transactions on Computer Systems,* 2(1), 39-59.

BLACK, U., [1995], *ATM: Foundation for Broadband Networks*, Prentice-Hall, Upper Saddle River, NJ.

BOGGS, D., J. SHOCH, E. TAFT, and R. METCALFE [April 1980], Pup: An Internetwork Architecture, *IEEE Transactions on Communications.*

BOGGS, D., J. MOGUL, and C. KENT [August 1988], Measured Capacity of an Ethernet: Myths and Reality, *Proceedings of ACM SIGCOMM '88*, 222-234.

BONNER, P. [1996], *Network Programming with Windows Sockets*, Prentice-Hall, Upper Saddle River, NJ.

BORMAN, D. [April 1989], Implementing TCP/IP on a Cray Computer, *Computer Communication Review,* 19(2), 11-15.

BROWN, M., K. KOLLING, and E. TAFT [November 1985], The Alpine File System, *ACM Transactions on Computer Systems,* 3(4), 261-293.

BROWNBRIDGE, D., L. MARSHALL, and B. RANDELL [December 1982], The Newcastle Connections or UNIXes of the World Unite!, *Software — Practice and Experience,* 12(12), 1147-1162.

CASNER, S., and S. DEERING [July 1992], First IETF Internet Audiocast, *Computer Communications Review,* 22(3), 92-97.

CERF, V., and E. CAIN [October 1983], The DOD Internet Architecture Model, *Computer Networks.*

CERF, V., and R. KAHN [May 1974], A Protocol for Packet Network Interconnection, *IEEE Transactions of Communications,* Com-22(5).

CERF, V. [October 1989], A History of the ARPANET, *ConneXions, The Interoperability Report,* 480 San Antonio Rd, Suite 100, Mountain View, CA.

CHERITON, D. R. [1983], Local Networking and Internetworking in the V-System, *Proceedings of the Eighth Data Communications Symposium.*

CHERITON, D. [August 1986], VMTP: A Transport Protocol for the Next Generation of Communication Systems, *Proceedings of ACM SIGCOMM '86,* 406-415.

CHESSON, G. [June 1987], Protocol Engine Design, *Proceedings of the 1987 Summer USENIX Conference,* Phoenix, AZ.

CHESWICK, W., and S. BELLOVIN [1998], *Firewalls And Internet Security: Repelling the Wiley Hacker,* 2nd edition, Addison-Wesley, Reading, MA.

CLARK, D., and W. FANG [August 1998], Explicit Allocation Of Best-Effort Packet Delivery Service, *IEEE/ACM Transactions On Networking,* 6(4).

CLARK, D., M. LAMBERT, and L. ZHANG [August 1987], NETBLT: A High Throughput Transport Protocol, *Proceedings of ACM SIGCOMM '87.*

CLARK, D., V. JACOBSON, J. ROMKEY, and H. SALWEN [June 1989], An Analysis of TCP Processing Overhead, *IEEE Communications,* 23-29.

COHEN, D., [1981], On Holy Wars and a Plea for Peace, *IEEE Computer,* 48-54.

COMER, D. E. [2000], *The Internet Book,* 3rd edition, Prentice-Hall, Upper Saddle River, NJ.

COMER, D. E. [2000], *Internetworking With TCP/IP Volume I: Principles, Protocols, and Architecture,* 4th edition, Prentice-Hall, Upper Saddle River, NJ.

COMER, D. E. and D. L. STEVENS [1999], *Internetworking With TCP/IP: Volume II: Design, Implementation, and Internals,* 3rd edition, Prentice-Hall, Upper Saddle River, NJ.

COMER, D. E., and D. L. STEVENS [2000], *Internetworking With TCP/IP Volume III: Client-Server Programming And Applications, LINUX/POSIX Sockets version,* Prentice-Hall, Upper Saddle River, NJ.

COMER, D. E. and D. L. STEVENS [1997], *Internetworking With TCP/IP Volume III — Client-Server Programming And Applications, Windows Sockets version,* Prentice-Hall, Upper Saddle River, NJ.

COMER, D. E. and D. L. STEVENS [1996], *Internetworking With TCP/IP Volume III — Client-Server Programming And Applications, BSD socket version,* 2nd edition, Prentice-Hall, Upper Saddle River, NJ.

COMER, D. E. and D. L. STEVENS [1994], *Internetworking With TCP/IP Volume III — Client-Server Programming And Applications, AT&T TLI version,* Prentice-Hall, Upper Saddle River, NJ.

COMER, D. E. and J. T. KORB [1983], CSNET Protocol Software: The IP-to-X25 Interface, *Computer Communications Review,* 13(2).

COMER, D. E., T. NARTEN, and R. YAVATKAR [April 1987], The Cypress Network: A Low-Cost Internet Connection Technology, *Technical Report TR-653,* Purdue University, West Lafayette, IN.

COMER, D. E., T. NARTEN, and R. YAVATKAR [1987], The Cypress Coaxial Packet Switch, *Computer Networks and ISDN Systems,* vol. 14:2-5, 383-388.

COTTON, I. [1979], Technologies for Local Area Computer Networks, *Proceedings of the Local Area Communications Network Symposium.*

DALAL Y. K., and R. S. PRINTIS [1981], 48-Bit Absolute Internet and Ethernet Host Numbers, *Proceedings of the Seventh Data Communications Symposium.*

DEERING S. E., and D. R. CHERITON [May 1990], Multicast Routing in Datagram Internetworks and Extended LANs, *ACM Transactions on Computer Systems,* 8(2), 85-110.

DEERING, S., D. ESTRIN, D. FARINACCI, V. JACOBSON, C-G LIU, and L. WEI [August 1994], An Architecture for Wide-Area Multicasting Routing, *Proceedings of ACM SIGCOMM '94,* 126-135.

DENNING P. J., [September-October 1989], *The Science of Computing: Worldnet,* in American Scientist, 432-434.

DENNING P. J., [November-December 1989], *The Science of Computing: The ARPANET After Twenty Years,* in American Scientist, 530-534.

DE PRYCKER, M. [1995], *Asynchronous Transfer Mode Solution for Broadband ISDN,* 3rd edition, Prentice-Hall, Upper Saddle River, NJ.

DIGITAL EQUIPMENT CORPORATION., INTEL CORPORATION, and XEROX CORPORATION [September 1980], *The Ethernet: A Local Area Network Data Link Layer and Physical Layer Specification.*

DION, J. [Oct. 1980], The Cambridge File Server, *Operating Systems Review,* 14(4), 26-35.

DRIVER, H., H. HOPEWELL, and J. IAQUINTO [September 1979], How the Gateway Regulates Information Control, *Data Communications.*

EDGE, S. W. [1979], Comparison of the Hop-by-Hop and Endpoint Approaches to Network Interconnection, in *Flow Control in Computer Networks,* J-L. GRANGE and M. GIEN (EDS.), North-Holland, Amsterdam, 359-373.

EDGE, S. [1983], An Adaptive Timeout Algorithm for Retransmission Across a Packet Switching Network, *Proceedings of ACM SIGCOMM '83.*

ENSLOW, P. [January 1978], What is a 'Distributed' Data Processing System? *Computer,* 13-21.

ERIKSSON, H. [August 1994], MBONE: The Multicast Backbone, *Communications of the ACM,* 37(8), 54-60.

FALK, G. [1983], The Structure and Function of Network Protocols, in *Computer Communications, Volume I: Principles,* CHOU, W. (ED.), Prentice-Hall, Upper Saddle River, NJ.

FARMER, W. D., and E. E. NEWHALL [1969], An Experimental Distributed Switching System to Handle Bursty Computer Traffic, *Proceedings of the ACM Symposium on Probabilistic Optimization of Data Communication Systems,* 1-33.

FEDOR, M. [June 1988], GATED: A Multi-Routing Protocol Daemon for UNIX, *Proceedings of the 1988 Summer USENIX Conference,* San Francisco, CA.

FLOYD, S. and V. JACOBSON [August 1993], Random Early Detection Gateways for Congestion Avoidance, *IEEE/ACM Transactions on Networking,* 1(4).

FRANK, H., and W. CHOU [1971], Routing in Computer Networks, *Networks,* 1(1), 99-112.

FULTZ, G. L., and L. KLEINROCK, [June 14-16, 1971], Adaptive Routing Techniques for Store-and-Forward Computer Communication Networks, presented at *IEEE International Conference on Communications,* Montreal, Canada.

GERLA, M., and L. KLEINROCK [April 1980], Flow Control: A Comparative Survey, *IEEE Transactions on Communications.*

HINDEN, R., J. HAVERTY, and A. SHELTZER [September 1983], The DARPA Internet: Interconnecting Heterogeneous Computer Networks with Gateways, *Computer.*

INTERNATIONAL ORGANIZATION FOR STANDARDIZATION [June 1986a], Information processing systems — Open Systems Interconnection — *Transport Service Definition,* International Standard number 8072, ISO, Switzerland.

INTERNATIONAL ORGANIZATION FOR STANDARDIZATION [July 1986b], Information processing systems — Open Systems Interconnection — *Connection Oriented Transport Protocol Specification,* International Standard number 8073, ISO, Switzerland.

INTERNATIONAL ORGANIZATION FOR STANDARDIZATION [May 1987a], Information processing systems — Open Systems Interconnection — *Specification of Basic Specification of Abstract Syntax Notation One (ASN.1),* International Standard number 8824, ISO, Switzerland.

INTERNATIONAL ORGANIZATION FOR STANDARDIZATION [May 1987b], Information processing systems — Open Systems Interconnection — *Specification of Basic Encoding Rules for Abstract Syntax Notation One (ASN.1),* International Standard number 8825, ISO, Switzerland.

INTERNATIONAL ORGANIZATION FOR STANDARDIZATION [May 1988a], Information processing systems — Open Systems Interconnection — *Management Information Service Definition, Part 2: Common Management Information Service,* Draft International Standard number 9595-2, ISO, Switzerland.

INTERNATIONAL ORGANIZATION FOR STANDARDIZATION [May 1988a], Information processing systems — Open Systems Interconnection — *Management Information Protocol Definition, Part 2: Common Management Information Protocol,* Draft International Standard number 9596-2.

JACOBSON, V. [August 1988], Congestion Avoidance and Control, *Proceedings ACM SIGCOMM '88.*

JAIN, R. [January 1985], On Caching Out-of-Order Packets in Window Flow Controlled Networks, *Technical Report,* DEC-TR-342, Digital Equipment Corporation.

JAIN, R. [March 1986], Divergence of Timeout Algorithms for Packet Retransmissions, *Proceedings Fifth Annual International Phoenix Conference on Computers and Communications,* Scottsdale, AZ.

JAIN, R. [October 1986], A Timeout-Based Congestion Control Scheme for Window Flow-Controlled Networks, *IEEE Journal on Selected Areas in Communications*, Vol. SAC-4, no. 7.

JAIN, R., K. RAMAKRISHNAN, and D-M. CHIU [August 1987], Congestion Avoidance in Computer Networks With a Connectionless Network Layer. *Technical Report*, DEC-TR-506, Digital Equipment Corporation.

JAIN, R. [1991], *The Art of Computer Systems Performance Analysis,* John Wiley & Sons, NY.

JAIN, R. [May 1992], Myths About Congestion Management in High-speed Networks, *Internetworking: Research and Experience*, 3(3), 101-113.

JAIN, R. [1994], *FDDI Handbook; High-Speed Networking Using Fiber and Other Media,* Addison Wesley, Reading, MA.

JENNINGS, D. M., L. H. LANDWEBER, and I. H. FUCHS [February 28, 1986], Computer Networking for Scientists and Engineers, *Science* Vol 231, 941-950.

JUBIN, J. and J. TORNOW [January 1987], The DARPA Packet Radio Network Protocols, *IEEE Proceedings.*

KAHN, R. [November 1972], Resource-Sharing Computer Communications Networks, *Proceedings of the IEEE,* 60(11), 1397-1407.

KARN, P., H. PRICE, and R. DIERSING [May 1985], Packet Radio in the Amateur Service, *IEEE Journal on Selected Areas in Communications,*

KARN, P., and C. PARTRIDGE [August 1987], Improving Round-Trip Time Estimates in Reliable Transport Protocols, *Proceedings of ACM SIGCOMM '87.*

KAUFMAN, C., PERLMAN, R., and SPECINER, M. [1995], *Network Security: Private Communication in a Public World,* Prentice-Hall, Upper Saddle River, NJ.

KENT, C., and J. MOGUL [August 1987], Fragmentation Considered Harmful, *Proceedings of ACM SIGCOMM '87.*

LAMPSON, B. W., M. PAUL, and H. J. SIEGERT (EDS.) [1981], *Distributed Systems - Architecture and Implementation (An Advanced Course),* Springer-Verlag, Berlin.

LAMPSON, B. W., V. SRINIVASAN, and G. VARGHESE [June 1999], IP Lookups Using Multiway and Multicolumn Search, *IEEE/ACM Transactions on Networking*, vol 7, 324-334.

LANZILLO, A. L., and C. PARTRIDGE [January 1989], Implementation of Dial-up IP for UNIX Systems, *Proceedings 1989 Winter USENIX Technical Conference,* San Diego, CA.

LEFFLER, S., M. McKUSICK, M. KARELS, and J. QUARTERMAN [1996], *The Design and Implementation of the 4.4BSD UNIX Operating System,* Addison Wesley, Reading, MA.

MARZULLO, K. and S. OWICKI [July 1985], Maintaining The Time In A Distributed System, *Operating Systems Review,* 19(3), 44-54.

MCNAMARA, J. [1998], *Technical Aspects of Data Communications,* 2nd edition, Digital Press, Digital Equipment Corporation, Bedford, MA.

MCQUILLAN, J. M., I. RICHER, and E. ROSEN [May 1980], The New Routing Algorithm for the ARPANET, *IEEE Transactions on Communications,* (COM-28), 711-719.

METCALFE, R. M., and D. R. BOGGS [July 1976], Ethernet: Distributed Packet Switching for Local Computer Networks, *Communications of the ACM,* 19(7), 395-404.

MILLS, D., and H-W. BRAUN [August 1987], The NSFNET Backbone Network, *Proceedings of ACM SIGCOMM '87.*

MORRIS, R. [1979], Fixing Timeout Intervals for Lost Packet Detection in Computer Communication Networks, *Proceedings AFIPS National Computer Conference,* AFIPS Press, Montvale, NJ.

NAGLE, J. [April 1987], On Packet Switches With Infinite Storage, *IEEE Transactions on Communications,* Vol. COM-35:4.

NARTEN, T. [Sept. 1989], Internet Routing, *Proceedings ACM SIGCOMM '89.*

NEEDHAM, R. M. [1979], System Aspects of the Cambridge Ring, *Proceedings of the ACM Seventh Symposium on Operating System Principles,* 82-85.

NEWMAN, P., G. MINSHALL, and T. L. LYON [April 1998], IP Switching — ATM Under IP, *IEEE Transactions on Networking,* Vol. 6:2, 117-129.

OPPEN, D., and Y. DALAL [October 1981], The Clearinghouse: A Decentralized Agent for Locating Named Objects, Office Products Division, XEROX Corporation.

PARTRIDGE, C. [June 1986], Mail Routing Using Domain Names: An Informal Tour, *Proceedings of the 1986 Summer USENIX Conference,* Atlanta, GA.

PARTRIDGE, C. [June 1987], Implementing the Reliable Data Protocol (RDP), *Proceedings of the 1987 Summer USENIX Conference,* Phoenix, Arizona.

PARTRIDGE, C. [1994], *Gigabit Networking,* Addison-Wesley, Reading, MA.

PARTRIDGE, C. and M. ROSE [June 1989], A Comparison of External Data Formats, in *Message Handling Systems and Distributed Applications,* E. STEFFERUD and O. JACOBSEN (EDS.) Elsevier-North Holland.

PELTON, J. [1995], *Wireless and Satellite Telecommunications,* Prentice-Hall, Upper Saddle River, NJ.

PERLMAN, R. [2000], *Interconnections: Bridges and Routers,* 2nd edition, Addison-Wesley, Reading, MA.

PETERSON, L., and B. DAVIE, [1999], *Computer Networks: A Systems Approach,* 2nd edition, Morgan Kaufmann, San Francisco, CA.

PIERCE, J. R. [1972], Networks for Block Switching of Data, *Bell System Technical Journal,* 51.

PLATT, D. [1996], *Windows 95 and NT: Win32 API from Scratch: A Programmer's Workbook,* Prentice-Hall, Upper Saddle River, NJ.

POSTEL, J. B. [April 1980], Internetwork Protocol Approaches, *IEEE Transactions on Communications,* COM-28, 604-611.

POSTEL, J. B., C. A. SUNSHINE, and D. CHEN [1981], The ARPA Internet Protocol, *Computer Networks.*

QUARTERMAN, J. S., and J. C. HOSKINS [October 1986], Notable Computer Networks, *Communications of the ACM,* 29(10).

RAMAKRISHNAN, K. and R. JAIN [May 1990], A Binary Feedback Scheme For Congestion Avoidance In Computer Networks, *ACM Transactions on Computer Systems,* 8(2), 158-181.

REYNOLDS, J., J. POSTEL, A. R. KATZ, G. G. FINN, and A. L. DESCHON [October 1985], The DARPA Experimental Multimedia Mail System, *IEEE Computer.*

RITCHIE, D. M., and K. THOMPSON [July 1974], The UNIX Time-Sharing System, *Communications of the ACM,* 17(7), 365-375; revised and reprinted in *Bell System Technical Journal,* 57(6), [July-August 1978], 1905-1929.

ROSE, M. [1993], *The Internet Message: Closing The Book with Electronic Mail,* Prentice-Hall, Upper Saddle River, NJ.

RYAN, T. [1996], *Distributed Object Technology,* Prentice-Hall, Upper Saddle River, NJ.

SALTZER, J. [1978], Naming and Binding of Objects, *Operating Systems, An Advanced Course,* Springer-Verlag, 99-208.

SALTZER, J. [April 1982], Naming and Binding of Network Destinations, *International Symposium on Local Computer Networks,* IFIP/T.C.6, 311-317.

SALTZER, J., D. REED, and D. CLARK [November 1984], End-to-End Arguments in System Design, *ACM Transactions on Computer Systems,* 2(4), 277-288.

SHOCH, J. F. [1978], Internetwork Naming, Addressing, and Routing, *Proceedings of COMPCON.*

SHOCH, J. F., Y. DALAL, and D. REDELL [August 1982], Evolution of the Ethernet Local Computer Network, *Computer.*

SNA [1975], *IBM System Network Architecture — General Information,* IBM System Development Division, Publications Center, Department E01, Research Triangle Park, North Carolina.

SOLOMON, J. [1997], *Mobile IP: The Internet Unplugged,* Prentice-Hall, Upper Saddle River, NJ.

SRINIVASAN, V., and G. VARGHESE [February 1999], Fast Address Lookups Using Controlled Prefix Expansion, *ACM Transactions on Computer Systems,* vol. 17, 1-40.

STALLINGS, W. [1997], *Local and Metropolitan Area Networks,* Prentice-Hall, Upper Saddle River, NJ.

STALLINGS, W. [1998], *High-Speed Networks: TCP/IP and ATM Design Principles,* Prentice-Hall, Upper Saddle River, NJ.

STEVENS, W. R. [1998], *UNIX Network Programming,* 2nd edition, Prentice-Hall, Upper Saddle River, NJ.

SWINEHART, D., G. MCDANIEL, and D. R. BOGGS [December 1979], WFS: A Simple Shared File System for a Distributed Environment, *Proceedings of the Seventh Symposium on Operating System Principles,* 9-17.

TICHY, W., and Z. RUAN [June 1984], Towards a Distributed File System, *Proceedings of Summer 84 USENIX Conference,* Salt Lake City, Utah, 87-97.

TOMLINSON. R. S. [1975], Selecting Sequence Numbers, *Proceedings ACM SIGOPS/SIGCOMM Interprocess Communication Workshop,* 11-23, 1975.

WATSON, R. [1981], Timer-Based Mechanisms in Reliable Transport Protocol Connection Management, *Computer Networks,* North-Holland Publishing Company.

WEINBERGER, P. J. [1985], The UNIX Eighth Edition Network File System, *Proceedings 1985 ACM Computer Science Conference,* 299-301.

WELCH, B., and J. OSTERHAUT [May 1986], Prefix Tables: A Simple Mechanism for Locating Files in a Distributed System, *Proceedings IEEE Sixth International Conference on Distributed Computing Systems,* 184-189.

WILKES, M. V., and D. J. WHEELER [May 1979], The Cambridge Digital Communication Ring, *Proceedings Local Area Computer Network Symposium.*

XEROX [1981], Internet Transport Protocols, *Report XSIS 028112,* Xerox Corporation, Office Products Division, Network Systems Administration Office, 3333 Coyote Hill Road, Palo Alto, CA.

ZHANG, L. [August 1986], Why TCP Timers Don't Work Well, *Proceedings of ACM SIGCOMM '86.*

Index

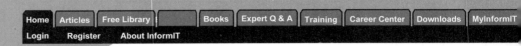